The Expression of Knowledge

Neurobehavioral Transformations of
Information into Action

The Expression of Knowledge

Neurobehavioral Transformations of
Information into Action

Edited by
Robert L. Isaacson
and Norman E. Spear

State University of New York
Binghamton, New York

PLENUM PRESS • NEW YORK AND LONDON

Library of Congress Cataloging in Publication Data

Main entry under title:

The Expression of knowledge.

Includes bibliographical references and index.
1. Comprehension. 2. Expression. 3. Performance. 4. Memory. 5. Psychology,
Physiological. I. Isaacson, Robert Lee, 1928 –   . II. Spear, Norman E.
BF325.E96 1928   153   82-13253
ISBN-13: 978-1-4684-7892-1   e-ISBN-13: 978-1-4684-7890-7
DOI: 10.1007/978-1-4684-7890-7

© 1982 Plenum Press, New York
Softcover reprint of the hardcover 1st edition 1982
A Division of Plenum Publishing Corporation
233 Spring Street, New York, N.Y. 10013

Contributors

Hymie Anisman, *Department of Psychology, Carleton University, Ottawa, Ontario, Canada*

Béla Bohus, *Rudolf Magnus Institute for Pharmacology, Vondellaan 6, Utrecht, The Netherlands*

Jeffrey W. Fagen, *Department of Psychology, St. John's University, Jamaica, New York*

Richard Hirsh, *Department of Psychiatry, McGill University, Montreal, Quebec, Canada*

Robert L. Isaacson, *Department of Psychology, State University of New York at Binghamton, Binghamton, New York*

Joel Krajden, *Department of Psychiatry, McGill University, Montreal, Quebec, Canada*

Donald R. Meyer, *Laboratory of Comparative and Physiological Psychology, Ohio State University, Columbus, Ohio*

Patricia Morgan Meyer, *Laboratory of Comparative and Physiological Psychology, Ohio State University, Columbus, Ohio*

Donald A. Overton, *Department of Psychiatry, Temple University School of Medicine, 3400 N. Broad St., Philadelphia, Pennsylvania*

GODFREY D. PEARLSON, *Department of Psychiatry and Behavioral Sciences, Johns Hopkins University School of Medicine, Baltimore, Maryland*

ROBERT G. ROBINSON, *Department of Psychiatry and Behavioral Sciences, Johns Hopkins University School of Medicine, Baltimore, Maryland*

CAROLYN K. ROVEE-COLLIER, *Department of Psychology, Rutgers University, New Brunswick, New Jersey*

NORMAN E. SPEAR, *Department of Psychology, State University of New York at Binghamton, Binghamton, New York*

DANIEL L. SCHACTER, *Department of Psychology, University of Toronto, Toronto, Ontario, Canada*

ENDEL TULVING, *Department of Psychology, University of Toronto, Toronto, Ontario, Canada*

DAVID L. WOLGIN, *Department of Psychology, Florida Atlantic University, Boca Raton, Florida*

Preface

What we know about the world and its opportunities limits what we do. If we do not know that there is a pot of gold at the end of the rainbow, we will not follow it. If we do not know that a desert cactus contains water, we will not cut into it for sustenance. Often, however, we do know things about the world and yet the knowledge does not seem to be reflected in behavior. Explaining this fact simply in terms of inadequate motivation for expression or incomplete memory for the important information does not really add much to our understanding. The expression of knowledge can be interrupted in very special ways by a variety of more specific conditions—fatigue, sources of forgetting that may include failure of memory retrieval, emotion, and various dysfunctions of brain and body systems—that are not satisfactorily incorporated by any current theories of motivation or memory. Also, a dissociation between knowledge and its expression can take the form of applying knowledge without apparent awareness of this action, a phenomenon that requires complicated assumptions for explanation in terms of either motivation or memory.

Dissociations between knowledge and action may be striking. After driving home on a familiar route we may not be able to report whether the last three traffic lights were red or green; yet we must have responded appropriately to them. Persons with brain dysfunction may switch rapidly between reports of fantasized and real experience without evidence of their discrimination between what is real and unreal. Such persons may even carry out complicated action patterns and later deny that they have done so. What is puzzling in a more general sense is why even our most relevant knowledge is often not expressed in what we do, even when our adaptation—or even our survival—requires it.

The chapters in this book illustrate what is becoming known about this topic.

The issue is hardly original. Why we do not behave in accordance with our knowledge has been debated for centuries. The advantage we have over our forbears is the accumulation of systematic, empirical evidence. Some of this evidence forms the core of the present book. It comes from laboratory studies of behavior that deal with either the environmental or physiological substrates of actions. But the origin of the problem is outside the laboratory, in daily life.

Some chapters in this book contain cases in which people with severe memory problems fail to realize that they can, in fact, remember; or in which knowledge apparently lost through brain damage can be readily expressed given the proper neurochemical treatment; or in which apparently inadequate expression of knowledge by infants can, under the proper circumstances, be manifested with an efficacy that approaches that of adults. Although this evidence is diverse, it centers on the problem of when and how acquired knowledge and behavioral dispositions become expressed in behavior.

Our particular interest in the topic we have labeled "expression of knowledge" arose from a series of conversations the editors held in each other's offices over a period of several months. Whatever the particular impetus for a conversation—whether an idea, problem, or discovery, and whether the source was the laboratory, a journal, or an article in the *New York Times*—the discussions seemed always to touch on, in some fashion, striking interdependences among knowing, thinking, and doing. We felt it would be useful to illustrate the generality of this problem and the varied ways of approaching it with a volume sampling a wide spectrum of neurobehavioral expertise. A difficulty with this approach is the transitions between chapters. We could have solved this problem in a number of ways: by adding a few pages between chapters to specify the relationships; by providing a final chapter summarizing the rest, or by insisting that the authors provide information specific to linking their chapter with the others. We found none of these solutions acceptable. Specifically, new relationships might be masked by ones that ultimately will be trivial. Furthermore, the reader will find that it does not take a great deal of insight to see interconnecting themes among the chapters. In fact, readers are likely to detect many relationships that we have not seen.

The great advantage of the diversity of the areas represented is to expose the reader to neurobehavioral approaches that might otherwise be missed. It is difficult enough these days to keep up with one specialty area; relevant investigations from other areas are easy to overlook. We feel that for such general issues as the expression of knowledge, a broad perspective is required. Therefore, these chapters are written so as to be accessible to students of neurobehavioral science even when their own area of expertise is not the particular subject matter of a chapter. The book is intended for neuroscientists, psychologists, and graduate students in these fields, as well as for advanced undergraduates. It will foster an appreciation for the broad scope of tools available to study problems in the neurobehavioral fields.

The subject matter of this book proceeds from emphasis on environmental variables and the measurement of behavior to concentration on physiological intervention for analysis of behavioral or neurophysiological consequences. The first chapter gives the gist of the general topic, emphasizing the scientific and not the philosophical approach. Examples are drawn largely from studies of learning and memory that have examined the expression of acquired knowledge in either humans or animals. The next two chapters deal exclusively with the expression of learning by people. Schacter and Tulving summarize evidence of dissociation between knowledge and its expression among persons with either acute or chronic amnesia. They show how these effects may be organized in terms of Tulving's distinction between episodic and semantic memory systems. Fagen and Rovee-Collier describe a series of their experiments assessing the retention and forgetting of instrumental learning acquired by 2- or 3-month-old infants. Contrary to long-standing generalizations held by most developmental psychologists, their studies show that infants of this age have a substantial capacity for remembering over long periods, although the expression of their acquired knowledge may require special circumstances for memory retrieval.

Chapters 4, 5, and 6 illustrate the control that drugs can exert over the expression of knowledge. Overton reviews the most recent evidence and interpretation of state-dependent retention, that is, the dependence of retention on the correspondence between drug states during original learning and later retention tests. The recently discovered role of neuropeptides in attention, learning, and memory is discussed by Bohus in Chapter 5. He concentrates on the evolution of this discovery in animal research conducted at the laboratories of the Rudolf Magnus Institute at the Medical School in Utrecht, the Netherlands, and describes some recent studies with humans. Donald and Patricia Meyer review the history and current status of their work on the importance of memory retrieval for the expression of knowledge, through experiments that reveal how brain-damaged animals can express previously acquired behaviors, contingent on the proper neurochemical context.

The chapters by Hirsh and Krajden and by Wolgin indicate the importance of the limbic system in the expression of knowledge. The former authors present a theoretical framework to account for the role of the hippocampus in learning and memory. Wolgin analyzes the changes in behavioral patterns after lateral hypothalamic damage in adults and finds them similar to the activation of behavioral patterns among immature organisms. The next two chapters are concerned with the neurochemical and neurophysiological determinants of affective or emotional responses. Anisman shows how behavior in general, and the expression of acquired knowledge in particular, can be profoundly influenced by the neurochemical consequences of extreme stress. Pearlson and Robinson appeal to data from brain-damaged human patients and from rats that undergo experimentally induced stroke. They show for both types of individuals that the expression of emotion is lateralized in the brain.

The final chapter considers the expression of knowledge following brain damage in terms of a reanalysis of some of Lashley's classical experiments and consideration of the sequence of recovery from brain damage. This chapter also submits a general conceptual framework for analyzing the determinants of the expression of knowledge.

In general, we hope that this book will stimulate readers to think somewhat differently about behavior and about the nervous system. It seems to us that the time has passed when we can think only about learning or memory without considering the conditions and mechanisms that translate knowledge into action, whether mental or behavioral.

ROBERT L. ISAACSON
NORMAN SPEAR

Contents

Chapter 1

The Problem of Expression

Norman E. Spear and Robert L. Isaacson

Chapter 2

Memory, Amnesia, and the Episodic/Semantic Distinction

Daniel L. Schacter and Endel Tulving

Chapter 3

A Conditioning Analysis of Infant Memory: How Do We Know They Know What We Know They Knew?

Jeffrey W. Fagen and Carolyn K. Rovee-Collier

Chapter 4

Memory Retrieval Failures Produced by Changes in Drug State

Donald A. Overton

Chapter 5

Neuropeptides and Memory

Béla Bohus

Chapter 6

Memory, Remembering, and Amnesia

Patricia Morgan Meyer and Donald R. Meyer

Chapter 7

The Hippocampus and the Expression of Knowledge

Richard Hirsh and Joel Krajden

Chapter 8

Motivation, Activation, and Behavioral Integration

David L. Wolgin

Chapter 9

Neurochemical Consequences of Stress: Intrusion of Nonassociative Factors in Behavioral Analysis

Hymie Anisman

Chapter 10

*Lateralization of Emotional or Behavioral Responses in Intact and
Hemisphere-Damaged Humans and Rats*

Godfrey D. Pearlson and Robert G. Robinson

Chapter 11

Neural and Mental Capacities

Robert L. Isaacson and Norman E. Spear

1

The Problem of Expression

Norman E. Spear and Robert L. Isaacson

1. INTRODUCTION

This book deals with a problem that has enormous significance for understanding behavior and is correspondingly broad in its scope. The problem is why at some times knowledge is readily available for adaptive application by an organism and yet at other times this same knowledge, whether in the form of learned relationships or the most elementary of species-specific motor patterns, is simply not expressed even though the individual's welfare, or even its survival, might require it. To say this another way, what is known is not always represented faithfully by what is expressed. Or, given what we know, why do we not always do what we should do?

Sometimes our potential for adaptive expression can be very low—which is a paradox, at least superficially. Why should we not express, without fail, acquired knowledge that could promote better adaptation? It would seem reasonable to expect at least this much from a machine–organism that has been shaped through millions of years of challenges to the survival of our predecessors' genes, the presumed selective elimination of less adaptive features, and the ultimate evolution of what seems, so far, to be the most adaptive genetic packaging for our contemporary environment. But this expectation is rarely realized. This book explores this puzzle.

Our thesis is that the problem of expression is not intractable. To

NORMAN E. SPEAR AND ROBERT L. ISAACSON • Department of Psychology, State University of New York at Binghamton, Binghamton, New York 13901.

consider it, however, we must deal with diverse topics in psychology and neuroscience. For instance, we must study a common observation that acquired memories are sometimes accessible but at other times quite inaccessible to the normal human, and consider at the same time that persons with temporal lobe brain damage, who regularly seem quite incapable of learning or expressing new knowledge, sometimes do acquire and retain knowledge quite well while at the same time denying their own ability to do so. The other extreme can be represented by three examples: (1) Acquired knowledge in animals can seem quite obliterated by brain damage but then be expressed upon certain neurochemical treatments; (2) species-specific motor patterns can be turned on or off depending on the activity of hormones having broad spectra of action; and (3) some, but not all, classes of knowledge that seem obliterated through any of various forms of brain insult later reappear, apparently spontaneously, following a period of recovery.

The problem of expression is found not only among individuals with neural dysfunctions or in the experimental laboratory. Probably everyone has observed, at one time or another, how others express their knowledge. We can hardly avoid being aware of this behavior in our children and our friends. Such observation leads, through curiosity or benevolent concern, to the question of *why* a person behaves as he or she did in a particular instance. We are then likely to explain the behavior, most often quite implicitly, in terms of two general factors. The first is the sum total of the individual's knowledge, the potential information or genetically programmed behaviors a person has at hand; the second is what the observed person was thinking or doing just before the behavior—his or her plans, intentions, or general "cognitions."

It is a convention, albeit an arrogant one, for us to believe that humans are rational in their behavior, that they know what they do and why they do it; that what they do is a simple product of which aspect of their accumulated knowledge is selected, after thought and planning, for manifestation in behavior. Another common explanation is based on how much the individual "cares" or is "motivated" about the affairs of the moment. This explanation may be only a special case of the second factor, cognition. For now, we shall forgo discussion of how much "caring" determines what one does and shall concentrate instead on the former two explanations, how "knowing" and "thinking" are related to "doing."

On the one hand, what we do or think is ultimately limited by an individual's total knowledge, that which is potentially available; on the other hand, by the immediate accessibility of a particular aspect of knowledge. This assertion as a whole may seem circular, and hence trivial, because evidence of knowledge can be found only in terms of what one does or thinks and hence, for practical purposes, knowledge is defined in this manner. But what is not trivial is the striking absence of a direct relationship between what an individual knows and he or she does in some circumstances. The scientific study of behavior has revealed that a person's specific knowledge and immediate thoughts can be a poor indication of their immediate behavior. The relationships frequently are of a kind not expected from our intuition. We shall see that appreciation of this independence between knowledge and behavior together with the single major constraint of the accessibility of knowledge, is central to understanding how and when our knowledge is expressed and how and when it is not.

Some aspects of knowledge that seem less "mental" are nevertheless important, such as individual motor actions and their integrated patterns, sensory preferences, or perceptual dispositions (perceptual learning) that are shaped through combinations of experiences and appear relatively "hard-wired." This side of knowledge is evident especially in nonhuman animals, but is nevertheless a pervasive core about which human behavior is organized. We take the view that this class of knowledge—habitual, overlearned, elicited, short-latency behaviors that might even be characterized as species-specific—is of vast importance for our topic. This type of knowledge seems largely to have been ignored in theories of how humans process information, in favor of knowledge derived from language-mediated, "higher-order" processing. We shall suggest, however, that it is the trade-off between both types of knowledge that largely determines what knowledge is expressed.

The central issue to be addressed, fundamental but also intriguing, is this: Once knowledge is acquired, once the potential for expressing "knowledge" is achieved, how and when will this knowledge affect behavior? To say this another way, what circumstances make a difference in whether or not a particular bit of knowledge will be expressed? Before an answer can be considered, we must first describe how we are using the term "knowledge," and next, how we determine that it has or has not been expressed.

2. KNOWLEDGE

What do we mean by knowledge? In a vague sense, the term refers to "all that has been perceived or grasped by the mind" (Webster's New World Dictionary of the American Language, 1978). Included would be the results of cognitive activities called perceiving, learning, judging, imagining, and so on. In some fashion, knowledge is the product of such mental actions or behavioral dispositions as are described in common language. But does identification of such activities in common language help us to understand what knowledge really is? Are we helped or hindered by everyday terms that are themselves poorly defined? In considering philosophical arguments about the special nature of knowledge, it appears that much of the difficulty arises from how words are used. For example, some have argued that not all cognitive activities produce knowledge. The products of our imagination may not be considered knowledge since what we imagine may not be in accordance with reality. Can knowledge be false or inaccurate? Logically, that is debatable; whereas knowing something correctly would be knowledge, believing in something that is not so could not be. Yet in a more practical sense, false beliefs might interact with "true knowledge" to help determine what is expressed. A growing research area has established that imagined events, even those founded largely in fantasy, are remembered in much the same way as real-life events and indeed may be mistaken for them or otherwise alter memory so as to affect their recall (Johnson & Raye, 1981).

An important point is that the gaining of knowledge is based on mental, cognitive activities that we believe are based in the collective operations of the neural tissues of the brain. But even though knowledge is based on mental-brain activities, that does not mean that consciousness or the semantic construction of languages is required for its attainment. It is appropriate to describe a dog as knowing its master, a cat knowing the location of its sandbox, or a rat knowing that certain tastes lead to sickness. These are legitimate uses of "knowing," even though we do not know if these animals are "aware" of their knowledge. Furthermore, the idea that they express knowledge in an internal linguistic format is most unlikely. Thus knowledge may be reflected in tendencies to behave in certain ways; knowledge can be inferred from performance. But, as will be emphasized in this book, although performance can indicate knowledge, the lack of performance need not indicate a lack of knowledge.

Knowledge may exist without being displayed in behavior or in thought. We all know vast amounts of things that may not be influencing our behavior at the moment. We know them even though our thoughts and actions are directed elsewhere. Our knowledge of the political circumstances in the Middle East is no less real when our attention is fully directed toward analysis of data from a recent experiment, grading of exams, or the Sunday-afternoon ballgame. Animals may know the location of food yet not express this knowledge in the presence of a predator. At least at the animal level, the appropriate behavior must be exhibited at least once to demonstrate unequivocally that something is known; and this requirement would seem to hold for humans also, although it is not inconceivable that one day knowledge might be measurable at the physiological level independently of behavior.

The "expression of knowledge" can mean many things. We want to be quite clear about what it means for this chapter and the remainder of this book. Our approach to this topic is to concentrate on what can be understood at the empirical level. We seek to determine what can be concluded generally, about animals as well as humans, regarding the necessary and sufficient conditions for the expression of knowledge. The approach is quite plainly a psychobiological one.

Generally speaking, our topic has been discussed for centuries by a variety of writers. Scores of books have addressed, formally and informally, the philosophical issue of what knowledge is and where it comes from. Scores of models have been developed to describe how knowledge is processed by humans. The widespread application of computers has in fact made the term "information processing" a household word. But although the classical approaches to knowledge and its expression must be acknowledged, they are not necessary considerations for this book; and they are in any case beyond its scope. The philosophical issues pertinent to identifying knowledge and its source will not be addressed here except in passing. Similarly, considerations of knowledge's structure and its processing, issues that have arisen from the perspective of how language is structured and used and that are addressed by models of human information processing, also will not be given much attention except for reference purposes.

The "knowledge" we wish to consider in this book is that commonly exhibited by animals and people in real-life or testing situations, including knowledge of what, when, and how to do things. In the present state of the science, the words "knowledge" and "information" are often used in a similar fashion. The root of the word "information" derives from a Latin word meaning "to represent." We use the word in many ways, including the description of those things about which we are informed.

With the introduction of mathematical information theory, however, the use of the term "information" has become identified with the degree to which the uncertainty of the observer is reduced by a particular message. The amount of information conveyed by any message depends on the message itself, the noise in the system, and the degree to which there is uncertainty about the situation ahead of time. Confirmation of an expected event conveys little information. The more predictable the event the less information a message of its confirmation conveys. Information in this sense refers to reduction of uncertainty as it might exist in games of chance, horseraces, and other situations with discrete outcomes. It is a number, a unit-free measure of an amount of theoretical entity. "Knowledge" means a bit more than this. "Knowledge" is a more general term used here to describe the entire set of an individual's potentially accessible representations of his or her experience. We shall call these representations "memories." Knowledge should also be understood to include the individual's set of stored inferences about these memories, together with species-typical dispositions. Knowledge includes motor skills, awareness of familiarity, beliefs (inferences from memories), and other activities in which the individual can demonstrate the ability to perform actions organized toward specific goals and aims. That would include actions based on beliefs about the environment, or even extraworldly events.

Some philosophers have struggled with the issue of special mental states associated with knowledge. We alluded earlier to a distinction sometimes drawn between knowing and believing. This issue brings up the topic of theories of truth. What do we say about the laboratory rat trained to go to a particular maze location to obtain food? Does the rat *know* the location of the food? Does the rat still know this if the experimenter stealthily changes the location of the food before the animal is tested on a particular trial? Within our framework, the answer is yes; the rat's memories and inferences would remain the same until it finds the food absent. The knowledge was not changed when the rat's belief was made incorrect or false.

Many of these issues deal with how we use words, the structure of common language, and what we mean by truth and falsity. Although these important issues deserve serious study, they are not of primary pertinence to the behavioral issues of this book. We are interested in what leads to an individual giving behavioral evidence of things that are believed. We will use the words "knowledge" and "knowing" freely, including beliefs that may be false and without assuming any necessary special conscious state uniquely associated with knowing as opposed to only believing.

3. ASSESSING KNOWLEDGE

Suppose our intentions were to provide integrative principles to clarify the thousands of discovered, but still disparate, relationships between brain function and the expression of knowledge. A major impediment to such integration would be the *amount* of empirical information at hand on this topic: There is too much. Attempts to reduce this information by generating equivalences through the application of hypothetical constructs have been hampered for lack of rules as to the transfer between knowledge and behavior. To say that these are insep-arable—that only that which is shown in behavior is known—entails an ultimately unacceptable level of analysis.

The generalizations that could serve to reduce the overload of em-pirical information are for the most part severely constrained by the particular experimental methods used to establish the relationships. For instance, it is undeniable that at the empirical level manipulations that affect passive avoidance "learning" do not always affect active avoid-ance "learning"; that those that alter discrimination "learning" with brightness as discriminanda do not always affect "learning" with spatial locations as the discriminanda; that "learning" to avoid taste is not always affected in the same way as "learning" to avoid places; that a "memory" assessed in terms of recall may be governed by different factors than is the same "memory" measured by recognition, and so on. Whether learning or remembering is said to occur depends (probably in a lawful manner) on what aspect of behavior is selected for assessing it.

The problem is not with the independent variables. For these, the physical referents are well established: milligrams of drug, histologically verified locus of lesion or stimulation, number of minutes or hours or days since CNS intervention, and so on. The real problem is not with the dependent variables either: The conventional physical referents of per-centage words recalled or recognized, response latency, its magnitude or its direction, and so on are objective and reasonable. The problem rests squarely in understanding precisely which of such operations con-verge meaningfully into the intervening variables of the acquisition and retrieval of knowledge, and how the execution of particular behaviors depends on the knowledge that is accessible.

A general issue, then, is what conceptualization will best summa-rize (reduce) the many data that in some way address the huge problem of when available knowledge will, or will not, be expressed when needed. As they are commonly used, the terms "learning" and "memo-ry" frequently seem inadequate to accommodate conflicting conclusions that arise from different ways of measuring learning or memory. It is nevertheless unlikely that an entirely new set of intervening variables will be necessary for each different event or episode. From an appropri-ate conceptual framework and set of intervening variables, much of the variation in expression that now accompanies different methods of mea-surement will be understood to reflect nontrivial issues, differences that are of substance for theory. An example is the distinction between rec-ognition and recall (Tulving, 1976; Tulving & Thomson, 1973). Second, it is likely that the bridging laws dictating the relationship between brain function and the expression of knowledge will accommodate the differ-ent amounts and different kinds of information required for an organism to solve the problem of expression in learning or remembering. On this basis we are not troubled by consideration of diverse manipulations and measurements of behavior under the general topic "expression of knowledge." Finally, it seems inevitable that knowledge-to-be-expressed will be multidimensional and, like multidimensional memories for representation of specific episodes (Spear, 1971; Underwood, 1969), will be expressible through any of several attributes or separable characteristics of what is known. All attributes need not be equally accessible for all forms of expression. Knowledge expressed readily through one behavioral mode might therefore seem quite available if a different measurement were taken.

How, in this circumstance, do we determine that an individual possesses certain knowledge? The issue is ancient. For behavioral scientists the methodological issues are all too familiar in reference to the classical problem of how to select the proper "unit of analysis" that will allow us to understand what has become known by a person or animal. For instance: How is a response defined? What is the nature of the "epistemic correlation," the relationship between the conceptual intentions of an experiment and the actual physical manipulations? Is it necessary to introduce a "mentalistic" concept like "knowledge" or even "memory" to understand evidence of a psychobiological nature? We choose not to focus on these important matters in order to avoid a digression into the philosophy of science and because, for practical purposes, the answers for many of them may ultimately be a matter of taste. But we shall not avoid the general problem of what unit of analysis is best for determing what knowledge is or can be expressed; this issue will arise throughout this book.

Generally speaking, it is fundamental if not trivial that verification of a memory (and hence, knowledge) depends on its physical manifestation in the behavioristic sense. Yet it seems clear, at least in theory, that a decision about the existence of knowledge might be reached through neurophysiological measures such as evoked potentials or biochemical change, as well as from inferences derived from the influence of the target knowledge on expression of other behavior (e.g., any test for transfer of training or of proactive or retroactive interference in retention; see Spear, 1978).

A final point is that the expression of knowledge can fail in several ways. Sometimes the knowledge seems not to exist; at other times inappropriate thoughts or behaviors occur instead of those more appropriate. In any case, some behavior occurs. It may merely be a "filler" activity, some constitutional or overlearned response such as grooming, drinking, or scratching one's head that requires little if any thinking. Yet these acts may be more than fillers. They may prepare us for significant events that act on the brain to promote memory retrieval mechanisms and help pry loose knowledge for expression. For example, in rats, grooming throughout excessively long bouts might allow the animal to decrease the attention being paid to external events and to de-arouse itself. This activity could enhance the ability to retrieve information after the grooming episode. Other acts that seem only to fill behavioral vacuums may serve a similar role. Paradoxically, behavioral research has taught us a good deal about when a particular bit of knowledge will probably not be expressed, but surprisingly little about what we can expect in its place.

4. WHAT DETERMINES EXPRESSION?

Within the past 10 to 20 years the form of many theories of memory has changed, perhaps more so than their content. Theories of memory are now most frequently represented by flow charts analogous to those that trace the processing of information within a computer. Other theories have principles held together mathematically or by conventional logic, and still others may depend on a few loosely linked metaphors. All such theories are about equally vague on one point: how the information is transferred into action—expressed—by the individual. It is common, even among the most important theories, to introduce an executor box, a "response operator" that translates new information and knowledge and converts it into behavior (e.g., Atkinson & Shiffrin, 1968; Wagner, 1981). How the response operator works is left unstated, though it could be argued that even so, this approach is better than ignoring the problem or assuming that the input information itself incorporates the instructions and mode for its expression (Spear, 1978). What cannot be easily dismissed, however, is evidence that how knowledge is to be expressed may influence, in very significant fashion, how new information is processed for incorporation into one's knowledge.

For instance, if normal persons are given visual presentation of a sequence of several letters and shortly thereafter are asked to remember them, their difficulty in remembering will correspond to the degree of phonetic similarity among the letters, or, in other words, how similar they sound when spoken. But for deaf persons, the difficulty in remembering letters shown in the same way corresponds to how similar are the hand motions used to represent these letters in sign language. Whereas vocalization is the mode of expression for persons with normal hearing, sign language is the corresponding mode for the deaf (for a review of such studies, see Crowder, 1976, pp. 73–87). As another example, it is now quite clear that persons who expect to be tested for full recall of newly acquired information will be more effective in recalling it and less effective in merely recognizing it than if they had expected a recognition test instead, and vice versa (e.g., Balota & Neely, 1980; Jacoby, 1973). Furthermore, there are indications that characteristics of the new knowledge itself—its meaningfulness, for instance—may determine how such expectations about the later requirements for expression will influence what is learned (Balota & Neely, 1980). Finally, expectations as to *when* expression of particular knowledge is to take place may influence what, and how, knowledge is acquired (Bellezza, Geiselman, & Aronovsky, 1975; Mazuryk, 1974; Watkins & Watkins, 1974). The point is that if anticipations of later expression requirements can influence how learning takes place and what aspects of knowledge are committed to memory, it may be dangerous for theories of learning and memory to relegate the problem of expression to an unspecified "response operator."

At another level of analysis, a common answer to when and how a particular memory will become accessible for expression might be, in two steps, something like this: (1) On the basis of evolutionary principles, the behaviors most likely to occur are those that are most adaptive for the ecological pressures through which they have evolved; (2) A consequence of ecological pressure is therefore to maximize the intelligence with which an animal or person approaches any circumstance requiring specific knowledge. By "maximizing of intelligence" is meant the recruiting of all available knowledge pertinent to a particular circumstance. From this reasoning it would follow that the "intelligent" behavior that must be expected will be available for expression whenever the circumstance is sufficiently urgent, and thus the individual can make knowledge accessible by, in effect, merely thinking hard about the particular circumstance.

But such is not the case. Expression simply does not work this way, either in humans or in animals. Everyone knows the exasperation of being unable to produce a particular bit of knowledge when it is of critical importance that one do so. Even when one's recent access to (use of) certain knowledge leaves one quite confident that the information could be produced at will, its expression may be blocked; and merely trying harder to think about it is unlikely to help, and may in fact hurt.

What, then, is wrong with the reasoning? Why has evolution not provided us a mechanism that will permit ready access to our knowledge when our survival depends on it? Why should pilots freeze at the controls of an airplane during moments of stress unless they are given much more training than would be needed to conduct all the flight operations under normal circumstances? Why is one unable to remember where the fire extinguisher is kept at the moment the kitchen curtains burst into flame? Within an evolutionary framework, two points help alleviate the paradox. First, what might be thought of as a capacity for "intelligent" tendencies or actions—a maximal plasticity in behavior and ready access to the acquired knowledge—is not *necessarily* important for survival. This point is well illustrated in a paper by Robin (1973) called "The Evolutionary Advantages of Being Stupid." For instance, the large brain that promotes this kind of intelligence in the dolphin carries with it a need for oxygen that limits this animal's submersion time to about 5 minutes before resurfacing is necessary. By comparison, the freshwater turtle has a far smaller brain and correspondingly less plasticity and memory capacity. The smaller brain, however, requires so little oxygen as to permit submersion for hours or even days. One can easily imagine that compared to this turtle, the dolphin is at a disadvantage in eluding predators and capturing prey because of the dolphin's relative inflexibility in where it must be every 5 minutes or so.

The second general point is related: Whereas evolutionary pressures might do a fine job in preparing an organism for survival in its ecological niche, this preparation might have quite drastic consequences when an organism finds itself in a place quite foreign to its "niche." The human is a prime example of an organism frequently outside its ecological niche. Consider, for instance, the survival value of the increased level of general activity that animals undergo when their nutritional resources become depleted. If an animal such as the wild rat spends more time moving from place to place when hungry, it increases its chances of encountering food; that much seems perfectly sensible. But consider a rat under different circumstances outside its ecological niche —for instance, in the laboratory. Suppose we provide this rat with an opportunity to run in a rotating wheel whenever it would like and we provide it with only as much food as would be sufficient for survival if it did no running. The way this rat now behaves is an example of the cruel quirks of evolution. As the rat runs in the wheel, its nutritional needs increase, the food ration becomes insufficient, and the rat becomes still hungrier. Because the rat is hungrier, it runs more in the wheel; because it runs more in the wheel, it becomes still hungrier. Eventually, the rat dies. The same mechanism that keeps the species thriving where it originated can be a disaster elsewhere.

That is not to suggest that evolution has failed, certainly not if the ultimate object of survival is the gene rather than that particular being that provides the packaging for the gene. Perhaps we are only confronting an example of the mercy of evolution toward the species but its disregard of the individual. On the average, increased activity by rats will pay off for the group as a whole; but it may be fatal in any particular instance. The point is only that evolution's apparent failure to provide adequately for inevitable perfection in the expression of knowledge is a failure only "on the average," and that this design has evolved because other aspects of information processing require it.

Generally, it appears that those behaviors necessary for survival are those heavily overlearned or perhaps even "hard-wired," that is, given a genetic priority such as to ensure their dominance by specific development in the nervous system. Such forms of knowledge are "of second nature" and inevitably accessible. The effort and operations applied to *acquiring* knowledge might therefore seem more important for expression than are those applied by an individual to promote expression when it is needed. Every athletic coach seems to assume as much: The player cannot depend on inspiration at game time, but must practice, practice, practice if proper execution is to occur.

Finally, we can note one obvious reason why our knowledge is not made more accessible by "trying harder," by general effort, general arousal, or general concentration at the time of expression: We have quite clear limitations in the amount of information that can be used once it is accessed. The adaptiveness of forgetting (in the sense of failure in retrieval of a memory) should not itself be forgotten. Calling up all possible knowledge in an emergency would be of no help at all; the individual would be lost in thought. What is needed is selectivity in what knowledge is accessed. The ultimate mechanism in controlling accessibility cannot, therefore, be internal except in the relatively trivial sense of becoming reasonably alert. We can "instruct ourselves" only indirectly, by providing access to stimuli that help promote retrieval of the knowledge we seek. We cannot gain access to X by giving ourselves a general instruction to remember X. Although we know of no direct tests for this assumption, it seems the most reasonable. What is accessed must therefore depend on the prevailing information, the memories or events that are somehow related to what is to be accessed. This fact would be especially important if capacities are limited (see Chapter 11). It is only through contemporary processing of such information that we can access knowledge.

5. EXAMPLES OF THE PROBLEM

What we know is not always what we do. For the experimental study of behavior, this problem means that measurement of what an individual does will not always assess accurately his or her disposition, that is, what the person remembers about what has been learned, his or her thoughts at the time—more simply, his or her knowledge. This is hardly an original observation. Probably everyone is aware of it in one sense or another. For experimental psychologists it is a maxim and therefore almost trivial. It is well-known that persons can and do dissociate responses, "say one thing and do another." We take it as no surprise that a practical problem of political polls is determining the likelihood that a person who says he will vote for X will actually do so. We easily accept that learning in the laboratory by either animals or humans might be measurable in terms of response latency but not in percentage of correct choices. Such differences are frequently dismissed as merely differential sensitivity in measurement, but this assumption can be misleading. An example is comparison between the measures of recognition and recall of words: When experiments determined that some items are more likely recalled than recognized, the matter took on substantive importance beyond a mere measurement problem (Tulving, 1976).

5.1. Normal Dissociation of Verbal Reports from Other Behaviors

In the experimental study of behavior, normal human subjects have been found notoriously poor in verbally reporting the basis of their behavior. We are speaking now of generally adaptive behavior that can reflect knowledge quite independently of a verbal report. For a variety of important psychological phenomena, such dissociation has been documented within the context of controlled experiments.

Nisbett and Wilson (1977) have reviewed and analyzed a variety of these cases of dissociation. They thoroughly illustrate how the expression of knowledge by subjects undergoing behavioral tests relevant to social psychology, problem solving, and behavior modification can occur for some behaviors without verbal acknowledgment or apparent awareness. In short, verbal expression often seems independent of other behavioral modes of expression.

In their conclusion Nisbett and Wilson put the matter succinctly:

> People often cannot report accurately on the effects of particular stimuli on higher order, inference-based responses. Indeed, sometimes they cannot report on the existence of critical stimuli, sometimes cannot report on the existence of their responses, and sometimes cannot even report that an inferential process of any kind has occurred. (p. 233)

Nisbett and Wilson describe studies that incite shifts in attitude; in spite of behavioral evidence that their attitudes have indeed changed, some subjects in these experiments do not acknowledge verbally any motivational or evaluative shifts. Other cases analyzed by Nisbett and Wilson include tests of subliminal perception and subjective reports of how creative processes occur, in which persons fail to acknowledge that a critical stimulus existed in spite of objective evidence that it did indeed influence their behavior. And they describe a variety of circumstances in which a response is explicitly elicited by a specific stimulus, yet the persons responding deny verbally any connection between the two.

The Nisbett and Wilson article illustrates that very systematic observation has confirmed a dissociation between verbal and other modes of behavioral expression of knowledge among normal humans. Notably, these examples involve prototypically "higher-order" mental processes, sometimes involving social interactions and sometimes not, but characteristically "human." This dissociation may not be different from that seen when skilled motor acts are not amenable to verbal description, and we believe it to be at least analogous to cases of persons suffering brain damage as well as some cases of dissociation in the expression of knowledge by animals.

There is, however, good reason to attend to the subjective reports of normal individuals serving in experiments. Ericsson and Simon (1980) defend this point well. But it must be done in spite of (and to a certain extent, because of) the frequent dissociation between what experimental subjects do and what they say they do. Ericsson and Simon themselves cite several classical instances of the dissociation between verbal and nonverbal expression. Some examples are: (1) Subjects can learn a general rule for a set of anagrams having a common solution yet fail to verbalize the nature of the similarity among the anagrams or their solutions. (2) Individuals may have their behavior controlled by explicit verbal conditioning contingencies—as when an experimenter replies "good" whenever members of a particular class of words are used in conversation and thus increases the subject's use of such words—and yet seem unaware of the contingencies and unable to verbalize their existence or nature. (3) People required to learn pairs of unrelated words may use a third word as a mnemonic mediator during this learning yet be unable to verbalize the particular mediator.

Other examples with important implications have appeared in a surprising variety of circumstances. We now turn to a few of these.

5.2. Amnesia

Dissociation between a subject's behavior and his or her verbal report of that behavior provides some of the most striking examples of dissociation in the expression of knowledge. For persons with global anterograde amnesia, remarkable dissociations of this kind have been identified and studied with increasing frequency, particularly by Weiskrantz and his colleagues (e.g., Weiskrantz, 1978). This amnesic syndrome is associated with etiology that includes brain damage to certain subcortical areas. Clinically it has the appearance of a complete absence of memory information. Experimental analysis over the past 15 years has established, however, that for some behaviors amnesic patients can acquire and express memories that represent new information. And yet, at the same time, these patients do not acknowledge verbally that they can do so. Weiskrantz (1978) characterizes this dissociated expression:

> By now it is known that amnesic subjects can learn and remember a variety of tasks when they are tested in particular ways. The only person who remains unconvinced about this is the amnesic subject himself, who persists in failing to acknowledge that his performance is based on specific past experience, or may occasionally confabulate about such aphasias. (p. 372)

Systematic verification of this dissociation has been frequent. Persons clinically diagnosed as amnesic can nevertheless show effective learning and good retention of motor skill learning, visual discrimination learning, cued recall of words or pictures, paired associative learning for word pairs having special cases of conceptual similarity, dispositions for the solution for particular kinds of puzzles involving pictures or words, and retention of certain visual events. But in spite of this variety of memory capability, the amnesics themselves remain unconvinced about their likelihood of expressing the memories they have acquired in these situations. The following examples bear out this point.

1. Weiskrantz and Warrington (1979) found that conditioning of an eyeblink response occurred in amnesic patients, who also showed quite effective retention of this conditioning over 10-minute rest pauses during conditioning and also over a 24-hour interval between experimental sessions. Yet, when interviewed, these patients not only failed to acknowledge that any learning had occurred, they also gave no indication of the significance of the conditioning apparatus and its role in producing the unconditioned stimulus, an air puff to the eye. Their verbal reports were as if they had not undergone the conditioning experience, whereas their conditioned eyeblinks unmistakably reflected an acquired and maintained memory for this experience.

2. The well-studied amnesic patient, H. M., has shown this characteristic in several situations. Milner (1962, 1965) found that H. M. progressively improved in reverse (mirror) drawing over a 3-day period and had significant retention over the 24-hour interval between daily tests. Yet H. M. did not acknowledge from day to day that he could remember ever having participated in this sort of test. Sidman, Stoddard, and Mohr (1968) found that H. M. consistently improved in discrimination among ellipses on a matching problem, and that retention of this discrimination learning was maintained over intervals of several minutes during which he was engaged in conversation. Following each conversational break, however, H. M. stated that he had no recollection of

having served in this kind of task before. Finally, after H. M. had learned, with difficulty, a tactile maze that included seven choice points, he was tested for retention 2 years later. Although he showed substantial retention in terms of accuracy on the maze (75% savings), he indicated that he did not remember his earlier tests with this problem (Milner, Corkin, & Teuber, 1968).

3. Two examples involve amnesics who were musicians. An amnesic patient studied by Starr and Phillips (1970) learned to play a new tune on the piano during a single practice session. Despite explicit denial the next day that any new tune had been learned, the patient proceeded to play the tune in its entirety when presented the first few notes. The other example is reported by Luria (1976) in reference to work by Kohnstamm (1917). This work described an amnesic patient who was quite capable of playing the accompaniment for singers, yet subsequently could recall nothing about having done so nor about the music itself.

4. Luria (1976, Chapter 5) describes a syndrome found among patients with tumors of the third ventricle. The symptoms include inevitable complaints about the deficiencies in their memory capacity ("I forget everything, I cannot retain anything," p. 234). Yet for many of these patients, when they are given objective tests involving the recall of words, there is little or no indication that any memory deficiency actually exists. They seem to behave normally on these memory tests. Notably, perhaps, such memory deficiency is shown to be extraordinary for these patients when retroactive interference of a specific or nonspecific nature is introduced.

5. Kinsbourne and Wood (1975, p. 280) were able to teach amnesics a principle for deriving a mathematical series ("start with two 1-digit numbers in immediately ascending sequence, e.g., 3, 4; the next number is the sum of the previous two, or 7; the next is the sum of the previous two, or 11; etc."). Retention was established after a 4-month period in terms of substantial savings in reacquiring the principle, but none of their subjects could remember ever doing the task before.

In Chapter 2 Schacter and Tulving present a theoretical analysis of such cases of behavioral dissociation among amnesics.

5.3. Blindsight

A different consequence of brain damage, perhaps analogous to this amnesic effect but involving sensation and perception rather than memory, has been identified and studied by Weiskrantz and his colleagues under the heading "blindsight" (Weiskrantz, 1980; Weiskrantz, Warrington, Sanders, & Marshall, 1974). Patients with extensive lesions of the visual cortex may explicitly deny seeing a particular object in space, yet accurately identify the location of the object when asked where it would be "if there were in fact something there." When monkeys have been tested for residual visual capabilities following complete removal of the striate cortex, an analogously surprising capability has been found. Like humans, these monkeys are capable of spatial discriminations, and under certain conditions they can also detect movement of distant objects and discriminate rates of movement; also, they can solve discrimination problems involving different geometric shapes, angles of line orientation, and multielement patterns or textures (Keating, 1980). Whether or not these individuals are "blind" depends entirely on the ways in which the information is tapped.

5.4. Normal Human Learning and Retention

In many situations there is a pronounced tendency for humans to exhibit learned behaviors that cannot be articulated. To illustrate, try to describe how you ride a bicycle or throw a baseball to someone 100 feet away. How often have you left your office for the evening and been quite incapable of verbalizing the last three things you did before shutting the door? Did you or did you not turn off the light?

Weiskrantz (1978) describes such effects in terms of a particular type of "access" to a memory. Here "access" is used differently, separately from its conventional use in the sense of retrieval of a memory for manifestation in behavior. For Weiskrantz, this second meaning of "access" refers "to *monitoring* of our own behavior and our own past experience" (p. 397). It only stands to reason that such "access"—the self-monitoring of behaviors at the level of verbalizable awareness—would be limited and focused. Weiskrantz explains why:

> It would be a very inefficient nervous system that had its monitoring system always connected to the whole stream of its activity. We are *not* aware of which eye we use in a particular situation. We don't know anything directly about the state of our lenses or many other bodily adjustments. In skilled behavior such as driving a car, the more skilled you become, the less able you are to give a commentary on what movements you have been making recently. It is efficient *not* to have that kind of information. (p. 405)

A useful example of variability in the expression of recently acquired knowledge is seen when human subjects are presented a set of 20 or so words to be recalled in any order they choose. We may consider the entire set of events, both the words themselves and the circumstances surrounding their presentation, as a new episode that theoretically adds to the subject's knowledge. What aspects of this episode can be expressed on demand? First, we know that humans will be extremely effective in expressing what was *not* a part of that episode. Rarely will an individual in this situation respond in recall with a word that was not in the list. For lists of 16 relatively familiar nouns, for instance, Underwood (1964) found that less than 1% of the words recalled were not in the list presented. In a slightly different experiment, testing learning of pairs of common words, only 1 of 1,424 errors was a word that did not appear somewhere in the list: A subject "imported" the word "yellow" when the correct response was "canary" (Underwood, 1964, p. 58).

Other characteristics of subjects' expression in these circumstances are of interest, particularly when there is some organization imposed in the list itself. Suppose, for instance, that a list of 16 nouns to be remembered includes four countries, four common birds, four common diseases, and four animals. In other words, the 16 items include four concepts of four exemplars each. Underwood (1964) summarizes what was expressed in one experiment by subjects asked to recall such a list after a single presentation. First of all, recall was quite proficient, with about 92% of the words recalled correctly; in over a third of the cases, all words were recalled correctly. But the subjects learned a good deal more than just what words to recall. They expressed the knowledge that there were four concepts represented in the list with four exemplars for each: In 86% of the cases all four words from a particular category were recalled before any from another; no subject ever gave five words from a particular category; on only about 1% of the occasions did anyone fail to recall at least one word from a particular category, and for the remainder of the cases, no fewer than three of the four exemplars were given for every category. It might be noted that what is expressed in such a test does not exhaust the subject's knowledge about what words were in it. When a longer list is given and the overall probability of recall is correspondingly decreased, it has been shown in many experiments that if subjects are reminded of the categories from which the words were derived, accuracy in recalling the words can be improved by 50% to 100%.

What happens to those words that are not recalled originally? Frequently there is evidence that some other aspect of knowledge about the words can be expressed, especially for words that subjects feel are "on the tip of the tongue." In such cases, Brown and McNeill (1966) found subjects quite accurate in providing information about such aspects as the number of syllables of the word, its first letter, its approximate meaning, and so on. When the correct first letter is supplied for such words their probability of recall doubles (Freedman & Landauer, 1966), and when items of this sort are tested for recognition in a multiple choice-test, recall has been found to be about 80% accurate (in comparison to a chance level, in this particular case, of about 18%; Hart, 1965).

Finally, there is increasing evidence that knowledge about incidental aspects of the environmental circumstances in learning such a set of words can be expressed and used to advantage if required. Smith (1979) analyzed the decrement that occurs when subjects are asked to recall words in a location that differs from that in which the words had been presented for learning. He found that subjects tested in a physically different environment could remember details of the physical features of their previous (learning) environment and could, if instructed, use these details to aid in retrieving the words themselves.

The evidence in this section indicates the selectivity with which knowledge is acquired and expressed by normal humans assigned the simple task of remembering a set of words shown to them. Although a great deal more is learned about the episode than just the words, it is extremely rare for subjects to respond with anything else, that is, any of the thousands of words they know that were not in the list (unless they are explicitly asked to do so). The residual knowledge acquired about the experimental task can, however, be used by the subjects to aid in further remembering if the opportunity arises.

5.5. Normals Can Be like Amnesics in Dissociating Their Modes of Expression

A dissociated expression of knowledge like that found in amnesics has been identified with normal subjects. Jacoby (1981) thoroughly analyzed this "normal" dissociation in expression. He starts from the view that recognition memory for a specific event is operationally equivalent to a judgment of its reoccurrence. Jacoby suggests that such a judgment can be based on either of two factors—perceptual fluency or respecification. Perceptual fluency refers to the subject's judged efficacy in perceiving a critical event. The notion is that because humans can realize when their perceptual fluency is relatively high for a particular item, they have a feeling of familiarity when this realization occurs and so judge that this item had occurred previously. Recognition based on perceptual fluency need not be accompanied by details of the prior occurrence; these details are provided in the process Jacoby labels "respecification." With this process the subject recovers a unique specification of the item that the subject had produced when he or she encountered the item on its earlier occurrence. The specification that was established through the subject's earlier processing includes what that occurrence of the item was related to, that is, any special semantic associates promoted by the circumstances, any contextual correlates, and so on.

Jacoby believes that where recognition memory is concerned, processing by amnesics (he specifies Korsakoff patients) is more routine and automatic than that of normals. Amnesics might therefore be expected to use the respecification process less than normals and so fail to establish a unique specification with regard to the context of other characteristics of the episode. This failure would obviously limit the information amnesics have available to aid in remembering the target item.

Jacoby's experiments illustrate that when conditions limit the use of the respecification process, normal people behave like amnesics: They deny, in effect, that they remember even though other aspects of their behavior show unmistakably that learning had occurred. In other words, performance indicating prior experience can be separated from the normal subject's ability to acknowledge the prior experience.

The gist of Jacoby's experimental method is to show that presentation of a word can alter later perceptual identification (perceptual fluency) in spite of a low probability that that item will be recognized as having been presented previously. Perceptual fluency was indicated by how well the subject identified a word presented both very rapidly (with a duration of 35 msec) and with a source of visual masking. As another index of perceptual fluency in other experiments, Jacoby measured how well the subject solved an anagram the solution of which was the word that had flashed on the screen. The index of recognition memory was the subjects' report of whether they had or had not previously seen the target item. In all of these experiments the words to be remembered differed in the level of processing required by specific orienting questions. For some words these questions required that the subject deal with their semantic qualities; for others, that they deal only with orthographic characteristics. For items given lower levels of processing (the latter kind), recognition memory was relatively poor, but the index of perceptual fluency was as high for such items as for those processed more deeply. In other words, with low levels of processing, the normal subjects, like amnesics, showed evidence of learning in terms of perceptual fluency, but did not acknowledge verbally, in terms of the recognition task, that they had in fact previously seen that item.

Kolers (1976), also with normal subjects, reports an analogous result. Kolers based his procedure on the fact that reading speed increases when the material has previously been read. He had subjects return a full year after they had read specific material. He measured both their speed of reading the material and their verbal recognition as to whether or not they remembered having ever read it before. As expected, reading speed was enhanced by the prior experience, indicating some memory for the prior reading. More important for our purposes, this indication of a memory for prior reading occurred regardless of whether the subjects did or did not show in other ways that they had seen the material previously.

The point is that for each of three different kinds of tasks used by

Jacoby and by Kolers, dissociation in the expression of knowledge was established with normal humans in a manner analogous to that found with amnesic patients, albeit in less dramatic fashion.

5.6. Source Amnesia

Source amnesia occurs when particular knowledge is accessible to an individual but the origin of that knowledge is not. Although this term could in principle be used to describe the sort of dissociated expression described in the previous two sections, its use has usually been restricted to an effect of posthypnotic amnesia. The best operational definition of posthypnotic amnesia is still a debatable matter, but this is not the place to elaborate the issues (for reviews of posthypnotic amnesia, see Hilgard, 1977, or Kihlstrom & Evans, 1979). Fundamentally, when hypnotized subjects are given new information followed by the suggestion that it be forgotten, and if this information is actually found less accessible than would have been expected otherwise, we say that posthypnotic amnesia has occurred. Source amnesia is said to occur in this situation when the individual can recall the new information but not where it was learned (Evans & Thorn, 1966).

Huesmann, Dorst, and Gruder (1979, Experiment 1) report a study of posthypnotic amnesia that provides a relevant example of dissociated expression. By presenting a series of Luchins water jar problems, a problem-solving set was induced in subjects who either were or were not under hypnosis. Following induction of this set, the hypnotized subjects were given an amnesia suggestion, that is, told to forget about the problems they had been presented. Half of these subjects were then instructed so as to "release" the amnesia ("Now you can remember about the problems"). On the subsequent transfer test, the problem-solving set influenced solutions to the test problems for all subjects. But unlike other subjects, those who had been given the amnesia suggestion without the release instruction were quite unable to verbalize the nature of the problem-solving rule—a case of dissociated expression. (For further examples in this vein together with a theoretical analysis, see Chapter 2, this volume.)

5.7. Expression during Infancy

Dissociated expression in infant humans (or animals) can hardly be between verbal and nonverbal modes of expressing knowledge. Nevertheless there are many indications that what the infant knows is expressed differently at different points in development. One example is the way infant humans respond to the dimension of depth. Pipp and Haith (1977) assessed the depth perception of 1- and 2-month-old infants when they were presented raised, recessed, or flat white bars on a black field. For the 1-month-olds, sensitivity to the depth cues was clearest in terms of how frequently they fixated visually near the bars. For the 2-month-olds, however, recognition of depth was clearest in terms of the particular course or "style" they used in scanning the objects that were presented. What the infants knew about the bars was expressed differently at 1 month than at 2 months.

5.8. Infantile Amnesia

The selective expression of knowledge of specific childhood episodes is a basic example of our topic. The recovery of childhood memories has long been a subject of particular interest for clinicians (White & Pillemer, 1979) and biographers (see Salaman, 1970), and it has come under increasing scrutiny in the laboratory through the application of animal models (Campbell & Spear, 1972; Spear & Campbell, 1979). The focus of these investigations has been the phenomenon of "infantile amnesia," wherein memories of childhood seem more likely forgotten by adults than are memories of adulthood (with length of the retention interval equated). Such an effect need not be attributable to ineffective memory retrieval or to a failure in appropriate expression, although modes of expression certainly change ontogenetically. Instead, the effect could reflect absolute differences in the quality of the memory in storage (Spear, 1979). This point, however, remains debatable, as does the precise role of memory retrieval processes in the recovery of childhood compared to adult memories. Although infantile amnesia seems evident in a number of altricial species, one obstacle to understanding this area has been the paucity of knowledge about how human infants process memories. However, research programs have begun to address this problem with human infants as subjects. One of the more innovative and promising of these is described in Chapter 3.

5.9. Expression of Knowledge in Animals

In the experimental study of animal learning and memory, the problem of the expression of knowledge arises when considering how an animal's knowledge might be structured. If behavior were regulated in the fundamental stimulus–response sense indicated by the reflexive model that was once conventional in American psychology, the problem of expression would be solved merely by proper identification of the stimulus—a quite different state of affairs than seems to exist. The general point is that to consider the structure of knowledge, whether at the level of the individual memory and whether for animals or humans, is to consider the problem of expression. At a more specific and analytic level, systematic consideration of how animal subjects organize their representations of experimentally controlled events has increased (Grant, 1981; Honig, 1981; Wagner, 1981).

This issue is well illustrated in studies conducted by Adams and Dickinson (1981) to test whether memorial representations held by rats are primarily "declarative" or "procedural" in form. For a rat that has learned to press a lever to obtain food, for instance, a declarative representation would take the form, "Lever pressing caused food delivery"; the procedural representation would be, "When in the operant chamber, press the lever." It is significant for our purposes that the declarative type of representation would require a "knowledge–action translator" or "response operator" of the sort alluded to earlier in this chapter, whereas the procedural representation would incorporate expression in relatively inflexible fashion.

Because several chapters in this book refer to "habitual" behavior or relatively "automatic" expression of knowledge, it is worth noting that Adams and Dickinson obtained evidence for instrumental activities that correspond to each of the alternative types of representations. They found that an instrumental activity seemed sometimes based on a declarative representation and resultant "actions" derived from a relatively flexible disposition; on other occasions this same instrumental activity could take the form of a "habit," a relatively automatic activity fairly insensitive to local reinforcement conditions, reflecting the operation of a procedural representation. The general notion of such habitlike behavior emerging from seemingly autonomous expression of knowledge will arise again with humans as well as animals.

6. RETRIEVAL OF MEMORIES

A paradigm for studying the expression of knowledge is the experimental investigation of how retrieval of discrete memories is accomplished. The bulk of such investigation has dealt with singular events learned for the first time relatively recently, a few minutes or at most several days before their retrieval is required. These tests have characteristically included a particular arrangement of otherwise familiar materials-to-be-remembered that is for the most part specific to the experimental context in which they are learned. For instance, the subject must learn and remember that the nonsense syllable DAX (a new arrangement of familiar letters) is the correct response whenever the number 29 occurs, that the words TABLE, DOG, and APPLE were among the items presented in the second list, or that the first sentence in the story to be remembered was "The man ran swiftly across the bridge." These materials are context-specific in that DAX is not inevitably the correct thing to say when one sees 29, the words TABLE, DOG, and APPLE are not always grouped together, and the first sentence in every story does not involve a man crossing a bridge. The point is that such materials differ from such knowledge as "Columbus discovered America," "Snow is white," or "The square root of 64 is 8." Distinctions between these two kinds of knowledge have been drawn frequently (e.g., Bergson, 1911), but the analysis of the difference by Tulving (1972) has unquestionably had the greatest influence on contemporary studies of how humans process memories. It is convenient to use Tulving's terminology, labeling the former type of materials "episodic" and the latter "semantic."

Tulving (1972) presents a good argument for treating the episodic and semantic memory systems separately when we try to understand how humans retrieve memories (see also Chapter 2, this volume). These are of course interdependent systems, constantly interacting and probably in at least some sense quite inseparable. Yet evidence such as that summarized by Tulving suggests that we might expect differing principles for the expression of episodic compared to semantic knowledge, that we should not proceed with Ebbinghaus's original belief that we could study the learning and retrieval of sequential sets of ideas drawn largely from semantic memory by assessing how persons learn and remember a serial list of discrete verbal units. That is not to say that sets of discrete verbal units might not be a satisfactory prototype for much of the new learning in which humans engage, but only that the retrieval and expression of knowledge derived from semantic memory may be expected to be governed by different factors than those associated with episodic memory. Nor do we mean to deny that there are functional similarities in the retrieval of episodic and semantic memories. For example, presenting subjects with exemplars of a set of conceptually related items to be remembered can affect retrieval of other exemplars from either system (e.g., Freedman & Loftus, 1971; Macht & Spear, 1977). Pragmatically speaking, however, retrieval from semantic memory has received far less systematic study than that from episodic memory, so that we can neither claim much about their similarities or differences nor assert much of substance for our purposes concerning semantic memory. Our subsequent reference to memory retrieval, therefore, concerns memories of the episodic type.

How important is retrieval for the expression of knowledge? If all acquired knowledge were potentially available but its accessibility and implementation depended on its retrieval, the importance would be quite complete. But can we assume all information is available, or is some knowledge permanently lost? This, of course, is a classic problem for scholars concerned with remembering and forgetting. Note that what is in question is the fate of information that has in fact been acquired. The question is not whether everything that is noticed is learned, but whether everything learned following initial filtering by attentional mechanisms could conceivably be remembered later on. That the latter is not a preposterous alternative is suggested by the uncounted anecdotes of adults reporting the recall of (often trivial) incidents of their childhood when they revisit the neighborhood in which they were raised, or who find an unexpected fluency in their native language along with a flood of apparently forgotten childhood memories when they revisit their native country after a long absence. What is perhaps more convincing are the numerous systematic studies showing that for a variety of sources of forgetting, from brain trauma to retention intervals that encompass a large chunk of one's life, special circumstances to promote retrieval have shown that the forgetting is not at all permanent (e.g., Riccio & Ebner, 1981; Spear, 1971, 1978).

But in a larger sense it is fruitless to try to convince anyone that all acquired knowledge is forever available (for a negative view, see E. F. Loftus & G. R. Loftus, 1980). The null hypothesis that there is no difference between what is acquired and what can possibly be retrieved is obviously impossible to prove. The point to be made, nevertheless, is that we need a working alternative to the assumption that memories can indeed decay or be destroyed and lost forever. This assumption cannot be established directly but only when memories fail to be retrieved. As a consequence, a position holding all acquired knowledge to be potentially available would seem more viable (for further recent discussion of this ancient issue, see Miller & Marlin, 1979; Spear, 1976, 1978).

A more central consideration for the expression of knowledge might be how knowledge changes from that originally acquired, once it is expressed. When we are to express what we know about automobiles, do we acknowledge them as loud, shiny things with large dark seats inside and running boards outside that took us to grandpa's when we were 3, or as the "wheels" with unlimited ornamental variations and potential for freedom that we knew as a teen-ager, or what we now know as the inordinately expensive, poorly constructed pollutant that uses too much gasoline? That our memories may seem to change with experience is inevitable and increasingly documented systematically, even for episodic memories (e.g., E. F. Loftus, 1979). The question, of course, is whether all variations of a memory are potentially available or only the most recent one. Does the original trace survive in spite of its modifications? Our intention is not to attempt an answer nor even to review the systematic studies that may lead to one, but only to provide a reminder of the ageless but still pervasive issues relating the topic of memory retrieval to the expression of knowledge.

6.1. How Are Memories Retrieved?

The extensive scientific literature addressing this problem is reviewed in some of the references cited above. To be sure, a formula that prescribes the necessary and sufficient conditions for inevitable retrieval is not available. The most viable working principles toward establishing such a formula have derived from the ancient intuition that retrieval of a particular (episodic) memory is best promoted when the circumstances that accompanied the acquisition of that memory are most closely matched. The most systematic extrapolation of this generalization to the modern study of human memory has undoubtedly been that of Tulving (e.g., Tulving, 1972, 1976, 1979) in terms of his "principle of encoding specificity."

This principle states that "what is stored is determined by what is perceived and how it is encoded, and what is stored determines what retrieval cues are effective in providing access to what is stored" (Tulving & Thompson, 1973, p. 353), and further "only that can be retrieved that has been stored, and . . . how it can be retrieved depends on how it was stored" (p. 359). In other words, cues responsible for memory retrieval are effective if and only if representation of them was encoded and stored originally, together with the target memory. According to this principle, the effectiveness of treatments that promote memory retrieval does not depend on their absolute properties but instead on their relationship with what was encoded and stored originally to represent the particular episode. Striking support for this contention has been obtained (e.g., Tulving, 1979). It is in one sense a strong form of the classic generalization that the more similar are the circumstances that comprise the episode originally learned and those present when memory retrieval is required, the more likely will the memory be retrieved. This general view has in some contexts permitted integration of a good deal of diverse evidence (Spear, 1971, 1978), and application of the principle of encoding specificity in the field of human memory has touched some of the most basic controversies (Tulving, 1979; Tulving & Watkins, 1975).

The foregoing considerations focus on when memory retrieval is effective and when it is not. What has not been addressed is the possibility that the retrieval process might itself vary in its functioning in spite of the presence of retrieval cues that might otherwise be sufficient to promote retrieval. It is to be expected that retrieval failure could be due to deficiencies in the retrieval *process* caused by aberrations in the central nervous system, independently of their effect on an organism's receipt and interpretation of potential retrieval cues, although for this topic there are relatively few hard facts.

The domain of memory retrieval as a determinant of behavior is theoretically huge, almost as encompassing as the expression of knowledge in general. Many studies of what determines memory retrieval have been conducted, some with animal subjects and others with humans. The considerable number of recent reviews on the data and theoretical issues pertaining to memory retrieval preclude, however, a need for extensive discussion of them here (e.g., Miller & Marlin, 1979; Spear, 1976, 1978, 1981; Spear & Mueller, 1982).

Two fundamental observations about memory retrieval can be stated simply. First, for both human and animal subjects, a variety of treatments have been found to enhance retention when presented just before or concurrent with a retention test. For animal subjects in particular, it is established that the effect of the pretest treatments is explicitly to alleviate "forgetting" in a broad sense, including that induced by such diverse sources as brain trauma from electroconvulsive shock or drugs, a long retention interval, or retroactive or proactive interference. We mentioned earlier that it is unclear precisely what it is about these treatments that is necessary or sufficient for the promotion of memory retrieval. Generally, however, it seems important that such treatments correspond in some manner to one or more of the events that made up the episode-to-be-remembered.

A second observation has indicated the value of a still sharper focus on the interaction between the circumstances of the original learning and those of the later test. This interaction may be the most important determinant of the expression of memory for specific episodes. The expression of learning may be more dependent on the relationship between the circumstances of learning and testing than on variables supposed to strengthen memory storage itself. There are good indications to that effect in the learning and memory of both humans (Tulving, 1979) and animals (Spear, 1981). To assert in such strong form that the expression of learning depends on the similarity between the conditions of training and those of testing is a significantly different orientation than has prevailed in the experimental study of conditioning and learning. The traditional assumption, most often only implicit, has been that the effects of training conditions on conditioning and learning are absolute and, provided the test occurs relatively soon thereafter, these conditions fully determine the likelihood that the learning will be expressed. It has been assumed, for instance, that if the conditioned stimulus is sufficiently intense and noticed by the subject, if the unconditioned stimulus is sufficient in quantity and quality and appropriate to the subject's motivation, if the contingency between the CS and UCS is appropriate, and so on, then learning will occur and its expression will be manifested in proportion to the values of these parameters. A quite different picture is suggested by the emphasis on the interaction between the conditions of learning and testing—between those of storage and of retrieval of the memory. It implies, for instance, that classical variables such as stimulus intensity or reward magnitude, and basic conditioning phenomena such as overshadowing and blocking may not have their effect solely at the time of initial learning and do not determine "memory strength" in an absolute sense. Instead, their effects are fully mediated by an interaction between the conditions of memory storage and those of retrieval (Spear, 1981).

6.2. Process Interference: Summary

The retrieval of memories depends, in important and unexpected ways, on how similar the prevailing circumstances are to those when the memories were acquired. This principle is of interest here because in one sense, tests of the retrieval of episodic memories within this framework provide a paradigmatic case for the expression of knowledge.

Suppose that animals or humans learn something in the laboratory and then are asked to remember it under quite different circumstances—a different room, among a group of people rather than alone, with a different experimenter, at a different time of day, and so on. We can be sure that because of this change, the individual will be less effective in expressing what was learned. Some of the reasons may be trivial for our present topic: that the individual simply fails to notice that a particular stimulus is presented; that a particular stimulus actually looks or sounds different than before; or that the subject fails to realize that the same "rules" apply here as when the original learning took place.

We begin to make substantive contact with the general problem of the expression of knowledge, however, when we consider some other reasons why learning is less likely exhibited under new circumstances. With retrieval circumstances different from those of learning, stimuli that otherwise might have helped promote retrieval of the original memory may be gone. Also, new stimulus events might promote retrieval of conflicting memories that interfere with the retrieval and expression of the critical learning. Either of these factors might also apply in a general sense to the expression of knowledge.

But there is another possible factor, more general in its implications but less studied empirically: namely, competition between the *process* of retrieving past memories and that of attending to and learning new ones. We may term this factor "process interference." We can reasonably assume that there is a limit to one's momentary capacity for cognitive activity in general. When old memories are to be retrieved and new ones acquired simultaneously, cognitive activity must be divided, perhaps leading to an inadequate allocation for completely effective retrieval. Although it is unclear what role, if any, this factor actually has for determining the retrieval of memories for specific episodes, process competition might provide a useful construct for the understanding of the expression of knowledge generally. We shall return to this notion in Chapter 11.

7. REFERENCES

Adams, C., & Dickinson, A. Actions and habits: Variation in associative representations during instrumental learning. In N. E. Spear & R. R. Miller (Eds.), *Information processing in animals: Memory mechanisms*. Hillsdale, N.J.: Lawrence Erlbaum, 1981.

Atkinson, R. C., & Shiffrin, R. M. Human memory: A proposed system and its control processes. In K. W. Spence & J. T. Spence (Eds.), *The psychology of learning and motivation* (Vol. 2). New York: Academic Press, 1968.

Balota, D. A., & Neely, J. H. Test-expectancy and word-frequency effects in recall and recognition. *Journal of Experimental Psychology: Human Learning and Memory*, 1980, 6, 576–587.

Bellezza, F. S., Geiselman, R. E., & Aronovsky, L. A. Eye movements under different rehearsal strategies. *Journal of Experimental Psychology: Human Learning and Memory*, 1975, 1, 673–679.

Bergson, H. *Matter and memory*. (N. M. Paul & W. S. Palmer, trans.). New York: Macmillan, 1911.

Brown, R., & McNeill, D. The "tip of the tongue" phenomenon. *Journal of Verbal Learning and Verbal Behavior*, 1966, 5, 325–337.

Campbell, B. A., & Spear, N. E. Ontogeny of memory. *Psychological Review*, 1972, 79, 215–236.

Crowder, R. G. *Principles of learning and memory*. Hillsdale, N.J.: Lawrence Erlbaum, 1976.

Ericsson, K. A., & Simon, H. A. Verbal reports as data. *Psychological Review*, 1980, 87, 215–251.

Evans, F. J., & Thorn, W. A. Two types of post-hypnotic amnesia: Recall amnesia and source amnesia. *International Journal of Clinical and Experimental Hypnosis*, 1966, 14, 162–179.

Freedman, J. L., & Landauer, T. K. Retrieval of long-term memory: "Tip of the tongue" phenomenon. *Psychonomic Science*, 1966, 4, 309–310.

Freedman, J. L., & Loftus, E. F. Retrieval of words from long-term memory. *Journal of Verbal Learning and Verbal Behavior*, 1971, 10, 107–115.

Grant, D. S. Short-term memory in the pigeon. In N. E. Spear & R. R. Miller (Eds.), *Information processing in animals: Memory mechanisms*. Hillsdale, N.J.: Lawrence Erlbaum, 1981.

Hart, J. T. Memory and the feeling-of-knowing experience. *Journal of Educational Psychology*, 1965, 56, 208–216.

Hilgard, E. R. *Divided consciousness: Multiple controls in human thought and action*. New York: Wiley, 1977.

Honing, W. K. Working memory in the temporal map. In N. E. Spear & R. R. Miller (Eds.), *Information processing in animals: Memory mechanisms.* Hillsdale, N.J.: Lawrence Erlbaum, 1981.

Huesmann, L. R., Dorst, G., & Gruder, C. L. *Inhibition of output in post-hypnotic amnesia.* Paper presented at the meeting of the Psychonomic Society, Phoenix, November 1979.

Jacoby, L. L. Test appropriate strategies in retention of categorized lists. *Journal of Verbal Learning and Verbal Behavior,* 1973, *12,* 675–682.

Jacoby, L. L. Some parallels between the behavior of Korsakoff patients and normals. In L. A. Cermak (Ed.), *Human memory and amnesia.* Hillsdale, N.J.: Lawrence Erlbaum, 1981.

Johnson, M. K., & Raye, C. L. Reality monitoring. *Psychological Review,* 1981, *88,* 67–85.

Keating, E. G. Residual spatial vision in the monkey after removal of striate and preoccipital cortex. *Brain Research,* 1980, *187,* 271–290.

Kihlstrom, J. F., & Evans, F. J. Memory retrieval processes during posthypnotic amnesia. In J. F. Kihlstrom & F. J. Evans (Eds.), *Functional disorders of memory.* Hillsdale, N.J.: Lawrence Erlbaum, 1979.

Kinsbourne, M., & Wood, F. Short-term memory processes in the amnesic syndrome. In D. Deutsch & J. A. Deutsch (Eds.), *Short-term memory.* New York: Academic Press, 1975.

Kolers, P. A. Reading a year later. *Journal of Experimental Psychology: Human Learning and Memory,* 1976, *2,* 554–565.

Kohnstamm, O. Über das Krankheitsbild der retro- und anterograden Amnesie und die Unterscheidung des spontanen und des lernenden Merkens. *Zeitschrift für Neurologie und Psychiatrie,* 1917, *41.*

Loftus, E. F. The malleability of human memory. *American Scientist,* 1979, *67,* 312–320.

Loftus, E. F., & Loftus, G. R. On the permanence of stored information in the human brain. *American Psychologist,* 1980, *35,* 409–420.

Luria, A. R. *The neuropsychology of memory.* New York: Wiley, 1976.

Macht, M. L., & Spear, N. E. Priming effects in episodic memory. *Journal of Experimental Psychology: Human Learning and Memory,* 1977, *3,* 333–341.

Mazuryk, G. F. Positive recency in final free recall. *Journal of Experimental Psychology,* 1974, *103,* 812–813.

Miller, R. R., & Marlin, N. A. Amnesia following electroconvulsive shock. In J. F. Kihlstrom & F. J. Evans (Eds.), *Functional disorders of memory.* Hillsdale, N.J.: Lawrence Erlbaum, 1979.

Milner, B. Memory disturbance after bilateral hippocampal lesions. In P. M. Milner & S. Glickman (Eds.), *Cognitive processes and the brain.* Princeton, N.J.: Van Nostrand, 1965. (Originally published, 1962.)

Milner, B., Corkin, S., & Teuber, H. L. Further analysis of the hippocampal-amnesic syndrome: Fourteen-year follow-up of H. M. *Neuropsychologia,* 1968, *6,* 215–234.

Nisbett, R. E., & Wilson, T. D. Telling more than we can know: Verbal reports on mental processes. *Psychological Review,* 1977, *84,* 231–259.

Pipp, S. L., & Haith, M. M. Infant visual scanning of two- and three-dimensional forms. *Child Development,* 1977, *48,* 1640–1644.

Riccio, D. C., & Ebner, D. L. Post-acquisition modifications of memory. In N. E. Spear & R. R. Miller (Eds.), *Information processing in animals: Memory mechanisms.* Hillsdale, N.J.: Lawrence Erlbaum, 1981.

Robin, E. D. The evolutionary advantages of being stupid. *Perspectives in Biology and Medicine,* 1973, *16,* 369–380.

Salaman, E. *A collection of moments.* London: Longman, 1970.

Sidman, M., Stoddard, L. T., & Mohr, J. P. Some additional quantitative observations of immediate memory in a patient with bilateral hippocampal lesions. *Neuropsychologia*, 1968, 6, 245–254.

Smith, S. M. Remembering in and out of context. *Journal of Experimental Psychology: Human Learning and Memory*, 1979, 5, 460–471.

Spear, N. E. Forgetting as a retrieval failure. In W. K. Honig & P. H. R. James (Eds.), *Animal memory*. New York: Academic Press, 1971.

Spear, N. E. Retrieval of memories. In W. K. Estes (Ed.), *Handbook of learning and cognitive processes. Vol. 4. Attention and memory*. Hillsdale, N.J.: Lawrence Erlbaum, 1976.

Spear, N. E. *The Processing of memories: Forgetting and retention*. Hillsdale, N.J.: Lawrence Erlbaum, 1978.

Spear, N. E. Memory storage factors leading to infantile amnesia. In G. H. Bower (Ed.), *The psychology of learning and motivation* (Vol. 13). New York: Academic Press, 1979.

Spear, N. E. Extending the domain of memory retrieval. In N. E. Spear & R. R. Miller (Eds.), *Information processing in animals: Memory mechanisms*. Hillsdale, N.J.: Lawrence Erlbaum, 1981.

Spear, N. E., & Campbell, B. A. (Eds.). *Ontogeny of learning and memory*. Hillsdale, N.J.: Lawrence Erlbaum, 1979.

Spear, N. E., & Mueller, C. On the meaning of consolidation during storage and retrieval. In H. Weingartner & E. S. Parker (Eds.), *Memory consolidation: Towards the psychobiology of cognition*. Hillsdale, N.J.: Lawrence Erlbaum, in press.

Starr, A., & Phillips, L. Verbal and motor memory in the amnesic syndrome. *Neuropsychologia*, 1970, 8, 75–88.

Tulving, E. Episodic and semantic memory. In E. Tulving & W. Donaldson (Eds.), *Organization of memory*. New York: Academic Press, 1972.

Tulving, E. Ecphoric processes in recall and recognition. In J. Brown (Ed.), *Recall and recognition*. London: Wiley, 1976.

Tulving, E. Relation between encoding specificity and levels of processing. In L. S. Cermak & F. I. M. Craik (Eds.), *Levels of processing in human memory*. New York: Wiley, 1979.

Tulving, E., & Thomson, D. M. Encoding specificity in retrieval processes in episodic memory. *Psychological Review*, 1973, 80, 352–357.

Tulving, E., & Watkins, M. J. Structure of memory traces. *Psychological Review*, 1975, 82, 261–275.

Underwood, B. J. The representativeness of rote verbal learning. In A. W. Melton (Ed.), *Categories of human learning*. New York: Academic Press, 1964.

Underwood, B. J. Attributes of memory. *Psychological Review*, 1969, 76, 559–573.

Wagner, A. R. SOP: A model of automatic memory processing in animal behavior. In. N. E. Spear & R. R. Miller (Eds.), *Information processing in animals: Memory mechanisms*. Hillsdale, N.J.: Lawrence Erlbaum, 1981.

Watkins, M. J., & Watkins, O. C. Processing of recency items for free recall. *Journal of Experimental Psychology*, 1974, 102, 488–493.

Webster's New World Dictionary of the American Language (Second College Edition). Cleveland, Ohio: William Collins & World Publishing Co., 1978.

Weiskrantz, L. A comparison of hippocampal pathology in man and other animals. In *Functions of the septo-hippocampal system* (CIBA Foundation Symposium No. 58). The Netherlands: Elsevier, 1978.

Weiskrantz, L. Varieties of residual experience. *Quarterly Journal of Experimental Psychology*, 1980, 32, 365–386.

Weiskrantz, L., & Warrington, E. K. Conditioning in amnesic patients. *Neuropsychologia*, 1979, 17, 187–194.

Weiskrantz, L., Warrington, E. K., Sanders, M. D., & Marshall, J. Visual capacity in the hemianopic field following a restricted occipital oblation. *Brain*, 1974, *97*, 709–728.

White, S. H., & Pillemer, D. B. Childhood amnesia and the development of a socially accessible memory system. In J. F. Kihlstrom & F. J. Evans (Eds.), *Functional disorders of memory*. Hillsdale, N.J.: Lawrence Erlbaum, 1979.

2

Memory, Amnesia, and the Episodic/Semantic Distinction

Daniel L. Schacter and Endel Tulving

1. INTRODUCTION

Imagine that our present civilization develops more or less peacefully and that the world is still intact a thousand years from now. Imagine further that you could visit the future world and bring back with you, among other things, the answer to one crucial question about human memory. What would be the question, and why?

Choosing "crucial" questions in any area of a developing science such as psychology is both easy and difficult. It is easy because crucial questions seem to abound; they are readily perceived anywhere and everywhere. Most contemporary students could rather easily make up a long list of apparently critical questions. The choice would be difficult, however, if it had to be guided by consensus. At present there is little agreement among practitioners as to what questions are important. In the discipline itself it is difficult to discern compelling, permanent developments that clearly point to a particular future. Today's crucial questions have a disconcerting habit of turning into tomorrow's historical curiosities. The time-traveler runs a real risk of disappointment at finding that his or her crucial question is meaningless to future generations.

DANIEL L. SCHACTER AND ENDEL TULVING • Department of Psychology, University of Toronto, Toronto, Ontario, Canada M5S, 1A1. This chapter was supported by a Special Research Program Grant from the Connaught Fund, University of Toronto, by an Ontario Graduate Fellowship to D. L. Schacter, and by the Natural Sciences and Engineering Research Council of Canada Grant No. A8632 to E. Tulving.

But science has always been a risky business; the possibility that the questions we ask are meaningless with respect to future developments should not deter us from taking a chance. The self-correcting nature of the enterprise guarantees that our mistakes of posing wrong questions will have no permanent effects. That is why we feel free to discuss one "crucial" question concerning human memory.

Our question has to do with the subdivisions of human memory. We assume, along with most other students of the subject, that memory is not a monolithic, unitary entity and that what we label memory in fact represents a number of separate but interacting systems. All these systems have a common function: They make possible the utilization of acquired and retained knowledge. It is their differences that are the subject of our crucial question: How can we characterize the various systems that comprise human memory?

The question implies, as well as leads to, others. How are the systems related to one another? How and to what extent do they interact? How are they similar to and how do they differ from the memory systems of other organisms and intelligent machines? What is the sequence of their development? To what extent do they serve strictly separate functions and to what extent can one substitute for another? All these and other related questions, too, can be regarded as critical to our understanding of memory. But they could not be raised unless we raise the first one concerning the nature of the systems; hence our present choice.

In this chapter we shall discuss the current status of one distinction between different memory systems—namely, the distinction between episodic and semantic memory. Our discussion will draw on observations of dissociations in memory function in individuals rendered amnesic through brain damage, hypnosis, or other, as yet little understood, psychological factors. The dissociations take the form of particular patterns of impaired and preserved abilities and skills of acquiring and subsequently utilizing new information or knowledge. We shall focus on data gathered in studies of pathological, rather than normal, populations because these data rather clearly—and sometimes dramatically—suggest the need for extending and revising the constructs of episodic and semantic memory.

2. EPISODIC AND SEMANTIC MEMORY

In speculations about the varieties of knowledge handled by human memory, the dichotomy between knowledge of personally experienced events and knowledge of the world at large has a long history. William James (1890), in presenting the distilled wisdom of a long series of keen observers of human nature, distinguishes between associations among ideas and memories of a person's own past as separate psychological phenomena. Henri Bergson (1911) also argues for the distinction between personal recollections of specific events and automatic or habitual memories that are built up through repetition. Reiff and Scheerer (1959) discuss in some detail the difference between *remembrances* and *memoria*. Remembrances are contextually specific memories for personally experienced events, and according to Reiff and Scheerer "are always accompanied by the experience of personal continuity through time . . . what is remembered is always experienced as 'being in my past'" (p. 25). Memoria, which include general knowledge of the world as well as habits and skills, lack this quality of self-reference. Schachtel (1947) argues for a separation of autobiographical and practical memory; Nielsen (1958) distinguishes between temporal and categorical memory; and Piaget and Inhelder (1973) contend that "memory in the strict sense" (autobiographical memory) should be demarcated from "memory in the wider sense" (general knowledge and skills).

The distinction between personal memories and general knowledge was brought into the focus of the experimental psychology of memory by the creation of a new field of study concerned with *semantic* memory (Quillian, 1968). The contrast between semantic memory and the kind that had been studied by psychologists since the time of Ebbinghaus (1885/1964) was in many ways similar to the earlier philosophical and psychiatric distinctions between personal and general memories. The two kinds of memory are discussed by Tulving (1972), who adopted the term "semantic" memory from Quillian and the term "episodic" memory from Munsat (1966).

According to Tulving's (1972) initial formulation, episodic memory is concerned with knowledge about a person's own past experiences, whereas semantic memory handles knowledge of language and what it represents, as well as knowledge of facts, concepts, and rules of various kinds. Episodic memories are unique to the individual; semantic memories may be shared by many. Episodic memories are "located" in particular places and "dated" at particular times: A person remembers doing something, there and then. Semantic memories are timeless and spaceless: If a person knows that Caesar crossed the Rubicon in 49 B.C., his or her *knowledge* (memory of the fact learned on an earlier occasion) does not have any temporal and spatial referents, although the statement itself refers to a particular dated event. Episodic memories are always embedded in a more or less rich, concrete context of other remembrances; semantic memories are related to other semantic memories but their truth value does not depend on any particular context. Finally, episodic memories are autobiographical, that is, they refer to a person's own past; an organism could not have any episodic memories if it was not aware of its personal identity and its continuity through space and time. Semantic memories, on the other hand, are generic; there is no necessary connection between a bit of semantic memory and the awareness of its relation to self. (By this criterion, computers could have semantic memories but not episodic ones.)

Despite the somewhat awkward terms and the somewhat uncertain status of the concepts, the distinction between episodic and semantic memory has become very popular. The strong philosophical flavor of the characterization of the two systems has not discouraged many people, not only in psychology but also in other fields, from adopting the distinction, at least for heuristic purposes (e.g., Berch, 1979; Eysenck, 1975; Hannigan, Shelton, Franks, & Bransford, 1980; Johnson, Klinger, & Williams, 1977; Kihlstrom, 1980; Kinsbourne & Wood, 1975; Nelson & Brown, 1978; Petrey, 1977; P. N. Russell & Beekhuis, 1976). A number of investigators have gone beyond this use of the distinction and have sought to establish the separate existence of the two memory systems in an empirically bound, functional sense (Herrmann & Harwood, 1980; Herrmann & McLaughlin, 1973; Moeser, 1976; Shoben, Wescourt, & Smith, 1978; Wood, Taylor, Penny, & Stump, 1980). And there have been critics who have argued against any need for a distinction between episodic and semantic memory, preferring what they regard as a more parsimonious view of unitary memory (e.g., Anderson & Ross, 1980; McKoon & Ratcliff, 1979; Muter, 1978).

Along with many other students of memory, we believe that the episodic/semantic distinction is a useful one. However, we also regard the initial formulation of the distinction (Tulving, 1972) as a beginning, and incomplete attempt to construct a taxonomy of memory systems. Accordingly, our major purpose in this chapter is to delineate and discuss some phenomena that are not easily accommodated by the distinction in its current form, with the hope that such discussion will help point the way to a more satisfactory taxonomy of memory systems.

Our discussion will be divided into three major sections, each concerned with observations of dissociations in memory function in one of three types of amnesia. First, we shall consider studies of amnesic syndromes that are due to various kinds of organic brain damage. Second, we shall discuss experiments in which amnesia is induced by hypnosis. Third, we shall consider observations made in cases of *functional* amnesia, in which memory disturbances appear after psychological trauma. We shall attempt to show how the patterns of impaired and preserved memory function observed in each type of amnesia suggest the need for revisions of the episodic/semantic distinction. Furthermore, we shall argue that the dissociations observed in the three kinds of amnesia are, in several respects, similar to one another.

3. ORGANIC AMNESIA

Both clinical and experimental studies of the organic amnesic syndrome have yielded data that bear on the episodic/semantic distinction. The amnesic syndrome can arise consequent to a variety of neurological malfunctions, including Korsakoff's syndrome, encephalitis, gas poisoning, closed-head injury, lesions of the medial temporal lobes, and Huntington's disease. The major clinical features of the amnesic syndrome, which have been thoroughly described in the literature (e.g., Grünthal, 1923; Korsakoff, 1889; Störring, 1931; Zangwill, 1946), are consistently observed from patient to patient. Amnesics' verbal skills are preserved, there is little impairment of general intelligence, they can adequately answer questions that tap their knowledge of the world, and their perceptual abilities and immediate memory are relatively unimpaired. However, these same patients demonstrate a striking inability to remember their recent personal experiences. Amnesics may not recall having met someone only minutes after seeing them, frequently fail to recognize physicians who have been treating them for months, and are often disoriented as to time and place.

It is possible to describe this general pattern of deficit as a selective impairment of episodic memory: In the amnesic syndrome, episodic memory is more severely affected than semantic memory. Some early clinical students of amnesia noted precisely this feature of the syndrome (Claparède, 1911/1951; Korsakoff, 1889), and more recent theorists, based on experimental as well as clinical observations, have argued that the amnesic syndrome represents a selective impairment of episodic memory (Kinsbourne, 1982; Kinsbourne & Wood, 1975; Rozin, 1976; Schacter & Tulving, 1982; Wood & Ebert, 1982). We shall now consider in some detail the pertinent evidence. We shall begin by discussing studies that have demonstrated retention of certain kinds of recently acquired information by amnesic patients, and then consider experiments that have provided evidence that amnesics can acquire a variety of skills much in the manner of normals. We shall then discuss some implications for the episodic/semantic distinction.

3.1. Retention of Recently Acquired Information

Let us first consider some clinical observations reported by the Swiss psychiatrist Claparède (1911/1951). Claparède's patient was a 47-year-old woman suffering from Korsakoff's syndrome. This patient presented a clinical picture entirely consistent with the conceptualization of amnesia as a selective impairment of episodic memory. She did not recognize the doctors who daily treated her, and forgot "from one minute to the next what she had been told" (p. 68); yet she could readily retrieve well-learned facts and adequately perform mental calculations. Claparède, however, was able to show that this patient could acquire and retain some information from a learning episode, even though she had no memory for the episode itself.

> When one told her a little story, read to her various items from a newspaper, three minutes later she remembered nothing, not even the fact that someone had read to her; but with certain questions one could elicit in a reflex fashion some of the details of those items. But when she found these details in her consciousness, she did not recognize them as memories but believed them to be something "that went through her mind" by chance, an idea she had "without knowing why," a product of her imagination of the moment, or even the result of reflection. (p. 69)

Claparède observed a similar phenomenon after pricking his patient with a pin hidden in his hand. When he again motioned toward her, the patient reflexively withdrew her hand. Claparède asked her why she did so, and she conjectured, "Is there perhaps a pin hidden in your hand?" (p. 69). When Claparède asked her why she thought he might have a pin hidden in his hand, she claimed that it was "an idea that went through my mind" (p. 70), and further suggested that "sometimes pins are hidden in people's hands" (p. 70). Although this patient retained some information about Claparède's behavior, she did not remember the episode in which she acquired it.

Observations reported by MacCurdy (1929) resemble those of Claparède. MacCurdy taught Korsakoff patients his full name and address; the patients failed to recall this information just minutes later. He then presented them with a series of 10 first names, 10 surnames, 10 street numbers, and 10 street names, and asked patients to "guess" which ones were his:

> To my surprise, the guesses were nearly as accurate as would be the conscious memory for such data of normal subjects. But the response remained to the subject a sheer guess, it was associated with no feeling of me-ness; on no occasion did the patient think that he had the slightest reason for picking one name rather than another from the list. (p. 121)

Weiskrantz and Warrington (1979) recently observed similar phenomena. These investigators studied the development of a classically conditioned response in amnesic subjects, using a compound auditory and visual signal as a conditioned stimulus and an air puff as the unconditioned stimulus. They assessed conditioning by measuring subjects' eyeblink latency at both 10-minute and 24-hour retention intervals. Weiskrantz and Warrington found that two severely amnesic patients showed evidence of conditioning at both retention intervals. However, when questioned during the delayed-retention sessions, these subjects expressed no memory for the events of the first conditioning sessions, although these events clearly affected their subsequent behavior;

Weiskrantz and Warrington observed that the amnesics did not even recognize the conditioning apparatus. Indeed, the sole reference to the air puff was made by a patient who claimed that he "had a weak right eye because someone had once blown some air into it" (p. 192).

Another example of amnesics' ability to retain information imparted to them during a learning episode, without conscious memory of the episode, is found in a case study of *source amnesia* that we recently completed (Schacter, Tulving, & Wang, 1981). Source amnesia occurs when subjects can retain an acquired fact without memory of how or when they learned it (e.g., Evans & Thorn, 1966). We developed two tasks for the investigation of source amnesia, and employed them in the study of a 34-year-old man (E. R.) who had developed amnesic symptoms after closed-head injury.

One of our tasks tapped the ability to retain newly acquired facts. The patient was asked a series of difficult questions about little-known facts and instructed to select an answer from five alternatives. For instance, the patient was asked, "Who holds the world's record for shaking hands?" and subsequently presented with the correct answer (Theodore Roosevelt) interspersed with four distractor items (Richard Nixon, Jimmy Carter, Woodrow Wilson, and Abraham Lincoln). When the patient selected the correct answer to a question, the item was eliminated from further consideration and a new question was substituted for it in the text. When an incorrect answer was selected, the experimenter informed the patient of the correct choice. Following a 20-minute interval, the patient was again asked all the questions that he answered incorrectly on the first pass, and was instructed to choose among the same five alternative responses. In addition, he was asked an equal number of new questions. After the patient chose an answer, the experimenter inquired about the source of the information by asking, "How do you know that?"

E. R. responded correctly to many of the questions that he had been asked, but had answered incorrectly, during acquisition. In contrast, the patient's performance on items that were presented for the first time during the test phase was at the chance level. These data suggest that E. R. was capable of acquiring, retaining, and utilizing some of the information imparted to him by the experimenter. However, E. R. was consistently unable to state accurately where or how he had acquired the new facts. He typically insisted that he knew a fact because he "read about it somewhere," "heard some people talking about it just recently," or because "my sister once told me about it." A 21-year-old hospitalized control subject with minor closed-head injury, matched for IQ and educational background, was able to retain the experimentally acquired facts and also to state accurately where he acquired them.

A second experimental task yielded a similar pattern of data. The patient viewed and described a series of photographs. After presentation of each photograph the experimenter related a bizarre story about it that would not be inferred from uninstructed viewing. Following a 20-minute delay, the patient was shown all of the previously presented photographs intermixed with an equal number of new ones. The patient's task was to select an appropriate title for each photograph from three alternatives. Two of these alternatives reflected the obvious physical characteristics of the picture; one of them reflected the theme of the unusual story associated with it. After the patient selected a title, he was asked why he chose it.

E. R. demonstrated a marked bias for choosing unusual titles when shown a photograph about which he had earlier been told the story, selecting the unusual title for a majority of the previously presented items. He demonstrated no such bias when selecting titles for new photographs; in fact, E. R. chose only one bizarre title for the 18 new pictures. However, the patient was frequently unable to report why he selected the unusual title, and typically insisted that "it just seemed right." For instance, when shown a picture of a man standing on a farm in front of his home and told that the man was a fugitive criminal, the patient later selected the title "Hiding from the Law" in preference to "Harvest Time on the Farm" or "A Man and His Home." Asked to state why, the patient could only suggest that "it looks like he's doing that [hiding from justice]." The control subject also selected many of the unusual titles, but in each case was able to state accurately why he did so.

Amnesics have shown an ability to retain experimenter-provided information, with impaired memory for when and where they acquired it, in other experimental situations. Experiment 2 of a study by Huppert and Piercy (1976) provides relevant data. Huppert and Piercy examined Korsakoff patients' recognition of familiar and unfamiliar pictures. Familiarity was manipulated by exposing subjects to a series of pictures in a training session. The following day the subjects studied a second set of pictures; half had been shown to them the previous day (familiar), and half had not (unfamiliar). Subjects' recognition memory was tested on the second day by asking them to indicate which picture they had seen during the *experimental* (vs. the training) session. An equal number of targets and lures were tested; half the lures were entirely new pictures, and half had been shown during the training session.

Huppert and Piercy found that Korsakoff patients, in comparison with alcoholic controls, displayed a greater tendency to say yes to familiar pictures than to unfamiliar pictures. That is, there was a significant interaction between patient groups and familiarity of material. Thus Korsakoff patients said yes to familiar lures (pictures they had seen during the training session but not during the experimental session) almost as often as they said yes to unfamiliar targets (pictures they had been exposed to only during the experimental session). Control subjects, in contrast, rarely said yes to familiar lures. These data suggest that Korsakoff patients' retention of information about the pictures' occurrence in *either* of the two sessions was relatively unimpaired, but their retention of information about the temporal context in which pictures occurred was severely impaired.

Owen and Williams (1980) report similar data using a somewhat different paradigm. They presented amnesic and control subjects with pictures of common and rare objects. Subjects were tested with sentence-frame cues that elicited the name of a target object, or an object that had not been experimentally presented, with a normative frequency of 90%. Subjects were asked to indicate, for each item generated, whether they remembered seeing a picture of the item on the experimental list. Owen and Williams found that amnesic patients experienced significantly greater difficulty distinguishing between new and old *common* objects than between new and old *rare* objects: The amnesics stated that pictures of almost all of the common objects had earlier been shown to them. Control subjects performed equally well in both cases. Thus amnesics' performance was controlled by preexperimental familiarity of the objects, rather than by contextual features of the study and test situations. Although the amnesics recalled nearly as many common objects as the controls, they could not remember the context in which the objects had occurred.

A series of important experiments by Warrington and Weiskrantz (1968, 1970, 1974) also contain relevant data. Warrington and Weiskrantz presented amnesic and control subjects with lists of common words and then probed their knowledge of these words with two different tests: (1) a yes/no recognition test in which subjects indicated which of a series of test items they *remembered* from the study session; and (2) a cued-recall test in which subjects were provided initial-letter fragments of list items and asked to try to *identify* the word. Although amnesics were severely impaired on the yes/no recognition test compared to controls, they performed as well as, and in some cases better than, control subjects on the fragmented-word prediction task. Amnesics' memory for the words they had studied during the learning episode was impaired, but they were able to use information acquired during the episode to successfully complete the fragment cues.

3.2. Acquisition and Retention of Skills

Some of the earliest evidence that amnesic patients are capable of new learning was provided by studies exploring acquisition and retention of motor skills. Milner (1962/1965), for instance, reports evidence of motor skill learning by the well-known amnesic patient H. M. Milner's observations were confirmed and extended in subsequent studies of H. M. by Corkin (1965, 1968), Milner (1970), and Milner, Corkin, and Teuber (1968). These investigators report that H. M. was able to improve his performance across trials on a variety of motor tasks, including pursuit rotor, mirror drawing, and maze learning. However, they also note that on each new trial H. M. failed to remember what happened on the previous trial: He had no episodic memory for the events that affected his motor skill performance. Similar observations were made by Starr and Phillips (1970) in their study of a densely amnesic encephalitis patient. This patient was successfully taught to play a new piece of music on the piano. On the following day he was able to play the piece by heart, but he did not remember the episode in which he learned it.

More recent evidence indicates that amnesics are capable of acquiring and retaining knowledge of a somewhat different nature. We shall refer to these kinds of knowledge as "cognitive skills": organized sets of procedures and operations that are used to perceive and encode information, formulate rules, and solve problems (Kolers, 1975). Kinsbourne and Wood (1975), for instance, report that they were able to teach amnesic subjects the Fibonacci rule (a rule for generating numbers with specified properties). Their patients showed substantial savings when they relearned the rule after a retention interval, but could not remember having previously performed the task. Brooks and Baddeley (1976) found that amnesic subjects were able to reassemble a jigsaw puzzle, and to arrange words into sentences, faster on the second trial than on the first trial; their savings scores were just as large as those of control subjects.

Cohen and Squire (1980) report a particularly striking instance of cognitive skill acquisition by amnesics. They presented amnesic and control subjects with sets of word triads that were printed in inverted script and asked them to read each triad aloud; some words appeared only once and some were repeated. Earlier work by Kolers (1975, 1976) with normal subjects had shown that time to read the inverted script systematically decreases with practice. Cohen and Squire observed a similar result with amnesics: Not only did they take progressively less time to decode the inverted script over the course of three daily sessions, the slope of their learning curve was just as steep as that of control subjects. In fact, amnesics, as well as controls, demonstrated significant savings on the inverted-script task after a 3-month retention interval.

Amnesics and controls, however, differed in two aspects of their performance. First, the amnesics' speed of reading *repeated* words was facilitated much less than that of control subjects; they benefited only slightly from the repetition of specific words. Second, when their memory for the occurrence of specific words was tested by yes/no recognition, amnesics performed extremely poorly with respect to controls. Cohen and Squire (p. 209) note that

> upon being questioned, none of the amnesic patients reported that words had been repeated during the task, even though by the end of session four the set of repeated words had been presented twenty times. All of the control subjects reported spontaneously that words were frequently repeated.

On the basis of their data, Cohen and Squire argue that the acquisition and expression of *procedural* knowledge—knowing how—was intact in their amnesic subjects.

3.3. Organic Amnesia and the Episodic/Semantic Distinction

The evidence that we have so far reviewed indicates that amnesic patients are capable of (1) retaining some of the information presented to them during a learning episode, even though they have little memory for the episode itself, and (2) improving a variety of skills—both motor and cognitive—with practice. Let us now consider the implications of these data for the episodic/semantic distinction.

The fact that amnesics can retain and utilize certain aspects of recently presented information raises an apparent difficulty for attempts to conceptualize amnesia in terms of the episodic/semantic distinction. If amnesia represents a selective impairment of episodic memory, why should amnesics be able to retain information presented during a learning episode? We believe that this problem can be at least partially resolved by circumscribing the precise meaning of the term "episodic memory." This term is frequently invoked to refer to situations entailing encoding, storage, and retrieval of any information that is presented to the subject by the experimenter. Thus experiments on paired-associate learning, recognition of recently presented pictures, or recall of prose passages might all be referred to as experiments concerned with episodic memory. Accordingly, subjects' retrieval of items, at the time of test, that correspond to the experimentally defined input units is generally regarded as evidence of episodic memory.

It is when episodic memory is viewed in this sense—as retention and utilization of *any* information presented to the subject by the experimenter—that the observations of amnesics' performance become problematic for theories that portray amnesia as a selective deficit of episodic memory: Amnesic patients clearly are able to retain and utilize some of the information that they have acquired during a learning episode. However, we suggest that amnesics' retention of isolated bits and pieces of knowledge acquired during the learning episode should not be taken as evidence of episodic memory. Recall the critical features of episodic memory as outlined by Tulving (1972). Episodic memory is characterized by retention and retrieval of spatial and temporal contextual information, as well as by autobiographical reference—integration of newly acquired information with the personal past of the rememberer. These are precisely the types of information that amnesics do *not* seem capable of retaining. Thus data concerning organic amnesics point to a sharp distinction between memory for the *factual content* of an episode and autobiographical memory for the episode itself. Memory performance of amnesic patients can be affected by the factual content of an episode, even though they may not remember when, where, or how they acquired it. Accordingly, it seems prudent to suggest that retrieval of information acquired during a unique learning episode does not constitute, by itself, evidence of episodic memory; autobiographical reference and memory for temporal and spatial context must also be present. The distinction between memory for the factual content of an episode and memory for the episode itself has not been explicitly made in previous discussion of episodic and semantic memory.

When the distinction was formulated in 1972, it seemed reasonable to assume that subjects' ability to reproduce the factual contents of an episode, such as a word on a list, would constitute direct evidence of their memory for the episode itself; if the subjects did not remember the episode, how could they recall the word? In light of the data we have discussed, this assumption no longer seems acceptable.

These data also raise an additional question concerning the episodic/semantic distinction. If amnesics' ability to retrieve information from a learning episode is not based on episodic memory, can we conclude that it is based on semantic memory? Although the data are too sparse to permit firm conclusions, there are reasons to suggest that something other than semantic memory may underlie amnesics' performance. As shown by many studies, semantic memory is a highly structured and organized system of interrelated facts and concepts (e.g., Collins & Loftus, 1975). It is not yet clear how new information becomes embedded in this complex structure, but common sense and experimental findings suggest that the acquisition of stable structures of new knowledge proceeds gradually over time (e.g., Homa, Rhoads, & Chambliss, 1979; Hull, 1920). It does not seem likely that the information retained by amnesics in the cases discussed earlier—acquired during one usually brief exposure—could have become instantaneously integrated into the existing structures of semantic memory. Indeed, one of the qualities of amnesics' memory that has been noted in the literature is that the retrieved information simply "pops into their minds." It does not serve as a cue that brings forth related information, as frequently happens when people generate information from semantic memory in tasks such as free association, but enters consciousness as an isolated fragment.

Another way to interpret amnesics' performance in terms of semantic memory is to argue that the experimental input "primes" existing knowledge in semantic memory (e.g., Colling & Loftus, 1975; Loftus, 1973) and that amnesics utilize the temporarily activated information at the time of recall. While this is an attractive hypothesis, it does entail a number of problems that have been discussed elsewhere (Tulving, Schacter, & Stark, 1982).

It seems clear, then, that amnesics' retention of information presented during a learning episode is not easily accommodated by the episodic/semantic distinction. Amnesics access kernels of information that have become detached from their episodic contexts, but are not, or not yet, integrated into the existing structures of semantic memory. We find it convenient to label these kernels of information "free fragments." Free fragments are, in a sense, somewhere "between" episodic and semantic memory. However, the episodic/semantic distinction, as it is currently formulated, makes no provision for the concept of free fragments. Research that systematically delineates the properties of free fragments is the next logical step: The knowledge that is gathered about free fragments in such research may provide a useful guide to revising the constructs of episodic and semantic memory.

The data on skill acquisition by amnesics likewise pose interpretive difficulties for the episodic/semantic distinction. The problem here is that the 1972 article focuses on *propositional* knowledge, and ignored *procedural* knowledge. The fact that amnesics' ability to improve their execution of skills as a function of experience can be dissociated from their memory for the content of the experience highlights the possibility that modification of procedural knowledge may be governed by different rules than modification of propositional knowledge. Accordingly, procedural knowledge should be specifically accounted for in a complete taxonomy of memory systems.

Unfortunately, we can do no better at present than to pose questions for future investigations that may help clarify how the acquisition of procedural knowledge fits with the constructs of episodic and semantic memory: Can skill acquisition be dissociated from utilization of semantic memory? For instance, are there patients who can acquire new skills but cannot access their general knowledge of the world, or vice versa? What kinds of cognitive skills are used in the encoding and retrieval of both episodic and semantic memories? Under what circumstances are cognitive skills modified as a function of experience (other than just by "practice")? How do variables that are known to affect episodic memory and semantic memory affect the modification of skills? When questions such as these are systematically addressed, and perhaps answered, we will be in a better position to revise the episodic/ semantic distinction in a way that takes account of procedural knowledge.

4. HYPNOTIC AMNESIA

In the previous section we reviewed studies of organic amnesic patients with an eye toward evaluating the ability of the episodic/semantic distinction to account for the observed patterns of preserved and impaired memory function. We shall now consider relevant studies of hypnotic amnesia. To anticipate our conclusions, we shall argue that (1) patterns of data observed in hypnotized subjects are qualitatively similar to the patterns found in organic amnesics, and (2) the hypnosis data and organic amnesic data have nearly identical theoretical implications for the episodic/semantic distinction.

4.1. Source Amnesia

We earlier described a case study of a concussion amnesia patient that provided evidence of *source amnesia:* The patient could acquire and retain experimenter-provided information, but could not remember the episode in which he learned it. This study was partially motivated by prior research that demonstrated the phenomenon in hypnotized subjects. Banister and Zangwill (1941) report perhaps the earliest experimental investigation of source amnesia; they label the phenomenon "restrictive paramnesia." Banister and Zangwill exposed subjects to series of picture postcards and simply asked them to describe what they saw. Each subject viewed a total of 12 pictures: Six were seen in the waking state on Day 1 of the experiment, and six were seen during hypnosis on Day 2. After viewing the pictures under hypnosis, subjects were given a suggestion to forget the events of the session. Subjects' recognition memory was tested on Day 3 by presenting them with the 12 old pictures, intermixed with 12 new ones, and asking them to indicate whether they had ever seen each picture, as well as to report anything the picture brought to mind.

Because Banister and Zangwill employed this procedure with only five subjects, their data are of interest for the qualitative rather than quantitative information they supply. Two of their subjects failed to respond to the amnesia suggestion and recalled all the events of hypnosis; one subject recalled most of the events. Two subjects did respond to the amnesia suggestion. Both of these subjects accurately recognized all pictures from the waking session, and correctly classified each of the new items. However, when presented with the six pictures from the hypnotic session, these subjects displayed unambiguous source amnesia for all but one of them. The following are representative responses (pp. 36–42):

> *Japanese Print:* "I've seen that before. On some exotic sort of Christmas card or Japanese lantern."
>
> *Egyptian Girl:* "I think I've seen that. In the National Geographical Magazine of American or an Egyptian State Railways poster . . ."
>
> *Reynolds' "Marquess of Crewe":* "I have seen a picture like that before. Probably in the National Gallery."
>
> *Nine Flints:* "I didn't see that card on Monday [the waking session] but I have seen it somewhere."

These responses are similar to phenomena observed in organic amnesic patients: Subjects retain some information about the experimental materials but do not remember when or where they acquired it. More recent studies of source amnesia in hypnotized subjects have provided data amenable to a similar interpretation. Evans and Thorn (1966), for instance, asked hypnotized subjects three difficult questions under the pretext of administering a "general knowledge test" (e.g., "An amethyst is a blue or purple gemstone. What color does it turn when exposed to heat?"). When subjects did not correctly answer, the experimenter provided the appropriate response (e.g., yellow). After hypnosis was terminated, the experimenter again asked the same questions. Evans and Thorn found evidence of source amnesia in about 10% of their 243 subjects: The subjects supplied the correct answer to at least one of the three questions, but could not accurately state when or where they acquired the new facts. Evans and Thorn also found that none of the control subjects who were instructed to *simulate* hypnosis developed source amnesia; they overplayed their role and "forgot" all events from the experimental session.

In the Evans and Thorn study, source amnesia was not explicitly suggested. Cooper (1966) specifically compared spontaneous and suggested source amnesia and found a small difference between the two. Nine percent of Cooper's subjects showed spontaneous source amnesia for at least one of the three experimental questions, whereas 14% displayed the phenomenon when source amnesia was suggested during hypnosis.

In the foregoing studies the incidence of source amnesia is relatively modest. Cooper (1966), however, reports that source amnesia occurred only in subjects who were also highly susceptible to hypnosis, a finding that suggests that the phenomenon might be more frequently observed by studying extremely susceptible subjects. Gheorghiu (1969) provides relevant data. He studied source amnesia in a selected group of highly susceptible neurotic subjects, who viewed a series of 10 pictures while under hypnosis (Gheorghiu does not indicate whether source amnesia was specifically suggested). Memory for the pictures was later tested in the waking state in three different ways: (1) Subjects were shown the 10 target pictures, plus 30 new ones, and asked to state if and when they had seen them previously; (2) subjects who denied having seen the pictures were required to select 10 from the set of 40 and "were told that these would be handed over for copying to a schoolboy" (p. 115); and (3) subjects who did not choose the target pictures were then asked to select those pictures that seemed familiar.

Gheorghiu found that 38% of his subjects selected only the 10 target pictures on the first test. However, these subjects, like subjects in other studies, did not know why they selected the target pictures and frequently confabulated a source: "They claimed to have seen them in a dream (sometimes they also made up a story), or that they had seen them upon some other occasion" (p. 116). Twenty-nine percent of the subjects denied having seen any pictures on the first test, but showed a marked bias for selecting the experimental pictures on the second (forced-choice) test: They chose 90% of the presented pictures and only 8% of the lures. The remaining 33% of the subjects, who neither recognized nor selected target pictures on the first two tests, chose 80% of them when asked to indicate a general sense of familiarity; in contrast, they indicated that 3% of the new pictures seemed familiar. Although these data pose interpretive problems—there were no control or simulator subjects and some of the testing methods are unorthodox—they do suggest that source amnesia may be more readily observed in highly susceptible subjects.

More recently, Evans (1979) reports data that also indicate that source amnesia is frequently observed in highly susceptible subjects. Evans selected subjects from the upper 5% of the susceptibility distribution, and compared their performance to that of simulating controls. He employed a task previously used by Evans and Thorn (1966), in which subjects are provided with answers to difficult questions and later asked about them. Source amnesia was not specifically suggested. Evans found evidence of source amnesia in about 33% of the susceptible subjects, and none of the simulating controls. Evans's subjects behaved much like those in other studies. When asked how they knew one of the experimentally acquired facts, the subjects often invented sources, suggesting that "my girlfriend must have told me" or "I guess I read it somewhere" (p. 560). As in the other studies, subjects were capable of retaining information presented during the hypnotic episode. They could not, however, remember when or where they acquired the new information.

Although not specifically directed at the problem of source amnesia, experiments by Williamsen, Johnson, and Eriksen (1965) and by Kihlstrom (1980) provide data that in many respects resemble the data in the foregoing studies.

In the Williamsen *et al.* experiment, hypnotized, simulating, and control subjects were instructed to remember a list of six common words. Their memory for these words was evaluated, in the waking state, by a series of four consecutive tests: (1) free recall, (2) identification of perceptually degraded fragments of study words, (3) free association to cues that elicited both target and nontarget words as primary associates, and (4) yes/no recognition of target and distractor items. Hypnotized subjects' free recall and recognition performance was significantly impaired with respect to controls. However, much as in the Warrington and Weiskrantz experiments with organic amnesics, the hypnotized subjects were able to identify word fragments just as accurately as were the control subjects. In addition, all subjects identified significantly more fragments of list words than of control words. The word association task yielded mixed results. Although hypnotized and control subjects did not differ on this task, list words were elicited only slightly more frequently than nonlist words. As in other experiments, the simulators overplayed their roles; they performed poorly on all memory tests.

Kihlstrom (1980) reports two experiments in which he replicated and extended some of the Williamsen *et al.* data. In his first experiment, Kihlstrom examined retention of strongly related word pairs in subject groups stratified according to level of hypnotic susceptibility (very high, high, medium, low). The word pairs were studied during hypnosis, and amnesia for the events of the hypnotic session was explicitly suggested. As in the Williamsen *et al.* experiment there were four sequential tests, all administered in the waking state: (1) free recall of word pairs, (2) free association to word stimuli, primary associates of which had appeared on the experimental list, (3) a second free recall test, and (4) after a cue reversing the posthypnotic amnesia suggestion was given, a third free recall test.

Kihlstrom found that subjects' free recall performance was graded according to their level of hypnotic susceptibility; the low susceptibles recalled the most words, the high susceptibles the fewest. However, the four subject groups did not differ on the word association task: All groups showed a relatively small but significant tendency to produce more list words than nonlist words. Performance on the second free recall task was nearly identical to performance on the first. Thus subjects' free recall performance did not benefit from their prior production of experimental words on the association task. After administration of the reversibility cue, however, free recall substantially improved in the high and very high susceptible subjects, though the performance did not differ among the four groups.

Kihlstrom's second experiment employed a similar sequence of experimental operations, except that only very high and low susceptible subjects were used, subjects studied lists of categorized materials, and a "category instance production" task was employed instead of a word association task: Subjects were presented with category names (half representing categories that appeared on the input list) and asked to generate instances of each category. The findings were entirely consistent with the results of Experiment 1. Very high-susceptible subjects were markedly worse than low susceptibles on the first free recall test, but they did not differ on the category instance production task; both groups retrieved more list items as category instances than would be produced in the absence of the experimental list. Neither group showed improvement in the subsequent free recall test—in spite of the fact that they produced many of those items on the category task—but the high susceptibles' free recall performance dramatically improved after the administration of the reversibility cue (low susceptibles were already at the ceiling).

The overall pattern of data in the Williamsen *et al.* and Kihlstrom experiments closely resembles data from the studies of source amnesia: Hypnotized subjects demonstrate retention of information imparted to them during the hypnotic episode when they are tested in ways that do not require them to remember contextual features of the episode itself.

4.2. The Hull Studies: Evidence for the Acquisition of Skills

The results of a series of experiments carried out in Clark Hull's Yale laboratory, which explored the extent of hypnotic amnesia, resemble in several respects data concerning preservation of skills in organic amnesics. Patten (1932), for instance, proposed to investigate the following question: "Do practice effects acquired in the hypnotic trance state carry over into the subsequent non-trance states even when the subject has a complete amnesia for the fact that practice has taken place?" (p. 196). Patten required hypnotized and control subjects to perform a continuous addition task during an experimental session for each of 18 consecutive days. For the first six sessions all subjects were in a normal state; during the second six half the subjects were hypnotized; and for the final six all the subjects were awake. Patten found that the hypnotized subjects showed about the same amount of improvement on the addition task during the hypnosis sessions as they did in the earlier and later sessions. Similarly, their practice increment while hypnotized was about as large as the control subjects' improvement during the comparable sessions. However, the hypnotized subjects reported no episodic memory for the events of the six hypnosis sessions. Using a similar experimental design, Life (cited in Hull, 1933, pp. 149–150) examined improvement in subjects' ability to learn successive lists of paired associates, a phenomenon that contemporary students of memory refer to as "learning to learn." Life found that hypnotized subjects showed as much improvement in performance across lists (learning to learn) when they were hypnotized as when they were not. The hypnotized subjects also showed as much learning to learn as control subjects.

Two other experiments from Hull's laboratory provide relevant data. Strickler (1929) taught hypnotized and control subjects paired associates consisting of line drawings and nonsense syllables. After a 15-minute retention interval, the line drawings were presented as cues for the nonsense syllables; all subjects were tested in the waking state. Hypnotized subjects were almost entirely amnesic for the experimental material: they recalled only 3% of the nonsense syllables compared to 84% for the controls. (It is interesting to note that Hull, commenting on Strickler's data, observed that when subjects did recall appropriate syllables, "they stated that the names seemed to come to mind from 'nowhere' and were not accompanied by any recollection that the character or symbol had ever been encountered before" [1933, p. 134].) Strickler's subjects then relearned the experimental list (in the waking state). Under this testing condition, the hypnosis group demonstrated large amounts of *savings:* They relearned the list in half the number of trials that were initially required. Although control subjects showed even more savings on the relearning trials, Strickler's data clearly indicate that exposure to the experimental list improved hypnotized subjects' ability to subsequently remaster the list, in spite of their dense amnesia for its contents. Coors (cited in Hull, pp. 141–145) used the savings method to evaluate the extent of maze learning in hypnotized and control subjects. Like Strickler, he found that the hypnosis group demonstrated significant savings upon relearning, although these savings were not as large as those of the control subjects.

In all of these studies from Hull's laboratory, subjects could not recall the events of the hypnotic episode. However, they were able to acquire some *procedural* knowledge during the hypnotic session that they later expressed when tested in the waking state: Subjects were faster to add numbers after hypnosis than before it, their processing of paired-associate lists improved during and after hypnosis, and they were able to relearn material presented during hypnosis more efficiently than when they initially acquired it. Although these tasks may not be directly comparable to those used in studies of organic amnesics, and the data require corroboration by future research, the dissociations between episodic memory and acquisiton of skills observed in studies of both hypnotic and organic amnesia are strikingly similar.

4.3. Hypnotic Amnesia and the Episodic/Semantic Distinction

Overall, the patterns of preserved and impaired memory reported in the foregoing studies of hypnotic amnesia closely resemble the patterns observed in organic amnesia. Hypnotized subjects who have no memory for the learning episode as such can retain decontextualized fragments of experimental input, and are able to improve their performance on tasks that require utilization of cognitive skills. It is not surprising, then, that the implications of these studies for the episodic/ semantic distinction are similar to those of the organic amnesia studies.

First, the studies of source amnesia in hypnosis reinforce the need to distinguish clearly between memory for the factual content of an episode and autobiographical memory for the episode itself. That hypnotized subjects, like organic amnesics, can sometimes retain the factual content of an episode does not imply the involvement of episodic memory: The factual content is not remembered as part of the personal past of the subject.

Second, attempts to account for hypnotized subjects' retention of free fragments in terms of utilization of the structured knowledge of semantic memory encounter some of the same problems enumerated with respect to organic amnesics. It is unlikely that the information imparted to hypnotized subjects during a single experimental session is immediately integrated with existing semantic structures, and the possibility that priming of existing knowledge structures accounts for retention of free fragments is limited because of the brief temporal intervals over which priming effects persist. The hypnosis data emphasize the need for elaboration of the episodic/semantic distinction in a way that satisfactorily addresses the free fragment phenomenon.

Third, the data on cognitive skill improvement in subjects undergoing hypnotic amnesia emphasize the need to clarify the place of procedural knowledge in the episodic/semantic distinction. Modifications of procedural knowledge can be dissociated from modifications of episodic memory: Hypnotized subjects improve their ability to utilize various skills, but express little episodic memory for the learning process. We do not yet know how such modifications of procedural knowledge can be accommodated by the episodic/semantic distinction. One purpose of this chapter is to call attention to the need for research on this problem.

5. FUNCTIONAL RETROGRADE AMNESIA

The bulk of contemporary research on amnesia is concerned with the analysis of organic amnesic syndromes and experimentally induced hypnotic amnesia. Relatively little attention has been paid to the category of pathological forgetting that we shall refer to as *functional retrograde amnesia*. This kind of amnesia typically occurs as a consequence of severe emotional trauma. The genesis of the amnesia is fairly consistent from case to case: Patients suddenly become aware that they cannot remember their name, where they live, and many other kinds of personal information. A fugue period often precedes awareness of the amnesia, during which the patient wanders about, unaware of his or her memory loss. After the fugue passes, the affected patient experiences little difficulty storing and retrieving information about ongoing events, but entire sections of his or her personal past remain inaccessible. The amnesia usually clears within a few days or a week, often in response to a cue that is associated with the precipitating emotional trauma.

Functional retrograde amnesia elicited considerable theoretical enthusiasm from late nineteenth- and early twentieth-century students of memory pathology. Azam (1876), who published perhaps the first case study of functional retrograde amnesia, boldly introduces his topic: "I am going to relate the history of a young woman whose existence is tormented by an impairment of memory, which is without a parallel in science" (p. 584). Coriat (1907) explicitly argues that students of memory pathology would do well to pay close attention to functional amnesias: "It is not the organic, but rather the functional amnesias, that display the most interesting and valuable phenomena" (p. 108). However, most subsequent research on functional retrograde amnesia was not concerned with its implications for theoretical analyses of memory or memory pathology. Instead these investigations pursued psychiatric issues, and attempted to distinguish between the various onset conditions of the amnesia (Abeles & Schilder, 1935; Kanzer, 1939; Kennedy & Neville, 1957; Sargant & Slater, 1941; Thom & Fenton, 1920), to relate it to different forms of psychopathology (Berrington, Liddell, & Foulds, 1956; Leavitt, 1935; Stengel, 1941; Wilson, Rupp, & Wilson 1950), to specify criteria for differentiating genuine amnesics from malingerers (Adatto, 1949; Hopwood & Snell, 1933; Lennox, 1943; Price & Terhune, 1919;

Siegal, 1951), to estimate the contribution of organic factors (Kennedy & Neville, 1957), to describe the duration of amnesia and the different forms of recovery (Abeles & Schilder, 1935; Kanzer, 1939; Wilson *et al.* , 1950), to suggest treatment methods (Sargant & Slater, 1941), and to clarify the psychodynamic functions of amnesia (Kennedy & Neville, 1957). Over the past 20 years there has been very little research of any kind concerning functional retrograde amnesia.

There are, however, some data in the literature that are of interest to us. These data derive from clinical observations that describe patterns of preserved and lost mnemonic abilities during functional retrograde amnesia. Although these observations lack experimental rigor, they provide a picture that is in general agreement with the previously described research on organic and hypnotic amnesia. It has been noted that in spite of patients' dense amnesia for personal experiences—including failure to recall and recognize their name, relatives, home, and place of work—their organized knowledge of the world is largely preserved (Jones, 1909; Wilson *et al.*, 1950), although it has been suggested that "general knowledge" remains intact only in some patients (Abeles & Schilder, 1935). But even in the most severe cases, when patients temporarily lose the ability to name and appropriately use familiar objects, access to this kind of knowledge returns rapidly, well before the amnesia for personally experienced episodes clears (Coriat, 1907). Patients' ability to use and comprehend language, read, write, and fluidly process new information—in short, their ability to employ a wide range of cognitive skills and procedures—is also frequently unaffected by the amnesia (Abeles & Schilder, 1935; Gillespie, 1937; Kanzer, 1939; Prince, 1910).

A number of turn-of-the-century clinical observers found that patients were able to access some memories related to their personal past if the method of retrieval was "indirect," and did not require patients consciously to attempt to retrieve their personal memories. Jones (1909) reports a case in which the patient could provide some accurate information about his personal past when asked to "guess" about it. For instance, the patient could not remember the names of his wife and daughter, but when asked to guess them he did so correctly (p. 221). However, the retrieved information was not recognized as part of his own past. Coriat (1907) reports similar observations. He asked patients to focus their attention on a monotonous stimulus and to report whatever came into their minds. Under such conditions, a patient suffering from a dense functional retrograde amnesia was able to retrieve information that accurately depicted parts of her past. But the retrieved contents seemed strange and unfamiliar to her. Coriat's description of these "distraction memories" resembles descriptions of the free fragments observed in organic amnesics and hypnotized subjects:

> These memory automatisms... are not looked upon as memories, but as strange, unfamiliar and isolated phenomena, which Susan N. [the patient] well expressed by the term "wonderments"....
>
> A prominent feature of all these distraction memories was their complete isolation; they did not act as a nucleus around which other memories grouped themselves by association.... They were the emerging into her mind of isolated memory images, such as a name, a face or a place, which seemed to come from out of nowhere, without any connection with anything else. They did not bring with them any extended associations. (p. 106–107)

Kanzer (1939) reports similar phenomena in his amnesic patients. For instance, one young woman became amnesic after a distressing telephone conversation with her boyfriend. During the amnesic period she recalled "someting about a telephone" (p. 115), but could not relate this fragmentary information to her personal past. Prince (1910), in his study of functional amnesia in a case of multiple personality, notes the occurrence of fragmentary "visions" of past events: "The visions were pure automatisms, excrescences in her mind, without conscious association with the other experiences of the life which they pictured. When seeing a vision she did not recognize the pictorial experiences as her own" (p. 265). Highly similar observations are reported by other students of functional retrograde amnesia (Gillespie, 1937; Janet, 1901; Sidis, 1914).

The unsystematic nature of these observations must be kept in mind, of course, when attempting to interpret them. However, it does seem appropriate to note the similarity between the "automatisms," "visions," and "distraction memories" of functional retrograde amnesia and the free fragments of organic and hypnotic amnesia: The qualitative resemblance is striking. In all three types of amnesia, people access isolated bits of information that were acquired during specific episodes but are not part of organized semantic structures, and are not experienced as part of the personal past of the rememberer. As noted earlier, it is not yet clear how the episodic/semantic distinction can make sense of this phenomenon.

5.1. Episodic/Semantic Dissociation: An Experiment with an N of 1

As noted earlier, the literature on functional retrograde amnesia primarily consists of clinical descriptions of memory processes during the amnesic period. We recently had the opportunity to perform an experiment with a single patient suffering from functional retrograde amnesia.*

The clinical course of this case resembles many others described in

---

*This research was conducted in collaboration with Dr. Paul Wang.

the literature. A patient whom we shall refer to as P. N., a 21-year-old man, entered Mount Sinai Hospital in Toronto unable to remember his name, address, or any other information about himself or his past. He also complained of back pains. The patient's picture was published in one of the Toronto newspapers, and a cousin who saw it came to Mount Sinai the next day (P. N. did not recognize this cousin). She reported that P. N.'s grandfather had died several days earlier; the funeral was held in Toronto. P. N.'s parents had separated when he was 10 months old, and P. N. was apparently closer to his grandfather than to any other person. When asked about his grandfather and the recent funeral, P. N. could recall nothing—not even the fact that he had a grandfather. The amnesia cleared, in dramatic fashion, four days after it had begun, while P. N. viewed the concluding episode of the television series *Shogun*. As he watched an elaborate cremation and funeral sequence, P. N. reported that an image of his grandfather gradually appeared in his mind. He subsequently remembered his grandfather's death and the recent funeral. He then regained his sense of personal identity, and over the next few hours, the large sections of his personal past that had been inaccessible for the previous 4 days also returned.

Neuropsychological testing revealed that P. N.'s ability to process information, access his general knowledge of the world, and utilize a variety of cognitive and motor skills was intact, or marginally impaired, during the amnesic episode. Clinical observations suggested that in spite of his inability to remember the events of his personal past, P. N.'s memory for "public" events was relatively preserved. Our study of P. N focussed on these two types of memory.

We tested the patient for episodic and semantic memory on two separate occasions: during the amnesic episode and three weeks after its termination. Semantic memory was represented by memory for public events. It was assessed by the famous-faces test of the Boston Veterans Administration retrograde amnesia battery (Albert, Butters, & Levin, 1979). P. N. was shown photographs of well-known people from each of the past 6 decades and asked to identify them. When he did not properly identify a face, he was provided with semantic cues related to it, and then asked to try and select the appropriate name from a set of four. We examined P. N.'s episodic memory by using the cuing procedures for personal experiences developed by Crovitz and Schiffman (1974) and Robinson (1976). The *episodic-cuing* task was given twice in succession under different conditions. In both tests, P. N. was given a series of common English words and asked to produce a discrete personal memory in response to each of them. He was also asked to date the memory temporally. In the initial, *unconstrained* condition, P. N. was instructed to retrieve a memory from any time in his personal past—minutes, days, weeks, months, or years ago. In the second, *constrained* condition, each cue was presented again, and P. N. was asked to retrieve a different memory in response to it. Now, however, P. N. was instructed to provide only memories that temporally preceded the onset of his amnesia. P. N. was tested on one form of both the famous-faces test and the episodic-cuing task during the amnesic period; a second form was administered after the amnesia had cleared.

P. N.'s performance on the famous-faces test was nearly identical across the two sessions. He was able to identify, or recognize the name of, 15 of the 24 faces tested during the amnesic period; he was correct on 16 of the 24 after the amnesic period. However, his performance on the episodic-cuing task substantially changed between test sessions. During the amnesic period, almost all (86%) of P. N.'s memory came from the 3 days that followed the onset of the amnesia. This pattern sharply contrasts with the performance of normals, who provide a relatively small proportion of memories (less than 25%) from the categories of minutes, hours, and days on the episodic-cuing task (Crovitz & Schiffman, 1974). When tested after the amnesia had cleared, P. N.'s performance drastically altered: Nearly all of his memories (92%) predated the onset of the amnesia. Similarly, the *median age* of P. N.'s memories in the unconstrained condition was much greater after the amnesic period than during it, and he was also much faster to retrieve episodic memories, in both the constrained and unconstrained conditions, after the amnesia passed.

P. N.'s performance in the constrained condition during the amnesic episode yielded some especially intriguing observations. When forced to retrieve memories predating the amnesic period, he recalled several pertaining to distinctive childhood episodes (e.g., that his finger was crushed in a door) and other isolated events. However, a large majority of his preamnesic memories derived from 2 months during 1979 when he worked for a Toronto courier service. P. N.'s descriptions indicated that this time was extremely happy for him. He was able to recall, in rich detail, many individual episodes associated with his courier job. Thus, although P. N. could not recall where he lived, what he was doing during the past year, who his family and friends were, or where he went to high school, he could recall the names and faces of his friends at the courier service, and many of the things they had done together. Observations of such "islands" of intact memory are common in studies of concussion amnesia (W. R. Russell, 1971), but have not yet been reported in cases of functional retrograde amnesia. When tested after the amnesic period, P. N. retrieved memories that were distributed across many temporal intervals; there were no comparable islands of memory.

Data obtained from a single subject must be treated with interpretive restraint. Accordingly, we shall not attempt to draw firm conclusions from this case study of functional retrograde amnesia, but shall instead raise several possibilities for exploration in future research.

First, P. N.'s stable performance on the public events test across sessions, in conjunction with the marked changes on the cuing test, suggest a selective impairment of episodic memory in functional retrograde amnesia. Second, that cuing procedures did elicit some memories from the time period covered by the amnesia suggests that functional retrograde amnesia need not be as uniformly dense as indicated by the clinical literature. Third, the finding of a memory "island," structured around a particular time in the subject's life, raises questions concerning the organization of episodic memories. What factors permitted P. N. to remember in detail the events nested within the island at the same time that he could not access almost all other sectors of his personal past? The positive emotions P. N. expressed concerning the events within the island suggest the possible importance of affective factors, but it is not yet clear how to assess the influence of affect on retrieval of episodic memories. In any case, our data suggest that quantitative exploration of functional retrograde amnesia may yield interesting insights concerning the operation of episodic memory, and also indicate that cuing procedures may provide a useful tool for studying the phenomenon.

6. CONCLUDING COMMENTS

We have reviewed evidence from studies of organic, hypnotic, and functional amnesia and have discussed the implications of this evidence for the distinction between episodic and semantic memory. Specifically, we have suggested that the observations of amnesics' memory performance highlight three difficulties with the distinction as it is currently formulated: (1) There may be a need to distinguish between memory for the factual content of a learning episode and autobiographical memory for the episode; (2) the distinction does not satisfactorily account for the phenomenon of free fragments—bits of retained information that have become detached from their episodic contexts but do not seem to be attached to organized knowledge structures in semantic memory; and (3) the episodic/semantic distinction is mute on the role of procedural knowledge in memory.

We have suggested directions for research that may help to elucidate these problems and, consequently, to stimulate revisions, and perhaps extensions, of the episodic/semantic distinction. We shall now address two issues likely to arise during the course of such research.

6.1. Dissociation between Systems or Loss of Information?

One of the fundamental properties of amnesics' memory impairment is that it is not uniform across all types of tasks or materials. The impairment—in the organic, hypnotic, and functional cases—is *selective;* amnesics perform better on some memory tasks than on others. When amnesics perform in a relatively intact fashion on tasks that are assumed to draw primarily on a particular memory system, but perform poorly on tasks that are largely dependent on a different system, we have evidence for the dissociation of the two systems. Using such logic, it is possible to move from observations of amnesics' patterns of performance on different tasks to more general statements about similarities and differences between underlying memory systems.

There is, however, a problem with this line of reasoning in the present context. It can be argued that the selectivity of amnesics' memory impairment does not provide evidence concerning the relation between underlying systems, but instead reflects the fact that some kinds of information are forgotten faster than others. Consider, for example, the case of source amnesia. Source amnesia occurs when subjects are tested sometime after presentation of information, and can retrieve the information without knowing when and where they acquired it. The problem is, however, that it would be difficult to observe source amnesia if testing were carried out *immediately* after study: Even amnesic subjects would probably be able to recall both the information and its source. It is plausible to argue, then, that observations of source amnesia simply reflect the fact that one kind of information (episodic information) is lost faster than another (semantic information). The same kind of argument could be applied to observations of skill acquisition by amnesics in the absence of memory for the events of the learning episode: Knowledge of the episode may be lost faster than knowledge about how to execute a particular skill.

The contention that apparent dissociations between memory systems are better interpreted in terms of differential rates of loss of information is difficult to refute convincingly at present. However, there are two strategies for handling this problem that might be fruitfully employed in future research. One is to attempt to specify conditions under which the "lost" information can be recovered. It is well-known that information that is not accessible under one set of retrieval conditions may be accessed under some others (Tulving & Pearlstone, 1966). For instance, if it could be shown that in the source amnesia task conditions exist under which subjects *can* retrieve information about the learning episode, then it would be difficult to contend that source amnesia is a consequence of rapid *loss* of episodic information. Indeed, this strategy has already been used in the work of Kihlstrom (1980), in which episodic amnesia was eliminated by the administering of a reversibility cue.

A second strategy is to look for *double dissociations* of memory function. In neuropsychology, double dissociations frequently take the form of crossover interactions between patient groups and tasks. If Patient Group A performs Task X better than Task Y, and Patient Group B performs Task Y better than Task X, then a double dissociation has occurred (cf. Shallice, 1979). In our context, it would be desirable to identify subject groups whose pattern of memory performance is *opposite* to the patterns of some of the subject groups discussed in this chapter. For example, if there are patients who retain information about the occurrence of an episode and its relation to their personal past but are pathologically unable to remember the factual content of the episode, then it would be difficult to maintain the argument that a phenomenon such as source amnesia reflects the fact that episodic information is lost faster than other kinds of information. In fact, Luria reports suggestive evidence along these lines (1976, p. 117).

6.2. How Many Memory Systems?

We have argued throughout that the distinction between episodic and semantic memory requires revision, and perhaps extension. We do not yet know if it is necessary to postulate additional systems beyond the two included in the distinction; and if additional systems are necessary, we do not know what they would be. Miller and Johnson-Laird (1976), for instance, have suggested the possibility of a fivefold classification: semantic, episodic, action, geographic, and person memories. Such a burgeoning of memory systems may be cause for concern to those who value parsimony in science: After one or two additional systems are suggested, the list may quickly become unmanagably long.

We acknowledge the possibility of an undesirable proliferation of memory systems. But we also recognize that it is a mistake to ignore distinctions that may have both heuristic and theoretical value. A taxonomy of memory systems, like taxonomies in other areas of science, should strike a balance between too many and too few distinctions. The problem is an old one, and was confronted by some of the founders of modern scientific taxonomy. Linnaeus, for instance, explicitly warned against the dangers of taxonomic excess: "If every minute difference, every trifling variation, is to establish a new species, why should I delay to exhibit ten thousand such species?" (Smith, 1978, p. 277). However, he also acknowledged that failure to make useful distinctions was an equally serious error: "If, then, genera be distinct, why should not their names be kept perfectly so likewise?" (Smith, p. 257).

There are no clear-cut rules for achieving a balance between the two undesirable extremes—too few distinctions or too many—and we suspect that the development of a suitable taxonomy of memory systems will be guided by the trial-and-error procedures that are characteristic of a developing science such as psychology. Perhaps it is not too much to hope that such procedures will help to provide a basis for answering the question with which we began: How can we characterize the systems that comprise human memory?

ACKNOWLEDGMENTS

We thank Michèle Stampp for comments on an earlier draft of the chapter, and Carol A. Macdonald for assistance in preparing the manuscript.

7. REFERENCES

Abeles, M., & Schilder, P. Psychogenic loss of personal identity. *Archives of Neurology and Psychiatry*, 1935, 34, 587–604.

Adatto, C. P. Observations on criminal patients during narcoanalysis. *Archives of Neurology and Psychiatry*, 1949, 62, 82–92.

Albert, M. S., Butters, N., & Levin, J. Memory for remote events in chronic alcoholics and alcoholic Korsakoff patients. In H. Begleiter & B. Kissen (Eds.), *Alcohol intoxication and withdrawal*. New York: Plenum Press, 1979.

Anderson, J. R., & Ross, B. H. Evidence against a semantic-episodic distinction. *Journal of Experimental Psychology: Human Learning and Memory*, 1980, 6, 441–466.

Azam, M. Periodical amnesia; or, double consciousness. *Journal of Nervous and Mental Disease*, 1876, 3, 584–612.

Banister, H., & Zangwill, O. L. Experimentally induced visual paramnesias. *British Journal of Psychology*, 1941, 32, 30–51.

Berch, D. B. Coding of spatial and temporal information in episodic memory. In H. W. Reese (Ed.), *Advances in child development and behavior* (Vol. 3). New York: Academic Press, 1979.

Bergson, H. *Matter and memory* (N. M. Paul & W. S. Palmer, trans.). New York: Macmillan, 1911.

Berrington, W. P., Liddell, D. W., & Foulds, G. A. A re-evaluation of the fugue. *Journal of Mental Science*, 1956, 102, 280–286.

Brooks, D. N., & Baddeley, A. D. What can amnesic patients learn? *Neuropsychologia*, 1976, 14, 111–122.

Claparède, E. Recognition and "me-ness." In D. Rapaport (Ed.), *Organization and pathology of thought*. New York: Columbia University Press, 1951. (Originally published, 1911.)

Cohen, N. J., & Squire, L. R. Preserved learning and retention of pattern-analyzing skill in amnesia: Dissociation of "knowing how" and "knowing that." *Science*, 1980, 210, 207–210.

Collins, A. M., & Loftus, E. F. A spreading-activation theory of semantic processing. *Psychological Review*, 1975, *82*, 407–428.

Cooper, L. M. Spontaneous and suggested posthypnotic source amnesia. *International Journal of Clinical and Experimental Hypnosis*, 1966, *14*, 180–193.

Coriat, I. H. The Lowell case of amnesia. *Journal of Abnormal Psychology*, 1907, *2*, 93–111.

Corkin, S. Tactually-guided maze learning in man: Effects of unilateral cortical excisions and bilateral hippocampal lesions. *Neuropsychologia*, 1965, *3*, 339–351.

Corkin, S. Acquisition of motor skill after bilateral medial temporal-lobe excision. *Neuropsychologia*, 1968, *6*, 255–265.

Crovitz, H. F., & Schiffman, H. Frequency of episodic memories as a function of their age. *Bulletin of the Psychonomic Society*, 1974, *4*, 517–518.

Ebbinghaus, H. *Memory*. (H. A. Ruger & C. E. Bussenius, Trans.). New York: Dover Press, 1964. (Originally published, 1885.)

Evans, F. J. Posthypnotic source amnesia. *Journal of Abnormal Psychology*, 1979, *88*, 556–563.

Evans, F. J., & Thorn, W. A. F. Two types of posthypnotic amnesia: Recall amnesia and source amnesia. *International Journal of Clinical and Experimental Hypnosis*, 1966, *14*, 162–179.

Eysenck, M. W. Retrieval from semantic memory as a function of age. *Journal of Gerontology*, 1975, *80*, 174–180.

Gheorghiu, V. Some peculiarities of posthypnotic source amnesia of information. In L. Chertok (Ed.), *Psychophysiological mechanisms of hypnosis*. New York: Springer, 1969.

Gillespie, R. D. Amnesia. *Archives of Neurology and Psychiatry*, 1937, *37*, 748–764.

Grünthal, E. Zur Kenntnis der Psycholopathologie des korsakowschen symptomen Komplexes. *Monatschrift für Psychiatrie und Neurologie*, 1923, *53*, 89–132.

Hannigan, M. L., Shelton, T. S., Franks, J. J., & Bransford, J. D. The effects of episodic and semantic memory on the identification of sentences masked by white noise. *Memory and Cognition*, 1980, *8*, 278–284.

Herrmann, D. J., & Harwood, J. R. More evidence for the existence of separate semantic and episodic stores in long-term memory. *Journal of Experimental Psychology: Human Learning and Memory*, 1980, *6*, 467–478.

Herrmann, D. J., & McLaughlin, J. P. Effects of experimental and preexperimental organization on recognition: Evidence for two storage systems in long-term memory. *Journal of Experimental Psychology*, 1973, *99*, 174–179.

Homa, D., Rhoads, D., & Chambliss, D. Evolution of conceptual structure. *Journal of Experimental Psychology: Human Learning and Memory*, 1979, *5*, 11–23.

Hopwood, J. S., & Snell, H. K. Amnesia in relation to crime. *Journal of Mental Science*, 1933, *79*, 27–41.

Hull, C. L. Quantitative aspects of the evolution of concepts. *Psychological Monographs*, 1920, *28* (1, Whole No. 123).

Hull, C. L. *Hypnosis and suggestibility*. New York: Appleton-Century, 1933.

Huppert, F. A., & Piercy, M. Recognition memory in amnesic patients: Effect of temporal context and familiarity of material. *Cortex*, 1976, *12*, 3–20.

James, W. *The principles of psychology* (Vol. 1). New York: Henry Holt, 1890.

Janet, P. *The mental state of hystericals*. New York: Putnam, 1901.

Johnson, J. H., Klinger, D. E., & Williams, T. A. Recognition in episodic long-term memory in schizophrenia. *Journal of Clinical Psychology*, 1977, *33*, 643–647.

Jones, E. Remarks on a case of complete autopsychic amnesia. *Journal of Abnormal Psychology*, 1909, *4*, 218–235.

Kanzer, M. Amnesia: A statistical study. *American Journal of Psychiatry*, 1939, *96*, 711–716.

Kennedy, A., & Neville, J. Sudden loss of memory. *British Medical Journal*, 1957, *2*, 428–433.

Kihlstrom, J. F. Posthypnotic amnesia for recently learned material: Interactions with "episodic" and "semantic" memory. *Cognitive Psychology*, 1980, *12*, 227–251.

Kinsbourne, M. Episodic-semantic distinction. In L. S. Cermak (Ed.), *Human memory and amnesia*. Hillsdale, N.J.: Lawrence Erlbaum, 1982.

Kinsbourne, M., & Wood, F. Short-term memory processes and the amnesic syndrome. In D. Deutsch & J. A. Deutsch (Eds.), *Short-term memory*. New York: Academic Press, 1975.

Kolers, P. A. Memorial consequences of automatized encoding. *Journal of Experimental Psychology: Human Learning and Memory*, 1975, *1*, 689–701.

Kolers, P. A. Reading a year later. *Journal of Experimental Psychology: Human Learning and Memory*, 1976, *2*, 554–565.

Korsakoff, S. S. Über eine besondere Form psychischer Störung kombiniert mit multiplen Neuritis. *Archiv für Psychiatrie und Nervenkrankheiten*, 1889, *21*, 669–704.

Leavitt, F. H. The etiology of temporary amnesia. *American Journal of Psychiatry*, 1935, *91*, 1079–1087.

Lennox, W. G. Amnesia, real and feigned. *American Journal of Psychiatry*, 1943, *99*, 732–743.

Loftus, E. F. Activation of semantic memory. *American Journal of Psychology*, 1973, *86*, 331–337.

Luria, A. R. *The neuropsychology of memory*. Washington: V. H. Winston, 1976.

MacCurdy, J. T. *Common principles in psychology and physiology*. Cambridge: Cambridge University Press, 1929.

McKoon, G., & Ratcliff, R. Priming in episodic and semantic memory. *Journal of Verbal Learning and Verbal Behavior*, 1979, *18*, 463–480.

Miller, G. A., & Johnson-Laird, P. N. *Language and perception*. Cambridge: Harvard University Press, 1976.

Milner, B. *Memory disturbances after bilateral hippocampal lesions*. In P. Milner & S. Glickman (Eds.), *Cognitive process and the brain*. Princeton, N. J.: Van Nostrand, 1965. (Originally published, 1962.)

Milner, B. Memory and the medial temporal regions of the brain. In K. H. Pribram & D. E. Broadbent (Eds.), *Biology of memory*. New York: Academic Press, 1970.

Milner, B., Corkin, S., & Teuber, H. L. Further analysis of the hippocampal-amnesic syndrome: Fourteen-year follow-up study of H. M. *Neuropsychologia*, 1968, *6*, 215–234.

Moeser, S. D. Inferential reasoning in episodic memory. *Journal of Verbal Learning and Verbal Behavior*, 1976, *15*, 193–212.

Munsat, S. *The concept of memory*. New York: Random House, 1966.

Muter, P. Recognition failure of recallable words in semantic memory. *Memory and Cognition*, 1978, *6*, 9–12.

Nelson, K., & Brown, A. L. The semantic-episodic distinction in memory development. In P. A. Ornstein (Ed.), *Memory development in children*. Hillsdale, N.J.: Lawrence Erlbaum, 1978.

Nielsen, J. M. *Memory and amnesia*. Los Angeles: San Lucas Press, 1958.

Owen, G., & Williams, M. Factors affecting the sense of familiarity with cue-elicited responses in amnesic patients. *Neuropsychologia*, 1980, *18*, 85–87.

Patten, E. F. Does post-hypnotic amnesia apply to practice effects? *Journal of General Psychology*, 1932, *7*, 196–201.

Petrey, S. Word associations and the development of lexical memory. *Cognition*, 1977, *5*, 57–72.

Piaget, J., & Inhelder, B. *Memory and intelligence*. London: Routledge & Kegan Paul, 1973.

Price, G. E., & Terhune, W. B. Feigned amnesia as a defense reaction. *Journal of the American Medical Association*, 1919, *72*, 565–567.

Prince, M. *The dissociation of a personality*. New York: Longmans, Green, 1910.

Quillian, M. R. Semantic memory. In M. Minsky (Ed.), *Semantic information processing.* Cambridge, Mass.: M.I.T. Press, 1968.

Reiff, R., & Scheerer, M. *Memory and hypnotic age regression.* New York: International Universities Press, 1959.

Robinson, J. A. Sampling autobiographical memory. *Cognitive Psychology,* 1976, *8,* 578–595.

Rozin, P. The psychobiological approach to human memory. In M. R. Rosenzweig & E. L. Bennett (Eds.), *Neural mechanisms of learning and memory.* Cambridge, Mass.: M.I.T. Press, 1976.

Russell, P. N., & Beekhuis, M. E. Organization in memory: A comparison of psychotics and normals. *Journal of Abnormal Psychology,* 1976, *85,* 527–534.

Russell, W. R. *The traumatic amnesias.* London: Oxford University Press, 1971.

Sargant, W., & Slater, E. Amnesic syndromes in war. *Proceedings in the Royal Society of Medicine,* 1941, *34,* 754–764.

Schachtel, E. G. On memory and childhood amnesia. *Psychiatry,* 1947, *10,* 1–26.

Schacter, D. L., & Tulving, E. Amnesia and memory reserach. In L. S. Cermak (Ed.), *Human memory and amnesia.* Hillsdale, N.J.: Lawrence Erlbaum, 1982.

Schacter, D. L., Tulving, E., & Wang, P. Source amnesia: New methods and illustrative data. Paper presented at the meeting of the International Neuropsychological Society, Atlanta, 1981.

Shallice, T. Neuropsychological research and the fractionation of memory systems. In L. G. Nilsson (Ed.), *Perspectives on memory reserach.* Hillsdale, N.J.: Lawrence Erlbaum, 1979.

Shoben, E. J., Wescourt, K. T., & Smith, E. E. Sentence verification, sentence recognition, and the semantic/episodic distinction. *Journal of Experimental Psychology: Human Learning and Memory,* 1978, *4,* 304–317.

Sidis, B. *Symptomatology, psychognosis, and diagnosis of psychopathic diseases.* Boston: Richard C. Bodger, 1914.

Siegal, L. J. Amnesia: Its integrative analysis in psychopathological orientation. *Archives of Neurology and Psychiatry,* 1951, *66,* 700–707.

Smith, J. E. *A selection of the correspondence of Linnaeus and other naturalists* (Vol. 2). New York: Arno Press, 1978.

Starr, A., & Phillips, L. Verbal and motor memory in the amnesic syndrome. *Neuropsychologia,* 1970, *8,* 75–88.

Stengel, E. On the aetiology of the fugue states. *Journal of Mental Science,* 1941, *87,* 572–599.

Störring, G. E. Über den ersten reinen Fall eines Menschen mit völligen, isolierten Verlust der Merkfähigkeit. *Archiv für die Gesamte Psychologie,* 1931, *81,* 257–384.

Strickler, C. B. A qualitative study of post-hypnotic amnesia. *Journal of Abnormal and Social Psychology,* 1929, *24,* 108–119.

Thom, D. A., & Fenton, W. Amnesia in war cases. *American Journal of Psychiatry,* 1920, *76,* 437–448.

Tulving, E. Episodic and semantic memory. In E. Tulving & W. Donaldson (Eds.), *Organization of memory.* New York: Academic Press, 1972.

Tulving, E., & Pearlstone, Z. Availability versus accessibility of information in memory for words. *Journal of Verbal Learning and Verbal Behavior,* 1966, *5,* 381–391.

Tulving, E., Schacter, D. L., & Stark, H. Priming effects in word-fragment completion are independent of recognition memory. *Journal of Experimental Psychology: Learning, Memory, and Cognition,* 1982, *8,* 336–342.

Warrington, E. K., & Weiskrantz, L. New method of testing long-term retention with special reference to amnesic patients. *Nature,* 1968, *217,* 972–974.

Warrington, E. K., & Weiskrantz, L. Amnesic syndrome: Consolidation or retrieval? *Nature,* 1970, *228,* 629–630.

Warrington, E. K., & Weiskrantz, L. The effect of prior learning on subsequent retention in amnesic patients. *Neuropsychologia*, 1974, *12*, 419–428.

Weiskrantz, L., & Warrington, E. K. Conditioning in amnesic patients. *Neuropsychologia*, 1979, *17*, 187–194.

Williamsen, J. A., Johnson, H. J., & Eriksen, C. W. Some characteristics of posthypnotic amnesia. *Journal of Abnormal Psychology*, 1965, *70*, 123–131.

Wilson, G., Rupp, C., & Wilson, W. W. Amnesia. *American Journal of Psychiatry*, 1950, *106*, 481–485.

Wood, F., & Ebert, V. The episodic-semantic memory distinction in memory and amnesia: Clinical and experimental observations. In L. S. Cermak (Ed.), *Human memory and amnesia*. Hillsdale, N.J.: Lawrence Erlbaum, 1982.

Wood, F., Taylor, B., Penny, R., & Stump, D. Regional cerebral blood flow response to recognition memory versus semantic classification tasks. *Brain and Language*, 1980, *9*, 113–122.

Zangwill, O. L. Some qualitative observations on verbal memory in cases of cerebral lesions. *British Journal of Psychology*, 1946, *37*, 8–19.

3

A Conditioning Analysis of Infant Memory

How Do We Know They Know What We Know They Knew?

Jeffrey W. Fagen and Carolyn K. Rovee-Collier

1. INTRODUCTION

In one of the most famous quotations in the field of developmental psychology, William James (1890) wrote that the world of the infant "is one great blooming, buzzing confusion" (p. 488). In the ensuing 90 years investigators have proved James two-thirds correct, that is, the world of the infant is indeed blooming and buzzing; it is not, however, one of confusion. Nowhere is this truth more evident than in the area of infant learning (Lipsitt, 1971). In spite of the fact, however, that demonstrations of learning are ex post facto demonstrations of memory (Bolles, 1976), research on infant memorial abilities has lagged far behind that on infant learning. We believe that this situation has resulted from a paradigmatic error. Infant memory researchers have overlooked the logical relation between learning and memory, focusing almost exclusively on the encoding and storage of information that may have no present rele-

JEFFREY W. FAGEN • Department of Psychology, St. John's University, Jamaica, New York 11439. CAROLYN K. ROVEE-COLLIER • Department of Psychology, Rutgers University, New Brunswick, New Jersey 08903. The research described in this chapter has been supported by Grant Nos. MH32307 and MH24711 from the National Institute of Mental Health to the second author.

vance for the infant (e.g., stimuli that lack signal value; cf. Thorpe, 1963) instead of on the subsequent utility of that which has previously been acquired. Underlying this research has been an allegiance to a multistore view of memory where information is believed to reside briefly (≤30 seconds) in a short-term memory store before either its transfer to a long-term store or its complete loss from the system. As a result, investigators of infant memory have found it convenient to use brief (2 to 8 minutes) single sessions to study long-term memory and have attributed performance deficits under these conditions to memory deficits arising from the permanent loss of information during either encoding, short-term storage, or transfer (Cohen & Gelber, 1975; Fagan, 1977; Olson, 1976; Werner & Perlmutter, 1979). In short, they have echoed the ancient biblical view that many are called but few are chosen: Only a small portion of the information in the short-term store is transferred to long-term memory; the rest is irrevocably lost.

In this chapter we shall describe an approach to the study of infant memory that focuses not on the encoding of information but on its subsequent retrieval. Consistent with this perspective, we discuss forgetting not as a permanent loss of information (i.e., a memory deficit) but as a retrieval failure (see also Chapter 6). Our assumptions are simple and follow those of Underwood (1969) and Spear (1973, 1976, 1978, 1979). We view memory as a multidimensional collection of attributes, each of which represents a characteristic of an event that the infant has noticed. Because these attributes are hypothetical representations and functionally independent, they may be forgotten at different rates. They include aspects of both the internal and external environment that were noticed at the time of acquisition and may be differentially coded as a function of the various factors known to affect an infant's attention (e.g., cue salience, biological predispositions, etc.).

Memory retrieval is also a hypothetical process. An attribute of a given memory is presumably aroused when the infant "notices an event sufficiently similar to that event represented by the attribute" (Spear, 1976, p. 35). Once aroused (noticed), any of the memory attributes may promote the arousal of others. The more attributes of the same memory that are noticed, the greater the probability that the target attribute (i.e., the one being measured by the experimenter) will be retrieved. We infer that retrieval has occurred as a result of performance in recognition, recall, or transfer tasks.

The working hypothesis of our research is that memories are permanent; that is, information acquired by the infant is assumed to be available to influence behavior at any time, although it may not always be accessible for retrieval. Thus by manipulating retrieval cues, we may be able to influence accessibility. We have arrived at this conclusion through the use of a relatively simple operant conditioning paradigm in which the infant is reinforced for legkicking by the movement of an overhead crib mobile (mobile conjugate reinforcement: Rovee-Collier & Gekoski, 1979). To determine whether the infant has acquired the footkick/mobile-movement contingency and can persist in "attempting to move the mobile" even in the absence of reinforcement, we assess retention immediately after the conclusion of training, as well as in some temporally distant session. A decrement in performance between the immediate and the long-term retention tests constitute an operational definition of forgetting (Spear, 1978).

As we shall demonstrate, immediate retention of infants for the contingency is excellent in the 3 minutes following the completion of training. Thus, we know that they "know" (how to make the mobile move). Two weeks later, however, when infants are returned to the original training context, performance has returned to their pretraining (baseline) levels. Does that mean they no longer "know"? Hardly. We shall also present evidence that the information necessary for the performance of the appropriate response is still available, but simply inaccessible. Through the use of reminders administered in a reactivation treatment (cf. Campbell & Jaynes, 1966; Spear, 1973) before the long-term retention test, performance can be returned to a level equivalent to that observed during the immediate retention test at the end of training. By assessing performance following a reactivation treatment and comparing it with performance immediately following training, we are led to conclude that information that appears forgotten is not gone. In short, that is how we know that the infants still know what we know they once knew.

2. THE INFERENCE OF MEMORY PROCESSING AND RETENTION

2.1. Methodologies

Research on infant "visual recognition" memory has been shaped by models of adult verbal learning and information processing. Measurement of retention has been indirect, inferred from the extent to which an infant does not fixate a familiarized stimulus. The starting point for this research was Sokolov's (1963) classic model of the habituation of the orienting reflex (Pavlov's "what is it" reflex; Pavlov, 1927). According to Sokolov, when an organism repeatedly encounters the same stimulus in the same context, an internal representation or *engram* of the stimulus is constructed. The infant continues to fixate the stimulus until the engram is complete. When that occurs, attention is directed elsewhere.

One derivative paradigm for studying infant visual recognition memory is the *habituation technique*. This technique involves the repeated presentation of a single stimulus until attention to it has declined to some absolute (e.g., McCall, Kennedy, & Dodds, 1977) or relative (e.g., Cohen, DeLoache, & Pearl, 1977) criterion. Following habituation, a novel stimulus is presented and a renewal of the attention to the novel stimulus is taken to indicate that the previous response diminution was not the result of effector or receptor fatigue. Subjects continuing to receive the original stimulus, however, do not show a resurgence of attention at this point in the trials. By varying the interval between the final habituation trial and the presentation of the novel target and seeking an interval after which different groups of infants fixate the novel and the familiar target equally on the test trial, investigators have tried to pinpoint the limits of infant long-term memory. That is, to the extent that the novel stimulus is fixated *more*, the infant is assumed to remember something about the familiar one. The current limit found with this procedure is approximately 5 minutes (cf. Cohen & Gelber, 1975; for review, see Werner & Perlmutter, 1979).

A common variation of this technique has been derived from the pioneering work of Fantz (1961). In the *paired-comparison technique*, the infant is simultaneously presented with two stimuli following a single familiarization trial with one of them. Again, retention ("recognition") is inferred from the extent to which the infant does not attend to the familiar stimulus. Instead, greater attention to the novel stimulus implies that the infant possesses a memory engram for the familiar stimulus. By varying the interval between the familiarization trial and the test pairing, the limits of retention are determined. Here, the limits appear to range from 8 minutes (Olson, 1976) to several days (Fagan, 1973). Although much research has been undertaken to compare these two methodologies (e.g., Caron, Caron, Minichiello, Weiss, & Friedman, 1977), the general consensus has been that both of these paradigms are effective for assessing the memorial capabilities of young infants (for review see Werner & Perlmutter, 1979; see also Sophian, 1980). Moreover, the *non*response to the familiarized stimulus has been called a "positive recognition response" (Bornstein, 1976, p. 189).

An obvious problem arises when the infant either looks longer at the familiarized stimulus on a test trial or looks at the two stimuli equally. Can such results be taken as an indication of a memory failure? That, in fact, is what previous researchers have inferred. Yet such an outcome can occur for a variety of reasons that have nothing whatsoever to do with memory. (In fact, we would argue that looking at a *novel* stimulus does not need to imply retention; see below.) Olson (1976) suggests that the determinants of looking on a paired-comparison trial can include discriminability factors (interstimulus contrasts, codability), preference factors (perceptual features, interpretation), and response biases (position habits, gaze-shifting criteria, state) in addition to familiarization/ novelty factors. In addition, infant attention may also be influenced by internal and/or external events that can neither be specified nor measured. In spite of Olson's realization that the infant's failure to look differentially at the two stimuli on a paired-comparison trial cannot be interpreted, he nevertheless claims that it "can be used as *circumstantial* evidence regarding coding abilities" (1976, p. 253, italics added). Others have asserted that the infant's failure to fixate a novel stimulus for longer than a familiar one reflects the fact that it is "too difficult" (Hopkins, Zelazo, Jacobson, & Kagan, 1976) or that the infant is simply making "false positive responses" (Bornstein, 1976, p. 189). The dilemma here is obvious. On the one hand, we have a "nonresponse" to familiar stimulus being taken as a "positive" response; on the other, the "nonresponse" to the novel stimulus is a "false positive." Given this a priori conviction, need we even study what the infant does?

Putting these considerations aside, we are still faced with accounting for the infant's initial habituation of the looking response. Again, the consensus has been to assume that the simple demonstration of any degree of habituation is evidence for memory. It is our position, however, that the concept of memory need not be invoked in situations that simply involve altered attention. Spear (1973), for example, describes the effect of novel cues that elicit orienting responses as distracting attention from effective (familiar) retrieval cues. In addition, Jeffrey (1976), in commenting on the widespread and uncritical use of the Sokolov model in infant visual recognition memory research, proposes that the infant's response to a novel stimulus is a simple, perceptual processing strategy devoid of memorial implications.

Many of the problems inherent in visual recognition memory research seem to arise from the measurement of a response that is maximally present in the normal waking infant. As such, all that can be measured in different experimental procedures is the extent to which attention appears to be differentially distributed among the various stimuli in the infant's environment. This distribution can occur reflexively as part of the orienting response (Cohen, 1972), or it may also occur as an operant (DeLoache, Rissman, & Cohen, 1978). In either instance, nonvisual as well as visual influences may alter the distribution (Clifton & Nelson, 1976; Horowitz, 1975).

Other measurement problems stem from the fact that the process of infant attention per se is not well understood (cf. Haith, 1980). This situation leads to the problem of the most appropriate means to index and quantify it. Although visual attention is typically indexed solely by fixation duration, it may vary along other immeasurable dimensions as well. For example, we have no way of quantifying whether looks of equal duration reflect equivalent "depths" of concentration. Furthermore, if attention is an all-or-none process, or if it reaches asymptote at a given point depending on the nature of the material, then duration of looking is not a meaningful measure. What, then, is one to infer from a duration measure of visual fixation? We agree with Haith (1980, p. 11) that "the important information is what a baby is doing or trying to do with his/her visual array, not how long the baby does it." In addition, although researchers using this technique assume that attention implies encoding, it cannot be known *what* an infant is encoding in the course of a visual fixation, or the *rate* at which the infant is encoding it. Indeed, there are large individual differences in both (McCall, 1971; McCall & Kagan, 1970; McCall *et al.*, 1977). Furthermore, Fagan (1972, 1973) has consistently reported negligible correlations between duration of fixation during familiarization exposure and later responsiveness to the novel stimulus in paired-comparison tests. In spite of these considerations, however, researchers have continued to cling hopefully to attention as an index of retention when clearly an overt, precisely quantifiable, index of retention is needed.

2.2. Direct and Implicit Tests of Infant Visual Recognition Memory

It is necessary to introduce an operational distinction between short- and long-term memory. Our purpose here is one of convenience and should not be confused with models of memory that propose the existence of short- and long-term memory stores. It is our position that studies conducted either within a single session or within a single day are short-term memory studies. The overwhelming majority of infant visual recognition memory studies are of this type. We shall define long-term memory studies as those involving a retention interval of at least 1 day.

2.2.1. Direct Tests of Infant Visual Recognition Memory

Few researchers have studied recognition memory over periods that meet our long-term memory criterion. Fagan (1973) used a paired-comparison procedure to study retention of 21- to 25-week-old infants for abstract black and white stimuli, facial photographs, and facial masks. In a series of experiments he exposed infants to the black and white stimuli, which varied either multidimensionally (contour and form, number of elements, etc.) or in pattern only (varying arrangements of black squares), and retested them during a 20-second session either 24 or 48 hours later. A reliably smaller percentage of total fixation time was allocated to the previously exposed stimulus after both retention intervals, whether stimuli differed multidimensionally or simply in pattern arrangement. Interestingly, the mean fixation time for both test stimuli was only 8.5 seconds of the 20-second test period. (One can only guess what the infants were looking at or doing for the remainder of the exposure period.) In a second experiment, Fagan assessed "recognition" of facial photographs following delays of 3 hours, 24 hours, 48 hours, 1 week, or 2 weeks. Again, recognition was inferred following all retention intervals. However, in Experiment 3, infants tested with lifelike facial masks of a man, a woman, and a baby did *not* show differential fixations of novel and preexposed masks after the 3-hour interval. Performance after the other intervals was not assessed.

Fagan described his paradigm as "the perfect 'incidental recall' conditions" (1973, p. 448), and concluded that recognition of pictorial stimuli after delays of 2 weeks must be a basic ability, particularly given its appearance in infants as young as 5 or 6 months. However, a series of recent studies has indicated that it is difficult to demonstrate interference effects within the visual recognition memory paradigm (Cohen *et al.*, 1977; Fagan, 1977; McCall *et al.*, 1977). Thus the poor "retention" reported by Fagan for the lifelike facial masks after only 3 hours remains unexplained.

Cornell (1979) used the Fagan paired-comparison paradigm to investigate the influence of a reminder (see also Section 4.) on recognition of briefly presented visual stimuli by 5- to 6-month-olds. After first determining the minimum exposure time necessary to obtain a significant response-to-novelty immediately following a familiarization trial, he then established that after an interval of 48 hours the infants fixated the novel and the preexposed stimuli equally (i.e., complete "forgetting"). However, if infants were reexposed to the familiar stimulus immediately before either the immediate or the long-term test, they once more exhibited a reliable preference for the stimulus that was *not* the reminder in both tests. The reminder treatment alone, however, without the prior familiarization trial, was ineffective in producing a reliable novelty preference at both intervals. Unfortunately, the data were inconsistent. Not only did the infants in the second experiment fail to evidence reliable "recognition" memory after 48 hours, they failed to do so after a short-term (40- to 105-second) interval as well. Cornell attributed this finding to one of two factors.

> A time interval between familiarization and recognition test may allow for partial recovery of response to the most salient cues of the familiar stimulus (Jeffrey, 1976). Or, the forgetting that occurred may have been the result of interference from visual events during the retention interval. (p. 367)

His first explanation echoes one of our concerns with this entire paradigm, namely, that changes in the distribution of visual attention between stimuli are not valid indicators of the memorial capabilities of young infants. The second explanation is inconsistent with findings of interference effects (cf. Cohen et al., 1977; Fagen, 1977; McCall et al., 1977).

The preceding results were elaborated to emphasize the frailties of paradigms that heretofore have comprised our sole means of measuring infant retention. Typically, researchers in this area claim that their results (or lack of them) reflect the extent to which the infant has encoded (or failed to encode) the target stimulus. Encoding, however, as a hypothetical construct, cannot be directly measured. In fact, one can speak only of retention and forgetting, both of which can be operationalized. The circularity of discussions that focus on encoding is exemplified by the McCall et al. (1977) study. As in the other studies of retroactive interference, this one failed to find any overall effect. However, when the data were reanalyzed for only those infants "who provided some sign that they had begun to encode the distracting stimulus (i.e., looking time declined over the five trials of distraction)" (p. 86), an interference effect was obtained. As discussed earlier, however, a decline in looking (habituation) cannot be considered evidence of encoding. We agree, then, with their ultimate conclusion that

> one must contend with the apparent requirement that the infant evidence some encoding of the distracting stimulus and the fact that *habituation even to asymptote may not be sufficiently precise to index this cognitive event*. (McCall et al., 1977, p. 87, italics added)

2.2.2. Implicit Tests of Infant Visual Recognition Memory

In the course of developing the familiarization/paired-comparison paradigm, Fagan (1970) used sets of three stimuli (e.g., A-B-C) in contrasting black and white patterns to define problems. On any given day, one member of the set (e.g., A) served as the familiarization stimulus and the two remaining members were novelty test stimuli. Each problem was tested once per day for 3 successive days, but on each occasion a different member served as the familiarization stimulus. Fagan found greater attention to test stimuli on the first day only; on subsequent tests with a given set of targets, infants did not differentially fixate stimuli.

This result implied that exposure to all of the stimuli on the first day made them equivalently familiar/novel, and that this effect persisted for 24 hours.

Studies by McCall and Kagan (1967) and McCall (1973) were not specifically designed to assess long-term memory, but were sequels to memory studies involving short-term familiarization techniques. Because in the earlier studies there were large individual differences in initial rates of habituation, the subsequent studies were designed to provide infants with periods of extended familiarization with the standard stimulus so that all might have sufficient exposure time to acquire a memory engram. In McCall (1973), for example, mothers were asked to expose their 3-month-old infants daily for 2 weeks to a stabile containing a given stimulus array. At the end of that time, infants were returned to the laboratory for discrimination tests with the same stimulus array and three variations of it, achieved by the rearrangement of its components. Unfortunately, the mothers turned out to be quite variable in their adherence to the familiarization regime. The median number of exposures was only 12, the distribution of exposures varied within and across days, and the interval between the final home exposure and the laboratory test varied, averaging 18 hours. Data were collected during only 80 seconds of a 180-second test session, with the total duration of the first fixation to two presentations each of the four test arrays constituting the response measure. A number of variables were reported to influence responding (age, sex, hypothetical pattern of habituation during home familiarization), both singly and in various interactions. Although specific conclusions regarding long-term memory were difficult to extract, it was clear that the home familiarization procedure did influence performance 18 hours later in the laboratory.

In a long-term familiarization study based on a preliminary report by Hunt and Uzgiris (1964), Kaplan (1967) sought to assess developmental changes in infant attention to novel and familiar stimuli. When their infants were 6 weeks old, mothers began exposing them twice daily to either a nonmoving stabile, a continuously moving mobile, or a mobile that moved in response to the activity of the infant. All familiarization stimuli were suspended within an experimental crib which remained in the home. Exposures varied in duration both within and across infants—infants were placed in the crib when they were alert and active and were removed when they either cried or fell asleep. Longitudinal assessments of infant preference for a familiar or novel nonmoving stabile were obtained during 4-minute paired-comparison tests after 2, 4, 6, and 8 weeks of familiarization (i.e., at 8, 10, 12, and 14 weeks of age). Each test occurred in the infant's own home, in the experimental crib, 24 hours following the last familiarization exposure.

Kaplan found no differential fixations of familiar and novel test stimuli no matter what type of familiarization stimulus was used until the infants were 12 weeks old. At that time they fixated the novel stimuli longer than the familiar stimuli, but the type of movement condition received during familiarization interacted with stimulus familiarity during testing. Specifically, fixations of infants familiarized with the automatically moving mobile were equally distributed over both test models. A slight preference was observed for novel stabiles by infants familiarized with nonmoving stabiles. Finally, a novelty preference of almost 2 : 1 was exhibited by the infants familiarized with the responsive mobile. Kaplan suggests that exposure to the continuously moving mobile might have resulted in any *nonmoving* test stimulus being regarded as novel, or that the movement might have impeded the discrimination of the details of the stimulus. Implicit in her findings, however, is evidence of 24-hour retention at 12 weeks of age, but not earlier.

Weizmann, Cohen, and Pratt (1971) modified Kaplan's design in a second long-term familiarization study of developmental changes in preferences for novel and familiar stimuli. They placed 4-week-olds in an experimental bassinet every day for 30 minutes. Suspended from the bassinet was a stabile containing either three colored-yarn tassels attached to a yellow disk or a cluster of pink plastic flowers affixed to the center of a red disk. Bassinets were of two types and differed in color of bedding and interior lining. Half of the sample were tested at both 6 and 8 weeks and half at 8 weeks only. The interval between the final home exposure and the test session was not indicated but presumably ranged from 12 to 24 hours. During test sessions, infants were placed in one of the bassinets and presented with both stabile models simultaneously. Visual fixation times to each model were recorded. After 4 minutes infants were switched to the other bassinet and testing was continued for an additional 4 minutes. At 6 weeks the infants fixated the familiar stabiles significantly longer than the novel stabiles, but at 8 weeks the difference in fixation times was not reliable. In addition, females tested in the novel bassinet fixated the novel stabile longer than the familiar stabile, and longer than females tested in the familiar bassinet. Fixations of 8-week-olds who had been tested 2 weeks earlier differed significantly from those of their first test counterparts. The direction of the difference, however, was a complicated function of infant sex. (Double-observation females fixated all test stimuli less than all double-observation males. Total mean fixations of the latter group, however, exceeded those of single-observation males.)

Although equivocal, these findings suggest that long-term home familiarization may influence test performance on a subsequent day. They also suggest that the effect of brief exposures may persist for 2 weeks, at least in females. These findings, however, must be viewed with caution. Not only are reports of sex differences in visual fixation measures erratic across procedures and laboratories (see Clifton & Nelson, 1976), but also at 6 weeks infants spent relatively little test time actually looking at the stabiles (only 155.6 seconds of 480 seconds of potential viewing time) and devoted only slightly more than a minute, on the average, to inspection of the novel stabile. In addition, these findings were not consistent with those of Kaplan (1967), who did not obtain differential fixation of familiar and novel stimuli on the part of 10-week-old infants who had been tested 2 weeks earlier and who never obtained significant differences in groups familiarized with a nonmoving stabile. Given the influence of test context, it would have been useful to know whether the infants were tested in their homes (a familiar context) or in the laboratory (an unfamiliar context).

2.3. Summary

Research in infant visual recognition memory has been shaped exclusively by models of adult verbal learning, and forgetting has been attributed to deficits in either encoding or storage. We argue that the procedures that have been used in memory studies have measured only the infant's ability to detect change in a stimulus array. In our view, the greater fixation time of a *novel* stimulus does not index the infant's memorial capabilities but constitutes a perceptual processing strategy (cf. Jeffrey, 1968, 1976). Thus a lack of differential response to novelty under these conditions, or a greater response to the familiar stimulus, cannot be interpreted as a memory deficit. This point is consistent with our view of memory as a collection of attributes, many of which represent contextual cues. To the extent that retention test context contains novel cues or cues not part of the context of the original experience, the number of potential retrieval cues will be reduced, and the probability of retrieval diminished. In studies of infant visual recognition memory, retention is assessed implicitly only; it is never directly or independently measured by the production of a specific, overt response to the familiar stimulus. It is difficult to see, therefore, how infants who do not look at familiar cues would be able to retrieve their representations and *use* the information about them that is presumably stored.

3. A CONDITIONING ANALYSIS OF INFANT MEMORY

A conditioning analysis of infant memory avoids the issue of perceptual processing versus memory by determining the extent to which infants can use what they have learned. This approach is modeled after studies of animal memory that have focused primarily on factors affecting retrieval and, in particular, on the role of context (see Jenkins, 1974). This emphasis reflects the fact that it is experimentally difficult, if not impossible, to measure encoding and storage independent of retrieval. If retrieval is prerequisite to demonstrations of retention, the possibility must remain that at a minimum, retrieval deficits are responsible for the poor retention. We concur, then, with Bruner (1964) that "the most important thing about memory is not storage of past experience, but rather the retrieval of what is relevant *in some usable form*" (p. 2, italics added).

The assumptions of our analysis are straightforward: (1) A memory is permanent; (2) context influences retrieval; and (3) accessibility of memory attributes is facilitated by cuing procedures. Because storage and retrieval cannot be assessed independently, our focus is on what behavior an infant can actually produce in the future rather than on what might have been encoded and lost from some inferred storage.

3.1. Methodology

The procedure we have used with young infants is known as mobile conjugate reinforcement (Rovee-Collier & Gekoski, 1979). As illustrated in Figure 3.1, an infant is placed supine in his or her crib and a length of ribbon is connected from the infant's ankle to one of two overhead mobile suspension bars. The ribbon permits the infant to draw and release the suspension bar, thereby moving the mobile in a manner commensurate with the vigor and rate of response. It is the *movement* of the mobile, and not simply its presence, that constitutes reinforcement. The reinforcing efficacy of this moving stimulus derives from the fact that young infants will fixate both moving and relatively novel stimuli for lengthy periods. Because each response produces a slightly different view of the suspended objects, satiation is not a problem. Moreover, the rapidity with which infants learn the response-reinforcement contingency (3 to 9 minutes, depending on age) precludes the necessity for lengthy training sessions.

To study infant memory, we have followed the general training and test procedures of Spear (1971, 1973, 1976, 1978) and Campbell (Campbell & Coulter, 1976; Campbell & Spear, 1972). The approach is straightforward: We train the infant to perform a specific response (a footkick) in a particular setting (the infant's home crib in the presence of distinctive mobile color/pattern cues), and at some future time return the infant to the same context to see if (1) the specific response will be produced at some level above pretraining baseline, and/or (2) the response is re-

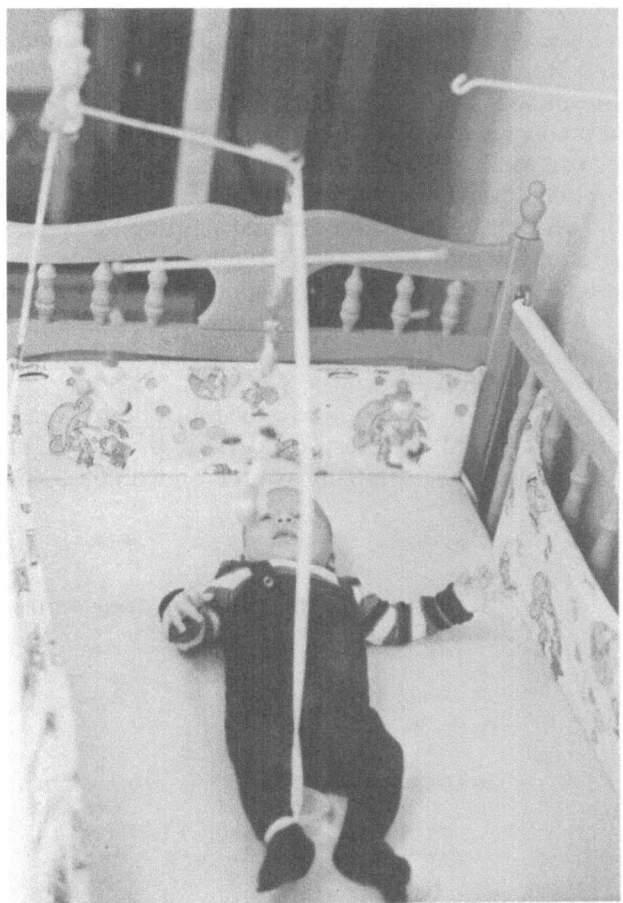

Fig. 3.1. The experimental arrangement of the mobile conjugate reinforcement paradigm. An 8-week-old infant is shown during a reinforcement phase. During nonreinforcement phases (baseline/long-term retention test; immediate retention test) the mobile is hung from the other mobile stand (upper right) to which no ribbon is attached.

learned more rapidly than if no prior learning had occurred. To be a test of "pure" retention (not relearning), reinforcement must be absent when the infant is initially returned to the training context. Only in this way can "recall" cued by the context be separated from reacquisition. Similarly, to provide a standard against which to assess recall in an identical context, retention should also be assessed immediately following training in a nonreinforcement period of comparable length, thus allowing a direct measure of the change in responding over the retention interval.

Our training and testing procedure is illustrated in Figure 3.2. During Phases 1 and 3 of each session, the mobile is in the infant's view but is suspended from the mobile stand to which the ankle ribbon is not attached. In this way, footkicks do not move the mobile; thus reinforcement is not present. However, the specific details of the mobile components per se can serve as contextual retrieval cues. In Session 1, Phase 1 is used to obtain the baseline rate of footkicking; in all subsequent sessions this phase serves as a long-term retention test. Here the visual characteristics of the mobile act as discriminative stimuli that can serve as retrieval cues for the conditioned response. Performance during the long-term retention test (Phase 1 of subsequent sessions) is assessed in relation to performance during Phase 3 of the preceding session, that is, the immediate retention test.

Sessions 1 and 2 are always separated by 24 hours, but the interval between Sessions 2 and 3 varies and defines the long-term retention interval under study. (Occasionally we have included a third training

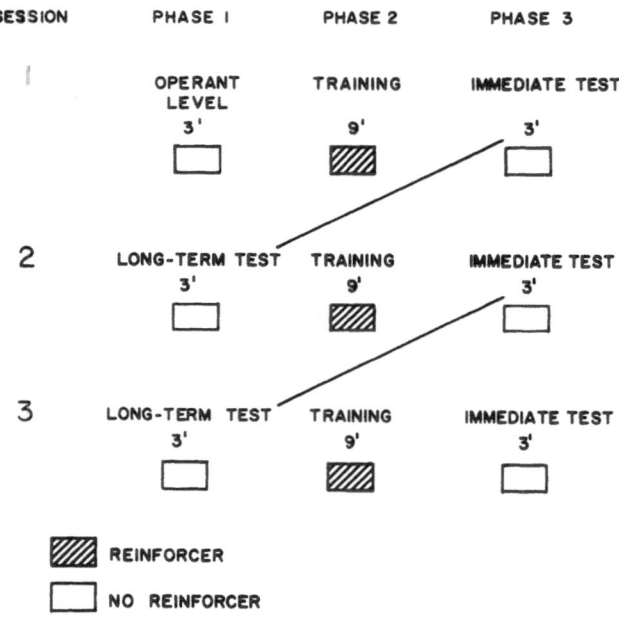

Fig. 3.2. The standard retention paradigm. Sessions 1 and 2 are separated by 24 hours, Sessions 2 and 3 by intervals ranging from 1 to 28 days, depending upon the study. Each session involves a 9-minute reinforcement phase preceded and followed by a 3-minute nonreinforcement phase. Performance during each long-term retention test is assessed in relation to performance during the procedurally identical immediate retention test of the preceding session (diagonal lines). During retention tests the mobile is suspended overhead but is nonmoving; its components serve as retrieval cues.

session 24 hours after the second one.) To assess retention of the conditioned response, we compare the change in response rate from the immediate retention test of one session to the long-term retention test of the next. The measures are either absolute numbers of footkicks, the difference in the number of footkicks in a long-term session of an experimental group relative to those of control group, or ratios derived from scores of each infant. One form of our "retention ratio" is B/A, where B is the response rate during the long-term retention test and A is the rate during the procedurally identical immediate retention test. Ratios of ≥ 1.00 indicate no forgetting over the retention interval; ratios of <1.00 reflect the particular fraction of conditioned responding that persisted after the retention interval. We prefer the ratio measure to our earlier procedure of simply comparing absolute numbers of footkicks because it eliminates problems arising from individual differences in response levels (which can be quite large) or shifts in momentary preferences for different reward values (see also Church, 1971, p. 713).

Occasionally, we have used another measure either because, for procedural reasons, an immediate retention test could not be given, or because response rates dramatically increased or decreased during the immediate retention test relative to the last 3 minutes of the preceding training period. This problem sometimes arises when very young infants (e.g., 8-week-olds) are tested. Under these conditions, we compute "baseline ratios" which reflect the extent to which an individual infant's performance during the long-term retention test continues to exceed his or her pretraining baseline (Session 1, Phase 1). This ratio is of the form B/P, where B is the response rate during the long-term test and P is the rate during the pretraining baseline. With the baseline ratio, ratios of 1.00 merely reflect performance that has returned to baseline. Because we typically define learning as a minimum increase in response rate of 1.5 times the (pretraining) operant level, retention of the contingency is inferred from baseline ratios ≥ 1.50.

After the reintroduction of reinforcement in Session 3, it is often interesting to determine the rapidity of reacquisition and to compare it to the rate of original learning. This is achieved through the use of "savings ratios" of the form $D-C/C$, where D represents the total number of footkicks during reacquisition (Session 3, Phase 2) and C represents the total number of footkicks during acquisition (Session 1, Phase 2). This ratio reflects the extent of each infant's net gain in responding during the retention test session relative to that same infant's response rate during training (Rovee-Collier & Fagen, 1981; Sullivan, Rovee-Collier, & Tynes, 1979). If past training has facilitated subsequent reacquisition, then the response asymptote should be reached more rapidly, and there would be a greater number of responses in the reacquisition phase than would be expected simply as a function of age-related increases in the speed of conditioning (Gekoski, 1977).

3.2. Initial Tests of Retention

3.2.1. The Retention Interval

To study infant memory using conditioning procedures, the logical starting point must be the question of what, if anything, an infant carries over from one training session to the next. In a pilot study using the mobile conjugate reinforcement technique, Smith (cited in Lipsitt, 1971, pp. 15–17) noted increasing rapidity of both conditioning and extinction across repeated training sessions with her infant son. In our initial study (Rovee & Fagen, 1976) we trained 3-month-olds for 15 minutes per day for 4 consecutive days. Each session followed our standard procedure of 9 minutes of reinforcement, immediately preceded and followed by a 3-minute nonreinforcement period (cf. Figure 3.2). Infants in this study were randomly assigned to experimental and control groups, but we need only concern ourselves here with the control group who received the same mobile on each of the 4 days. What we sought to determine was the extent to which performance of these infants at the end of each day was reflected in their performance at the outset of the next daily session (i.e., the initial nonreinforcement phase). As shown in Figure 3.3, on each succeeding day they essentially picked up where they had left off on the previous day. This was the first direct demonstration of long-term (24-hour) retention of an acquired association involving a "cued-recall" task. In addition, the infants were half the age of those tested in previous visual recognition memory studies.

Having found excellent retention over 24-hour periods, we next asked what was the maximum retention interval over which these training effects would persist. Sullivan et al. (1979) trained infants for 2 days and administered a third session after retention intervals of 48, 72, 96, 120, 192, or 336 hours (cf. Figure 3.2). Here, significant forgetting (i.e., a decrement in performance between Sessions 2 and 3) was observed only in infants tested after 14 days, when their long-term retention test performance was indistinguishable from their Session 1 operant level. This study also indicated that the forgetting of a newly acquired memory, expressed in terms of group retention ratios, declined gradually as a function of time since training.

3.2.2. The Training and Test Contexts

If one views memory as a collection of attributes representing that which was originally noticed about an event, then the context in which a

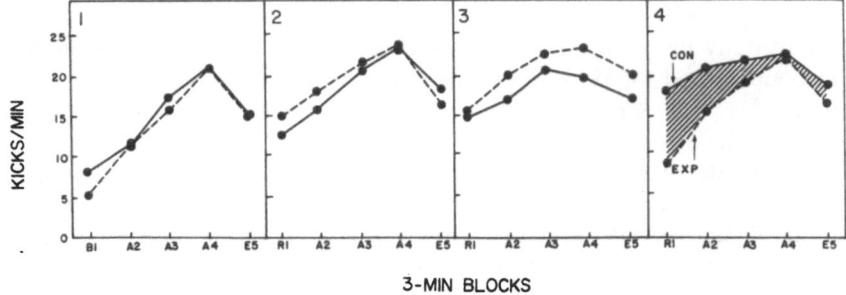

3-MIN BLOCKS

Fig. 3.3. Conditioning curves of 3-month-old infants over four consecutive training sessions spaced by 24 hours each. During Sessions 1 to 3 all infants received the "same" mobile model; during Session 4 infants in the control group (CON) were tested with the original mobile, but infants in the experimental group (EXP) were tested with a different model. The decrement in performance attributable to the altered test context is indicated by diagonal lines. Note the high level of retention during each successive long-term retention test (RI) relative to performance during the immediate retention test (E5) of the preceding session. B indicates baseline; A indicates acquisition phases. (From "Extended Conditioning and 24-hr Retention in Infants" by C. K. Rovee and J. W. Fagen, *Journal of Experimental Child Psychology*, 1976, 21, p. 5. Fig. 1 [redrawn]. Copyright 1976 by Academic Press. Reprinted by permission.)

memory is acquired as well as that in which retention is tested are critical aspects of any assessment of retention. If contextual cues are potential retrieval cues, then any change between the context in which a memory was acquired and that in which retention is assessed may contribute to an apparent memory deficit through retrieval deficits. In our preceding studies, infants were tested in an experimental context identical to that of training. In other words, the same mobile components were present as retrieval cues during the immediate and long-term retention tests. If, however, we alter the context in which retention is assessed, then we have created a generalization test with the number of common attributes in the two contexts determining the probability of retrieval. Although there are a number of ways in which this can be accomplished, we have chosen to vary the characteristics of the mobile per se and/or its consequences, insofar as the infant's attention to the reinforcer is usually high and sustained.

In the Rovee and Fagen (1976) study, one group of infants (the "experimental" group) received a novel mobile on their fourth training day. Instead of exhibiting the characteristic session-to-session response carry-over of the control infants, these infants exhibited little or no conditioned responding during the initial 3-minute long-term retention test of Session 4. Furthermore, although their reattainment of asymptotic responding appeared to be gradual, individual infants in the experimental group actually produced discontinuous response functions, resuming high and stable footkicking at different points into the session. This result suggested that the novel attributes of the unfamiliar test mobile may initially have distracted the infants from the familiar retrieval cues for conditioned responding. However, when the cues in the novel mobile that were similar to those in the familiar one were finally noticed, retrieval occurred.

This interpretation was supported in a subsequent study in which the number of novel components in the Day 4 mobile was varied (Fagen, Rovee, & Kaplan, 1976). Thus, after 3 days of training with a particular five-component mobile, infants were tested on a fourth day with a five-component mobile containing either zero, one, two, three, or four "new" elements substituted for "old" ones. As shown in Figure 3.4, performance during the Day 4 long-term retention test was a power function of the number of novel components with a slope of −0.90. Given that 3-month-olds show a strong attentional response to novelty, we think the number of novel components influenced the latency for the infant to notice familiar retrieval cues. Interestingly, adults who scaled the similarity of each Day 4 mobile with respect to the training mobile yielded a similar power function.

In the preceding studies, the Day 4 mobile differed from the mobile seen on Days 1 to 3 along a number of dimensions (color, shape, etc.). Thus it was not clear which of these, either singly or in combination, influenced infant behavior during the long-term retention test. Previous research with visual recognition paradigms had demonstrated that in-

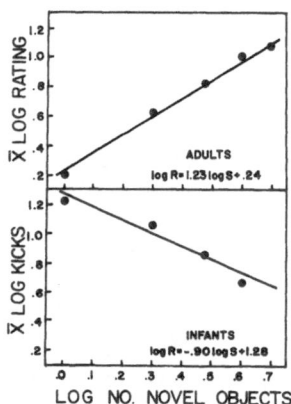

Fig. 3.4. Power functions showing adult ratings of dissimilarity (top) and infant conditioned footkicks during the Day 4 long-term retention test (bottom) as a function of the number of substituted mobile elements. (From "Psychophysical Scaling of Stimulus Similarity in 3-Month-Old Infants and Adults" by J. W. Fagen *et al., Journal of Experimental Child Psychology*, 1976, 22, pp. 349–360. Copyright 1976 by Academic Press. Reprinted by permission.)

creasing numbers of changes in the dimensions of a stimulus array elicited increasing durations of visual attention (Welch, 1974), and Olson (1976) had concluded that infants under 4 months old could detect stimulus differences only when stimuli varied multidimensionally.

In our initial studies we assessed the effects of changes in component numerosity in a paradigm borrowed from the animal literature on shifts in the amount of reinforcement (cf. Crespi, 1942; Zeaman, 1949). We began by training infants with mobiles containing either 10, 6, or 2 identical components and subsequently switching all mobiles to the two-element type (Fagen & Rovee, 1976). When the reinforcer was shifted from 6 to 2 components, infants immediately doubled their previous response rate, but infants experiencing the 10- to 2-component shift, after an initial vigorous burst, ceased responding altogether, instead either crying or falling asleep. This outcome suggested that the *absolute* number of components during testing was not the factor determining response: Both shift groups viewed the same number of components during testing, yet their behavior differed dramatically. Moreover, infants were able to detect differences in a single dimension of reinforcement, namely, numerosity.

In a follow-up study (Mast, Fagen, Rovee-Collier, & Sullivan, 1980) we hypothesized that during the course of training infants acquired certain expectancies about how their footkicks would affect the mobile movement (see also Bolles, 1972, 1976). When the number of components contained in the mobile was reduced, this expectancy was violated, resulting in the behavioral changes observed by Fagen and Rovee (1976). Moreover, if these expectancies are learned, they should continue to influence the infant's behavior for a relatively extended period. To evaluate this hypothesis we again trained infants with mobiles containing either 6 or 10 identical components and subsequently shifted them to a mobile containing only two components. Emotional and operant behaviors were assessed as before but were reassessed after a 24-hour retention interval. During the 24-hour retention test, infants were exposed to either the 2-component mobile or their original 6- or 10-component mobile. Relative to a control group that received reinforcement from the two-component mobile throughout, infants shifted to this "smaller" mobile exhibited the same pattern of responding observed previously; however, these effects were not transient, persisting 24 hours later on the part of infants in the 10- to 2-component group who continued to receive the "smaller" mobile during the test session. This finding strongly suggests that infants develop expectancies about their rewards that influence their behavior over periods as long as 24 hours.

In the studies by Fagen and Rovee (1976) and Mast *et al.* (1980), the pre- and postshift mobiles varied along only one of the many possible dimensions, numerosity. Although this pattern produced robust changes in behavior when mobiles were switched following experience with one of them, infants responded similarly to the three mobiles when they had no prior mobile reinforcement experience. Fagen (1980) varied mobiles along the color dimension and observed differences in response rate both before and after the shift. Specifically, infants were trained for 2 days with mobiles containing either blue-only or green-only objects and were then shifted to the "novel" mobile color partway into the session on the third day. On Day 4, half of the infants continued to receive the postshift mobile whereas the remaining half were returned to the original (preshift) mobile. Even before the shift, infants kicked more in the presence of the blue than the green mobile, which implied that they "preferred" the blue mobile; in fact, following the shift, 80% of the infants switched from blue to green cried. This behavior was not seen in infants switched from green to blue. Also on the fourth day, 40% to 60% of the infants who had been shifted to the green mobile on the day before cried. Again, however, crying never occurred in the presence of the blue postshift mobile. Along with the data on numerosity shifts, these findings reaffirm our belief that both "psychological" as well as physical attributes are represented as a part of the infant's memory of an event.

Finally, we have recently begun to investigate the functional organization of infant memory and the temporal parameters of such organization. We questioned why retrieval ever occurred in the experimental infants tested by Rovee and Fagen (1976), given that they were experiencing a completely novel mobile on the fourth day of training. In short, what were the retrieval cues that these infants noticed and that permitted them to produce the conditioned response? Because both adults (Loftus & Kallman, 1979) and children (Williams, Fryer, & Aiken, 1977) appear to code both the general and specific details of a situation, it seemed entirely possible that infants did too. In this way the infant, upon receiving a novel stimulus (mobile) in a situation highly similar to that existing when the memory was originally acquired, could eventually retrieve the appropriate response through noticing the more general features shared by the original and novel mobiles. That such retrieval did not occur immediately in the earlier study suggests that although both types of retrieval cues are available, the specific (novel) details are more salient. Although that may be the case shortly following training, it has been suggested that the general features should be accessible to retrieval over longer periods (Hasher & Griffin, 1978).

Rovee-Collier and Sullivan (1980) differentiated between the general and specific details of the mobile conjugate reinforcement situation by investigating the "distractibility-by-novelty" phenomenon after increasingly lengthy intervals. Infants were trained for two sessions with one five-component mobile (cf. Figure 3.2) and were exposed to a completely novel five-component mobile during a third session after retention intervals of 24, 48, 72, or 96 hours (see Figure 3.5). The typical session-to-session response carry-over (cf. Rovee & Fagen, Figure 2) occurred in all infants as long as the mobile remained unchanged. The introduction of the novel mobile impaired performance when Session 3 followed Session 2 by 24, 48, and 72 hours. However, the novel mobile had no effect on conditioned responding after 96 hours, suggesting that after this temporal interval, infants no longer differentiated the specific details of "novel" and "familiar" mobiles. Instead they showed complete generalization (high and stable response rates to the novel mobile), suggesting that they had retrieved attributes corresponding to features defining the general class "mobile." Thus it appears that the general attributes of a situation can influence behavior over a lengthier period than can the specific attributes, and that infants can exhibit positive

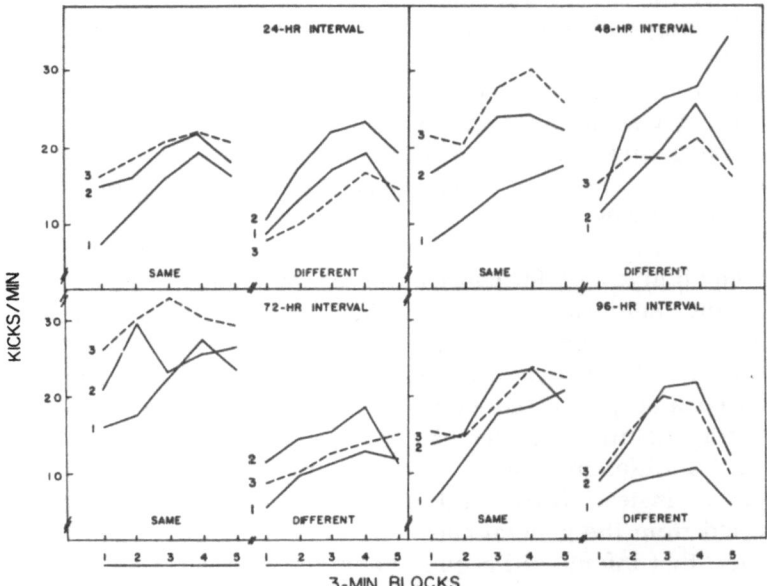

Fig. 3.5. Conditioning curves of independent groups of infants receiving the "same" mobile for three consecutive sessions or the "same" mobile for two sessions only a "different" mobile in Session 3 (dashed line). Blocks 1 and 5 in each session are nonreinforcement phases; Blocks 2 to 4 are reinforcement phases. The interval between Sessions 1 and 2 was 24 hours; that between Sessions 2 and 3 varied from 24 to 96 hours, as indicated in each panel. (From "Organization of Infant Memory" by C. K. Rovee-Collier and M. W. Sullivan, *Journal of Experimental Psychology: Human Learning and Memory*, 1980, *6*, 798–807. Copyright 1980 by the American Psychological Association. Reprinted by permission.)

transfer from one situation to another by noticing their shared or general features while selectively forgetting their specific details at a faster rate. These data further suggest that young infants can and do spontaneously categorize stimuli into classes, much the same as older children do (Flavell, 1970).

Given that attributes representing both general features and specific details comprise the infant's memory of an event, we next asked the following: (1) Could infants learn to ignore the otherwise salient novel details of a test stimulus and learn to use general or shared features as a basis of responding? (2) If they could do so, could they still respond to the distinctive features? (3) What are the minimal conditions for the occurrence of one or both of these?

To address these questions, we began by training infants for 4 consecutive days in the standard mobile conjugate reinforcement procedure (Fagen, Rovee-Collier, Morrongiello, & Gekoski, 1980). Infants were randomly assigned to one of three groups defined by the particular five-component mobile model (A, B, C, or D) received on each test day. One group (Group AAAA) received the same mobile every day whereas a second group (ABCD) always received a novel mobile. Finally, Group ABCA received a different mobile on each of the first 3 days but was returned to the Day 1 mobile (A) on Day 4. Conditioning performance on each day was not different among the groups; that is, infants receiving a novel mobile each day (ABCD) had the same response functions as those receiving the same model (AAAA). This finding indicated that Group ABCD was treating each new mobile as a member of the same general class, ignoring the novel distinctive details. The successive 24-hour retention test performance of these infants (Figure 3.6) highlighted this result. There was a progressive increase in conditioned responding during long-term retention tests at the outset of each session *before the reintroduction of reinforcement*. Notably, however, on Day 4 Group ABCA evidenced a response reduction during the long-term retention test, suggesting that these infants, like those in Group ABCD, had learned to "expect" a different mobile on each day. When the (Day 1) mobile reappeared instead, it constituted a "novel" occurrence and they were distracted from the general cues by its details. This outcome showed, however, that infants did acquire enough about the (Day 1) mobile in that single session to respond differentially to it, by a response suppression, 3 days later.

Comparing these data (Figure 3.7, left panel) with portions of those collected by Rovee and Fagen (1976; Figure 3.7, right panel) and Rovee-Collier and Sullivan (1980; Figure 3.7, middle panel), we see that two encounters with a given mobile may be sufficient for the abstraction of the general features as the principal attributes by which the mobile is

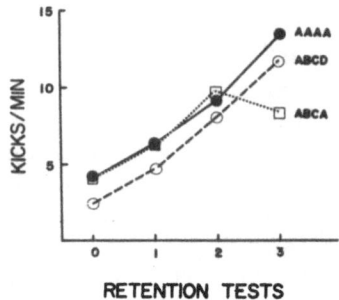

Fig. 3.6. Performance of three groups of infants over successive long-term retention tests of four sessions each separated by 24 hours. Session 1 performance actually reflects operant level. Infants received either the Session 1 mobile for all sessions (Group AAAA), a different mobile in every session (Group ABCD), or a different mobile in each of the first three sessions but the Session 1 mobile in Session 4 (Group ABCA). (From Fagen *et al.*, 1980.)

represented. Retrieval deficits accompanied the introduction of a novel mobile at the outset of sessions following both three and two prior encounters with another mobile, but not following only a single encounter. Thus what is abstracted as "the same" (prototype or general features) and what is "novel" or distinctive appears to depend on the nature of the invariance from episode to episode. A simple frequency rule might define this relation.

In a second experiment infants were assigned to one of four groups defined as before by the mobile model received on each training day (Groups AAA, ABC, AAB, ABA). We hypothesized that if 2 days of exposure to a given mobile condition (either the same mobile twice or a different mobile twice) were necessary to define the rule for "same" so

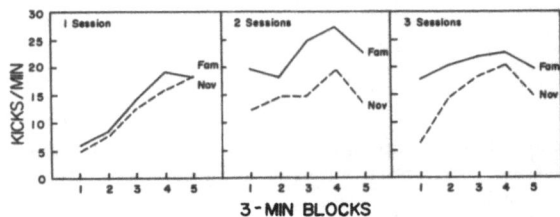

Fig. 3.7. A composite showing the effect of introducing a novel (Nov) mobile as a function of the number of previous training sessions with an alternative model (one, two, or three prior sessions). The difference in conditioned footkicks between infants continuing to receive the same mobile (Fam) and those receiving the novel one is significant in the first block (nonreinforced), but only when two or more sessions with an alternative model have been received (middle and right panels). Blocks 1 and 5 are nonreinforcement phases; Blocks 2 to 4 are reinforcement phases. (From Fagen *et al.*, 1980.)

that attention to the other (novel) features would not cue retrieval, then both Groups AAB and ABA should show a reduction in the number of footkicks emitted during the long-term retention test of Session 3. The hypothesized necessity of two encounters was further examined by seeking evidence of reduced Day 2 responding in Groups ABC and ABA, that is, in those infants receiving a novel mobile on the second training day. As in the first experiment, there were no differences in conditioned responding among the four groups at any point during acquisition in the three sessions. However, during long-term retention tests (Figure 3.8), (1) infants who received a novel mobile on Day 2 showed the same amount of response carry-over as did those infants who continued to receive the same mobile, but (2) infants who received a "different" mobile on Day 3 than predicted by that experienced on Days 1 and 2 (Groups AAB and ABA) showed a response reduction relative to the other two groups, who continued to receive the "same" mobile condition (Groups AAA and ABC). These data, then, demonstrate that the memory processing of young infants is both highly efficient and adaptive, permitting infants to respond appropriately to multiple variations of recurring stimuli while simultaneously permitting appropriate, differential response to those stimuli that remain invariant over successive encounters. A system thus organized according to a

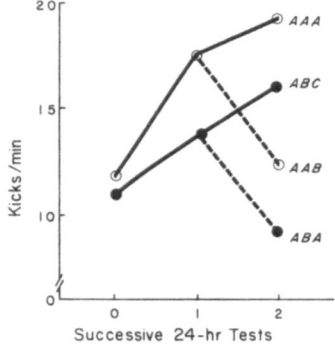

Fig. 3.8. Performance of four groups of infants over successive long-term retention tests of three sessions. Session 1 performance represents operant level. Infants in Group AAA received the same mobile in every session whereas those in Group ABC received a different one in every session. Group AAB infants received the same mobile for the first two sessions and a novel one in the third. Finally, infants in Group ABA were reexposed to their Session 1 mobile in Session 3, after having received a different one during the intervening session. Performance during the first retention test (Session 2) has been combined for those infants who were either reexposed to their Day 1 mobile (Groups AAA and AAB) or who received a different mobile (Groups ABC and ABA). The dashed lines reflect the change in performance of infants receiving a deviation from the "pattern" established by the first 2 training days. (From Fagen et al., 1980.)

(few) simple rule(s) of frequency reduces to a manageable amount the large amount of information the infant must keep relatively accessible for retrieval.

3.2.3. Acquisition Factors

The history of experimental psychology is replete with examples of independent variables that affect acquisition. Many of the variables that affect original conditioning may also affect retention. Moreover, their effect on retention may be only indirect, mediated by their effect on level of acquisition and so on. Because our own investigation of these problems in infancy has just begun, only two of the many possible independent variables will be discussed here: age, and distribution of training.

Ontogenetic differences in learning and memory have received a good deal of attention in both the human and animal literature (e.g., Ornstein, 1978; Rovee-Collier & Lipsitt, 1982; Spear & Campbell, 1979). The underlying assumption appears to be that young organisms learn either more slowly or less efficiently and forget more rapidly than do adults. Gekoski (1977) tested infants longitudinally in the mobile conjugate reinforcement paradigm and obtained age-related differences in acquisition. Only 50% of infants tested at 9 weeks successfully acquired the contingency by the conclusion of a first daily session. Compared to their performance at 12 and 15 weeks, they were slower to exceed operant level, attained a lower asymptote of conditioning, and continued to increase responding during extinction. At 12 weeks all learned rapidly within one session, achieved a higher level of conditioning, and their responding leveled off during extinction; these trends were even more pronounced at 15 weeks.

The learning differences reported by Gekoski suggest that infants of various ages might also differ in retention. Although they did eventually acquire the contingency at 9 weeks, if the younger infants learned the task less completely or less efficiently, poor retention might be the result (see also Gordon, 1979). Davis (1980) tested a group of 8-week-olds and found that they did not acquire the contingency until the fifth 3-minute block of acquisition. In contrast, 12-week-olds typically acquire the contingency by the end of the first (Fagen *et al.*, 1976; Sullivan, 1980) or second (Rovee & Fagen, 1976; Rovee-Collier & Sullivan, 1980) block of acquisition. Because these infants continued to increase responding during the immediate retention test at the end of their second session, long-term retention was assessed in terms of baseline ratios (see Section 3.1.) after a 14-day retention interval. However, it was not clear that infants had forgotten the contingency after that interval. Although group performance did not significantly exceed the pretraining (operant) level, the mean baseline ratio was 1.59 and half of the infants exhibited high kick rates, indicative of remembering the contingency, during the long-term retention test. When Davis trained a second group of 8-week-olds and assessed their retention after 18 days, however, there was no evidence of retention on any index in spite of the fact that these infants acquired the contingency more rapidly than did those in her initial study. Thus infants at 8 weeks of age show equivocal retention after an interval of 2 weeks but none after 2½ weeks, when they have been trained in two sessions. Older (13-week-old) infants show no evidence of retention after 2 weeks when trained in two sessions (cf. Sullivan, 1980; Sullivan et al., 1979).

It is likely, however, that such factors as number or distribution of sessions influence retention differently at different points in ontogeny. For example, Franklin, in a dissertation currently in progress in our laboratory, has found that presenting 6, 12, or 18 minutes of conjugate reinforcement to 8- and 13-week-olds in a *single* session produces little evidence of retention in 8-week-olds after 1 week, when retention of 13-week-olds is excellent. This effect is seen in spite of the fact that age groups did not differ in acquisition. In the Davis (1980) study we saw that 8-week-olds receiving 18 minutes of training distributed into *two* sessions exhibited equivocal evidence of retention after 2 weeks, and only after 2½ weeks was forgetting clearly complete. Finally, Franklin has found that 18 minutes of training distributed into *three* sessions produces robust retention (i.e., virtually no forgetting) in 8-week-olds tested after 2 weeks. Therefore it appears that more episodes, rather than their absolute duration, are critical for good retention in very young infants. These findings are consistent with findings that distributed practice facilitates performance in retention tests with preweanling rats (Bryan, 1980; Coulter, 1979).

The same effects of distributed practice, however, have not been obtained in our paradigm with 13-week-olds (Caniglia, Fagen, & Enright, 1980). When 18 minutes of conjugate reinforcement were distributed over one, two, or three sessions with these older infants, performance of the three-session group evidenced no retention after just 1 week. Infants receiving two 9-minute acquisition periods exhibited good retention after 1 but not 2 weeks; those receiving all reinforcement in a single (massed) 18-minute session evidenced high levels of performance during retention tests following intervals of both 1 and 2 weeks. Both multisession groups exhibited a "warm-up" decrement at the outset of each session—an observation also made by Franklin in her study of 8-week-olds.

These findings challenge the view that distributed practice usually facilitates both learning and retention (Hintzman, 1974, 1976). Although distributed training did impede acquisition, all eventually acquired the contingency. However, the higher response rate of the one-session group cannot be taken to indicate that this group "learned better"; instead it is likely that infants in this group increased response rate over time in order to *maintain* the relative novelty of the reinforcing (moving) mobile. This, in turn, may have increased the number of cues, both motoric and visual, that were represented as part of the memory and that could serve as retrieval cues weeks later. It is interesting that retention performance was inversely related to the speed of acquisition, raising another acquisition factor as deserving of attention. In any event, these data reaffirm the fact that traditional conclusions about learning and memory may be modified as new research paradigms are explored and the range of ages of subjects is extended.

4. FORGOTTEN BUT NOT GONE: THE REACTIVATION OF INFANT MEMORY

The research we have been discussing indicates that, although the memory of human infants at 3 months old is quite robust, after a sufficient period following acquisition infants will no longer exhibit evidence of conditioned responding in the retention test. Does the fact that the prior training no longer influences behavior mean that the information that was previously acquired is irrevocably lost? If not, are there any conditions under which this knowledge can be expressed?

Indirectly, we have already seen how such expression might be accomplished. Recall that alterations in the test context had detrimental effects on retention (Fagen *et al.*, 1976; Rovee & Fagen, 1976). This finding was attributed to the increase in unlearned exploratory tendencies by novel stimuli, which distracted the infant from familiar retrieval cues. In short, the fewer the number of contextual cues present during the retention test that were noticed during the original acquisition of the memory, the lower the probability that the target attribute will be aroused (Spear, 1976). Conversely, to improve the probability that the previous learning or knowledge will be expressed, the training and test contexts should be made as similar as possible.

Intervention procedures can also be used to demonstrate the expression of knowledge that would not otherwise influence behavior. One type of intervention involves presenting the organism with aspects of the original training context ("reminders") before (but not during) the retention test (Spear, 1973, 1976, 1978). Presumably, reencountering or renoticing these aspects reactivates or arouses their memory representations, which then become more accessible to retrieval. Once aroused, a given memory attribute can presumably arouse other attributes that comprise the same memory, thereby increasing the probability that the target attribute (i.e., the one being measured) will be among those that have been "stirred up" or primed (cf. Spear, 1976).

The effectiveness of "prior cuing" procedures in permitting the expression of knowledge that otherwise appeared lost was originally suggested by Campbell and Jaynes (1966). They attributed the superior retention of adults to a greater opportunity for intermittent reexposure to the conditions of original training, and proposed that the reinstatement of an earlier context was the mechanism by which the effects of early learning, for example, could be maintained over relatively lengthy retention intervals. Reinstatement was hypothesized to occur only if the organism had been previously trained and then reencountered some of the original conditions of training. Training alone (i.e., without the reencounters) or the reencounters only (i.e., without prior training) was deemed insufficient for evidence of retention after extended intervals.

Although Campbell and Jaynes used complete training trials (CS–UCS pairings) spaced throughout the retention interval as the reinstatement treatment, recent research has shown that only a fractional component of original training (e.g., CS, the UCS, the training apparatus) administered once, at the end of the retention interval, can be effective (Spear & Parsons, 1976; see also Riccio & Haroutunian, 1979).

The hypothetical priming effects of a reinstatement procedure are described by Spear (1973) as "reactivation"; subsequently both terms— reinstatement and reactivation—have been applied to reminder procedures.

4.1. Methodology

Spear and Parsons (1976) trained rats in a Pavlovian fear conditioning paradigm to avoid footshock (UCS) by hurdling a barrier into an adjacent (safe) compartment in the presence of a light or tone (CS). This avoidance response is learned rapidly and retained well for 24 hours; however, it is forgotten after 28 days. If, however, rats are placed in a neutral apparatus and given a *single* footshock (the reinforcer, or UCS) 24 hours before the 28-day retention test, forgetting is significantly alleviated and avoidance performance returns to the 24-hour posttraining level. Control groups that receive no reactivation treatment before the 28-day retention test or that receive the "reactivation" treatment with no previous training do not exhibit the avoidance response when the CS alone is presented during the retention test. Thus the alleviation of forgetting is neither artifactual nor the result of new learning during the reactivation treatment.

Our basic reactivation procedure is similar to that of Spear and Parsons but modified to accommodate our appetitive conditioning and retention paradigm (see Figure 3.2). We train infants for 2 successive days in the mobile conjugate reinforcement paradigm and then administer a third session after a given retention interval. Infants in the reactivation treatment condition are reexposed to a portion of their original training context before the retention test session and after forgetting is presumably complete—typically, 24 hours before the third session, as in the Spear and Parsons (1976) procedure. Also as in their study, we use a brief (3-minute) exposure to the reinforcer (i.e., the moving mobile) as the reminder. Because infants vary considerably in their rate of footkicking during training, we try to reproduce the visual reinforcer as previously seen by each infant by moving the mobile at the rate that each infant had kicked at the end of acquisition. During the reactivation treatments the ribbon from the mobile suspension bar is not attached to the infant's ankle but is draped over the side of the crib where it is drawn and released by an experimenter, hidden from view. Finally, to ensure that infants do not practice the response during the reactivation treatment, each is placed in an infant seat within the crib (see Figure 3.9). The infant's weight is thus redistributed, making footkicking difficult at best. Actual counts of the number of footkicks emitted during the reactivation treatment have ranged from 0 to 2 per minute for infants aged 14 weeks (Sullivan, 1980).

4.2. Analysis of Reactivation Effects

The first study of the reactivation procedure with infants was conducted in a dissertation by Sullivan (1980; see also Rovee-Collier, Sullivan, Enright, Lucas, & Fagen, 1980). Because her earlier research (Sullivan et al., 1979) had indicated that, after a 2-week retention interval, 12-week-olds had forgotten the response-reinforcer contingency, she attempted to alleviaite forgetting after this interval. Sullivan administered a reactivation treatment to a group of infants 13 days following the completion of 2 days of training and assessed their retention on the following day. Two control groups were also included. A "no-reactivation" control group received the training and the final retention test without the interpolated reactivation treatment, and a "familiarization/reactivation/age-control" group received a reactivation procedure with no formal prior contingency experience. During the initial two "training" sessions these infants were removed from their cribs during the 9-minute reinforcement periods but were allowed to view the *nonmoving* mobile during nonreinforcement periods. As expected, these infants showed low levels of footkicking during the long-term retention test at

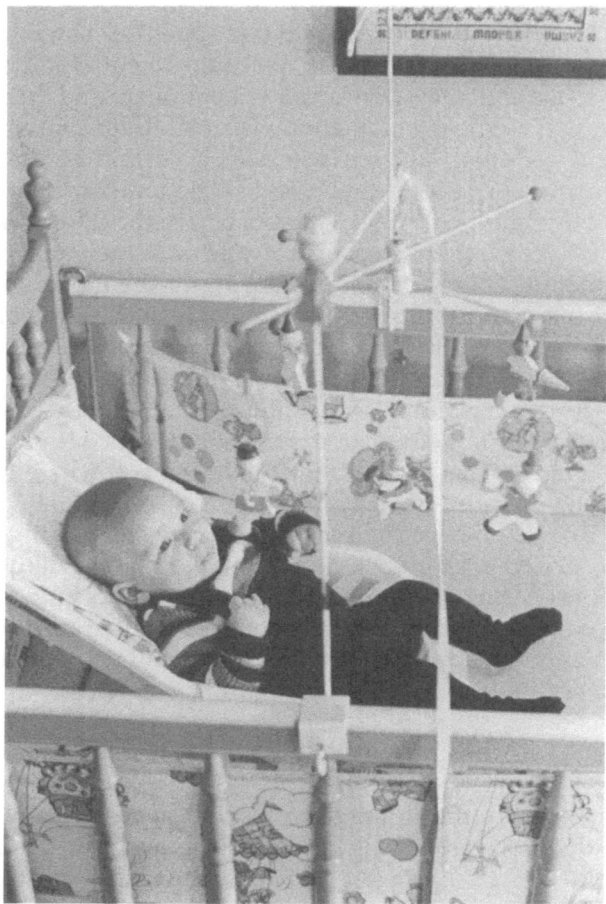

Fig. 3.9. An 8-week-old infant receiving a reactivation treatment. Notice that the ribbon is not attached to the infant's ankle (cf. Figure 3.1) but is draped over the side of the crib where it is drawn and released by the experimenter who is hidden from view.

the outset of Session 3, indicating that the high level of kicking seen in the experimental group was not simply a result of (1) familiarization with the mobile, (2) the reactivation treatment per se, and/or (3) age-related increases in activity (i.e., they were 2 weeks older than when they were trained).

The session-to-session performance of the reactivation and no-reactivation groups is illustrated in Figure 3.10. As expected, these groups did not differ at any point during training and both evidenced excellent 24-hour retention at the outset of Session 2. After 2 weeks, however,

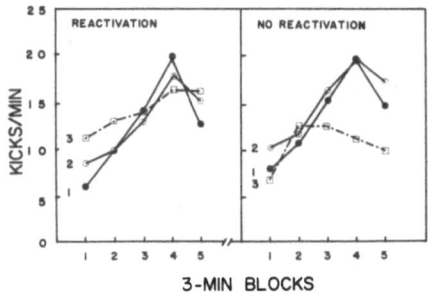

3-MIN BLOCKS

Fig. 3.10. Conditioning curves of two groups of infants over three 15-minute sessions. The interval between Sessions 1 and 2 was 1 day; that between Sessions 2 and 3, 14 days. Infants in the reactivation group received a reactivation treatment 24 hours before Session 3. Blocks 1 and 5 in each session are nonreinforcement phases; Blocks 2 to 4 are reinforcement phases. Note that infants who did not receive the reactivation treatment began Session 3 at operant level (Block 1, Session 1), whereas those who received the reminder were performing at a level not different from that of the immediate retention test administered at the conclusion of training (Block 5, Session 2). (From Sullivan, 1980. Reprinted by permission.)

infants in the no-reactivation group evidenced complete forgetting during the long-term retention test, performing at a level not different from their Session 1 pretraining level. Coupled with the data from the other control group, this finding confirms both that infants do not simply become more active over the 2-week retention interval and that prior familiarity, even with a moving mobile, is insufficient to promote evidence of cued-recall 2 weeks later. The reactivation group, on the other hand, showed excellent retention of the contingency, with response rates during the long-term retention test equivalent to their performance during the immediate retention test at the conclusion of training 2 weeks earlier.

In a follow-up study, we administered the reactivation treatment to a group of 11-week-olds 27 days following the completion of training and assessed retention 24 hours later (Rovee-Collier et al., 1980; see Figure 3.11). As before, reactivation and no-reactivation groups did not differ in either training or 24-hour retention, but marked differences were again observed during the 28-day long-term retention test when only the reactivation group exhibited retention.

Finally, Davis (1980) repeated the Sullivan procedure with 8-week-old infants tested 18 days after training and 24 hours after reactivation treatment, obtaining reliable retention only in the reactivation group. These studies clearly demonstrate that reactivation " works" with human infants, just as it does with human children (Hoving, Coates, Bertucci, & Riccio, 1972) and with rats (e.g., Spear & Parsons, 1976). A brief reminder from the original training context can restore perform-

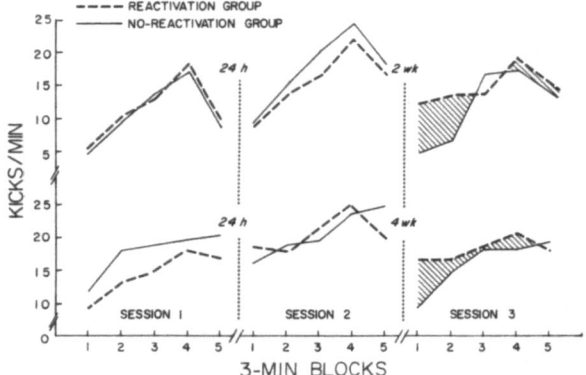

Fig. 3.11. A composite showing the conditioning and retention performance of infants who received a reactivation treatment 24 hours before Session 3 (dashed line) in relation to the performance of a control group who received no reactivation treatment between the final training session (Session 2) and the long-term retention test (Block 1) of Session 3. Note that infants who did not receive the reactivation treatment began Session 3 at operant level (Block 1, Session 1), whereas those who received a reminder were performing the condition response at a level consistent with that of the immediate retention test (Block 5) of Session 2. (From "Reactivation of Infant Memory" by C. K. Rovee-Collier et al., *Science*, 1980, *208*, 1159–1161. Copyright 1980 by the American Association for the Advancement of Science. Reprinted by permission.)

ance of infants as young as 8 weeks to a level commensurate with that observed at the conclusion of training. Presumably this occurs as a result of increasing the accessibility of memory attributes. Moreover, within the limits of the parameters tested so far, it appears that the effectiveness of reactivation is not constrained by either the age of the memory or the age of the infant.

Having previously described the course of forgetting of a newly acquired memory in our paradigm (Sullivan et al., 1979; see Section 3.2.1.), we sought to compare this process with the resilience of a reactivated memory (see also Feldman & Gordon, 1979; Mactutus, Riccio, & Ferek, 1979; Miller & Springer, 1973). To make this comparison, we extended Sullivan's (1980) original finding of alleviated forgetting 1 day after a reactivation treatment (14 days after training) to include evidence of retention 3, 6, 9, or 15 days after a reactivation treatment (i.e., the Session 3 long-term retention test occurred either 16, 19, 22, or 28 days, respectively, following training). Figure 3.12 presents the retention ratios of independent groups of infants tested at various intervals following either the completion of original training (newly acquired or original memory) or the presentation of a reminder 13 days after training was complete (reactivated memory). The most striking aspect of this figure is that the forgetting function following a reactivation treatment is

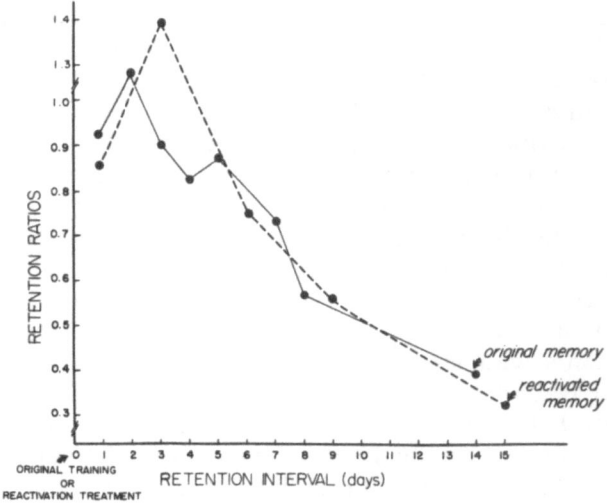

Fig. 3.12. A composite summarizing the data of a number of studies conducted with the procedure of Figure 3.2. Retention ratios reflect the fraction of Session 2 immediate retention test performance that is exhibited during the initial 3-minute cued-recall long-term retention test given at the outset (Block 1) of the third session. The retention interval between either training or the reactivation treatment and the long-term retention test is indicated on the X axis. The forgetting curve of infants who received no reactivation treatment between training and testing (solid line) describes the temporal course of the newly acquired or "original memory"; the forgetting curve of infants who received the reminder 13 days following training (dashed line) describes the temporal course of the "reactivated memory." Note that the reactivation treatment returned performance to a level not different from that observed following original training and that the course of forgetting was highly similar for both memories. (From "The Forgetting of Newly Acquired and Reactivated Memories of 3-Month-Old Infants" by C. K. Rovee-Collier, M. K. Enright, D. Lucas, J. W. Fagen, and M. J. Gekoski, *Infant Behavior and Development*, 1981, 4, 317–331. Copyright 1981 by Infant Behavior and Development. Reprinted by permission.)

highly similar to that following original acquisition (Rovee-Collier *et al.*, 1980; Rovee-Collier, Enright, Lucas, Fagen, & Gekoski, 1981).

The preceding data indicate that a brief reactivation treatment is not only effective in restoring performance to a level as high as that immediately following original training but also has a relatively enduring effect on behavior for some time thereafter. In addition, it appears that both the reactivated and newly acquired memory attributes become progressively less accessible over time. There is, however, an interesting anomaly in each forgetting function. Notice in Figure 3.12 that the value of the retention ratio is actually *greater than 1.00* at 2 days following original learning and at 3 days following a reactivation treatment. Although we do not as yet understand why that occurred, we suspect that this *hypermnesia* (Erdelyi & Becker, 1974) reflects some underlying organizational process akin to that reported by Rovee-Collier and Sullivan

(1980; see Section 3.2.2.). To explore this phenomenon further, we have recently administered the mobile reactivation treatment 13 days follow-ing training but this time have assessed retention of independent groups of infants either ¼, 1, 8, or 24 hours later. Surprisingly, we have found retention following a reactivation treatment to be a *linear increasing* func-tion of time since reactivation (see Figure 3.13). Infants tested 24 hours after the reactivation treatment performed at a level equivalent to that observed during the immediate retention test 2 weeks earlier, whereas those tested just 15 minutes or 1 hour after the reactivation treatment still evidenced complete forgetting! Inspection of individual retention ratios of infants tested 8 hours following a reminder indicated that some of these infants evidenced excellent retention (maximum retention ratio = 1.20) whereas others still evidenced complete forgetting or, in fact, performance below the pretraining level (minimum retention ratio = 0.05). We had asked mothers of the infants in the 8-hour test group to record the amount of time that their infants spent sleeping between the reactivation treatment and the retention test. (This group was the only one other than the 24-hour group in which any significant sleeping

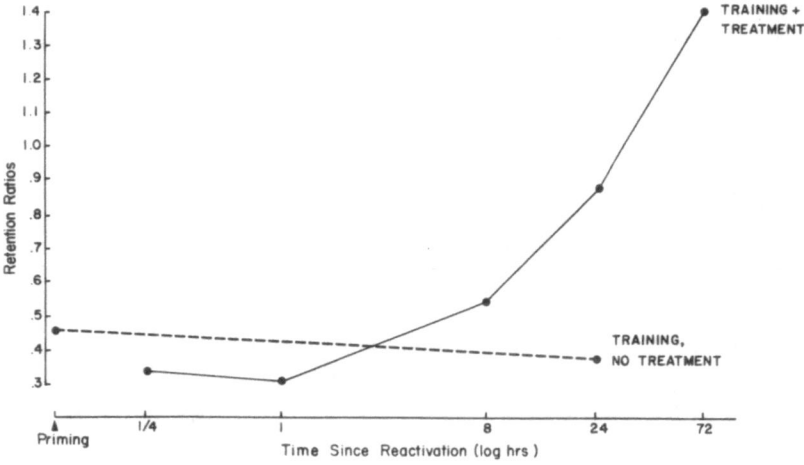

Fig. 3.13. Retention ratios of independent groups of infants tested for retention at various intervals following a reactivation treatment administered 13 days after training (solid line). For comparison purposes, the performance of infants not receiving the reactivation treat-ment but tested for retention 13 or 14 days after training (i.e., either at an interval follow-ing original training equivalent to when the other groups received the reactivation treat-ment, or 24 hours later) is included to indicate that retention ratios of 0.3 to 0.5 reflect a return to pretraining levels. Note that the X axis is plotted in log hours. Note also that beginning 1 hour after the priming event, performance is a linear increasing function of the time since reactivation and that it actually exceeds a retention ratio of 1.00 at 72 hours.

occurred.) Remarkably, the resulting correlation between the percentage of sleep and the retention ratio was 0.75 ($p < .05$)!

These data together with those indicating enhanced retention after 2 to 3 days suggest that the "recruitment" of the sufficient number or kind of stored memory attributes necessary to "reactivate" the target memory attributes is a time-locked process. Even if the cues noticed during the reactivation treatment are identical to those present when the memory was originally acquired, they are insufficient for the behavioral expression of the memory. That is, *the priming process takes time.* The noticed attributes continue to be "active" after the reactivation treatment has ended and may continue to recruit more and more attributes. Whether the phenomenon is a threshold phenomenon, and discontinuous, or a progressive, continuous function of the number of aroused attributes remains to be seen. That this recruitment process is facilitated by sleep suggests that the rate at which various attributes once more become accessible increases during periods of minimal interference. Miller and Springer (1973) presented an interesting analogy that can be extended to these data. They likened memory consolidation to the placement of a newly acquired book on a library shelf. Memory (or book) retrieval, on the other hand, cannot occur unless the appropriate entries are made in the library's card catalog. If the librarian fails to make the card-catalog entries, the book, although present in the library, would not be accessible to prospective borrowers. Thus a reactivation treatment may only provide the infant with enough information as to the general vicinity in which to search for the appropriate entry (i.e., the target memory attribute); the precise location of the correct entry takes time. The more cues (clues) there are, the faster the entry can be found. On the other hand, our reactivation paradigm involves returning infants to their complete original context—the only "different" aspects are the infant seat (which is the infant's *own* seat, hence familiar and presumably not distracting) and the detachment of the ankle ribbon. However, infants are observed to fixate the moving mobile (their own previous reinforcer) continuously during the reactivation treatment. In fact, it is difficult to imagine a more complete array of cues. Thus it is possible that our reminder provides 100% of the necessary information required to locate the stored memory but that recycling the memory (retrieval per se) simply takes time. One might further speculate that more recently forgotten memories would be retrieved more rapidly than memories forgotten much longer in the past. These speculations are the focus of our current research.

We have also recently found that forgetting is selectively alleviated, that is, the infant must reencounter a highly similar or identical contextual cue in order for reactivation to work. Fagen, Yengo, Rovee-

Collier, and Enright (1981) asked whether a reactivation treatment with a discriminative stimulus (S+) would affect the memory attributes. We trained infants for 3 days in a behavioral contrast paradigm (Fagen, 1979; Rovee-Collier & Capatides, 1979) in order to produce reliable differences in responding to two mobiles (S+ and S−) with components of different colors and patterns. Twenty days following training, infants received a reactivation treatment with either S+ or S− and were tested for long-term retention 24 hours later. Infants in a control group received no reactivation treatment. The data showed that a *particular reminder* was necessary for the alleviation of forgetting. Specifically, the S+/S− discrimination was maintained during the 21-day cued-recall test only by infants reactivated with S+; reactivation with S− proved no more effective in alleviating forgetting than no reactivation treatment at all (see Figure 3.14). The ineffectiveness of the S− stimulus as a reactivator suggests that the attributes of S+ and S− acquired during training become differentially accessible over time, possibly as a result of declining attention to those cues that do not predict reinforcement (i.e., attributes of S−). Given that an attribute of memory is retrieved when the subject subsequently "notices an event sufficiently similar to that event represented by the attribute" (Spear, 1976, p. 35), it is likely that noticing S−

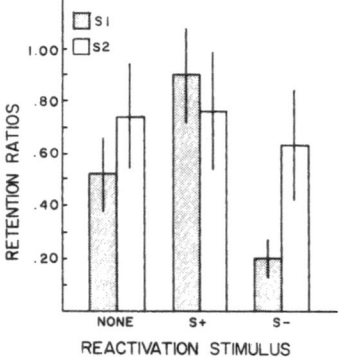

Fig. 3.14. Retention ratios 21 days following discrimination training for S1 (S+) and S2 (S−) as a function of the reactivation treatment received 24 hours earlier. Infants reactivated with S+ received the moving S1 during the 3-minute reactivation treatment; those reactivated with S− were exposed to the nonmoving S2 mobile. The high rentention ratios of all groups to S2 reflect the continuation of the low rate of responding to this mobile over the 3-week retention interval. Note, however, that only infants reactivated with S+ continued to exhibit a high rate of responding in its presence 24 hours following the reminder. Vertical bars represent ±1 standard error. (From "Reactivation of a Visual Discrimination in Early Infancy" by J. W. Fagen *et al.*, *Developmental Psychology*, 1981, 17, pp. 266–274. Copyright by the American Psychological Association. Reprinted by permission.)

may only reactivate attributes associated with S− (i.e., nonresponse). If S+ only arouses attributes associated with the S+ (i.e., footkicking to S+) and did not affect S− attributes, the present result would also be obtained.

The preceding data indicate that a *nonmoving* mobile, presented after an interval after which infants no longer differentiate the specific details of mobiles (Rovee-Collier & Sullivan, 1980), does not enhance conditioned responding to either test mobile 24 hours later, whereas the *moving* mobile differentially facilitates retention. Is it, however, that the mobile is moving only, or would only the *original* moving mobile be effective in alleviating forgetting? Some interesting insights into this problem were recently obtained by Enright in a dissertation in our laboratory. She found that the original cues of the training mobile continued to influence retention selectively, even after periods at which discrimination is not observed. Infants reactivated with a *moving but novel* mobile 13 days after training showed no evidence of retention when exposed to either the reactivation or the training mobile 24 hours later. Instead, forgetting was alleviated only when the infants were reactivated with their original training mobile. However, the memory reactivated by this stimulus generalized to a novel mobile. Thus, although infants do not differentiate between a mobile presented 4 days earlier and a current novel one, they do selectively use the familiar and the novel cues as retrieval cues! This fact reemphasizes the importance of the similarity among the training, reactivation, and test contexts and suggests that the infant's memory is both highly organized and adaptive (see Section 5.2.). Moreover, that generalization is complete following the reactivation treatment but not following original training emphasizes important differences in newly acquired and reactivated memories (see Mactutus *et al.*, 1979). We currently think that the infant has remembered a "rule" of action that is stored in an instance of that rule.

5. SUMMARY AND CONCLUSIONS

5.1. The Utility of Using Motivated Infants

We began by discussing how current knowledge about infant memory has been based almost exclusively on a Sokolovian (1963) model of the habituation of the orienting reflex. We argued that the use of implicit indexes of retention obtained in a context different from that in which the memory was acquired makes this model inappropriate for the analysis of how the infant can retrieve and use stored information. We proposed that a conditioning analysis was more suitable because it yields a sensitive and direct index of retention, as well as direct evidence of the way past experiences influence future performance, with and without intervention.

There is, however, another, equally important aspect of our conditioning procedure with young infants that undoubtedly has contributed to its fruitfulness. Researchers studying infant visual "recognition memory" have literally placed their infants in boxes, effectively removing all sources of environmental stimulation other than the stimuli arbitrarily permitted by the experimenter. This practice has left the infant with only two choices: to look at those stimuli, or to attempt to remove oneself (or get removed) from the situation. That subject loss due to crying is typically 50% suggests that there is truly something noxious and "unnatural" about this otherwise apparently innocuous procedure. Indeed, recent studies that have allowed the infant some measure of control over the onset and/or offset of the visual stimuli (e.g., Horowitz, 1975) have partially alleviated the subject loss problem.

Unlike the classic drive reduction view of Hull (1943), current thinking views most organisms, including human infants, as active seekers of both stimulation and environmental control (see Haith 1980; Rovee-Collier, in press; Ruff, 1980). If we hope to understand how infants acquire and use knowledge, that is, if we hope to understand infant cognition, then we must observe infants who are both motivated to solve the problem(s) of the experimental paradigm and who also are allowed to do so. Indeed, it may be difficult, if not impossible, adequately to separate the concepts of cognition and motivation in early infancy (Ulvand, 1980; Yarrow & Pedersen, 1976). This problem leads directly to a consideration of infant competence, which has been defined as *"knowing how* rather than *knowing that*. For competence implies action, changing the environment as well as adapting to the environment" (Connolly & Bruner, 1974, p. 3). Studies of infant visual recognition memory, with its reliance on response-to-novelty, can only tell us that the infant *knows that* there has been a change in a stimulus. A conditioning analysis, on the other hand, tells us that the infant *knows how* to use the information he or she has previously acquired. Furthermore, the evidence gathered in regard to the reactivation of infant memory convinces us that infants continue to know how to do so long after they have apparently forgotten how.

5.2. The Organization of Infant Memory

In the tradition of Underwood (1969) and Spear (1971, 1973, 1976, 1978), we view memory as a multidimensional collection of attributes that represent events or stimuli that the organism noticed during initial learning. The organism can retrieve this memory by noticing contextual cues that are similar, in number and/or kind, to those represented as attributes of the memory.

Our data permit us to hypothesize about how the infant's memory attributes are organized. At present, we think that the attributes corresponding to the specific details of a particular event are stored together and hence equally accessible. However, we think that infants abstract general features from repeated encounters or episodes that are highly similar, and that these are stored separately as "rules" or higher-order attributes. These are more accessible for longer periods than are specific details. However, when all access is lost, the rules can be retrieved only through a previous specific instance. Tulving (1972) has proposed a very similar organization. This sort of organization produces the desirable redundancy without necessitating immediate access to many details. It may also account for both the time-locked retrieval function and the hypermnesia (reminiscence) that has been observed.

Finally, the success of reactivation treatments with human infants underlines the necessity of distinguishing between the knowledge and its expression. Failure to observe retention in young infants can no longer be taken as evidence that previously acquired information has been irrevocably lost from storage. Instead, it is now more parsimonious to interpret such a retention failure as a *retrieval failure*. The evidence for this position is the fact that in many cases a reactivation treatment, in the form of exposing specific contextual cues that were present during original training, can successfully alleviate forgetting.

5.3. The Significance of Reactivation for Theories of Development

Most theories of development are based on the premise of the continuity of behavior and, as such, place varying emphasis on early experiences and learning. Even discontinuous or stage theories such as those of Piaget (1952) and Kagan (1979), though arguing that differences in the organization of abilities characterize each stage of development, assume that the structures of one stage are prerequisite for those of the next. Although Kagan (1976) argued metaphorically that the butterfly is not simply a better caterpillar but a different creature, we know from the work of Miller and Berk (1977) that behavioral continuity can persist even over such extreme forms of discontinuous development as metamorphosis.

Although the importance of the effects of early experience on later behavior has recently been seriously questioned (e.g., Clarke & Clarke, 1979; Kagan & Klein, 1973), it has generally been accepted that early experiences *do* in fact influence behavior for periods extending from infancy into childhood, adolescence, and beyond. The mechanism by which this occurs has, however, remained elusive (see Clarke & Clarke, 1979; Hunt, 1979; Thompson & Grusec, 1970). This problem has been exacerbated by the accruing evidence about infantile amnesia (see Coulter, 1979). We are in agreement with Campbell and Jaynes (1966), who originally proposed that reexposure to certain of the cues present at the time of an original event is sufficient to maintain the memory of that event. Our research demonstrates that reinstatement is a feasible mechanism by which the effects of prior experiences can affect subsequent behaviors. The importance of this mechanism was anticipated by Cicero more than 2,050 years ago:

> History is the witness that testifies to the passing of time; it illumines reality, vitalizes memory, provides guidance in daily life, and brings us tidings of antiquity. (Marcus Tullius Cicero, *De oratore* 2. 36)

In short, as students of memory, we must be historians as well as psychologists.

ACKNOWLEDGMENTS

We are grateful to Byron A. Campbell and Norman E. Spear, whose research provided much of the framework for our own, and to the many dedicated students who have contributed to our research. In particular, we wish to thank Mary Enright, Marcy Gekoski, and Marge Sullivan.

6. REFERENCES

Bolles, R. C. Reinforcement, expectancy, and learning. *Psychological Review*, 1972, 79, 394–409.

Bolles, R. C. Some relationships between learning and memory. In D. L. Medin, W. A. Roberts, & R. T. Davis (Eds.), *Processes of animal memory*. Hillsdale, N.J.: Lawrence Erlbaum, 1976.

Bornstein, M. H. Infants' recognition memory for hue. *Developmental Psychology*, 1976, 12, 185–191.

Bruner, J. The course of cognitive growth. *American Psychologist*, 1964, 19, 1–15.

Bryan, R. G. *Retention of odor-shock conditioning in neonatal rats: Effects of distribution of practice*. Unpublished doctoral dissertation, Rutgers University, 1980.

Campbell, B. A., & Coulter, X. Neural and psychological processes underlying the development of learning and memory. In T. J. Tighe & R. N. Leaton (Eds.), *Habituation*. Hillsdale, N.J.: Lawrence Erlbaum, 1976.

Campbell, B. A., & Jaynes, J. Reinstatement. *Psychological Review*, 1966, 73, 478–480.

Campbell, B. A., & Spear, N. E. Ontogeny of memory. *Psychological Review*, 1972, 79, 215–236.

Caniglia, K., Fagen, J. W., & Enright, M. K. *The effects of distribution of training on condition-

ing and retention in three-month-old infants. Paper presented at the meeting of the Eastern Psychological Association, Hartford, Connecticut, April 1980.

Caron, A. J., Caron, R. F., Minchiello, M. D., Weiss, S. J., & Friedman, S. L. Constraints on the use of the familiarization-novelty method in the assessment of infant discrimination. *Child Development,* 1977, *48,* 747–762.

Church, R. W. Aversive bahavior. In L. W. Kling & L. A. Riggs (Eds.), *Woodworth and Schlosberg's experimental psychology* (Vol. 2). New York: Holt, Rinehart & Winston, 1971.

Clarke, A. M., & Clarke, A. D. B. *Early experience: Myth and evidence.* New York: Free Press, 1976.

Clarke, A. M., & Clarke, A. D. B. Early experience: Its limited effect upon later development. In D. Shaffer & J. Dunn (Eds.), *The first year of life.* London: Wiley, 1979.

Clifton, R. K., & Nelson, M. N. Developmental study of habituation in infants: The importance of paradigm, response system, and state. In T. J. Tighe & R. N. Leaton (Eds.), *Habituation.* Hillsdale, N.J.: Lawrence Erlbaum, 1976.

Cohen, L. B. Attention-getting and attention-holding processes of infant visual preference. *Child Development,* 1972, *43,* 869–879.

Cohen, L. B., & Gelber, E. R. Infant visual memory. In L. B. Cohen & P. Salapatek (Eds.), *Infant perception: From sensation to cognition* (Vol. 1). New York: Academic Press, 1975.

Cohen, L. B., DeLoache, J. S., & Pearl, R. A. An examination of interference effects in infants' memory for faces. *Child Development,* 1977, *48,* 88–96.

Connolly, K. J., & Bruner, J. S. Competence: Its nature and nurture. In K. J. Connolly & J. S. Bruner (Eds.), *The growth of competence.* London: Wiley, 1974.

Cornell, E. H. Infants' recognition memory, forgetting, and savings. *Journal of Experimental Child Psychology,* 1979, *28,* 359–374.

Coulter, X. The determinants of infantile amnesia. In N. E. Spear & B. A. Campbell (Eds.), *Ontogeny of learning and memory.* Hillsdale, N.J.: Lawrence Erlbaum, 1979.

Crespi, L. P. Quantitative variations of incentive and performance in the white rat. *American Journal of Psychology,* 1942, *55,* 467–515.

Davis, J. M. *Facilitated retrieval of a learned contingency in 8-week-old infants.* Unpublished master's thesis, Rutgers University, 1980.

DeLoache, J. S., Rissman, M. D., & Cohen, L. B. An investigation of the attention-getting process in infants. *Infant Behavior and Development,* 1978, *1,* 11–25.

Erdelyi, M.H., & Becker, J. Hypermnesia for pictures. *Cognitive Psychology,* 1974, *6,* 159–171.

Fagan, J. F. Memory in the infant. *Journal of Experimental Child Psychology,* 1970, *9,* 217–226.

Fagan, J. F. Infants' recognition memory for faces. *Journal of Experimental Child Psychology,* 1972, *14,* 453–476.

Fagan, J. F. Infants' delayed recognition memory and forgetting. *Journal of Experimental Child Psychology,* 1973, *16,* 424–450.

Fagan, J. F. Infant recognition memory: Studies in forgetting. *Child Development,* 1977, *48,* 68–78.

Fagen, J. W. Behavioral contrast in infants. *Infant Behavior and Development,* 1979, *2,* 101–112.

Fagen, J. W. Stimulus preference, reinforcer effectiveness, and relational responding in infants. *Child Development,* 1980, *51,* 372–378.

Fagen, J. W., & Rovee, C. K. Effects of quantitative shifts in a visual reinforcer on the instrumental response of infants. *Journal of Experimental Child Psychology,* 1976, *21,* 349–360.

Fagen, J. W., Rovee, C. K., & Kaplan, M. G. Psychophysical scaling of stimulus similarity in 3-month-old infants and adults. *Journal of Experimental Child Psychology*, 1976, 22, 272–281.

Fagen, J. W., Rovee-Collier, C. K., Morrongiello, B. A., & Gekoski, M. J. *The use of abstracted and distinctive features as retrieval cues by young infants.* Unpublished manuscript, Rutgers University, 1980.

Fagen, J. W., Yengo, L. A., Rovee-Collier, C. K., & Enright, M. K. Reactivation of a visual discrimination in early infancy. *Developmental Psychology*, 1981, 17, 266–274.

Fantz, R. L. The origin of form perception. *Scientific American*, 1961, 204, 66–72.

Feldman, D. T., & Gordon, W. C. The alleviation of short-term retention decrements with reactivation. *Learning and Motivation*, 1979, 10, 198–210.

Flavell, J. Concept development. In P. H. Mussen (Ed.), *Carmichael's manual of child psychology* (Vol. 1). New York: Wiley, 1970.

Gekoski, M. J. Visual attention and operant conditioning in infancy: A second look (Doctoral dissertation, Rutgers University, 1977). *Dissertation Abstracts International*, 1977, 38, 875B. (University Microfilms No. 77-17, 533)

Gordon, W. C. Age: Is it a constraint on memory content? In N. E. Spear & B. A. Campbell (Eds.), *The ontogeny of learning and memory.* Hillsdale, N.J.: Lawrence Erlbaum, 1979.

Haith, M. M. *Rules that babies look by.* Hillsdale, N.J.: Lawrence Erlbaum, 1980.

Hasher, L., & Griffin, M. Reconstructive and reproductive processes in memory. *Journal of Experimental Psychology: Human Learning and Memory*, 1978, 4, 318–330.

Hintzman, D. L. Theoretical implications of the spacing effect. In R. Solso (Ed.), *Theories in cognitive psychology: The Loyola symposium.* Potomac, Md.: Lawrence Erlbaum, 1974.

Hintzman, D. L. Repetition and memory. In G. H. Bower (Ed.), *The psychology of learning and motivation* (Vol. 10). New York: Academic Press, 1976.

Hopkins, J. R., Zelazo, P. R., Jacobson, S. W., & Kagan, J. Infant sensitivity to stimulus schema discrepancy. *Genetic Psychology Monographs*, 1976, 93, 27–62.

Horowitz, F. D. (Ed.). Visual attention, auditory stimulation, and language development in young infants. *Monographs of the Society for Research in Child Development*, 1975, 39 (5/6, Serial No. 158).

Hoving, K. L., Coates, L., Bertucci, M., & Riccio, D. C. Reinstatement effects in children. *Developmental Psychology*, 1972, 6, 426–429.

Hull, C. L. *Principles of behavior.* New York: Appleton-Century-Crofts, 1943.

Hunt, J. McV. Psychological development: Early experience. In M. R. Rosenzweig & L. W. Porter (Eds.), *Annual review of psychology* (Vol. 30). Palo Alto, Calif.: Annual Reviews, 1979.

Hunt, J., & Uzgiris, I. C. *Cathexis from recognitive familiarity.* Paper presented at the meeting of the American Psychological Association, Los Angeles, September 1964.

James, W. *The principles of psychology.* New York: Henry Holt, 1890.

Jeffrey, W. E. The orienting reflex in cognitive development. *Psychological Review*, 1968, 75, 323–334.

Jeffrey, W. E. Habituation as a mechanism for perceptual development. In T. J. Tighe & R. N. Leaton (Eds.), *Habituation.* Hillsdale, N.J.: Lawrence Erlbaum, 1976.

Jenkins, J. J. Remember that old theory of memory? Well, forget it! *American Psychologist*, 1974, 29, 785–795.

Kagan, J. Resilience and continuity in psychological development. In A. M. Clarke & D. B. Clarke (Eds.), *Early experience: Myth and evidence.* New York: Free Press, 1967.

Kagan, J. Growing by leaps: The form of early cognitive development. *The Sciences*, 1979, 19, 8–12, 32.

Kagan, J., & Klein, R. E. Cross-cultural perspectives on early development. *American Psychologist*, 1973, 28, 947–961.

Kaplan, M. G. *Infant visual preferences: The role of familiarity and responsiveness.* Unpublished master's thesis, University of Illinois, 1967.

Lipsitt, L. P. Infant learning: The blooming, buzzing confusion revisited. In M. E. Meyer (Ed.), *Second western symposium on learning: Early learning.* Bellingham, Wash.: Western Washington State College, 1971.

Loftus, G. R., & Kallman, H. J. Encoding and the use of detail information in picture recognition. *Journal of Experimental Psychology: Human Learning and Memory,* 1979, *5,* 197–211.

Mactutus, C. F., Riccio, D. C., & Ferek, J. M. Retrograde amnesia for old (reactivated) memory: Some anomolous characteristics. *Science,* 1979, *204,* 1319–1320.

Mast, V. K., Fagen, J. W., Rovee-Collier, C.K., & Sullivan, M. W. Immediate and long-term memory for reinforcement context: The development of learned expectations in early infancy. *Child Development,* 1980, *51,* 700–707.

McCall, R. B. Attention in the infant: Avenue to the study of cognitive development. In D. N. Walcher & D. L. Peters (Eds.), *Early childhood: The development of self-regulatory mechanisms.* New York: Academic Press, 1971.

McCall, R. B. Encoding and retrieval of perceptual memories after long-term familiarization and the infant's response to discrepancy. *Developmental Psychology,* 1973, *9,* 310–318.

McCall, R. B., & Kagan, J. Stimulus-schema discrepancy and attention in the infant. *Journal of Experimental Child Psychology,* 1967, *5,* 381–390.

McCall, R. B., & Kagan, J. Individual differences in the infant's distribution of attention to stimulus discrepancy. *Developmental Psychology,* 1970, *2,* 90–98.

McCall, R. B., Kennedy, C. B., & Dodds, C. The interfering effect of distracting stimuli on the infant's memory. *Child Development,* 1977, *48,* 79–87.

Miller, R. R., & Berk, A. M. Retention over metamorphosis in the African claw-toed frog. *Journal of Experimental Psychology: Animal Behavior Processes,* 1977, *3,* 343–356.

Miller, R. R., & Springer, A. D. Amnesia, consolidation, and retrieval. *Psychological Reveiw,* 1973, *80,* 69–79.

Olson, G. M. An information-processing analysis of visual memory and habituation in infants. In T. J. Tighe & R. N. Leaton (Eds.), *Habituation.* Hillsdale, N.J.: Lawrence Erlbaum, 1976.

Ornstein, P. A. (Ed.). *Memory development in children.* Hillsdale, N.J.: Lawrence Erlbaum, 1978.

Pavlov, I. P. *Conditioned reflexes.* London: Oxford University Press, 1927.

Piaget, J. *Origins of intelligence in children.* New York: W. W. Norton, 1952.

Riccio, D. C., & Haroutunian, V. Some approaches to the alleviation of ontogenetic memory deficits. In N. E. Spear & B. A. Campbell (Eds.), *Ontogeny of learning and memory.* Hillsdale, N.J.: Lawrence Erlbaum, 1979.

Rovee, C. K., & Fagen, J. W. Extended conditioning and 24-hr retention in infants. *Journal of Experimental Child Psychology,* 1976, *21,* 1–11.

Rovee-Collier, C. K. Infants as problem solvers: A psychobiological approach. In M. D. Zeiler & P. Harzem (Eds.), *Advances in the analysis of behavior.* Vol. 3. *Biological factors in learning.* London: Wiley, in press.

Rovee-Collier, C. K., & Capatides, J. B. Positive behavioral contrast in 3-month-old infants on multiple conjugate reinforcement schedules. *Journal of the Experimental Analysis of Behavior,* 1979, *32,* 15–27.

Rovee-Collier, C. K., & Fagen, J. W. The retrieval of memory in early infancy. In L. P. Lipsitt (Ed.), *Advances in infancy research* (Vol. 1). Norwood, N.J.: Ablex, 1981.

Rovee-Collier, C. K., & Gekoski, M. J. The economics of infancy: A review of conjugate reinforcement. In H. W. Reese & L. P. Lipsitt (Eds.), *Advances in child development and behavior* (Vol. 13). New York: Academic Press, 1979.

Rovee-Collier, C. K., & Lipsitt, L. P. Learning, adaptation, and memory. In P. Stratton (Ed.), *Psychobiology of the newborn*. London: Wiley, 1982.

Rovee-Collier, C. K., & Sullivan, M. W. Organization of infant memory. *Journal of Experimental Psychology: Human Learning and Memory*, 1980, *6*, 798–807.

Rovee-Collier, C. K., Sullivan, M. W., Enright, M. K., Lucas, D., & Fagen, J. W. Reactivation of infant memory. *Science*, 1980, *208*, 1159–1161.

Rovee-Collier, C. K., Enright, M. K., Lucas, D., Fagen, J. W., & Gekoski, M. J. The forgetting of newly acquired and reactivated memories of 3-month-old infants. *Infant Behavior and Development*, 1981, *4*, 317–331.

Ruff, H. A. The development of perception and recognition of objects. *Child Development*, 1980, *51*, 981–992.

Sokolov, E. N. *Perception and the conditioned reflex*. New York: Macmillan, 1963.

Sophian, C. Habituation is not enough: Novelty preferences, search, and memory in infancy. *Merrill-Palmer Quarterly*, 1980, *26*, 239–257.

Spear, N. E. Forgetting as retrieval failure. In W. K. Honig & P. H. R. James (Eds.), *Animal memory*. New York: Academic Press, 1971.

Spear, N. E. Retrieval of memory in animals. *Psychological Review*, 1973, *80*, 163–194.

Spear, N. E. Retrieval of memories. In W. K. Estes (Ed.), *Handbook of learning and cognitive processes*. Vol. 4. *Attention and memory*. Hillsdale, N.J.: Lawrence Erlbaum, 1976.

Spear, N. E. *The processing of memories: Forgetting and retention*. Hillsdale, N.J.: Lawrence Erlbaum, 1978.

Spear, N. E. Memory storage factors leading to infantile amnesia. In G. H. Bower (Ed.), *The psychology of learning and motivation* (Vol. 13). New York: Academic Press, 1979.

Spear, N. E., & Campbell, B. A. (Eds.). *Ontogeny of learning and memory*. Hillsdale, N.J.: Lawrence Erlbaum, 1979.

Spear, N. E., & Parsons, P. J. Analysis of a reactivation treatment: Ontogenetic determinants of alleviated forgetting. In D. L. Medin, W. A. Roberts, & R. T. Davis (Eds.), *Processing of animal memory*. Hillsdale, N.J.: Lawrence Erlbaum, 1976.

Sullivan, M. W. Infant learning in a memory paradigm: Long-term retention and alleviated forgetting (Doctoral dissertation, Rutgers University, 1980). *Dissertation Abstracts International*, 1980, *40*, 5259B. (University Microfilms No. 80-8923)

Sullivan, M. W., Rovee-Collier, C. K., & Tynes, D. M. A conditioning analysis of infant long-term memory. *Child Development*, 1979, *50*, 152–162.

Thompson, R. W., & Grusec, J. E. Studies of early experience. In P. H. Mussen (Ed.), *Carmichael's manual of child psychology* (Vol. 1). New York: Wiley, 1970.

Thorpe, W. H. *Learning and instinct in animals*. Cambridge: Harvard University Press, 1963.

Tulving, E. Episodic and semantic memory. In E. Tulving & W. Donaldson (Eds.), *Organization of memory*. New York: Academic Press, 1972.

Ulvand, S. E. Cognition and motivation in early infancy: An interactionist approach. *Human Development*, 1980, *23*, 17–32.

Underwood, B. J. Attributes of memory. *Psychological Review*, 1969, *76*, 559–573.

Weizmann, F., Cohen, L. B., & Pratt, R. J. Novelty, familiarity, and the development of infant attention. *Developmental Psychology*, 1971, *4*, 149–154.

Welch, M. M. Infants' visual attention to varying degrees of novelty. *Child Development*, 1974, *45*, 344–350.

Werner, J. S., & Perlmutter, M. Development of visual memory in infants. In H. W. Reese & L. P. Lipsitt (Eds.), *Advances in child development and behavior* (Vol. 14). New York: Academic Press, 1979.

Williams, T. M., Fryer, M. L., & Aiken, L. S. Development of visual pattern classification in preschool children: Prototypes and distinctive features. *Developmental Psychology,* 1977, *13,* 577–584.

Yarrow, L. J., & Pedersen, F. A. The interplay between cognition and motivation in infancy. In M. Lewis (Ed.), *Origins of intelligence.* New York: Plenum Press, 1976.

Zeaman, D. Response latency as a function of the amount of reinforcement. *Journal of Experimental Psychology,* 1949, *39,* 466–483.

4

Memory Retrieval Failures Produced by Changes in Drug State

Donald A. Overton

1. INTRODUCTION

This chapter will discuss the effects of drugs on the expression of knowledge as indicated by the performance of learned responses by animals. I shall begin with a brief description of the major types of effects of drugs on the acquisition and/or expression of knowledge. I shall then review the available evidence about the effects of changes in drug state on memory retrieval, that is, evidence about state-dependent learning.

2. COMMON DRUG EFFECTS ON LEARNING AND RETENTION

Most scientific information about the acquisition and expression of knowledge in animals is based on learned motor behaviors and on analysis of the circumstances in which such behaviors do and do not occur. Such studies usually involve two major phases: acquisition and retrieval. During the acquisition phase, contingencies are arranged so that the animal learns something—typically, a response that can subse-

DONALD A. OVERTON • Department of Psychiatry, Temple University School of Medicine, 3400 N. Broad St., Philadelphia, Pennsylvania 19140.

quently be observed. During the retrieval phase, the animals are tested under various conditions to determine the circumstances in which the response will occur, that is, in which knowledge of the the response will be expressed.

Drugs influence the acquisition of new knowledge and the performance of previously learned responses by a variety of mechanisms. Table 4.1 shows several of these drug effects on memorization and memory retrieval, suggesting the pattern of results than can be expected in four different groups of animals that are initially trained and subsequently tested for retention of a learned response. Group 1 is both trained and subsequently tested for retention without drug (N), animals in Group 2 are trained while drugged (D) and tested without drug, Group 3 animals are trained without drug and tested while under the influence of drug, and Group 4 is both trained and tested while drugged. Aided by this table, we can proceed with a discussion of the major effects of drugs on learning and on memory retrieval.

Table 4.1. Major Effects of Drugs on the Acquisition and Performance of Learned Responses

		Group			
		1	2	3	4
		Drug state during acquisition			
		N	D	N	D
Type of drug effect	Phase of experiment	Drug state during retention test			
		N	N	D	D
1. Memorization deficit	Train	C[a]	C(or–)[b]	C	C(or–)
	Test	C	–	C	–
2. Retrieval deficit	Train	C	C(or –)	C	C(or –)
	Test	C	C	–	–
3. Performance deficit	Train	C	–	C	–
	Test	C	C	–	–
4. State-dependent retrieval	Train	C	C	C	C
	Test	C	–	–	C
5. Combined effects	Train	C	–	C	–
	Test	C	–	–	–

[a] C = control-level (unimpaired) performance.
[b] – = impaired performance.

2.1. Impairment of Memorization

Many drugs can interfere with or prevent the formation of new memories. In such cases no learning takes place even though the animal is exposed to conditions that would lead to learning in an undrugged animal. The deficit is in the acquisition rather than in the expression of knowledge. Drugs can also facilitate the acquisition of knowledge (McGaugh & Petrinovich, 1965), but only under special circumstances, whereas impairment of acquisition is almost universally observed when sufficiently high doses of psychoactive drugs are used.

The top panel in Table 4.1 shows the expected pattern of results if a drug produces a deficit in the formation of new memories and has no other effects on learning, retrieval, or performance. Group 1 shows control-level (C) performance during both the training and retention testing sessions; that is, subjects acquire and perform the response normally when not drugged. Group 2 shows impaired performance (–) during the N test session; subjects do not perform the response because drug prevented the formation of permanent engrams during the preceding D training session. Group 2 may also show impaired performance by the end of the training session in comparison to the control group, where performance gradually improves during the training session as permanent engrams are formed. Group 3 shows control-level performance during both acquisition and retention testing. This group's performance is crucial for distinguishing a drug effect on memorization from other drug effects on learning and retention, as unimpaired retrieval shows that presence of drug during retention testing does not impair either the retrieval of old memories or the performance of the response. Thus it can be inferred that the drug acts exclusively to block the formation of new memories. Group 4's performance is identical to that of Group 2; the impaired performance during training and testing is based on a failure to form permanent memories during the D training session.

2.2. Drug-Induced Retrieval Deficits

We have seen the results obtained when drugs impede the formation of memories without preventing normal retrieval of previously formed engrams. The term "retrieval deficit" refers to the converse situation, in which drugs prevent the retrieval of previously formed engrams without preventing the consolidation of new memories. This situation leads to the pattern of performance shown in the second panel of Table 4.1, in which poor performance is observed during testing only in Groups 3 and 4—the two groups in which memory retrieval is attempted while the animal is drugged. Groups 2 and 4 may also show impaired performance toward the end of the training session, since they will have difficulty remembering material that was learned early in the training session.

Impairment of memory retrieval by drugs has been demonstrated in only a few studies (Oliverio, 1967, 1968; Pazzagli & Pepeu, 1964). Because this effect usually occurs in combination with drug effects on memorization and/or performance, the impairment of retrieval is difficult to isolate in most experimental paradigms. However, this problem appears to be only a practical one of experimental design. It is generally accepted that the formation of memories and their subsequent retrieval are two separate processes (Spear, 1973). Hence it is reasonable to expect that drugs will have effects on memory retrieval that are distinct from their effects on the formation of memories.

2.3. Drug Impairment of Performance

Let us next consider the case in which a drug affects the performance of a learned response without impairing either the acquisition or the retrieval of engrams. For example, curare prevents responding by paralyzing the musculature. However, reports of human volunteers tell us that the drug does not prevent either the acquisition of new knowledge or the recollection of old memories (Harvey & Masland, 1941; Smith, Brown, Toman, & Goodman, 1947), it simply prevents the motoric expression of knowledge by blocking muscle movements. The third panel in Table 4.1 diagrams the expected consequences of such a drug effect. Performance is impaired during sessions when the drug is present, that is, in Groups 2 and 4 during training and in Groups 3 and 4 during the retrieval test. Normal performance by Group 2 during the test session demonstrates that normal learning took place during the training session even though performance was inhibited by drug during that session.

2.4. State-Dependent Retrieval

In addition to drug-induced retrieval deficits, there is another effect of drugs on memory retrieval that can best be termed state-dependent retrieval (SDR). When SDR occurs, efficient retrieval and performance of a learned response occur only if the drug conditions are identical during training and retention testing. SDR is depicted in the fourth panel of Table 4.1. Control-level performance occurs during the retrieval test in Group 1 where both training and testing occur in the N state, and also in Group 4 where both training and testing occur in the D state. Memory retrieval is impaired in Groups 2 and 3 where retention testing takes place in a drug state different from that present during initial acquisition of the response.

Girden and Culler (1937) referred to this phenomenon as "dissociation" of learning—a usage that is congruent with the use of the same term to describe such psychiatric syndromes as multiple personality, in which certain memories are intermittently irretrievable or dissociated from consciousness. Many subsequent authors have used the term "state-dependent learning." However, we shall use the phrase "state-dependent retrieval" because it most accurately describes the phenomenon; it is the retrieval of memories that is state-dependent, rather than the process of learning.

As we shall see, the mechanism responsible for SDR is subject to some dispute. One possibility is that drug effects constitute an important part of the stimulus context when the response is learned. Efficient retrieval (or at least performance) of the response occurs only when the stimulus conditions present during acquisition are reinstated, that is, when the animal is again placed in the training apparatus and the drug condition present during training is reestablished.

2.5. Combined Effects

In a few experimental paradigms one or another of the aforementioned drug effects will predominate and the others will be relatively insignificant. However, a more common observation is that a drug simultaneously produces several of the these effects. The fifth panel of Table 4.1 shows the expected results if a drug prevents the acquisition of new memories, blocks the retrieval of old memories, impairs performance, and produces SDR. Because the various drug actions produce overlapping effects that are confounded with one another, such data provide little information about the relative strengths of the individual effects the drug produces (Overton, 1974). To appreciate this point, note that any one of the four drug effects can entirely fail to occur, and yet the pattern of results during test sessions will still be the same as that shown in the table. Much of our progress in the investigation of drug effects on learning and memory retrieval has resulted from the development of paradigms in which one or another of the drug effects predominates.

2.6. Drug Discrimination Performance

Finally, to provide a suitable background for this chapter, we need to describe drug discriminations (DDs). To obtain DDs, an animal is usually trained in a task in which two different behavioral responses are possible. The animal is required to perform one response during all training sessions when drug is present, and to perform the other response during sessions when drug is not present. After the D versus N discrimination is learned, the N response regularly occurs during N sessions and the D response during D sessions. We can say that during D sessions, the animals retrieve the D response and show an apparent amnesia for the N response. Conversely, during N sessions it appears that the animal only "knows" the N response. DDs do not reflect a major drug effect on learning or retention distinct from those previously described; instead they are a variant of SDR. However, we describe DDs separately because of the different behavioral procedures that are used to demonstate them. DDs have been an important source of information about the mechanisms and properties of SDR.

3. A CONCEPTUAL HISTORY OF STATE-DEPENDENT RETRIEVAL

The movie *City Lights* depicts a character who is drunk when he first meets Charlie Chaplin, and who thereafter only recognizes Chaplin when he is again intoxicated. Apparently this character illustrates SDR, inasmuch as alcohol facilitates the retrieval of memories for events that happened while the subject was previously intoxicated. Even earlier anecdotal and clinical reports of SDR can be found (e.g., Collins, 1868/1966; Semon, 1904/1921).

3.1. Early Drug SDR Experiments

The first experimental demonstration of SDR was reported by Girden and Culler (1937). They observed that a conditional leg flexion response learned by a dog while it was drugged with curare would, thereafter, only be performed when the dog was once again curarized. In subsequent experiments Girden tested for SDR of conditioned pupillary responses and conditioned blood pressure responses, and he investigated the effects of brain lesions on SDR (Girden, 1940, 1942a,b,c). In spite of his unprecedented results, Girden's line of investigation was not immediately followed up by other investigators.

Heistad and Torres (1959) reported SDR of a conditioned emotional response produced by the drug thioridazine in the rat. Although this study is rarely cited, it marked the beginning of a period of active investigation of drug-induced SDR. Sachs (1961) reported that intraventricularly administered calcium or potassium would produce SDR of a conditioned avoidance response in cats; Overton (1961, 1964) reported that pentobarbital would produce SDR of learned escape responses in a T-maze task. Other investigators found that drugs would produce SDR in rats in active avoidance tasks (Holmgren, 1964a,b; Otis, 1964; Sachs, Weingarten, & Klein, 1966), in approach–avoidance conflict tasks (Barry, Miller, & Tidd, 1962), and in operant bar-pressing tasks (Belleville, 1964).

Taken as a group, these studies clearly established the existence of SDR. They also initiated a lively debate about its causes, with some investigators concluding that SDR resulted from a change in sensory context, and others postulating novel neural mechanisms as responsible.

3.2. Contextual Stimulus Effects on Retrieval: Early Experiments

Because of the importance attributed to contextual stimuli in many theories of learning, investigations of the effects of changes in context have been carried out throughout the twentieth century. A few early studies using animal subjects reported moderately robust effects (e.g., Carr, 1917; Hunter, 1911; Patrick & Anderson, 1930; Watson, 1907). However, the majority of these studies were carried out with human subjects, and they reported relatively weak effects. These experiments with human subjects investigated the effects of changes in a variety of contextual stimuli including the proprioceptive stimuli produced by changes in bodily posture (Rand & Wapner, 1967; Reed, 1931), the effects of changing the verbal context surrounding a to-be-remembered word (Pan, 1926), the effects of changing the color of the paper on which words to be recalled were printed (Dulsky, 1935), the effects of moving from indoors to outdoors or from one room to another between training and retention (Bilodeau & Schlosberg, 1951; Farnsworth, 1934; Greenspoon & Ranyard, 1957), as well as the effects of other environmental manipulations (Pessin, 1932). Evidence of contextual effects was obtained in many of these experiments, but the detrimental effects on retrieval produced by changes in stimulus context were generally quite small. The subjects could recall most of the to-be-remembered materials in spite of changes in stimulus context. Thus, although the experiments showed that changes in stimulus context could somewhat impair retrieval, they also showed that engrams were quite robust and could be retrieved rather effectively in spite of substantial changes in stimulus context. Nowhere in this literature are there data suggesting that a contextual change can produce a total amnesia for an entire learning experience.

3.3. Neurological Theories of SDR

Investigators who observed relatively weak drug-induced SDR effects had no particular difficulty in explaining their results. Response decrements of similar size had been observed to follow changes in environmental or proprioceptive stimuli, and it seemed reasonable to postulate that drugs produced sensory effects, and that changes in such "drug stimuli" were responsible for the observed SDR effects (Barry *et al.*, 1962; Belleville, 1964; Heistad, 1957; Otis, 1964). However, investigators who chanced to work with preparations that produced strong SDR effects found their results more difficult to explain. In several experiments virtually complete amnesias for apparently well-learned responses were observed, even under circumstances that presumably produced a high motivation to perform (e.g., escape or avoidance of shock). Investigators who obtained such results concluded, without exception, that their findings could not be explained on the basis of changes in sensory context. Confronted with data that appeared inexplicable in terms of previously demonstrated mechanisms, they speculated about new hypothetical brain mechanisms that could account for their results (Bliss, 1974; Girden & Culler, 1937; John, 1967; Overton, 1964; Sachs, 1967).

It will be informative to describe a few of the resulting "neurological" theories of SDR.

3.3.1. Decortication

Girden and Culler (1937) postulated that the drug curare renders the cortex nonfunctional. They also suggest that in the undrugged animal, the cortex inhibits the subcortical regions. When an undrugged animal is conditioned, learning takes place in the cortex and subsequently the learned response cannot be performed when the animal is drugged and its cortex is depressed. When a drugged animal is conditioned, subcortical regions learn the conditioned response; if the animal is subsequently tested while undrugged, the educated subcortex is inhibited by the cortex and so the animal appears untrained.

3.3.2. State-Dependent Cell Assemblies

Overton (1964) proposed a completely different theory that departed from the concept that cell assemblies are formed during learning. Following Hebb (1949, p. 201), Overton argued that cell assemblies developed in a particular physiological condition will function efficiently only as long as that physiological condition is maintained; if a change in brain excitability is induced by a drug or other intervention, then the cell assembly will function inefficiently or not at all. More concretely, cell assemblies formed in the absence of drug will be disorganized by drug actions. Conversely, cell assemblies formed while drug is present will not function effectively when drug is absent.

3.3.3. Addition or Deletion of Brain Functions

According to a model proposed by Overton (1978), each different drug disables a different subset of brain functions. If an animal is capable of learning a task under a particular drug, it does so by utilizing the remaining subset of brain functions. When a different drug is present and different brain functions are intact, they may not suffice to mediate the previously learned response. When the animal is undrugged, brain functions that did not operate during task acquisition are now functional and may cause behaviors that interfere with performance of the learned response. Essentially this model is an extension of Girden's decortication model adapted to accommodate the fact that several different drugs can produce SDR, and that responses learned under one drug are often unavailable under the influence of other drugs.

In addition to these three theories, at least half a dozen additional mechanisms have been postulated as responsible for drug-induced SDR (see Overton, 1978). All of these models seem to be attempts by investigators to explain data that appear inexplicable on the basis of the effects of changes in stimulus context.

3.4. Early Drug-Discrimination Experiments

Conger (1951) carried out the first DD experiment. In a telescope alley task, rats were trained to run down the alley to obtain food when drugged and to refuse to progress down the alley in order to avoid shock when undrugged. Other rats learned the reverse task. The authors concluded that ethanol must be producing discriminable stimuli that provided a basis for differential responding.

Overton (1961, 1966) reported DDs in a T-maze task in which rats were reinforced for left turns when drugged and for right turns when undrugged. Subsequently, Barry (1968) and many other investigators reported DDs in a variety of tasks (Overton, 1971). By 1970 the following properties of DDs had been demonstrated.

1. Drug versus no-drug discriminations can be learned with increasing rapidity as dosage is increased (Overton, 1964). Apparently the degree of "discriminability" of a drug increases with dosage.

2. Drug versus no-drug discriminations can be learned with several types of drugs, including anesthetics, antimuscarinics, nicotinics, and stimulants (Overton, 1964, 1966, 1967, 1969).

3. Animals can also discriminate between two different drugs (i.e., D1 vs. D2) or two different doses of a single drug (Overton, 1966, 1968).

4. At least two and probably several different types of discriminable effects can be produced by various drugs (Overton, 1966, 1967, 1969).

3.5. Sensory Interpretations of DDs and SDR

Investigators studying DDs have been almost unanimous in concluding that the phenomenon is based on the sensory consequences of drug action. The basic idea has been that drugs produce some discriminable alterations in the total sensory experience of the animal, and that during DD training the rats learn to attend to—and base their response selection on—the current state of these stimuli. Apparently, I am the only investigator who has worked extensively with DDs without concluding that they were based on drug-induced stimuli, and even I have acknowledged that most of the properties of DDs are congruent with the idea that DDs are based on drug stimuli (Overton, 1972).

3.6. Experimental Tests of Sensory Models for DDs

Several experiments have tested specific sensory events to see if they might be involved as mediators for drug discriminations. We can easily review these experiments by stating the hypothesis that each was designed to test, and the results obtained.

The first experiment of this type tested the hypothesis that pentobarbital versus no-drug discriminations might be based on the unusual proprioceptive stimuli resulting from drug-induced ataxia. Overton (1964) trained rats to discriminate gallamine versus no drug using doses high enough to produce obvious muscular weakness and uncoordination. Gallamine, a drug similar to curare, partially or completely paralyzes striate muscles but has few direct actions on the central nervous system. Rats were not able to discriminate presence versus absence of gallamine, suggesting that abnormal proprioceptive cues were not mediators for pentobarbital's discriminability.

Overton (1971) next tested whether DDs might be based on unusual autonomic afferent stimuli caused by drug effects on the autonomic nervous system or on autonomically innervated organs. He was not able to demonstrate DDs using drugs that acted exclusively on the peripheral autonomic nervous system, which suggests that drug actions on the autonomic nervous system are not readily discriminated.

Another hypothesis stated that DDs were based on some sort of drug-induced alteration of normal visual perception—for example, on drug-induced blurring of vision. Overton (1968) demonstrated that surgically blinded rats could discriminate pentobarbital versus no drug just as easily as could sighted rats. In addition, if sighted rats were trained to discriminate pentobarbital versus no drug and then blinded, only a transient disruption of the pentobarbital discrimination resulted. These findings indicate that drug-induced alterations of visual perception play either a small role or no role at all in the mediation of DDs.

It was also suggested that DDs in the shock escape task might be mediated by drug-induced analgesia, which altered the rat's perception of a particularly salient cue (pain). Overton (1968) tested this hypothesis indirectly by requiring rats to discriminate between high and low shock levels in the T-maze task. These discriminations were formed slowly, suggesting that variations in the amount of pain produced by shock were not mediating the rapid discriminative control produced by pentobarbital. This hypothesis was later tested more directly by comparing the ease of discriminability of pentobarbital to that of narcotics. Pentobarbital was considerably more discriminable than narcotics, even though its analgesic effects were presumably less profound (Overton, 1966; Overton & Batta, 1979). Again, the results indicate that drug-induced analgesia is not responsible for the discriminability of pentobarbital.

Several additional studies have simply tested whether sensory stimuli can be discriminated more rapidly or less rapidly than drugs. Depending on the drug and the sensory conditions selected, drugs produced either more or less rapid discriminative control than that achieved by sensory events (Duncan, Phillips, Reints, & Schechter, 1979; Kilbey, Harris, & Aigner, 1971; Overton, 1971).

In summary, sensory stimuli appear to be as effective as drugs in providing a basis for control of discriminative responding, and hence could mediate DDs at least in principle. However, it has not been possible to find sensory events that demonstrably mediate discriminations based on drug states. The more obvious sensory candidates have been tested and were shown not to be involved.

3.7. Logical Positivism as Applied to DDs

Although the phenomenology of DDs resembles that of sensory discriminations in a variety of respects, there are no data that prove that DDs are mediated by sensory events. Logical positivism suggests that it may be unwise to use terminology suggesting such causation unless it can be proved. In this context, it should be noted that DDs differ from sensory discriminations in one important respect. In the case of the latter, the controlling sensory events are operationally definable, and whatever internal prceptions the animals may have of these events are

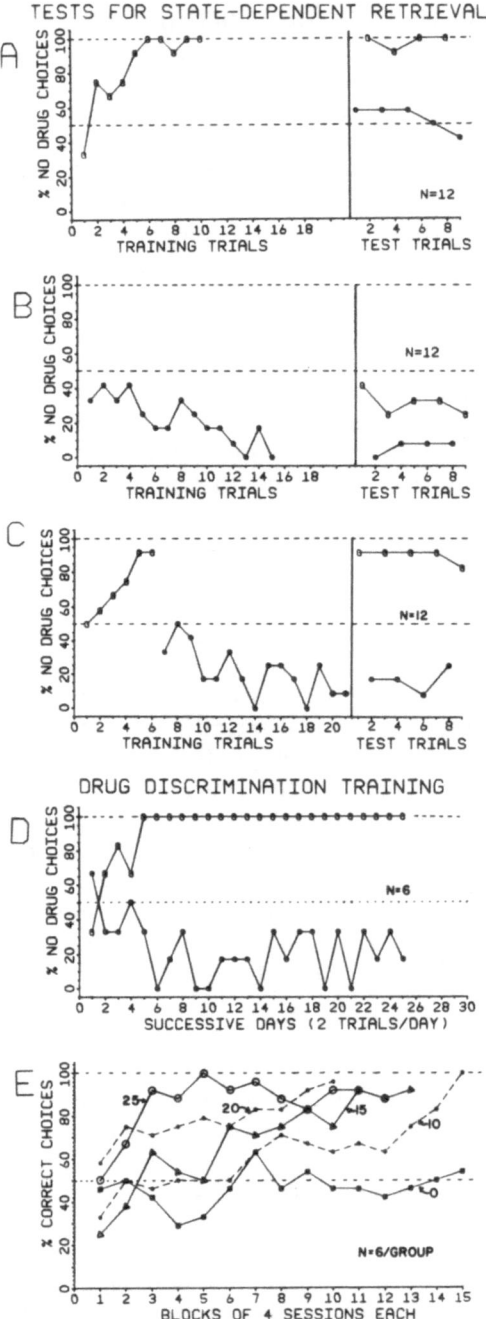

TESTS FOR STATE-DEPENDENT RETRIEVAL

DRUG DISCRIMINATION TRAINING

inferred. Hence it is parsimonious to speak of stimulus control of behavior and undesirable to speak of the internal states and sensations that may be produced by these stimuli. However, in the case of DDs, the situation is more or less reversed. An altered drug state is operationally definable whereas any resulting sensory events are inferred. Hence logical positivism suggests that it may be preferable to use the noninferential phrase "drug state" rather than a hypothetical construct such as "drug stimulus" to describe the event that provides the basis for DDs.

3.8. Relationships of SDR to DDs

Our review of research on SDR and DDs must also mention the important fact that the same drug actions appear to be responsible for both SDR and DDs. Because of the importance of this conclusion, we will review here the original data on which it was based.

Three groups of rats were used to demonstrate SDR in a T-maze task, as shown in Figures 4.1A, 4.1B, and 4.1C. Group 1 received 10 training trials without drug during which a right turn was required to escape from shock; the correct response was learned in three to six trials (Fig. 4.1A). During subsequent D and N test trials, this response was reliably performed only on N-trials. Group 2 was trained while drugged to run to the left goal box. Learning was somewhat slower than in Group 1, because of the debilitating effects of the high dose of pentobarbital, and these rats required six to twelve trials to learn the correct response. In subsequent tests, the left-turn response occurred more frequently during D sessions than during N sessions. Group 3 was first trained to turn right when undrugged (six trials), then trained to turn left when drugged (fifteen trials), and finally received a series of test trials during which retrieval of both responses was state dependent, that is, on test trials without drug, most animals in Group 3 performed the initially learned no-drug response and, conversely, on drug trials most performed the drug-state response (Overton, 1964).

Fig. 4.1. T-maze results showing SDR and DDs produced by pentobarbital. Rats were trained to run to the left (or right) goal box during sessions when they were drugged and/ or to run to the right (or left) goal box during sessions when undrugged to escape from shock. In some groups, subsequent test trials were conducted during which both goal boxes were accessible. The no-drug (N) state was produced by isotonic saline injection and the drug (D) state by intraperitoneal pentobaribital injection 15 minutes prior to training. Dosage was 25 mg/kg in panels A to D, and differed for each group in panel E as shown in the figure. Panels A to D show the percentage of rats making the N choice during training and/or test trials (solid circles are D trials; open circles are N trials). Panel E shows percentage of correct turns during D versus N discrimination training (D and N trials pooled) in five groups of rats.

Analysis of performance during acquisition gave additional evidence of SDR. The number of errors during acquisition of the drug-state response (left turn) was no higher in Group 3 (which had previously learned to turn right) than in Group 2 (which learned only the left-turn response), indicating that the right-turn response learned in the no drug state by rats in Group 3 did not interfere with subsequent acquisition of the left-turn habit in the drug state.

Another five groups of rats were required to learn DDs in the T-maze. These rats received a series of alternating N and D trials (two trials per day). They were reinforced for right turns when drugged and for left turns when undrugged. As the bottom panel of Figure 4.1 shows, approximately 10, 25, 40, and 60 training trials, respectively, were required to discriminate pentobarbital doses of 25, 20, 15, and 10 mg/kg from no injection, accepting 80% accuracy as evidence of discrimination. The lowest curve in Fig. 4.1E was a control group (dose = 0) testing whether rats could learn to alternate their choice or discriminate time of day in this task—they did not.

Performance by the rats trained to discriminate 10 or 15 mg/kg versus no drug was rather uninformative; except for drug-induced ataxia, the behavior of these rats was in all visible respects indistinguishable from that of rats learning sensory discriminations in the same maze. Performance by the 25-mg/kg DD group is replotted in Fig. 4.1D to allow detailed inspection. Note that acquisition of the right-turn habit did not differ from N-state acquisition in Groups 1 or 3 as shown in Figures 4.1A and 4.1C. Similarly, performance during the D sessions of discrimination training in Figure 4.1D did not differ from performance of Groups 2 or 3 during D training sessions. This suggests that during 25 mg/kg versus no-drug discrimination training, acquisition of the N-state response did not measurably interfere with concurrent acquisition of the opposite response in the D state, and vice versa. This result appears to indicate that the rats, when drugged, did not remember the N-state habit, and vice versa.

The results of this experiment strongly suggested that SDR and DDs were closely related. At low doses the relevant drug effects were weak, and comparatively prolonged training was required to establish DDs. The acquisition of these DDs resembled the acquisition of other sensory discriminations. As dosage was increased, the strength of the relevant (discriminable) drug effects appeared to increase monotonically, and DDs were more and more rapidly acquired. During DD training with very high doses, SDR prevented the no-drug response from being recalled during drug training sessions, and vice versa. Hence state-appropriate responding was acquired as rapidly as the individual right- and left-turn responses could be learned. The apparent conclusion is that SDR and DDs are based on the same drug effects. Whatever these effects are, they have to be present in rather large amounts to produce SDR amnesias. However, rats are capable of learning DDs based on the weaker effects of low doses if training is sufficiently prolonged.

This conclusion clearly has important theroretical consequences. It means that any mechanism proposed to mediate DDs must also be capable of mediating SDR. Conversely, any mechanism proposed to mediate SDR must be capable of mediating DDs.

3.9. Status circa 1970

The 1960s were the first decade of serious research on SDR and DDs. Many of the major properties of both phenomena were demonstrated. By the end of the decade there were two major schools of thought regarding the causes of SDR and DDs. A sensory interpretation of these phenomena was accepted by most investigators who studied the DD phenomenon, and by those who had observed relatively weak SDR amnesias. However, investigators who had observed relatively complete SDR amnesias all believed that some nonsensory mechanism must underlie the results they had obtained. There was no agreement among these investigators on the particular mechanism that might be responsible for SDR, and a variety of theories had been advanced. No investigators had been able to produce any data that convincingly supported their theoretical models.

4. RECENT EVIDENCE ABOUT THE MECHANISM OF SDR AND DDS

The 1970s have witnessed a dramatic increase in the number of publications dealing with SDR and DDs; but there has not been a correspondingly increased interest in the mechanisms responsible for these phenomena. DDs have been adopted as a research tool in many studies dealing with pharmacological questions, but most of these experiments have not been designed to investigate the mechanisms that underlie DDs. Among the SDR studies conducted with human subjects, most have been simply intended to determine drug and task variables that would allow SDR to occur. Only a relatively few studies have been explicitly designed to test theoretically interesting questions about the mechanisms responsible for SDR and DDs (e.g., Eich, 1977; Modrow & Bliss, 1979; Weingartner, Walker, Eich, & Murphy, 1976). Nevertheless, there have been several theoretically important findings during the decade, and these mandate an appreciable revision of our theoretical concepts about SDR and DDs.

4.1. Multiplicity of Drug States

Perhaps the most important new finding is that many discriminably different drug states are produced by available drugs. Data suggesting the existence of a multitude of drug states were first reported in 1971 (Harris & Balster, 1971; Overton, 1971) and have since been confirmed repeatedly. Indeed, there appear to be about as many discriminably different drug conditions as there are major classes of psychoactive drugs (Barry, 1974; Colpaert & Rosecrans, 1978; Ho, Richards, & Chute, 1978; Lal, 1977; Overton, 1973, 1975, 1982). Recalling the continuity between SDR and DDs, we can infer that psychoactive drugs produce more than a dozen different states in which learning is partially dissociated, and that responses learned in any one of these states generalize only incompletely to the other states, or to the no-drug condition. The strength of the SDR effects of many of these drugs is too small to be measured directly, and we know of the SDR effects of these drugs only indirectly from the results of DD experiments.

The demonstration that there are several discriminably different drug states was not intended as a test of any theory; nevertheless it has important theoretical consequences. Consider, for example, Girden's decortication model for SDR. Curare was postulated to produce SDR by decorticating the animal. Hence, according to that theory, there could be only two dissociated states—the normal (no-drug) state and the decorticated (drug) state. If new evidence shows that phenobarbital produces a third state dissociated from both the curare state and the no-drug state, then the model is unable to accommodate such a finding. Analogously, perhaps half of the extant "neurological" theories of SDR are not capable of mediating multiple SDR effects (Bliss, 1974; Overton, 1978).

From a broader perspective, we can say that some classes of theories have more difficulty accommodating the multiplicity of demonstrated drug states than do other classes of theories. For example, sensory theories have no difficulty at all. It is intuitively acceptable to postulate that the rat is capable of differentiating a variety of qualitatively different drug-induced sensations. Similarly, the "state-specific cell assembly" theory (Overton, 1964) has no difficulty dealing with the existence of several different drug states. One need only postulate that each drug produces a somewhat different pattern of synaptic excitability changes. The resulting cell assemblies formed in each drug state will then be specific to the drug state in which they were formed, and will operate at reduced efficiency with all other drugs. However, "lesion" theories that postulate that the drug disables a particular brain structure do, intrinsically, have difficulty with multiple drug states. For each new discriminably different state that is demonstrated, a new locus of action in the brain must be postulated. Soon there are more discriminably different drug states than there are brain structures that can reasonably be thought to be affected by these drugs. Overall, the demonstration of multiple drug states has reduced the number of tenable hypothetical mechanisms that could possibly be responsible for SDR and DD—an improvement in our state of knowledge.

4.2. Robustness of SDR

Data collected during the 1970s have rather sharply delimited the circumstances under which strong SDR effects can be expected. For example, results obtained before 1970 allowed one to postulate that SDR amnesias might be produced by almost any change in drug state (e.g., Heistad, 1957). However, it is now apparent that only a relatively restricted set of drug conditions can produce strong SDR effects. These conditions are produced by high doses of only three or four types of drugs—most notably by depressant drugs (Overton, 1975, 1977, 1982). Additionally, it has been found that strong retrieval cues tend to override SDR retrieval deficits (Eich, 1977; Petersen, 1977). Furthermore, it has been repeatedly shown that overtraining can abolish SDR amnesias (Bliss, 1972; Iwahara, 1971; Iwahara & Noguchi, 1972, 1974; Modrow & Bliss, 1979).

Taken together, these results show that drug-induced SDR amnesias can be observed only under a rather restricted set of conditions. The theoretical consequences of this finding will become clear after we discuss recent experiments on the effects of changes in stimulus context.

4.3. Contextual Stimuli: Recent Experiments

Several recent experiments have tested the effects of changes in contextual cues. Although the results have not fundamentally changed our understanding of the effects of stimulus context on memory retrieval, they have shown that retrieval deficits induced by changes in sensory context can sometimes be quite substantial—especially in animal subjects.

In several studies the impairment of retrieval produced by changes in context has been about as large as can be produced by changes in drug state. For example, several studies have used the contextual conditions "lights on" versus "lights off," and have found that responses learned with lights on generalize quite poorly the lights-off condition, and vice versa (Moffett & Ettlinger, 1966, 1967). Other related studies required animals to learn different S+/S− discriminations in the lights-on and lights-off conditions (Hickis, Robles, & Thomas, 1977); these compound discriminations were learned without difficulty. The results of these experiments indicate that learning that occurs with lights on is partially "dissociated" (i.e., irretrievable) when the rat is in the dark, and vice versa. The impairment of retrieval produced by a change from light to dark (or vice versa) appears to be quantitatively comparable to that produced by a switch into or out of the pentobarbital state (Duncan, 1977; Overton, 1971).

Several studies have used the wall color and/or floor texture of mazes as contextual stimuli. Both Chiszar and Spear (1969) and Zentall (1970) convincingly showed that responses learned in one context only partially transferred into a second context, and vice versa. In a similar study, Spear, Smith, Bryan, Gordon, Timmons, and Chiszar (1980) directly compared the strong SDR effects of pentobarbital to the only slightly weaker effects of a change in stimulus context, using two different experimental rooms as the two contexts. Essentially these studies tested the degree to which responses learned in one maze would generalize into another, similar maze; hence they are less directly comparable to SDR studies than are the light versus dark studies, in which all training took place in the same apparatus.

Generally, there has been a resurgence of interest in the effects of contextual cues (Nadel & Willner, 1980; Rescorla & Wagner, 1972; Welker, Tomie, Davitt, & Thomas, 1974), and a variety of experiments have shown that contextual stimuli can have strong effects on retrieval (Archer & Sjoden, 1980; Archer, Sjoden, Nilsson, & Carter, 1979; Chiszar & Spear, 1969; Godden & Baddeley, 1975; Tomie, 1976). The effects of a change in context have been especially large in the case of minimally learned or partially forgotten responses (Deweer, Sara, & Hars, 1980; Gatti, Pais, & Weeks, 1975; Spear, 1971), which is reminiscent of the fact that drug-induced SDR amnesias are most apparent if overtraining has not occurred and if retrieval cues are minimal (Petersen, 1977).

The results of these experiments on the effects of changes in stimulus context clearly make it easier to believe that drug-induced SDR may be mediated by drug-induced stimuli. Previously, we were in the awkward situation of postulating that changes in hypothesized drug-induced stimuli could produce large SDR impairments in retrieval even though changes in directly observable sensory stimuli usually produced only small impairments of retrieval. However, the recent literature shows that changes in stimulus context can produce substantial response decrements under circumstances similar to those that produce robust SDR amnesias after changes in drug state. These results, finally, make it reasonable to postulate a sensory mechanism for SDR.

4.4. Threshold Dosages for SDR and DDs

It appears that a determination of the threshold doses capable of producing SDR and DDs, respectively, may provide a relatively definitive test of whether the mechanism underlying these effects is sensory in nature or involves one of the postulated neurological mechanisms. The argument is as follows.

A sensory interpretation of SDR and DDs appears to predict that the threshold for discriminative control will be considerably lower than the threshold required to produce SDR decrements. Our discussion of contextual stimuli suggests that moderately large sensory changes should be necessary to produce retrieval failures secondary to a change in stimulus context, that is, relatively high drug doses should be necessary to produce SDR. In contrast, during DD training it is reasonable to expect that an animal will be able to discriminate much smaller differences between states, because prolonged training will allow the animal gradually to learn to attend to the relevant stimulus attributes of the drug. Unfortunately, the literature provides little evidence regarding the relative magnitude of the sensory changes that are required to produce (1) retrieval deficits based on changes in sensory context, and (2) an adequate basis for discriminative control. However, some evidence suggests that the threshold for discriminative control is considerably lower than that for contextual retrieval effects—perhaps an order of magnitude lower (Riccio, Urda, & Thomas, 1966).

In contrast, all neurological models for SDR predict that the thresholds for DDs and for SDR will be equal. According to these theories, DDs are based on weak (but measurable) SDR effects. During DD training, the animal is assumed to learn two responses that have approximately equal habit strengths. During each DD trial, both habits are believed to be retrieved from memory. However, the habit that was learned in the currently imposed drug state is retrieved somewhat more efficiently, and dominates the overt behavior of the animal (Spear et al., 1980). Clearly, in such a situation where two responses are competing for expression, if the state-appropriate response is consistently performed then its engram must be appreciably (measurably) more retrievable than that of the other response. Hence the lowest drug dosage that is capable of controlling differential responding should be no lower than the lowest dosage at which a measurable SDR effect will result from D-to-N or N-to-D state changes.

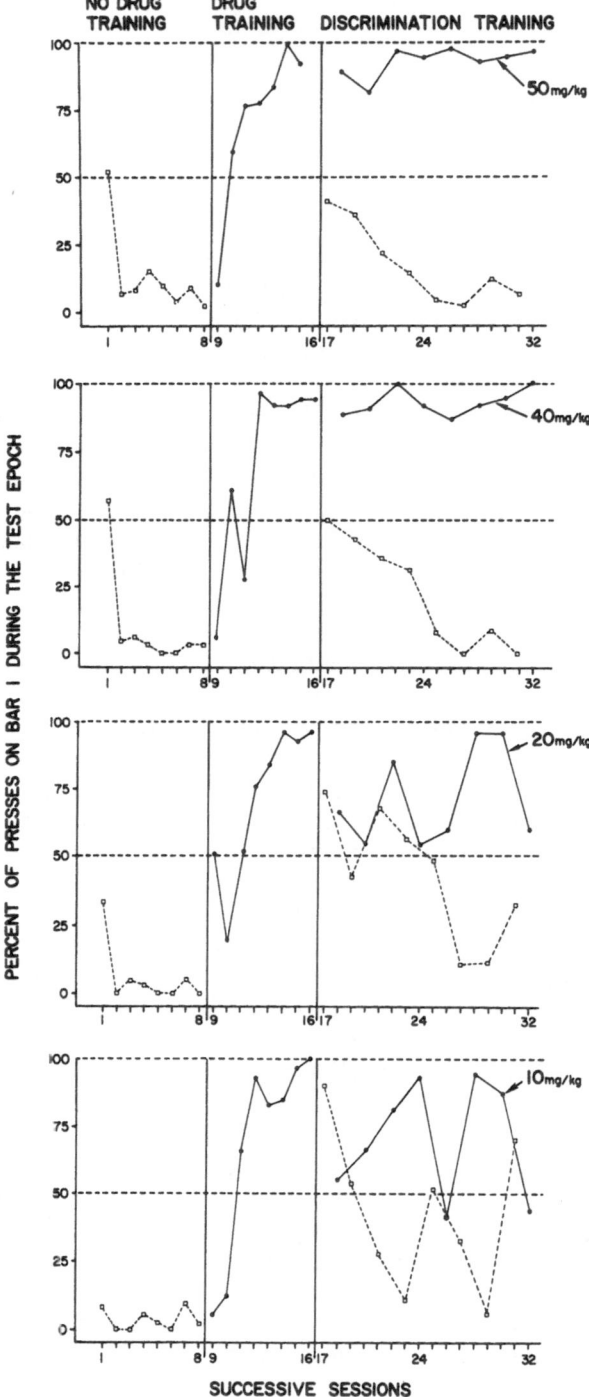

The time seems right for a test that could reject either the sensory or the neurological interpretations of SDR. Unfortunately, no such experiment has been performed, and at this point only pilot data are available regarding the threshold dosages for SDR and DDs. Nevertheless, because of the importance of the issue, we will present the data that are available.

We recently developed a DD dosage titration method for determining the lowest dosage of a drug that could be discriminated from no drug. Initially, animals were trained to discriminate a high dose versus no drug. After they learned this discrimination, a lower dose was substituted as the training condition. Successive dosage reductions occurred until the animal could no longer discriminate the presence of the drug. Next, the training dosage was gradually raised until discimination reappeared. Then dosage was again decreased until discrimination disappeared. Using this procedure it was possible to define for each of several training drugs a relatively stable "threshold" dose below which the drug could not maintain control of discriminative behavior. For several of the drugs we tested, the threshold discriminable doses were quite low—probably considerably lower than the threshold doses at which noticeable SDR effects would have disappeared if they had been directly measured. In the one rat tested with phenobarbital, the lowest dose that could be reliably discriminated was 5 mg/kg (Overton, 1979).

This DD threshold can be compared to the lowest dose capable of producing a measurable degree of SDR. Although we have not yet performed an ideally designed SDR threshold experiment, data from one of our recent studies do provide an initial estimate of the minimum dose of phenobarbital that can produce SDR. In that study, four groups of rats were trained to bar press in an operant compartment containing two levers mounted side by side on one wall of the chamber. Initially, they were trained to press Bar 2 during eight sessions while undrugged. During these sessions presses on Bar 2 were reinforced with 0.1 ml of 1% saccharine solution, using reinforcement schedules of increasing difficulty until an interlocked FR-10/FI-90 second schedule was reached;

Fig. 4.2. Test for the lowest dose of phenobarbital capable of producing SDR. Rats were trained to bar press in a two-lever operant compartment. The X axis represents successive daily training sessions. The Y axis shows the percentage of presses on the drug lever during the "test epoch" before the first reinforcement of each session. These test epochs lasted until the rat pressed 10 times on either Bar 1 or Bar 2. Eight no-drug sessions with reinforcement of Bar 2 presses were followed by 8 drug sessions during which presses on Bar 1 were reinforced. On Day 17 (no drug) in Groups 1 to 4, five, one, zero, and zero rats, respectively, pressed more times on the N lever than on the D lever during the test epoch, thus showing retrieval of the initially learned bar 2 response. This result suggests that the lowest dose of phenobarbital capable of producing SDR in this task is slightly below 40 mg/kg.

presses on Bar 1 had no programmed consequence. Drug injection preceded Sessions 9 to 16, and during these sessions presses on Bar 1 were
reinforced using similar schedules of reinforcement. Thereafter DD
training commenced, and the D and N conditions alternated from day to
day, as did the reinforced lever. Each session lasted 15 minutes. Groups
1 to 4 contained eight, three, three, and three rats, respectively, which
were injected with phenobarbital 50, 40, 20, and 10 mg/kg, 20 minutes
before the beginning of D sessions (solid circles). Figure 4.2 shows the
percentage of presses on Bar 1 prior to the first reinforcement of each
session. The test for SDR occurred on Session 17 (no drug) when an
attempt was made to retrieve the initially learned Bar 2 response. In
Groups 1 to 4, respectively, 63, 33, 0.0, and 0.0 percent of the rats
pressed predominantly on Bar 2, suggesting that the threshold for SDR
was only slightly below 40 mg/kg. The weak point of the study, of
course, is that the Bar 1 (drug) response may have been overtained.
Possibly if fewer Bar 1 sessions had occurred during the second phase of
training, SDR would have been apparent in more rats at lower doses.

Our pilot data suggest that the threshold discriminable dose of phenobarbital is somewhat lower than the threshold dose capable of producing SDR. This result tentatively supports a sensory interpretation of
both SDR and DDs. Unfortunately, the SDR threshold detection procedure may have yielded an artifactually high estimate of threshold.
Also, the DD titration study was run in only a single rat. A definitive
study has not yet been completed.

4.5. Summary

Several recent findings provide increased support for a sensory interpretation of SDR and DDs: (1) As more and more drugs have been
shown to be discriminable, some of the postulated neurological mechanisms for SDR have been unable to accommodate the demonstrated
complexity of the DD phenomenon. (2) The size of the decrements in
response strength that can result from changes in contextual stimuli has
been shown to be larger than was indicated by the previous literature.
(3) SDR deficits have been shown to occur in a relatively restricted set of
circumstances, usually involving minimally-learned responses and high
doses of depressant drugs. (4) Preliminary data suggest that the threshold dosage for DDs may be lower than the threshold for SDR. Clearly
the issue is not closed, and a definitive demonstration of the mechanism
responsible for SDR is yet to be reported. Nevertheless, the accumulat-
ing evidence increasingly suggests that a sensory mechanism may underlie SDR and DDs. This raises the question of just why drug stimuli

provide such potent cues. Persuasive answers to this question have not yet been formulated.

5. REFERENCES

Archer, T., & Sjoden, P. Context-dependent taste-aversion learning with a familiar conditioning context. *Physiological Psychology*, 1980, 8, 40–46.

Archer, T., Sjoden, P., Nilsson, L., & Carter, N. Role of exteroceptive background context in taste-aversion conditioning and extinction. *Animal Learning and Behavior*, 1979, 7, 17–22.

Barry, H., III. Prolonged measurements of discrimination between alcohol and nondrug states. *Journal of Comparative and Physiological Psychology*, 1968, 65, 349–352.

Barry, H., III. Classification of drugs according to their discriminable effects in rats. *Federation Proceedings*, 1974, 33, 1814–1824.

Barry, H., III, Miller, N. E., & Tidd, G. E. Control for stimulus change while testing effects of amobarbital on conflict. *Journal of Comparative and Physiological Psychology*, 1962, 55, 1071–1074.

Belleville, R. E. Control of behavior by drug-produced internal stimuli. *Psychopharmacology (Berl.)*, 1964, 5, 95–105.

Bilodeau, I. McD., & Schlosberg, H. Similarity in stimulating conditions as a variable in retroactive inhibition. *Journal of Experimental Psychology*, 1951, 41, 199–204.

Bliss, D. K. Dissociated learning and state-dependent retention induced by pentobarbital in Rhesus monkeys. *Journal of Comparative and Physiological Psychology*, 1972, 84, 149–161.

Bliss, D. K. Theoretical explanations of drug-dissociated behaviors. *Federation Proceedings*, 1974, 33, 1787–1796.

Carr, H. Maze studies with the white rat. I. Normal animals. *Journal of Animal Behavior*, 1917, 7, 259–275.

Chiszar, D. A., & Spear, N. E. Stimulus change, reversal learning and retention in the rat. *Journal of Comparative and Physiological Psychology*, 1969, 69, 190–195.

Collins, W. *The moonstone*. Harmondsworth, England: Penquin Books, 1966. (Originally published, 1868.)

Colpaert, F. C., & Rosecrans, J. A. (Eds.). *Stimulus properties of drugs: Ten years of progress*. Amsterdam: Elsevier/North-Holland, 1978.

Conger, J. J. The effects of alcohol on conflict behavior in the albino rat. *Quarterly Journal of Studies on Alcohol*, 1951, 12, 1–29.

Deweer, B., Sara, S. J., & Hars, B. Contextual cues and memory retrieval in rats: Alleviation of forgetting by a pretest exposure to background stimuli. *Animal Learning and Behavior*, 1980, 8, 265–272.

Dulsky, S. G. The effect of a change in background on recall and relearning. *Journal of Experimental Psychology*, 1935, 18, 725–740.

Duncan, P. M. The effects of external stimulus change on ethanol-produced dissociation. *Pharmacology, Biochemistry and Behavior*, 1977, 11, 377–381.

Duncan, P. M., Phillips, J., Reints, J., & Schechter, M. D. Interaction between discrimination of drug states and external stimuli. *Psychopharmacology*, 1979, 61, 105–106.

Eich, J. E. State-dependent retrieval of information in human episodic memory. In I. M. Birnbaum & E. S. Parker (Eds.), *Alcohol and human memory*. Hillsdale, N.J.: Lawrence Erlbaum, 1977.

Farnsworth, P. R. Examinations in familiar and unfamiliar surroundings. *Journal of Social Psychology*, 1934, 5, 128–129.

Gatti, S. V., Pais, N., & Weeks, J. R. Effect of reinstatement procedure on retention of differential appetitive responding. *Bulletin of the Psychonomic Society*, 1975, 6, 57–60.

Girden, E. Cerebral mechanisms in conditioning under curare. *American Journal of Psychology*, 1940, 53, 397–406.

Girden, E. Generalized conditioned responses under curare and erythroidine. *Journal of Experimental Psychology*, 1942, 31, 105–119. (a)

Girden, E. The dissociation of blood pressure conditioned responses under erythroidine. *Journal of Experimental Psychology*, 1942, 31, 219–231. (b)

Girden, E. The dissociation of pupillary conditioned reflexes under erythroidine and curare. *Journal of Experimental Psychology*, 1942, 31, 322–332. (c)

Girden, E., & Culler, E. A. Conditioned responses in curarized striate muscle in dogs. *Journal of Comparative Psychology*, 1937, 23, 261–274.

Godden, D. R., & Baddeley, A. D. Context-dependent memory in two natural environments: On land and underwater. *British Journal of Psychology*, 1975, 66, 325–331.

Greenspoon, J., & Ranyard, R. Stimulus conditions and retroactive inhibition. *Journal of Experimental Psychology*, 1957, 53, 55–59.

Harris, R. T., & Balster, R. L. An analysis of the function of drugs in the stimulus control of operant behavior. In T. Thompson & R. Pickens (Eds.), *Stimulus properties of drugs*. New York: Appleton-Century-Crofts, 1971.

Harvey, A. M., & Masland, R. L. Actions of curarizing preparations in the human. *Journal of Pharmacology and Experimental Therapeutics*, 1941, 73, 304–311.

Hebb, D. O. *The organization of behavior: A neuropsychological theory*. New York: Wiley, 1949.

Heistad, G. T. A bio-psychological approach to somatic treatments in psychiatry. *American Journal of Psychiatry*, 1957, 114, 540–545.

Heistad, G. T., & Torres, A. A. A mechanism for the effect of a tranquilizing drug on learned emotional responses. *University of Minnesota Medical Bulletin*, 1959, 30, 518–527.

Hickis, C. F., Robles, L., & Thomas, D. R. Contextual stimuli and memory retrieval in pigeons. *Animal Learning and Behavior*, 1977, 5, 161–168.

Ho, B. T., Richards, D. W., III; & Chute, D. L. (Eds.). *Drug discrimination and state dependent learning*. New York: Academic Press, 1978.

Holmgren, B. Nivel de vigilia y reflejos condicionados. *Boletin del Instituto de Investigaciones de la Actividad Nerviosa Superior*, 1964, 1, 33–50. (a)

Holmgren, B. Conditional avoidance reflex under pentobarbital. *Boletin del Instituto de Estudios Medicos y Biologicos*, 1964, 22, 21–38. (b)

Hunter, W. S. Some labyrinth habits of the domestic pigeon. *Journal of Animal Behavior*, 1911, 1, 278–304.

Iwahara, S. Effects of drug-state changes upon two-way shuttle avoidance responses in rats treated with chlordiazepoxide or placebo. *Japanese Psychological Research*, 1971, 13, 207–218.

Iwahara, S., & Noguchi, S. Drug-state dependency as a function of overtraining in rats. *Japanese Psychological Research*, 1972, 14, 141–144.

Iwahara, S., & Noguchi, S. Effects of overtraining upon drug-state dependency in discrimination learning in white rats. *Japanese Psychological Research*, 1974, 16, 59–64.

John, E. R. *Mechanisms of memory*. New York: Academic Press, 1967.

Kilbey, M. M., Harris, R. T., & Aigner, T. G. Establishment of equivalent external and internal stimulus control of an operant behavior and its reversal. *Proceedings of the American Psychological Association*, 1971, 6, 767–768.

Lal, H. (Ed.). *Discriminative stimulus properties of drugs.* Vol. 22. *Advances in behavioral biology.* New York: Plenum Press, 1977.

McGaugh, J. L., & Petrinovich, L. E. Effects of drugs on learning and memory. *International Review of Neurobiology,* 1965, *8,* 139–196.

Modrow, H. E., & Bliss, D. K. Electrophysiological correlates of state-dependent learning. *Physiological Psychology,* 1979, *7,* 259–262.

Moffett, A., & Ettlinger, G. Opposite responding in two sense modalities. *Science,* 1966, *153,* 205–206.

Moffett, A., & Ettlinger, G. Opposite responding to position in the light and dark. *Neuropsychologia,* 1967, *5,* 59–62.

Nadel, L., & Willner, J. Context and conditioning: A place for space. *Physiological Psychology,* 1980, *8,* 218–228.

Oliverio, A. Contrasting effects of scopolamine on mice trained simultaneously with two different schedules of avoidance conditioning. *Psychopharmacology (Berl.),* 1967, *11,* 39–51.

Oliverio, A. Effects of scopolamine on avoidance conditioning of mice. *Psychopharmacology (Berl.),* 1968, *12,* 214–226.

Otis, L. S. Dissociation and recovery of a response learned under the influence of chlorpromazine or saline. *Science,* 1964, *143,* 1347–1348.

Overton, D. A. Discriminative behavior based on the presence or absence of drug effects. *American Psychologist,* 1961, *16,* 453–454. (Abstract)

Overton, D. A. State dependent or "dissociated" learning produced with pentobarbital. *Journal of Comparative and Physiological Psychology,* 1964, *57,* 3–12.

Overton, D. A. State dependent learning produced by depressant and atropine-like drugs. *Psychopharmacology (Berl.),* 1966, *10,* 6–31.

Overton, D. A. Differential responding in a three choice maze controlled by three drug states. *Psychopharmacology (Berl.),* 1967, *11,* 376–378.

Overton, D. A. Visual cues and shock sensitivity in the control of T-maze choice by drug conditions. *Journal of Comparative and Physiological Psychology,* 1968, *66,* 216–219.

Overton, D. A. Control of T-maze choice by nicotinic, antinicotinic, and antimuscarinic drugs. *Proceedings of the American Psychological Association,* 1969, *4,* 869–870.

Overton, D. A. Discriminative control of behavior by drug states. In T. Thompson & R. Pickens (Eds.), *Stimulus properties of drugs.* New York: Appleton-Century-Crofts, 1971.

Overton, D. A. State-dependent learning produced by alcohol and its relevance to alcoholism. In B. Kissen & H. Begleiter (Eds.), *The biology of alcoholism.* Vol. 2. *Physiology and behavior.* New York: Plenum Press, 1972.

Overton, D. A. State-dependent learning produced by addicting drugs. In S. Fisher & A. M. Freedman (Eds.), *Opiate addiction: Origins and treatment.* Washington, D.C.: V. H. Winston, 1973.

Overton, D. A. Experimental methods for the study of state-dependent learning. *Federation Proceedings,* 1974, *33,* 1800–1813.

Overton, D. A. Comparative efficacy of various drugs in a T-maze drug discrimination task. *Neuroscience Abstracts,* 1975, *5,* 335.

Overton, D. A. Drug state–dependent learning. In M. E. Jarvik (Ed.), *Psychopharmacology in the practice of medicine.* New York: Appleton-Century-Crofts, 1977.

Overton, D. A. Major theories of state dependent learning. In B. T. Ho, D. W. Richards, III, & D. L. Chute (Eds.), *Drug discrimination and state dependent learning.* New York: Academic Press, 1978.

Overton, D. A. Drug discrimination training with progressively lowered doses. *Science.* 1979, *205*, 720–721.

Overton, D. A. Comparison of the degree of discriminability of various drugs using the T-maze drug discrimination paradigm. *Psychopharmacology,* in press.

Overton, D. A., & Batta, S. K. Investigation of narcotics and antitussives using drug discrimination techniques. *Journal of Pharmacology and Experimental Therapeutics, 1979, 211,* 401–408.

Pan, S. The influence of context upon learning and recall. *Journal of Experimental Psychology,* 1926, *9,* 468–491.

Patrick, J. R., & Anderson, A. C. Incidental stimuli and maze learning. *Journal of Comparative Psychology,* 1930, *10,* 295–307.

Pazzagli, A., & Pepeu, G. Amnesic properties of scopolamine and brain acetylcholine in the rat. *International Journal of Neuropharmacology,* 1964, *4,* 291–299.

Pessin, J. The effect of similar and dissimilar conditions upon learning and relearning. *Journal of Experimental Psychology,* 1932, *15,* 427–435.

Petersen, R. C. Retrieval failures in alcohol state-dependent learning. *Psychopharmacology (Berl.),* 1977, *55,* 141–146.

Rand, G., & Wapner, S. Postural status as a factor in memory. *Journal of Verbal Learning and Verbal Behavior,* 1967, *6,* 268–271.

Reed, H. J. The influence of a change in conditions upon the amount recalled. *Journal of Experimental Psychology,* 1931, *14,* 632–649.

Rescorla, R. A., & Wagner, A. R. A theory of Pavlovian conditioning: Variations in the effectiveness of reinforcement and non-reinforcement. In A. H. Black & W. F. Prokasy (Eds.), *Classical conditioning.* Vol. 2. *Current research and theory.* New York: Appleton-Century-Crofts, 1972.

Riccio, D. C., Urda, M., & Thomas, D. R. Stimulus control in pigeons based on proprioceptive stimuli from floor inclination. *Science,* 1966, *153,* 434–436.

Sachs, E. The role of brain electrolytes in learning and retention. *Federation Proceedings,* 1961, *20,* 339. (Abstract)

Sachs, E. Dissociation of learning in rats and its similarities to dissociative states in man. In J. Zubin & H. Hunt (Eds.), *Comparative psychopathology.* New York: Grune & Stratton, 1967.

Sachs, E., Weingarten, M., & Klein, N. W., Jr. Effects of chlordiazepoxide on the acquisition of avoidance learning and its transfer to the normal state and other drug conditions. *Psychopharmacology (Berl.),* 1966, *9,* 17–30.

Semon, R. *Die Mneme* (L. Simon, trans.).London: George Allen & Unwin, 1921. (Originally published, 1904)

Smith, S. M., Brown, H. O., Toman, J. E. P., & Goodman, L. S. The lack of cerebral effects of d-tubocurarine. *Anesthesiology,* 1947, *8,* 1–14.

Spear, N. E. Forgetting as retrieval failure. In W. K. Honig & P. H. R. James (Eds.), *Animal memory.* New York: Academic Press, 1971.

Spear, N. E. Retrieval of memory in animals. *Psychological Review,* 1973, *80,* 163–194.

Spear, N. E., Smith, G. J., Bryan, R. G., Gordon, W. C., Timmons, R., & Chiszar, D. A. Contextual influences on the interaction between conflicting memories in the rat. *Animal Learning and Behavior,* 1980, *8,* 273–281.

Tomie, A. Retardation of autoshaping: Control by contextual stimuli. *Science,* 1976, *192,* 1244–1246.

Watson, J. B. Kinaesthetic and organic sensations: Their role in the reactions of the white rat to the maze. *Psychological Review Monographs* 1907, *8*(33).

Weingartner, H., Walker, T., Eich, J. E., & Murphy, D. L. Storage and recall of verbal and pictorial information. *Bulletin of the Psychonomic Society,* 1976, *7,* 349–351.

Welker, R. L., Tomie, A., Davitt, G. A., & Thomas, D. R. Contextual stimulus control over operant responding in pigeons. *Journal of Comparative and Physiological Psychology*, 1974, *86*, 549–562.

Zentall, T. R. Effects of context change on forgetting in rats. *Journal of Experimental Psychology*, 1970, *86*, 440–448.

5

Neuropeptides and Memory

Béla Bohus

1. INTRODUCTION

The notion that peptide hormones of pituitary or brain origin are important modulators of behavioral adaptation stems from a unified endocrine and behavioral view of coping with environmental demands. Adaptive changes include a chain of physiological events such as cardiovascular, thermoregulatory, immunologic, and hormonal responses. The stress theory of Selye (1950) suggested that pituitary-adrenal response to "noxious" stimuli facilitates coping with environmental challenges, the theory also emphasized physically damaging stressors.

From the 1950s onward, observations of both animals and people led to the recognition that environmental stimuli that induce fear, anxiety, rage, disappointment, and so on are among the most powerful stimuli for activating pituitary adrenocorticotropinhormone (ACTH) release. The recognition of the central nervous control of the pituitary gland, in particular of the role of limbic system in the control of pituitary ACTH release, was an important step in linking endocrine activity and behaviors that are closely related to the limbic system function. Learning and memory may be considered the most efficient way for an organism to assure survival. The idea that the brain is a target of "adaptive" hormones received support from a few experimental studies demonstrating behavioral changes following the removal of the pituitary or the adrenal gland. In addition, clinical observations suggested mood altera-

BÉLA BOHUS • Rudolf Magnus Institute for Pharmacology, Vondellaan 6, Utrecht, The Netherlands.

tions and changes in the electrical activity of the brain following ACTH or corticosteroid therapy. Extensive research on the influences of peptide hormones on brain functions has been going on for almost 20 years. However, the neuropeptide concept, which suggests that the pituitary gland manufactures peptides that affect the acquisition and maintenance of new behavioral patterns (de Wied, 1969), has received general acceptance only recently.

This chapter will stress the importance of two "families" of peptide hormones, the pro-opio-melanocortin fragments (ACTH and related peptides and endorphins) and the neurohypophyseal hormones (vasopressin and oxytocin), in the modulation of memory and cognition. The aim is to summarize the knowledge obtained from animal experiments, but the relevance of these findings for the physiology and pathology of human memory will also be discussed.

1.1. Terminology and Methodology

My working hypothesis is that peptide hormones are important modulators of behavioral performance. Performance, as measured by the retention of a learned response, depends on the consolidation (establishment of the memory trace), storage (passive maintenance of memory traces), and retrieval (recall) processes. My study of the influences of various peptides on consolidation processes has led me to accept McGaugh's (1961) proposition, namely, that treatments given shortly after learning affect brain processes that are related to the consolidation of memory. An important criterion of effects on consolidation is time dependence: The shorter the interval between learning and treatment, the more profound is the facilitation or attenuation of the later retention of the newly acquired behavior (McGaugh, Zornetzer, Gold, & Landfield, 1972). Treatments given shortly before the retention test are considered to influence retrieval of memory. The effects of postlearning treatments have been ascribed exclusively to influences on memory processes. Effects on learning, motivation, attention, motor activity, and so on cannot play a role. It is, however, debatable whether changes in performance during retention test as the consequence of preretention treatments are all retrieval effects. It is not always easy to differentiate between "true" and "nonspecific" retrieval effects.

Another important criterion for memorial effects of peptide hormones is that such influences are generalized across aversive and appetitive conditions. Applying this criterion entails accepting the existence of a single memory process (with several attributes; see Spear, 1973) as opposed to multiple memories.

The separation of cognitive from memorial effects is operational rather than theoretical. Hilgard (1980) argues that cognition is a generic term that designates all processes involved in knowing; hence it covers everything from perception to reasoning. Cognitive behavior refers here to the performance of the rat in a problem-solving situation. It is felt that in contrast to simple retention tests, problem-solving behavior contains reasoning (i.e., the recognition of) elements necessary for the solution embedded in changing environments. These elements include the use of information acquired during pretraining.

Spear (1973) emphasizes that the measurement of retention may profoundly affect retrieval processes. When some relearning criteria are used, the contingencies that were present during learning have to be reinstated on the first test trial. However, when performance measures other than relearning are used, it is not necessary to exactly reinstate the previous reinforcement contingencies. Extinction tests in which reinforcement contingencies are omitted or recall tests in passive (inhibitory) avoidance paradigms may be representative of such retention tests.

Studies on the influence of peptide hormones on the extinction of avoidance behavior represent the early phase of neuropeptide research. In particular the use of an extinction paradigm after spaced-trial pole-jumping avoidance behavior is still an extremely helpful technique in determining psychoactive properties of various neuropeptides (de Wied, 1980). However, it is not always clear whether improved or attenuated retention performance is due to effects on consolidation, retrieval, or a combination of both. Effects on extinction behavior have been observed when the peptides were given after acquisition training, before or just after the first extinction session.

In the majority of the experiments that will be outlined in this chapter, a one-trial learning, passive (inhibitory) avoidance paradigm was used. A step-through-type paradigm was applied that includes pretraining trials as described by Ader, Weijnen, and Moleman (1972). An important variable in this paradigm is the relatively low intensity of inescapable footshock used on the learning trial: 0.25 mA for 2 seconds or 0.75 mA for 3 seconds in the amnesia studies. The latency to reenter the area in which shocks have been received formerly was used as the measure of retention, mostly 24 hours after shock. Straight runways or a T-maze were used in appetitive paradigms.

Problem-solving behaviors were investigated in a Rabinowith-Rosvold-type maze situation. The rats were deprived of food for 19.5 hours, and following an adaptation and three pretraining sessions the performance in three problem situations was studied over 3 consecutive days. These runs were made for each problem, with an intertrial interval of 30 minutes. The number of errors served as the measure of performance.

2. PRO-OPIO-MELANOCORTIN FRAGMENTS, MEMORY, AND COGNITION

As we have seen, effects of ACTH and related peptides on behavior were the first recognized actions of neuropeptides on brain function. The discovery of endorphins, endogenous peptides with opioid activities, has opened a new chapter in the hormonal modulation of behavior. The behavioral activities of ACTH-related peptides are different in many respects. The rather recent recognition that these peptides originate from a common precursor molecule named pro-opio-melanocortin stresses that their behavioral activities cannot be envisaged separately.

2.1. Pro-opio-melanocortin Fragments in the Pituitary and the Brain

The coexistence of ACTH and β-lipotropic hormone (β-LPH), from which endorphins originate, within the same cells in the anterior pituitary (Phifer, Orth, & Spicer, 1974) presupposed a common origin of these peptides. In 1977 it was shown that ACTH and β-LPH originate from a common precursor protein with high molecular weight (Mains, Eipper, & Ling, 1977; J. L. Roberts & Herbert, 1977). This precursor molecule contains several pairs of basic amino acid residues that may be attacked by proteolytic enzymes; thereby several small peptides are produced. ACTH and β-LPH are the first products of proteolysis. ACTH and β-LPH are then further processed in the anterior lobe of the pituitary into α-melanocyte stimulating hormone (α-MSH or Acetyl-ACTH 1-13-amide), CLIP (ACTH 18-39), β-MSH (β-LPH 41-58), β-endorphin (β-LPH 61-91), γ-endorphin (β-LPH 61-77), and α-endorphin (β-LPH 61-76). The sequence of formation of these peptides as proposed by several investigators (Chrétien, Benjanett, Gossard, Gianoulakis, Crine, Lis, & Seidah, 1979; Lowry, Silman, Jackson, & Estivariz, 1979) is shown schematically in Figure 5.1. Recently, the amino acid structure of the N-terminus of the pro-opio-melanocortin molecule has also been recognized by determining the nucleotide sequence of cloned cDNA for bovine pro-opio-melanocortin (Nakanishi, Inoue, Kita, Nakamura, Chang, Cohen, & Numa, 1979) and by isolating the amino terminal glucopeptide from pig pituitary material (Hakanson, Ekman, Sundler, & Nilsson, 1980). The amino acid sequence of the N-terminus of the precursor molecule indicates the presence of a further MSH-like moiety in pro-opiocortin, which is named γ-MSH by Nakanishi et al. (1979). The

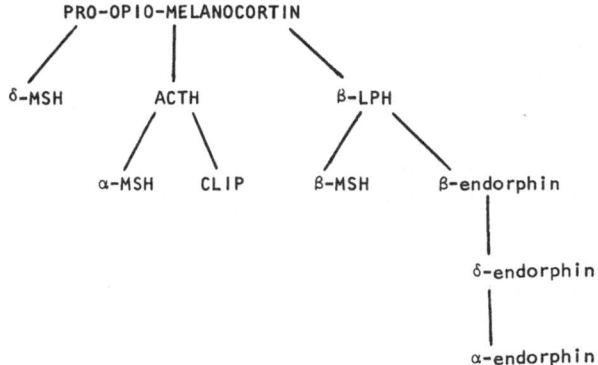

Fig. 5.1. Formation of peptide sequences from pro-opio-melanocortin.

occurrence of immunoreactive γ-MSH-like peptides in bovine pituitary has been demonstrated (Shibasaki, Ling, & Guillemin, 1980).

In addition to the pituitary gland, the brain is also a source of pro-opio-melanocortin-related peptides. Immuno- and bioreactive ACTH, α-MSH, and endophins have all been detected in the brains of intact and hypophysectomized rats (Krieger & Liotta, 1979; Verhoef, Loeber, Burbach, Gispen, Witter, & de Wied, 1980). A discrete pro-opio-melanocortin containing peptidergic system exists in the brain. The cell bodies of this system are located in the arcuate region of the hypothalamus and the nerves terminate in many limbic and midbrain areas (Watson & Akil, 1981).

2.2. ACTH-Related Peptides and Memory

Observations of the influence of ACTH-related peptides on extinction behavior in active avoidance paradigms represent the early phase of peptide research on retention. ACTH, α-MSH, β-MSH, and such fragments as ACTH 4-10 are referred to here as ACTH-related because of their rather uniform behavioral effects (see Bohus & de Wied, 1980). In general, spaced-trial, one- or two-way active avoidance paradigms were used (10 or 20 trials per session), and the peptides were administered as long-acting preparations every other day from the last acquisition session onward or as short-acting preparations before each extinction session. The findings that ACTH-related peptides delay extinction of conditioned avoidance response (Bohus, Nyakas, & Eñdröczi, 1968; de Wied, 1966) first suggested that retention of a behavioral response is enhanced by these peptides. This effect, however, seemed to be brief. Termination of treatment during extinction resulted in a rapid decline of avoidance performance (Bohus *et al.*, 1968). In another experiment, α-MSH was administered throughout a 14-day extinction period; after a 3-week interval the rats were retested again in three extinction sessions. Although the peptide-treated rats displayed an almost 100% avoidance performance during the first extinction period, during the retest their behavior did not differ from that of the controls (almost completely extinguished during the first extinction training). It was proposed that the ACTH-related peptides might have enhanced "trial-to-trial" memory (de Wied & Bohus, 1966).

It was subsequently found that ACTH-related peptides enhance retention of appetitive responses motivated by hunger or sex (Bohus, Hendricks, van Kolfschoten, & Krediet, 1975; Garrud, Gray, & de Wied, 1974). These observations suggest that influences on retention can be generalized across avoidance and appetitive behavior, although it was not clear whether consolidation or retrieval processes were affected. Long-acting preparations of ACTH or related peptides administered immediately after the last acquisition session might have affected both consolidation and retrieval as well as increasing resistance to extinction (de Wied, 1969).

There are few observations in which the influence of ACTH-related peptides on consolidation of memory was studied by administering the peptides as short-acting preparations. P. E. Gold and van Buskirk (1976a,b) found that postlearning ACTH administration influences the later retention of a passive avoidance response. The direction of the peptide effect depended on the intensity of aversive experience (shock level) and the dose of the peptide. A low dose of ACTH facilitated later retention at low footshock levels, whereas impairment was observed with higher footshock. Increasing the dose of ACTH at low footshock levels also led to an impairment. Sands and Wright (1979) report similar findings. In addition, P. E. Gold and van Buskirk (1976a) found a time-dependent effect: The shorter the interval between training and treatment, the more profound are the effects on later retention. Similarly, Flood, Jarvik, Bennett, and Orme (1976) found facilitation of retention of both active and passive avoidance responses in mice by administration of the ACTH fragment ACTH 4-10.

In contrast to these studies, van Wimersma Greidanus (1977) failed to observe an effect of ACTH 4-10 when administered immediately after learning on the retention of a passive avoidance response. Martinez, Vasquez, Jensen, Soumireu-Mouret, and McGaugh (1979) report a similar negative finding with a potentiated ACTH 4-9 analog. We recently replicated these studies by using ACTH 4-10 (Bohus & de Wied, 1981). Although an effect of another pro-opio-melanocortin fragment was apparent, no effect of ACTH 4-10 was found (see Table 5.1).

Effects of ACTH-related peptides on retrieval of memory have been clearly demonstrated by a number of studies. Administration of various ACTH fragments before the first retention test of a step-through passive avoidance response facilitated retention (Bohus & de Wied, 1981; Greven & de Wied, 1973; van Wimersma Greidanus, 1977; see Table 5.1). Similar effects have been reported in studies using conditioned taste aversion paradigms (Levine, Smotherman, & Hennessy, 1977; Rigter & Popping, 1976).

The influence of ACTH-related peptides on "cognitive" types of behaviors has been noted in few observations. Isaacson, Dunn, Rees, and Waldock (1976) found that ACTH 4-10 improves performance in a four-table choice test, but only during the first trial. We recently investigated the influence of ACTH 4-10 on problem-solving behavior. A tendency to reduce the number of errors during the first trials was observed after the repeated administration of ACTH 4-10 in a dose of 50 µg per rat subcutaneously, but the differences did not reach statistical significance.

Overall, the reported studies reveal marked effects of ACTH-related peptides on retention. Influences on retrieval are more likely than on consolidation.

There are two ways to explain the contradictory findings on the effects on memory consolidation: The first relates to differences in structural requirements for effects on consolidation and retrieval, the second to behavioral factors. Experiments using the avoidance extinction paradigm suggest that the 4-10 fragment of ACTH contains the essential information for this type of behavior. This fragment contains two "active sites": ACTH 4-7 and ACTH 7-9 (de Wied, Witter, & Greven, 1975; Greven & de Wied, 1973). Dose-dependent enhancement or disruption of later performance by postlearning peptide administration was found

Table 5.1. *Comparative Effects of Pro-opio-melanocortin Fragments on Memory Processes*

Peptides	Consolidation	Retrieval	Reversal of amnesia
β-endorphin	$+$[a]	$+/-$[c]	n.d.[d]
γ-endorphin	$-$[b]	$-$	n.d.
α-endorphin	$+$	$+$	0[e]
ACTH/α-MSH	0	$+$	$+$
γ-MSH	$-$	$-$	n.d.

[a] $+$ = facilitation.
[b] $-$ = attenuation.
[c] $+/-$ = dose-related effects.
[d] n.d. = not determined.
[e] 0 = no effect.

in those studies where the whole molecule of ACTH was administered. Therefore, it may be that the active sequence in the ACTH that affects consolidation resides outside the 4-10 sequence. Interestingly, the ACTH 11-24 sequence also contains an active site as suggested by the extinction studies (Greven & de Wied, 1977). The behavioral explanation involves the degree of conditioning of the particular response as reflected in the retention performance of the control animals. In the study by Flood et al. (1976), control mice showed rather poor performance during retention. ACTH 4-10, therefore, might have improved weak memory storage. Observations of vasopressin-deficient rats support this alternative. Impaired retention behavior of rats suffering from hereditary hypothalamic diabetes insipidus can be corrected by postlearning administration of ACTH 4-10 (Bohus, 1979a). Furthermore, hypophysectomy-induced retention deficits can also be improved by postlearning ACTH administration (P. E. Gold, Rose, Spanis, & Hankins, 1977).

That ACTH-related peptides administered before the test improve retention whether the measure is an extinction (active avoidance, running in straight alleys for reward) or a recall (passive avoidance, conditioned taste aversion) is the strongest suggestion of effects on retrieval of memory. The finding that ACTH-related peptides reverse or alleviate experimental amnesias caused by postlearning carbon dioxide inhalation (Rigter & van Riezen, 1975) or administration of protein synthesis inhibitors (Flexner & Flexner, 1971; Flood et al., 1976) further corroborates a retrieval hypothesis. Furthermore, the improvement of performance by ACTH 4-10 in the four-table test (Isaacson et al., 1976) is also consonant with the retrieval hypothesis.

There are, however, some observations that question whether the effects of preretention test treatments are due to memory retrieval improvement by ACTH-related peptides. We saw earlier that termination of treatment is followed by a rapid decline in performance of avoidance responding during extinction (Bohus et al., 1968; de Wied & Bohus, 1966). Passive avoidance retention is facilitated by ACTH-related peptides, but this effect did not carry over into the test without pretreatment that took place 24 hours later (de Wied, 1974). It may be, therefore, that the temporary superior performance under the influence of the peptides is due to other factors, such as motivational (de Wied, 1974) or attentional (Kastin, Sandman, Stratton, Schally, & Miller, 1975) alterations. Enhancement of performance by ACTH-related peptides under low levels of incentive motivation has been reported (Guth, Levine, & Seward, 1971; Nyakas, Bohus, & de Wied, 1980).

Bohus et al. (1968) investigated the influence of ACTH treatment given during different phases of extinction training of an active avoidance response. Reinstatement of almost 100% response performance by ACTH was observed when the controls were performing at about the 70% level. ACTH administration during later phases of extinction was not effective. It is worth mentioning that a single footshock would have reactivated the response performance from even a 0% performance level.

Overall, it is not unreasonable to assume that the influences of ACTH-related peptides on preretention treatment involve different mechanisms in nonamnesic and amnesic rats.

2.3. Effects of β-endorphin and Fragments on Consolidation and Retrieval of Memory and on Problem-Solving Behavior

The discovery of endorphins and enkephalins, which are endogenous peptides with opiatelike activities, has initiated major efforts to determine their physiological functions in behavior. It appears that β-endorphin has the greatest affinity for opiate receptors and induces the most potent morphinelike actions such as catatonia, antinociception, and excessive grooming (Guillemin, Ling, Lazarus, Burgus, Minick, Bloom, Nicoll, Siggins, & Segal, 1977; Gispen, Wiegant, Bradbury, Hulme, Smyth, Snell, & de Wied, 1976). Shorter fragments of β-endorphin such as γ-endorphin and α-endorphin, which are formed in discrete stages by cleaving brain enzymes associated with synaptosomal plasma membrane fraction (Burbach, Loeber, Verhoef, Wiegant, de Kloet, & de Wied, 1980), display less morphinelike activities than does β-endorphin itself (Gispen et al., 1976; Guillemin et al., 1977). A general feature of the opiatelike behavioral effects is that they are primarily evoked by central administration and that such opiate antagonists as naloxone or naltrexone block the peptide-induced responses.

The recognition that β-endorphin and related fragments may profoundly affect active avoidance extinction and passive avoidance retention following the administration of subanalgesic amounts given subcutaneously or intracerebraventricularly (de Wied, Bohus, van Ree, & Urban, 1978; de Wied, Kovács, Bohus, van Ree, & Greven, 1978) has prompted us to investigate the effects of these peptides on memory and cognitive processes.

Observations in passive avoidance situations indicate a profound effect of β-endorphin on both memory consolidation and retrieval. Administration of β-endorphin shortly after learning facilitates later retention of the passive avoidance response. This facilitation is not dependent on the analgesic property of the peptide. Removal of the C-terminal amino acid residue tyrosine, which yields the fragment Des-Tyr^1-β-endophin (β-LPH$_{62-91}$), abolishes analgesic activity but does not prevent the effect on memory consolidation (Table 5.1).

The influence of β-endorphin on retrieval of memory depends on the dose of the peptide. Small doses given before the retention test either peripherally or intracerebroventricularly improve retention. This influence of β-endorphin cannot be prevented by pretreatment with the opiate antagonist naltrexone (Bohus, 1980). Higher doses of the peptide (10 ng subcutaneously or 100 ng intracerebroventricularly), however, suppress passive avoidance retention in 50% of the subject population, whereas they facilitate it in the rest of the rats. The suppressive effect of the peptide is totally prevented by pretreatment with the opiate antagonist naltrexone (Table 5.1).

These observations suggest that the influence of β-endorphin on memory processes involves multiple mechanisms. Facilitation of both consolidation and retrieval is clearly independent of the classic opiatelike (analgesic) properties of the peptide. Suppression of memory or, at least, of retrieval, by β-endorphin is possibly mediated by a certain class of opiate receptors, which are sensitive to the opiate antagonist naltrexone. Induction of retrograde amnesia in the rat by β-endorphin following postlearning administration has been reported by Izquierdo (1980a,b). Izquierdo (1980b) also found that preretention-test administration of the peptide facilitates retention performance of an active avoidance and a habituation task. According, facilitation of memory by β-endorphin is not restricted to a single task. We shall deal later with the question whether the nonopioid or opioid effects of the peptide represent a physiological memory-modulating mechanism.

Our first observations on the behavioral effects of peripherally administered endorphins showed that fragments of β-endorphin such as α-endorphin are more potent than the parent peptide in affecting extinction behavior in the rat (de Wied, Bohus, van Ree, & Urban, 1978). We therefore assumed that the less potent behavioral activity of β-endorphin may be due to the presence of some fragment(s) in the molecule with opposite behavioral activities. Indeed, it appears that γ-endorphin (β-LPH$_{61-77}$) attenuates the maintenance of passive and active avoidance responses (de Wied, Kovács, Bohus, van Ree, & Greven, 1978; LeMoal, Koob, & Bloom, 1979). Since α-endorphin (β-LPH$_{61-76}$) has an opposite effect—that is, it facilitates active and passive avoidance retention (de Wied, Bohus, van Ree, & Urban, 1978; LeMoal, Koob, & Bloom, 1979)—the presence or absence of a single amino acid residue (leucine in Position 77) determines the direction of the behavioral effects of these β-endorphin fragments.

Memory for aversive experiences is profoundly influenced by α- and γ- endorphin (Bohus, 1980; Kovács, Bohus, & de Wied, 1981). Administration of α-endorphin immediately after the learning trial in a passive avoidance paradigm results in facilitated later retention. This facilitation appears to be a time-dependent effect: The shorter the interval between training and treatment, the stronger is the peptide effect. The γ-endorphin has an opposite effect on later retention performance in a time-dependent manner. Preretention administration of these endorphin fragments also influences passive avoidance retention: α-endorphin facilitates it whereas γ-endorphin attenuates it.

These observations favor the notion that α- and γ-endorphin affect both memory consolidation and retrieval. An absence of changes in later retention following a 6-hour training–treatment interval suggests that postlearning treatment effects are due to the modulation of memory consolidation rather than a consequence of proactive retrieval influences. There are, however, some observations that question whether the influences of preretention treatments are true retrieval effects. First, LeMoal et al. (1979) found that α- and γ-endorphin exert a similar effect on a runway response as measured in an extinction paradigm in water-deprived rats. Both peptides attenuate the extinction of the response. Grossi and Bohus, in an unpublished work, observed that Des-Tyr[1]-γ-endorphin facilitates extinction of a runway response in food-deprived rats. Des-Tyr[1]-α-endorphin has similar but less potent effect. In addition, Haller & Bohus, in an unpublished work, observed that Des-Tyr[1]-α-endorphin fails to reverse pentylenetetrazol-induced amnesia in the rat. Thus it seems more likely that α- and γ-type endorphins affect performance rather than retrieval processes.

Pharmacological characteristics of these peptides may partially explain effects on performance versus retrieval of memory. Opiatelike activities of α- and γ-endorphin are relatively low (Gispen et al., 1976; Guillemin et al., 1977); the Des-Tyr[1] fragments are practically devoid of opioid properties. The γ-endorphin and Des-Tyr[1]-γ-endorphin, however, have behavioral activities that resemble the action of neuroleptic drugs. Both of these peptides and the neuroleptic haloperidol induce cataleptic states after peripheral or central administration (de Wied, Kovács, Bohus, van Ree, & Greven, 1978), and attenuate ACTH-induced excessive grooming behavior after administration into the neostriatum or the nucleus accumbens (Cools, Wiegant, & Gispen, 1978; Gispen, Ormond, ten Haaf, & de Wied, 1980; Wiegant, Cools, & Gispen, 1977). The effects of neuroleptics and the peptides on exploratory and motor behavior are, however, dissimilar. Unlike neuroleptics, the peptides fail to suppress locomotor and exploratory behavior (de Wied, Kovács, Bohus, van Ree, & Greven, 1978; Pedigo, Ling, Reisine, & Yamamura, 1979; Weinberger, Arnstein, & Segal, 1979). The α-endorphin and Des-Tyr[1]-α-endorphin, on the other hand, share a number of behavioral actions with the psychostimulant amphetamine. Both α-endorphin and amphetamine attenuate catalepsy induced by the destruction of the thalamic parafascicular nuclei in the rat (van Ree, Bohus, & de Wied, 1980). Des-Tyr^1-α-endorphin and amphetamine suppress food intake, but the effect of the peptide is short-term (Bohus, van Ree, & de Wied, 1980). However, in contrast to amphetamine, the peptides fail to induce an increase in locomotor behavior or in stereotypy (van Ree *et al.*, 1980).

Although β-endorphin fails to influence problem-solving behavior significantly, at least at the dose levels studied here, its fragments have profound effects (Table 5.2). Des-Tyr^1-α-endorphin impairs this behavior, as indicated by the higher number of errors during the first trials and also by the total errors. Des-Tyr^1-γ-endorphin has a less profound effect on this behavior: It reduces the number of errors, but only during the first trials. Accordingly, α- and γ-type endorphins also have opposite effects on problem solving. The psychostimulant amphetamine, like Des-Tyr^1-α-endorphin, impairs problem solving; the most pronounced effects are on the first trials. Haloperidol affects this behavior less profoundly and in an opposite manner. As with Des-Tyr^1-γ-endorphin, the number of errors during the first trials is reduced slightly by the drug.

Taken together, β-endorphin and fragments such as γ- and α-endorphin affect consolidation of memory, and the peptides are also effective with preretention administration. These latter effects involve multiple mechanisms and may be related to the pharmacological properties of the peptides. The influences of γ- and α-type endorphins on problem-solving behavior are also similar to the influences of neuroleptic or psychostimulant drugs. Since these drugs may influence performance, and α-type endorphins are unable to reverse experimental amnesia, it is questionable whether retrieval of memory and cognitions *per se* is affected.

2.4. The γ-MSH: A Functional Antagonist of Endorphins and ACTH-Related Peptides on Memory Processes?

The recognition of a melanotroplike amino acid sequence in the N-terminal portion of the pro-opio-melanocortin precursor molecule, which was named γ-MSH (Nakanishi *et al.*, 1979), has prompted us to study the behavioral actions of this sequence because of the structural similarity to ACTH-like peptides. The proposed γ-MSH sequence contains a methionine residue at the N-terminus (Position 3) and His-Phe-Arg-Trp tetrapeptide sequence (Position 5-8). The residue and the tetrapeptide sequence are common for ACTH-related peptides. It has been shown that the 4-10 fragment of ACTH (Met-Glu-His-Phe-Arg-Trp-Gly; ACTH$_{4-10}$) contains the essential information for increasing resistance to extinction of active avoidance responding (de Wied, Witter, & Greven, 1975).

Despite the structural similarities, the influences of γ-MSH on memory function appear to be the opposite of those of ACTH-related peptides (Bohus & de Wied, 1981). Furthermore, in some aspects, γ-MSH may also be considered a functional antagonist of β-endorphin. As shown in Table 5.1. The γ-MSH attenuates later retention of a passive avoidance response. This attenuation can be observed following post-learning and preretention administration of various doses of the peptide. Accordingly, γ-MSH seems to influence both consolidation and retrieval of memory for the aversive experience.

Problem-solving behavior of rats is slightly impaired by γ-MSH, but only after repeated administration (Table 5.1).

Analysis of the behavioral profile and other biological actions of γ-MSH suggests that the peptide resembles opiate antagonists in certain respects (van Ree, Bohus, Csontos, Gispen, Greven, Nijkamp, Opmeer, de Rotte, van Wimersma Greidanus, Witter, & de Wied, 1981). For example, behavioral symptoms that are reminiscent of opiate withdrawal can be elicited by administering γ-MSH into the periaqueductal gray in opiate-naïve rats. Peptide treatment attenuates the development of heroin self-administration in the rat, and reduces analgesic and thermic actions of β-endorphin. Additionally, ACTH-induced excessive grooming is also blocked by γ-MSH.

The position of pairs of basic amino acids in the γ-MSH region of the pro-opio-melanocortin suggests that γ-MSH-like peptides may be formed by enzymatic cleavage. It is not yet clear whether γ-MSH exists as an end product of biotransformation. Hakanson *et al.* (1980) failed to find γ-MSH or similar fragments during the isolation of the N-terminus of the precursor molecule. Shibasaki *et al.* (1980), on the other hand, found immunoreactive γ-MSH in the whole bovine pituitary extract. Accordingly, it remains to be resolved whether the so-called γ-MSH is an end product or if it only represents a behaviorally active site within a larger peptide molecule. However, the importance of such a peptide as an antagonist of β-endorphin and ACTH-related peptides is obvious.

2.5. Multiplicity of Behavioral Information in Pro-opio-melanocortin: An Integration

Neuropeptides originating from the common precursor molecule modulate a number of behavioral processes, including memory and cognition. As Table 5.1 shows, ACTH-related peptides, β-endorphin, and γ-MSH may have opposite effects on these behavioral processes, but overlapping information may also be encoded in the molecule. These areas of overlap may represent dormant sites in the molecule (Gispen, van Ree, & de Wied, 1977), but an alternative hypothesis of a coopera- tive action cannot be excluded. Obviously, the potential information content of the molecule is further enlarged by the cleavage of β-en- dorphin into γ- and α-endorphins. The occurrence of the various pro- opio-melanocortin fragments within the same neuronal pool in the brain, or their parallel release from the pituitary and subsequent retro- grade transport to the brain, stresses the significance of enzymatic cleav- ing of the precursor molecule as a physiologically significant modulatory mechanism in the brain.

These observations suggest that pro-opio-melanocortin fragments affect memory and cognitive functions in the rat. However, a number of issues must be resolved before the exact nature of their actions will be understood. Enhancement or attenuation of memory consolidation by the various neuropeptides is clear in avoidance paradigms, but their generality is still an open question. Retrieval-type actions seem to be on performance rather than memory. The multiplicity of interactions of endorphins with different well-described, putative receptor systems in the brain stresses the necessity of using a multiple dose range of the peptides and multiple behavioral assays.

Problem-solving behavior, which is used here as a measure of more complex cognitive functions, is not profoundly affected by pro-opio- melanocortin fragments. Some of the effects may be related to changes in performance, but the final word cannot be given at this point. Ex- tended observations with various dose levels and the use of more varia- tions of deprivation conditions are essential.

2.6. Pro-opio-melanocortin Fragments, Memory, and Cognition in Man

Data available on the influence of pro-opio-melanocortin fragments are entirely restricted to ACTH-related peptides. The effects of ACTH 4-10 on short-term recall of verbal memory have been studied by a number of researchers. In healthy volunteers, no effect of the peptide was found in short-term recall of paired-associate verbal material (Mil- ler, Harris, van Riezen, & Kastin, 1976) and of auditorily or visually presented consonant trigrams (Dornbush & Nikolski, 1976). Ashton, Millman, Telford, Thompson, Davies, Hall, Shuster, Thody, Coy, and Kastin (1977) report that α-MSH facilitates and β-MSH 1-22 disrupts performance on verbal scales of the Wechsler Memory Scale; the pep- tides failed to affect performance on the Benton Visual Retention Test. ACTH 4-10 facilitates verbal memory without an effect on visual memo- ry, but only in women (Veith, Sandman, George, & Stevens, 1978). Although Miller *et al.* (1976) report a beneficial effect on visual memory,

Sandman, George, McCanne, Nolan, Kaswan, and Kastin (1977) and Veith *et al.* (1978) report a negative one.

In elderly patients with mild cognitive impairments, delayed recall for visual material was impaired by ACTH 4-10, whereas the recognition of visual material was improved by ACTH 4-10 in severely impaired patients (Ferris, Sathananthan, Gershon, Clark, & Moshinsky, 1976). The influence of ACTH 4-10 on delayed recall in psychiatric patients following electroconvulsive-shock-induced memory impairment has been studied by Small, Small, Milstein, and Dian (1977). Although the peptide caused some improvement in patients who received an electroconvulsive shock, no effect was found in between five or six shock treatments. Branconnier, Cole, and Gardos (1979) report a slight improvement of memory retrieval by ACTH 4-10 in patients with senile organic brain syndrome.

In sum, despite the fact that most of these studies followed an acceptable experimental design, the data are far from conclusive. Positive effects of the peptides in healthy volunteers are rather marginal and often unreplicable. Almost optimal, "ceiling" performance of young volunteers may mask peptide effects, if there are any present. Clinical data are even harder to evaluate because of the limited observations. It seems, therefore, that the peptides have no dramatic effects on memory functions in healthy people, and that reversal of cognitive deficits by ACTH 4-10 is a rather subtle effect.

Profound changes in rats' behavior following administration of various endorphins led a number of researchers to assume that these neuropeptides are involved in the etiology of certain mental disorders. Bloom, Segal, Ling, and Guillemin (1976) hypothesize that derangements in β-endorphin homeostasis may have etiologic significance in such mental disorders as schizophrenia. On the basis of neurolepticlike activities of Des-Tyr^1-γ-endorphin and the amphetaminelike properties of α-type endorphins, de Wied (1979) hypothesizes that an excess or lack of one of the potent endorphins may change the interpretation of environmental events and thereby alter the adequacy of the behavioral responses. Although animal experiments suggest that a number of behavioral activities of endorphins can be interpreted as influences on memory and cognition, it remains to be elucidated how these are applicable to humans.

3. HYPOTHALAMIC NEUROSECRETORY PEPTIDES IN MEMORY AND COGNITION

The concept that neurosecretory peptides of hypothalamic origin influence memory processes stems from the observation that administration of pitressin, a relatively crude extract of the posterior pituitary, the storage organ of neurosecretory peptides, resulted in long-term maintenance of a conditioned avoidance response (de Wied & Bohus, 1966). This experiment was designed on the basis of some endocrine and behavioral findings. Removal of the posterior pituitary appeared to abolish pituitary-adrenocortical stress response to "emotional" stimuli, whereas the response to "systemic" stressors remained unaffected. Administration of pitressin restored the response to "emotional" stimuli (de Wied, 1961). It was assumed that neurosecretory principles may have been involved in the organization of emotional responses. In accordance with this assumption, de Wied (1965) found that although the acquisition of an avoidance response was normal in rats, once the posterior lobe of the pituitary was removed rapid extinction occurred. Pitressin administration normalized the extinction deficit. De Wied and Bohus (1966) trained rats to acquire a shuttle-box active avoidance response and then subjected them to extinction training of 14 days. Ten trials of avoidance and extinction were given each day. Twenty-four days later, retention of the response was tested again during extinction conditions. Rats treated with pitressin during either acquisition or the first extinction period displayed resistance to extinction. Substantial retention of the avoidance response was found during the second extinction test in the pitressin-treated rats, whereas the controls were almost entirely extinguished. Since the duration of the action of pitressin outlasted the presence of exogenously administered peptide(s), it was assumed that pitressin influenced long-term memory formation.

Subsequent observations showed that vasopressin (Table 5.2) was responsible for long-term effect on avoidance behavior in rats (Bohus, 1971; de Wied, 1971). This behavioral activity of vasopressin is independent of its classic endocrine effects such as antidiuresis and increased blood pressure. Removal of the C-terminal amino acid residue, glycine, which results in an almost complete loss of endocrine effects, does not affect the behavioral activity (de Wied, Greven, Lande, & Witter, 1972).

Table 5.2. *Comparative Effects of Vasopressin and Oxytocin on Memory Processes*

	Consolidation	Retrieval
Cys-Tyr-Phe-Gln-Asn-Cys-Pro-Arg-Gly-NH$_2$ (arginine vasopressin)	$+$[a]	$+$
Cys-Tyr-Ile-Gln-Asn-Cys-Pro-Leu-Gly-NH$_2$ (oxytocin)	$-$[b]	$-$

[a] $+$ = facilitation.
[b] $-$ = attenuation.

The specificity of vasopressin in long-term behavioral effects has been further corroborated by observations that oxytocin often has effects on behaviors that are opposite to those of vasopressin: It attenuates the maintenance of avoidance responses (Bohus, Urban, van Wimersma Greidanus, & de Wied, 1978; Kovács, Vécsei, & Telegdy, 1978; Schulz, Kovács, & Telegdy, 1974). Like vasopressin, oxytocin is also produced by the hypothalamic neurosecretory nuclei. Structurally it is slightly different from vasopressin (Table 5.2), but it has different biological activities such as contracting the uterus during labor and inducing milk ejection during nursing.

3.1. Vasopressin and Oxytocin Affect Consolidation and Retrieval of Memory

Long-term resistance of extinction of an active avoidance response by a single dose of vasopressin administered after the last acquisition session suggests an influence on memory consolidation. If the peptide was administered 3 hours after the training, it appeared to be less effective, and it is ineffective if the treatment is postponed for 6 hours (de Wied, 1971). A similar time-dependent effect of vasopressin is observed when the peptide is given intracerebroventricularly immediately, 3, or 6 hours after the learning trial in a passive avoidance task. Later retention of the behavioral response is facilitated by the immediate and 3-hour treatments, but not by the 6-hour one; this observation excludes a proactive retrieval effect (Bohus, Kovács, & de Wied, 1978).

The effect of postlearning administration of vasopressin on later retention can be generalized across avoidance and appetitive behaviors, and even the maintenance of such species-typical behaviors as sexual behavior in male rats is affected by this neuropeptide. Administration in the male rat of Des-glycineamide-lysine vasopressin (DGLVP) immediately after a training session in a T-maze facilitates later retention (Bohus, 1977). In this experiment copulation with a receptive female served as the reward. If the males were not rewarded with copulation—that is, a receptive female—correct-choice behavior failed to develop and DGLVP had no effect on later performance. Another experiment focused on the influence of posttest administration of DGLVP on the maintenance of copulatory activity following castration (Bohus, 1979b). If the castrated males once initiated mounting behavior, the full copulatory pattern—that is, intromission and ejaculationlike behavior—was maintained longer in peptide-treated rats.

The importance of the anomalous time–dose interactions with posttraining vasopressin treatment in later retention has been recognized by Hagan, Bohus, and de Wied (1980). In these experiments rats were trained to learn a shuttle-box avoidance task in a single training session.

Retention of the response was studied in a single extinction session given 24 hours later. A rapid decrease in avoidance responding within the early extinction trials suggested that the response was weakly established. Administration of lysine vasopressin in a low dose (0.11 ng/rat, s.c.) immediately or 60 minutes after training increased extinction responding, whereas a higher dose (2.97 ng) was ineffective where injected immediately afterward and facilitated avoidance responding during extinction when injected 60 minutes after training. The influence of the peptide on extinction performance varied as an inverted-U-shaped function of the vasopressin dose when injected 30 minutes after training. For example, 0.11 ng increased whereas 2.97 ng reduced responding. The low response strength, as observed in the control rats, has been associated with susceptibility to amnesic treatments (Flood, Bennett, Rosenzweig, & Orme, 1973, 1974) and may be a contributing factor to the sensitivity of this behavioral paradigm. Changes in the direction of high-dose effects as a function of training–injection intervals may suggest changes in the substrate that mediates the behavioral effects of vasopressin. It cannot be ruled out that the peptide influences labile memory (Gibbs & Ng, 1976) differentially depending on the dose.

The influence of oxytocin on memory consolidation is the opposite of that of vasopressin (Bohus, Kovács, & de Wied, 1978; Bohus, Urban, van Wiersma Greidanus, & de Wied, 1978). Intracerebroventricular administration of oxytocin immediately after the learning trial of a one-trial passive avoidance response attenuates later retention. The longer the interval between training and treatment, the less effective is the treatment on retention. It therefore seems that oxytocin is a naturally occurring neuropeptide influencing performance in memory tasks.

Effects of vasopressin on retention of various behavioral responses following administration shortly before the retention tests suggest an influence on retrieval of memory. Vasopressin treatment increases resistance to extinction of active avoidance responding (Bohus, Ader, & de Wied, 1972; de Wied, Bohus, & van Wimersma Greidanus, 1974; Schulz et al., 1974). In addition to active avoidance behavior, vasopressin facilitates passive (inhibitory) avoidance retention (Bohus et al., 1972; Kovács et al., 1978; Krejči, Kupková, Metys, Barth, & Jost, 1979). As in these treatments, which used peripheral injection of the peptide, intraventricularly administered vasopressin also facilitates retrieval (Bohus, Kovács, & de Wied, 1978). DGLVP also increases resistence to extinction of a conditioned taste aversion (Vawter & Green, 1980). In addition, vasopressin treatment antagonizes the retention deficit of a taste aversion in aged rats (R. L. Cooper, McNamara, & Thompson, 1980).

Although Garrud et al. (1974) failed to observe an effect of DGVLP on the extinction of a food-rewarded runway task, subsequent studies demonstrate peptide-induced resistance to extinction of appetitive responses. Hostetter, Jubb, and Kozlowski (1977) report that vasopressin delayed extinction of a food-reinforced discriminative response. DGLVP also increases resistance to extinction of a sweet preference response in nondeprived rats (Bohus, unpublished). These observations may be explained as a retrieval effect of vasopressin, an explanation further corroborated by the findings that the peptide reverses experimental amnesia (see the following section).

Oxytocin administered intracerebroventricularly before the retention test attenuates retention of a passive avoidance (Bohus, Kovács, & de Wied, 1978). A similar observation has been reported following peripheral administration of the peptide (Kovács, Vécsei, & Telegdy, 1978). Rapid extinction of an active avoidance response was also found (Schulz et al., 1974). It is not yet known whether this peptide produces amnesic effects in appetitive situations.

Vasopressin administration before each test substantially improves problem-solving behavior. The most prominent effect is on the first trial performance in each problem. The peptide particularly reduces the number of errors made during the first trials, but also the total number of errors. Since the trial-to-trial improvement of this behavior is not affected by the peptide, it is likely that the retrieval of information obtained during practice is improved by vasopressin. Interestingly, a vasopressin analog impaired short-term working memory in a 12-arm radial maze (Buresová & Skopková, 1980). The authors theorize that the peptide may reduce flexibility of behavior that is required for an efficient working memory.

3.2. Antiamnesic Effect of Vasopressin in the Rat

Lande, Flexner, and Flexner (1972) were the first to report that vasopressin pretreatment prevents amnesia induced by puromycin. Similar findings have been reported by Walter, Hoffman, Flexner, and Flexner (1975); protection against carbon-dioxide-induced amnesia by vasopressin pretreatment has been observed by Rigter, van Riezen, and de Wied (1974). Amnesia induced by posttraining electroconvulsive shock or pentylenetetrazol could also be prevented by vasopressin administration before the acquisition (Bookin & Pfeifer, 1977; Pfeifer & Bookin, 1978). These observations, however, do not allow the conclusion that the antiamnesic effect of the peptide was due to an influence on memory processes. In these experiments the peptide was administered before learning. It may have enhanced the acquisition of the response thereby resulting in less susceptibility for amnesic treatments.

However, postlearning administration of vasopressin can also reverse the impairment of later retention of a passive avoidance response that was induced by pretreatment with the catecholamine synthesis inhibitor α-methyl-paratyrosine (Moberg, Bohus, & de Wied, unpublished). Since vasopressin could not affect the original learning in this paradigm, it is likely that the peptide either prevented the deleterious effect of the catecholamine synthesis inhibitor or activated some eventually peripheral mechanism that was able to counteract the consequences of brain catecholamine depletion on memory formation.

Vasopressin administration before the retention test reverses amnesia induced by postlearning carbon dioxide inhalation (Bookin & Pfeifer, 1977) or electroconvulsive shock (Pfeifer & Bookin, 1978). We recently showed that peripherally administered vasopressin and its Desglycineamide analog reverse pentylenetetrazol-induced amnesia in the rat when administered before the retention test. In addition, intracerebroventricular administration of vasopressin has similar antiamnesic effect indicating a direct action on the brain (Bohus, Conti, Kovács, & Versteeg, 1982).

These observations reinforce the notion that vasopressin enhances the retrieval of memory. Additionally, vasopressin or its analogs may be an important tool in the treatment of memory disorders. Consistent with this suggestion, improvement of passive avoidance performance and retention of conditioned taste aversion in aged rats by pretest vasopressin administration was observed. As compared to young control rats, the aged subjects without peptide treatment showed a deficit in retention behavior (R. L. Cooper et al., 1980).

3.3. Vasopressin, Oxytocin, and Memory Processes: Localization of the Effects

Behavioral, electrophysiological, and neurochemical findings have suggested the involvement of the limbic-midbrain system in the effect of vasopressin on brain mechanisms. Electrolytic lesions in the septal area or the dorsal hippocampus prevented the effect of vasopressin on active avoidance extinction (van Wimersma Greidanus & de Wied, 1976a; van Wimersma Greidanus, Bohus, & de Wied, 1974). Vasopressin and oxytocin affected theta activity in the hippocampus during paradoxical sleep episodes in an opposite manner (Bohus et al., 1978; Urban & de Wied, 1978). Peripheral or intracerebroventricular administration of vasopressin affected the steady-state levels and turnover rates of noradrenaline and dopamine in some limbic and brainstem areas (Kovács, Vécsei, Szabó, & Telegdy, 1977; Tanaska, de Kloet, de Wied, & Versteeg, 1977).

The exact localizations of the influence of vasopressin on memory consolidation and reversal of amnesia and of oxytocin's effects in inducing amnesia have been investigated by local microinjection of the peptides into the brain (Bohus et al., 1982; Kovács, Bohus, Versteeg, de Kloet, & de Wied, 1979). The observations are summarized in Table 5.3. Microinjection of vasopressin (25-25 pg) into the dentate gyrus of the hippocampus or 50 pg of the peptide in the dorsal raphe nucleus immediately after the learning trial facilitated later retention of a passive avoidance response. The same amounts of oxytocin have the opposite effect: passive avoidance retention is attenuated. Injections into the subiculum, central nuclei of amygdala, and locus coeruleus were ineffective. Vasopressin and oxytocin were also effective when injected in the dorsal septal area. An opposite effect on consolidation processes was absent, since both peptides facilitated the retention of the passive avoidance response. Why oxytocin affects behavior in a vasopressinlike manner in this region is not yet understood.

Table 5.3 also shows the localization of the antiamnesic effect of vasopressin. Reversal of pentylenetetrazol-induced amnesia was not achieved by local peptide injection, but microinjection of vasopressin improved retention when injected in the central amygdala or dentate gyrus of the hippocampus shortly before the retention test. Local injections of the peptide in the dorsal septum and the dorsal raphe nuclei were ineffective (Bohus et al., 1982).

These observations suggest that the effects of vasopressin and oxytocin are localized in more than one limbic-midbrain region, and that the influences of vasopressin on memory consolidation and retrieval (reversal of amnesia) are differentially localized. The effect of vasopressin microinjections on amnesic rats is only partial. Kesner (1975) suggests that the amygdala and the hippocampus are equally involved in memory processing. Whereas the amygdala seems to subserve the emotional aspects of memory, the hippocampus may be involved in the readout of

Table 5.3. *Localization of the Effects on Memory of Vasopressin and Oxytocin*

| | Consolidation | | Antiamnesia |
	Vasopressin	Oxytocin	vasopressin
Hippocampal dentate gyrus	$+$[a]	$-$[b]	$+$
Dorsal septum	$+$	$-$	0[c]
Amygdala	0	0	$+$
Dorsal raphe nucleus	$+$	$-$	$+$
Locus coeruleus	$-$	n.d.[d]	n.d.

[a] $+$ = facilitation.
[b] $-$ = attenuation.
[c] 0 = no effect.
[d] n.d. = not determined.

information. It is therefore possible that a concerted action of vasopressin on both these areas or even additional ones is necessary for a complete reversal of amnesia.

3.4. Brain Amines and the Action of Vasopressin on Memory Processes

The involvement of noradrenergic mechanisms, particularly the coerules-telencephalic noradrenergic pathway (dorsal noradrenergic bundle system, or DNB), in memory processes has been emphasized (Crow, 1968; McGaugh, Gold, van Buskirk, & Haycock, 1975). Observations concerning the influence of vasopressin on noradrenaline levels and turnover rate (Kovács et al., 1977; Tanaka et al., 1977) suggest that this transmitter is a likely candidate for a pre- or postsynaptic regulatory effect of vasopressin. The effective sites from which vasopressin affects memory processes coincide with the brain regions where the fibers of the DNB terminate (Lindvall & Björklund, 1974). Additionally, local injections of vasopressin into the dentate gyrus and the dorsal septum resulted in local changes of noradrenaline turnover rate (Kovács, Bohus, Versteeg, de Kloet, & de Wied, 1979). It was therefore postulated that vasopressin may act on the cerulotelencephalic noradrenergic system in influencing memory processes.

To investigate this hypothesis, the effects of vasopressin on consolidation and retrieval of memory have been studied in rats with selective chemical lesions in the various aminergic systems of the brain. 6-hydroxydopamine (6-OHDA) injection into the neurons of the DNB results in a selective degeneration of the forebrain and brainstem noradrenergic (but not dopaminergic) system (D. C. Roberts, Price, & Fibiger, 1976). Chemical destruction of the DNB prevented the influence of vasopressin on memory consolidation. Destruction of the dopaminergic terminals in the nucleus accumbens by local 6-OHDA microinjection, or of the serotinergic system arising from the dorsal raphe nucleus, by 5,6-dihydroxytryptamine (5,6-DHT) failed to prevent the facilitation of later retention of the passive avoidance response by postlearning systemic administration of vasopressin. Accordingly, modulation of noradrenergic transmission by vasopressin, most probably at the level of the presynaptic terminals of the cerulotelencephalic system, is of primary importance in the effect of the peptide on the consolidation of memory (Kovács, Bohus, & Versteeg, 1979).

The ascending serotonergic system seems to be involved in the facilitation of retrieval processes by vasopressin. The effect of the peptide administered before the retention test was prevented by the selective destruction of serotonergic cell bodies in the dorsal raphe nucleus.

Destruction of the DNB terminals by 6-OHDA only slightly attenuated the effect of vasopressin on the retrieval of memory.

As summarized in Table 5.4, the observations with selective chemical lesions suggest that the influences of vasopressin on consolidation and retrieval of memory involve interactions with different transmitter systems. Facilitation of consolidation by vasopressin may be the consequence of an increased noradrenergic transmission, particularly in the dentate gyrus on the hippocampus. This suggestion receives support from recent observations by Kovács, de Kloet, Versteeg, and Bohus (1981). A correlation was observed in rats of an unselected population between the retention performance in a passive avoidance task and the noradrenaline turnover rate, but only in the dorsal hippocampus. The longer the passive avoidance latencies, the higher were noradrenaline turnover rates in the dentate gyrus.

It is not yet clear how vasopressin interacts with the serotonergic system in the modulation of retrieval processes. It is likely that vasopressin acts at the presynaptic terminal level or interacts with serotonin binding at postsynaptic receptors. Partial reversal of amnesia was observed after microinjection of vasopressin in some of the terminal areas of the ascending serotonergic system—that is, in the central amygdala and the dentate gyri of the hippocampus. Injection of the peptide in the serotonergic cell body region failed to affect amnesia. It is worth noting that correlations exist among passive avoidance learning, carbon-dioxide-induced amnesia, and hippocampal serotonin concentration in the rat. Passive avoidance learning was accompanied by a rise in hippocampal serotonin level 24 hours later; amnesia treatment immediately after learning prevented this increase (Leonard & Rigter, 1975; Rigter, van Eys, & Leonard, 1974). Vasopressin pretreatment that prevents the development of amnesia also resulted in a reoccurrence of the serotonin rise in the hippocampus (Ramaekers, Rigter, & Leonard, 1978).

Less is known about the neurochemical basis of the effect of oxytocin on memory processes. This neuropeptide does not affect nor-

Table 5.4. *Selective Destruction of Neurotransmitter Systems in the Brain Modify the Influence of Vasopressin on Memory Processes*

			Effect of arginine-vasopressin on	
Neurotoxin	Site of lesion	Monoamine	Consolidation	Retrieval
6-OH-dopamine	Dorsal noradrenergic bundle	Noradrenaline	Absent	Partially present
5,6-DHT	Dorsal raphe	Serotonin	Present	Absent
6-OH-dopamine	Nucleus accumbens	Dopamine	Present	Not studied

adrenergic transmission (Versteeg, unpublished). It seems, therefore, that the amnesic effect of oxytocin on postlearning administration is not due to a competitive antagonism between oxytocin and vasopressin on the same (noradrenergic) mechanism.

3.5. Vasopressin and Memory Functions in Man

Legros, Gilot, Seron, Claessens, Adam, Moeglen, Audibert, and Berchier (1978) and Oliveros, Jandali, Timsit-Berthier, Remy, Benghezal, Audibert, and Moeglen (1978) were the first to report evidence with humans to support the hypothesis that vasopressin affects memory functions. Improved immediate memory, learning, and recognition, which were judged by psychometric tests involving attention, concentration, and motor rapidity in elderly volunteers, were observed by applying lysine-vasopressin in nasal spray (Legros et al., 1978). Oliveros et al. (1978) report improved memory by lysine-vasopressin treatment in patients suffering from traumatic or alcoholic amnesia. Subsequently, memory improvements have been observed in patients with Korsakoff syndrome (LeBoeuf, Lodge, & Eames, 1978) and traumatic amnesia (Timsit-Berthier, Mantanus, Jacques, & Legros, 1980). The effect of vasopressin outlasted the termination of peptide treatment. Improvement of disturbed passive avoidance learning in children with Lesch-Nyhan disease was found by Anderson, David, Bonnet, and Dancis (1979). Vasopressin improved cognitive functions in patients suffering from primary affect disorder without affecting other symptoms of the disease (Gold, Weingartner, Ballenger, Goodwin, & Post, 1979; Weingartner, Gold, Ballenger, Smallberg, Summers, Rubinow, Post, & Goodwin, 1981). Significant vasopressin effects on serial learning, prompted free recall, and the recall of semantically related words have been reported in young college students. A long-term memory effect was not observed, but performance under placebo treatment was almost apparent for long-term recall (Weingartner et al., 1981). These authors also investigated verbal memory before and after electroconvulsive shock therapy in patients with mood disorders. Retrograde amnesia induced by the convulsive shock was partially reversed by vasopressin. Negative findings have been reported, however, in patients with the Wernicke-Korsakoff syndrome or traumatic amnesia (Blake, Dodd, & Grimley Evans, 1978; Jenkins, Mather, Coughlan, & Jenkins, 1979).

Vasopressin deficiency (central idiopathic hereditary diabetes insipidus—Gilot, Crabbe, & Legros, 1980; or vasopressin-sensitive diabetes insipidus—Wagner, Járdánházy, Laczi, Szilárd, Telegdy, & László,

1979) is accompanied by memory impairments. Beneficial effects of vasopressin were observed in these patients.

Most of the observations reviewed here are consonant with the hypothesis that vasopressin influences memory processes, and the peptide may be beneficial in patients with memory disorders. These encouraging findings clearly need further support, and more elaborate memory studies are required to understand the nature of the effects of vasopressin on memory and cognition in humans.

4. ARE NEUROPEPTIDES INDISPENSABLE FOR MEMORY AND COGNITION?

Research on peptide effects on brain and behavior stems mainly from endocrine studies. It is a classical endocrine approach to study the significance of hormones by removing the source of given hormones and then correcting for the resulting deficits by a supplementary hormonal therapy. Removal of the pituitary gland as the source of peptide hormones served as an endocrine model in studying the effect of peptides on behavior. De Wied (1964) found that hypophysectomy results in a deficit of active avoidance acquisition in the rat. This deficit could be corrected by supplementary therapy with ACTH (de Wied, 1964) or fragments of this peptide (de Wied, 1969).

The observations of Bohus and de Wied (1966) suggest the involvement of pituitary peptides in the retention of avoidance behavior. Rats were trained to acquire an active avoidance response, and were subsequently subjected to hypophysectomy. Following retraining, extinction behavior was studied. Hypophysectomized rats displayed a rapid extinction of the response; administration of ACTH 1-10 prevented such extinction. Accordingly, hypophysectomized rats were able to recall the previously learned response in the presence of punishment, but not when the unconditioned stimulus was omitted. These observations suggest that retrieval processes are deficient in the absence of pituitary peptides and that ACTH-related peptides that have been shown to influence these processes can correct this deficiency. Bohus, Gispen, and de Wied (1973) emphasize another aspect of the involvement of the pituitary peptides in performance. Hypophysectomized rats receiving either ACTH 4-10 or vasopressin were trained to acquire an active avoidance response. Peptide-treated rats displayed normal avoidance behavior. After termination of treatments, the behavior of the ACTH-4-10-treated rats deteriorated despite the footshock punishment, whereas those animals that had received vasopressin still displayed efficient avoidance behavior. These findings again suggest a short-term, probably retrieval-type action of ACTH fragments and a long-term, consolidation-type effect of vasopressin.

Retention of one-trial learning passive avoidance response is also disturbed in hypophysectomized rats. However, normal passive avoidance behavior was observed if the intensity of footshock punishment was increased. (Lissák & Bohus, 1972). It must be pointed out that the behavioral reactivity of hypophysectomized rats to electric footshock is not decreased, but instead increased (Gispen, van Wimersma Greidanus, & de Wied, 1970). Thus the retention deficit of the hypophysectomized rats is not due to a reduced perception of the punishment. High-intensity footshock might have mobilized some other mechanisms that were able to compensate for the absence of the pituitary.

The effect of hypophysectomy on problem-solving behavior of rats was investigated (Bohus, unpublished). In order to avoid a deleterious effect of food deprivation, pieces of milk chocolate served as reward. As Figure 5.2 shows, hypophysectomized rats made more errors than sham-operated rats. Thus cognitive functions are also disturbed in the absence of the pituitary. It is not yet known which peptides can restore this behavioral deficit.

These observations suggest that pituitary peptides, most likely ACTH or its fragments, play a significant role in memory processes.

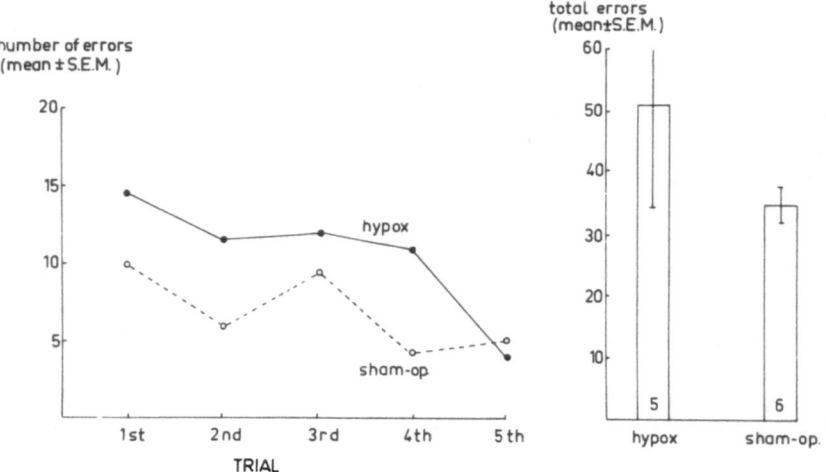

Fig. 5.2. Maze performance of hypophysectomized rats. The rats were operated 10 days before the onset of pretraining in a Rabinowitch-Rosvold-type maze. Nondeprived rats were rewarded with pieces of milk chocolate.

Observations that hypophysectomized rats show retention behavior when the intensity of punishment is very high (Lissák & Bohus, 1972) and that retention of appetitive responses is not severely impaired by pituitary removal (Stone & Obias, 1955) suggest that the pituitary is not absolutely indispensable for these processes. It appears that fine-tuned modulation of memory is absent in hypophysectomized rats.

The discovery of the pro-opio-melanocortin system in the brain and the recognition that the pituitary is not the only source of these peptides may raise doubts about the usefulness of hypophysectomy in determining whether these peptides are indispensable for memory processes. The evidence reviewed, however, suggests a greater justification for the question, Where do the pro-opio-melanocortin peptides originate? A final answer is not yet possible, but it seems that fine-tuned regulation of memory processes is likely served by peptides of pituitary origin. The peptides may reach the brain by retrograde transport (see de Kloet, Palkovits, & Mezey, 1981).

The neurohypophyseal peptides vasopressin and oxytocin are manufactured in the neurosecretory nuclei of the hypothalamus (supraoptic, paraventricular, and suprachiasmatic nuclei). The peptides are transported to the posterior pituitary through the hypothalamohypophyseal tract. The release of the peptide to the peripheral circulation occurs from the posterior pituitary. Additional transport routes are directed to the brain. The peptides are secreted into the cerebral ventricles; recently, vasopressinergic and oxytocinergic neurons have been discovered that terminate in several limbic, midbrain, and hindbrain areas including the amygdala, lateral septum, and hippocampus (Buijs, Swaab, Dogterom, & van Leeuwen, 1978; Sofroniew & Weindl, 1978).

Evidence for a physiological role of vasopressin in memory processes has been obtained in rats suffering from hereditary hypothalamic diabetes insipidus (Brattleboro strain). Rats homozygous for this disease lack the ability to synthesize vasopressin (Valtin & Schroeder, 1964). Impaired retention behavior in passive avoidance situations suggested memory deficits in diabetes insipidus rats (Bailey & Weiss, 1979; de Wied, Bohus, & van Wimerma Greidanus, 1975). The deficit is most prominent for the long-term retention. Normal avoidance behavior was observed shortly after learning, but not 24 or more hours later (Bohus, van Wimersma Greidanus, & de Wied, 1975). In addition, retention of active avoidance responses appeared to be deficient (Bohus, van Wimersma Greidanus, & de Weid, 1975). The behavioral deficit in the passive avoidance response could be normalized by administering vasopressin either immediately after learning (de Wied et al., 1975) or before the retention test (Bohus, 1979a). Administration of ACTH 4-10 before the retention also normalizes the behavior (Bohus, 1979a). These findings suggest that retrieval of information is more severely impaired than consolidation in the absence of vasopressin.

Another way to determine the physiological role of neurohypophyseal peptides in memory processes is to decrease the availability of endogenous peptides in the brain by intracerebroventricular administration of specific antisera against vasopressin and oxytocin. Intracerebroventricular administration of antisera may act on the peptidergic neuronal network or may block the transport of these peptides in the cerebrospinal fluid. Vasopressin antiserum administered either immediately after learning (van Wimersma Greidanus, Dogterom, & de Wied, 1975) or before the retention test of a passive avoidance response (van Wimersma Greidanus & de Wied, 1976b) resulted in a behavioral deficit similar to that observed in diabetes insipidus rats. On the other hand, antiserum against oxytocin given immediately after learning resulted in an enhanced retention of the passive avoidance response (Bohus, Urban, van Wimersma Greidanus, & de Wied, 1978).

Because of the amnesic properties of oxytocin, it may well be that the behavioral deficits of Brattleboro rats with diabetes insipidus and of Wistar rats with decreased availability of brain vasopressin are due to an oxytocin effect that becomes prominent in the absence or reduction of vasopressin. However, oxytocin antiserum given intracerebroventricularly to rats with diabetes insipidus failed to normalize the behavior of these rats (Bohus, 1979a). Hence the presence of vasopressin in the brain is essential for oxytocin to have an effect on memory. It is therefore assumed that the formation and expression of memory are modulated physiologically by these two neurosecretory peptides, which act in opposition to each other. Any departure from the balance between vasopressin and oxytocin results in altered memory.

5. CONCLUSION

An adaptive view of the relations and interactions between hormones and brain functions has always been prominent in psychoneuroendocrine research. The abilities to remember and to forget are important for adapting to the environment. Peptides hormones play an important role in modulating brain processes involved in information storage, remembering, and forgetting in animals. A number of observations with humans (which, admittedly, have not yet dealt with sufficient numbers of healthy subjects) suggest that neuropeptides may be important for their memorial functions as well.

Studies on the memorial effects of neuropeptides suggest that multiple, behavior-related informational units are encoded in peptide molecules. When similar information is encoded in more than part of a peptide molecule, one of the sites may be redundant and dormant; but cooperative actions among such sites cannot be excluded. The multiplicity of information content of peptide molecules may assure a dynamic modulation of memory in relation to environmental demands. Selective formation or release of the "appropriate" peptide fragments is a possible way that a dynamic modulation can be assured. However, selective actions may also be determined by a specific sensitivity of the ongoing brain processes toward a certain neuropeptide fragment.

Vasopressin and oxytocin seem to be more specifically memory-related neuropeptides than are the pro-opio-melanocortin-related peptides. Fragments of pro-opio-melanocortin often affect retention performance in ways that seem unrelated to an action on memory processes.

Although neuropeptides do not seem absolutely indispensable for memory processing, a dynamic modulation of the expression of knowledge is missing when the neuroendocrine mechanisms dysfunction. For example, vasopressin-deficient animals and people display memory disturbances (hypoamnesia). Vasopressin administration results in unusually effective memory processing (hyperamnesia). Thus it may be that this neuropeptide is of etiologic significance in certain memory disorders. The antiamnesic properties of vasopressin and amnesic action of oxytocin may be useful in the treatment of memory impairments, even when these treatments are given for the symptoms rather than for the underlying disorder.

Finally, neuropeptides may serve as important attributes of memory. Spear (1973) emphasizes that arousal of a number of attributes that belong to the same memory is presumably necessary and sufficient for retrieval of a given target attribute. Changes in the internal environment (e.g., hormonal alterations) may also be attributes of a given memory set. Bohus et al. (1972) found that the administration of vasopressin affected retention performance of a behavioral response that was tested at least once shortly after the administration of the peptide. Vasopressin increased resistance to extinction of an active avoidance response 1 hour after peptide treatment, but failed to influence the retention of a passive avoidance task that was tested 6 hours later. The authors suggest that the effect of exogenous vasopressin in maintaining behavior may be related to the relative ease with which a given behavioral response is elicited when situation-specific cues reoccur. An association between the endogenous release of vasopressin or related peptides and specific environmental cues may be of pysiological significance in the maintenance of new behavior patterns in spite of the "nonspecific" nature of the release of the peptide. Klein (1972) reports that water stress, stimulation of the lateral anterior hypothalamus, and direct implantation of

ACTH in the lateral anterior hypothalamus reinstated avoidance memory in rats at a short interval after learning (alleviation of the Kamin effect). Since pituitary-adrenal activation is low at this interval (Brush & Levine, 1966), Klein (1972) suggests that ACTH is probably associated with avoidance training as "the consequence of the rat's normal attention to its internal state." P. E. Gold and van Buskirk (1976a) suggest that postlearning administration of ACTH may affect memory processes by mimicking the hormonal correlate of punishment. The recent findings outlined here add further support to an attribute hypothesis. It is, however, a novel view of present research that the peptides may serve not only as arousing factors, that is, activating a memory, but may also act to dearouse memories leading to repression of the retrieval of information.

6. REFERENCES

Ader, R., Weijnen, J. A. W. M., & Moleman, P. Retention of passive avoidance response as a function of the intensity and duration of electric shock. *Psychonomic Sciences*, 1972, *26*, 125–128.

Anderson, L. T., David, R., Bonnet, K., & Dancis, J. Passive avoidance learning in Lesch-Nyhan disease: Effect of 1-desamino-8-arginine-vasopressin. *Life Sciences*, 1979, *24*, 905–910.

Ashton, H., Millman, J. E., Telford, R., Thompson, J. W., Davies, T. F., Hall, R., Shuster, S., Thody, A. J., Coy, D. H., & Kastin, A. J. Psychopharmacological and endocrinological effects of melanocyte stimulating hormones in normal man. *Psychopharmacology*, 1977, *55*, 165–172.

Bailey, W. H., & Weiss, J. M. Evaluation of a "memory deficit" in vasopressin-deficient rats. *Brain Research*, 1979, *162*, 174–178.

Blake, D. R., Dodd, M. J., & Grimley Evans, J. Vasopressin in amnesia. *Lancet*, 1978, *1*, 608.

Bloom, F., Segal, D., Ling, N., & Guillemin, R. Endorphins: Profound behavioral effects in rats suggest new etiological factors in mental illness. *Science*, 1976, *194*, 630–632.

Bohus, B. Effect of hypophyseal peptides on memory functions in rats. In G. Ádám & J. Szentágothai (Eds.), *The biology of memory*. Budapest: Akadémiai Kiadó, 1971.

Bohus, B. Effect of desglycinamide-lysine vasopressin (DG-LVP) on sexually motivated T-maze behavior on the male rat. *Hormones and Behavior*, 1977, *8*, 52–61.

Bohus, B. Inappropriate synthesis and release of vasopressin in rats: Behavioral consequences and effects of neuropeptides. *Neuroscience Letters*, 1979, *3*, 329. (Suppl.) (a)

Bohus, B. Neuropeptide influences on sexual and reproductive behavior. In L. Zichella & P. Pancheri (Eds.), *Psychoneuroendocrinology in reproduction*. Vol. 5. *Developmental endocrinology*. Amsterdam: Elsevier/North-Holland, 1979. (b)

Bohus, B. Endorphins and behavioral adaptation. *Advances in Biological Psychiatry*, 1980, *5*, 7–18.

Bohus, B., & de Wied, D. Inhibitory and facilitatory effect of two related peptides on extinction and avoidance behavior. *Science*, 1966, *153*, 318–320.

Bohus, B., & de Wied, D. Pituitary-adrenal system hormones and adaptive behaviour. In I. Chester-Jones & I. W. Henderson (Eds.), *General, comparative and clinical endocrinology of the adrenal cortex*. (Vol. 3). London: Academic Press, 1980.

Bohus, B., & de Wied, D. Actions of ACTH- and MSH-like peptides on learning, performance, and retention. In J. L. Martinez, Jr., R. A. Jensen, R. B. Messing, H. Rigter & J. L. McGaugh (Eds.) *Endogenous peptides and learning and memory processes*, Academic Press, New York, 1981.

Bohus, B., Nyakas, C. S., & Eñdröczi, E. Effects of adrenocorticotropic hormone on avoidance behavior of intact and adrenalectomized rats. *International Journal of Neuropharmacology*, 1968, *7*, 307–314.

Bohus, B., Ader, R., & de Wied, D. Effects of vasopressin on active and passive avoidance behavior. *Hormones and Behavior*, 1972, *3*, 191–197.

Bohus, B., Gispen, W. H., & de Wied, D. Effect of lysine vasopressin and $ACTH_{4-10}$ on conditioned avoidance behavior of hypophysectomized rats. *Neuroendocrinology*, 1973, *11*, 137–143.

Bohus, B., Hendricks, H. H. L., van Kolfschoten, A. A., & Krediet, T. G. The effect of $ACTH_{4-10}$ on copulatory and sexually motivated approach behavior in the male rat. In M. Sandler & G. L. Gessa (Eds.), *Sexual Behavior: Pharmacology and biochemistry*. New York: Raven Press, 1975.

Bohus, B., van Wimersma Greidanus, T. J. B., & de Wied, D. Behavioral and endocrine responses of rats with hereditary hypothalamic diabetes insipidus (Brattleboro strain). *Physiology and Behavior*, 1975, *14*, 609–615.

Bohus, B., Kovács, G. L., & de Wied, D. Oxytocin and vasopressin and memory: Opposite effects on consolidation and retrieval processes. *Brain Research*, 1978, *157*, 414–417.

Bohus, B., Urban, I., van Wimersma Greidanus, T. J. B., & de Wied, D. Opposite effects of oxytocin and vasopressin on avoidance behavior and hippocampal theta rhythm in the rat. *Neuropharmacology*, 1978, *17*, 239–247.

Bohus, B., van Ree, J. M., & de Wied, D. Psychostimulant-like behavioral activities of α-endorphin and Des-Tyr[1]-α-endorphin. *Neuroscience Letters*, 1980, *Suppl. 5*, S352.

Bohus, B., Conti, L., Kovács, G. L., & Versteeg, D. H. G. Modulation of memory processes by neuropeptides: Interaction with neurotransmitter systems. In H. Matthies & M. A. Brazieur (Eds.), *Mechanisms and models of neural plasticity: The role of hippocampal structures*. New York: Raven Press, 1982.

Bookin, H. B., & Pfeifer, W. D. Effect of lysine vasopressin on pentylenetetrazol-induced retrograde amnesia in rats. *Pharmacology, Biochemistry and Behavior*, 1977, *7*, 51–54.

Branconnier, R. J., Cole, J. O., & Gardos, G. $ACTH_{4-10}$ in the amelioration of neuropsychological symptomatology associated with senile organic brain syndrome. *Psychopharmacology*, 1979, *61*, 161–165.

Buijs, R. M., Swaab, D. F., Dogterom, J., & van Leeuwen, F. W. Intra- and extra-hypothalamic vasopressin and oxytocin pathways in the rat. *Cell Tissue Research*, 1978, *186*, 423–433.

Brush, F. R., & Levine, S. Adrenocortical activity and avoidance learning as a function of time after fear conditioning. *Physiology and Behavior*, 1966, *1*, 309–311.

Burbach, J. P. H., Loeber, J. G., Verhoef, J., Wiegant, V. M., de Kloet, E. R., & de Wied, D. Selective conversion of β-endorphin into peptides related to γ-and α-endorphin. *Nature*, 1980, *238*, 96–97.

Buresová, O., & Skopková, J. Vasopressin analogues and spatial short-term memory in rats. *Peptides*, 1980, *1*, 261–263.

Chrétien, M., Benjannet, S., Gossard, R., Gianoulakis, C., Crine, P., Lis, M., & Seidah, N. G. From β-lipotropin to β-endorphin and "pro-opiomelanocortin." *Canadian Journal of Biochemistry*, 1979, *57*, 1111–1121.

Cools, A. R., Wiegant, V. M., & Gispen, W. H. Distinct dopaminergic systems in ACTH-induced grooming. *European Journal of Pharmacology*, 1978, *50*, 265–268.

Cooper, R. L., McNamara, M. C., & Thompson, W. Vasopressin and conditioned flavor aversion in aged rats. *Neurobiology of Aging*, 1980, *1*, 53–57.

Crow, T. J. Cortical synapses and reinforcement: A hypothesis. *Nature*, 1968, *219*, 736–737.

de Kloet, E. R., Palkovits, M., & Mezey, E. Opiocortin peptides: Localization, source and avenues of transport. *Pharmacology, Therapeutics*, 1981, *12*, 321–351.

de Wied, D. The significance of the antidiuretic hormone in the release mechanism of corticotropin. *Endocrinology*, 1961, *68*, 956–970.

de Wied, D. Influence of anterior pituitary on avoidance learning and escape behavior. *American Journal of Physiology*, 1964, *207*, 255–259.

de Wied, D. The influence of the posterior and intermediate lobe of the pituitary and pituitary peptides on the maintenance of a conditioned avoidance response in rats. *International Journal of Neuropharmacology*, 1965, *4*, 157–167.

de Wied, D. Inhibitory effect of ACTH and related peptides on extinction of conditioned avoidance behavior. *Proceedings of the Society of Experimental Biology and Medicine*, 1966, *122*, 28–32.

de Wied, D. Effects of peptide hormones on behavior. In W. F. Ganong & L. Martini (Eds.), *Frontiers in neuroendocrinology*. New York: Oxford University Press, 1969.

de Wied, D. Long term effect of vasopressin on the maintenance of a conditioned avoidance response in rats. *Nature*, 1971, *232*, 58–60.

de Wied, D. Pituitary-adrenal system hormones and behavior. In F. O. Schmidt & F. G. Worden (Eds.), *The neurosciences*. Cambridge, Mass.: MIT Press, 1974.

de Wied, D. Schizophrenia as an inborn error in the degradation of β-endorphin: A hypothesis. *Trends in Neuroscience*, 1979, *2*, 79–82.

de Wied, D. Pituitary neuropeptides and behavior. In K. Fuxe, T. Hökfelt, R. Luft (Eds.), *Central regulation of the endocrine system*. New York: Plenum Press, 1980.

de Wied, D., & Bohus, B. Long term and short term effects on retention of a conditioned avoidance response in rats by treatment with long acting pitressin and α-MSH. *Nature*, 1966, *212*, 1484–1486.

de Wied, D., Greven, H. M., Lande, S., & Witter, A. Dissociation of the behavioral and endocrine effects of lysine vasopressin by tryptic digestion. *British Journal of Pharmacology*, 1972, *45*, 118–122.

de Wied, D., Bohus, B., & van Wimersma Greidanus, T. J. B. The hypothalamo-neurohypophyseal system and the preservation of conditioned avoidance behavior in rats. In D. F. Swaab & J. P. Schadé (Eds.), *Progress in brain research* (Vol. 41). Amsterdam: Elsevier, 1974.

de Wied, D., Bohus, B., & van Wimersma Greidanus, T. J. B. Memory deficit in rats with hereditary diabetes insipidus. *Brain Research*, 1975, *85*, 152–156.

de Wied, D., Witter, A. & Greven, H. M. Behaviourally active ACTH analogues. *Biochemical Pharmacology*, 1975, *24*, 1463–1468.

de Wied, D., Kovács, G. L., Bohus, B., van Ree, J. M., & Greven, H. M. Neuroleptic activity of the neuropeptide β-LPH 62-77 (Des-Tyr[1]-γ-endorphin: DTγE). *European Journal of Pharmacology*, 1978, *49*, 427–436.

de Wied, D., Bohus, B., van Ree, J. M., & Urban, I. Behavioral and electrophysiological effects of peptides related to lipotropin (β-LPH). *Journal of Pharmacological and Experimental Therapy*, 1978, *204*, 570–580.

Dornbush, R. L., & Nikolovski, O. ACTH$_{4-10}$ and short-term memory. *Pharmacology, Biochemistry and Behavior*, 1976, *5* (Suppl. 1), 69–72.

Ferris, S. H., Sathananthan, G., Gershon, S., Clark, C., & Moshinsky, J. Cognitive effects of ACTH$_{4-10}$ in the elderly. *Pharmacology, Biochemistry and Behavior*, 1976, *5* (Suppl. 1), 73–78.

Flexner, J. B., & Flexner, L. B. Pituitary peptides and the suppression of memory by puromycin. *Proceedings of the National Academy of Sciences*, 1971, *68*, 2519–2521.

Flood, J. F., Bennett, E. L., Rosenzweig, M. R., & Orme, A. E. The influence of duration of protein synthesis inhibition on memory. *Physiology and Behavior*, 1973, *10*, 555–562.

Flood, J. F., Bennett, E. L., Rosenzweig, M. R., & Orme, A. E. Comparison of the effects of anisomycin on memory across six strains of mice. *Behavioral Biology*, 1974, *10*, 147–160.

Flood, J. F., Jarvik, M. E., Bennett, E. L., & Orme, A. E. Effects of ACTH peptide fragments on memory formation. *Pharmacology, Biochemistry and Behavior*, 1976, *5* (Suppl. 1), 41–51.

Garrud, P., Gray, J. A., & de Wied, D. Pituitary-adrenal hormones and extinction of rewarded behaviour in the rat. *Physiology and Behavior*, 1974, *12*, 109–119.

Gibbs, M. E., Ng, K. T. Memory: A new three phases model. *Neuroscience Letters*, 1976, *2*, 165–169.

Gilot, P., Crabbe, J., & Legros, J. J. Bilan mnesique chez 5 patients souffrant d'un diabete insipide central idiopathique. *Acta Psychiatrica Belgica*, 1980, *80*, 755–780.

Gispen, W. H., van Wimersma Greidanus, T. J. B., & de Wied, D. Effects of hypophysectomy and $ACTH_{4-10}$ on responsiveness to electric shock in rats. *Physiology and Behavior*, 1970, *5*, 143–146.

Gispen, W. H., van Ree, J. M., & de Wied, D. Lipotropin and the central nervous system. *International Review of Neurobiology*, 1977, *20*, 209–250.

Gispen, W. H., Ormond, D., ten Haaf, J., & de Wied, D. Modulation of ACTH-induced grooming by Des-Tyr^1-γ-endorphin and haloperidol. *European Journal of Pharmacology*, 1980, *63*, 203–207.

Gispen, W. H., Wiegant, V. M., Bradbury, A. F., Hulme, E. C., Smyth, D. G., Snell, C. R. & de Wied, D. Induction of excessive grooming in the rat by fragments of lipotropin. *Nature*, 1976, *264*, 794–795.

Gold, P. E., & van Buskirk, R. Effects of posttrial injections on memory processes. *Hormones and Behavior*, 1976, *7*, 509–517. (a)

Gold, P. E., & van Buskirk, R. Enhancement and impairment of memory processes with post-trial injections of adrenocorticotropic hormone. *Behavioral Biology*, 1976, *16*, 387–400. (b)

Gold, P. E., Rose, R. P., Spanis, C. W., & Hankins, L. L. Retention deficit for avoidance training in hypophysectomized rats: Time-dependent enhancement of retention performance with ACTH injections. *Hormones and Behavior*, 1977, *8*, 363–371.

Gold, P. W., Weingartner, H., Ballenger, J. C., Goodwin, F. K., & Post, R. M. Effects of 1-desamino-8-D-arginine vasopressin on behaviour and cognition in primary affective disorder. *Lancet*, 1979, *2*, 992–994.

Greven, H. M., & de Wied, D. The influence of peptides derived from corticotrophin (ACTH) on performance. Structure activity studies. In E. Zimmermann, W. H. Gispen, B. H. Marks, & D. de Wied (Eds.), *Drug effects on neuroendocrine regulation*. Vol. 39. *Progress in brain research*. Amsterdam: Elsevier, 1973.

Greven, H. M., & de Wied, D. Influence of peptides structurally related to ACTH and MSH on active avoidance behavior in rats. A structure-activity relationship study. In Tj. B. van Wimersma Greidanus (Ed.), *Frontiers of hormone research* (Vol. 4). Basel: Karger, 1977.

Guillemin, R., Ling, N., Lazarus, L., Burgus, R., Minick, S., Bloom, F., Nicoll, R., Siggins, G., & Segal, D. The endorphins, novel peptides of brain and hypophysial origin, with opiate-like activity: Biochemical and biological studies. *Annual New York Academy of Science*, 1977, *297*, 131–156.

Guth, S., Levine, S., & Seward, J. P. Appetitive acquisition and extinction effects with exogenous ACTH. *Physiology and Behavior*, 1971, *7*, 195–200.

Hagan, J. J., Bohus, B., & de Wied, D. Post training lysine vasopressin (LVP) may facilitate or delay shuttle box avoidance extinction. *Neuroscience Letters*, 1980, *5*, 352.

Hakanson, R., Ekman, R., Sundler, F., & Nilsson, R. A novel fragment of the corticotrophin-β-lipotropin precursor. *Nature*, 1980, *283*, 789–792.

Hilgard, E. R. Consciousness in contemporary psychology. *Annual Review of Psychology*, 1980, *31*, 1–26.

Hostetter, G., Jubb, S. L., & Kozlowski, G. P. Vasopressin affects the behavior of rats in a positively-rewarded discrimination task. *Life Sciences*, 1977, *21*, 1323–1328.

Isaacson, R. L., Dunn, A. J., Rees, H. D., & Waldock, B. $ACTH_{4-10}$ and improved use of information in rats. *Physiological Psychology*, 1976, *4*, 159–162.

Izquierdo, I. Effect of β-endorphin and naloxone on acquisition, memory and retrieval of shuttle avoidance and habituation learning in rats. *Psychopharmacology*, 1980, *69*, 111–115. (a)

Izquierdo, I. Effects of a low and a high dose of β-endorphin on acquisition and retention in the rat. *Behavioral and Neural Biology*, 1980, *30*, 460–466. (b)

Jenkins, J. S., Mather, H. M., Coughlan, A. K., & Jenkins, D. G. Desmopressin in post-traumatic amnesia. *Lancet*, 1979, *2*, 1245–1246.

Kastin, A. J., Sandman, C. A., Stratton, L. O., Schally, A. V., & Miller, L. H. Behavioral and electrographic changes in rat and man after MSH. In W. H. Gispen, T. J. B. van Wimersma Greidanus, B. Bohus, & D. de Wied (Eds.), *Hormones homeostasis and the brain*. Vol. 42. *Progressive brain research*. Amsterdam: Elsevier, 1975.

Kesner, R. P. A neural system approach to the study of memory storage and retrieval. In R. R. Drucker-Colin & J. L. McGaugh (Eds.), *Neurobiology of sleep and memory*. New York: Academic Press, 1975.

Keyes, J. B. Effect of ACTH on ECS-produced amnesia of a passive avoidance task. *Physiological Psychology*, 1974, *2*, 307–309.

Klein, S. B. Adrenal-pituitary influence in reactivation of avoidance-learning memory in the rat after immediate intervals. *Journal of Comparative and Physiological Psychology*, 1972, *3*, 341–359.

Kovács, G. L., Vécsei, L., Szabó, G., & Telegdy, G. The involvement of catecholaminergic mechanisms in the behavioural action of vasopressin. *Neuroscience Letters*, 1977, *5*, 337–344.

Kovács, G. L., Vécsei, L., & Telegdy, G. Opposite action of oxytocin to vasopressin in passive avoidance behavior in rats. *Physiology and Behavior*, 1978, *20*, 801–802.

Kovács, G. L., Bohus, B., & Versteeg, D. H. G. Facilitation of memory consolidation by vasopressin: Mediation by terminals of the dorsal noradrenergic bundle? *Brain Research*, 1979, *172*, 73–85.

Kovács, G. L., Bohus, B., Versteeg, D. H. G., de Kloet, E. R., & de Wied, D. Effect of oxytocin and vasopressin on memory consolidation: Sites of action and catecholaminergic correlates after local microinjection into limbic-midbrain structures. *Brain Research*, 1979, *175*, 303–314.

Kovács, G. L., Bohus, B., & de Wied, D. Retention of passive avoidance behavior in rats following α- and γ-endorphin administration: Effects of postlearning treatments. *Neuroscience Letters*, 1981, *22*, 79–82.

Kovács, G. L., Versteeg, D. H. G., de Kloet, E. R., & Bohus, B. Passive avoidance performance correlates with catecholamine turnover in discrete limbic regions. *Life Sciences*, 1981, *28*, 1109–1116.

Krejči, I., Kupková, B., Metys, J., Barth, T., & Jost, K. Vasopressin analogs: Sedative properties and passive avoidance behavior in rats. *European Journal of Pharmacology*, 1979, *56*, 347–353.

Krieger, D. T., & Liotta, A. S. Pituitary hormones in brain: Where, how and why? *Science*, 1979, *205*, 366–372.

Lande, S., Flexner, J. B., & Flexner, L. B. Effect of corticotropin and desglycinamide[9]-lysine vasopressin on suppression of memory by puromycin. *Proceedings of the National Academy of Sciences*, 1972, *69*, 558–560.

LeBoeuf, A., Lodge, J., & Eames, P. G. Vasopressin and memory in Korsakoff syndrome. *Lancet*, 1978, 2, 1370.

Legros, J. J., Gilot, P., Seron, X., Claessens, J., Adam, A., Moeglen, J. M., Audibert, A., & Berchier, P. Influence of vasopressin on learning and memory. *Lancet*, 1978, 1, 41–42.

LeMoal, M., Koob, G. F., & Bloom, F. E. Endorphins and extinction: Differential actions on appetitive and adversive tasks. *Life Sciences*, 1979, 24, 1631–1636.

Leonard, B. E., & Rigter, H. Changes in brain monoamine metabolism and carbon dioxide amnesia in the rat. *Pharmacology, Biochemistry and Behavior*, 1975, 3, 775–780.

Levine, S., Smotherman, W. P., & Hennessy, J. W. Pituitary-adrenal hormones and learned taste aversion. In L. H. Miller, C. A. Sandman, & A. J. Kastin (Eds.), *Neuropeptide influences on the brain and behavior*. New York: Raven Press, 1977.

Lindvall, O., & Björklund, A. The organization of the ascending catecholamine neuron systems in the rat brain. *Acta Physiologica Scandinavica*, 1974, suppl. 412, 1–48.

Lissák, K. & Bohus, B. Pituitary hormones and avoidance behavior of the rat. *International Journal of Psychobiology*, 1972, 2, 103–115.

Lowry, P. J., Silman, R., Jackson, S., & Estivariz, F. The lipotropin- and corticotropin-related peptides of the mammalian pituitary. In M. T. Jones, B. Gilham, M. F. Dallman, & S. Chattopadhyay (Eds.), *Interaction within the brain-pituitary-adrenocortical System*. London: Academic Press, 1979.

Mains, R. E., Eipper, B. A., & Ling, N. Common precursor to corticotrophins and endorphins. *Proceedings of the National Academy of Sciences*, 1977, 74, 3014–3018.

Martinez, J. L., Jr., Vasquez, B. J., Jensen, R. A. Soumireu-Mouret, B., & McGaugh, J. L. $ACTH_{4-9}$ analog (Org 2766) facilitates acquisition of an inhibitory avoidance response in rats. *Pharmacology, Biochemistry and Behavior*, 1979, 10, 145–147.

McGaugh, J. L. Facilitative and disruptive effects of strychnine sulphate on maze learning. *Psychological Reports*, 1961, 8, 99–104.

McGaugh, J. L., Zornetzer, S. F., Gold, P. E., & Landfield, P. W. Modification of memory systems: Some neurobiological aspects. *Quarterly Review of Biophysics*, 1972, 5, 163–186.

McGaugh, J. L., Gold, P. E., van Buskirk, R., & Haycock, J. Modulating influences of hormones and catecholamines on memory storage processes. In W. H. Gispen, T. J. B. van Wimersma Greidanus, B. Bohus, & D. de Wied (Eds.), *Hormones homeostasis and the brain*. Vol. 42. *Progress in brain research*. Amsterdam: Elsevier, 1975.

Miller, L. H., Harris, L. C., van Riezen, H., & Kastin, A. J. Neuroheptapeptide influence on attention and memory in man. *Pharmacology, Biochemistry and Behavior*, 1976, 5, 17–21. (Suppl. 1)

Nakanishi, S., Inoue, A., Kita, T., Nakamura, M., Chang, A. C. Y., Cohen, S. N., & Numa, S. Nucleotide sequence of cloned cDNA for bovine corticotrophin-β-lipotropin precursor. *Nature*, 1979, 278, 423–427.

Nyakas, C., Bohus, B., & de Wied, D. Effects of $ACTH_{4-10}$ on self-stimulation behavior in the rat. *Physiology and Behavior*, 1980, 24, 759–764.

Oliveros, J. C., Jandali, M. K., Timsit-Berthier, M., Remy, R., Benghezal, A., Audibert, A., & Moeglen, J. M. Vasopressin in amnesia. *Lancet*, 1978, 1, 42.

Pedigo, N. W., Ling, N. C., Reisine, T. D., & Yamamura, H. I. Examination of Des-Tyrosine[1]-γ-endorphin activity at 3H-spiroperidol binding sites in rat brain. *Life Sciences*, 1979, 24, 1645–1650.

Pfeifer, W. D., & Bookin, H. B. Vasopressin antagonizes retrograde amnesia in rats following electroconvulsive shock. *Pharmacology, Biochemistry and Behavior*, 1978, 9, 261–263.

Phifer, R. F., Orth, D. N., & Spicer, S. S. Specific demonstration of the human hypophyseal adrenocortico-melanotropic (ACTH/MSH) cell. *Journal of Clinical Endocrinology and Metabolism*, 1974, 39, 684–692.

Ramaekers, F., Rigter, H., & Leonard, B. E. Parallel changes in behaviour and hippocampal monoamine metabolism in rats after administration of ACTH-analogues. *Pharmacology, Biochemistry and Behavior*, 1978, *8*, 547–551.

Rigter, H., & Popping, A. Hormonal influences on the extinction of conditioned taste aversion. *Psychopharmacologia*, 1976, *46*, 255–261.

Rigter, H., & van Riezen, H. Anti-amnesic effect of $ACTH_{4-10}$: Its independence of the nature of the amnesic agent and the behavioral test. *Physiology and Behavior*, 1975, *14*, 563–566.

Rigter, H., van Riezen, H., & de Wied, D. The effects of ACTH- and vasopressin-analogues on CO_2-induced retrograde amnesia in rats. *Physiology and Behavior*, 1974, *13*, 381–388.

Rigter, H., van Eys, G., & Leonard, B. E. Hippocampal monoamine metabolism and the CO_2-induced retrograde amnesia in rats. *Physiology and Behavior*, 1974, *13*, 381–388.

Roberts, J. L., & Herbert, E. Characterization of a common precursor to corticotropin and β-lipotropin: Cell-free synthesis of the precursor and identification of corticotropin peptides in the molecule. *Proceedings of the National Academy of Sciences*, 1977, *74*, 4826–4830.

Roberts, D. C., Price, M. T. C., & Fibiger, H. C. The dorsal tegmental noradrenergic projection: An analysis of its role in maze learning. *Journal of Comparative and Physiological Psychology*, 1976, *90*, 363–372.

Sandman, C. A., George, J., McCanne, T. R., Nolan, J. D., Kaswan, J., & Kastin, A. J. MSH/ACTH 4-10 influences behavioral and physiological measures of attention. *Journal of Clinical Endocrinology and Metabolism*, 1977, *44*, 884–891.

Sands, S. F., & Wright, A. A. Enhancement and disruption of retention performance by ACTH in a choice task. *Behavioral and Neural Biology*, 1979, *27*, 413–422.

Schulz, H., Kovács, G. L., & Telegdy, G. Effect of physiological doses of vasopressin and oxytocin on avoidance and exploratory behaviour in rats. *Acta Physiologica Academiae Scientiarum Hungaricae*, 1974, *45*, 211–215.

Selye, H. Stress. The physiology and pathology of exposure to stress. *Acta Medica Publication*, Montreal, 1950.

Shibasaki, T., Ling, N., & Guillemin, R. A radioimmunoassay for g-melanocyte stimulating hormone. *Life Sciences*, 1980, *26*, 1781–1785.

Small, J. G., Small, I. F. Milstein, V., & Dian, D. A. Effects of ACTH 4-10 on ECT-induced memory dysfunctions. *Acta Psychiatrica Scandinavica*, 1977, *55*, 241–250.

Sofroniew, M. V., & Weindl, A. Projection from the parvocellular vasopressin and neurophysin-containing neurons of the suprachiasmatic nucleus. *American Journal of Anatomy*, 1978, *153*, 391.

Spear, N. E. Retrieval of memory in animals. *Psychological Review*, 1973, *80*, 163–164.

Stone, C. P., & Obias, M. D. Effects of hypophysectomy on behavior in rats. II. Maze and discrimination learning. *Journal of Comparative and Physiological Psychology*, 1955, *48*, 404–411.

Tanaka, M., de Kloet, E. R., de Wied, D., & Versteeg, D. H. G. Arginine[8]-vasopressin affects catecholamine metabolism in specific brain nuclei. *Life Sciences*, 1977, *20*, 1799–1808.

Timsit-Berthier, M., Mantanus, H., Jacques, C., & Legros, J. J. Utilité de la lysine-vasopressine dans le traitment de l'amnésie post-traumatique. *Acta Psychiatrica Belgica*, 1980, *80*, 728–747.

Urban, I., & de Wied, D. Neuropeptides: Effects on paradoxical sleep and theta rhythm in rats. *Pharmacology, Biochemistry and Behavior*, 1978, *8*, 51–59.

Valtin, H., & Schroeder, H. A. Familial diabetes insipidus in rats (Brattleboro strain). *American Journal of Physiology*, 1964, *206*, 425–430.

van Ree, J. M., Bohus, B., & de Wied, D. Similarity between behavioral effects of Des-Tyr[1]-γ-endorphin and haloperidol and of α-endorphin and amphetamine. In E. L.

Way (Ed.), *Endogenous and exogenous opiate agonists and antagonists*. New York: Pergamon Press, 1980.

van Ree, J. M., Bohus, B., Csontos, K. M., Gispen, W. H., Greven, H. M., Nijkamp, F. P., Opmeer, F. A., de Rotte, G. A. A., van Wimersma Greidanus, T. J. B., Witter, A., & de Wied, D. Behavioral profile of γ-MSH: Relationship with ACTH and β-endorphin. *Life Sciences*, 1981, *28*, 2875–2888.

van Wimersma Greidanus, Tj. B. Effects of MSH and related peptides on avoidance behavior in rats. In Tj. B. van Wimersma Greidanus (Ed.), *Frontiers in hormone research* (Vol. 4). Basel: Karger, 1977.

van Wimersma Greidanus, Tj. B., & de Wied, D. Dorsal hippocampus: A site of action of neuropeptides on avoidance behavior? *Pharmacology, Biochemistry and Behavior*, 1975 (Suppl. 1), 29–33. (a)

van Wimersma Greidanus, Tj. B., & de Wied, D. Modulation of passive avoidance behavior of rats by intracerebroventricular administration of antivasopressin serum. *Behavioral Biology*, 1976, *18*, 325–333. (b)

van Wimersma Greidanus, Tj. B., Bohus, B., & de Wied, D. CNS sites of action of ACTH, MSH and vasopressin in relation to avoidance behavior. In W. E. Stumpf & L. D. Grant (Eds.), *Anatomical neuroendocrinology*. Karger: Basel, 1974.

van Wimersma Greidanus, Tj. B., Dogterom, J., & de Wied, D. Intraventricular administration of anti-vasopressin serum inhibits memory in rats. *Life Sciences*, 1975, *16*, 637–644.

Vawter, M. P., & Green, K. F. Effects of Desglycinamide-lysine vasopressin on a conditioned taste aversion in rats. *Physiology and Behavior*, 1980, *25*, 851–854.

Veith, J. L., Sandman, C. A., George, J. M., & Stevens, V. C. Effects of MSH/ACTH 4-10 on memory, attention and endogenous hormone levels in women. *Physiology and Behavior*, 1978, *20*, 43–50.

Verhoef, J., Loeber, J. G., Burbach, J. P. H., Gispen, W. H., Witter, A., & de Wied, D. a-endorphin, g-endorphin and their Des-Tyrosine fragments in rat pituitary and brain tissue. *Life Sciences*. 1980, *26*, 851–859.

Wagner, Á., Járdánházy, T., Laczi, F., Szilárd, J., Telegdy, G., & László, F. Study of the psychological effects of lysine vasopressin and DDAVP in diabetes insipidus patients *Acta Medica Academiae Scientiarum Hungaricae*, 1979, *36*, 81.

Walter, R., Hoffman, P. L., Flexner, J. B., & Flexner, L. B. Neurohypophyseal hormones, analogs, and fragments: Their effect on puromycin-induced amnesia. *Proceedings of the National Academy of Sciences*, 1975, *72*, 4180–4184.

Watson, S. J., & Akil, H. On the multiplicity of active substances in single neurons: b-endorphin and a-melanocyte stimulating hormone as a model system. In D. de Wied & P. A. van Keep (Eds.), *Hormones and the brain*. Cambridge, Mass.: M.I.T. Press, 1981.

Weinberger, S. B., Arnsten, A., & Segal, D. S. Des-Tyrosine[1]-g-endorphin and haloperidol: Behavioral and biochemical differentiation. *Life Sciences*, 1979, *24*, 1637–1644.

Weingartner, H., Gold, P., Ballenger, J. C., Smallberg, S. A., Summers, R., Rubinow, D. R., Post, R., & Goodwin, F. K. Effects of vasopressin on human memory functions. *Science*, 1981, *211*, 601–603.

Wiegant, W. M., Cools, A. R., & Gispen, W. H. ACTH-induced excessive grooming involves brain dopamine. *European Journal of Pharmacology*, 1977, *41*, 343–345.

6

Memory, Remembering, and Amnesia

Patricia Morgan Meyer and Donald R. Meyer

1. INTRODUCTION

Memories, and particularly long-term memories, are the basic ingredients of knowledge. Hence it is important that we ask where their traces, or engrams, are stored within the brain, and also that we understand the possible fates of the engrams while they are in storage. Moreover, inasmuch as knowledge is worthless if it cannot be expressed, it is equally important that we understand the variables that govern the remembering of memories.

In this chapter we shall review investigations that suggest that the engrams of long-term memories are temporally stable and resilient. Also, we shall argue that whatever they may be, they are stored by mechanisms below the level of the cerebral cortex. We do not wish to tarry on the question whether dynamical encoding is a necessary aspect of the process of formation of an engram, for it has now been established that structural encoding is complete within a few milliseconds (cf. Hebb, 1975; Lewis, 1979; D. R. Meyer & Beattie, 1977). Instead, we shall be exclusively concerned with the properties of memories that were

PATRICIA MORGAN MEYER AND DONALD R. MEYER ● Laboratory of Comparative and Physiological Psychology, Ohio State University, Columbus, Ohio 43212. Many of the studies described in this chapter were conducted with support from the United States Public Health Service, and primarily with funds supplied by Grant No. MH06211 from 1960 through 1980.

learned days, weeks, months, or even years before their fates while in long-term storage were assessed.

2. ON RIBOT'S AND ROBBINS'S PRINCIPLES

In general, a memory that is relatively old is harder to remember than a new one. However, there are numerous exceptions to the rule, and perhaps the most dramatic are those that are observed in patients with injuries to the brain. Thus, as Ribot (1885) first pointed out a century ago, these patients tend to have greater problems in recalling comparatively recent memories. Ritchie Russell (1959) came to a similar conclusion from his studies of soldiers in World War II with amnesias from wounds to the head, and suggested that his findings implied that the traces of long-term memories become more resilient as they age. The question we shall first address is whether Ribot's law, with which we do not propose to quarrel, is attributable to alterations of properties of engrams or, instead, to impairments of remembering.

We have explored the question in a series of experiments with rats. The first of these was reported by Robbins and D. R. Meyer (1970). They trained groups of rats on sets of three discrimination problems; two of the problems were learned for one incentive and the other for a different incentive. The incentives were food while the animals were hungry, and avoidance of very mild shocks to the feet while the animals were satiated. The tasks were presented in succession. Hence, when the training was completed, each rat had learned a habit that by then was approximately 2 weeks old, a second habit that by then was nearly 1 week old, and a third habit that had just been mastered.

Thereafter, each rat, as soon as it had reached a stringent criterion of performance of the third and last problem, was given a single electroconvulsive shock (ECS) treatment. On the following day, it was tested for performance of its oldest or next-oldest problem. None of the rats had any difficulty remembering either of the problems provided that the problem had been learned for a different incentive than had the third and last problem. Thus, for example, if the third task had been food related, and the subject was tested for performance of either a first or second shock-related problem, it had no difficulty remembering the problem and despite the fact that one of the problems was older than the other. The converse was also true for first or second food-related problems, which were both well remembered by subjects that were trained on shock-related problems immediately before they were given single ECS treatments. However, if either the first or second problem had been learned for the same incentive as the third and newest problem, the ECS treatment selectively affected recall of that particular problem.

Subsequently, C. I. Thompson and Grossman (1972) showed that the treatments did not affect the animals' memories for the first and second problems in the series. They used an $S_1F_2S_3$ (shock, food, shock) paradigm. That is, their subjects learned the first and final problems in the series as shock avoidance tasks, and learned the second problem in the series while hungry and for food. Thompson and Grossman confirmed the observation of Robbins and D. R. Meyer that an ECS treatment, if given immediately after completion of training on an S_3 problem, will impair performance of an S_1 problem but will have no effect on retention of a newer F_2 problem. But they also observed that if the animals were given a second ECS on the following day and before the test for retention, the subjects that were tested for S_1 retention performed that problem very well. Although the mechanism of the latter reinstatement is unclear, the result was reminiscent of the notion that amnesias that result from traumata to the head are sometimes dramatically corrected by subsequent blows.

In similar studies (Howard & D. R. Meyer, 1971; Howard, Glendenning, & Meyer, 1974), we found that a single ECS treatment will not impair remembering of the most recent problem and does not make the animal forget the motivational condition under which it was being trained immediately before the treatment. For example, if the animal is trained on the $S_1F_2S_3$ paradigm, it will exit very slowly from the goal box when tested for retention of any of the problems. Conversely, if the animal is trained on the $F_1S_2F_3$ paradigm, it will exit very quickly from the goal box when tested for retention of any of the problems. But under both conditions, it will show no impairment of performance of the second or the third tasks, and under both conditions it will only very slowly relearn the first tasks in the series.

We have also observed that an ECS treatment's effect on remembering of older memories is much the same regardless of whether the memories are relatively older or newer. For example, if animals are trained on an $F_1S_2F_3$ paradigm, and others are trained on an $S_1F_2F_3$ paradigm, the treatment's selective effect on performance of an older, motivationally related problem is approximately the same for the F_1 and F_2 problems. The same thing is true for S_1 and S_2 problems when the paradigms are $S_1F_2S_3$ and $F_1S_2S_3$, respectively. Food-related problems are not relearned as rapidly as shock avoidance problems, but within the two classes the effect is the same regardless of whether the problem is learned 2 weeks or 1 week before the time of the treatment.

We believe, from the results of the foregoing studies, that Ribot's principle does not imply that engrams of memories in long-term storage become more resilient as they age. Instead, the observations indicate that structural engrams are temporally stable, and also that contexts are powerful determinants of whether they will be rememberable. Thus, if one manipulates the contexts within which a memory is formed and an injury to the brain is sustained, one can easily produce a pattern of amnesia in which an older memory is forgotten by a subject that can still recall a newer memory.

In a recent, elegantly conceived set of studies, Squire, Slater, and Chace (1975) observed that mental patients who were treated with ECS had greater impairments of remembering of television shows of the preceding season than of older television shows. The results were exactly as expected from Ribot's principle, and Squire *et al.* interpreted them as supporting the notion that engrams in long-term storage undergo continuous alterations. Importantly, however, the patients' recall of memories that were older than about 1 year were not intermediately affected; instead, the only significant effect was suppression of remembering of memories for shows from the preceding season. We suggest that the diseases for which the patients were treated were in progress by that time, and hence that Robbins's principle accounts for their impairments without an appeal to the concept that relatively recent memories are more vulnerable than older memories.

3. ON THE THEORY OF LONG-TERM DECAY

We shall now turn to the question whether the substrates of long-term memories decay while in storage. As Gleitman (1971) observes, the concept is difficult to test. However, in the popular use-it-or-lose-it version of the theory of decay, the concept is coupled with the notion that disuse accelerates the rate of decay. Hence we shall describe investigations in which we assessed the resiliencies of disused memories. The subjects were cats and rats with injuries to the cerebral cortex; the animals were tested for performances of visual placing.* A cat with an injury to the visual neocortex will not ordinarily exhibit the placing reaction (Bard & Brooks, 1934), and the same is true for rats that are prepared with complete neocortical ablations (Braun, 1966).

It may seem at first glance that impairments of placing, though perhaps of some interest to students of the substrates of vision, can hardly be regarded as the business of students of memory. However, as

---

*Visual placing refers to an animal extending its forepaws on a flat surface when it is being held just in front of the surface.

Held and Hein (1963) showed, the placing reaction is a habit, and close examinations of impairments of placing have shown that the impairments are amnesias.

A visually decorticated cat, for example, will show no recovery of the placing reaction within a period of many months. However, it will then perform the reaction if given treatments with amphetamine (P. M. Meyer, Horel, & Meyer, 1963). And so will a rat that has undergone a one-stage ablation of the entire neocortex (Braun, 1966). But treatments with amphetamine will not permit a rat with a posterior injury to learn a form discrimination problem (Jonason, Lauber, Robbins, Meyer, & Meyer, 1970), although such a subject will exhibit visual placing whether it is treated or not (Braun, 1966). Hence visual placing is not a test of visual-form perception, and both rats and cats with visual-cortical ablations are evidently able to see well enough to perform the visual placing reaction.

It has also been shown that if rats are prepared with two-stage ablations of the entire visual neocortex, they have the same profound and permanent impairments of visual-form discrimination learning as do subjects with comparable one-stage injuries (Lavond & Dewberry, 1980; Lavond, Hata, Gray, Geckler, Meyer, & Meyer, 1978). And that is so regardless of whether the animals are given interoperative training. However, rats prepared with two-stage ablations of the entire dorsal pallial cortex exhibit very rapid recoveries of placing following the second injuries to their brains if given interoperative practice with the visual placing task (Braun, 1966; cf. Braun, 1978). Such results are uninterpretable in terms of the concept that placing impairments are perceptual impairments—even though the deficits are brought by injuries that result in perceptual impairments.

Another set of findings that shows very clearly that placing impairments are amnesias has come from recent studies of cats that were prepared with small visual-cortical ablations (Ritchie, Meyer, & Meyer, 1976). The animals with injuries that were reasonably complete, like subjects we had previously prepared with massive posterior injuries (P. M. Meyer *et al.*, 1963), failed to exhibit spontaneous recoveries of placing for many months thereafter. However, when the aniamls were treated with amphetamine and then were given many tests of placing, their capacities for placing returned and then persisted for periods of many days or weeks.

There is one disadvantage to the use of visual placing in assessments of the properties of engrams of disused memories. It is difficult to put a number on a pattern, and the placing reaction is a pattern. However, Amassian, Ross, Wertenbaker, & Weiner (1972) studied recoveries of tactile placing, a reaction that is not ordinarily elicitable in cats with bilateral ablations of the somesthetic cortex. Amassian *et al.* report that the reaction reappears if subjects thus prepared are treated with amphetamine, and thereby provided a cross-confirmation of our findings with respect to visual placing. Also, with the aid of an array of instruments, they found that the only difference between the reinstated pattern and the normal pattern was a very small change in latency.

Such results are difficult to square with the notion that disused memories decay. We have personally observed a number of cats that had failed to place for more than 1 year, but nevertheless recovered their capacities for placing within a few minutes after treatment. A year is a very large fraction of the lifetime of a cat. On the basis of a decay theory, there ought to be substantial differences between the placing reactions of normal animals and those of cats with long-chronic injuries to the cerebral cortex. But the differences are small indeed, and hence we suggest that the theory of decay is plausible but is without other merit.

4. ON THE THEORY OF MEMORIAL DISPLACEMENT

We have thus far considered our reasons for believing that engrams are temporally stable. Now we shall discuss the question whether, as Loftus and Loftus (1980) propose, a memory in storage is sometimes destroyed when a contradictory memory is formed. The experiments to be described were carried out with rats as subjects, and the animals were tested for performance of the black-white or "brightness" discrimination problem.

The black-white problem is a very useful tool for students of the functions of the brain because it is one of a handful of tasks whose performances are cortically dependent if the cortex is intact. To illustrate, a rat that is trained with our procedures and is then subjected to a one-stage bilateral ablation of the posterior cortex will relearn a white-plus version of the problem in approximately 25 trials. A preoperatively naïve posterior perparation will learn the same problem in approximately 29 trials. Those numbers replicate, in principle, the outcomes of classical experiments by Lashley (1935), who thought his findings meant that the engram for the black-white memory is stored by the cortex provided the cortex is intact.

Lashley's observations are significant because they served for many years as the principal support for the notion that at least some varieties of memories are stored as modifications of the cortex. Thus, although Pavlov (1927) had proposed the theory in its strongest form, his own observations with respect to the effects of injuries to the cortex on performances of classically conditioned responses were that the responses were suppressed by ablations of the cortex, but nevertheless could be reinstated and with savings if the animals were trained after surgery. But Lashley's results suggested that the trace of a memory can be obliterated, and also with methods that will not prevent a subject from forming a compensatory memory.

However, in a study by Braun, Meyer, and Meyer (1966), we found that if rats that are trained on the problem before operation and are treated with amphetamine before they are tested for retention, they will relearn the problem with considerable savings. We also observed that the treatments would not accelerate the rate at which the problem is learned by preoperatively naïve subjects. The results thus suggested that untreated rats given preoperative training on the problem still have a memory for the problem, even though their rates of postoperative relearning will not reveal the fact that it exists.

These findings were crossed-validated in a study by LeVere and Morlock (1973). Essentially, their method was to train rats to choose a brighter or a dimmer stimulus and then, when the animals had been prepared with injuries to the visual neocortex, to train them on reversals of the tasks they had learned before surgery. LeVere and Morlock found that the reversals were learned very slowly; hence they concluded that even though preoperative black-white memories are not retrievable by subjects with posterior injuries, the traces still exist and will strongly interfere with postoperative learning of a contradictory discrimination.

In unpublished experiments with Patsch and Gibson, we have studied the findings of LeVere and Morlock from a quantitative point of view. Under our conditions, the white-plus problem is learned before surgery in approximately 25 trials, and normal rats will also learn the black-plus problem in approximately 25 trials. If, after surgery, the white-plus subjects are retrained on the white-plus problem, they require about 25 more trials to relearn the problem. However, if black-plus subjects are trained on the white-plus problem after surgery, it takes them approximately 50 trials to learn the white-plus problem. Such results suggest not only that the injuries to the cortex spared the black-plus engrams, but also that the engrams had not been affected in the slightest by these injuries.

LeVere and Davis (1977) recently discovered a feature of the black-white reversal paradigm that has greatly enhanced its potential usefulness for studies of memory and remembering. They examined the effects of injuries to the cortex on the rates at which postoperative reversals are learned when the subjects are trained on those tasks for a different incentive than the one that was employed when the contradictory problems were presented before operation. The incentives were water while the animals were thirsty and avoidance of shocks while they were water satiated. LeVere and Davis found that a brain-damaged rat can learn a postoperative reversal without interference from an earlier memory that was learned for a different incentive. That result was highly reminiscent of the findings of the Robbins and Meyer (1970) investigation, and the two studies suggest to us at least that transituational utilizations of memories in storage are profoundly affected by injuries to the cerebral cortex.

Davis and LeVere (1979) employed the paradigms for studies of the bases of postoperative recoveries from amnesias for brightness habits. Dingman and Sporn (1961) had observed that 8-azaguanine, an antimetabolite of RNA, impairs acquisiion of maze-learning tasks but has no effect on remembering of the tasks if they are learned before treatments with the drug. LeVere and Fontaine (1978) confirmed that result for learning and retention of brightness tasks by normal animals, and Davis and LeVere, in their first experiment, showed that it also holds for subjects prepared with injuries to the visual neocortex. Thus they report that operated rats given azaguanine before being trained take about twice as long to learn a brightness habit as do saline control animals, but that such treatments have no effect whatever on retention scores if given 2 days after training.

Davis and LeVere observed, in addition, that if rats are first trained on a water-going bright-plus problem and are treated with the drug after having been prepared with injuries to the posterior cortex, they are very slow to learn a shock avoidance version of the same task after surgery. But they found that if rats are trained on a shock avoidance bright-plus problem before surgery, and are treated with the drug before they are retrained on the same task and for the same incentive, the animals will make only half as many errors in reaching the preoperative criterion of performance as will saline control preparations.

We have employed a bright-plus, bright-plus shock avoidance training in most of our studies of recoveries from black-white amnesias (cf. D. R. Meyer & P. M. Meyer, 1977). We once believed that an untreated rat, when given retraining after surgery, is forced to form a substitutive memory that replaces its still intact but nevertheless completely inaccessible preoperative memory for the task (cf. D. R. Meyer, 1972a). However, Davis and LeVere's findings for same-incentive, same-task conditions show clearly that postoperative retraining does not induce recovery of performance of the problem by developing another memory. If that were so, the 8-azaguanine treatments should have had a deleterious effect, and regardless of whether the preoperative and postoperative incentives were the same or not the same. Hence we now believe that the function of retraining is largely, and perhaps exclusively, to serve as a reminder to the subjects of the memories they learned when they were normal animals.

However, it seems that a subject with a posterior cortex lesion cannot be reminded by postoperative retraining of a task it learned before surgery for a different incentive. Thus the effects of azaguanine suggest that under such conditions, the animal recovers by forming a new memory. That conclusion is consistent with LeVere and Davis's (1977) findings for reversal paradigms, and especially with the fact that a preoperative memory will not interfere with postoperative learning of a contradictory memory unless the same incentives are used before and after operation.

Such observations reinforce our belief that engrams are hard to destroy. They also reinforce our belief that impairments of recall can be profound and enduring without necessarily implying that a subject has lost its memory for a problem. In addition, they have shown that contradictory memories can be entered into long-term storage, and will then be independently recoverable through changes in a subject's incentives for performance.

Loftus and Loftus (1980) argue that failures of recall can reasonably be viewed as memorial impairments if the deficits persist in the face of strenuous efforts to reverse them. We are able to imagine that under some conditions, the acquisition of a new memory will obliterate an older memory. However, we know of no proof for such a concept, including the one that they have offered; namely, that persons who are shown slides depicting events in an automobile–pedestrian accident will refuse to believe that they have been misled by subsequent misleading information. In our opinion, that their subjects preferred a newer to an older memory is readily interpretable as another instance of a state-related failure of retrieval.

5. ON THE THEORY OF TRACE AMALGAMATION

We have described three procedures for detection of memories that are not ordinarily rememberable by animals with injuries to the brain. The first involves treatments with amphetamine, which reinstate performances of placing reactions and accelerate the rate of relearning of the black-white problem. The second is to study the effects of the memories on the rate at which posterior preparations will form contradictory memories. The third is to suppress postoperative learning through treatments with 8-azaguanine, and thereafter to remind the subjects of the task through postoperative retraining on the task.

Those findings have prompted us to ask if there are methods for inducing postoperative remembering that do not involve the use of drugs in conjunction with retraining. As we have observed, the positive effects of treatments with amphetamine on visual placing will soon disappear unless the animals are regularly tested for performances of placing. Similarly, Kircher, Braun, Meyer, and Meyer (1970) found that amphetamine treatments by themselves are worthless as procedures for protecting postoperative remembering of the black-white problem. Hence, since the actions of the drugs are adjunctive and are not necessary for induced reinstatements to endure, it has seemed to us at least that the memories ought to be retrievable through suitable, purely behavioral procedures.

We have already given our reasons for believing that long-term memories in storage are classified according to the motives of the subjects at the times that the memories were formed. We note once again that ECS treatments, if administered to rats while they are working for a given incentive, will selectively suppress recall of older memories that were learned for the same incentive. That result, when taken in conjunction with results from a classical experiment by Chow (1952), led us to suspect that there might be a converse principle. Chow observed that monkeys with temporal lobe injuries that are trained on new discrimination problems after surgery are thereby enabled to remember older problems that the injuries would otherwise have caused them to forget completely. Hence we were prompted to think that induction of postoperative remembering of one visual problem by rats prepared with posterior injuries would also permit them to retrieve other memories that were learned for the same incentives before the operations.

There were several limitations on our choice of methods for assessing such a concept. First, inasmuch as we had an understanding of many of the variables that govern recoveries of performance of the black-white problem, we believe that our projected tests would have the greatest power if the task was included in the set. Second, we believed that the methods' sensitivities would also be enhanced if the other tasks were visual problems that the subjects could learn in the same apparatus and for the same incentive. However, it is not easy to devise a set of visual problems that will have those features and will also be learnable by animals prepared with injuries to the visual neocortex.

When, in Gray and Meyer (1981), we undertook the task, we already knew that the posterior subjects are capable of learning certain kinds of visuospatial problems. For example, decorticated rats will readily discriminate between a deep and a shallow visual alley (Braun, Lundy, & McCarthy, 1970), and cats with injuries to the visual neocortex can solve a large variety of "visual-pattern" tasks provided the cues are different with respect to overall amounts of visual contour (e.g., Dalby, Meyer, & Meyer, 1970; Ritchie *et al.*, 1976; Wetzel, 1969).

We were also aware that such subjects are completely and permanently form-blind. That is, if presented with a task in which the cues are carefully equated with respect to amounts of flux and contour, the animals will fail the task no matter how long they are retrained (cf. Horel, Bettinger, Royce, & Meyer, 1966; Jonason *et al.*, 1970; Lavond & Dewberry, 1980; Lavond *et al.*, 1978). The gist of the foregoing studies was that rats with ablations of the posterior cortex are unable to detect the orientations of static visual contours and therefore, in principle, will fail any rigorously controlled test of shape recognition.

A subject with posterior cortical lesion, despite its form-blindness, can nevertheless discriminate between arrays of black-and-white squares of different spatial frequencies. Hence, in the Gray and Meyer (1981) study, we studied the effects of the checks-problem training on recoveries of performance of the black-white problem, and vice versa. However, a coarse versus fine checks problem and the black-white problem, as we usually present it, share a common mode of solution. Thus, as we have noted, a posterior subject discriminates amounts of edginess, and a white door on black background presents a contour cue that a black door does not if it is also on a black background. Hence, if an animal is given checks training, and is thereby forced to discriminate amounts of visual contour, it will then learn the black-white problem with substantial savings. Similarly, training on the black-white problem facilitates checks-problem learning, although the amount of transfer of training is considerably less than that which is observed when the subjects first learn the checks problem.

Our method of coping with the problem posed by transfer between the two discrimination problems was to train normal rats on both problems. Different groups of subjects were trained on the tasks in different orders. Thereafter, the subjects were prepared with bilateral ablations of visual neocortex, and were trained on both problems once again. The principal questions were whether the rats that were first retrained on the black-white problem would profit from their having had mixed or "broad" preoperative training, and whether they would then relearn the checks discrimination at a faster rate than could be accounted for in terms of postoperative transfer. Remarkably, the answer to both of the questions was no. Rats with black-white preoperative training relearned the black-white problem after surgery at about the same rate as subjects trained on both problems before surgery. Moreover, even though there was postoperative transfer of training between the two problems, the subjects' performance of a second checks problem after they had first relearned the black-white problem was approximately the same as that for subjects that had not learned the checks problem before surgery.

In Gray and Meyer (1981), we also searched for crossed inductions of retrieval with serial paradigms. First, we must note that if normal rats are trained on the black-white discrimination problem, successive uni-lateral posterior ablations produce the same postoperative amnesias for the task as do one-stage bilateral ablations (Kircher *et al.*, 1970; Pe-trinovich & Carew, 1969). However, if two-stage subjects are retrained on the problem between the operations, they exhibit considerable amounts of savings when tested for ultimate retention (Glendenning, 1972; R. F. Thompson, 1960b; cf. D. R. Meyer & P. M. Meyer, 1977). The Thompson effect is not observed in rats that have had no preoperative training (Bodart, Hata, Meyer, & Meyer, 1980); hence the protection of ultimate retention implies that the subjects are enabled by the training to utilize memories that were formed before the first operations.

Although, as we have noted, rats with bilateral ablations of the visual neocortex are permanently and absolutely form-blind, subjects with unilateral posterior injuries can master form discrimination prob-lems. Hence we asked if serial posterior perparations that are trained on a form task between the two surgeries will thereby be enabled to remem-ber a black-white problem they learned when they were normal. We found, once again to our surprise, that the training had no effect what-ever; that is, the ultimate impairments of the subjects were no less severe than those produced by one-stage bilateral ablations.

In Gray and Meyer (1981), we also observed that if rats are given enormous amounts of overtraining on the black-white problem before surgery, the overtraining lessens the effects on recall that are noted after one-stage ablations of the posterior cortex. However, preoperative over-training does not produce as much protection of remembering as does interoperative retraining. Why that should be is still unclear, but we can say with considerable assurance that neither form of training has sa-lubrious effects because an overtrained or a retrained subject has a better acquaintance with the testing situation than does a rat that is not over-trained. Thus, of the several methods we have tried, only two were found to make a difference, and both involved explicit training or re-training on the black-white discrimination problem.

The findings have made us dubious about the concept of trace amal-gamation, that is, the notion that as memories are formed their engrams become incorporated with the engrams of older memories. We would not have been surprised to find that visual-form training is useless as a method for protecting retrieval of a memory for a black-white problem if the subjects had been trained on the two tasks for different incentives.

However, the motive was the same for both problems, and the training situations were identical except for the stimuli to be discriminated. Hence we suggest that if traces do become amalgamated under some conditions, our conditions were ripe for amalgamation of at least some components of the memories for the black-white and visual-form discrimination problems. However, our inferences are somewhat tentative, and thus far we have found it very difficult to think of other ways to get at the question.

6. ON THE THEORY OF DISTRIBUTED STORAGE

From this point on, our principal concern will be with the problem of the role of the cortex in storage. We begin with the question whether the memory for the black-white problem is stored at the level of the cortex. As we have observed, performance of the problem is cortically dependent provided that the cortex is intact, and posterior subjects will not ordinarily exhibit any signs of the fact that they still have a memory for the task that was formed when they were trained before surgery. Now we shall ask if it is reasonable to think that the still-surviving trace was stored at the level of the cortex, and hence is retained by posterior subjects because the extravisual regions of the cortex are intact (cf. Hughes, 1977, for definition).

If a posterior subject is trained on the problem by what we term Glendenning's (1972) method, it will relearn the problem in approximately 25 trials; a subject that has lost its extravisual cortex, in approximately 17 trials. These numbers have standard errors of about 10%. Had Pavlov (1927) been aware of the outcomes, we think he would have viewed them as a confirmation of his theory that the visual analyzer of the cortex has a posterior focus and a fringe in the anterior cortex. According to the theory, the traces of memories are stored throughout the cerebral cortex, and hence are not destroyable by any subtotal injury to the cerebral cortex.

However, if naïve subjects are prepared with bilateral anterior injuries, are trained on the problem, and are subsequently prepared with second-stage posterior cortex injuries, their rate of relearning is exactly the same as that of subjects trained on the problem as normal animals and then prepared with bilateral posterior ablations (Hata, Diaz, Gibson, Jacobs, Meyer, & Meyer, 1980; Horel et al., 1966). Conversely, if rats are prepared with bilateral posterior ablations, are trained on the problem, and are then subjected to second-stage anterior injuries, their rate of relearning of the problem is the same as that of subjects trained on the problem as normal animals and then prepared with anterior injuries

(Horel *et al.*, 1966; Howarth, Meyer, & Meyer, 1979). The findings are for subjects that sustained both injuries in adulthood. Hence, inasmuch as the recoveries that occur after injuries to either subsector of the cortex are completely independent of whether or not the rest of the cortex is intact, it is plain that the memories that are inaccessible to posterior subjects are stored below the level of the cortex.

However, although the foregoing findings led us to reject the notion that the trace is stored throughout the cerebral cortex, our observation that anterior injuries have substantial effects on performance of the problem was at variance with a finding of Lashley (1921). For that and other reasons, we assessed the effects on retention of other kinds of injuries to the cortex. The results of those studies have led us to believe that a function exists for which the cortex is equipotential, and also that impairments of performance of the function need to be discounted if we wish to understand the properties of long-term traces.

If performance of the black-white problem is the measure of behavior, the cost of an injury to a quadrant of the cortex is approximately eight to nine trials. With only one exception that we know of, injuries to more than one quadrant have additive effects. Thus, for example, $2 \times 8.5 = 17$ trials, and that is the number of trials that it takes a bilateral anterior preparation to relearn the problem. It is also very close to the number of trials that it takes for relearning of the problem by a subject with a hemidecortication, that is, with a unilateral injury to both the visual and the extravisual cortex (D. R. Meyer & P. M. Meyer, 1977).

Perhaps that is pseudomathematics. However, even though bilateral ablations of the posterior cortex have a greater cost than bilateral anterior ablations, the costs of unilateral posterior or anterior ablations are essentially the same. Also, if a unilateral posterior injury is combined with a contralateral injury to the anterior cortex, the effect on relearning is within a trial or two of the cost of a bilateral anterior ablation or a hemidecortication (D. R. Meyer & P. M. Meyer, 1977).

The exception to the rule of additivity is that one-stage bilateral posterior ablations have a greater effect than other two-quadrant injuries. The number is the same regardless of whether the subjects are prepared with one-stage or two-stage ablations (Kircher *et al.*, 1970). Nor can it be reduced by interoperative training of two-stage subjects unless they have been trained on the problem as normal animals (Bodart *et al.*, 1980). Therefore, a bilateral posterior injury has a cost of about eight trials that cannot be accounted for in terms of the nonspecific costs of an injury of that scope.

We have studied the effects on performance of the problem of complete ablations of the neocortex in one stage (P. M. Meyer, Yutzey,

Dalby,& D. R. Meyer, 1968). The experiment was carried out with what we now describe as the massed-trial procedure of Horel *et al.* (1966). The scores thus obtained can be readily converted through the use of what we term Glendenning's (1972) rule into scores of the kinds we have been considering in this discussion (cf. Gray & Meyer, 1981). According to the present analysis, the subjects should have relearned the problem in (8.5 × 4) + 8 spaced trials, or 42 trials. In fact, the subjects relearned the problem in an estimated 38 trials.

Significantly, a one-stage posterior preparation, if treated with amphetamine, will relearn the problem approximately as fast as a bilateral anterior subject (cf. Braun *et al.*, 1966; Horel *et al.*, 1966). The estimated spaced-trial number is 15 trials. Also, the treatments do not significantly affect the rate at which the black-white problem is relearned by bilateral anterior preparations (Jonason *et al.*, 1970). And two-stage posterior preparations given training on the problem before surgery will relearn the problem in eight to nine trials provided they are also retrained on the task between the first and second operations (D. R. Meyer & P. M. Meyer, 1977). Therefore, treatments with the drug are effective for reducing the posteriorly specific impairments of performance of the black-white problem, and interoperative retraining on the problem corrects both impairments but conveys no protection against the nonspecific consequences of a second-stage posterior injury.

At present, we have no convictions about the nature of the regionally nonspecific function except that it is not memorial. Thus, although the only known procedures that will serve to induce compensations for impairments of the function are training or retraining of the subject, the compensations are completely independent of whether or not the injured subsectors were intact at the time the animal was first given training on the black-white problem. Moreover, if the nonspecific costs of the injuries are discounted, there is no impairment of retention of the problem by posterior preparations given treatments with amphetamine. Hence, on those grounds, and also on the grounds provided by the studies of LaVere and his colleagues with respect to the effects of posterior injuries on postoperative reversal learning (LeVere & Davis, 1977; LeVere & Morlock, 1973), we see no reason to believe that any part of the engram of the memory for the black-white problem is stored at the level of the cortex.

7. ON STORAGE OF COMPLETELY LATENT MEMORIES

Our reasons for believing that the cortex is not a memory bank include a proof that an injury to the cerebral cotex will not necessarily prevent the formation of a memory for a task that the brain-damaged subject is completely unable to perform. This finding is the clearest demonstration we know of that the systems that mediate storage and retrieval obey completely different sets of laws. It is also another illustration of the fact that long-term memories are resilient, and that failures of performance are likelier than not to be impairments of remembering.

In these studies the rats' task was buzzer-signaled shuttle-avoidance learning. In the first investigation (P. M. Meyer, Johnson, & Vaughn, 1970), we found that the task is relatively easy for rats prepared with either bilateral anterior or posterior injuries. However, we also observed that a rat with a one-stage ablation of the entire neocortex will not ordinarily be able to perform it within 300 trials of training. That is more than four times as many training trials as it takes normal rats to learn the problem, and thus we concluded that performance of the task is cortically dependent under ordinary circumstances.

However, in the same investigation, we found that neodecorticated rats have little difficulty with the shuttle-box problem, if they are also prepared with injuires to the septum of the forebrain. Indeed, such subjects, like animals with injuries to the septum alone (King, 1958), will learn the shuttle problem at a somewhat faster rate than normal control animals. Hence it was apparent that the neocortex is not required for shuttle-box learning, even though complete neocortical ablations by themselves suppress performance of the problem.

We were prompted by these findings to ask if treatments with amphetamine would also correct the impairment (Beattie, Gray, Rosenfeld, Meyer, & Meyer, 1978). We found that if the treatments were given every day for 10 days, and the animals were given 30 trials of training each day, the animals made a few avoidance responses during the first few sessions. However, they then stopped responding to the signal, and by the end of training were escaping but were not avoiding. Hence, at that point, the animals' levels of performance of the task were almost indistinguishable from those of subjects with comparable injuries that had served as a saline control group.

Thereafter the treatments of the groups were reversed, and the animals were given further training. The subjects that had previously been treated with amphetamine but were then given dialy injuections of saline continued to fail to avoid. Thus their median avoidance scores were quite close to zero during each of 10 additional sessions of 30 training trails. By the end of that phase the subjects had been given a total of 600 trials, or nine times as many trials as are required by normal rats for mastery of the problem

However, the subjects that were first given saline while being trained for 300 trials and that previously had not exhibited avoidance responses reacted to their subsequent treatments with amphetamine by rapidly starting to avoid. Indeed, in the first few sessions with the treatment, their levels of performance were substantially higher than those of normal subjects with no previous training on the problem. This finding was startling because, before treatment, the median avoidance score for the group had been zero during each of its previous 10 sessions with the problem.

We interpreted the outcomes as similar to those of Braun *et al.* (1966), even though the studies were carried out with different behavioral procedures. As we have observed, Braun *et al.* found that treatments with amphetamine will not facilitate the rate of acquisition of the black-white problem by naïve posterior cortex lesion preparations, but nevertheless will have an effect on the rate of relearning of the problem by subjects trained on the task as normal animals. Hence we proposed that the decorticated subjects trained on the shuttle-box problem for 300 trials before the treatments began had formed a latent memory for the problem that had not been expressible until these delayed treatments began. We attributed the finding that the treatments had been ineffective for the other animals to their not having had a memory to recall at the time the treatments with the drug were begun.

In a third training phase, we once again reversed the treatments of the two groups of subjects. We found that the levels of performance of the group first trained with saline and then amphetamine underwent a precipitious decline. However, contrary to our expectations, the treatments did not permit the subjects trained with amphetamine first and then with saline to perform when the signals were presented. Conceivably the subjects had developed a learned helplessness (cf. Overmier & Seligman, 1967), for by that time they had failed to avoid nearly 600 shocks to their feet.

In the same investigation, but with subjects whose behaviors are described by D. R. Meyer and Beattie (1977), we studied the effects of daily alternations of saline and amphetamine treatments. Initially, the animals were trained on the problem for 300 trials with saline. We then observed, as had Braun (1966) in his studies of inductions of recoveries of placing, that alternating treatments with amphetamine and saline resulted in a seesaw improvement of the subjects' performance of the problem over days. Moreover, as in Ritchie *et al.*'s (1976) investigation of recoveries of placing in the cat, we observed that the subjects, if given further practice, would continue to avoid when treatments with the drug were discontinued.

As a group, the findings offer very strong support for Tolman's (1932) theory that memory formation has nothing necessarily to do with performance of a task. They also suggest that the systems involved in conveying information into storage are not necessarily the systems that mediate retrieval of memories from storage. And third, inasmuch as the studies were performed with neodecorticated subjects, they are evidently in keeping with our proposition that the cerebral cortex is not a good place to look for engrams (cf. D. R. Meyer, 1972a).

8. ON THE FUNCTIONS OF THE PREFRONTAL CORTEX

Still other impairments of animals with injuries to the cortex have prompted some investigators to conclude that the organ is a memory-storage bank. Although it may well come as a surprise to workers not directly concerned with assessments of the functions of the cortex, deficits of placing, of black–white retention, and of learning of the shuttle-box problem constitute a very large fraction of the set of permanent impairments that have thus far been produced by either subtotal or total neocortical ablations. And the set is even smaller than it would otherwise be if one excludes impairments of performance of tasks that, if properly designed and presented, are measures of visual-perceptual deficits (cf. Lavond & Dewberry, 1980; Lavond et al., 1978).

Of the other rare birds whose plumage we have not yet described, there are only three or four with markings which suggest that they might be memorial impairments. The set includes (1) the classical delayed response impairment of monkeys with prefrontal injuries (e.g., Jacobsen, 1936; D. R. Meyer, Harlow, & Settlage, 1951), which is usually observed in association with impairments of delayed alternation (e.g., Jacobsen & Nissen, 1937; Mishkin & Pribram, 1955); (2) impairments of performance of certain kinds of visual learning tasks, which constitute a part of the Klüver-Bucy syndrome of monkeys with temporal lobe ablations (e.g., Klüver & Bucy, 1937, 1939; Mishkin, 1972; Mishkin & Pribram, 1954); and (3) impairments of conditioned discriminations of temporally spaced groups of cues, which, however, we shall not discuss because we believe they are evidently impairments of short-term and not of long-term memory (cf. Konorski, 1959; D. R. Meyer & Woolsey, 1952; Neff & Diamond, 1958; R. F. Thompson, 1960a).

We begin with the delayed response impairment. In the commonest version of this problem, the monkey is first shown a small piece of food. The food is then dropped into one of two food wells, and both food wells are then covered with identical small objects. After a delay, the monkey is permitted to displace one object or the other, and is then permitted to pick up the food provided its choice was correct. Although the task is simple, monkeys with complete bilateral dorsolateral prefrontal injuries are usually unable to perform it, and will not recover their abilities to do so for periods of up to several years (cf. D. R. Meyer, Hughes, Buchholz, Dalhouse, Enloe, & Meyer, 1976).

The preparations nevertheless can learn to discriminate between pairs of small common objects. Discrimination problems are arranged while the subject is not watching. A piece of food is placed in one of two food wells, and two dissimilar objects are then placed above the food wells. Thereafter, the monkey is permitted to choose between the objects, and learns over trials to select the object that has a piece of food concealed beneath it. Prefrontal monkeys are likelier than normals to persist in their choices of the objects they selected on their first training trials with a problem (cf. D. R. Meyer, Treichler, Yutzey, & P. M. Meyer, 1965), but their perseverative deficits in such a situation are modest when compared with their impairments of delayed responding.

The use of common objects as discriminative cues for studies in the field of primate learning began with the experiments of Harlow (1949). He showed that if monkeys are trained on many instances of two-choice discrimination problems, that is, with replacement of old pairs of cues with novel cues, the animals will soon learn the rules of the game and will then solve further novel problems essentially at once. Harlow describes the effect as the formation of an object-learning set. Monkeys with bilateral prefontal ablations can still form an object-learning set (e.g., Harlow, Davis, Settlage, & Meyer, 1952; D. R. Meyer, 1972b), and after having done so exhibit both conceptual and habitual approaches to new discrimination learning problems (cf. D. R. Meyer, 1971).

A set-trained monkey is a useful animal for studies of delayed response impairments. In the DR problem, a prefrontal monkey must choose between one of two identical objects on the basis of the information it receives when it sees the experimenter drop a piece of food into a food well. In a two-trial object discrimination problem, it receives information as to which of the objects it should choose on the second, or test trial from the outcomes of its choices of one of two objects that it has not yet seen. In both situations the measure of performance is obtained following a delay, that is, the delay of the DR task and the intertrial interval between the first and second trials of a two-trial object discrimination problem. Therefore, that a prefrontal monkey, if set-trained, will fail the first problem but will pass the second suggests that delay has nothing whatsoever to do with the DR impairment.

Many years ago, D. R. Meyer et al. (1951) asked if the difference was a function of the fact that the DR problem is a test of spatial memory and the two-trial object discrimination problem a test of nonspatial memory. They observed that if DR procedures are employed but the food wells are covered after placement of the food with markedly dissimilar objects, the use of such objects results in a small but significant improvement in performance of the DR problem by prefrontal monkeys. However, because that procedure did not by any means permit them to perform the task at a near-normal level, it was apparent that the DR impairment was not a spatial memory impairment.

Subsequently, D. R. Meyer and Settlage (1958) observed that if prefrontal monkeys are presented with a row of four identical boxes, and one of the boxes contains a food reward that must be searched for, the operated animals are less systematic than normals in their patterns of searching. Thus a normal monkey will start at one end of the row and go down it until the food reward is encountered, but a prefrontal monkey will often skip a box in the process. Importantly, however, although their searching styles are quite abnormal, prefrontal monkeys are no more likely to reopen a box they have opened before and found empty than are animals whose brains are intact. That result was also inconsistent with the notion that the subjects fail the spatial DR problem because they are unable to remember where the food was put at the beginning of the test.

It was therefore plain that the impairment had something to do with the mode of presentation of the information a prefrontal subject must be able to remember in order to perform the DR problem. Hence in Blake, Meyer, and Meyer (1966), we examined the performances of set-trained monkeys with prefrontal injuries of three varieties of two-choice nonspatial problems. In the first variety, the DR procedure was employed. The animal was shown a food reward, and then the two food wells were covered with dissimilar objects the subject had never seen before. In the second variety, the subject was permitted to displace the objects on the first trial of a two-trial discrimination problem and, after having thus discovered where the food was, to pick up the food and eat it. The third variety was like the second except that when the objects were displaced, the subject could see where a food reward was placed but could not obtain it because the food well was covered with a thin transparent lid. In all three varieties, the test consisted of a re-presentation, following a delay, of the pair of dissimilar objects. Of the three tasks, only the DR problem was failed by the prefrontal monkeys.

We knew, at that point, that a prefrontal monkey can remember the outcomes of its choices but will fail to remember what experimenters do at the beginning of a DR test. The riddle thus presented proved unsolvable until the development of testing procedures that permitted close control of times of presentation of pairs of visual stimuli to monkeys. Such procedures were devised by LeVere and Bartus (1969, 1971, 1972); they involved automatic presentations of the cues when the monkey being tested through a window at a screen. The monkey was prevented from responding to the cues for varying intervals of time, and within those intervals the cues could be changed while the monkey was watching through the window.

Bartus and LeVere (1977) used these methods in a study of pattern discrimination learning by monkeys with prefrontal injuries. The paradigms involved successive presentations, within each trial, of pairs of visual patterns that were relevant or not relevant to solution of the problems by the monkeys. The positions of the members of the relevant pairs indicated which of two positional responses would yield a food reinforcement. The time of presentation of each pair of patterns was 500 milliseconds, and the monkeys were forced to observe both pairs before they were permitted to respond.

Bartus and LeVere (1977) found that their subjects with injuries to the prefrontal cortex could readily learn the visual-pattern problem if the last pair of cues presented on a trial were relevant discriminative cues. However, when the relevant cues were first presented, and were followed by a brief presentation of irrelevant cues, the prefrontal monkeys learned the pattern problem very slowly. Thus the results suggest that frontal preparations are unusually susceptible to retroactive interference, and provided what we view as having been the key to the nature of the DR impairment.

In the DR test, the monkey must remember where a small piece of food has been put. However, after having shown the monkey where the food is, the experimenter covers the food wells; hence the presentation of the relevant cue is immediately succeeded by another event before the arrangement is completed. Before Bartus and LeVere's (1977) study, we had found it very hard to imagine that such a seemingly trivial feature of the DR procedure as the covering of the food wells could yield a blanking of the prefrontal subject's remembrance of where the food had been. However, that feature distinguishes the test from others that the animals can solve, regardless of whether the cues to be remembered are spatial or nonspatial cues.

Our theory that the DR deficit is due to interference before the delay, and is not a consequential function of the fact that the test involves periods of delay, is contrary to Goldman and Rosvold's (1970), theory that monkeys with injuries to the prefrontal cortex have spatial-memorial impairments. We think our theory provides a simple explanation for a number of classical results, including those of Malmo (1942), Spaet and Harlow (1943), Mishkin and Pribram (1955, 1956), Glick, Goldfarb, and Jarvik (1969), and Glick and Jarvik (1970). The gist of these studies was that prefrontal monkeys have little difficulty performing what are termed indirect delayed reactions or go-no-go delayed reactions, and also that the animals have only transitory impairments of performance of matching-from-sample problems that involve a period of delay. We cannot go into the specifics of these studies, but we will note that without exception, the last information the subject received on every trial before the period of delay was relevant information.

Recently, Fuster (1980), after having reviewed a large fraction of the literature on monkeys with prefrontal injuries, concluded that the "studies taken together seriously challenge the notion that the prefrontal cortex is the storage site of any memory, transient or otherwise." That is close to the conclusion we have come to. Prefrontal monkeys, as Ferrier (1886) first observed, are temporally chaotic preparations; they are hyperreactive to and slow to habituate to changes in their environments (cf. French & Harlow, 1955). In quiet situations they exhibit perseverative tendencies (e.g., Mishkin, 1964; Settlage, Zable, & Harlow, 1948), which we view as the reason they are unable to perform delayed alternations (cf. Pribram & Tubbs, 1967). However, so far as we can see, their spatial and nonspatial memories are substantially intact, and hence we reject the concept that the frontal cortex is a memory-storage bank.

9. ON THE FUNCTIONS OF THE TEMPORAL NEOCORTEX

As we have observed, if monkeys are prepared with injuries to both temporal lobes, they exhibit impairments of learning and remembering of certain kinds of simple visual tasks. In the last 30 years many studies of the variables that govern the impairments have appeared. However, the experiments have mainly been concerned with attempts at differentiation of the functions of various subregions of the temporal neocortex and the deep structures of the temporal lobes, and have been carried out with remarkably limited numbers of behavioral procedures. It seems to us that the results obtained thus far with these procedures have not shown that memories are affected by temporal injuries.

The procedures used by Mishkin and Pribram (1954) have been used in many experiments with temporal preparations. The subjects were baboons that were given preoperative training on a plus-square problem. The animals were then prepared with lesions of the ventral temporal cortex. After operation, they were tested for postoperative retention of the plus-square habit, and then for their abilities to learn circle–square, stripes–diamond, red-green, and two-grays discrimination problems. Mishkin and Pribram found that the baboons were unable to relearn the plus-square problem within 1,000 trials of training, and were usually unable to learn the other problems except for the red-green problem.

Significantly, however, the patterns between which the monkeys were asked to discriminate were mounted in the centers of the lids of

small boxes that the animals opened from the front. In such an arrangement the subject makes its choice by grasping the lid's nearest edge, and
its behavior is then primarily controlled by cues presented on that edge.
The bias is termed the "stimulus–response spatial contiguity effect." It is
readily detectable in normal animals as well as in temporal preparations,
and implies that a visual discrimination problem will be difficult for
monkeys if the cues are surrounded by identical manipulable borders
(cf. D. R. Meyer, Treichler, & Meyer, 1965).

We have found that the bias is enormously enhanced by injuries to
the temporal neocortex (cf. D. R. Meyer, 1958, 1972b). Thus it is virtually
impossible to train a bitemporal monkey on a two-color problem if the
colors are surrounded by borders—in contrast to the findings of Mishkin
and Pribram (1954) with respect to their red–green problem. However,
in their study the colors extended to the forward edges of the box lids
and hence were well within the spatial regions to which their baboons
were attending. Under such conditions, bitemporal subjects will learn
the task as fast as normal subjects, although they will still have impairments of remembering of preoperatively learned color problems (cf.
Chow, 1952).

That impairments of attending, and not of memory, account for the
deficits of temporal preparations in visual-habit learning situations is
also demonstrated by the animals' behaviors when the cues are small,
common objects. Bitemporal monkeys can learn such problems as readily as normal animals provided the training arrangement is such that
they touch the cues when they respond (cf. Mishkin, 1972). However, if
the objects are attached to bases and the animals manipulate the bases,
even object problems are very hard for temporal preparations (cf. Ungerleider & Pribram, 1977). The reason, again, is that the animals attend
to the bases and not to the cues, even though the objects are only an
inch or so away from the animals' response sites.

We stress that it matters very little if the cues have been attached to
cards or to other kinds of bases, provided the monkey is forced to touch
the cues when it responds. Schrier and Harlow's (1957) findings are a
case in point. If white cards are anchored to the surface of a test tray, or
form board, and the cards surround the food wells of the form board,
and the cues are smaller and displaceable cards of different colors, the
problem is virtually as easy for a monkey as one in which larger, colored
cues without borders are used as the discriminative cues. However, if
the colored cards are glued to white cards that are movable when touched on their edges, the problem is then very different indeed, even for a
normal animal.

Another demonstration of the fact that temporal subjects are even
more affected than normal monkeys by S–R discontiguities can be found

in Butter and Hirtzel (1970). In their study, the subjects were forced to respond to the nearest edges of a pair of small plaques. First, the near halves of the plaques were red or blue, and the far halves of both plaques were gray. Under those conditions, temporal preparations learned the color problem as rapidly as normal animals. However, when the plaques were reversed, and the color cues were then on the far halves of the plaques instead of the near halves, the temporal preparations made four times as many errors as the normal animals.

It is worth noting that although temporal monkeys have little difficulty learning visual problems under S–R contiguous conditions, they are very much inferior to normal animals in terms of acquisition and retention of object-learning sets (D. R. Meyer, 1972b; Riopelle, Alper, Strong, & Ades, 1953; cf. Horel & Keating, 1972). In that respect, they differ from frontal preparations with injuries of equivalent scopes (Harlow et al., 1952; D. R. Meyer, 1972b). However, our present concern is with memories for habits, and not with the neural mechanisms of conceptual behaviors (cf. D. R. Meyer, 1971). And neither bitemporal nor bifrontal preparations are impaired in their abilities to learn visual problems provided, once again, that attending to the cues to be discriminated is enforced.

With those points established, we return to the fact that temporal preparations have selective impairments of postoperative performance of preoperatively learned visual problems. The one remaining question is whether those impairments, which are noted regardless of whether the problems are S–R contiguous or not, are due to the destruction of preoperative engrams or, instead, are impairments of retrieval.

The impairments are reduced by overtraining, and can be eliminated through cross-induction procedures (Chow, 1952; Chow & Survis, 1958; Orbach & Fantz, 1958). As we have observed, we have been unsuccessful in obtaining crossed induction of retrieval of the black–white engram. But in both situations overtraining is effective, as it is also effective in reducing impairments of postoperative retention of tactile habits by rats with somatosensory injuries (Weese, Neimand, & Finger, 1973). Hence, although the question deserves further study, we concur with Chow's (1952) judgment that the "deficit is not a simple loss of memory traces, but rather the result of the specific habits being temporarily suppressed."

10. CONCLUSION

We have found that it is easy to show that injuries to the cortex will bring about impairments of remembering. Indeed, such impairments are the commonest effects of the injuries, and have been observed by every student of the cortex who has ever used a formal behavioral procedure for assessment of its role in memory. Thus Franz (1902), who first employed what would now be described as operant or instrumental methods, had much the same experience as all of his successors when he found that frontal subjects will forget simple habits, but will then promptly relearn them.

However, neither Franz (1902) nor Pavlov (1927) nor Lashley (1935) was able to arrive at a proof that the engram for any memory is stored at the level of the cerebral cortex. In our own investigations, we have looked for such a proof for approximately a quarter of a century; and while we have been working, we have witnessed an enormous expansion in the field of brain research. Yet so far as we know not a single paper has appeared in our professional lifetimes that has lent any credence whatsoever to the notion that the cortex has memorial functions. We say this despite of our awareness of the fact that experiential factors have been shown to modify the microstructure of the cerebral cortex (see Greenough, 1976), which we find very interesting but think of as related to the role of the cortex in retrieval.

Why, then, has the theory gone unchallenged? First, it has survived for as long as it has for other theoretical reasons, particularly the notion that humans and other mammals are behaviorally superior to other organisms because of their capacities for learning. When such a supposition is coupled with the fact that expansion of the cortex is by far the most significant event in the process of mammalian evolution, it seems plausible that this expansion permits the storage of a larger and more varied aggregate of memories. However, we know of no convincing evidence for such a view; the only established distinction among the behavioral capacities of mammals with brains of various sizes is in their abilities to learn rules or concepts, and not to learn particular habits (cf. Warren, 1965).

The theory has also gone unchallenged because it seemed supported by at least a few studies. Of those the most convincing was Lashley's (1935), for his findings indicated that posterior injuries will permanently suppress remembering of a problem that subjects thus prepared are capable of learning or relearning. However, in experiments with Lashley's paradigms we have shown that the memory for the black–white problem is intact after injuries to the cortex, and hence that his results could be interpreted in terms of a very strong form of von Monakow's (1914) theory of impairments and recoveries of functions. We say a strong form because although von Monakow believed that the proper functions of a central neural system are revealed by impairments that persist for long periods, our own investigations have also revealed the existence of latent capacities that will never be expressed unless active steps are taken to induce their expression.

And the theory has also gone unchallenged because of the seeming plausibilities of theories that engrams are stored throughout the cerebral cortex and sometimes at several neural levels. Pribram's (1971) holographic theory is a recent example. In our own investigations we have found what we regard as support for the concept that the cortex is equipotential for a function, but we have yet to encounter a suggestion that the function has anything to do with memory storage.

Our theory that the cortex is not involved in storage is silent with respect to the question of where, if not within the cortex, the engrams of memories for cortically dependent performances are stored. However, we have studied the effects on performance of the black–white problem of combined ablations of the posterior cortex and a number of subcortical structures (Gray, Lavond, Meyer, & Meyer, 1979; D. R. Meyer & P. M. Meyer, 1977). We have found that the latter kinds of injuries by themselves have relatively modest consequences, but that lesions of the pretectal region of the brainstem result in a marked potentiation of the deficits of subjects with second-stage injuries to the cortex. Hence we suspect that the memory is encoded by centrencephalic mechanisms, but we know of no survivable injury to those systems that will block the formation of the memory.

Our conclusion about the dynamics of engrams, wherever and however they are formed, is that they are almost incredibly tough and invariant as a function of time. Hence our views are basically the same as those of Penfield (1958), who based his own theory of the stability of memories on his findings concerning the effects of stimulation of the temporal lobes of epileptic patients. We consider the conclusions valid regardless of how long a memory has been stored, and in that respect our notions are at variance with two-stage or multistage theories of encoding (cf. D. R. Meyer & Beattie, 1977).

A few years ago, in his now classic treatise on forgetting, Spear (1971) began by saying that the purpose of his paper was "not to present a case for retrieval failure as a source of forgetting to the unqualified exclusion of decay in storage"; that instead he had

> the more modest intention of attributing some diverse cases of retention loss to a common source, namely, retrieval failure. Surely the existence of memory decay in some form is quite plausible, although perhaps limited to chemical or anatomical changes in brain sites linked with memory, and insignificant in terms of behavior.

We think it is now abundantly clear that his emphasis was not misplaced. Indeed, at this juncture, we know of no procedure for selective destruction of a memory, and so far as we can see there is not a single shred of support for the theory of decay.

We believe our results have important implications for approaches to therapies for strokes, and particularly strokes that involve the cerebral cortex and bring about impairments of remembering. We think their most important message for clinicians is that memories can be permanently and absolutely latent and yet substantially intact. The second message is that failures of remembering are correctable with pharmacotherapies, even when the failures of retrieval have persisted for the human equivalent of years. The third is that the therapies are not very likely to be effective by themselves, but only when employed in conjunction with behavioral procedures for inductions of retrieval.

We make no suggestions as to what kinds of agents should be tried. The studies in which we first employed amphetamine were carried out before the field of neurochemistry was well advanced, and were prompted by a finding of Maling and Acheson (1946) that treatments with the drug will induce recoveries of righting by pontine preparations. Thereafter our concern was not with the drug's mode of action but with the question whether its effects were effects on learning or on remembering. We believe our answer is important because, in our opinion, it would make little sense for a physician to attempt to treat an old amnesic patient if the patient has no memories to remember. We are not so rash as to claim that all amnesias are impairments of retrieval or recall, but we think our results suggest that a clinician should at least begin with that hypothesis.

At present, we are exploring behavioral procedures for inductions of recoveries from amnesias. Although it is apparent that treatments with drugs will fascilitate the process, it is equally clear that the treatments are not essential for the maintenance of access. Hence we suspect that pharmacotherapies, which are only now beginning to be actively considered and primarily by workers in Europe (e.g., de Wied, 1980; but see also Weingartner, Gold, Ballenger, Smallberg, Summers, Rubinow, Post, & Goodwin, 1981), will flourish for about the next 20 years and will then be displaced by other methods.

Hints as to what sorts of methods these will be are gradually beginning to emerge. One is that remembering is more state-specific when the brain has been damaged than when it is intact. Moreover, recent findings by LeVere and Davis (1977) and Davis and LeVere (1979) were so striking as to lead us to believe that memories in long-term storage are stored in different state-related bins. But whether that is so or not, the implication for practice is that therapists should try to reconstruct the contexts within which the memories to be reinstated were established. We think successful therapists will be instructors for the patient's relatives, for the principle suggests that a hospital suite is not a good setting for inductions of recoveries except via substitutive learning.

We continue to hope that Gray and Meyer's (1981) negative results with respect to crossed inductions will in the long run prove an exception to the rule. We would like to believe that if during a visit to familiar surroundings, one's amnesic grandmother could be prompted to recognize Fred, it would then be easier to help her recall the names of Uncle Bert and Uncle Harry. We are baffled by the fact that it is easy to show that ECS treatments will suppress retrieval of groups of state-related memories, and yet it is difficult to show that procedures that facilitate remembering of a given memory will have a salubrious effect on recall of another state-related memory. We consider this problem to be of considerable practical importance, and believe its resolution would also enhance our present understanding of the organization of storage and of the process of retrieval. Because we think we have studied the problem as closely as we can with our customary methods of inquiry, we are now looking for alternative approaches.

11. REFERENCES

Amassian, V. E., Ross, R., Wertenbaker, C., & Weiner, H. Cerebello-thalamocortical interrelations in contact placing and other movements in rats. In T. L. Frigyesi, E. Rinvik, & M. D. Yahr (Eds.), *Cortico-thalamal projections and sensorimotor activities*. New York: Raven Press, 1972.

Bard, P., & Brooks, C. M. Localized cortical control of some postural reactions in the cat and rat together with evidence that small cortical remnants may function normally. *Research Publications of the Society for the Study of Nervous and Mental Disease*, 1934, *13*, 107–157.

Bartus, R. T., & LeVere, T. E. Frontal decortication in rhesus monkeys: A test of the interference hypothesis. *Brain Research*, 1977, *119*, 233–248.

Beattie, M. S., Gray, T. S., Rosenfeld, J. A., Meyer, P. M., & Meyer, D. R. Residual capacity for avoidance learning in decorticate rats: Enhancement of performance and demonstration of latent learning with d-amphetamine treatments. *Physiological Psychology*, 1978, *6*, 279–287.

Blake, M. O., Meyer, D. R., & Meyer, P. M. Enforced observation in delayed response learning by frontal monkeys. *Journal of Comparative and Physiological Psychology*, 1966, *61*, 374–379.

Bodart, D. J., Hata, M. G., Meyer, D. R., & Meyer, P. M. The Thompson effect is a function of the presence or absence of preoperative memories. *Physiological Psychology*, 1980, *8*, 15–19.

Braun, J. J. The neocortex and visual placing in rats. *Brain Research*, 1966, *1*, 381–394.

Braun, J. J. Time and recovery from brain damage. In S. Finger (Ed.), *Recovery from brain damage*. New York: Plenum Press, 1978.

Braun, J. J., Meyer, P. M., & Meyer, D. R. Sparing of a brightness habit in rats following visual decortication. *Journal of Comparative and Physiological Psychology*, 1966, *61*, 79–82.

Braun, J. J., Lundy, E. G., & McCarthy, F. V. Depth discrimination in rats following removal of the visual neocortex. *Brain Research*, 1970, *20*, 283–291.

Butter, C. M., & Hirtzel, M. Impairment in sampling visual stimuli in monkeys with inferotemporal lesions. *Physiology and Behavior*, 1970, *5*, 369–370.

Chow, K. L. Conditions influencing the recovery of visual discriminative habits in monkeys following temporal neocortical ablations. *Journal of Comparative and Physiological Psychology*, 1952, *45*, 430–437.

Chow, K. L., & Survis, J. Retention of overlearned visual habit after temporal cortical ablation in monkey. *Archives of Neurology and Psychiatry*, 1958, *79*, 640–646.

Dalby, D. A., Meyer, D. R., & Meyer, P. M. Effects of occipital neocortical lesions upon visual discriminations in the cat. *Physiology and Behavior*, 1970, *5*, 727–734.

Davis, N., & LeVere, T. E. Recovery of function after brain damage: Different processes and facilitation of one. *Physiological Psychology*, 1979, *7*, 233–240.

de Wied, D. Hormonal influences on motivation, learning, memory and psychosis. In D. T. Krieger & J. C. Hughes (Eds.), *Neuroendocrinology*. Sunderland, Mass.: Sinauer, 1980.

Dingman, W., & Sporn, M. B. The incorporation of 8-azaguanine into rat brain RNA and its effect on maze learning by the rat: An inquiry into the biochemical basis of memory. *Journal of Psychiatric Research*, 1961, *1*, 1–11.

Ferrier, D. *The functions of the brain*. London: Smith & Elder, 1886.

Franz, S. I. On the functions of the cerebrum. I. The frontal lobes in relation to the production and retention of simple sensory-motor habits. *American Journal of Physiology*, 1902, *8*, 1–22.

French, G. M., & Harlow, H. F. Locomotor reaction decrement in normal and brain-damaged monkeys. *Journal of Comparative and Physiological Psychology*, 1955, *48*, 496–501.

Fuster, J. M. *The prefrontal cortex: Anatomy, physiology and neuropsychology of the frontal lobe*. New York: Raven Press, 1980.

Gleitman, H. Forgetting of long-term memories in animals. In W. K. Honig & P. H. R. James (Eds.), *Animal memory*. New York: Academic Press, 1971.

Glendenning, R. L. Effects of training between two unilateral lesions of visual cortex upon ultimate retention of black-white habits by rats. *Journal of Comparative and Physiological Psychology*, 1972, *80*, 216–229.

Glick, S. D., & Jarvik, M. E. Differential effects of amphetamine and scopolamine on matching performance of monkeys with lateral frontal lesions. *Journal of Comparative and Physiological Psychology*, 1970, *73*, 307–312.

Glick, S. D., Goldfarb, T. L., & Jarvik, M. E. Recovery of delayed matching performance following lateral frontal lesions in monkeys. *Communications in Behavioral Biology*, 1969, *3*, 299–303.

Goldman, P. S., & Rosvold, H. E. Localization of function within the dorsolateral prefrontal cortex of the rhesus monkey. *Experimental Neurology*, 1970, *27*, 291–304.

Gray, T. S., & Meyer, D. R. Effects of mixed training and overtraining on recoveries from amnesias in rats with visual cortical ablations. *Physiological Psychology*, 1981, *9*, 54–62.

Gray, T. S., Lavond, D. G., Meyer, P. M., & Meyer, D. R. Comparative significance of pretectal and ventral lateral geniculate systems in functional recoveries after injuries to the posterior cortex. *Physiological Psychology*, 1979, *7*, 22–28.

Greenough, W. T. Enduring effects of differential experience and training. In M. R. Rosenszweig & E. L. Bennett (Eds.), *Neural mechanisms of learning and memory*. Cambridge, Mass.: M.I.T. Press, 1976.

Harlow, H. F. The formation of learning sets. *Psychological Review*, 1949, *56*, 51–65.

Harlow, H. F., Davis, R. T., Settlage, P. H., & Meyer, D. R. Analysis of frontal and posterior association syndromes in brain-damaged monkeys. *Journal of Comparative and Physiological Psychology*, 1952, *45*, 419–429.

Hata, M. G., Diaz, C. L., Gibson, C. F., Jacobs, C. E., Meyer, P. M., & Meyer, D. R. Perinatal injuries to extravisual cortex enhance the significance of visual cortex for performance of a visual habit. *Physiological Psychology*, 1980, *8*, 9–14.

Hebb, D. O. Science and the world of imagination. *Canadian Psychological Review*, 1975, *16*, 4–11.

Held, R., & Hein, A. Movement-produced stimualtion in the development of visually-guided behavior. *Journal of Comparative and Physiological Psychology*, 1963, *56*, 872–876.

Horel, J. A., & Keating, E. G. Recovery from a partial Klüver-Bucy syndrome in the monkey produced by disconnection. *Journal of Comparative and Physiological Psychology*, 1972, *79*, 105–114.

Horel, J. A., Bettinger, L. A., Royce, G. J., & Meyer, D. R. Role of neocortex in the learning and relearning of two visual habits by the rat. *Journal of Comparative and Physiological Psychology*, 1966, *61*, 66–78.

Howard, R. L., & Meyer, D. R. Motivational control of retrograde amnesia in rats: A replication and extension. *Journal of Comparative and Physiological Psychology*, 1971, *74*, 37–40.

Howard, R. L., Glendenning, R. L., & Meyer, D. R. Motivational control of retrograde amnesia: Further explorations and effects. *Journal of Comparative and Physiological Psychology*, 1974, *86*, 187–192.

Howarth, H., Meyer, D. R., & Meyer, P. M. Perinatal injuries to the visual cortex enhance the significance of extravisual cortex for performance of a visual habit. *Physiological Psychology*, 1979, *7*, 163–166.

Hughes, H. C. Anatomical and neurobehavioral investigations concerning the thalamo-cortical organization of the rat's visual system. *Journal of Comparative Neurology*, 1977, *175*, 311–336.

Jacobsen, C. F. Studies of cerebral functions in primates. I. The functions of the frontal association areas in monkeys. *Comparative Psychology Monographs*, 1936, *23*, 101–112.

Jacobsen, C. F., & Nissen, H. W. Studies of cerebral functions in primates. IV. The effects of frontal lobe lesions on the delayed alternation habit in monkeys. *Journal of Comparative Psychology*, 1937, *23*, 101–112.

Jonason, K. R., Lauber, S., Robbins, M. J., Meyer, P. M., & Meyer, D. R. The effects of dl-amphetamine upon discrimination behaviors in rats with cortical lesions. *Journal of Comparative and Physiological Psychology*, 1970, *73*, 47–55.

King, F. A. Effects of septal and amygdaloid lesions on emotional behavior and conditioned avoidance in the rat. *Journal of Nervous and Mental Diseases*, 1958, *126*, 57–63.

Kircher, K. A., Braun, J. J., Meyer, D. R., & Meyer, P. M. Equivalence of simultaneous and successive neocortical ablations in production of impairments of retention of black-white habits in rats. *Journal of Comparative and Physiological Psychology*, 1970, *71*, 420–425.

Klüver, H., & Bucy, P. C. "Psychic blindness" and other symptoms following bilateral temporal lobectomy in rhesus monkeys. *American Journal of Physiology*, 1937, *119*, 352–353.

Klüver, H., & Bucy, P. C. Preliminary analysis of functions of the temporal lobes in monkeys. *Archives of Neurology and Psychiatry*, 1939, *42*, 979–1000.

Konorski, J. A new method of physiological investigation of recent memory in animals. *Bulletin of the Polish Academy of Science*, 1959, *7*, 115–117.

Lashley, K. S. Studies of cerebral function in learning. III. The motor areas. *Brain*, 1921, *44*, 255–286.

Lashley, K. S. The mechanisms of vision. XII. Nervous structures concerned in habits based upon reactions to light. *Comparative Psychology Monographs*, 1935, *11*, 43–79.

Lavond, D., & Dewberry, R. G. Visual form perception is a function of the visual cortex. II. The rotated horizontal-vertical and oblique-stripes pattern problems. *Physiological Psychology*, 1980, *8*, 1–8.

Lavond, D., Hata, M. G., Gray, T. S., Geckler, C. L., Meyer, P. M., & Meyer, D. R. Visual form perception is a function of the visual cortex. *Physiological Psychology*, 1978, *6*, 471–477.

LeVere, T. E., & Bartus, R. T. APDA: A discontiguous S-R automated primate discrimination apparatus. *Behavioral Research Methods and Instrumentation*, 1969, *1*, 250–262.

LeVere, T. E., & Bartus, R. T. Stimulus information and primate discrimination learning: Pre-response utilization of stimulus information. *Journal of Comparative and Physiological Psychology*, 1971, *77*, 200–205.

LeVere, T. E., & Bartus, R. T. Stimulus information and primate discrimination learning: Utilization of pre-response information following acquisition. *Journal of Comparative and Physiological Psychology*, 1972, *79*, 432–437.

LeVere, T. E., & Davis, N. Recovery of function after brain damage: The motivational specificity of spared neural traces. *Experimental Neurology*, 1977, *57*, 883–899.

LeVere, T. E., & Fontaine, C. W. A demonstration of the importance of RNA metabolism for the acquisition but not performance of learned behaviors. *Experimental Neurology*, 1978, *59*, 444–449.

LeVere, T. E., & Morlock, G. W. The nature of visual recovery following posterior decortication in the hooded rat. *Journal of Comparative and Physiological Psychology*, 1973, *83*, 62–67.

Lewis, D. G. Psychobiology of active and inactive memory. *Psychological Bulletin*, 1979, *86*, 1054–1083.

Loftus, E. F., & Loftus, G. R. On the permanence of information in the brain. *American Psychologist*, 1980, *35*, 409–420.

Maling, H. M., & Acheson, G. H. Righting and other postural activity in low decerebrate cats after d-amphetamine. *Journal of Neurophysiology*, 1946, *9*, 379–386.

Malmo, R. B. Interference factors in delayed response in monkeys after removal of the frontal lobes. *Journal of Neurophysiology*, 1942, *5*, 292–308.

Meyer, D. R. Some psychological determinants of sparing and loss following damage to the brain. In H. F. Harlow & C. N. Woolsey (Eds.), *Biological and biochemical bases of behavior*. Madison: University of Wisconsin Press, 1958.

Meyer, D. R. The habits and concepts of monkeys. In L. E. Jarrard (Ed.), *Cognitive processes of non-human primates*. New York: Academic Press, 1971.

Meyer, D. R. Access to engrams. *American Psychologist*, 1972, *27*, 124–133. (a)

Meyer, D. R. Some features of the dorsolateral frontal and inferotemporal syndromes in monkeys. *Acta Neurobiologia Experimentalis*, 1972, *32*, 235–260. (b)

Meyer, D. R., & Beattie, M. S. Some properties of substrates of memory. In L. H. Miller, C. A. Sandman, & A. J. Kastin (Eds.), *Neuropeptide influences on brain and behavior*. New York: Raven Press, 1977.

Meyer, D. R., & Meyer, P. M. Dynamics and bases of recoveries of functions after injuries to the cerebral cortex. *Physiological Psychology*, 1977, *5*, 133–165.

Meyer, D. R., & Settlage, P. H. Analysis of simple searching behavior in the frontal monkey. *Journal of Comparative and Physiological Psychology*, 1958, *51*, 408–410.

Meyer, D. R., & Woolsey, C. N. Effects of localized cortical destruction on auditory discriminative conditioning in cat. *Journal of Neurophysiology*, 1952, *15*, 149–162.

Meyer, D. R., Harlow, H. F., & Settlage, P. H. A survey of delayed-response performance by normal and brain-damaged monkeys. *Journal of Comparative and Physiological Psychology*, 1951, *44*, 17–25.

Meyer, D. R., Treichler, F. R., & Meyer, P. M. Discret-trial training techniques and stimulus variables. In A. M. Schrier & H. F. Harlow (Eds.), *Behavior of non-human primates.* New York: Academic Press, 1965.

Meyer, D. R., Treichler, F. R., Yutzey, D. A., & Meyer, P. M. Precedence effects in discrimination learning by normal and frontal monkeys. *Journal of Comparative and Physiological Psychology*, 1965, *58*, 472–474.

Meyer, D. R., Hughes, H. C., Buchholz, D. J., Dalhouse, A. D., Enloe, L. J., & Meyer, P. M. Effects of successive unilateral ablations of principalis cortex upon performances of delayed alternation and delayed response by monkeys. *Brain Research*, 1976, *108*, 397–412.

Meyer, P. M. Analysis of visual behavior in cats with extensive neocortical ablations. *Journal of Comparative and Physiological Psychology*, 1963, *56*, 397–401.

Meyer, P. M., Horel, J. A., & Meyer, D. R. Effects of dl-amphetamine upon placing responses in neodecorticate cats. *Journal of Comparative and Physiological Psychology*, 1963, *56*, 402–414.

Meyer, P. M., Yutzey, D. A., Dalby, D. A., & Meyer, D. R. Effects of simultaneous septal-visual, septal-anterior, and anterior-posterior lesions upon relearning a black-white discrimination. *Brain Research*, 1968, *8*, 281–290.

Meyer, P. M., Johnson, D., & Vaughn, D. The consequences of septal and neocortical ablations upon learning a two-way avoidance response. *Brain Research*, 1970, *22*, 113–120.

Mishkin, M. Perseveration of central sets after frontal lesions in monkeys. In J. M. Warren & K. Akert (Eds.), *The frontal granular cortex and behavior.* New York: McGraw-Hill, 1964.

Mishkin, M. Cortical visual areas and their interactions. In A. G. Karczmar (Ed.), *The brain and human behavior.* New York: Springer, 1972.

Mishkin, M., & Pribram, K. H. Visual discrimination performance following partial ablations of the temporal lobe. I. Ventral vs. lateral. *Journal of Comparative and Physiological Psychology*, 1954, *47*, 14–20.

Mishkin, M., & Pribram, K. H. Analysis of the effects of frontal lesions in monkeys. I. Variations of delayed alternation. *Journal of Comparative and Physiological Psychology*, 1955, *48*, 492–495.

Mishkin, M., & Pribram, K. H. Analysis of the effects of frontal lesions in monkeys. II. Variations of delayed response. *Journal of Comparative and Physiological Psychology*, 1956, *49*, 36–40.

Neff, W. D., & Diamond, I. T. The neural basis of auditory discrimination. In H. F. Harlow & C. N. Woolsey (Eds.), *Biological and biochemical bases of behavior.* Madison: University of Wisconsin Press, 1958.

Orbach, J., & Frantz, R. L. Differential effects of temporal neocortical resections on overtrained and non-overtrained monkeys. *Journal of Comparative and Physiological Psychology*, 1958, *51*, 126–129.

Overmier, J. B., & Seligman, M. E. P. Effects of inescapable shock upon subsequent escape and avoidance responding. *Journal of Comparative and Physiological Psychology*, 1967, *63*, 28–33.

Pavlov, I. P. *Conditioned reflexes.* London: Oxford University Press, 1927.

Penfield, W. *The excitable cortex in conscious man.* Liverpool: Liverpool University Press, 1958.

Petrinovich, L., & Carew, T. J. Interaction of neocortical lesion size and interoperative experience in retention of a learned brightness discrimination. *Journal of Comparative and Physiological Psychology*, 1969, *68*, 451–454.

Pribram, K. H. *Languages of the brain*. Englewood Cliffs, N.J.: Prentice-Hall, 1971.

Pribram, K. H., & Tubbs, W. E. Short-term memory, parsing, and the primate frontal cortex. *Science*, 1967, *156*, 1765–1767.

Ribot, T. *Diseases of memory*. London: Kegan Paul, 1885.

Riopelle, A. J., Alper, R. G., Strong, P. N., & Ades, H. W. Multiple discrimination and patterned string performance of normal and temporal-lobectomized monkeys. *Journal of Comparative and Physiological Psychology*, 1953, *46*, 145–149.

Ritchie, G. D.., Meyer, P. M., & Meyer, D. R. Residual spatial vision of cats with lesions of the visual cortex. *Experimental Nuerology*, 1976, *53*, 227–253.

Ritchie, R., W. *Brain, memory, learning: A neurologist's view*. Oxford: Clarendon Press, 1959.

Robbins, M. J., & Meyer, D. R. Motivational control of retrograde amnesia. *Journal of Experimental Psychology*, 1970, *84*, 220–225.

Schrier, A. M., & Harlow, H. F. Direct manipulation of the relevant cue and difficulty of discrimination. *Journal of Comparative and Physiological Psychology*, 1957, *50*, 576–580.

Settlage, P. H., Zable, M., & Harlow, H. F. Problem solution by monkeys following bilateral removal of the prefrontal areas. VI. Performance on tests requiring contradictory reactions to similar and to identical stimuli. *Journal of Experimental Psychology*, 1948, *38*, 50–65.

Spaet, T., & Harlow, H. F. Problem solution by monkeys following bilateral removal of the prefrontal areas. II. Delayed reaction problems involving the use of the matching-from-sample method. *Journal of Experimental Psychology*, 1943, *32*, 424–434.

Spear, N. E. Forgetting as retrieval failure. In W. K. Honig & P. H. R. James (Eds.), *Animal memory*. New York: Academic Press, 1971.

Squire, L. R., Slater, P. C., & Chace, P. M. Retrograde amnesia: Temporal gradient in very long-term memory following electroconvulsive therapy. *Science*, 1975, *187*, 77–79.

Thompson, C. I., & Grossman, L. B. Loss and recovery of long-term memories after ECS in rats: Evidence for state-dependent recall. *Journal of Comparative and Physiological Psychology*, 1972, *78*, 248–254.

Thompson, R. F. Function of auditory cortex in frequency discrimination. *Journal of Neurophysiology*, 1960, *23*, 321–334. (a)

Thompson, R. F. Retention of a brightness discrimination following neocortical damage in the rat. *Journal of Comparative and Physiological Psychology*, 1960, *53*, 212–215. (b)

Tolman, E. C. *Purposive behavior in animals and men*. New York: Appleton-Century, 1932.

Ungerleider, L. G., & Pribram, K. L. Inferotemporal versus combined pulvinar-prestriate lesions in the rhesus monkey: Effects on color, object and pattern discrimination. *Neuropsychologia*, 1977, *15*, 481–498.

von Monakow, C. *Die Lokalisation im Grosshirn und der Abbau der Funktion durch kortikale Herde*. Wiesbaden: Bergmann, 1914.

Warren, J. M. Primate learning in comparative perspective. In A. M. Schrier, H. F. Harlow, & F. Stollnitz (Eds.), *Behavior of non-human primates* (Vol. 1). New York: Academic Press, 1965.

Weese, G. D., Neimand, D., & Finger, S. Cortical lesions somesthesis in rats: Effects of training and overtraining prior to surgery. *Experimental Brain Research*, 1973, *16*, 542–550.

Weingartner, H., Gold, P., Ballenger, J. C., Smallberg, S. A., Summers, R., Rubinow, D. R., Post, R. M., & Goodwin, F. K. Effects of vasopressin on human memory functions. *Science*, 1981, *211*, 601–603.

Wetzel, A. B. Visual cortial lesions in the cat: A study of depth and pattern discrimination. *Journal of Comparative and Physiological Psychology*, 1969, *68*, 580–588.

Yutzey, D. A., Meyer, D. R., & Meyer, P. M. Effects of simultaneous septal and neo- or limbic-cortical lesions upon emotionality in the rat. *Brain Research*, 1967, *5*, 452–458.

7

The Hippocampus and the Expression of Knowledge

Richard Hirsh and Joel Krajden

1. INTRODUCTION: SUMMATIONAL AND RETRIEVAL PROCESSES

This chapter will have three major themes. The first is that the attainment and expression of knowledge depend on the hippocampus by virtue of its involvement in retrieval processes. We shall define retrieval somewhat more restrictively than is normally the case. By retrieval we mean the selection of a single or small set of memories from among a larger set having some common content. Knowledge of any one object or stimulus can be only as rich or diverse as retrieval processes allow. We think retrieval processes are central to the kinds of processes that were thought to be responsible for learning by theorists in the cognitive tradition, as exemplified by Tolman (1948). We think a cognitive learning system, which includes the hippocampus, is present in the brain.

Following hippocampal ablation, animals have substantial capacities for learning. This residual learning appears to conform fairly closely to the theories espoused by the initiators of the associative tradition in experimental psychology, as exemplified by Hull (1943). Thus the second major theme of this chapter is that a purely associative learning system is also present in the brain. Over the years the associationists and the cognitivists have engaged in arduous debate. We will not re-

RICHARD HIRSH AND JOEL KRAJDEN • Department of Psychiatry, McGill University, Montreal, Quebec, Canada, H3A 1B1.

count that history except to say that associative theories were modified
to account for the phenomena that cognitivists used to support their
position. Eventually many learning theorists came to think there was no
fundamental difference between the two traditions. However, the effects of hippocampal lesions indicate that this conclusion is false. Cognitive learning processes require parts of the brain that are not necessary
for associative learning. To us this fact suggests that very different processes underlie each.

We have just postulated, in effect, that two systems capable of
learning are present in the brain. When two different systems appearing
to address the same substantive matters are present, it is worthwhile to
ponder how they might interact. This interaction is our third major
theme. We think that on some occasions the two systems compete; on
others they cooperate. Once the fundamental differences between the
two systems are understood, their differing capacities become clear.
Each has capabilities that the other does not. There are certain features
of knowledge that cannot be attained without using the capacities of
both.

Associative theories vary considerably in detail, but all subscribe to
the central tenet that the relation between the stimulus and the response
is evocative. Associative theories hold that learning is the linking of the
neural entity activated by the stimulus to the neural entity that generates
the response, so that the stimulus comes to evoke the response. Such
links will operate whenever the stimulus occurs, without any other possible recourse. A strong link or association serves, in effect, to fuse the
neural entities together.

Because the stimulus evokes the response, the stimulus, according
to associative theories, cannot be simultaneously incorporated into more
than one strong association. If the stimulus has been incorporated into
two or more learned relations only one of them can be strong. Otherwise, the occurrence of the stimulus would evoke conflicting responses.

In order to form evocative relations and also to prevent gains in
influence on the part of associations incorporating the same stimulus,
associative theories employ a summational process that consists entirely
of addition and subtraction in the ordinary sense. For example, according to Hull's (1943) S–R theory, reinforcement strengthens associative
bonds, nonreinforcement weakens them, and the effects of the two are
cumulative. That is, they are summed over experience of the stimulus,
S. Should the stimulus S_1 be incorporated into both S_1–R_1 and S_1–R_2, R_1
will occur on some occasions when only R_2 is reinforced and vice versa.
As a result of the summation of the effects of reinforcement and nonreinforcement, the associations S_1–R_1 and S_1–R_2 will be neither particularly strong nor particularly weak. Neither association will be particularly influential in ruling in or ruling out the occurrence of R_1 or R_2.

Associative processes are summational in an additional way. In every constellation of input there are elements that unequivocally elicit the appropriate response and those that are more equivocal in doing so. Associative theory holds that the effects of the former are consistent so that they will gain or maintain influence, whereas the effects of the later are inconsistent so that they will lose influence. For this principle to work, it is necessary to assume that the elements comprising the input are independent, that is, they do not influence each other. Thus their combined influence in determining behavior is strictly a function of their sum, an assumption made explicit by Estes (1950).

According to associative theories of learning, a strong association or memory involving a given stimulus can exist only when the representation of that stimulus is incorporated into no more than one association. When such a monolithic association is present, there is no more information about the stimulus present in the nervous system than is apparent in behavior; hence the appellation "behaviorism." The occurrence of the stimulus is sufficient to ensure the activation of the appropriate memory. There is no need for selection among many possibilities.

Associative theories, then, employ summational logic to form evocative relations between stimuli and responses. Because the learned relation is evocative and summational logic is employed, an associative system can "know" only one thing about any stimulus at any given time.

In contrast, cognitive theories hold that the relations acquired during learning are not evocative but instead describe how parts of the world, or stimuli, are related to each other. Because the relations are not evocative, a given stimulus can be simultaneously described within many different relations. For example, an animal may learn how one place is spatially related to any number of other places. Thus more than one thing may be known about the same object or stimulus at the same time. When a variety of things are known about the same stimulus, a selective process is necessary to determine which of the many potentially relevant pieces of knowledge, or memories, will control behavior. Because the stimulus is described in all of them, something else must supplement its actions in the selection or retrieval process. We shall discuss this additional factor later.

Tolman's (1948) treatment of latent learning exemplifies the cognitive approach. In latent learning experiments animals, usually rats, are allowed to wander through a maze in the absence of explicitly produced motivational conditions. Subsequently the animal is made hungry and is shown food in another, arbitrarily selected, location. Aminals that have had an opportunity to explore the maze obtain the food with fewer errors than do animals that have not explored the maze.

Tolman holds that during exploration the rats have acquired a cognitive map of the maze, that is, the spatial relations among the various parts of the maze have been apprehended. Since the rats appear to know something about a path arbitrarily chosen by the experimenter, it is necessary to assume that each part of the maze has been spatially related to many other parts of the maze. That is, the same part of the maze has been incorporated into many different spatial relations. Because the part of the maze, the stimulus, is described in many different relations, a selective process involving something in addition to the stimulus must be employed. According to Tolman the additional information is provided by the motivational state, in this case hunger. The hunger endows the food with value, or, in Tolman's terminology, valence. Because the food has been related to a place, value is transferred to that location and information describing how that location might be reached is selected. Note that the influence of the motivational state differs in kind from that of the stimulus.

In sum, cognitive learning processes result in descriptive relations. Because the relations are descriptive, many different things may be simultaneously known about the same stimulus or object. Because many different things may be simultaneously known about a stimulus, a selective or retrieval process in which the influence of the stimulus is supplemented by some other type of input is necessary.

We shall describe the logic underlying selection or retrieval, which we shall term "conditional," in detail below. For now it suffices to say that it is quite different from the summational logic underlying associative processes. As we indicated earlier, attainment of certain kinds of knowledge requires both summational and conditional logic.

2. THE HIPPOCAMPUS AND MEMORY

Today, most workers interested in the hippocampus hold that it is involved in some mnemonic process, although there is debate as to the specific nature of the process in question. The main support for this position is still the clinical finding that surgical ablation of the hippocampus* affects memory quite severely, while leaving other faculties untouched (Penfield & Milner, 1958) as assessed by the nonmnemonic scales of IQ tests.[†]

Experience occurring as much as 1 year before surgery cannot be recalled, although partial recovery is observed in some cases. Anterograde amnesia is dramatic. Permanent acquisition of new information,

---

*Performed as a therapy for epilepsy that was otherwise intractable.
[†]A reader who wishes to subject our ideas to a severe test should bear this fact in mind.

for example, that required by most occupations, is nil, although motor skills are normally acquired. Only rarely does a patient remember events that took place after surgery.

Some prima facie evidence of hippocampal involvement in mnemonic processes in animals has been obtained in studies of the activity of single or small groups of neurons in the hippocampus and related structures during learning. In these experiments, animals learn one thing about a stimulus so that behavior and hippocampal unit activity enter characteristic modes. For example, a period of pseudoconditioning is run as a control before the start of conditioning. As a result of pseudoconditioning, both the animals and the hippocampal neurons sampled cease to respond to the presentation of the stimulus that will be

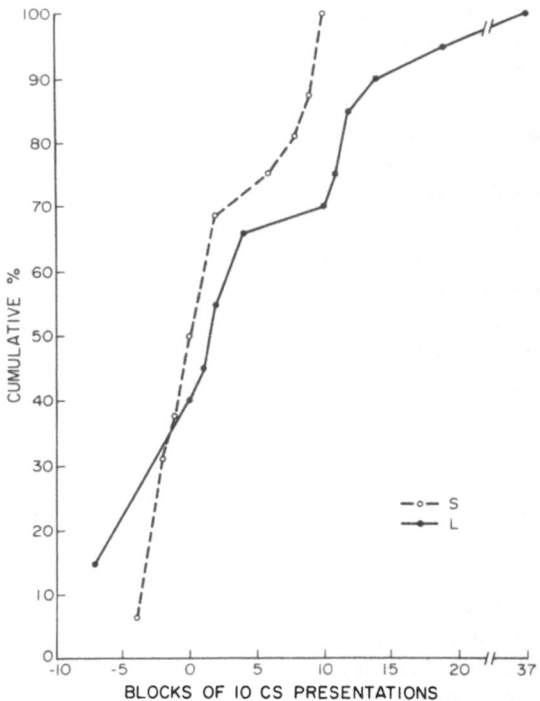

Fig. 7.1. Data illustrating the lag between behavioral conditioning and the appearance of conditioning-induced responses in a majority of hippocampal units. The abscissa represents the block in which the unit response reached conditioning criterion minus the block in which the behavioral response reached the criterion. A negative number on this scale indicates that the unit response was conditioned before the behavioral one; a positive number indicates that the behavioral conditioning preceded unit conditioning. The ordinate represents the cumulative percentages of conditionable units reaching the conditioning criteria. S is a group receiving a short period of pseudoconditioning.

used as the conditioned stimulus. Experimental conditions are then changed so that the initial learning is modified. For example, the stimulus is now paired with the unconditioned stimulus. When that is done, behavioral conditioning occurs well before the majority of hippocampal neurons respond to the conditioned stimulus (Hirsh, 1973). The lag between behavioral conditioning and the appearance of conditioning-induced unit responses in the hippocampus increases as the amount of pseudoconditioning is increased, as illustrated in Figure 7.1.

Studies of unit activity during discrimination reversal provide confirmatory evidence of a lag between changes in overt behavior and unit activity. Units in the hippocampus and related structures respond differentially to the CS+ and CS− after differential conditioning. Typically a tone, indicating that the US will occur, is followed by an increase in the firing rate of the unit, whereas a tone indicating that no US will occur does not alter or decrease the firing rate. When the roles of the tones serving as CS+ and CS− are reversed, the behavioral responses are switched before the reversal of unit responses in the hippocampus (Disterhoft & Segal, 1978) and in structures receiving efferents from the hippocampal gyrus, the anterior thalamic nuclei and cingulate cortex (Gabriel, Miller, & Saltwick, 1977). For considerable periods both tones elicit accelerated firing rates, even though behavorial responses to the new CS− have ceased (Disterhoft & Segal, 1978).

During the lag between the change in overt behavior and the change in the unit response, the unit responses cannot be said to reflect present behavior or factors responsible for it. Instead the nature of the unit responses reflects the presence of some residue of past experience, that is, a memory of some kind.

3. HIPPOCAMPAL ABLATION IN ANIMALS: AN OVERVIEW

Early studies on the effect of hippocampal ablation in animals appeared to contradict the conclusion that the hippocampus is involved in memory. Today, those and subsequent studies are taken as indications that ideas about the nature of memory in animals and about the involvement of the hippocampus in memory are in need of refinement.

The clinical report of Penfield and Milner (1958) precipitated a flood of experimentation with animals on the effects of hippocampal ablation on learning. Much to the chagrin of everyone involved, hippocampally ablated animals learn and retain at normal rates in such time-honored paradigms as classical conditioning, runway learning, simultaneous discrimination, and acquisition of operant behavior in Skinner boxes. Abnormalities on the part of hippocampally ablated animals are not observed in these paradigms until modification of initially established behavior is induced, as, for example, in the case of extinction or discrimination reversal (Douglas, 1967). Suggestions were made that the hippocampus, at least in animals, was not involved in memory but instead was necessary for inhibitory processes that were only tangentially involved in learning (Douglas, 1967; Kimble, 1968).

These suggestions can be rejected for three reasons. One is that the hypothesis that hippocampal ablation incapacitates inhibitory processes in a global fashion has been disconfirmed in several experiments (Blanchard, Blanchard, & Fial, 1970; Kaplan, 1968; Olton, 1972). Second, there is evidence that the residual learning capacities of humans and animals suffering from hippocampal lesions are not all that different. In a Skinner box scaled for humans, a patient with clinically obvious and severe anterograde amnesia was able to learn and retain a simultaneous discrimination at normal rates (Sidman, Stoddard, & Mohr, 1968). At the same time the patient was unable to recall past experience in the test situation or to predict what would happen in the coming session; nor could he explain why he was behaving as he was, despite having entirely normal linguistic capacities. Finally, animals in which hippocampal function has been incapacitated display far from subtle abnormalities during cognitive forms of learning such as latent learning (Herrmann, Black, Anchel, & Ellen, 1978; Rabe & Haddad, 1969). Thus while hippocampal ablation spares some forms of learning, it incapacitates others.

Although the psychology of learning has contemplated a variety of learning mechanisms, associative theories have been dominant. Elementary associative theories have had little trouble explaining the behavior in such paradigms as classical conditioning, runway learning, and simultaneous discrimination—those in which the behavior of hippocampally ablated animals is apparently normal. Nevertheless, a considerable number of learning theorists, unhappy with the associative position, demanded fundamental revisions. Others have advocated abandoning associationism in favor of more cognitive theories. Both groups developed elegant paradigms for demonstrating their cases. More recently, the effects of hippocampal ablation have been increasingly assayed in their paradigms in the absence of any clear understanding of hippocampal function. A rather dazzling array of abnormalities and deficiencies have been reported (see Hirsh, 1974). Hirsh (1974) and others (O'Keefe & Nadel, 1978) suggest that the hippocampus is involved in cognitive forms of memory but not in associative forms. To us, the hippocampus appears to be necessary for the acquisition, retention, and/or expression of knowledge of some kind; at the same time the brain also appears to contain an associative learning system that can function quite well without the hippocampus. According to this formulation, hippocampal dysfunction eliminates cognition, and thus ablated animals are expected to be deficient in the relatively sophisticated learning paradigms. At the same time no deficits are expected in paradigms, such as the more basic learning ones for which associative theories have adequately accounted. Modification of previously established learning, even in the basic paradigms, as in the case of extinction or reversal of a simultaneous discrimination, is held to be a case in which intact animals exercise an option to learn and know more than one thing about the same situation. Hippocampal ablation would eliminate this option and the ablated animals would appear to be abnormal.

We shall develop the idea that the hippocampus is necessary for knowledge but not necessary for associative learning in more detail below. We shall argue that the hippocampus is involved in selective retrieval, retrieval in which the effective stimulus is the result of an interaction between, rather than the sum of, component inputs. Selective retrieval, as we conceive it, is a conditional operation.

4. CONDITIONAL OPERATIONS

In a conditional operation, as we define it, a preestablished set is constrained as a result of an asymmetrical interaction between a categorical and a local operator. As illustrated in Figure 7.2, the categorical operator specifies a preestablished set or category, which is then constrained by a local condition or operator. This relation is asymmetrical in that the categorical operator does not constrain the local one. In the example of the conditional probabilities, X_1 and X_2 constrain or operate on pA; pA does not operate on X_1 and X_2.

Different local conditions can constrain the same set differently. A conditional operation allows *what may be considered the same entity* to be treated quite differently. For example, consider the statements:

$$\text{Given } X_1, pA = 0.5$$
$$\text{Given } X_2, pA = 0.01$$

where pA is the probability of the same event, A in both cases. The statements need not be considered contradictory; pA may be regarded as a set of values that includes 0.5 and 0.01. X_1 and X_2 act to constrain or qualify this set. Because X_1 and X_2 are different constraints on the same set, there is no contradiction.

As we envision them, conditional operations may involve external stimuli, motivational states, items in short-term memory, or items in long-term memory.

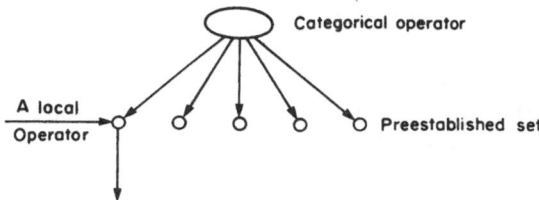

Fig. 7.2. A conditional operation. The arrows represent active channels. Inactive channels have been omitted.

4.1. Motivational States

A recent series of experiments in our laboratory modeled conditional relations between motivational states and knowledge of external stimuli. Rats were required to learn to behave differently in the presence of the same external stimuli as motivational state varied. Food was placed in one arm of a T-maze, water in the other arm. On odd-numbered days the animals were deprived of one incentive, for example, water; on even-numbered days they were deprived of the other, food.* Maximally adaptive behavior thus required opposing responses in the same external environment.

A cognitive view of this paradigm is that the animals will learn the spatial relationship between the choice point and end boxes, and that one end box contains food whereas the other contains water. The maze cues may be cast as a categorical operator activating the entire set of memories describing the choice point. Each of the motivational states may be cast as a local operator constraining this set in a different way, that is, selecting a different set of items from it. According to this view, learning in one motivational condition will be independent of learning in the other.

The associative view is that the motivational states will act as stimuli like any other stimulus. Rather than biasing the influence of the maze cues, the influence of the motivational states will be pooled with or added to that of the maze cues. The sum of these influences will determine which response occurs. During the first learning session the maze cues will become somewhat attached to the response that is reinforced during that session. In the next session they will tend to evoke the same response, regardless of which motivational state is present. Now, however, the response attached to the maze cues is incorrect. The commonality of the maze cues to both conditions is a hindrance to learning

---

*Only three widely separated trials were run each day. Between trials water was freely available to thirsty animals and food to hungry ones.

in this situation. This hindrance will cease only when the maze cues become equally attached to both responses, thereby nullifying the effect of their presence. As the influence of the maze cues is nullified there is an increase in the relative influence of motivational state. Because each of the motivational states was present only when the response satisfying it was reinforced, learning will eventually occur.

The presence of conditional operators can be assessed by plotting success in obtaining food and in obtaining water as a function of trials on the same axes for each individual animal. If conditional operations are occurring, the two curves will be independent. If summational or associative processes are operating, behavior will be similar in both conditions. Because the paradigm requires opposing responses for success in obtaining food and water, similar behavior will result in negatively correlated performance levels.

As shown in Figure 7.3, the control animals behave as if they are confronting two more or less separate problems, that is, conditionally. When control animals first learn to obtain one incentive, their performance in obtaining the other, as observed in three separate experiments, remains at chance levels. When the animals subsequently learned to obtain the other incentive, the initially achieved success was sustained. Independence between the learning curves was quantitatively assessed by computing Pearson r correlation coefficients for success rates during the first 12 sessions for each individual.* The median coefficients for control groups in three separate experiments range between $r = -0.33$ and $r = 0.45$.†

Three separate disruptions of hippocampal function have been found to produce a nonconditional form of learning. Transection of all fornix fibers (Hirsh, Leber, & Gillman, 1978), neonatal destruction of dentate granule cells by means of irradiation (Hirsh, Holt, & Mosseri, 1978), and transection of only those fornix fibers bound for the anterior thalamus (Hirsh, Davis, & Holt, 1979) all produce results typified by those in Figure 7.3B. These experimental animals behave as if they are confronting a single problem responding similarly in both deprivation conditions. At the outset of learning they tend to make just one response, so that whereas performance level in obtaining one incentive is high, the other is low. There is some indication that this stereotypy is learned (Hirsh, Holt, & Mosseri, 1978). Furthermore, even as response bias disappears, as between Trials 48 and 84 in Figure 7.3B, there is little differentiation between motivational conditions. The median correlation

---

*At any given instant different animals are behaving differently. Thus even though negative correlation was consistently observed it would be masked in group curves.
†r^2 yields an estimate of the portion of the variance in one curve that can be attributed to variance in the other.

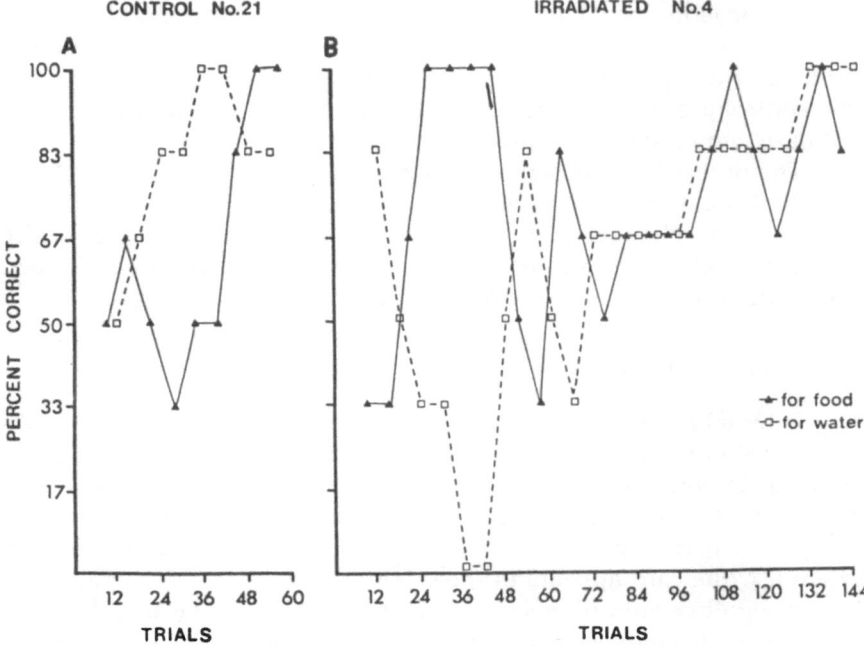

Fig. 7.3. Performance levels in obtaining food and water from different parts of the same maze are plotted on the same axes as a function of trials for an individual control animal (A) and an individual suffering from hippocampal incapacitation (B). Both of these animals used the median number of trials in reaching criterion in their respective groups. Each point on the curve represents performance during six trials. Each successive point represents the last three trials included in the preceding point plus the next three trials of that type.

coefficients for three lesional groups ranged between $r = 0.80$ and $r = -0.91$.

The similarity of the behavior of the animals with lesions in the two motivational conditions indicates that in their case the maze cues are exerting a direct or unmodulated influence over response selection, as associative theories would predict. According to associative theory the animals will be simultaneously successful in obtaining food and water only when the influence of the maze cues is nullified. Nullification will occur as the associations into which the maze cues have been incorporated are successively reinforced and nonreinforced. The effects of reinforcement and nonreinforcement will accumulate and be summed; nullification will be gradual.

The prediction that the influence of the maze cues over the behavior of the animals with lesions would be gradually nullified was assessed in the study of the effects of transsecting fornicothalamic fibers. Correlation coefficients were computed for performance levels during the last 36 trials before the beginning of criterion-level performance. The median value for the experimental group was approximately the same as that for the control group at the outset of learning, indicating a gradual decline in maze cue influence, as predicted by associative theory.

The necessity for nullification of maze cues can be relieved by placing the food and water in different mazes. Under such conditions an associative mechanism is no longer disadvantaged. The rates at which hippocampally damaged animals learn simultaneously to obtain food and water are not detectably different from those for controls.

4.2. External Stimuli

External stimuli may operate conditionally on the influence of other external stimuli. Conditional discriminations are an example. In a conditional discrimination an animal may be required to enter one end box to obtain an incentive when a black card is present in the choice point of a T-maze, and to enter the other end box to obtain the same incentive when a white card appears in the otherwise identical choice point.

A cognitive view of this paradigm is that the animal learns that each of the paths from the choice point may lead to the incentive. The choice point may be cast as the categorical operator eliciting the activation of the full set of possibilities. The cards may be cast as local operators constraining the set of memories with potential for controlling behavior one way or the other.

In contrast, the basic associative view is that the influence of the card present and the choice point are added together on every trial. The influence of the latter will be gradually nullified as the choice point is not consistently related to reinforcement. Nullification will be gradual because the effects of inconsistency must be accumulated and summed. An associative system can be expected to learn more slowly than one capable of conditional operations.

Hippocampally ablated animals are deficient in acquiring conditional discriminations, at least one involving black and white cards (Kimble, 1963). This result may be taken as an indication that hippocampal dysfunction incapacitates conditional operations forcing reliance on associative or summational processes.

In contrast to conditional discrimination, simultaneous discrimination is a paradigm that does not place summational processes at an obvious disadvantage. A simultaneous discrimination differs from a conditional one in that both discriminanda are always present, with each being placed within one of the two choices open to the animal.

Thus a correct response involves approaching one of the discriminanda, and an incorrect one involves approaching the other. The maze cues are not given the opportunity to be at odds with the discriminanda. Approach to the positive discriminanda is reinforced and so is the association between the maze cues and that response. Conversely, approaching the negative discriminanda is not reinforced and the association between maze cues and that response is weakened. Therefore, nullification of the influence of the maze cues is not necessary for the attainment of criterion. Thus an animal employing a summational strategy should not appear to be deficient in the initial acquisition of a simultaneous discrimination. As mentioned earlier, hippocampally ablated animals acquire simultaneous discriminations at normal rates, including one involving black-and-white cards (Kimble, 1963).

4.3. Short-Term or Working Memory

Information in short-term or working memory may operate conditionally upon the influence of external stimuli. Solving of sequential problems is a case in point. Sequential problems were initially intended as demonstrations of ideation. An animal was required to choose among a set of available options and then to choose another. The external stimulus was held as constant as possible in order to show that behavior was being influenced by an internal representation of what had just been done. A cognitive view is that the animals learn that on some occasions each of the choices may lead to an incentive and that on others it does not. Each option acts as a categorical operator calling forth an extensive set of memories in which it is described. A description of what has just been done, residing in working memory, acts as a local operator and constrains this set.

In contrast, the associative position is to deny that the sequential paradigm is in any way special. It holds that all inputs are added together or summed. However, the options themselves contain no information because they have been both reinforced and nonreinforced. The only possible sources of information are additional stimuli. Thus the associationists hold that each preceding response generates new stimuli, just as would moving from one part of a maze to a different part. When all else fails, kinesthetic stimuli are postulated. The associative view rejects the claim that stimuli are constant, replying that stimulus changes are simply unacknowledged by the sequential paradigm.

The literature on the effects of hippocampal lesions on the acquisition and performance of sequences is divided. There are many reports of deficits, and an approximately equal number of reports of no effect

(Hirsh, 1974). Normal acquisition appears to occur in those cases in which mediating stimuli can be detected; deficits appear in experiments where the presence of response-generated stimuli are less obvious.

In a recent series of experiments, (Pisa, 1978) the number of by-products that could result from responses was explicitly manipulated. For example, in one experiment the animal was fed in the rather wide stem of a T-shaped maze. Each arm of the maze contained a lever. Food delivery was contingent on the animal alternating between the levers on successive trials. To eliminate the possibility that kinesthetic cues arising from the last response might serve to indicate the next, baffles were inserted in the stem. In negotiating the baffles the animal had to make the same movements before every response; thus kinesthetic cues could not indicate the correct choice. The ability of hippocampally ablated rats to acquire and perform sequences dropped as the number of stimuli that could serve as mediators was reduced. These results support the interpretation that hippocampally ablated animals must rely on summational operations in the absence of conditional ones.

4.4. Long-Term Memory

Perhaps the most interesting case of conditional interaction is that between information residing in long-term memory and the influence of external stimuli. Suppose an animal is required to modify previously established learning, as in the case of reversal of a simultaneous discrimination. Conditional operations would allow retention of the initial learning under a tag or label indicating it was true in the past, whereas the new learning would be labeled as presently true. The discriminanda would serve as categorical operators calling out an extensive set of memories. This set would be constrained by whether the past or present was of interest. Retention of the previously gained knowledge is necessary for the formation of reversal sets, which are quite within the capacities of normal rats.*

In contrast, associative or summational processes would require that initial learning would have to be undone before reversal could occur. The tendency to approach the initially positive cue, which became strong during acquisition, would have to be made particularly weak; the tendency to approach the initially negative cue, which was weakened during acquisition, would have to be made particularly strong. The process would necessarily be slow.

---

*A reversal set is said to form when an animal becomes increasingly proficient at adjusting its behavior over successive reversals of the same discrimination.

Despite having no apparent problems in acquiring simultaneous discriminations, hippocampally ablated animals are severely deficient in reversing them (Hirsh, 1974; Olton, Becker, Handelmann, & Mitchell, 1980). The course followed by the lesioned animals in attaining reversal is quite different from the one they follow during the extinction of simultaneous discrimination (Kimble & Kimble, 1970; Silveira & Kimble, 1968). An associative explanation of learning by hippocampally ablated animals accounts quite well for this difference (see Hirsh, 1974, p. 435). Furthermore, when tested, hippocampally ablated animals have demonstrated no ability to form reversal (Kimble & Kimble, 1970) or extinction–reacquisition sets (Schmaltz & Theios, 1972), indicating that they are not retaining information acquired before modification of reinforcement contingencies as would be expected when summational processes are employed.

4.5. Episodic Memory

Episodic memory may be regarded as the ultimate case of a conditional operation. As defined by Schacter and Tulving in Chapter 2, episodic memories are those for events that occurred at a particular time and in a particular context. Semantic memories—facts, rules, concepts, and so on—are defined as not having this characteristic; a semantic memory is a general truth.

Semantic memories, much like episodic memories, must be constrained by context. The world is a highly variable place and there are few things that are true across all conditions. In Sections 4.1, 4.2, and 4.3, we gave examples of the conditional or contextual constraints of what appear to be semantic memories. Correct performance requires the selection of one particular truth about the stimulus among the many that the animal has learned. The last example of a conditional operation given in Section 4.4 appears to be a case of episodic memory. After initial learning, one discrimination rule was valid. After reversal, another rule was valid and both were remembered. The constraining or selective process can be the same in all four cases; a conditional operation will suffice for each. The only difference is that in the first three cases either an external stimulus, or information in short-term memory, or a motivational state acted as the local operator, whereas in the fourth case time of performance acted as the local operator. In our intuition time is just another aspect of life. Therefore we do not regard a selective process that used time as a constraining factor as being formally different from an otherwise analogous process that employed some other constraining factor. We think that semantic and episodic memories are formally alike.

5. RETRIEVEL DURING ACQUISITION

In the following sections we shall argue that the selective capacities of conditional retrieval operations are necessary for the acquisition of knowledge. These arguments may prove unsettling to those accustomed to defining retrieval as the mnemonic process that follows encoding and storage in the course of learning. Defining retrieval in this way, however, is wrong for at least three reasons.

1. The proposition that information can be retrieved only after encoding and storage are completed is true only in regard to a particular piece of information. There is no logical reason why previously acquired knowledge cannot be retrieved and employed in gaining further knowledge. Indeed, in most situations anything else is less than efficient.

2. One of the ways previously acquired knowledge can be employed is in determining which aspects of current input may be relevant to current problems, a process often termed "encoding." In most usages "encoding" implies that the code used to characterize a given input can vary radically from trial to trial. Such variation requires selection or retrieval from a group of available and potentially relevant codes. Furthermore, the selection process must incorporate at least one degree of freedom over and above those inherent in the occurrence of the input to be encoded.

3. There is little value to simply dumping information into a store. It must be entered in such a way as to be accessible under appropriate conditions. This filing of newly acquired information and subsequent retrieval of it are likely to involve many of the same operations. Thus a part of the brain carrying out one of these operations is likely to be involved in both storage and retrieval.

We shall show how retrieval or selective processes might be involved in the formation or acquisition of knowledge.

6. DIMENSIONS

Conditional operations are necessary for constructing *dimensions* from experience. A dimension is a set of mutually exclusive and exhaustive event classes or values (Hays, 1973). In particular, conditional operations are necessary to determine which values are mutually exclusive.

As an example, we will show how a set of values comprising a dimension can be determined from experiencing circles that may be red or blue and 5 or 25 square inches in area. The first step is to ascertain which properties are common to all items being considered, which, in this example, is being round. The property defines the category to which all of the items being considered belong. The second step is to ascertain the properties of the individual items. Examining one of the items requires that the category be constrained to one particular item. The selected item may be round, blue, and 5 square inches in area. The other individual items may be round, blue, and 25 square inches; or round, red, and 5 square inches; or round, red, and 25 square inches. The properties that are not common to all items are red, blue, 5 square inches, and 25 square inches.

The next step is to select one of these properties, for example, blue, and use it to define a subcategory, "blue circles." This step requires two instances of constraint on preestablished sets or categories. One is the selection of the property "blue" from the set properties that are not common to the circles; the other is the constraint of the category "circles" to the subcategory "blue circles." Now, the properties not common to the items in the subcategory "blue circles" must be ascertained. Examining the individuals within the subcategory requires constraining it to individual members. The individual items in the subcategory may be round, blue, and 5 square inches or round, blue, and 25 square inches. Note that none of the members of the subcategory "blue circles" is red, whereas some of the members of the more inclusive "category" circles are. The converse result will be obtained after the subcategory "red circles" has been selected. Blue and red may thus be regarded as mutually exclusive alternatives and thus as different values along the same dimension. Similarly, the subcategories "5-square-inch circles" and "25-square-inch circles" may be used to determine whether 5 square inches and 25 square inches are mutually exclusive, and thus whether they are values along a dimension. Furthermore, because a member of the subcategories "blue circles" or "red circles" can be either 5 or 25 square inches, it can be concluded that the latter values are not alternatives to blue or red and are thus values along a different dimension.

We do not wish to be misleading. Note that red and blue have been established as mutually exclusive alternatives only in the context of the category "circles". If they are to be considered values along a more generally applicable dimension, they must be shown to be mutually exclusive in the context of other categories.

The values along a dimension are in one way the same and in another way different. For example, 5 square inches is not 25 square inches, but both are values along the same dimension "area." To say that two or more items are at once the same and different is no small trick.

Conditional operations permit items in a set to be considered the same in one way and different in another, because they have the capacity to constrain categories. A category is a set of items having properties in common. The criteria for inclusion in the category make no reference to the variation among the members. Within the boundaries of the category all of the members are equivalent. Within a conditional process, the categorical operator names or specifies the set of equivalent items. The available local operators have the capacity to name or specify individuals within the category. The interaction between a particular categorical and a particular local operator will select one of the members of the category. Comparison is now possible between the properties of the selected member and the properties listed within the criteria for inclusion in the category. Such comparison in turn permits the way in which the items differ to be distinguished from the way in which they are the same.

Summational processes discard variation. For example, the sum 27 can result from any number of possible sets of values that are to be added together. Thus summational processes are incapable of selecting a particular individual from a preestablished set. Consequently, they are insufficient for determining how a particular member of a preestablished set differs from the other members of that set. This is, because they cannot specify individuals, summational processes alone are not able to establish that certain values are mutually exclusive alternatives along the same dimension.

However, precisely because summational processes discard variation between entries they are capable of determining the way in which they are the same. In doing so, they are capable of establishing a category. An established category is a prerequisite for a conditional operation.

The presence and utilization of dimensions in this sense was not contemplated in the earliest versions of associationism. Dimensions as such were introduced into the psychology of learning by opponents of associationism who held that discrimination learning involves apprehension of the relation between the cues rather than the development of an approach or an avoidance response to one particular dimension cue. To prove their point, these theorists developed the transposition paradigm (Kohler, 1929). In one version of transposition, animals learn that a large circle indicates the position of the incentive whereas a small one indicates no incentive. After the discrimination is learned, the animal is presented with a choice between an even larger circle and the largest of the two previously employed circles. If the animal has learned to go to the larger of the circles, it will approach the novel circle, or transpose. Conversely, when presented with a choice between the small circle and an even smaller one, it will reject the novel stimulus and go to the larger of the two, even though that particular circle initially indicated no incentive. Normal animals do indeed transpose.

Although basic associative theories such as those of Spence (1940) were subsequently adjusted to account for transposition, they held and continue to hold that the animal has learned to approach one discriminandum and not to approach the other. The developers of the transposition paradigm interpreted the associative position as predicting that the animal would favor the positive cue when it was pared with the novel circle and not favor the negative one. That is, in fact, what hippocampally ablated animals do (Winocur & Mills, 1970).

7. TRANSFORMATIONS

In constructing a dimension from experience it is necessary to distinguish the way in which a set of objects differ from the way in which they are the same. Our intuition is that an analogous requirement must be met in constructing transformation rules from experience. Thus we think conditional operations are also necessary in the latter case.

A transformation rule describes how the state of some object or entity can be changed. Constructing a transformation rule requires distinguishing the way in which the object changes during some action from the way in which it remains the same. That is, throughout the course of the action some properties of the object remain unchanged, whereas others are present only at one particular phase of the action. For example, the color and shape of a door do not change during the course of pushing it. However, the door is open only at the beginning of the push and closed only at the end of it. Those properties that remain constant throughout the action identify the object. Those that are present only during particular phases of the action constitute a transformation. Because the latter properties are mutually exclusive (a closed door is never open, and vice versa), a transformation can be considered to be related to dimensions. Determining whether the properties of the object are common to all phases of the action requires listing its properties during each particular phase. To list the properties during one phase, it is necessary to select that phase. To determine whether a property that appears in one list is present in the other, it is necessary to select that property. Both selections are constraints on established sets; they are conditional operations.

As we have noted, summational processes are incapable of selecting individuals within a category. Thus by themselves they are incapable of formulating transformation rules from experience. At the same time, transformation rules cannot be formulated until the entity involved is identified. Here, discarding variation is extremely useful. The summational process may be thought of as isolating the entity from the states it assumes.

The early versions of associationism did not contemplate transformations. Responses were defined in terms of the movements involved. This view was first challenged by Lashley (1921), who demonstrated that maze learning survived crippling of the means of locomotion employed during its acquisition. The animal had learned to go from one place to another, to change its position in space rather than make particular limb movements. It learned to transform its location from one position in space to another. This and other experiments eventually led both associationists and cognitivists to define learned responses in terms of the changes that resulted from them.

The ability to generate and/or utilize relatively abstract transformations is diminished by hippocampal ablation. The learned responses of hippocampally ablated animals are in many instances more aptly described in terms of their constituent movements than in terms of the consequences they engender (Hirsh, 1974). For example, hippocampally ablated animals that have experienced electric shocks on a grid following conditioned stimulus presentations learn to run rather than leave the grid. If the conditioned stimulus is presented while such an animal is out of the way of harm, it will run, a response that often carries the animal onto the grid (Black, Nadel, & O'Keefe, 1977).

8. RELATIONS BETWEEN CONDITIONAL AND SUMMATIONAL SYSTEMS

Up to now, we have been attributing the difference between hippocampally ablated and intact animals to the loss of conditional or cognitive processes. At the same time, we have attributed the residual learning capacities of the ablated animals to the presence of a summational or associative system, which in some cases is capable of addressing the same problems as the cognitive one. This approach, as Abe Black first realized, implies that both cognitive and associative systems are present within a normal brain. Hippocampal ablation does not somehow inject the associative system into the brain. Instead it incapacitates the cognitive one, leaving the associative one free to dominate the field.

When two systems addressing the same substantive matters are thought to be present in the nervous system, it is wise to consider how they might be related to each other. There are two, not necessarily mutually exclusive, possibilities. One is that, on occasion, the two systems compete, supplanting one another. Indeed, there is some evidence that the two systems do compete; this possibility is discussed below. The second possibility is that the two systems can, on occasion, cooperate with and complement each other. As we discussed earlier, the formation or identification of dimensions and transformations requires both conditional and summational systems. An interplay between conditional and summational processes is particularly crucial to the formation of hierarchies.

8.1. Complementarity during the Formation of Hierarchies

Forming hierarchies requires the addition of categories that are both more inclusive and more abstract than those already present. Summational processes are capable of increasing inclusivity but not abstractness. However, once summational processes have produced a more inclusive category, conditional operations may be employed to produce more abstract dimensions that can be used to define more abstract categories.

8.1.1. Inclusivity as Opposed to Abstractness

Summational processes are effective as a result of isolating consistencies. The constancy across two categories, for example, one defined by the properties "round," "blue" and the other by the properties "round," "red," is the property "round." The category of round items is indeed more inclusive than either the category of round, red items or that of round, blue items. However, the more inclusive category is in no way on a higher level of organization. The properties that define it are also used to define the less inclusive categories. The only change has been a deletion of properties, in this case red and blue. Thus the addition of the new category does not contribute any information not already present in the system. Note that the properties that define a category are independent of each other, which is why some of them can be retained whereas others are deleted in forming a more inclusive category.

In contrast to summational processes, conditional ones allow the properties "red" and "blue" to be considered mutually exclusive within the category "round." By virtue of being exclusive alternatives, they can be considered to be related as values along a dimension. Because a dimension rests on a relation between values, it can be considered to be on a *new,* higher-order, or more abstract level of organization than are the properties corresponding to the values. Thus it is possible to say that the dimension "color" is more abstract than the properties of being red or blue. The construction of the dimension provides the system with additional information. For example, the term "color" refers to something quite different from shape, another equally abstract dimension. "Red," in contrast, may refer to any shape with that attribute.

8.1.2. *Construction of Hierarchies*

Constructing a hierarchy from experience requires increases in both inclusivity and abstraction. A hierarchy is a stratified system in which the elements on each successively higher level operate in domains that are both more inclusive and more abstract than do elements at the lower level. For example, in a military hierarchy, generals are responsible for armies, colonels for regiments. The information-processing capacity of an element at a higher level is not necessarily greater than that of a lower-level element. When a colonel becomes a general, his capacity for processing information is not changed. Therefore, if the elements at a higher level are to operate in a more inclusive domain, they must leave details to elements at lower levels. The more detailed operations of the lower-level element must, therefore, be determined by factors local to the lower level as well as input from the highest level.

In order to add a still higher level to an already existing hierarchy, it is necessary to ensure that the categories present at the new level will be more inclusive than those already present. One way to increase inclusivity is to isolate those properties that are common to the lists of criteria for inclusion in categories existing at a lower level of the hierarchy, presumably by means of a summational process. However, isolating the properties of categories that have already been built into the hierarchy adds nothing new to the hierarchy. The categories in the layer to be added to the top of an existing hierarchy must not only be more inclusive but also more abstract. For example, generals base their decisions on considerably more than those items that are common to the reports of their colonels.

More abstract categories may be obtained once dimensions have been drawn from those categories present at the highest already existing level. As a result of applying conditional operations, some of the properties that differentiate the members of a particular category will be found to be mutually exclusive alternatives to each other. These properties can be considered to be values along the same dimension. Because the dimension is a relational term, it is not a property of any one member of the existing category. The dimension is a new term because it relates items within the category to each other; it can thus be considered a higher-order property of the category. Let us suppose the same dimension can be drawn from other categories at the highest existing level of the hierarchy. This dimension can then be considered a higher-order property common to those categories and can serve as a criterion for inclusion in a category that is both more abstract and more inclusive.

For example, the members of the category "cheese" do not all taste the same, but taste is an important dimension of cheese. Similarly, the members of the category "fruit" do not taste the same, but taste is an important dimension or attribute of both this category and the category "cheese." Thus it can serve as a criterion for including these categories within the category "food." More abstract dimensions in turn may be formed comparing the members of the newer, more abstract category to each other. The pleasure in eating different foods varies considerably more than that in eating different fruits or cheeses. Thus the dimension "pleasure" may be used to define the category "incentives." In this way, a hierarchy of any number of levels may be erected.

Doubtless much if not most of the hierarchical organization of the nervous system is embodied in its innate structure.* However, innate stratification cannot account for the degree of abstraction that at least one species, Homo sapiens, can attain. The human mind appears capable of an infinite degree of abstraction. In contrast, the innate stratification of the nervous system is limited by the skull.

A system with a limited number of structurally defined strata can attain an infinite degree of abstraction only by resorting to recursive operations on memory. A recursive system is able to use items already retained in memory to generate new, more abstract items that will also be retained and available for use in generating still more abstract items. An interplay between conditional and summational systems using dimensions and categories acquired during the erection of hierarchies is an example of recursion. To us the hippocampus appears to be operating conditionally on memory at the level of abstraction at which memory must be utilized in generating further hierarchical organization.

8.2. Some Asides

Dimensions and transformations are usually thought of as either more abstract, more inclusive, or of a higher order than particular values or states. For example, the dimension "color" is more abstract or general than the color red in that it relates red, green, blue, and so on. The concept of dimension was employed by both associationists and cognitivists to account for observations of a higher order of perceptual learning. Certain species, for example, are capable of forming discrimination sets based on color. Having learned to discriminate between red and blue squares, for instance, they will pay attention to differences between colors, even those not involving red and blue, in future discriminations.

Similarly, transformations are considered to be either somewhat abstract or general. The transformation of going to one place from an-

---

*We would argue that in these cases an interplay between conditional and summational processes occurred within the realm of the genetic information.

other applies equally well to running, swimming, or climbing. The concept of transformation was employed by both the associationists and the cognitivists to explain observations of higher-order responses. For example, rats that have learned to negotiate a dry maze, which involves running, have no navigational problems when it is flooded and they must swim (MacFarland, 1930). It is concluded that a higher-order response has been learned that encompasses both running and swimming, namely, going to a particular place.

8.2.1. Control of Behavior

Conditional operations are necessary if already formed hierarchies are to accomplish anything. The chief obstacle for the expression of hierarchical organization is that by definition the details of operation of a lower hierarchical level are not represented within the operations of a higher level. Thus the higher level cannot completely determine the operations of the lower level, raising the question of how the lower level does operate. For example, learning that instructs the animal to transform geographic location by going from one place to another says nothing explicit about limb movements or muscle contractions; yet the transformation cannot occur without them.

The answer to this problem lies in treating the input from the more abstract level as a command that is supplemented by input local to the operational sphere of the lower level. The interaction between the command from the higher level and the local input determines the operations of the lower level.

Because the categorical and local operators play different roles with respect to each other, the conditional operation is ideal for supplementary abstract commands with local information. The abstract command may be cast as a categorical operator, specifying a set of various movements that all produce a particular kind of transformation. For example, transformation of geographic locations specifies locomotory movements, a set that includes running, swimming, climbing, and so on. This set would be further constrained by an input that was local to the less abstract level. For instance, in the presence of a dry, flat surface, running is the appropriate method of achieving locomotion. When the space to be traversed is inundated, swimming is the appropriate method for transforming geographic position. In effect, the conditional operation translates the abstract command into more detailed terms.

8.2.2. Hierarchical Perception

Once dimensions are present in a hierarchy, both summational and conditional processes are capable of determining which dimension will encode input, for example, shape rather than some other dimension is to be treated as the important aspect of particular discrimination cues.

A tenable associative theory, embodying summational logic, of how input comes to be encoded in terms of a particular dimension has been advanced by Sutherland and MacKintosh (1971). According to this theory, for example, the influence of an analyzer that is sensitive to each of the values along a particular dimension is changed during the course of discrimination. When the operation of the analyzer is followed by reinforcement, the tendency of the analyzer to encode the input increases. When nonreinforcement follows, the tendency of the analyzer to encode the input decreases. The cumulative effects of reinforcement and nonreinforcement can lead to a strong differential among the influence of the various analyzers present.

A predominant analyzer will operate when values along the dimension to which it is responsive are present. When subsequent discriminations involve new values along the previously relevant dimension, positive transfer occurs. However, when a previously irrelevant dimension is made relevant (and the previously relevant dimension irrelevant), the effects of the subsequent learning will necessarily undo those of the previous learning. Thus associative or summational processes operating on the level of dimensions are as inflexible as they are on the level of simple stimuli (see Section 3.).

Using a conditional process to select the dimension that will encode input allows preservation of flexibility, as well as efferent control. Only a certain number of dimensions are relevant to an input. The input can be cast as a categorical operator specifying a set of dimensions. Efferent signals, originating centrally and going to more peripheral parts of a perceptual system, can be cast as local operators. Each efferent signal would constrain the set of dimensions to one, which would be applied to encoding the input. Different efferent signals would select different dimensions. When the efferent signal changed, the replaced dimension would momentarily lose its influence on behavior. However, its potential for influencing behavior over the long term would not be diminished.

8.2.3. The Engram

An interplay between conditional and summational mnemonic systems has important implications for those interested in the neural basis of information storage or memory. The division of this field, not unnaturally, reflects the fact that the cognitive and associative schools advocate different forms of or formats for acquired information. This argument, however, is irrelevant to those trying to determine its form within the nervous system. Once one appreciates that the output of a cognitive-conditional process can serve as the input to an associative-summational one and vice versa, it is .clear that at the very least the information produced by one kind of system has to be in a format that can be translated into a form that can be utilized by the other kind of system. The didactic argument between the cognitive and associative theorists is sustained only by ignorance of the roles played by conditional and summational operations and thus of their complementarity.

8.3. Summational Systems as an Alternative to Conditional Ones

It is logically possible, however, for the most abstract hierachy to be subverted by associative processes. In some situations, options as to how the lower level is to go about its business are not necessary. In these cases the signal from the higher level is sufficient to elicit the lower level's response and thus associative proceses are adequate.

There is some evidence that such subversion actually occurs. Maier (1929) developed a number of paradigms in which the use of knowledge of spatial relations within a triangular maze was pitted against the tendency to perform habits based on movements. The results of these experiments were not clear-cut. The behavior of some animals appeared to be in a cognitive mode, that of others in an associative mode, with the balance being subject to experimental conditions. This situation was recently reexamined. Early in learning the animals are likely to employ spatial relations, particularly when correction procedures are used. If during training the same movements are allowed to be repeatedly successful, they will be employed by the animal when habit is pitted against cognition.* Incapacitation of hippocampal function not only eliminates the occurrence of cognitive behavior in Maier paradigms (Herrman et al., 1978; Rabe & Haddad, 1969) but also eliminates the advantage that correction procedures bestow in some instances of learning (Hirsh, 1974).

One of us (R. H.) has observed a similar phenomenon in his own behavior. I am generally good about learning geographic relations and generally use them in finding my way. When I first came to Montreal I lived in an area separated from the rest of the city by Mount Royal. Consequently the first part of the route to all destinations within the city was always the same. The overwhelming majority of my trips were to work. On several occasions when I was intending to go elsewhere my mind wandered to other topics; I was surprised to find that I had not diverged from the route to the campus.

A similar subversion of cognitive-conditional processes by associative-summational ones could account for the survival (in humans who

*Abe Black, personal communication, 1978.

have undergone hippocampal ablation) of long-established memories and of intellectual skills, as assessed in IQ tests, for adults. Long-established memories and certain intellectual skills are in some senses highly practiced and dominant.

9. SUMMARY

From our vantage point, the hippocampus appears very important for the acquisition and expression of knowledge by virtue of its involvement in conditional retrieval. However, the hippocampus does not appear necessary for the operation of a summational-associative learning system that is also present in the brain.

In some cases the conditional-cognitive system and the summational-associative one appear to compete with one another for control over behavior. However, it is also clear that the computational capabilities of conditional and summational operations are complementary. In forming dimensions and transformations, summational operations are necessary precursors of conditional ones. Furthermore, both types of logic are necessary if extensive abstraction is to be achieved.

Finally, it should be noted that conditional operations do not make exotic demands on neurophysiology. The interactions discussed by Bohus in Chapter 5 between influences that elicit excitative or inhibitive postsynaptic potentials and those that are modulatory are asymmetrical in the same way as is the interaction between the categorical and local operators. Within a conditional operation, one operator can be regarded as being the immediate cause of output; the other operator may be thought of as exerting a powerful selective bias on it.

10. REFERENCES

Black, A. H., Nadel, L., & O'Keefe, J. Hippocampal function in avoidance learning and punishment. *Psychological Bulletin*, 1977, *84*, 1107–1129.

Blanchard, R. J., Blanchard, D. C., & Fial, R. A. Hippocampal lesions in rats and their effects on activity avoidance, and aggression. *Journal of Comparative and Physiological Psychology*, 1970, *71*, 92–102.

Disterhoft, J. F., & Segal, M. Neuron activity in rat hippocampus and motor activity during discrimination reversal. *Brain Research Bulletin*, 1978, *3*, 583–588.

Douglas, R. J. The hippocampus and behavior. *Psychological Bulletin*, 1967, *67*, 416–442.

Estes, W. K. Toward a statistical theory of learning. *Psychological Review*, 1950, *57*, 94–109.

Gabriel, M., Miller, J. D., & Saltwick, S. E. Unit activity in cingulate cortex and antero-ventral thalamus of the rabbit during different conditioning and reversal. *Journal of Comparative and Physiological Psychology*, 1977, *91*, 423–433.

Hays, W. L. *Statistics for the social sciences.* New York: Holt, Rinehart & Winston, 1973.

Herrman, T., Black, A. H., Anchel, H., & Ellen, P. Comparison of septal and fornical lesioned rats' performance on the Maier three-table reasoning task. *Physiology and behavior*, 1978, *20*, 297–302.

Hirsh, R. Previous stimulus experience delays conditioning induced changes in hippocampal unit responses in rats. *Journal of Comparative and Physiological Psychology*, 1973, *83*, 337–345.

Hirsh, R. The hippocampus and contextual retrieval of information from memory: A theory. *Behavioral Biology*, 1974, *12*, 421–444.

Hirsh, R., Leber, B., & Gillman, K. Fornix fibers and motivational states as controls of behavior: A study stimulated by the contextual retrieval theory. *Behavioral Biology*, 1978, *22*, 463–478.

Hirsh, R., Davis, R., & Holt, L. Fornico-thalamus fibers, motivational states, and contextual retrieval. *Experimental Neurology*, 1979, *65*, 373–390.

Hirsh, R., Holt, L., & Mosseri, A. Hippocampal mossy fibers, motivational states, and contextual retrieval. *Experimental Neurology*, 1978, *62*, 68–79.

Hull, C. L. *Principles of behavior*. New York: Appleton-Century-Crofts, 1943.

Kaplan, J. Approach and inhibitory reaction in rats after bilateral hippocampal lesions. *Journal of Comparative and Physiological Psychology*, 1968, *65*, 279–281.

Kimble, D. P. The effects of bilateral hippocampal lesions in rats. *Journal of Comparative and Physiological Psychology*, 1963, *56*, 272–283.

Kimble, D. P. Hippocampus and internal inhibition. *Psychological Bulletin*, 1968, *70*, 285–295.

Kimble, D. P., & Kimble, R. J. The effect of hippocampal lesions on extinction and "hypothesis" behavior in rats. *Physiology and Behavior*, 1970, *5*, 735–738.

Kohler, W. *Gestalt psychology*. New York: Liverwright, 1929.

Lashley, K. S. Studies of cerebral function in learning. III. The motor areas. *Brain*, 1921, *44*, 255–286.

MacFarland, D. A. The role of kinesthesis in maze learning. *University of California Publications in Psychology*, 1930, *4*, 277–305.

Maier, N. R. F. Reasoning in white rats. *Comparative and Physiological Monograph*, 1929, *6*, 1–93.

O'Keefe, J., & Nadel, L. *The hippocampus as a cognitive map*. New York: Oxford University Press, 1978.

Olton, D. S. Behavioral and neuroanatomical differentiation of response-suppression and response-shift mechanisms in the rat. *Journal of Comparative and Physiological Psychology*, 1972, *78*, 450–456.

Olton, D. S., Becker, J. T., Handelmann, G. E., & Mitchell, S. J. Hippocampal function: Working memory on cognitive mapping. *Physiological Psychology*, 1980, *8*, 239–246.

Penfield, W., & Milner, B. Memory deficit produced by bilateral lesions in the hippocampal zone. *Archives of Neurology and Psychiatry*, 1958, *79*, 475–497.

Pisa, M. A. *On the role of the hippocampus in episodic memory*. Unpublished doctoral dissertation, McGill University, 1978.

Rabe, A., & Haddad, R. K. Integration deficit after hippocampal lesions. *Proceedings of the 77th Annual Convention of the American Psychological Association*, 1969, *4*, 213–214.

Schmaltz, L. W., & Theios, J. Acquisition and extinction of a classically conditioned response in hippocampectomized rabbits (Oryctologous cuniculus). *Journal of Comparative and Physiological Psychology*, 1972, *79*, 328–334.

Sidman, M., Stoddard, L. T., & Mohr, J. P. Some additional quantitative observations of immediate memory in a patient with bilateral hippocampal lesions. *Neuropsychologia*, 1968, *6*, 245–254.

Silveira, J. M., & Kimble, D. P. Brightness discrimination and reversal in hippocampally lesioned rats. *Physiology and Behavior*, 1968, *3*, 625–630.

Spence, K. W. Continuous versus non-continuous interpretations of discrimination learning. *Psychological Review*, 1940, *47*, 271–288.

Sutherland, N. S., & MacKintosh, N. J. *Mechanisms of animal discrimination learning.* New York: Academic Press, 1971.

Tolman, E. C. Cognitive maps in rats and men. *Psychological Review*, 1948, *55*, 189–208.

Winocur, G., & Mills, J. A. Transfer between related and unrelated problems following hippocampal lesions in rats. *Journal of Comparative and Physiological Psychology*, 1970, *73*, 162–169.

8

Motivation, Activation, and Behavioral Integration

David L. Wolgin

1. INTRODUCTION

The lateral hypothalamus has long been regarded as an important neural substrate for the expression of motivated behavior. Electrical or chemical stimulation of the hypothalamus can elicit a wide range of species-typical responses, including feeding, drinking, attack, and mating (see, e.g., Myers, 1974; Roberts, 1970). Conversely, ablation of the hypothalamus disrupts the natural counterparts of these elicited behaviors (Anand & Brobeck, 1951; Brookhart & Dey, 1941; Caggiula, Antelman, & Zigmond, 1973; Hitt, Hendricks, Ginsberg, & Lewis, 1970; Karli & Vergnes, 1964; Teitelbaum & Epstein, 1962; Teitelbaum & Stellar, 1954; Wolgin & Teitelbaum, 1978). Historically, these results have been attributed to the direct manipulation of hypothalamic circuits mediating specific motivational states (e.g., Hoebel, 1975; Roberts, 1969, 1970; Stellar, 1954). However, during the past decade three lines of evidence have suggested that circuits subserving relatively nonspecific functions are also importantly involved. First, Valenstein and his colleagues have shown that the hypothalamic circuits mediating feeding and drinking are more "plastic" than previously thought (Valenstein, Cox, & Kakolewski, 1970). For example, feeding elicited by electrical stimulation of the hypothalamus can be transformed to drinking simply by replacing

DAVID L. WOLGIN ● Department of Psychology, Florida Atlantic University, Boca Raton, Florida 33431.

the rat's food with a drinking tube containing water (Valenstein, Cox, & Kakolewski, 1968). A second line of evidence comes from recent analyses of the effects of lateral hypothalamic lesions. This work has shown that the loss of motivated behavior that results from such lesions is accompanied by impairments in sensorimotor capacities and tonic arousal (Levitt & Teitelbaum, 1975; Marshall & Teitelbaum, 1974; Marshall, Turner, & Teitelbaum, 1971; Wolgin & Teitelbaum, 1978). The third line of evidence is perhaps the most telling, because it provides a neuroanatomic substrate for these "nonspecific" effects of lateral hypothalamic damage. This is Ungerstedt's discovery that many of the behavioral deficits that result from destruction of the lateral hypothalamus can be attributed to interruption of the nigrostriatal bundle, which connects the substantia nigra with the striatum and passes through the lateral hypothalamus (Ungerstedt, 1970, 1971).*

Taken together, these findings have prompted a reassessment of earlier views regarding the contribution of the hypothalamus to the expression of motivated behavior (cf. Marshall & Teitelbaum, 1977; Mogenson & Phillips, 1976; Stricker & Zigmond, 1976; Teitelbaum, Schallert, De Ryck, Whishaw, & Golani, 1980; Teitelbaum, Schallert, Whishaw, & Golani, 1983; Valenstein et al., 1970). As a consequence, there is now less emphasis on the role of the hypothalamus in the integration of homeostatic signals and greater emphasis on the role of hypothalamic circuits in the integration of behavior. In the first part of this chapter, I shall review some of the evidence for this new perspective, giving particular emphasis to the effects of lateral hypothalamic lesions. In brief, the data suggest that the destruction of neural circuits running through the hypothalamus can temporarily abolish the expression of all forms of motivated behavior. During the ensuing period of recovery, the animal's responses are initially very fragmented, but gradually become more integrated. In succeeding sections I shall suggest that the underlying basis for such behavioral fragmentation is the loss of endogenous activation. I shall then discuss the role of activation in recovery and in normal infantile development. In the final section, I shall turn to some recent developments regarding the neurophysiological basis of activation. It is often assumed that activation is mediated by the brainstem reticular formation and reflected in cortical electroen-

*That is not to deny that cells intrinsic to the lateral hypothalamus are specifically involved in feeding and drinking. For example, several studies have shown that intrahypothalamic injections of kainic acid, which destroys cell bodies but not fibers of passage, produce an initial aphagia and adipsia after which the animals recover but display persistent regulatory deficits. Impairments in sensorimotor capacities and tonic arousal are not found in such animals (Grossman, Dacey, Halaris, Collier, & Routtenberg, 1978; Stricker, Swerdloff, & Zigmond, 1978).

cephalographic desynchronization and hippocampal theta (Green & Arduini, 1954; Moruzzi & Magoun, 1949). However, recent findings have challenged these long-standing beliefs. As we shall see, the data suggest that both the reticular formation and the electroencephalographic activity it generates are more directly involved with the expression of behavior than previously recognized.

2. BEHAVIORAL FRAGMENTATION AND REINTEGRATION FOLLOWING LATERAL HYPOTHALAMIC DAMAGE

2.1. Ingestive Behavior

A prototypical example of behavioral fragmentation and reintegration following lateral hypothalamic damage is the "lateral hypothalamic syndrome." Bilateral lesions of the lateral hypothalamus (Teitelbaum & Epstein, 1962) or more selective destruction of the dopaminergic nigrostriatal bundle (Stricker & Zigmond, 1976; Ungerstedt, 1971) results in the complete cessation of feeding (aphagia) and drinking (adipsia), followed by recovery of ingestion in four stages. In Stage 1, the animals refuse water and all foods, no matter how palatable, and steadily lose weight. Some animals will chew and swallow food placed in their mouths, but they will not initiate feeding even if the food is located nearby. During this stage they must be force-fed and hydrated, or they will die of starvation. In Stage 2, fragmentary feeding occurs. The animals eat small amounts of palatable foods and fluids but they do not eat long enough to ingest sufficient calories to maintain their body weight, and they continue to refuse water. They are therefore anorexic and adipsic. In Stage 3, feeding becomes more integrated. The animals now eat sufficient quantities of palatable foods and fluids to maintain and, later, to increase their body weight, and they adjust their caloric intake when their diet is diluted. However, because they still do not drink water, they do not eat dry chow, which is itself dehydrating, unless provided with acceptable fluids or hydrated by injections of saline. Finally, in Stage 4, drinking returns. Even then, however, more subtle "regulatory" deficits persist. For example, unlike normal animals, "recovered" lateral hypothalamic rats do not increase their food intake in response to large decreases in glucose utilization produced by injections of insulin or 2-deoxyglucose (Epstein & Teitelbaum, 1967; Kanner & Balagura, 1971; Miselis & Epstein, 1971; Wayner, Cott, Millner, & Tartaglione, 1971; but see Stricker, Friedman, & Zigmond, 1975). Furthermore, such rats do not drink in response to a variety of hydrational challenges (e.g., injection of hypertonic saline or polyethylene glycol) under conditions that evoke substantial drinking in normal rats (Epstein & Teitelbaum, 1964; Stricker & Wolf, 1967; but see Rowland, 1976; Stricker, 1976). Thus, even in Stage 4, the neural controls of ingestive behavior are not fully reintegrated.

2.2. Predatory Attack

Feeding and drinking are not the only motivated behaviors disrupted by lateral hypothalamic lesions. Predatory attack shows similar fragmentation and reintegration (Wolgin & Teitelbaum, 1978; see also Gybels, Meulders, Callens, & Colle, 1967; Jimerson & Reis, 1973). In the early postoperative period, cats with lateral hypothalamic lesions totally ignore a mouse, even when it walks directly across their path. If prodded on the snout with the mouse, such cats can sometimes be induced to grasp it by the scruff of the neck, but they then lapse into somnolence with the mouse still dangling from their jaws (Figure 8.1). However, as they begin to recover, elements of the integrated sequence of attack gradually reappear. At first the cats only track the mouse with their eyes and head, but do not approach it. Later in recovery, they approach and briefly stalk the mouse, but quickly lose interest, particularly if the mouse remains stationary. Still later they stalk, pounce on, and trap the mouse with their forepaws, but they do not make a killing bite. Eventually, the integrated pattern of orienting, stalking, trapping, biting, and eating returns.

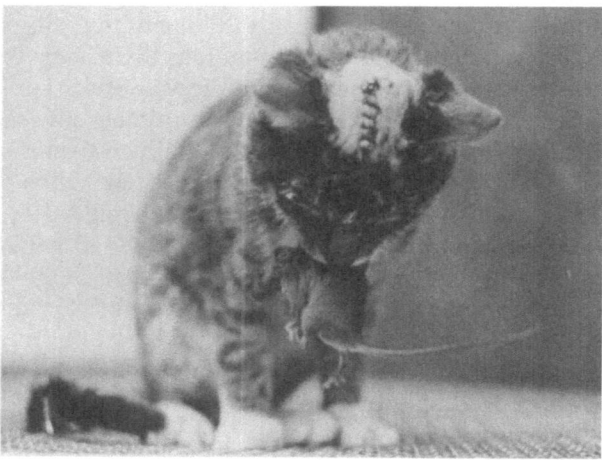

Fig. 8.1. Cat with lateral hypothalamic damage falls asleep with mouse dangling from its jaws.

2.3. Sensorimotor Dysfunctions

These disturbances in motivated behavior are accompanied by the disintegration of more basic sensorimotor capacities. For example, early in recovery, animals with lateral hypothalamic lesions or nigrostriatal bundle damage display multimodal sensory neglect. This impairment has several facets. First, the animals do not orient to auditory, visual, tactile, or olfactory stimuli (Feeney & Wier, 1979; Levitt & Teitelbaum, 1975; Ljungberg & Ungerstedt, 1976a; Marshall & Teitelbaum, 1974; Marshall, Turner, & Teitelbaum, 1971; Marshall, Richardson, & Teitelbaum, 1974; Schallert & Whishaw, 1978; Turner, 1973; Wolgin & Teitelbaum, 1978). Second, they do not show forelimb placing reflexes in response to proprioceptive, tactile, or visual stimulation (Grijalva & Lindholm, 1980; Ljungberg & Ungerstedt, 1976a; Marshall & Teitelbaum, 1974; Marshall et al., 1971; Marshall et al., 1974; Sechzer, Ervin, & Smith, 1973; Turner, 1973; Wolgin & Teitelbaum, 1978; Wolgin, Hein, & Teitelbaum, 1980). Finally, the animals are cataleptic; that is, they do not make postural adjustments when their limbs or bodies are placed in awkward positions (kinesthetic neglect; see Figure 8.2; Balagura, Wilcox, & Coscina, 1969; Levitt & Teitelbaum, 1975; Marshall, Levitan, & Stricker, 1976; Schallert, Whishaw, De Ryck, & Teitelbaum, 1978; Teitelbaum & Wolgin, 1975; Wolgin & Teitelbaum, 1978). However, as with feeding and attack, sensorimotor capacities gradually recover during the ensuing weeks.

2.4. Akinesia

Animals with lateral hypothalamic damage are also akinetic (Golani, Wolgin, & Teitelbaum, 1979; Levitt & Teitelbaum, 1975; Marshall et al., 1976; Robinson & Whishaw, 1974; Wolgin & Teitelbaum, 1978).* Although akinesia is often viewed as a unitary phenomenon (i.e., lack of movement), it too represents a state of behavioral fragmentation. Thus quantitative analysis of recovery from akinesia using the Eshkol-Wachmann movement notation system has shown that akinesia involves deficits along several dimensions of movement. During recovery, movements in each dimension return independently at different rates (Golani et al., 1979). Lateral movement recovers first. Initially the rat makes only small-amplitude movements of the head along the floor. Later in recovery, the amplitude of these lateral scans increases and

*Similarly, akinesia is produced by more selective destruction of the nigrostriatal bundle (Ungerstedt, 1971). However, recent evidence suggests that the mesolimbocortical dopamine system is also involved in sustaining movement (Ervin, Fink, Young, & Smith, 1977; Fink & Smith, 1979, 1980; Jeste & Smith, 1980).

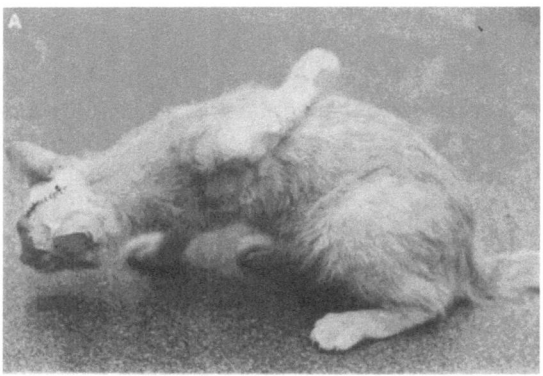

Fig. 8.2. Cataleptic postures maintained by cats with lateral hypothalamic damage: (A) limb in retroflexion; (B) limbs in abduction; (C) limb dangling from a table; (D) clinging to the back of a chair.

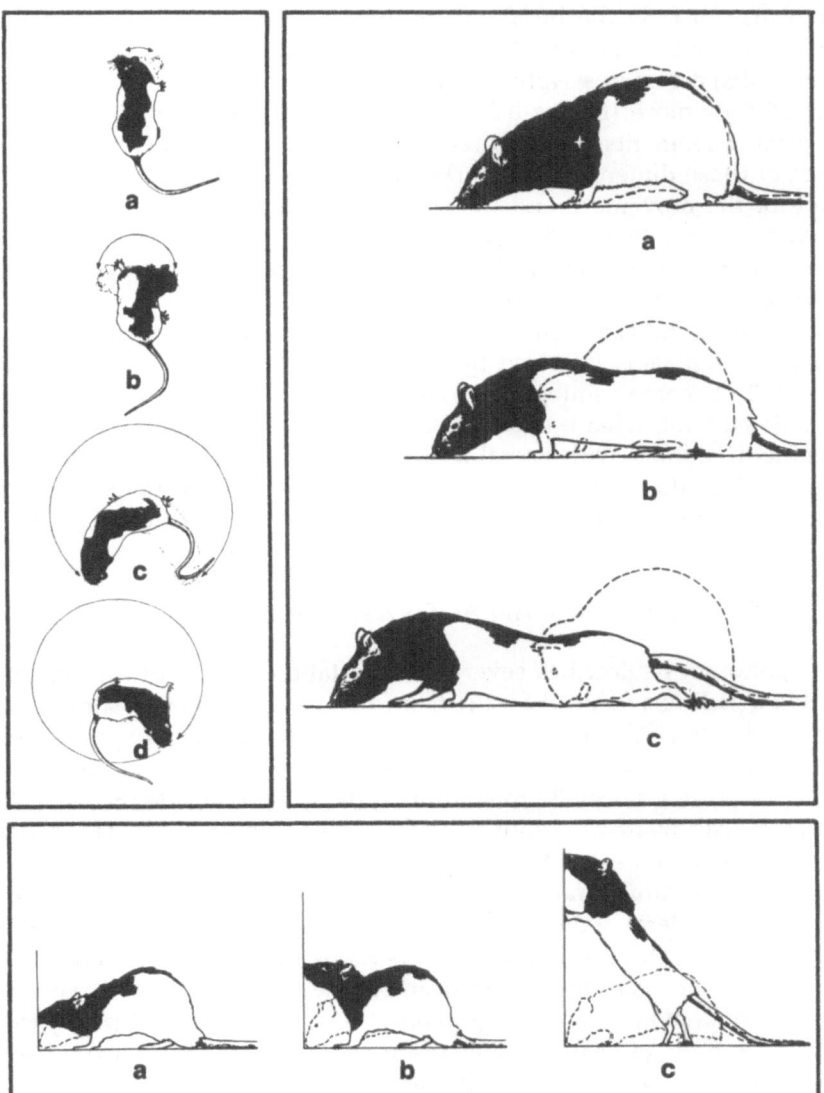

Fig. 8.3. Recovery of movement following lateral hypothalamic damage (left: in the lateral dimension; right: in the longitudinal dimension; bottom: in the vertical dimension). (From "A Proprosed Natural Geometry of Recovery from Akinesia in the Lateral Hypothalmic Rat" by I. Goloni *et al. Brain Research*, 1979, *164*, 237–267, Figs. 2, 3, and 4. Copyright 1979 by Elsevier/North Holland Biomedical-Press, Amsterdam. Reprinted by permission.)

involves not only the head but the upper torso as well. With further recovery, more caudal body segments (forelimbs, whole torso, pelvis, hindlimbs) are successively recruited until ultimately the rat can circle a full 360° or more (Figure 8.3, left). Somewhat later, longitudinal and vertical movements begin to recover as well. Once again, recovery in each of these dimensions is marked by a gradual increase in the amplitude of the movement and the successive recruitment of more caudal body segments (Figure 8.3, right and bottom). With recovery of movement in the longitudinal and vertical dimensions, normal-appearing exploratory locomotion returns.

In sum, damage to the lateral hypothalamus results in the fragmentation of behavior, followed by recovery during which the fragments gradually become reintegrated. These findings raise two fundamental questions: First, what ingredient, essential for behavioral integration, is lacking in animals with lateral hypothalamic lesions? Second, what are the variables that control recovery? To answer these questions, we must examine in more detail the phenomenon of sensory neglect.

3. SENSORY NEGLECT: AN ACTIVATIONAL DEFICIT

Although neglect has several manifestations, much of the analysis of this deficit has focused on the failure to orient to sensory stimuli. As Marshall *et al.* (1971) first showed, animals with unilateral hypothalamic lesions do not orient to stimuli presented on the contralateral side of the body, but orient normally to stimuli on the ipsilateral side (Figure 8.4). Animals with bilateral lesions neglect stimuli on both sides. The deficit does not seem to be due to impaired sensory or motor capacities per se. Thus rats with unilateral neglect that do not orient to tactile stimulation of the contralateral body surface often make skeletomotor or autonomic responses to such stimulation, demonstrating that they are not anesthetic. Because they can move their heads to the contralateral body surface during bouts of spontaneous grooming, they are clearly not paralyzed. Moreover, even after they recover orientation to somatonsensory stimuli, such rats still do not orient to visual stimuli for 1 to 2 weeks (Marshall & Teitelbaum, 1974; Marshall *et al.*, 1971). Turner (1973) has shown that rats with unilateral damage can be conditioned to orient toward the contralateral side to escape electric shocks presented to the ipsilateral foot, or to orient toward the ipsilateral side to escape shocks to the contralateral foot. Thus the rats can perceive the stimulus (shock) on the contralateral side and can orient their heads in the contralateral direction (but see Hoyman, Weese, & Frommer, 1979). Yet such rats do not make a contralateral orientation to escape contralateral shock. There-

IPSILATERAL
SIDE

CONTRALATERAL
SIDE

WHISKER
TOUCH

ODOR

BODY
TOUCH

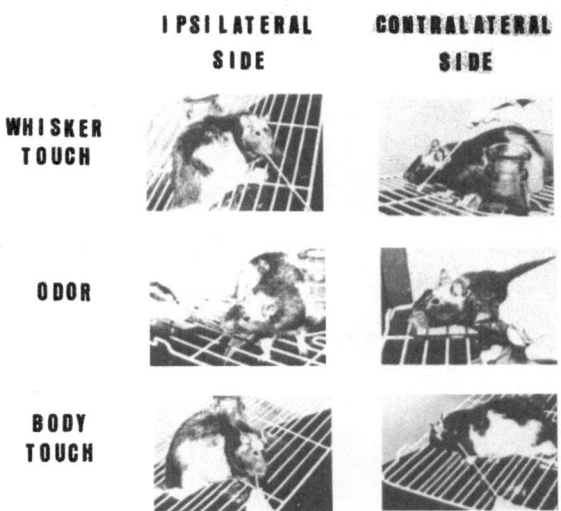

Fig. 8.4. Rat with unilateral hypothalamic lesion orients to stimuli on the ipsilateral side, but neglects the same stimuli on the contralateral side. (From "Sensory Neglect Produced by Lateral Hypothalmic Damage" by J. F. Marshall *et al.*, *Science*, 1971, *174*, 523–525, Fig. 1. Copyright 1971 by American Association for the Advancement of Science. Reprinted by permission.)

fore, neglect seems to reflect an inability to link sensory information with appropriate response systems.

We can gain further insight into the nature of this integrative deficit by considering sensory neglect from a human perspective. Neglect is sometimes observed in patients who have suffered a stroke affecting the parietal or frontal lobes (Denny-Brown & Banker, 1954; Heilman & Valenstein, 1972). For example, Heilman and Watson (1977a) describe a prototypical example of left-sided neglect in one such patient, who was otherwise alert and oriented to time, place, and person. The patient failed to put on clothing on the left side of his body, to shave the left side of his face, or to eat food from the left side of his plate. When given a book, he read words only on the right side of the page. Presented with compound words like "baseball" and "toothpick," he read "ball" and "pick." Asked to bisect a line, he divided the right half of it. Another particularly vivid illustration of human neglect may be found in some of the later drawings of Lovis Corinth, an artist who displayed left-sided neglect following a stroke. As can be seen in Figure 8.5, the left halves of his drawings are blurry or lack detail and contours, whereas the right halves are accurately drawn and sharply delineated. Such deficits demonstrate the impact of neglect on more "encephalized" human capaci-

Fig. 8.5. Portraits made by Lovis Corinth about 10 months after suffering a stroke that affected his right hemisphere. The drawings reveal a neglect of the left side. (From Singer, 1921.)

ties. (For further discussion of Corinth's neglect, see Jung, in Zülch, Creutzfeldt, & Galbraith, 1975.)

What is the underlying basis of this disorder? Recent analyses suggest that neglect is the result of deficient endogenous activation. Thus, when activated by stressful stimuli or stimulant drugs, animals with lesions of the lateral hypothalamus or nigrostriatal bundle exhibit a remarkable improvement in their sensorimotor capacities. For example, when their tails are pinched, brain-damaged cats orient briskly and precisely to stimuli they otherwise neglect. When their limbs are placed in cataleptic postures, they immediately return them to a normal position and begin to walk around (Teitelbaum & Wolgin, 1975; Wolgin & Teitelbaum, 1978). Similar improvement has been found in brain-damaged rats immersed in cool water or an ice bath, or placed in a cage with cats or other rats (Levitt & Teitelbaum, 1975; Marshall *et al.*, 1976; Robinson & Whishaw, 1974). Injections of stimulant drugs such as amphetamine, apomorphine, amantadine, or L-DOPA also counteract neglect and akinesia in such brain-damaged animals (Butterworth,

Belanger, & Barbeau, 1978; D. F. Lindsley, Ranf, Fernandez, & Wyr-wicka, 1975; Marshall & Gotthelf, 1979; Marshall, Berrios, & Sawyer, 1980; Wolgin & Teitelbaum, 1978; Wolgin et al., 1980).*

Electroencephalographic disturbances in the neglectful (ipsilateral) hemisphere have also been cited as evidence that neglect represents an activational deficit (but see Section 7.2.) For example, split-brain cats with unilateral lateral hypothalamic lesions display increased cortical synchrony in the hemisphere ipsilateral to the lesion. With recovery from neglect, the disparity in the electroencephalogram (EEG) between the two hemispheres disappears (Wright & Craggs, 1978, 1979). Because no consistent changes in visually evoked potentials in the two hemi-spheres have been found in such animals (Wright, Craggs, & Sergejew, 1979), visual neglect does not seem to be due to asymmetrical visual input. Unilateral neglect with ipsilateral cortical slowing has also been found in animals with unilateral lesions of the midbrain reticular forma-tion and caudate nucleus (Reeves & Hagamen, 1971; Watson, Heilman, Miller, & King, 1974), and in humans with parietal lobe damage (Heil-man & Watson, 1977b). Although neglect produced by unilateral de-struction of the substantia nigra is not accompanied by ipsilateral cortical slowing, tactile stimuli produce briefer durations of cortical desynchro-nization when applied to the contralateral body surface of animals with such lesions than when applied on the ipsilateral side (Siegfried & Bures, 1978, 1979). Interestingly, both hemispheres are activated to the same degree, whichever side is stimulated (see also Wright & Craggs, 1979). Also of interest is the finding that the duration of EEG desynchro-nization varies with the site of somatosensory stimulation: Rostral sites evoke longer durations of cortical desynchronization than caudal sites, irrespective of the side stimulated (Siegfried & Bures, 1978). This finding may be related to the fact that orientation to somatosensory stimuli recovers in a rostrocaudal sequence (Marshall, 1979; Marshall & Teitelbaum, 1974; Marshall et al., 1971; see also Marshall et al., 1980; Schallert & Whishaw, 1978).

Following bilateral hypothalamic lesions, both hemispheres show continuous cortical synchronization (De Ryck & Teitelbaum, 1978; Kolb & Whishaw, 1977; Kolb, Dodic, & Whishaw, 1979; Lindsley et al., 1975; Robinson & Whishaw, 1974). Early in recovery, such synchronization may persist even when the rat grooms, or when its tail is pinched (Dan-guir & Nicolaidis, 1980; De Ryck & Teitelbaum, 1978; Kolb & Whishaw,

---

*Recently, it has been demonstrated that intravenous injection of L-DOPA enhances the discharge of dorsal horn cells in response to cutaneous stimulation and increases the size of their receptive fields. This effect is found in intact cats as well as in cats with spinal transections (Hodge, Woods, & Delatizky, 1979). Thus L-DOPA has both peripheral and central effects on responsiveness to stimuli.

1977). Later, in Stage 2, the EEG is still largely synchronized, but tail pinch or stimulant drugs now evoke cortical activation (desynchronization; De Ryck & Teitelbaum, 1978; Lindsley *et al.*, 1975). With further recovery, the cortical EEG becomes desynchronized spontaneously, even during immobility, as in normal rats (De Ryck & Teitelbaum, 1978; Kolb & Whishaw, 1977).

4. RECOVERY OF MOTIVATED BEHAVIOR

4.1. The Role of Activation

Just as they counteract neglect, external activators also reinstate more integrated patterns of motivated behavior. For example, when their tails are pinched, aphagic cats (Stage 1) will approach and briefly ingest palatable foods. Later, when they eat limited quantities of such foods spontaneously (Stage 2), activation by tail pinch prompts more sustained feeding (Teitelbaum & Wolgin, 1975; Wolgin & Teitelbaum, 1978; see also Marshall *et al.*, 1974; Mufson, Balagura, & Riss, 1976). If the pinch is applied chronically, animals in Stage 1 or 2 will eat sufficient quantities of food to gain weight (Antelman, Rowland, & Fisher, 1976a; Wolgin, Cytawa, & Teitelbaum, 1976), a milestone that is not otherwise reached until Stage 3.

Similarly, more integrated feeding behavior can be elicited following activation by amphetamine (Teitelbaum & Wolgin, 1975; Wolgin & Teitelbaum, 1978). Although it produces marked suppression of feeding in normal animals, amphetamine evokes a dramatic increase in food intake and weight gain in anorexic cats in Stage 2 (Figure 8.6; see also Berger, Wise, & Stein, 1971; Stricker & Zigmond, 1976; Wolgin *et al.*, 1976). As shown in Figure 8.6, when injected with saline, cats in this stage eat very little. Typically, they approach the food dish, eat at a slow rate for several minutes, and then walk away. However, when injected with amphetamine the cats eat avidly, consuming most of the food in 30 minutes of nonstop feeding. Later in recovery, when more integrated feeding occurs spontaneously (Stage 3), the drug is less efficacious, and by Stage 4 it produces anorexia, but in milder form than in normal cats (see also Blundell & Leshem, 1974; Carlisle, 1964; Russek, Rodriguez-Zendejas, & Teitelbaum, 1973). Feeding and drinking are also reinstated in animals with nigrostriatal bundle damage following injection of dopaminergic agonists (Ljungberg & Ungerstedt, 1976b; Marshall & Ungerstedt, 1976).

Activating stimuli can reinstate other motivated behaviors disrupted by lateral hypothalamic damage as well. For example, cats that

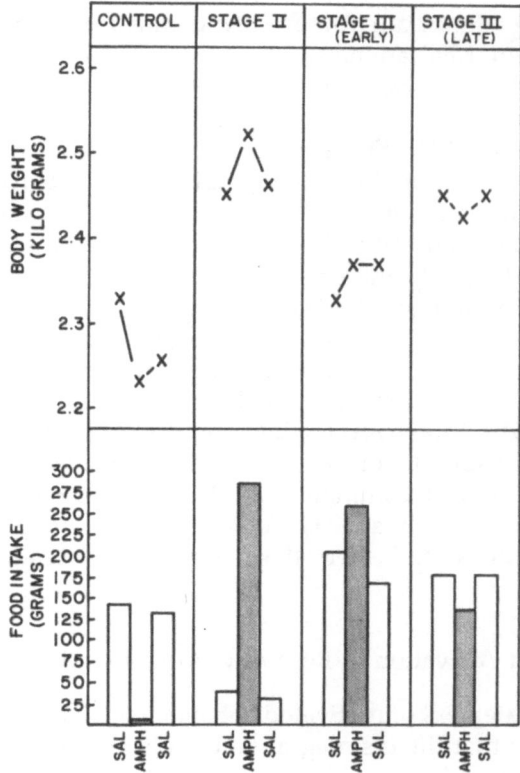

Fig. 8.6. Effect of amphetamine on food intake and body weight in normal (control) and lateral hypothalamic cat. Control: Amphetamine (AMPH) decreases food intake and body weight in control cat. Stage 2: activation of feeding with consequent weight gain by same dose of amphetamine in anorexic lateral hypothalamic cat. Stage 3 (early): With recovery of spontaneous feeding, amphetamine is less efficacious. Stage 3 (late): Later in Stage 3 and thereafter, amphetamine produces mild anorexia. (SAL = saline.) (From "Neurotransmitters and the Regulation of Food Intake" by P. Teitelbaum and D. L. Wolgin in W. H. Gispen et al. (Eds.), Hormones, Homeostasis and the Brain. Progress in Brain Research (Vol. 42), 1975, p. 243, Fig. 2. Copyright 1975 by Elsevier, Amsterdam. Reprinted by permission.)

do not spontaneously attack a mouse can be induced to do so by pinching their tails. Cats that stalk and trap a mouse but do not bite it will stalk, trap, kill, and eat the mouse when activated by tail pinch or amphetamine (Wolgin & Teitelbaum, 1978; Wolgin et al., 1976; see also Ellison & Flynn, 1968). Similarly, sexual receptivity is reinstated by amphetamine in female rats with hypothalamic damage (Herndon & Neill, 1973), and copulation is reinstated by tail pinch in male rats with catecholamine depletions, which mimic many of the effects of lateral hypothalamic damage (Caggiula, Shaw, Antelman, & Edwards, 1976).

Activating stimuli can also evoke integrated patterns of behavior in neurologically normal animals. For example, electric shock or stimuli associated with shock can induce or facilitate mating in noncopulating rats (Barfield & Sachs, 1968; Caggiula & Eibergen, 1969; Crowley, Popolow, & Ward, 1973; Sachs & Barfield, 1974). Similarly, pinching the tail evokes feeding, drinking, mating, and maternal behavior in normal rats (Antelman, Szechtman, Chin, & Fisher, 1975; Marques, Fisher, Okrutny, & Rowland, 1979; Rowland & Antelman, 1976; Szechtman, Siegel, Rosenblatt, & Komisaruk, 1977; Wang & Hull, 1980). Such stimulation can also motivate the learning of an instrumental task through which the rat gains access to the goal object (Koob, Fray, & Iversen, 1976). These effects are similar to those produced by electrical stimulation of the hypothalamus (cf. Antelman, Rowland, & Fisher, 1976b; Valenstein, 1976). Moreover, feeding and drinking elicited by tail pinch or hypothalamic stimulation are abolished by damage to the nigrostriatal system, suggesting a common underlying mechanism (Antelman & Szechtman, 1975; Antelman *et al.*, 1975; Phillips & Fibiger, 1976; but see Rowland, Marques, & Fisher, 1980; Shipley, Rowland, & Antelman, 1980).

4.2. Sources of Activation in Recovery: Afference and Reafference

The reinstatement of motivated behavior by tail pinch and stimulant drugs suggests that the disintegration of behavior following lateral hypothalamic damage is caused by inadequate levels of tonic activation. It follows that the reintegration of behavior during recovery must reflect the return of endogenous activation. How does this come about? One might view such recovery in terms of a quantitative increase in the capacity of the damaged brain to sustain an activated state. For example, Stricker and Zigmond (1976) suggest that compensatory processes such as denervation supersensitivity and increased synthesis of neurotransmitter may contribute to recovery from lateral hypothalamic damage. Because these are gradual processes, the functional capacity of the damaged activating system would be expected to improve slowly during the course of recovery and only gradually to support more integrated forms of behavior. Because only a fraction of the original system is functional, however, we would expect such a compensated system to remain susceptible to disruption if demands on the animal are too great. Indeed, rats that have recovered from lateral hypothalamic or nigrostriatal damage revert to a state of aphagia, adipsia, and sensorimotor dysfunction when subjected to stressful homeostatic challenges or when the functional capacity of their activating system is slightly reduced by low doses of dopaminergic antagonists that have little effect in normal rats (Epstein & Teitelbaum, 1967; Heffner, Zigmond, & Stricker, 1977; Stricker 1976; Stricker, Cooper, Marshall, & Zigmond, 1979; Zigmond & Stricker, 1973). The inability to tolerate excessive stress seems to underlie the apparent regulatory deficits in feeding and drinking that are found in recovered lateral hypothalamic animals. When less severe testing procedures are used such deficits are not found (Rowland, 1976; Stricker, 1976; Stricker et al., 1975).

However, there are qualitative differences in the sources of activation during the course of recovery as well. For example, the recovery of feeding in cats is extraordinarily dependent on activation from specific sensory modalities (Wolgin & Teitelbaum, 1978). When the cats begin to eat for the first time (Stage 2), feeding is controlled by sight of the food. If opaque contact occluders are placed in their eyes, the cats do not eat even when food is held directly in front of their mouths (Figure 8.7, bottom) or brought into contact with their snouts. Such visually deprived cats are also less responsive to other ambient stimuli in the laboratory. In contrast, normal cats are not at all affected by the loss of vision (Figure 8.7, top). These results suggest that in Stage 2, feeding in lateral hypothalamic cats is activated by the sight of food. Somewhat later, touching the snout with food elicits brief ingestion when the eyes are occluded, suggesting the recovery of tactile control of feeding. However, even with vision, feeding in this stage is very fragmentary; that is, the cats do not eat enough to regulate their body weight. Sustained feeding and maintenance of body weight appear to require additional activation from olfactory stimuli. Thus when the cats regain the ability to localize food by olfaction alone, with their eyes occluded, food intake and body weight increase dramatically (Stage 3). This fact implies that, like tail pinch, vision and olfaction promote more integrated feeding during the course of recovery by virtue of their activating properties.

Indeed, the activating effect of sensory stimuli can be seen in other situations as well (Wolgin & Teitelbaum, 1978). For example, during the first few postoperative days, cats with lateral hypothalamic damage are often profoundly somnolent. Although unresponsive to gentle prodding or even nociceptive stimuli (tail pinch, pinprick), such cats can be aroused by auditory stimuli (hand clap, a truck rumbling by outside). Later in recovery, sensory stimuli in one modality can facilitate orientation to stimuli in another modality. For instance, when the cats begin to recover from sensory neglect, the sound of a piece of paper sliding across the floor (out of sight of the cat) greatly facilitates orientation to visual stimuli. Similarly, vision seems to provide activation for orientation to touch, even when the tactile stimulus is not initially visible. Thus

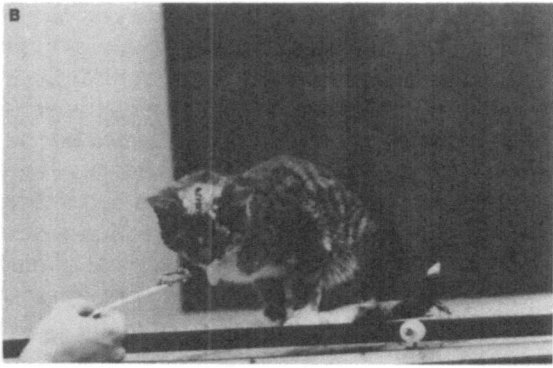

Fig. 8.7. (A) Normal cat with occluders in its eyes orients to food and begins to eat it. (B) In Stage 2, anorexic lateral hypothalamic cat with occluders does not respond to food even when it is held close to its face. (From "The Role of Activation in the Regulation of Food Intake" by D. L. Wolgin *et al.*, in D. Novin *et al.* (Eds.), *Hunger: Basic Mechanisms and Clinical Implications,* 1976, Figs. 2 & 4. Copyright 1976 by Raven Press, New York. Reprinted by permission.)

cats that orient briskly to touch of the body may fail to do so when tested with occluders in their eyes. In contrast, normal cats often respond more briskly when their eyes are occluded.

Interoceptive stimuli also provide activation in such brain-damaged animals. For example, otherwise akinetic cats will suddenly arise and walk around just before urinating or defecating (Wolgin & Teitelbaum, 1978). Similarly, in Stage 2 (anorexia), lateral hypothalamic rats move about quite actively when deprived of food for several hours. However, when given 10 to 15 cc of liquid diet intragastrically, they become akinetic and completely unresponsive to sensory stimuli. In contrast, normal rats are not as severely affected (Levitt & Teitelbaum, 1975). Thus locomotion in these brain-damaged animals seems to be activated by stimuli originating from the viscera.

Activation can also be generated reafferently as a result of the animal's own movements. For example, when a partially recovered lateral hypothalamic rat is removed from its cage and placed on a table it first appears to be akinetic. Shortly thereafter, however, it begins to move. At first it makes only small-amplitude head movements along the floor in the lateral or longitudinal dimensions. As these movements are repeated, they gradually grow in amplitude, ultimately recruiting more caudal body segments. Finally, forward locomotion occurs, but the rat initially maintains snout contact with the floor even when it encounters a vertical surface. Later, vertical scans occur as well, and gradually increase in amplitude. This warm-up of movement, which recapitulates the animal's previous history of recovery from akinesia, occurs each time the rat is placed on the table (Golani et al., 1979). (A similar warm-up occurs when totally akinetic rats are given apomorphine; Marshall & Gotthelf, 1979.) This finding suggests that repetition of the smaller-amplitude movements generates "reafferent activation," which then sustains more integrated movements (Teitelbaum et al., 1983).*

A related phenomenon has been observed in aphagic rats with posterior hypothalamic lesions (Wolgin et al., 1976). Although they are typically somnolent, such rats will groom themselves if their fur is sprayed with water (cf. Robinson & Whishaw, 1974). If the water is repeatedly dripped onto their snouts, the rats display frenzied face wiping and paw licking. If they then encounter a pellet of food, they begin to lick and eat the food, somewhat tentatively at first, but then more vigorously. Although at this point such feeding appears quite normal, it is critically dependent on the release of repetitive movements elicited by the dripping water. When the water stops, feeding gradually declines and the rats revert back to a somnolent state.

A recent study by Schallert, De Ryck, and Teitelbaum (1980) suggests that reafferent activation also contributes to drug-induced stereotypy. When rats are injected with atropine and placed in a blind alleyway, they walk to the end of the enclosure and then make stereotyped head movements along the vertical surfaces of the alley. As the movements are repeated they gradually grow in amplitude so that the forelimbs, shoulders, and torso are successively recruited in the upward scans. In many respects this phenomenon resembles the warm-up of

---

*Alternatively, warm-up could result from a corollary discharge from efferent neurons (efference copy). In principle, this issue could be resolved by testing deafferented animals.

vertical movements in recovering lateral hypothalamic rats (cf. Figure 8.3, bottom). However, when such stereotyped movements are precluded by inserting a low roof over the alley, the atropinized rats rapidly lapse into immobility and appear to fall asleep. Moreover, their EEG changes from an activated desynchronized pattern to a deactivated synchronized one. These results suggest that the stereotyped movements induced by atropine are sustained by reafferent activation generated by the movements themselves.

4.3. Activation and Parkinsonism

There are many striking similarities between rats and cats with lateral hypothalamic damage and humans suffering from Parkinsonism. As in brain-damaged animals, parkinsonian patients exhibit anorexia, akinesia, and sensorimotor disturbances (Martin, 1967; Sacks, 1973; Schwab, England, & Peterson, 1959). Moreover, these deficits can be counteracted by activating stimuli or dopaminergic drugs (Hornykiewicz, 1966; Martin, 1967; Sacks, 1973; Schwab, 1972; Schwab & Zieper, 1965). Such similarities stem from a common etiology: Parkinsonism is the result of degeneration in the nigrostriatal system. Unlike the lateral hypothalamic rat or cat, however, the parkinsonian patient also demonstrates the importance of activation for more "encephalized" functions. For example, postencephalitic patients with severe degeneration exhibit not only poverty of movement but also poverty of speech, of motivation, and of affect. When activated by L-DOPA, such patients show dramatic improvement in all of these spheres (Sacks, 1973). Similar improvement can sometimes be achieved by reafferent self-activation, as Sacks (1973) describes in the following passage:

> Although very rigid and bradykinetic at the start of an examination, Miss A. showed a remarkable ability to "activate" and loosen herself by exercise (her functional state before and after physiotherapy were strikingly different). Her mood, if depressed, would show dramatic improvement *pari passu* with her motor activation. (pp. 185–186)

It is possible, of course, that the correlated improvement in movement, motivation, and mood in these examples is artifactual. One might argue that a chronically institutionalized patient who cannot initiate movement voluntarily is likely to lack both motivation and emotional expression. If suddenly able to move as a result of medication or physiotherapy, such a patient might well feel elated and highly motivated. It is interesting, however, that when given L-DOPA on a chronic basis, side effects appear in all three spheres simultaneously. Moreover, the side effects are polar opposites of the initial parkinsonian symptoms. For example, akinesia is replaced by compulsive movements and thoughts; muted speech and mood by echolalia and maniclike affect (cf. Sacks, 1973). These results suggest a state of overactivation that simultaneously affects multiple central processes (for a discussion of parallel dopaminergic controls of movement and mental function, see Matthysse, 1974).

5. HYPOTHALAMIC ACTIVATION OF PATTERNED REFLEXES

We can gain further insight into the mechanisms by which the hypothalamus contributes to behavioral integration by considering the effects of hypothalamic stimulation. As previously mentioned, electrical stimulation of the hypothalamus elicits a wide range of species-typical responses. For example, hypothalamic stimulation can elicit predatory attack in cats that will not attack a rat spontaneously (Wasman & Flynn, 1962). Such elicited attack is similar in all major respects to natural feline attack (Berntson, Hughes, & Beattie, 1976; Levison & Flynn, 1965; Roberts & Kiess, 1964). In analyzing this phenomenon, Flynn and his colleagues have found that hypothalamic stimulation opens up lateralized sensory fields for stimuli associated with the prey. During unilateral stimulation, touch of the snout on the contralateral side of the face elicits orientation of the head toward the stimulated side; touch on the ipsilateral side of the face is ineffective (MacDonnell & Flynn, 1966). Similarly, touch of the contralateral lip during hypothalamic stimulation elicits jaw opening (MacDonnell & Flynn, 1966), touch of the contralateral limb elicits swiping (Bandler & Flynn, 1972), and sight of a mouse in the contralateral visual field elicits lunging (Bandler & Flynn, 1971). Increasing the intensity of the stimulating current causes the sensory fields for these reflexes to expand, whereas in the absence of hypothalamic stimulation no response is elicited. Thus the hypothalamus "motivates" predatory attack by selectively facilitating sensorimotor mechanisms for relatively independent response components ("patterned reflexes"; Flynn, 1972). In many respects this is similar to the effect of hormones, which facilitate sexual behavior, in part, by opening up sensory fields for sexual reflexes (Komisaruk, Adler, & Hutchinson, 1972; Kow & Pfaff, 1973).

It should be noted that the patterned reflexes themselves are not localized in the lateral hypothalamus. Even when the hypothalamus is destroyed or surgically isolated from the rest of the brain, predatory attack can still be elicited by pinching the tail or stimulating the midbrain (Ellison & Flynn, 1968; Proshansky, Bandler, & Flynn, 1974; Wolgin &

Teitelbaum, 1978). Several studies have traced the neural circuits for attack from the hypothalamus to these midbrain areas (Berntson, 1972; Chi & Flynn, 1971a,b; Chi, Bandler, & Flynn, 1976; Smith & Flynn, 1979). Indeed, there is considerable evidence that the brainstem contains sensorimotor mechanisms not only for attack, but for other species-typical responses as well (see Berntson & Micco, 1976). These findings are consistent with the view that the neural mechanisms that control motivated behavior are hierarchically organized within the nervous system (cf. Gallistel, 1980; Teitelbaum, 1977).

Gallistel (1975) proposes a schema for conceptualizing the functional relationship between the hypothalamus and "lower" brainstem mechanisms (Figure 8.8). He suggests that we can conceive of the hypothalamus as sitting atop a hierarchy of sensorimotor mechanisms (see also Gallistel, 1980). Hypothalamic control of behavioral integration is achieved by selective facilitation of appropriate lower-level circuits (e.g., those involved in approach to the prey) and suppression of inappropriate ones (e.g., those involved in withdrawal from prey).* Presumably, the selection of what is appropriate at any given time is determined by several factors including internal state, external stimuli, and past experience. From this perspective, lateral hypothalamic damage would produce a state in which lower-level sensorimotor mechanisms are disconnected from higher-level facilitating influences. This conception fits with our previous analysis of sensory neglect. In a sense, neglect represents an inability to activate patterned reflexes.

To recapitulate, during recovery from lateral hypothalamic damage there is a gradual transition from fragmentary responses to more integrated ones. The fragmentation of behavior seems to be caused by deficient endogenous activation since more integrated sequences of behavior can be elicited by providing external sources of activation, such as tail pinch. This fact confirms that animals with lateral hypothalamic damage have the competence to respond, but lack the motivation/activation to express that competence. Throughout the early postoperative period, motivationally specific sources of activation (e.g., homeostatic signals associated with hunger) do not seem to contribute to the expression of behavior, except in a relatively nonspecific way (e.g., by modulating general responsiveness; cf. Levitt & Teitelbaum, 1975; Schallert & Whishaw, 1978). Later in recovery, more integrated patterns of behavior occur "spontaneously." However, they are critically dependent on ac-

---

*It is not clear how the ascending nigrostriatal system interacts with the descending circuits mediating predatory attack; mapping studies have failed to reveal direct connections between hypothalamic attack sites and the nigrostriatal bundle or the striatum (cf. Chi & Flynn, 1971a,b; Smith & Flynn, 1980).

tivation from sensory stimuli, both exteroceptive and interoceptive, afferent and reafferent. Because animals with lateral hypothalamic damage are so dependent on activation from sensory stimuli, their behavior appears to be more reflexive than that of normal animals (see also Teitelbaum *et al.*, 1980).

6. THE ROLE OF ACTIVATION IN DEVELOPMENT

In several respects, normal infantile development resembles recovery from lateral hypothalamic damage. Early in ontogeny, behavior is highly fragmented compared to adult standards, and only gradually becomes more integrated. Specific examples of this transition can be found in developmental studies of locomotion, posture, and movement (Altman & Sudarshan, 1975; Blanck, Hard, & Larsson, 1967; Bolles & Woods, 1964; Frederickson & Frederickson, 1979; Gard, Hard, Larsson, & Petersson, 1967; Golani, Bronchti, Moualem, & Teitelbaum, 1981; Levine, Hull, & Buchwald, 1980; Tilney, 1933), sensorimotor capacities (Almli & Fisher, 1977; Altman & Sudarshan, 1975; Fox, 1970; Hein, Gower, & Diamond, 1970; Villablanca & Olmstead, 1979; Wolgin *et al.*, 1980), play (Barrett & Bateson, 1978; West, 1974), predatory attack (Leyhausen, 1956, 1973, 1979), and ingestive behavior (Adolph, 1957; Bolles & Woods, 1964; Cheng, Rozin, & Teitelbaum, 1971; Hall, 1979b; Hall & Bryan, 1980; Johanson & Hall, 1980; Teitelbaum, Cheng, & Rozin, 1969). Furthermore, early in ontogeny, behavior is often critically dependent on specific sensory stimuli, but only indirectly affected by internal state (see, e.g., Blass, Hall, & Teicher, 1979; Rosenblatt, 1976, 1979). Are these phenomena related to the immaturity of the infant's activating system? In the following sections I shall review some recent studies on the ontogeny of ingestion and predatory attack that speak to this question.

6.1. Ingestive Behavior

The earliest form of ingestive behavior in mammals is suckling. As recent work has shown, this distinctly infantile response is highly dependent on olfactory and tactile stimuli. Thus suckling is eliminated by washing the mother's nipples, but is immediately reinstated by coating them with either amniotic fluid or the mother's saliva (Blass, Teicher, Cramer, Bruno, & Hall, 1977; Bruno, Teicher, & Blass, 1980; Teicher & Blass, 1976, 1977; see also Hofer, Shair, & Singh, 1976). Although altering thermal and tactile cues associated with the mother does not eliminate suckling (Blass, *et al.*, 1977; Bruno *et al.*, 1980), deafferenting the

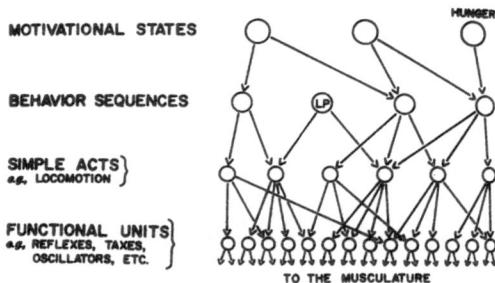

Fig. 8.8. Schema representing hierarchical relationship between hypothalamic motivating system and lower-level sensorimotor mechanisms. During a specific motivational state (e.g., hunger), the hypothalamus selectively facilitates appropriate circuits and inhibits inappropriate ones. (From "Motivation as Central Organizing Process: The Psychophysical Approach to Its Functional and Neurophysiological Analysis" by C. R. Gallistel in J. K. Cole and T. B. Sonderegger (Eds.), *Nebraska Symposium on Motivation* (Vol. 22), 1975, p. 190, Fig. 1. Copyright 1975 by University of Nebraska Press. Reprinted by permission.)

pup's snout either surgically (Hofer, Fisher, & Shair, 1981) or pharmacologically (Kenyon, Cronin, & Malinek, 1981) has catastrophic effects, even when the pup is placed at the nipple. The disruption of suckling by removal of olfactory and tactile cues is reminiscent of the loss of feeding following removal of vision in adult cats with lateral hypothalamic lesions. In both cases, ingestion is highly dependent on specific sensory modalities.

Surprisingly, internal controls over hunger do not regulate suckling in young infants. For example, deprived and nondeprived rat pups under 2 weeks old do not differ in their latencies to attach to the nipples of nonlactating mothers (Cramer, Blass, & Hall, 1980; Hall, Cramer, & Blass, 1975, 1977; Henning, Chang, & Gisel, 1979). Similarly, stomach distension does not terminate attachment to the nipple in young animals unless it is extreme, in which case the animals stop suckling only because they become lethargic and generally unresponsive (Hall & Rosenblatt, 1977; James & Rollins, 1965; Koepke & Pribram, 1971; Satinoff & Stanley, 1963). Older infants stop suckling before reaching such extreme levels of distension, then explore and groom before going to sleep (Hall & Rosenblatt, 1977), as adult animals do (Antin, Gibbs, Holt, Young, & Smith, 1975). Furthermore, nutritive stomach preloads are no more effective than nonnutritive preloads in limiting the intake of young rat pups, whereas in older pups nutritive preloads are more effective (Hall & Rosenblatt, 1978). Finally, cholecystokinin, a gut hormone that has a powerful satiating effect in adult rats (Antin *et al.*, 1975; Gibbs, Young, & Smith, 1973), does not inhibit intake in rat pups less than 2 weeks old (Blass, Beardsley, & Hall, 1979).

Thus, as in adult animals with lateral hypothalamic damage, ingestion (suckling) in young infants is relatively unaffected by homeostatic
signals that control intake in older infants and adults. That is not to say
that food deprivation has no effect on suckling in young infants. Both
deprivation and satiation profoundly affect the pup's level of activation,
and this, rather than the infant's nutritional state, seems to be the determining factor in whether or not the infant will nurse (cf. Blass, Hall, &
Teicher, 1979). As Blass, Hall, and Teicher, (1979) point out, handling the
subjects before testing ensures that they are in an activated state when
given the opportunity to nurse. Under natural conditions the stimulus
characteristics of the mother, including her behavior vis-a-vis the pups,
provide activation for suckling.

Of course, suckling is a unique form of ingestive behavior and differs from the adult form in several respects (cf. Blass *et al.*, 1979).
Adultlike feeding does not normally appear until about 3 weeks of age,
when the rat is already quite mature. As Teitelbaum and his colleagues
have shown, the emergence of such ingestion during ontogeny bears
several striking similarities to the recovery of feeding and drinking in
adult animals with lateral hypothalamic lesions (Cheng *et al.*, 1971;
Teitelbaum *et al.*, 1969). As we saw in previous sections, early in recovery, feeding in such brain-damaged animals is contingent on sensory
sources of activation. Would preweanling infants also show normal
adultlike ingestion if properly activated? A recent series of experiments
by Hall bears on this point. Hall has demonstrated that when rat pups as
young as 1 day old are deprived and tested in a warm environment
(33°C), adultlike ingestive responses can be elicited by infusing milk
directly into the front of their mouths, or spreading milk or other foods
in a thin layer on the floor (Hall, 1979a,b; Hall & Bryan, 1980). Such
responses resemble adult feeding in three ways. First, the motor patterns are topographically similar, consisting of mouthing, licking, and
probing along the floor. Second, like ingestion in adults, intake increases with increasing levels of deprivation. Finally, like adults (cf.
Antin *et al.*, 1975), the pups terminate feeding by gradually decreasing
the frequency of ingestive responses and becoming progressively less
active.

At the same time, there are several important differences in the
ingestive behavior of infants and adults. First, infantile ingestive responses are only one manifestation of a more general behavioral activation elicited by the testing conditions. Thus, in addition to mouthing
and probing, there is a general increase in movement as well as the
appearance of other, more specific motor patterns (Hall, 1979a,b). Some
of these (rooting, rolling over, reaching in the air) resemble motor patterns used in suckling. Others include walking, crawling, burrowing,

climbing, grooming, and posturing (which resembles lordosis). There are two developmental trends associated with these responses. Younger pups typically exhibit suckling-related motor patterns, but rarely show licking or grooming responses. On the other hand, older pups frequently groom and lick (as do adults), but never exhibit suckling-related postures. Furthermore, in young infants the ingestive responses themselves are relatively diffuse. While probing, such infants make lateral head scans from side to side while moving forward. When food is placed in a specific location on the floor they are unable to focus their activity, and consequently eat less. In contrast, older pups, like adults, are able to confine their probing to one area of the floor if that is where food is located (Hall, 1979b; Hall & Bryan, 1980). Thus, during the course of development, there is a trend toward greater specificity of response and increased attentiveness to environmental stimuli.

A second difference between infants and adults is that feeding in the infant is highly dependent on the testing conditions. Specifically, the pups must be severely deprived and tests must be conducted in a warm environment (Hall, 1979a,b). At room temperature, for example, young pups show little ingestive behavior and no behavioral activation. Johanson and Hall (1980) examined the role of temperature in more detail. They found that *even in the absence of food*, young pups (3 to 6 days old) display high levels of ingestive responses and behavioral activation when tested in a warm environment. The higher the temperature, the more active the pups. Moreover, the effect is greater in deprived pups than in nondeprived pups. On the other hand, the behavior of older pups (12 days old) is not as sensitive to either temperature or deprivation.

In the same study, Johanson and Hall also reexamined the effect of temperature when infusions of milk are given. They found that when tested in a cool environment (22–24°C), young pups allow the milk to spill out of their mouths, and show no behavioral activation. In a warm environment, active ingestion and behavioral activation occur. By manipulating the pups' core temperature independently of ambient temperature, they showed that the critical factor is the temperature in which the tests are conducted. Thus feeding and behavioral activation in young pups are contingent on a warm environment, not on the pup's core temperature. The dependence of infantile feeding on warmth points up another difference between infants and adults: In the adult, feeding is increased in the cold and depressed in the heat (Brobeck, 1948).

Taken together, these findings demonstrate that the sensorimotor mechanisms for adult ingestive behavior are present in newborn rat pups (see also Wirth & Epstein, 1976), just as they are present in adults with lateral hypothalamic damage. Such mechanisms are probably represented at quite low levels of the neuraxis (cf. Berntson & Micco, 1976; Grill, 1980). Yet, under normal circumstances, they are not observed until much later in ontogeny. This is because, in the infant, the stimuli that activate adult ingestive responses are rarely encountered under natural conditions. Rat pups are not normally severely deprived, and if they are, they are not likely to be warm. Moreover, many environmental stimuli have a deactivating effect on the infant (e.g., thermotactile and olfactory cues associated with the mother, siblings, or the nest; cf. Rosenblatt, 1976). Such stimuli help to maintain a low or moderate level of activation under natural conditions.

As in adults with lateral hypothalamic damage, ingestive responses in infants seem to result from nonspecific activation provided by the sensory environment in which the tests are conducted, not by homeostatic signals. This conclusion is supported by three facts. First, the stimuli that elicit ingestive responses also evoke increased activity as well as a variety of motor patterns that are not related to feeding (Hall, 1979a,b). Second, food is not necessary for such behavioral activation; warmth alone is sufficient (Johanson & Hall, 1980). Third, although deprivation influences intake, this effect does not appear to be specific. Even in the absence of food, deprivation increases the frequency of both ingestive responses (mouthing and probing) and general activity, provided the pups are tested in a warm environment (Johanson & Hall, 1980).

Further support for this conclusion comes from a recent study by Szechtman and Hall (1980) showing that oral behavior can be elicited in preweanling rats by tail pinch. This study also demonstrates that there are both qualitative and quantitative changes in the effect of tail pinch during the course of development. First, there is a change in the type of behavior elicited. At 5 days old, tail pinch elicits only licking; at 15 days old, licking, gnawing, and eating are elicited, as in adults (cf. Antelman et al., 1975). Second, during ontogeny, the pups' responses become more integrated. In the youngest animals the elicited response is short-lived; in older infants it is sustained throughout the duration of the pinch. Third, the behavior elicited by tail pinch becomes more focused during development. For example, when their tails are pinched, 5-day-old pups lick in the air and only rarely lick an object; 10-day-olds lick nonfood objects; 15-day-olds lick both food and nonfood objects; and 20- to 30-day-olds direct most of their activity to food. Finally, the "threshold" for elicited behavior decreases during ontogeny. Because a cross-sectional paradigm was used (i.e., pups were tested at only one age), these results cannot be attributed to experience with tail pinch. Instead, they suggest that during the course of ontogeny, the infant's activating system becomes capable of mediating more focused and integrated responses.

6.2. Predatory Attack

The ontogeny of predatory attack provides another illustration of the importance of activation for behavioral integration during development. In analyzing the ontogeny of predatory behavior, Leyhausen (1956, 1973, 1979) has found that most of the components of attack (e.g., stalking, pouncing, use of the forelimbs) are present in the kitten by 6 weeks, when the mother cat first provides dead prey for her litter. However, development of the killing bite often lags behind. The problem is that inexperienced kittens typically fail to bite the prey with sufficient force to kill it. According to Leyhausen, this is because the killing bite requires a higher level of activation than do the other components. During the development of attack, such activation comes from three main sources: the mother, competition from littermates, and from "play" with the prey. Play refers to the repetition of other appetitive components of attack, such as chasing, swiping, and throwing, and is a particularly important source of activation. "For the first elicitation of the killing bite . . . *the exciting, self-intensifying performance of the associated instinctive movements is a necessary condition*" (Leyhausen, 1973, p. 212,).

In certain respects, this phenomenon seems to be analogous to "reafferent activation" observed in lateral hypothalamic rats recovering from akinesia. That is, the repetition of components with lower activational thresholds generates activation for higher-threshold components.* In order to analyze this phenomenon in more detail, we have recently begun to study the development of attack in kittens (Wolgin & Servidio, 1979). Our procedure is to test kittens from a given litter collectively in an observation box, first without the mother present and then again with the mother. Testing begins when the kittens are 2 weeks old, by which time their eyes are open, and continues two or three times per week until the development of attack is complete. Live albino mice are used as prey.

Our first aim was to identify the motor patterns used by kittens in their interactions with a mouse. In the adult cat, predatory attack often

---

*Reafferent activation derives from the phenomenon of warm-up observed during recovery from akinesia following lateral hypothalamic damage (Golani *et al.*, 1979). As originally defined, warm-up consists of an orderly buildup in the amplitude of movement *in a specific dimension*. I use the term "reafferent activation" in a more general sense to refer to a buildup in the amplitude or vigor of a movement (e.g., biting) as a result of the repetition of that as well as other movements (e.g., chasing and swiping).

consists of a highly stereotyped pattern that includes stalking approach, pouncing on the prey, trapping or cuffing with the forelimbs, seizing the prey in the mouth, and biting (cf. Berntson et al., 1976; Leyhausen, 1973). In a sense, these may be viewed as components of approach, in that they bring the cat closer to the prey. After observing the attack behavior of young kittens, however, we realized that a good deal of their interaction with the mouse consists of withdrawal, that is, retracting the head and upper torso or the whole body. Components of approach tend to occur when the mouse is stationary or moving its head or body away from the kitten; components of withdrawal occur when the mouse moves its head or body toward the kitten, and when it vocalizes (Figure 8.9). These latter components are often quite exaggerated in young kittens, and probably reflect fear of the mouse. Adult cats that are inefficient killers also show such withdrawal (Adamec, 1975; Biben, 1979; Leyhausen, 1973). Indeed, the tendency to withdraw is greatly reduced if such cats are pretreated with an anxiolytic drug such as chlordiazepoxide or oxazepam (Apfelbach, 1978; Wolgin & Servidio, 1979). As I shall document more fully below, it is the superimposition of approach and withdrawal that creates the illusion of playfulness in the kitten's attack of a mouse and that generates the activation necessary for the killing bite.

In analyzing the ontogeny of attack, we identified three stages. In the first stage (2 to 3 weeks) the kittens totally ignore the mouse, even when it climbs over or burrows under them. Throughout the session they remain huddled together in a corner of the box, asleep. Later, when the mother is introduced, they instantly become aroused, but most of their activity is then directed toward her rather than toward the mouse.

The second stage (3 to 5 weeks) is a transitional one marked by dramatic changes in the kittens' coordination and arousal (cf. Frederickson & Frederickson, 1979; Levine et al., 1980). During this period the kittens orient toward the mouse, approach it, sniff it, and occasionally pursue it briefly. However, their interest in the mouse is not sustained and they are easily distracted. For example, if, while approaching the mouse, their view of it is briefly obstructed, they seem to forget the mouse and do not pursue it further (see also Gruber, Girgus, & Banuazizi, 1971). Seizing in the mouth and biting do not generally occur during this period.

Components of withdrawal are also observed in this stage. When approached by a mouse, the kittens retract their head and upper torso and raise a forelimb defensively. If the mouse persists in its approach, the kittens back away from it in a very defensive posture and sometimes hiss.

Throughout this stage the mother has a profound activating effect

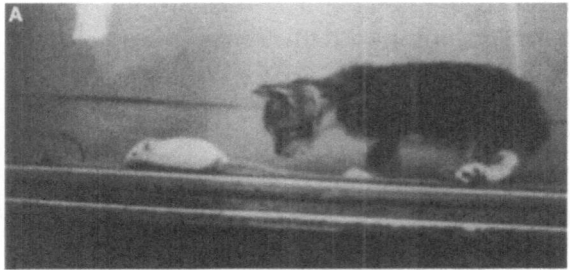

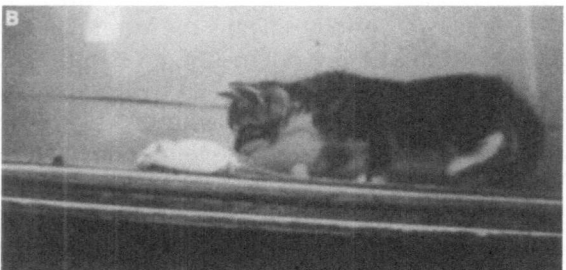

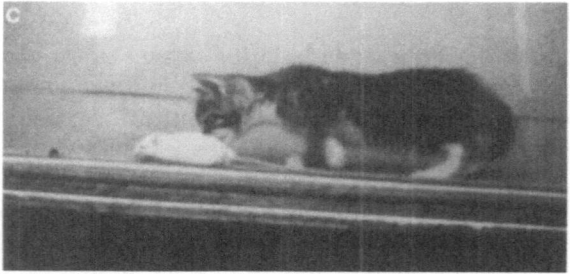

Fig. 8.9. (A–C): 6-week-old kitten approaches and extends its head toward a stationary mouse. (D) When the mouse turns, the kitten retracts its head and raises its forelimb defensively.

on the kittens. For example, when the kittens are first tested without the mother, they typically spend the final minutes of their session asleep. When the mother is then placed in the box, they immediately become highly aroused and show renewed interest in the mouse. Moreover, seizing the mouse in the mouth and biting it, which are rarely observed in the absence of the mother, occur frequently in her presence. The importance of the mother in activating attack is underlined by the finding that when the mother is removed while the kittens are attacking the mouse, they immediately stop and then ignore it. When the mother is reinstated several minutes later, they promptly return to the mouse and attack it. In addition, the kittens often stalk and swipe at objects placed in the box, or swipe in vacuo, when the mother is present, but rarely do so when she is absent. Littermates also provide activation (social facilitation) for attack in this stage. If the kittens are tested individually, they spend very little time interacting with the mouse. Instead they first pace about the box meowing and then lie down and fall asleep.

In the third stage (5 to 8 weeks), predatory attack is sustained even in the absence of the mother. It is in this stage that reafferent self-activation from "play" becomes prominent. The following sequence illustrates the temporal dynamics of attack during this period: When the mouse is presented, the kitten slowly follows and swipes it gently several times, which causes the mouse to run away. The kitten then pursues the mouse more quickly and swipes it more intensely. If the mouse freezes, the kitten lowers its snout to bite, but abruptly withdraws its head before making mouth contact if the mouse moves or vocalizes. After additional chasing, swiping, and aborted attempts to bite, the kitten's movements become faster and more intense. It now occasionally seizes the mouse in its teeth and then abruptly retracts its head and releases its grasp, which results in throwing or dropping the mouse.

At this point kittens that have had relatively little previous experience (e.g., at the beginning of this stage) often lapse into frenzied throwing and swiping, which persists even after the mouse has died. In such a hyperactivated state, the kitten's responses seem to have become independent of the stimuli (movements and vocalizations) that elicited them initially (for other examples of rapidly executed movement patterns becoming independent of external sensory control and a discussion of their theoretical significance see Fentress, 1976, 1983). More experienced kittens, after throwing the mouse several times, ultimately seize the mouse in their teeth and hold it for several seconds (often with head retracted and/or while backing up several steps) before releasing their grasp. Invariably, this period of increased mouth contact is soon followed by a deep, crunching bite through the skull or neck.

Thus, during the course of ontogeny, the tendency to attack a mouse is highly correlated with the kitten's ability to maintain an aroused state. In addition, there is a transformation in the source of activation for attack: Activation first derives from the mother or from littermates (social activation); later in development it is generated by the repetition of components of approach and withdrawal (reafferent self-activation); and finally, in kittens that become efficient killers, activation is generated "spontaneously" by central processes responsive to both external stimuli and internal state (endogenous activation).

7. ACTIVATION AND CHANGING CONCEPTS OF THE RETICULAR FORMATION

7.1. Activation versus Waking: Independent Dimensions

It is interesting to note that the importance of activation for behavioral integration was recognized a quarter of a century ago in Hebb's (1955) classic paper. Hebb recognizes that sensory stimuli have two properties: a "cue function," which guides behavior, and a "vigilance function," which provides activation or arousal. "Without a foundation of arousal," Hebb adds "the cue function cannot exist" (p. 249). Hebb further proposes that there is an optimal level of arousal at which cues will be most effective in eliciting and guiding behavior (Figure 8.10), thus implying that in addition to enhancing responsiveness to sensory stimuli, activation also increases the vigor or completeness of the response (Andrew, 1974). It follows that if arousal is too low, integrated patterns of behavior will not be possible. In these respects, Hebb's views are strongly supported by the data presented in earlier sections.

Like other activation theorists (e.g., Lindsley, 1951; Moruzzi, 1969), Hebb equates arousal with diffuse cortical desynchronization generated by the reticular formation (cf. Moruzzi & Magoun, 1949). Conceptually, sleep, waking, and levels of vigilance are viewed as falling along a single continuum of arousal (cf. Figure 8.10). Although this view has been widely accepted, it now appears to be incorrect. One problem arises from the assumption that activation (vigilance) and sleep are at opposite ends of the same dimension, which implies that the converse of activation is sleep. As we have seen, however, the absence of activation is not sleep, but neglect. Thus a cat that does not spontaneously attack a mouse may be quite awake; it simply lacks "hypothalamic" facilitation/ activation of the patterned reflexes for attack. This fact suggests that sleep–waking and neglect–activation are independent dimensions.

Dramatic support for this view can be found in recent work on the effects of lesions in the dorsal pontine tegmentum on paradoxical sleep

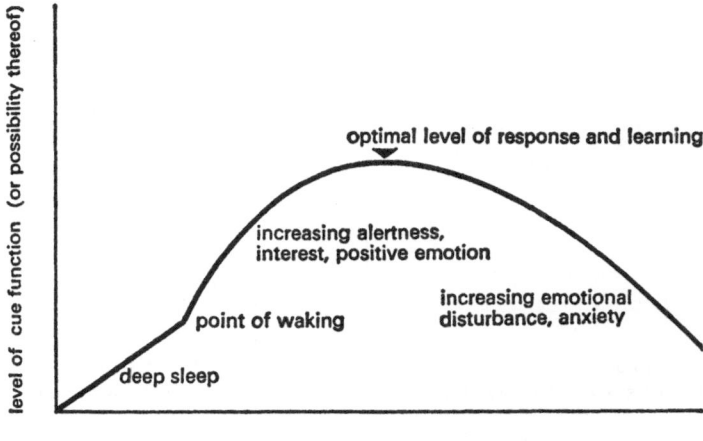

level of arousal function (nonspecific cortical bombardment)

Fig. 8.10. Relationship among arousal, cue function, and behavior. (From "Drives and the CNS (Conceptual Nervous System)" by D. O. Hebb, *Psychological Review*, 1955, 62, p. 129. Fig. 2. Copyright 1955 by American Psychological Association. Reprinted by permission.)

in cats (see Morrison, 1979). The term "paradoxical" is used because this stage of sleep is characterized by electrographic signs (cortical desynchronization, hippocampal theta) similar to those observed during waking. Accompanying these signs is profound muscular atonia due to postsynaptic inhibition of alpha motoneurons (Gassel, Marchiafava, & Pompeiano, 1965; Morrison & Pompeiano, 1965). Following dorsal tegmental lesions, muscular atonia is abolished (Henley & Morrison, 1974; Jouvet & Delorme, 1965). When a cat with such lesions passes from slow-wave sleep into paradoxical sleep, a remarkable phenomenon occurs: The cat performs integrated responses ranging from orientation of the head and postural adjustments, to grooming, exploration, and even predatory attack of an imaginary mouse (Henley & Morrison, 1974; Sastre & Jouvet, 1979). Such attack includes stalking approach, trapping with the forelimbs, and biting (Sastre & Jouvet, 1979). Yet, by a variety of criteria, the cat is asleep. For example, although the eyes are open, the pupils are miotic and the nictitating membranes are relaxed (when the cat awakens, the pupils dilate and the nictitating membranes retract); the episodes always follow slow-wave sleep; ponto-geniculo-occipital spikes occur; rapid eye movements are observed if the cat is restrained; brain temperature rises; there is a loss of thermoregulatory mechanisms; and the cat is unresponsive to external sensory stimuli (Hendricks, Bowker, & Morrison, 1977; Jouvet & Delorme, 1965; Parmeggiani, 1977; Sastre & Jouvet, 1979).

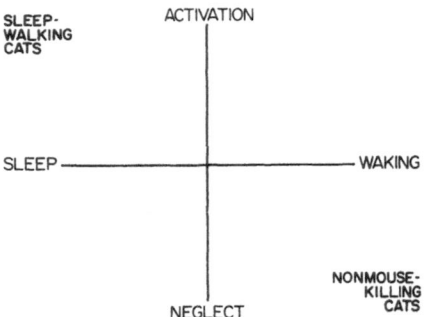

Fig. 8.11. Relationship between the sleep–waking and neglect–activation dimensions. Sleepwalking cats are activated, but asleep; nonmouse-killing cats are awake, but not activated.

These findings lead to several conclusions. First, they provide an explanation for the "paradox" of paradoxical sleep. As in waking, the EEG desynchronization accompanying this stage of sleep represents an activated behavioral state; unlike waking, however, it is normally masked by tonic inhibition of spinal motoneurons. Second, although there may be alternative explanations, it seems reasonable to conclude that during paradoxical sleep without atonia (and presumably during waking), the cat's behavior (e.g., attack) can be guided by cognitive representations of stimuli. Viewed from the context of the neural mechanisms of predatory attack, this fact implies a cognitive level of control in addition to the more reflexive mechanisms (i.e., patterned reflexes) discovered by Flynn and his colleagues (for a discussion of levels of control, see Teitelbaum, 1977). Finally, these results provide additional evidence that sleep–waking and neglect–activation are independent dimensions. Just as Flynn's "unmotivated" (i.e., unstimulated) cats are awake but not activated, these "sleepwalking" cats are activated but not awake (Figure 8.11).

7.2. Activation versus Movement

As previously mentioned, Hebb's views on the importance of arousal for behavioral integration were predicated on the then current conception of the reticular formation as an activating system. This assumption derived in large part from the discovery that electrical stimulation of the reticular formation elicits diffuse cortical desynchronization and behavioral alerting similar to that produced by peripheral stimuli (Moruzzi & Magoun, 1949; Segundo, Arana, & French, 1955), whereas lesions of the reticular formation that spare the classical sensory pathways result in sustained cortical synchrony and behavioral inertia (Lindsley, Schreiner, Knowles, & Magoun, 1950). However, the conclusion that arousal is mediated by the reticular formation and reflected in cortical desynchronization has recently been questioned. One challenge has come from analysis of the behavioral correlates of single-unit activity in the reticular formation (see Siegel, 1979a). The results of earlier studies had suggested that such units discharge in response to a variety of sensory stimuli as well as during increased levels of arousal (for references, see Siegel, 1979a). By studying the activity of these cells in unrestrained cats, however, Siegel and his colleagues have shown that their discharge is actually correlated with directionally specific types of movements or postures (Siegel, 1979b; Siegel & McGinty, 1977; Siegel, Wheeler, & McGinty, 1979; see also Bambridge & Gijsbers, 1977; Malmo & Malmo, 1977; Schwartzbaum, 1975). The primacy of movement, rather than sensory input or arousal, is suggested by several observations. For example, unit discharge is more closely associated with phasic electromyographic activity associated with the presentation of a stimulus than with the stimulus itself. When sensory input to given units is eliminated (e.g., by applying lidocaine to receptive fields of tactile cells, blocking the ear canals with wax for auditory cells, or placing the cat in a dark box to eliminate vision), the units continue to discharge during motor activity (Siegel, 1979a; Siegel & McGinty, 1977). Interestingly, such units are also active during paradoxical sleep (Siegel, McGinty, & Breedlove, 1977; Siegel et al., 1979; Vertes, 1977, 1979). This finding implies that it is the central patterning of movement rather than movement itself that is reflected in the activity of these cells.

Because the pontine and medullary reticular formation give rise primarily to descending reticulospinal fibers (Castiglioni, Gallaway, & Coulter, 1978; Eccles, Nicoll, Taborikova, & Willey, 1975; Torvik & Brodal, 1957), it might be argued that the units studied by Siegel and his colleagues (which were located in those areas) are not the ones involved in electrographic activation of the cortex. It is possible, for example, that units located more rostrally in the midbrain reticular formation mediate EEG desynchronization and behavioral arousal (cf. Steriade, Ropert, Kitsikis, & Oakson, 1980). However, even if we accept this explanation, there is another, more fundamental challenge to the reticular-activating concept that is more difficult to dismiss: namely, Vanderwolf's contention that cortical desynchronization and hippocampal theta, both of which have traditionally been associated with arousal (Green & Arduini, 1954; Moruzzi & Magoun, 1949), are in fact electrographic correlates of *movement* (see Vanderwolf, 1983; Vanderwolf & Robinson, 1981).

In brief, Vanderwolf and his colleagues have demonstrated that there are two pharmacologically distinct types of cortical desynchronization and hippocampal theta having different behavioral correlates (Kramis, Vanderwolf, & Bland, 1975; Robinson, Kramis, & Vanderwolf, 1977; Vanderwolf, 1975; Vanderwolf & Pappas, 1980; Vanderwolf, Kramis, Gillespie, & Bland, 1975; Vanderwolf, Kramis, & Robinson, 1978; Whishaw, 1976). One form occurs only during what Vanderwolf refers to as "voluntary" or "Type 1" behaviors such as walking, swimming, or moving the head, and, interestingly, during the phasic muscle twitches of paradoxical sleep. It does not occur during more stereotyped "automatic" activities ("Type 2" behaviors) such as chewing, licking, face washing, and shivering, or during immobility. (These latter activities are accompanied by large-amplitude, irregular activity in the hippocampus.) Cortical desynchronization and hippocampal theta accompanying voluntary behavior are resistant to disruption by atropine, but are abolished by anesthetics and by reserpine. Recent evidence suggests that the cortical response is mediated by a trace amine (Vanderwolf, Robinson, & Pappas, 1980). A second form of such activity sometimes occurs during complete immobility. This form differs from the first in two important respects. First, it seems to be mediated by a cholinergic system because it can be induced by eserine and abolished by antimuscarinic drugs such as atropine, but is unaffected by anesthetics. Second, the hippocampal theta has a lower frequency than that accompanying "voluntary" behavior (4 to 7 Hz vs. 7 to 12 Hz; Kramis et al., 1975).

In a normal undrugged rat, the correlation between hippocampal theta and "voluntary" behavior is quite compelling (cf. Leblanc & Bland, 1979; Vanderwolf, 1969). On the other hand, cortical desynchronization is normally observed in the awake animal both during movement and during alert immobility. However, if the rat is given atropine, cortical desynchronization during immobility is abolished. In such an atropinized animal, diffuse cortical desynchronization (and hippocampal theta) occurs only during "voluntary" movements, whether initiated spontaneously or induced by electrical stimulation of the hypothalamus or reticular formation. At all other times, the cortex shows EEG synchrony, as during slow-wave sleep in undrugged animals (Robinson & Vanderwolf, 1978; Vanderwolf, 1975; Vanderwolf, Bland, & Whishaw, 1973). As with unit activity in the reticular formation, cortical desynchronization and hippocampal theta are also observed in response to sensory stimuli, but only when such stimuli initiate "voluntary" movement (Vanderwolf et al., 1978). One implication of this finding is that the cortical synchrony observed in animals with sensory neglect (cf. Section 3.) may be a result of the failure to orient to the stimulus, rather than of deficient arousal per se.

The contention that EEG activity reflects movement, and not activation, has other implications as well. For example, EEG criteria are traditionally used to define the sleep–waking continuum (e.g., Dement & Kleitman, 1957; Jouvet, 1969). Thus progressively deeper stages of sleep are inferred from increasingly more synchronous EEG activity. However, if, as Vanderwolf proposes, the EEG reflects activity in movement-related neural circuits, then the primary basis for defining a sleep–waking continuum would be eliminated. Perhaps, instead, sleep and waking should be viewed as discrete states in which different levels of *behavioral* activation (or its central representation, as in paradoxical sleep) are possible (cf. Figure 8.11).

At the present time, the Vanderwolf theory must be regarded as controversial, as a recent open peer commentary testifies (see *The Behavioral and Brain Sciences*, 1981, *4*, 459–514). Many questions remain regarding the relationship between the reticular formation, EEG activity, and behavior, and further research will be required before the theory can be properly evaluated. Nevertheless, the approach taken by Vanderwolf (and by Siegel) in addressing this issue represents an important advance because it focuses attention on the need for a *behavioral* definition of activation.

8. CONCLUSIONS

Psychologists have long recognized that knowledge or competence can only be assessed indirectly, by means of overt behavior. For example, we infer learning and memory capacities only when the subject indicates *through its behavior* that it has learned or remembered. Similarly, we assess an animal's competence to regulate its body weight or to catch a mouse by providing it with relevant cues (e.g., food, a mouse) and observing its behavior. If the subject fails to respond appropriately, we infer a lack of competence. As physiological psychologists, however, we often go one step further and infer from the animal's behavior (or lack thereof) something about the state of its nervous system. Thus a rat with lateral hypothalamic damage that does not eat very much is assumed to have lost the neural mechanisms for maintaining nutritional homeostasis. Similarly, a rat pup that normally obtains its food only by suckling and continues to suckle even when satiated is thought to lack the neural mechanisms for adult ingestion. However, the absence of adult patterns of integrated behavior does not necessarily imply a lack of competence at either the behavioral or the neural level. As we have seen, subjects may fail to express their competence if they are not sufficiently activated.

Therefore, in analyzing the neurological capacities of either brain-damaged adults or normal infants, careful consideration must be given to the activational requirements of the subjects.

ACKNOWLEDGMENTS

I am grateful to Elliott Blass, John Fentress, Gregory Lockhead, John Marshall, and Philip Teitelbaum for their helpful comments on an earlier version of this chapter.

9. REFERENCES

Adamec, R. The behavioral bases of prolonged suppression of predatory attack in cats. *Aggressive Behavior*, 1975, *1*, 297–314.

Adolph, G. F. Ontogeny of physiological regulations in the rat. *Quarterly Review of Biology*, 1957, *32*, 80–137.

Almli, C. R., & Fisher, R. S. Infant rats: Sensorimotor ontogeny and effects of substantia nigra destruction. *Brain Research Bulletin*, 1977, *2*, 425–459.

Altman, J., & Sudarshan, K. Postnatal development of locomotion in the laboratory rat. *Animal Behaviour*, 1975, *23*, 896–920.

Anand, B. K., & Brobeck, J. R. Hypothalamic control of food intake in rats and cats. *Yale Journal of Biology and Medicine*, 1951, *24*, 123–140.

Andrew, R. J. Arousal and the causation of behaviour. *Behaviour*, 1974, *51*, 135–165.

Antelman, S. M., & Szechtman, H. Tail pinch induces eating in sated rats which appears to depend on nigrostriatal dopamine. *Science*, 1975, *189*, 731–733.

Antelman, S. M., Szechtman, H., Chin, P., & Fisher, A. E. Tail pinch-induced eating, gnawing and licking behavior in rats: Dependence on the nigrostriatal dopamine system. *Brain Research*, 1975, *99*, 319–337.

Antelman, S. M., Rowland, N. E., & Fisher, A. E. Stress related recovery from lateral hypothalamic aphagia. *Brain Research*, 1976, *102*, 346–351. (a)

Antelman, S. M., Rowland, N. E., & Fisher, A. E. Stimulation bound ingestive behavior: A view from the tail. *Physiology and Behavior*, 1976, *17*, 743–748. (b)

Antin, J., Gibbs, J., Holt, J., Young, R. C., & Smith, G. P. Cholecystokinin elicits the complete behavioral sequence of satiety in rats. *Journal of Comparative and Physiological Psychology*, 1975, *89*, 784–790.

Apfelbach, R. Instinctive predatory behavior of the ferret (*Putorius putorius furo* L.) modified by chlordiazepoxide hydrochloride (Librium®). *Psychopharmacology*, 1978, *59*, 179–182.

Balagura, S., Wilcox, R. H., & Coscina, D. V. The effect of diencephalic lesions on food intake and motor activity. *Physiology and Behavior*, 1969, *4*, 629–633.

Bambridge, R., & Gijsbers, K. The role of tonic neural activity in motivational processes. *Experimental Neurology*, 1977, *56*, 370–385.

Bandler, R. J., & Flynn, J. P. Visual patterned reflex present during hypothalamically elicited attack. *Science*, 1971, *171*, 703–706.

Bandler, R. J., & Flynn, J. P. Control of somatosensory fields for striking during hypothalamically elicited attack. *Brain Research*, 1972, *38*, 197–201.

Barfield, R. J., & Sachs, B. D. Sexual behavior: Stimulation by painful electrical shock to skin in male rats. *Science*, 1968, *161*, 392–395.

Barrett, P., & Bateson, P. The development of play in cats. *Behaviour*, 1978, *66*, 106–120.

Berger, B. D., Wise, C. D., & Stein, L. Norepinephrine: Reversal of anorexia in rats with lateral hypothalamic damage. *Science*, 1971, *172*, 281–284.

Berntson, G. G. Blockade and release of hypothalamically and naturally elicited aggressive behaviors in cats following midbrain lesions. *Journal of Comparative and Physiological Psychology*, 1972, *81*, 541–554.

Berntson, G. G., & Micco, D. J. Organization of brainstem behavioral systems. *Brain Research Bulletin*, 1976, *1*, 471–483.

Berntson, G. G., Hughes, H. C., & Beattie, M. S. A comparison of hypothalamically induced biting attack with natural predatory behavior in the cat. *Journal of Comparative and Physiological Psychology*, 1976, *90*, 167–178.

Biben, M. Predation and predatory play behaviour of domestic cats. *Animal Behaviour*, 1979, *27*, 81–94.

Blanck, A., Hard, E., & Larsson, K. Ontogenetic development of orienting behavior in the rat. *Journal of Comparative and Physiological Psychology*, 1967, *63*, 327–328.

Blass, E. M., Teicher, M. H., Cramer, C. P., Bruno, J. P., & Hall, W. G. Olfactory, thermal, and tactile controls of suckling in preauditory and previsual rats. *Journal of Comparative and Physiological Psychology*, 1977, *91*, 1248–1260.

Blass, E. M., Beardsley, W., & Hall, W. G. Age-dependent inhibition of suckling by cholecystokinin. *American Journal of Physiology*, 1979, *236*, E567–E570.

Blass, E. M., Hall, W. G., & Teicher, M. H. The ontogeny of suckling and ingestive behavior. In J. M. Sprague & A. N. Epstein (Eds.), *Progress in psychobiology and physiological psychology* (Vol. 8). New York: Academic Press, 1979.

Blundell, J. E., & Leshem, M. B. Central action of anorexic agents: Effects of amphetamine and fenfluramine in rats with lateral hypothalamic lesions. *European Journal of Pharmacology*, 1974, *28*, 81–88.

Bolles, R. C., & Woods, P. J. The ontogeny of behaviour in the albino rat. *Animal Behaviour*, 1964, *12*, 427–441.

Brobeck, J. R. Food intake as a mechanism of temperature regulation. *Yale Journal of Biology and Medicine*, 1948, *20*, 545–552.

Brookhart, J. M., & Dey, F. L. Reduction of sexual behavior in male guinea pigs by hypothalamic lesions. *American Journal of Physiology*, 1941, *133*, 551–554.

Bruno, J. P., Teicher, M. H., & Blass, E. M. Sensory determinants of suckling behavior in weanling rats. *Journal of Comparative and Physiological Psychology*, 1980, *94*, 115–127.

Butterworth, R. F., Belanger, F., & Barbeau, A. Hypokinesia produced by anterolateral hypothalamic 6-hydroxydopamine lesions and its reversal by some antiparkinson drugs. *Pharmacology, Biochemistry and Behavior*, 1978, *8*, 41–45.

Caggiula, A. R., & Eibergen, R. Copulation of virgin male rats evoked by painful peripheral stimulation. *Journal of Comparative and Physiological Psychology*, 1969, *69*, 414–419.

Caggiula, A. R., Antelman, S. M., & Zigmond, M. J. Disruption of copulation in male rats after hypothalamic lesions: A behavioral, anatomical and neurochemical analysis. *Brain Research*, 1973, *59*, 273–287.

Caggiula, A. R., Shaw, D. H., Antelman, S. M., & Edwards, D. J. Interactive effects of brain catecholamines and variations in sexual and non-sexual arousal on copulatory behavior of male rats. *Brain Research*, 1976, *111*, 321–336.

Carlisle, H. J. Differential effects of amphetamine on food and water intake in rats with lateral hypothalamic lesions. *Journal of Comparative and Physiological Psychology*, 1964, *58*, 47–54.

Castiglioni, A. J., Gallaway, M. C., & Coulter, J. D. Spinal projections from the midbrain in monkeys. *Journal of Comparative Neurology*, 1978, *178*, 329–346.

Cheng, M. F., Rozin, P., & Teitelbaum, P. Semi-starvation retards the development of food and water regulations in infant rats. *Journal of Comparative and Physiological Psychology*, 1971, *76*, 206–218.

Chi, C. C., & Flynn, J. P. Neural pathways associated with hypothalamically elicited attack behavior in cats. *Science*, 1971, *171*, 703–706. (a)

Chi, C. C., & Flynn, J. P. Neuroanatomic projections related to biting attack elicited from hypothalamus in cats. *Brain Research*, 1971, *35*, 49–66. (b)

Chi, C. C., Bandler, R. J., & Flynn, J. P. Neuroanatomic projections related to biting attack elicited from ventral midbrain in cats. *Brain, Behavior and Evolution*, 1976, *13*, 91–110.

Cramer, C. P., Blass, E. M., & Hall, W. G. The ontogeny of nipple-shifting behavior in albino rats: Mechanisms of control and possible significance. *Developmental Psychobiology*, 1980, *13*, 165–180.

Crowley, W. R., Popolow, H. B., & Ward, O. B. From dud to stud: Copulatory behavior elicited through conditioned arousal in sexually inactive male rats. *Physiology and Behavior*, 1973, *10*, 391–394.

Danguir, J., & Nicolaidis, S. Cortical activity and sleep in the rat lateral hypothalamic syndrome. *Brain Research*, 1980, *185*, 305–321.

Dement, W., & Kleitman, N. Cyclic variations in EEG during sleep and their relation to eye movements, body motility, and dreaming. *Electroencephalography and Clinical Neurophysiology*, 1957, *9*, 673–690.

Denny-Brown, D., & Banker, B. Q. Amorphosynthesis from left parietal lesions. *Archives of Neurology and Psychiatry*, 1954, *71*, 302–313.

De Ryck, M., & Teitelbaum, P. Neocortical and hippocampal EEG in normal and lateral hypothalamic-damaged rats. *Physiology and Behavior*, 1978, *20*, 403–409.

Eccles, J. C., Nicoll, R. A., Taborikova, H., & Willey, T. J. Medial reticular neurons projecting rostrally. *Journal of Neurophysiology*, 1975, *38*, 531–538.

Ellison, G. D., & Flynn, J. P. Organized aggressive behavior in cats after surgical isolation of the hypothalamus. *Archives Italiennes de Biologie*, 1968, *106*, 1–20.

Epstein, A. N., & Teitelbaum, P. Severe and persistent deficits in thirst produced by lateral hypothalamic damage. In M. J. Wayner (Ed.), *Thirst in the regulation of body water*. Oxford: Pergamon Press, 1964.

Epstein, A. N., & Teitelbaum, P. Specific loss of the hypoglycemic control of feeding in recovered lateral rats. *American Journal of Physiology*, 1967, *213*, 1159–1167.

Ervin, G. N., Fink, J. S., Young, R. C., & Smith, G. P. Different behavioral responses to L-DOPA after anterolateral or posterolateral hypothalamic injections of 6-hydroxydopamine. *Brain Research*, 1977, *132*, 507–520.

Feeney, D. M., & Weir, C. S. Sensory neglect after lesions of substantia nigra or lateral hypothalamus: Differential severity and recovery of function. *Brain Research*, 1979, *178*, 329–346.

Fentress, J. C. Dynamic boundaries of patterned behaviour: Interaction and self-organization. In P. P. G. Bateson & R. A. Hinde (Eds.), *Growing points in ethology*. Cambridge: Cambridge University Press, 1976.

Fentress, J. C. Ethological models of hierarchy and patterning of species specific behavior. In E. Satinoff & P. Teitelbaum (Eds.), *Handbook of behavioral neurobiology: Motivation*. New York: Plenum Press, 1983.

Fink, J. S., & Smith, G. P. Decreased locomotor and investigatory exploration after denervation of catecholamine terminal fields in the forebrain of rats. *Journal of Comparative and Physiological Psychology*, 1979, *93*, 34–65.

Fink, J. S., & Smith, G. P. Mesolimbocortical dopamine terminal fields are necessary for normal locomotor and investigating exploration in rats. *Brain Research*, 1980, *199*, 359–384.

Flynn, J. P. Patterning mechanisms, patterned reflexes, and attack behavior in cats. In J. K. Cole & D. D. Jensen (Eds.), *Nebraska symposium on motivation* (Vol. 20). Lincoln: University of Nebraska Press, 1972.

Fox, M. W. Reflex development and behavioral organization. In W. A. Himwich (Ed.), *Developmental neurobiology*. Springfield, Ill.: Charles C Thomas, 1970.

Frederickson, C. J., & Frederickson, M. H. Developmental changes in open-field behavior in the kitten. *Developmental Psychobiology*, 1979, *12*, 623–628.

Gallistel, C. R. Motivation as central organizing process: The psychophysical approach to its functional and neurophysiological analysis. In J. K. Cole & T. B. Sonderegger (Eds.), *Nebraska symposium on motivation 1974* (Vol. 22). Lincoln: University of Nebraska Press, 1975.

Gallistel, C. R. *The organization of action: A new synthesis*. Hillsdale, N.J.: Lawrence Erlbaum, 1980.

Gard, C., Hard, E., Larsson, K., & Petersson, V. The relationship between sensory stimulation and gross motor behaviour during the postnatal development in the rat. *Animal Behaviour*, 1967, *15*, 563–567.

Gassel, M. M., Marchiafava, P. L., & Pompeiano, O. An analysis of supraspinal influences acting on motoneurons during sleep in the unrestrained cat: Modification of the recurrent discharge of the alpha motoneurons during sleep. *Archives Italiennes de Biologie*, 1965, *103*, 25–44.

Gibbs, J., Young, R. C., & Smith, G. P. Cholecystokinin decreases food intake in rats. *Journal of Comparative and Physiological Psychology*, 1973, *84*, 488–495.

Golani, I., Bronchti, G., Moualem, D., & Teitelbaum, P. "Warm-up" along dimensions of movement in the ontogeny of exploration in rats and other infant mammals. *Proceedings of the National Academy of Sciences*, 1981, *78*, 7226–7229.

Golani, I., Wolgin, D. L., & Teitelbaum, P. A proposed natural geometry of recovery from akinesia in the lateral hypothalamic rat. *Brain Research*, 1979, *164*, 237–267.

Green, J. D., & Arduini, A. A. Hippocampal electrical activity in arousal. *Journal of Neurophysiology*, 1954, *17*, 533–557.

Grijalva, C. V., & Lindholm, E. Restricted feeding and its effects on aphagia and ingestion-related disorders following lateral hypothalamic damage. *Journal of Comparative and Physiological Psychology*, 1980, *94*, 164–177.

Grill, H. J. Production and regulation of ingestive consummatory behavior in the chronic decerebrate rat. *Brain Research Bulletin*, 1980, *5*, 79–87. (Suppl. 4)

Grossman, S. P., Dacey, D., Halaris, A. E., Collier, T., & Routtenberg, A. Aphagia and adipsia after preferential destruction of nerve cell bodies in hypothalamus. *Science*, 1978, *202*, 537–539.

Gruber, H. E., Girgus, J. S., & Banuazizi, A. The development of object permanence in the cat. *Developmental Psychology*, 1971, *4*, 9–15.

Gybels, J., Meulders, M., Callens, M., & Colle, J. Disturbances of visuo-motor integration in cats with small lesions of the caudate nucleus. *Archives Internationales de Physiologie et de Biochimie*, 1967, *75*, 283–302.

Hall, W. G. Feeding and behavioral activation in infant rats. *Science*, 1979, *205*, 206–209. (a)

Hall, W. G. The ontogeny of feeding in rats. I. Ingestive and behavioral responses to oral infusions. *Journal of Comparative and Physiological Psychology*, 1979, *93*, 977–1000. (b)

Hall, W. G., & Bryan, T. E. The ontogeny of feeding in rats. II. Independent ingestive behavior. *Journal of Comparative and Physiological Psychology*, 1980, *94*, 746–756.

Hall, W. G., & Rosenblatt, J. S. Suckling behavior and intake control in the developing rat pup. *Journal of Comparative and Physiological Psychology*, 1977, *91*, 1232–1247.

Hall, W. G., & Rosenblatt, J. S. Development of nutritional control of food intake in suckling rat pups. *Behavioral Biology*, 1978, *24*, 413–427.

Hall, W. G., Cramer, C. P., & Blass, E. M. Developmental changes in suckling of rat pups. *Nature*, 1975, *258*, 318–320.

Hall, W. G., Cramer, C. P., & Blass, E. M. Ontogeny of suckling in rats: Transitions toward adult ingestion. *Journal of Comparative and Physiological Psychology*, 1977, *91*, 1141–1155.

Hebb, D. O. Drives and the CNS (conceptual nervous system). *Psychological Review*, 1955, *62*, 243–254.

Heffner, T. G., Zigmond, M. J., & Stricker, E. M. Effects of dopaminergic agonists and antagonists on feeding in intact and 6-hydroxydopamine-treated rats. *Journal of Pharmacology and Experimental Therapeutics*, 1977, *201*, 386–399.

Heilman, K. M., & Valenstein, E. Frontal lobe neglect in man. *Neurology*, 1972, *22*, 660–664.

Heilman, K. M., & Watson, R. T. The neglect syndrome: A unilateral defect of the orienting response. In S. Harnad, R. W. Doty, L. Goldstein, J. Jaynes, & G. Krauthamer (Eds.). *Lateralization in the nervous system*. New York: Academic Press, 1977. (a)

Heilman, K. M., & Watson, R. T. Mechanisms underlying the unilateral neglect syndrome. In E. A. Weinstein & R. P. Friedland (Eds.), *Advances in neurology* (Vol. 18). New York: Raven Press, 1977. (b)

Hein, A., Gower, E., & Diamond, R. Exposure requirements for developing the triggered component of the visual-placing response. *Journal of Comparative and Physiological Psychology*, 1970, *73*, 188–192.

Hendricks, J. C., Bowker, R. M., & Morrison, A. R. Functional characteristics of cats with pontine lesions during sleep and wakefulness and their usefulness for sleep research. In W. Koella & P. Levin (Eds.), *Sleep 1976*. Basel: Karger, 1977.

Henley, K., & Morrison, A. R. A re-evaluation of the effects of lesions of the pontine tegmentum and locus coeruleus on phenomena of paradoxical sleep in the cat. *Acta Neurobiologiae Experimentalis*, 1974, *34*, 215–232.

Henning, S. J., Chang, S. S. P., & Gisel, E. G. Ontogeny of feeding controls in suckling and weanling rats. *American Journal of Physiology*, 1979, *237*, R187–R191.

Herndon, J. G., & Neill, D. B. Amphetamine reversal of sexual impairment following anterior hypothalamic lesions in female rats. *Pharmacology, Biochemistry and Behavior*, 1973, *1*, 285–288.

Hitt, J. C., Hendricks, S. E., Ginsberg, S. I., & Lewis, J. H. Disruption of male, but not female, sexual behavior in rats by medial forebrain bundle lesions. *Journal of Comparative and Physiological Psychology*, 1970, *73*, 377–384.

Hodge, C. J., Woods, C. I., & Delatizky, I. The effects of L-DOPA on dorsal horn cell responses to innocuous skin stimulation. *Brain Research*, 1979, *173*, 271–285.

Hoebel, B. G. Brain reward and aversion systems in the control of feeding and sexual behavior. In J. K. Cole & T. B. Sonderegger (Eds.), *Nebraska symposium on motivation 1974* (Vol. 22). Lincoln: University of Nebraska Press, 1975.

Hofer, M. A., Shair, H., & Singh, P. Evidence that maternal ventral skin substances promote suckling in infant rats. *Physiology and Behavior*, 1976, *17*, 131–136.

Hofer, M. A., Fisher, A., & Shair, H. Effects of infraorbital nerve section on survival, growth, and suckling behaviors of developing rats. *Journal of Comparative and Physiological Psychology*, 1981, *95*, 123–133.

Hornykiewicz, O. Dopamine (3-hydroxytyramine) and brain function. *Pharmacological Reviews*, 1966, *18*, 925–964.

Hoyman, L., Weese, G. D., & Frommer, G. P. Tactile discrimination performance deficits following neglect-producing unilateral lateral hypothalamic lesions in the rat. *Physiology and Behavior*, 1979, *22*, 139–147.

James, W. T., & Rollins, J. Effect of various degrees of stomach loading on the sucking response in puppies. *Psychological Reports*, 1965, *17*, 844–846.

Jeste, D. V., & Smith, G. P. Unilateral mesolimbocortical dopamine denervation decreases locomotion in the open field and after amphetamine. *Pharmacology, Biochemistry and Behavior*, 1980, *12*, 453–457.

Jimerson, D., & Reis, D. J. Effects of intrahypothalamic injection of 6-hydroxydopamine on predatory aggression in rat. *Brain Research*, 1973, *61*, 141–152.

Johanson, I. B., & Hall, W. G. The ontogeny of feeding in rats: III. Thermal determinants of early ingestive responding. *Journal of Comparative and Physiological Psychology*, 1980, *94*, 977–992.

Jouvet, M. Biogenic amines and the states of sleep. *Science*, 1969, *163*, 32–41.

Jouvet, M., & Delorme, F. Locus coeruleus et sommeil paradoxal. *Comptes Rendus des Seances de la Societe de Biologie*, 1965, *159*, 895–899.

Kanner, M., & Balagura, S. Loss of feeding response to 2-deoxy-D-glucose by recovered lateral hypothalamic rats. *American Zoologist*, 1971, *11*, 624.

Karli, P., & Vergnes, M. Dissociation experimentale du comportement d'agression interspecifique rat-souris et du comportement alimentaire. *Comptes Rendus des Seances de la Societe de Biologie*, 1964, *158*, 650–653.

Kenyon, C. A. P., Cronin, P., & Malinek, P. Effects of lidocaine on nipple attachment and home orientation by rat pups. *Behavioral and Neural Biology*, 1981, *32*, 261–264.

Koepke, J. E., & Pribram, K. H. Effect of milk on the maintenance of sucking behavior in kittens from birth to six months. *Journal of Comparative and Physiological Psychology*, 1971, *75*, 363–377.

Kolb, B., & Whishaw, I. Q. Effects of brain lesions and atropine on hippocampal and neocortical electroencephalograms in the rat. *Experimental Neurology*, 1977, *56*, 1–22.

Kolb, B., Dodic, R., & Whishaw, I. Q. Effects of serial lateral hypothalamic destruction on feeding behavior, body weight, and neocortical and hippocampal EEG activity. *Experimental Neurology*, 1979, *66*, 263–276.

Koob, G. F., Fray, P. J., & Iversen, S. D. Tail pinch stimulation: Sufficient motivation for learning. *Science*, 1976, *194*, 637–639.

Komisaruk, B. R., Adler, N. T., & Hutchinson, J. Genital sensory field: Enlargement by estrogen treatment in female rats. *Science*, 1972, *178*, 1295–1298.

Kow, L. M., & Pfaff, D. W. Estrogen effect on pudendal nerve receptive field size in the female rat. *Anatomical Record*, 1973, *175*, 362–363.

Kramis, R., Vanderwolf, C. H., & Bland, B. H. Two types of hippocampal rhythmical slow activity in both the rabbit and the rat: Relations to behavior and effects of atropine, diethyl ether, urethane, and pentobarbital. *Experimental Neurology*, 1975, *49*, 58–85.

Leblanc, M. O., & Bland, B. H. Developmental aspects of hippocampal electrical activity and motor behavior in the rat. *Experimental Neurology*, 1979, *66*, 220–237.

Levine, M. S., Hull, C. D., & Buchwald, N. A. Development of motor activity in kittens. *Developmental Psychobiology*, 1980, *13*, 357–371.

Levison, P. K., & Flynn, J. P. The objects attacked by cats during stimulation of the hypothalamus. *Animal Behavior*, 1965, *13*, 217–220.

Levitt, D. R., & Teitelbaum, P. Somnolence, akinesia, and sensory activation of motivated behavior in the lateral hypothalamic syndrome. *Proceedings of the National Academy of Sciences*, 1975, *72*, 2819–2823.

Leyhausen, P. Verhaltensstudien an Katzen. *Zeitschrift für Tierpsychologie*, 1956, Suppl. 2, 1–120.

Leyhausen, P. On the function of the relative hierarchy of moods (as exemplified by the phylogenetic and ontogenetic development of prey-catching in carnivores). In K. Lorenz & P. Leyhausen (Eds.), *Motivation of human and animal behavior*. London: Van Nostrand Reinhold, 1973.

Leyhausen, P. *Cat behavior: The predatory and social behavior of domestic and wild cats* (B. A. Tonkin, Trans.). New York: Garland STPM Press, 1979.

Lindsley, D. B. Emotion. In S. S. Stevens (Ed.), *Handbook of experimental psychology*. New York: Wiley, 1951.

Lindsley, D. B., Schreiner, L. H., Knowles, W. B., & Magoun, H. W. Behavioral and EEG changes following chronic brain stem lesions in the cat. *Electroencephalography and Clinical Neurophysiology*, 1950, *2*, 483–498.

Lindsley, D. F., Ranf, S. K., Fernandez, F. C., & Wyrwicka, W. Effects of anti-Parkinsonian drugs on the motor activity and EEG of cats with subthalamic lesions. *Experimental Neurology*, 1975, *47*, 404–418.

Ljungberg, T., & Ungerstedt, U. Sensory inattention produced by 6-hydroxydopamine-induced degeneration of ascending dopamine neurons in the brain. *Experimental Neurology*, 1976, *53*, 585–600. (a)

Ljungberg, T., & Ungerstedt, U. Reinstatement of eating by dopamine agonists in aphagic dopamine denervated rats. *Physiology and Behavior*, 1976, *16*, 277–283. (b)

MacDonnell, M. F., & Flynn, J. P. Control of sensory fields by stimulation of hypothalamus. *Science*, 1966, *152*, 1406–1408.

Malmo, H. P., & Malmo, R. B. Movement-related forebrain and midbrain multiple unit activity in rats. *Electroencephalography and Clinical Neurophysiology*, 1977, *42*, 501–509.

Marques, D. M., Fisher, A. E., Okrutny, M. S., & Rowland, N. E. Tail pinch induced fluid ingestion: Interactions of taste and deprivation. *Physiology and Behavior*, 1979, *22*, 37–41.

Marshall, J. F. Somatosensory inattention after dopamine-depleting intracerebral 6-OHDA injections: Spontaneous recovery and pharmacological control. *Brain Research*, 1979, *177*, 311–324.

Marshall, J. F., & Gotthelf, T. Sensory inattention in rats with 6-hydroxydopamine-induced degeneration of ascending dopaminergic neurons: Apomorphine-induced reversal of deficits. *Experimental Neurology*, 1979, *65*, 398–411.

Marshall, J. F., & Teitelbaum, P. Further analysis of sensory inattention following lateral hypothalamic damage in rats. *Journal of Comparative and Physiological Psychology*, 1974, *86*, 375–395.

Marshall, J. F., & Teitelbaum, P. New considerations in the neuropsychology of motivated behaviors. In L. L. Iversen, S. D. Iversen, & S. H. Snyder (Eds.), *Handbook of psychopharmacology* (Vol. 7). New York: Plenum Press, 1977.

Marshall, J. F., & Ungerstedt, U. Apomorphine-induced restoration of drinking to thirst challenges in 6-hydroxydopamine-treated rats. *Physiology and Behavior*, 1976, *17*, 817–822.

Marshall, J. F., Turner, B. H., & Teitelbaum, P. Sensory neglect produced by lateral hypothalamic damage. *Science*, 1971, *174*, 523–525.

Marshall, J. F., Richardson, J. S., & Teitelbaum, P. Nigrostriatal bundle damage and the lateral hypothalamic syndrome. *Journal of Comparative and Physiological Psychology*, 1974, *87*, 808–830.

Marshall, J. F., Levitan, D., & Stricker, E. M. Activation-induced restoration of sensorimotor functions in rats with dopamine-depleting brain lesions. *Journal of Comparative and Physiological Psychology*, 1976, *90*, 536–546.

Marshall, J. F., Berrios, N., & Sawyer, S. Neostriatal dopamine and sensory inattention. *Journal of Comparative and Physiological Psychology*, 1980, *94*, 833–846.

Martin, J. P. *The basal ganglia and posture*. Philadelphia: J. B. Lippincott, 1967.

Matthysse, S. Schizophrenia: Relationships to dopamine transmission, motor control, and feature extraction. In F. O. Schmitt & F. G. Worden (Eds.), *The neurosciences: Third study program*. Cambridge, Mass.: MIT Press, 1974.

Miselis, R. R., & Epstein, A. N. Preoptic-hypothalamic mediation of feeding induced by cerebral glucoprivation. *American Zoologist*, 1971, *11*, 624.

Mogenson, G. J., & Phillips, A. G. Motivation: A psychological construct in search of a physiological substrate. In J. M. Sprague & A. N. Epstein (Eds.), *Progress in psychobiology and physiological psychology* (Vol. 6). New York: Academic Press, 1976.

Morrison, A. R. Brain-stem regulation of behavior during sleep and wakefulness. In J. M. Sprague & A. N. Epstein (Eds.), *Progress in psychobiology and physiological psychology* (Vol. 8). New York: Academic Press, 1979.

Morrison, A. R., & Pompeiano, O. An analysis of supraspinal influences acting on motoneurons during sleep in the unrestrained cat: Responses of the alpha motoneurons to direct electrical stimulation during sleep. *Archives Italiennes de Biologie*, 1965, *103*, 497–516.

Moruzzi, G. Sleep and instinctive behavior. *Archives Italiennes de Biologie*, 1969, *107*, 175–216.

Moruzzi, G., & Magoun, H. W. Brain stem reticular formation and activation of the EEG. *Electroencephalography and Clinical Neurophysiology*, 1949, *1*, 455–473.

Mufson, E. J., Balagura, S., & Riss, W. Tail pinch-induced arousal and stimulus bound behavior in rats with lateral hypothalamic lesions. *Brain, Behavior and Evolution*, 1976, *13*, 154–164.

Myers, R. D. *Handbook of drug and chemical stimulation of the brain*. New York: Van Nostrand Reinhold, 1974.

Parmeggiani, P. L. Interaction between sleep and thermoregulation. *Waking and Sleeping*, 1977, *1*, 123–132.

Phillips, A. G., & Fibiger, H. C. Long-term deficits in stimulation-induced behaviors and self-stimulation after 6-hydroxydopamine administration in rats. *Behavioral Biology*, 1976, *16*, 127–143.

Proshansky, E., & Bandler, R. J. Midbrain-hypothalamic interrelationships in the control of aggressive behavior. *Aggressive Behavior*, 1975, *1*, 135–155.

Proshansky, E., Bandler, R. J., & Flynn, J. P. Elimination of hypothalamically elicited biting attack by unilateral lesion of the ventral midbrain tegmentum of cats. *Brain Research*, 1974, *77*, 309–313.

Reeves, A. G., & Hagamen, W. D. Behavioral and EEG asymmetry following unilateral lesions of the forebrain and midbrain in cats. *Electroencephalography and Clinical Neurophysiology*, 1971, *30*, 83–86.

Roberts, W. W. Are hypothalamic motivational mechanisms functionally and anatomically specific? *Brain, Behavior and Evolution*, 1969, *2*, 317–342.

Roberts, W. W. Hypothalamic mechanisms for motivational and species-typical behavior. In R. E. Whalen, R. F. Thompson, M. Verzeano, & M. M. Weinberger (Eds.), *The neural control of behavior*. New York: Academic Press, 1970.

Roberts, W. W., & Kiess, H. O. Motivational properties of hypothalamic aggression in cats. *Journal of Comparative and Physiological Psychology*, 1964, *58*, 187–193.

Robinson, T. E. Electrical stimulation of the brain stem in freely moving rats: I. Effects on behavior. *Physiology and Behavior*, 1978, *21*, 223–231.

Robinson, T. E., & Vanderwolf, C. H. Electrical stimulation of the brain stem in freely moving rats: II. Effects on hippocampal and neocortical electrical activity, and relations to behavior. *Experimental Neurology*, 1978, *61*, 485–515.

Robinson, T. E., & Whishaw, I. Q. Effects of posterior hypothalamic lesions on voluntary behavior and hippocampal electroencephalograms in the rat. *Journal of Comparative and Physiological Psychology*, 1974, *86*, 768–786.

Robinson, T. E., Kramis, R. C., & Vanderwolf, C. H. Two types of cerebral activation during active sleep: Relations to behavior. *Brain Research*, 1977, *124*, 544–549.

Rosenblatt, J. S. Stages in the early behavioural development of altricial young of selected species of non-primate mammmals. In P. P. G. Bateson & R. A. Hinde (Eds.), *Growing points in ethology*. Cambridge: Cambridge University Press, 1976.

Rosenblatt, J. S. The sensorimotor and motivational bases of early behavioral development of selected altricial mammals. In N. E. Spear & B. A. Campbell (Eds.), *The ontogeny of learning and memory*. Hillsdale, N.J.: Lawrence Erlbaum, 1979.

Rowland, N. E. Recovery of regulatory drinking following lateral hypothalamic lesions: Nature of residual deficits analyzed by NaCl and water infusions. *Experimental Neurology*, 1976, *53*, 488–507.

Rowland, N. E., & Antelman, S. M. Stress-induced hyperphagia and obesity in rats: A possible model for understanding human obesity. *Science*, 1976, *191*, 310–312.

Rowland, N. E., Marques, D. M., & Fisher, A. E. Comparison of the effects of brain dopamine-depleting lesions upon oral behaviors elicited by tail pinch and electrical brain stimulation. *Physiology and Behavior*, 1980, *24*, 273–281.

Russek, M., Rodriguez-Zendejas, A. M., & Teitelbaum, P. The action of adrenergic anorexigenic substances on rats recovered from lateral hypothalamic lesions. *Physiology and Behavior*, 1973, *10*, 329–333.

Sachs, B. D., & Barfield, R. J. Copulatory behavior of male rats given intermittent electric shocks: Theoretical implications. *Journal of Comparative and Physiological Psychology*, 1974, *86*, 607–615.

Sacks, O. W. *Awakenings*. New York: Vintage Books, 1973.

Sastre, J. P., & Jouvet, M. Le comportement onirique du chat. *Physiology and Behavior*, 1979, *22*, 979–989.

Satinoff, E., & Stanley, W. C. Effect of stomach loading on sucking behavior in neonatal puppies. *Journal of Comparative and Physiological Psychology*, 1963, *56*, 66–68.

Schallert, T., & Whishaw, I. Q. Two types of aphagia and two types of sensorimotor impairment after lateral hypothalamic lesions: Observations in normal weight, dieted, and fattened rats. *Journal of Comparative and Physiological Psychology*, 1978, *92*, 720–741.

Schallert, T., Whishaw, I. Q., De Ryck, M., & Teitelbaum, P. The postures of catecholamine-depletion catalepsy: Their possible adaptive value in thermoregulation. *Physiology and Behavior*, 1978, *21*, 817–820.

Schallert, T., De Ryck, M., & Teitelbaum, P. Atropine stereotypy as a behavioral trap: A movement subsystem and electroencephalographic analysis. *Journal of Comparative and Physiological Psychology*, 1980, *94*, 1–24.

Schwab, R. S. Akinisia paradoxica. *Electroencephalography and Clinical Neurophysiology*, 1972, *Suppl. 31*, 87–92.

Schwab, R. S., England, A. C., & Peterson, E. Akinesia in Parkinson's disease. *Neurology*, 1959, *9*, 65–74.

Schwab, R. S., & Zieper, I. Effects of mood, motivation, stress and alertness on the performance in Parkinson's disease. *Psychiatria et Neurologia*, 1965, *150*, 345–357.

Schwartzbaum, J. S. Interrelationship among multiunit activity of the midbrain reticular formation and lateral geniculate nucleus, thalamocortical arousal, and behavior in rats. *Journal of Comparative and Physiological Psychology*, 1975, *89*, 131–157.

Sechzer, J. A., Ervin, G. N., & Smith, G. P. Loss of visual placing in rats after lateral hypothalamic microinjections of 6-hydroxydopamine. *Experimental Neurology*, 1973, *41*, 723–737.

Segundo, J. P., Arana, R., & French, J. D. Behavioral arousal by stimulation of the brain in the monkey. *Journal of Neurosurgery*, 1955, *12*, 601–613.

Shipley, J. E., Rowland, N., & Antelman, S. M. Orbital or medial frontal cortical lesions have different effects on tail pressure-elicited oral behaviors in rats. *Physiology and Behavior*, 1980, *24*, 1091–1094.

Siegel, J. M. Behavioral functions of the reticular formation. *Brain Research Reviews*, 1979, *1*, 69–105. (a)

Siegel, J. M. Behavioral relations of medullary reticular formation cells. *Experimental Neurology*, 1979, *65*, 691–698. (b)

Siegel, J. M., & McGinty, D. J. Pontine reticular formation neurons: Relationship of discharge to motor activity. *Science*, 1977, *196*, 678–680.

Siegel, J. M., McGinty, D. J., & Breedlove, S. M. Sleep and waking activity of pontine gigantocellular field neurons. *Experimental Neurology*, 1977, *56*, 553–573.

Siegel, J. M., Wheeler, R. L., & McGinty, D. J. Activity of medullary reticular formation neurons in the unrestrained cat during waking and sleep. *Brain Research*, 1979, *179*, 49–60.

Siegfried, B., & Bures, J. Asymmetry of EEG arousal in rats with unilateral 6-hydroxydopamine lesions in substantia nigra: Quantification of neglect. *Experimental Neurology*, 1978, *62*, 173–190.

Siegfried, B., & Bures, J. Conditioning compensates the neglect due to unilateral 6-OHDA lesions of substantia nigra in rats. *Brain Research*, 1979, *167*, 139–155.

Singer, H. W. *Meister der Zeichnung: Zeichnungen von Lovis Corinth.* Leipzig: A. Schumann's Verlag, 1921.

Smith, D. A., & Flynn, J. P. Afferent projections related to attack sites in the pontine tegmentum. *Brain Research*, 1979, *164*, 103–119.

Smith, D. A., & Flynn, J. P. Afferent projections to quiet attack sites in cat hypothalamus. *Brain Research*, 1980, *194*, 29–40.

Stellar, E. The physiology of motivation. *Psychological Review*, 1954, *61*, 5–22.

Steriade, M., Ropert, N., Kitsikis, A., & Oakson, G. Ascending activating neuronal networks in midbrain reticular core and related rostral systems. In J. A. Hobson & M. A. B. Brazier (Eds.), *The reticular formation revisited.* New York: Raven Press, 1980.

Stricker, E. M. Drinking by rats after lateral hypothalamic lesions: A new look at the lateral hypothalamic syndrome. *Journal of Comparative and Physiological Psychology*, 1976, *90*, 127–143.

Stricker, E. M., & Wolf, G. The effects of hypovolemia on drinking in rats with lateral hypothalamic damage. *Proceedings of the Society for Experimental Biology and Medicine*, 1967, *124*, 816–820.

Stricker, E. M., & Zigmond, M. J. Recovery of function after damage to central catecholamine-containing neurons: A neurochemical model for the lateral hypothalamic syndrome. In J. M. Sprague & A. N. Epstein (Eds.), *Progress in psychobiology and physiological psychology* (Vol. 6). New York: Academic Press, 1976.

Stricker, E. M., Friedman, M. I., & Zigmond, M. J. Glucoregulatory feeding by rats after intraventricular 6-hydroxydopamine or lateral hypothalamic lesions. *Science*, 1975, *189*, 895–897.

Stricker, E. M., Swerdloff, A. F., & Zigmond, M. J. Intrahypothalamic injections of kainic acid produce feeding and drinking deficits in rats. *Brain Research*, 1978, *158*, 470–473.

Stricker, E. M., Cooper, P. H., Marshall, J. F., & Zigmond, M. J. Acute homeostatic imbalances reinstate sensorimotor dysfunctions in rats with lateral hypothalamic lesions. *Journal of Comparative and Physiological Psychology*, 1979, *93*, 512–521.

Szechtman, H., & Hall, W. G. Ontogeny of oral behavior induced by tail pinch and electrical stimulation of the tail in rats. *Journal of Comparative and Physiological Psychology*, 1980, *94*, 436–445.

Szechtman, H., Siegel, H. I., Rosenblatt, J. S., & Komisaruk, B. R. Tail-pinch facilitates onset of maternal behavior in rats. *Physiology and Behavior*, 1977, *19*, 807–809.

Teicher, M. H., & Blass, E. M. Suckling in newborn rats: Eliminated by nipple lavage, reinstated by pup saliva. *Science*, 1976, *193*, 422–425.

Teicher, M. H., & Blass, E. M. First suckling response of the newborn albino rat: The roles of olfaction and amniotic fluid. *Science*, 1977, *198*, 635–636.

Teitelbaum, P. The encephalization of hunger. In J. M. Sprague & A. N. Epstein (Eds.), *Progress in physiological psychology* (Vol. 4). New York: Academic Press, 1971.

Teitelbaum, P. Levels of integration of the operant. In W. K. Honig & J. E. R. Staddon (Eds.), *Handbook of operant behavior*. Englewood Cliffs, N.J.: Prentice-Hall, 1977.

Teitelbaum, P., & Epstein, A. N. The lateral hypothalamic syndrome: Recovery of feeding and drinking after lateral hypothalamic lesions. *Psychological Review*, 1962, *69*, 74–90.

Teitelbaum, P., & Stellar, E. Recovery from the failure to eat produced by hypothalamic lesions. *Science*, 1954, *120*, 894–895.

Teitelbaum, P., & Wolgin, D. L. Neurotransmitters and the regulation of food intake. In W. H. Gispen, Tj. B. van Wimersma Greidanus, B. Bohus, & D. de Wied (Eds.), *Progress in brain research*. Vol. 42. *Hormones, homeostasis and the brain*. Amsterdam: Elsevier, 1975.

Teitelbaum, P., Cheng, M. F., & Rozin, P. Development of feeding parallels its recovery after hypothalamic damage. *Journal of Comparative and Physiological Psychology*, 1969, *67*, 430–441.

Teitelbaum, P., Schallert, T., De Ryck, M., Whishaw, I. Q., & Golani, I. Motor subsystems in motivated behavior. In R. F. Thompson, L. H. Hicks, & V. B. Shvyrkov (Eds.), *Neural mechanisms of goal-directed behavior and learning*. New York: Academic Press, 1980.

Teitelbaum, P., Schallert, T., Whishaw, I. Q., & Golani, I. Sources of spontaneity in motivated behavior. In E. Satinoff & P. Teitelbaum (Eds.), *Handbook of behavioral neurobiology: Motivation*. New York: Plenum Press, 1983.

Tilney, F. Behavior in its relation to the development of the brain. II. Correlation between the development of the brain and behavior in the albino rat from embryonic states to maturity. *Bulletin of the Neurological Institute of New York*, 1933, *3*, 252–358.

Torvik, A., & Brodal, A. The origin of reticulospinal fibers in the cat. *Anatomical Record*, 1957, *128*, 113–137.

Turner, B. H. Sensorimotor syndrome produced by lesions of the amygdala and lateral hypothalamus. *Journal of Comparative and Physiological Psychology*, 1973, *82*, 37–47.

Ungerstedt, U. Is interruption of the nigro-striatal dopamine system producing the "lateral hypothalamus syndrome"? *Acta Physiologica Scandinavica*, 1970, *80*, 35A–36A.

Ungerstedt, U. Adipsia and aphagia after 6-hydroxydopamine induced degeneration of the nigro-striatal dopamine system. *Acta Physiologica Scandinavica*, 1971, *Suppl. 367*, 95–122.

Valenstein, E. S. Stereotyped behavior and stress. In G. Serban (Ed.), *Psychopathology of human adaptation*. New York: Plenum Press, 1976.

Valenstein, E. S., Cox, V. C., & Kakolewski, J. W. Modification of motivated behavior elicited by electrical stimulation of the hypothalamus. *Science*, 1968, *159*, 1119–1121.

Valenstein, E. S., Cox, V. C., & Kakolewski, J. W. Reexamination of the role of the hypothalamus in motivation. *Psychological Review*, 1970, *77*, 16–31.

Vanderwolf, C. H. Hippocampal electrical activity and voluntary movement in the rat. *Electroencephalography and Clinical Neurophysiology*, 1969, *26*, 407–418.

Vanderwolf, C. H. Neocortical and hippocampal activation in relation to behavior: Effects of atropine, eserine, phenothiazines, and amphetamine. *Journal of Comparative and Physiological Psychology*, 1975, *88*, 300–323.

Vanderwolf, C. H. The role of the cerebral cortex and ascending activating systems in the control of behavior. In E. Satinoff & P. Teitelbaum (Eds.), *Handbook of behavioral neurobiology: Motivation*. New York: Plenum Press, 1983.

Vanderwolf, C. H., & Pappas, B. A. Reserpine abolishes movement-correlated atropine-resistant neocortical low voltage fast activity. *Brain Research*, 1980, 202, 79–94.

Vanderwolf, C. H., & Robinson, T. E. Retico-cortical activity and behavior: A critique of the arousal theory and a new synthesis. *The Behavioral and Brain Sciences*, 1981, 4, 459–514.

Vanderwolf, C. H., Bland, B. H., & Whishaw, I. Q. Diencephalic, hippocampal, and neocortical mechanisms in voluntary movement. In J. D. Maser (Ed.), *Efferent organization and the integration of behavior*. New York: Academic Press, 1973.

Vanderwolf, C. H., Kramis, R., Gillespie, L. A., & Bland, B. H. Hippocampal rhythmical slow activity and neocortical low voltage fast activity: Relations to behavior. In K. H. Pribram & R. L. Isaacson (Eds.), *The hippocampus: A comprehensive treatise*. New York: Plenum Press, 1975.

Vanderwolf, C. H., Kramis, R., & Robinson, T. E. Hippocampal electrical activity during waking behaviour and sleep: Analyses using centrally acting drugs. In *CIBA Foundation Symposium 58: Functions of the Septo-Hippocampal System*. Amsterdam: Elsevier, 1978.

Vanderwolf, C. H., Robinson, T. E., & Pappas, B. A. Monoamine replacement after reserpine: Catecholaminergic agonists restore motor activity but phenylethylamine restores atropine-resistant neocortical low voltage fast activity. *Brain Research*, 1980, 202, 65–77.

Vertes, R. P. Selective firing of rat pontine gigantocellular neurons during movement and REM sleep. *Brain Research*, 1977, 128, 146–152.

Vertes, R. P. Brain stem gigantocellular neurons: Patterns of activity during behavior and sleep in the freely moving rat. *Journal of Neurophysiology*, 1979, 42, 215–228.

Villablanca, J. R., & Olmstead, C. E. Neurological development of kittens. *Developmental Psychobiology*, 1979, 12, 101–127.

Wang, L., & Hull, E. M. Tail pinch induces sexual behavior in olfactory bulbectomized male rats. *Physiology and Behavior*, 1980, 24, 211–215.

Wasman, M., & Flynn, J. P. Directed attack elicited from the hypothalamus. *Archives of Neurology*, 1962, 6, 220–227.

Watson, R. T., Heilman, K. M., Miller, B. D., & King, F. A. Neglect after mesencephalic reticular formation lesions. *Neurology*, 1974, 24, 294–298.

Wayner, M. J., Cott, A., Millner, J., & Tartaglione, R. Loss of 2-deoxy-D-glucose induced eating in recovered lateral rats. *Physiology and Behavior*, 1971, 7, 881–884.

West, M. Social play in the domestic cat. *American Zoologist*, 1974, 14, 427–436.

Whishaw, I. Q. The effects of alcohol and atropine on EEG and behavior in the rabbit. *Psychopharmacologia*, 1976, 48, 83–90.

Wirth, J. B., & Epstein, A. N. Ontogeny of thirst in the infant rat. *American Journal of Physiology*, 1976, 230, 188–198.

Wolgin, D. L., & Servidio, S. Disinhibition of predatory attack in kittens by oxazepam. *Society for Neuroscience Abstracts*, 1979, 5, 667.

Wolgin, D. L., & Teitelbaum, P. Role of activation and sensory stimuli in recovery from lateral hypothalamic damage in the cat. *Journal of Comparative and Physiological Psychology*, 1978, 92, 474–500.

Wolgin, D. L., Cytawa, J., & Teitelbaum, P. The role of activation in the regulation of food intake. In D. Novin, W. Wyrwicka, & G. Bray (Eds.), *Hunger: Basic mechanisms and clinical implications*. New York: Raven Press, 1976.

Wolgin, D. L., Hein, A., & Teitelbaum, P. Recovery of forelimb placing after lateral hypothalamic lesions in the cat: Parallels and contrasts with development. *Journal of Comparative and Physiological Psychology*, 1980, 94, 795–807.

Wright, J. J., & Craggs, M. D. Changed cortical activation and the lateral hypothalamic syndrome: A study in the split-brain cat. *Brain Research*, 1978, *151*, 632–636.

Wright, J. J., & Craggs, M. D. Intracranial self-stimulation, cortical arousal, and the sensorimotor neglect syndrome. *Experimental Neurology*, 1979, *65*, 42–52.

Wright, J. J., Craggs, M. D., & Sergejew, A. A. Visual evoked response in lateral hypothalamic neglect. *Experimental Neurology*, 1979, *65*, 178–185.

Zigmond, M. J., & Stricker, E. M. Recovery of feeding and drinking by rats after intraventricular 6-hydroxydopamine or lateral hypothalamic lesions. *Science*, 1973, *182*, 717–720.

Zülch, K. J., Creutzfeldt, O., & Galbraith, G. L. *Cerebral localization*. New York: Springer, 1975.

9

Neurochemical Consequences of Stress
Intrusion of Nonassociative Factors in Behavioral Analysis

Hymie Anisman

1. INTRODUCTION

Physical or psychological insults or the threat of such insults will insti-
gate a series of behavioral changes that can be viewed as adaptive alterations to meet environmental demands. That is, these behavioral acts
minimize the impact of the stress or promote either escape or avoidance
from the aversive stimuli. Concurrently, several physiological changes
occur, including neurochemical, hormonal, and immunologic alterations, that likely have adaptive significance (see Amkraut & Solomon,
1975; Anisman, Kokkinidis, & Sklar, 1981a; Miline, 1980; Sklar & Anisman, 1981; Yuwiler, 1976). For example, the physiological alterations
may reduce the aversiveness of the stimuli (Chance, White, Krynock, &
Rosecrans, 1977, 1978; Maier and Jackson, 1979), blunt the affect associated with the stress (Abramson & Sackeim, 1977), prevent or minimize
physical pathologies or illness (see Sklar & Anisman, 1981), prepare the
organism for further encounters with stress (Anisman & Sklar, 1979),

HYMIE ANISMAN ● Department of Psychology, Carleton University, Ottawa, Ontario,
Canada K1S 5B6. This chapter was supported by Grants No. A9845 from the Natural
Sciences and Engineering Research Council and No. MT6486 from the Medical Research
Council.

and they may be instrumental in eliciting the behavioral sequence culminating in evasion of the stressful stimuli (Anisman, Kokkinidis, & Sklar, 1981b).

As will be seen later, the range of physiological and behavioral changes that occur in response to stress is fairly extensive. It is naïve to assume that a one-to-one correspondence exists between physiological and behavioral alterations. Several neurochemical/hormonal changes may be responsible for a given behavioral change, and conversely, a single neurochemical/hormonal event may directly or indirectly influence several behaviors. Accordingly, learning and memory processes cannot be adequately assessed through evaluation of any single endogenous substrate or brain region. Moreover, identification of the processes that subserve learning and memory is hampered by the fact that the expression of learned behaviors is influenced in great measure by the intrusion of nonassociative factors. Indeed, it is often the case that pharmacological or surgical treatments employed to discern the neuronal substrates of learning and memory modify behavior through effects on nonassociative mechanisms.

This chapter will outline the contributions of associative and nonassociative factors to avoidance and escape behaviors, and some of the conditions under which nonassociative events influence the expression of previously formed or to-be-formed associations. There will follow an analysis of the neurochemical consequences of stress and their potential contribution to behavior.

2. STRESS AND AVOIDANCE BEHAVIOR

Within the laboratory situation two forms of avoidance behavior have been assessed most often: those tasks where the animal must emit a particular response for successful avoidance (active avoidance), and those tasks that require the animal to withhold responding (passive avoidance). Although numerous avoidance paradigms are available, they all require one or the other of these responses.

Despite the apparent simplicity of avoidance tasks, several variables will profoundly influence behavior, including not only organismic and experiential factors but nonassociative factors related to the stressor itself. In general, the major elements that contribute to avoidance are *associative processes* such as (1) stimulus–shock association, and (2) response–shock association, and *nonassociative processes* such as (1) response factors, (2) stimulus factors, (3) stimulus–response interface, (4) attentional factors, (5) motivation, and (6) preparatory responses.

2.1. Associative Processes

In order for an avoidance response to be acquired, a *drive* state and a source for reinforcement must be established. The processes involved have been discussed at length (e.g., Bolles, 1971; Herrnstein, 1969; Rescorla & Solomon, 1967); suffice it to say that according to some investigators the drive is established through Pavlovian conditioning of fear of the conditioned stimulus paired with shock, and reinforcement is derived from fear reduction that occurs upon CS termination following emission of an appropriate response (Rescorla & Solomon, 1967). Others have argued that the motive for responding is to avoid shock. The pairing of a CS with shock results in "expectancy" of shock when the CS is subsequently presented, whereas offset of the CS, which occurs when an appropriate response is emitted, serves as a feedback or safety signal (Bolles, 1970, 1971).

In an active avoidance task the animal must not only learn that a particular stimulus precedes shock, but also that an *active response*, appropriately directed, is necessary to prevent or terminate the aversive stimulus. Thus the organism must be able to *initiate* a response, *direct* this response appropriately, and *sustain* this response through to completion of the sequence. It is often difficult to determine how a particular treatment disrupts performance since alterations of any one of the various components involved in avoidance may ultimately modify responding. Conversely, facilitation of a single component may not necessarily result in enhanced avoidance since some other component may represent a rate-limiting step for the learning process. For example, facilitating response initiation may not guarantee enhanced performance if the response cannot be appropriately directed. Likewise, treatments that improve an organism's ability to learn response–outcome contingencies may not enhance performance if the appropriate response cannot readily be initiated.

An important and often overlooked consideration is that there is no a priori reason to believe that the processes that govern stimulus–shock and response–shock associations are identical. After all, an organism may be well equipped for the establishment of stimulus–shock association (e.g., through Pavlovian processes) and yet be deficient in acquiring response–shock associations. Campbell and Spear (1972), for example, indicate that young animals may be inferior to adults in the retention of aversively motivated responses and yet be as greatly affected as adults by early life trauma. In effect, the cue–stress association may have been well established, but the response–stress contingency may not have been adequately retained. Furthermore, Izquierdo and Elisabetsky

(1978) indicate that several "memory channels" exist, each subserved by different neurochemical systems.

2.2. Nonassociative Processes

The behavior of an organism in an aversive situation is determined in large measure by its defensive style, together with the requirements of the avoidance task. Bolles (1970) indicates that when an animal is exposed to an aversive stimulus, its response repertoire becomes restricted to a narrow range such that defensive response patterns predominate. Whereas some animals are most reliant on camouflage or mimicry, other organisms may adopt various threatening postures or may attempt varied forms of flight. The nature of the defense style adopted varies not only among species but among strains within a species. Presumably, such environmental factors as land topography and the nature of predators in the vicinity would have contributed to the selection factors that acted on the species in the development of defensive styles.

With respect to laboratory-assessed avoidance behavior, Bolles (1970) argues that if the response requirement of the avoidance task coincides with the organism's defensive style, avoidance can be readily established. If the designated response is not part of the organism's defensive repertoire, it will be established through instrumental processes once the more potent defensive behaviors have been suppressed. As a result these behaviors will be established exceedingly slowly.

Several investigators have expressed views similar to that advanced by Bolles. For instance, Seligman (1970) suggests that animals may be prepared, unprepared, or contraprepared to learn certain responses. Essentially, predispositions for particular responses, established through genetic or experiential processes, determine the rate at which responses will be acquired. Indeed, it has been shown that strains of rats will differ in anticipatory responding (i.e., in a classical conditioning paradigm) and that the frequency of such responses is related to avoidance response rate (Katzev & Mills, 1974; Shurman & Katzev, 1975). Likewise, Izquierdo (1976) reports that pharmacological treatments that influence anticipatory responding and pseudoconditioned responses have parallel effects on avoidance performance.

In addition to response factors, the nature of the stimulus employed may influence avoidance. Certainly, salience or discriminability of the CS would be expected to influence performance. Moreover, it seems that some stimuli are more apt to elicit particular responses than others. For example, a loud buzzer will increase the likelihood of a startle reaction (or a pseudoconditioned response), which aids in response initiation and hence in completion of a successful avoidance. Furthermore, it has been hypothesized that the associability of events may be related to location and the temporal aspects of the to-be-associated stimuli (Testa, 1974). Just as animals may be better equipped to complete particular responses, they may also be better prepared to associate a response with some stimuli than with others (Shettleworth, 1972).

2.3. Dissociation of Associative and Nonassociative Factors

2.3.1. Activity–Reactivity

In order to assess fully the processes that contribute to avoidance and escape behavior, it is appropriate to examine behavior in various tasks that reflect the components of the more complex learning situation. Among rats and mice the level of general activity (or exploratory behavior) displayed in the absence of a stressor is not predictive of the behavior exhibited in aversive tasks. However, the response changes that are displayed once a stressor has been applied may foretell the performance levels that can be expected in avoidance situations (Anisman & Waller, 1972; Anisman, Grimmer, Irwin, Remington, & Sklar, 1979). It seems that under nonthreatening circumstances animals will not display their defensive repertoire. Once a stressor is applied animals will exhibit their particular defensive styles; thus it should be possible to determine to what extent the response requirements of the avoidance tasks are compatible with the prepotent response in the organism's defensive repertoire.

Exposure to aversive stimuli will induce both behavioral excitation and inhibition. The extent of these behavioral outcomes varies with numerous factors such as stress severity, previous stress history, and so on (see Anisman, 1975). Among naïve animals, exposure to an aversive stimulus results in a transient period of response excitation that may persist for as long as 10 minutes (Pinel & Mucha, 1973). The source for the initial excitation is not known, but it has been suggested that the efflux of catecholamines prompted by the stress is responsible for this stress reaction (Anisman, 1975).

The initial period of excitation is followed by a more protracted period of behavioral inhibition that will persist for 1 to 4 hours after stress exposure (see Anisman, 1975; Brush, 1971). It seems that one essential requirement for the aforementioned changes to occur is that the initial stressor be inescapable or that the animal receive an insufficient number of trials for avoidance to have been acquired (see Brush,

1971). If animals receive a sufficiently large number of escapable/avoidable shocks, the resulting responses established through instrumental means will mask these nonassociative consequences of the stress.

Assuming that nonassociative factors influence avoidance behavior, and that stress has predictable nonassociative effects, several deductions can be made concerning treatment effects on avoidance behavior. In particular, provided that associative capacities are unimpeded, the occurrence of nonassociative factors compatible with the required response will enhance performance, whereas incompatible tendencies will hinder it. The rate of acquiring a response that is incompatible with nonassociative response tendencies will be inversely related to the strength of the incompatible response and directly related to the ease with which these tendencies are suppressed.

2.3.2. Passive (Inhibitory) Avoidance

In a passive avoidance task animals are punished for emitting a particular response. Subsequently, animals are reintroduced to the test chamber and the latency of emitting the punished response is recorded. Although the passive avoidance task has been widely employed in learning/memory tasks, it is questionable whether valid conclusions about these processes can be derived from the passive avoidance procedure. Animals may withhold responding because an active response was previously punished or because of a reluctance to approach cues previously associated with shock. However, the nonassociative effects of shock (i.e., freezing) also influence performance. Indeed, manipulations that reduce freezing tend to disrupt passive avoidance (e.g., treatment with scopolamine and amphetamine, or septal and hippocampal lesions), whereas treatments that enhance freezing have the opposite effect (see Bignami, 1976; Bignami & Michalek, 1978; Peters, Anisman, & Pappas, 1978).

The approach–avoidance conflict task bears resemblance to the passive avoidance task in that both involve suppression of responding. However, because the conflict task involves positive reinforcement, thereby maintaining the active response, repeated testing may be possible without total cessation of responding. Like the passive avoidance task, performance in the conflict situation may be subject to nonassociative effects related to motor functions. The use of procedures such as the Geller paradigm (Geller, 1962) may allow for assessment of nonassociative influences. In particular, animals are trained on a multiple operant task in which punishment is delivered on only one of the two reinforcement schedules, resulting in selective response suppression. If a particular treatment influences performance on both schedules, then this treatment probably influences behavior through nonassociative mechanisms. In contrast, if the treatment effect is exclusive to punished responding it is likely that the behavioral change is not due to general effects such as variations in anxiety.

Like the conflict and passive avoidance tasks, behavioral suppression can be determined through the conditioned emotional response (CER). In this task animals are trained to emit an operant until stable response rates are reached. In one form of the task a CS is paired with noncontingent shock; in a second form, shock is presented after response emission. The rate of responding is subsequently gauged as some proportion of responses emitted during CS and non-CS periods. Since in either paradigm performance in the CER task is evaluated against baseline responding, it can be determined whether the effects of various treatments are restricted to periods during which a CS is present (see, e.g., Barry & Buckley, 1966; Miczek, 1973a,b). Unfortunately, this task does not readily allow for differentiation between changes in learning/memory and emotionality.

With respect to the CER task, treatment effects are dependent on whether the tasks involve contingent or noncontingent shock presentation. Several investigators, for example, reported that such treatments as chlordiazepoxide alleviated response suppression in the contingent

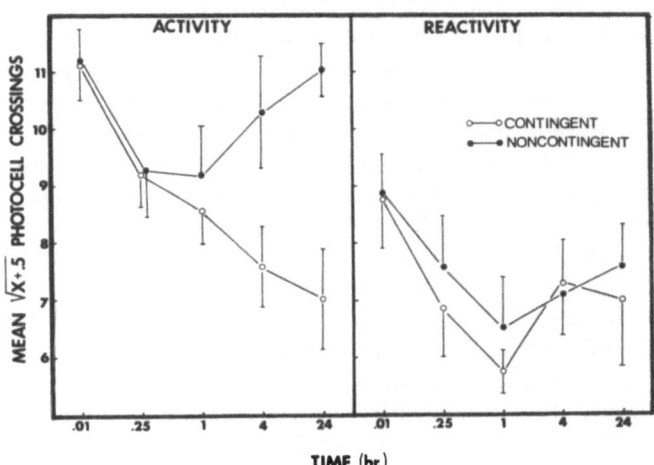

Fig. 9.1. Photocell crossings (±SEM) in mice at several intervals after exposure to movement-contingent shock and among yoked (noncontingent shock) controls. The left-hand panel (activity) shows the number of photocell crossings that occurred over the initial 5 minute of the test session. The right-hand panel shows the number of photocell crossings over the 5-minute period following reexposure to a single shock 2.5 seconds long. (From Anisman, 1977.)

but not in the noncontingent paradigm (Huppert & Iversen, 1965; McMillan & Leander, 1975). Furthermore, as indicated earlier, activity following shock varies as a U-shaped function over time. As shown in the left-hand panel of Figure 9.1, such an effect occurs after noncontingent shock, but after contingent shock activity tends to decline monotonically over the initial 24-hour period. If animals are reexposed to a single shock, then levels of reactivity (right-hand panel) resemble a U-shaped function in both instances (Anisman, 1977). Clearly, contingent and noncontingent shock may lead to similar outcomes in some instances but not in others. Accordingly, the contribution of associative processes to behavioral change may be dubious when assessing response suppression.

2.3.3. Active Avoidance

As we have seen, an active avoidance task requires that the animal be able to initiate an active response at the appropriate time, and then to direct this response to a particular locale. Accordingly, it would be expected that the presence of a strong immobility response (freezing) that hinders response initiation would disrupt performance. However, it is important in this respect to differentiate between different types of active avoidance tasks. In the one-way avoidance task a unidirectional running response is necessary for successful performance. In this task, one compartment always serves as a safe (nonshock) area and the other always serves as a danger (shock) area. Because the response requirements are relatively unambiguous, and because animals are always required to run *away* from the compartment associated with shock, the immobility response can be readily suppressed and the running response is rapidly established. In contrast to the one-way task, the shuttle task requires that animals run from one compartment to the next on one trial, and then back again on the next trial. Consequently, the shock–cue relationship is more ambiguous, freezing is not suppressed as readily, and avoidance performance thus progresses slowly (Anisman & Waller, 1972; McAllister & McAllister, 1971). To be sure, in some strains of rats and mice high rates of shuttle avoidance are observed, but typically these strains exhibit low levels of response immobility (e.g., Anisman, 1975; Wahlsten, 1972,a,b). Likewise, high rates of avoidance are typical in some species (e.g., the gerbil) where the defensive style of the organism is not predicated on directionality (Ashe & McCain, 1972).

In considering one-way avoidance responding, it is important to distinguish between tasks that require a running response for successful avoidance and tasks that require the animal to jump out of a box to avoid shock. Although both tasks involve functionally effective responses (i.e., the response takes the animal out of the danger situation, and freezing is suppressed quickly), interesting strain differences have been observed that speak to the importance of defensive style in analyzing learning processes. That is, some inbred strains of mice tend to perform well in a locomotor avoidance task, whereas others are more adept at jump-out avoidance. These differences appear to be related to the defensive style of the organism (Wahlsten, 1972b). Similarly, arboreal and terrestrial strains of mice have been reported to display differential performance rates in the two tasks. Whereas the terrestrial strain exhibits high levels of performance in the running task and poor performance in the jump-out task, for the arboreal strain it is just the opposite (see Bignami & Michalek, 1978). Given these differential results, one would be hard pressed to believe that the strains differ in their associative ability; it seems more likely that the mice are more inclined to respond in a species-typical style.

Even when jump-out avoidance is considered alone, it is important to assess subtle defensive characteristics of the species. For instance, among rats a jump-out avoidance is acquired readily when the response entails jumping onto a ledge placed against a wall of the shock chamber. Much slower avoidance is seen when the ledge is located in the center of the apparatus (Grossen & Kelley, 1972). Inasmuch as the rat is a thigmotaxic animal, staying close to walls particularly in potentially threatening situations, it is less prepared to emit a response that entails venturing to the central portion of the chamber.

In view of the contribution made by nonassociative factors to avoidance performance, it should be clear that the effects of a given treatment in any one task is not indicative of associative processing. Some hint concerning the mechanisms that subserve a treatment effect can be gained from the analysis of behavioral changes in several different tasks. Specifically, if a treatment is suspected of enhancing associative ability, performance should be improved in both active and passive avoidance tasks. Alternatively, if the treatment is suspected of improving performance because of nonassociative changes, task-specific outcomes should result. That is, if the treatment reduces freezing, disruption of passive avoidance should occur, shuttle avoidance should be enhanced, and one-way avoidance (where freezing is minimal) should be either unaffected or even disrupted.

Thus, for example, Figure 9.2 shows the effect of pairing a CS with shock in a classical conditioning paradigm on later acquisition of a one-way and a shuttle avoidance response. Rats that received shock of 1 mA during initial training and were tested with 1 mA in either a one-way or shuttle task showed facilitated performance relative to naïve animals (upper panel). Presumably, preshock facilitated performance by estab-

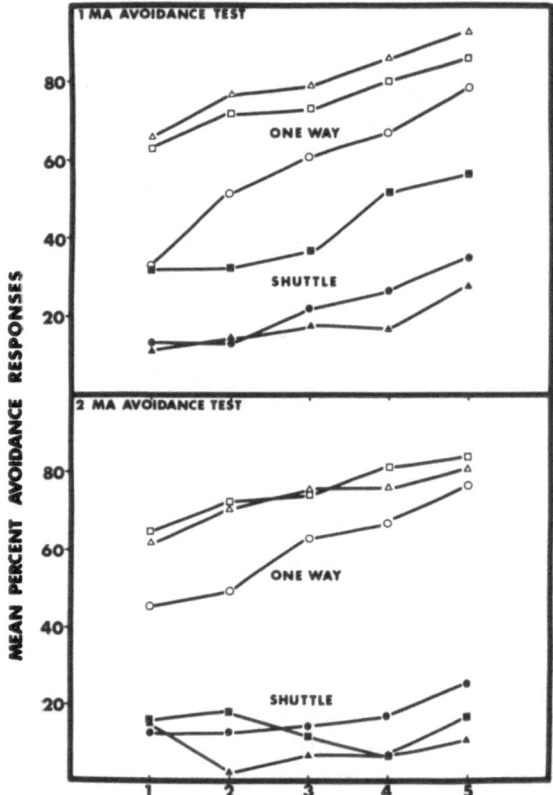

Fig. 9.2. Mean percentage avoidance responses over blocks of 10 trials in a one-way or a shuttle task. Holtzman rats received pretraining consisting of either 10 CS–shock pairings involving 1-mA shock (squares) or 2-mA shock (triangles) or no shock (circles). Twenty-four hours afterward, rats were tested in either a one-way or a shuttle avoidance test using shock of 1 mA (upper panel) or 2 mA (lower panel). (From Anisman & Waller, 1972.)

lishing the drive to avoid the aversive stimulus. Interestingly, if rats received preshock of 2 mA, which substantially increased the immobility response, facilitated performance was still seen in the one-way task but was absent in the shuttle task (upper panel). Indeed, if rats were tested with shock of 2 mA, one-way avoidance was facilitated but shuttle performance was actually disrupted (lower panel). It seems the initial training produced not only a drive (or expectancy of shock) but an immobility response as well. When the immobility response could not be readily suppressed, as in the case of the shuttle task under the condition of intense shock, the beneficial effects of the CS–shock pairings (seen in the one-way task) were outweighed by the adverse effects of the strong immobility response.

Although the interplay between running and freezing responses certainly contributes to avoidance behavior, data are available that are not readily interpretable by the foregoing type of analysis. In particular, shuttle avoidance is presumed to progress slowly because animals are required to return to those locales that had been associated with shock, thereby exacerbating existing freezing tendencies. Yet Anisman and Wahlsten (1974) found that when rats were permitted to make either unidirectional or bidirectional types of responses to avoid shock (anyway avoidance), they initially chose the unidirectional response mode (oneway) but then frequently adopted a bidirectional (shuttle) response style. Evidently, once they had acquired the response contingency, directionality of the response was neither an important element in determining response selection nor predictive of avoidance response rate.

Using a novel paradigm, Pinel and Treit (1978) also found that animals would return to locales associated with shock. In their experiments shock was administered to rats when contact was made with an electrified prod that protruded into the test chamber. Rather than keeping a maximal distance from the prod, rats quickly approached the prod and buried it with material at hand (at paw). It seems that the defensive style of the animal is predicated on situational cues, and interpretations toward learning and memory processes must consider such factors.

2.3.4. Discriminated Avoidance

Rather than independently evaluating one-way and shuttle avoidance to determine whether a treatment modifies behavior through associative processes, the concurrent measurement of several behaviors may provide a better indication for the source of treatment effects. Bignami and his colleagues (Bignami, 1976; Frontali, Amorico, De Acetis, & Bignami, 1976; Rosić & Bignami, 1970a) have extensively evaluated associative and nonassociative factors through the use of the go–no go paradigm. That is, in response to one stimulus animals were required to emit an active response to avoid shock, whereas a passive response was required to avoid shock in response to a second stimulus. These investigators found that a variety of treatments known to eliminate response suppression resulted in decreased errors of omission but increased errors of comission. Essentially, this task yielded results comparable to those seen in the independent analysis of active and passive avoidance performance. Interestingly, however, it was also found that the nature of some drug effects was dependent on the particular stimulus complex that served as go and no-go signals. These investigators argue that some drug treatments modify behavior by influencing the stimulus–response interface rather than response style per se (Bignami & Michalek, 1978; Frontali *et al.*, 1976).

A second fruitful approach for assessing associative and non-associative processes is the Y-maze discrimination task. Here it can be determined whether animals are able to initiate a response upon CS onset, and whether they are able to direct this response to the correct arm of the maze. A treatment that enhances active avoidance performance by reducing immobility should increase the frequency of response initiation upon CS onset, but without increasing the proportion of correct discriminations. In contrast, if beneficial effects on avoidance are due to associative factors, changes in discrimination performance might also be expected. Barrett, Leith, and Ray (1972, 1974) used this technique extensively and found that those treatments that seem to have their effects through nonassociative mechanisms (vis-à-vis the aforementioned studies by Bignami) modified response initiation and hence avoidance performance, without altering the frequency of correct discriminations.

2.3.5. Reversal Learning

In evaluating retention of avoidance behavior, the caveats discussed in the preceding sections must of course be considered. In addition, however, it should be remembered that the nonassociative effects of stress may vary in a nonmonotonic fashion over the 24-hour interval following incomplete avoidance training (see Figure 9.1). Thus it comes as no surprise that shuttle avoidance performance varies as a U-shaped function of time since initial training.

Given the various nonassociative consequences of aversive stimulation that influence the expression of behavior, it follows that an analysis of memory function must be conducted over a broad range of tasks that adequately assess the precise contribution of nonassociative change. Furthermore, in attempting to assess the substrates of learning and memory through surgical or pharmacological techniques, it should be recognized that these manipulations may likewise have nonassociative consequences. For example, a treatment that might potentially affect learning and memory might also alter performance through any number of nonassociative changes. These may range from motor effects to changes in attention, arousal, and even toxic side effects of the treatment. One method that reduces the extent of these problems, although by no means eliminating them, is a multiple testing procedure in which animals are trained in a drug state and then later retested in the nondrug state. It can thus be determined whether the effects of the manipulation applied during initial training would modify behavior under conditions where immediate nonassociative effects of the treatment were absent. Alternatively, if one were interested in assessing the mechanisms involved in memory consolidation, the treatment could be applied immediately after the initial training session. Assuming that the treatment is without proactive effects and does not induce state-dependent performance changes, these techniques may provide useful information for the analysis of memory processes.

Although these procedures minimize the nonassociative consequences of the drug or surgical treatments, it is still possible that some of the nonassociative effects of the initial shock experience may persist (see Section 4.). A reversal learning procedure may permit fracture lines to be drawn between associative and nonassociative contributions to memory change. For example, when animals are tested in an avoidance task in which they are required to run toward stimuli previously associated with danger or when they are required to make a response opposite that which previously led to successful avoidance (e.g., train in active avoidance and test in passive, or vice versa), negative transfer should arise. Conversely, if testing parameters are compatible with those of initial training, positive transfer would be expected. If a particular treatment disrupts memory processes it should eliminate both the negative and positive transfer effects. Importantly, both stimulus and response reversal procedures should be assessed since the treatment that influences response learning may not influence stimulus learning and memory (for the effects of CS–shock pairings on later escape from the CS, see McAllister & McAllister, 1971; for effects on later avoidance training, see Anisman, 1978).

2.4. Limitations in the Analysis of Associative-Nonassociative Processes

The caveats that follow represent some of the limitations of methods for identifying associative and nonassociative contributions to avoidance.

1. A treatment that influences behavior through nonassociative processes does not necessarily do so to the exclusion of associative processes, and vice versa. Treatments may have parallel or serial effects, thereby influencing both associative and nonassociative processes. For instance, a drug treatment such as amphetamine may enhance avoidance by virtue of its capacity to reduce freezing responses. However, some portion of the performance enhancement may be due to the increase of "attention" and hence associative ability produced by the drug

(parallel effects of the drug). Alternatively, the reduction of freezing may facilitate the establishment of the response–shock association simply because it is more likely that the correct response will occur more often during the early training trials (serial effects of the drug).

2. If a treatment has both associative and nonassociative consequences, it is not necessarily the case that they will act in concert in determining avoidance performance. That is, the associative and nonassociative effects of a treatment may be complementary or they may be antagonistic to one another. For instance, in an active avoidance task a treatment may enhance performance by (a) reducing response suppression elicited by shock, and (b) increasing the animal's ability to attend to relevant environmental cues (amphetamine treatment is a possible case in point), thereby maximizing the probability of associations being formed. In a passive avoidance task the increased attention resulting from the treatment may serve to enhance performance, but the reduction in response immobility may have an opposite effect.

3. Just as a treatment may have independent effects on associative and nonassociative processes, a treatment may have multiple nonassociative effects. These may act agonistically or antagonistically depending on the parameters of the task.

4. Given that response–shock and stimulus–shock contingencies may be subserved by different mechanisms, a particular treatment may influence the establishment of only one of these associations. Enhancing the establishment of one of these associations (e.g., response–shock association) does not assure enhancement of performance (e.g., when the cue–shock association is not readily established).

5. Furthermore, eliminating a nonassociative effect that ordinarily hinders performance may not result in enhanced avoidance if associative difficulties are present. For instance, minimizing immobility responses or aggressive posturing will be of dubious benefit if the animal fails to learn that a particular cue precedes the primary aversive stimulus. Likewise, little benefit will be gained by increasing the probability of an active response being emitted if this response cannot be appropriately directed.

6. The effectiveness of treatments that modify nonassociative processes is dependent on various task parameters. As we have seen, if the task is associatively too demanding, reducing the immobility response may have little effect. Indeed, it may well be that a task that is associatively too demanding will result in the exacerbation of the immobility response (with successive failures to avoid shock the freezing response may become strengthened), thereby further reducing the probability of the avoidance response being acquired. The elimination of the immobility tendency in this instance will not necessarily assure high rates of

avoidance, but will reduce the number of factors the organism must contend with for successful performance to progress.

7. As noted earlier, eliminating the immobility tendency in a task where response suppression is intense may yield facilitated active avoidance performance. However, if the task is one that allows for rapid avoidance acquisition because nonassociative competing tendencies can be readily eliminated, treatments that reduce nonassociative tendencies may contribute little to avoidance acquisition. On the contrary, under these conditions performance may actually be disrupted owing to the intrusion of other behaviors (e.g., excessive exploration, inattention, hyperactivity).

8. It follows that the organism's previous experience may influence the effects of a given treatment. For instance, a drug or surgical treatment that results in response disinhibition will facilitate performance in a task where responding is hampered by a potent inhibitory tendency. If the animal was previously trained in the task, thus minimizing the inhibitory tendency, the effectiveness of a drug or surgical treatment may be negligible. Conversely, the effectiveness of a drug or surgical treatment that induces response inhibition will vary with task and experiential factors. If the task is one that can be readily acquired or if the animal was previously trained in the task (see, e.g., Anisman, 1973; Fibiger, Zis, & Phillips, 1975), the disruptive effects of the treatment may not be evident. As the task employed becomes motorically more demanding, the treatment effect will become more pronounced.

9. Different treatments may produce similar outcomes on a given task because these treatments elicit comparable types of nonassociative effects. However, the nature of these nonassociative effects could differ subtly, thus differentially influencing performance in another task. The example of a treatment that produces response disinhibition (i.e., elimination of response suppression) versus one that produces response excitation beyond that of disinhibition per se is a case in point. That is, in the presence of a strong inhibitory tendency either treatment may augment active responding. In the absence of response inhibition a disinhibitory treatment may be of little consequence, whereas a treatment that produces response excitation may enhance active avoidance performance.

10. Just as the effectiveness of various manipulations varies with the organism's previous history, it would be expected that performance would vary among species as well as strains within a species. If, for whatever reason, a given strain encounters associative difficulties in a task (ranging from retinal degeneration to genuine learning impairment; see Wahlsten, 1978), reductions of nonassociative tendencies will not culminate in performance enhancement. Likewise, if the task demands

responses foreign to the animal's repertoire, alterations of nonassociative tendencies will not augment performance. Finally, the degree of response suppression induced by stress, as well as the immediate reaction to aversive stimuli will vary considerably across strains of animals; consequently, treatments that modify nonassociative processes will differentially influence performance across these strains (see Wahlsten, 1978).

11. As Wahlsten (1978) discusses in detail, where inferences are to be drawn to learning and memory ability, behavioral assessment must necessarily be conducted across a broad assortment of tasks. Since treatments with nonassociative consequences may have differential effects across tasks, it is not appropriate to draw conclusions about associative ability on the basis of a single task.

12. At this point it should come as no surprise that evaluation of cognitive abilities among infrahuman animals is exceedingly difficult. As will be seen later in this chapter, cognitive interpretations have been offered for several behavioral phenomena (e.g., helplessness; see Maier & Seligman, 1976). It is premature either to accept or to reject explanations that are based on cognitive processes; however, given the broad range of physiological changes that are induced by stressors (e.g., neurochemical, hormonal, or immunologic alterations), it is probably best to explore the contribution of these variables to behavioral change before relying on cognitive types of hypotheses. Indeed, owing to the multiple effects of stress, aversive paradigms might be inappropriate for analyzing cognitive phenomena.

13. Experiments involving pharmacological or lesion techniques need to consider that such manipulations, when applied in aversive paradigms, might interact with the effects of the US. For instance, the effects of a drug such as α methyl-p-tyrosine may be exacerbated in an avoidance task since the stress of shock will enhance the depletion of brain catecholamines induced by the drug. By the same token, the motor effects of reserpine can be modified by aversive stimuli (see Welch & Welch, 1970), thus obfuscating the effects on learning that might be seen in tasks that do not involve aversive motivation.

14. The choice of warning stimuli used in an avoidance task is known to influence performance. In addition, the effects of a number of pharmacological treatments have been shown to vary not only as a function of task but also as a function of the CS used in that particular task (see Frontali et al., 1976).

15. Although the nonassociative effects of stress are typically thought to wane over time following stress exposure, data are available (see the ensuing sections) that suggest that nonassociative effects may last over fairly long intervals.

3. ESCAPE BEHAVIOR

3.1. Shock-Elicited Activity

Shock-elicited activity must be distinguished from reactivity. Whereas reactivity refers to motor changes that occur after exposure to a stressor (shock), shock-elicited activity refers to levels of activity observed during shock. With extended shock presentations (6 seconds), high levels of shock-elicited activity are seen initially but decrease rapidly as shock continues. As shown in Figure 9.3, within several seconds shock-elicited activity is reduced to less than 50% of the initial level. Moreover, the extent of the decline is more marked among mice that had received inescapable shock 24 hours earlier than among mice that had received either escapable shock or no shock. Whereas reactivity to a CS may be indicative of response initiation ability, the activity during protracted shock may reflect the organism's ability to *sustain* active responses to strong stimulation.

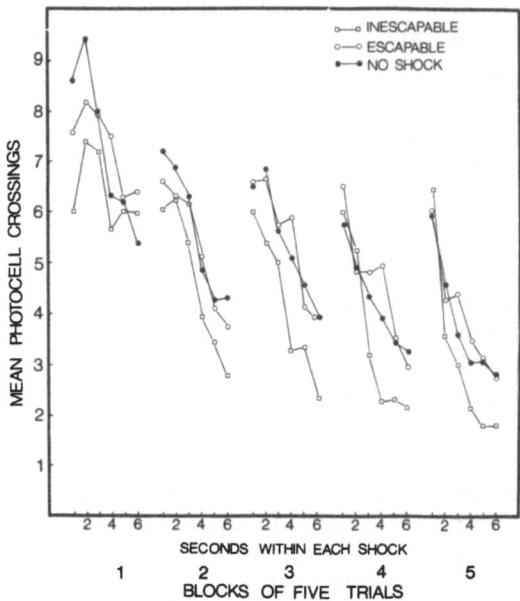

Fig. 9.3. Mean levels of shock-elicited activity among Swiss-Webster mice previously exposed to 60 escapable shocks (150 μA), yoked inescapable shock, or no shock. Shock-elicited activity was monitored on a second-by-second basis. Each curve describes levels of shock-elicited activity over 6-second shock presentations averaged over five trials. (From Anisman, deCatanzaro, & Remington, 1978.)

3.2. Escape

At least at first blush, escape behavior appears to be less complex than avoidance behavior. In the escape task animals need simply initiate a response and direct it appropriately in order to escape rapidly. Of course, the nature of the task is an important element in determining performance. Whereas running responses are established with apparent ease, bar-press responses are less readily established. Likewise, by increasing the complexity of the task (i.e., motoric or associative difficulty), performance may be retarded (Anisman, deCatanzaro, & Remington, 1978; Glazer & Weiss, 1976a; Maier & Testa, 1975) and may also be more susceptible to disruption by various pharmacological and nonpharmacological manipulations (Anisman, Remington, & Sklar, 1979; Glazer & Weiss, 1976a,b).

It has been suggested that the simple escape task is principally a reflection of response initiation to strong stimulation, whereas in more complex tasks the organism's ability to sustain active and vigorous responding is being tapped (Anisman et al., 1978). Given the reflexive nature of response initiation to strong stimulation, behavior in a simple escape task is robust and not readily subject to disruption. Response maintenance in more complex escape tasks, on the other hand, appears to be less reflexive and hence more susceptible to disruption. As in the case of avoidance, such factors as stress severity, line or strain of animal, as well as the species may determine levels of performance and disruptibility of the response by experimental manipulations.

3.3. Effects of Uncontrollable Stress

In recent years escape performance has been used as an index of cognitive change in animals. In particular, following exposure to controllable stress, later escape behavior progresses readily. However, animals initially exposed to equivalent amounts of uncontrollable stress (administered in a yoked paradigm) later display pronounced deficits of escape behavior, characterized by frequent failures to escape from shock. Maier and Seligman (1976) suggest that during inescapable shock animals learn that shock offset is independent of their responses. That is, they learn that they are "helpless" in determining shock offset, and thus on subsequent encounters with stress they attempt neither to escape nor to avoid. In contrast to dogs, where the escape deficits induced by uncontrollable shock are evident in a simple shuttle task, in rodents the interference effect is not as readily apparent. It has been argued (Maier & Testa, 1975; Maier, Albin, & Testa, 1973) that because running is very high in the rodent's repertoire, the "helplessness" induced by the uncontrollable stress will be masked. If the associative difficulty of the task is increased, say by testing animals in an FR-2 shuttle task (where animals must run from one compartment to the next and back again on a single trial), the interference will become evident.

Several alternative explanations to the helplessness hypothesis have been offered; for a detailed review, see Anisman, Kokkinidis, and Sklar (1981a). According to one hypothesis the interference arises because animals learn unauthorized responses during inescapable shock that are incompatible with the response required for successful escape during the subsequent test session (Bracewell & Black, 1974; Glazer & Weiss, 1976a,b). A second alternative is that uncontrollable shock results in nonassociative motor deficits that hinder later escape behavior (Anisman et al., 1978; Weiss, Glazer, & Pohorecky, 1976). Indeed, as Figure 9.3 shows, levels of shock-elicited activity decline dramatically during the course of extended shock presentations and this effect is more pronounced among animals that had previously been exposed to uncontrollable shock. Although animals appear deficient in initiating responses to weak stimuli after being exposed to inescapable shock (Anisman & Waller, 1973), it seems that responses can be readily initiated to strong stimuli (e.g., shock). However, after inescapable shock animals seem unable to sustain active vigorous responding for protracted periods (Anisman et al., 1978). According to the motor hypothesis, the high levels of shock-elicited activity that are typical at shock inception will favor rapid response latencies in a simple shuttle escape task. However, if the task is motorically more demanding, or if the associative difficulty of the task is increased thereby increasing the latency to complete the response, the low levels of shock-elicited activity evident 5 to 6 seconds after shock onset will favor poor performance. Among animals that had been exposed to inescapable shock, frequent escape failures might occur owing to the relatively marked decline in shock-elicited activity.

Consistent with this explanation, it has been reported that increasing the height of the hurdle that separates the compartments of the shuttle box will enhance the magnitude of the interference effect, whereas requiring a simple response, such as nose poke, will not result in behavioral deficits after inescapable shock (Glazer & Weiss, 1976a,b). Anisman et al. (1978), in fact, showed that the interference effect could be induced in a simple shuttle task where sustained active responding was required of the animal. Figure 9.4 demonstrates the effects of uncontrollable shock in a shuttle task where escape was possible either immediately upon shock onset or at various times after shock onset. When escape was possible immediately after shock onset, behavioral disruption was not evident; however, the disruptive effects of inescapa-

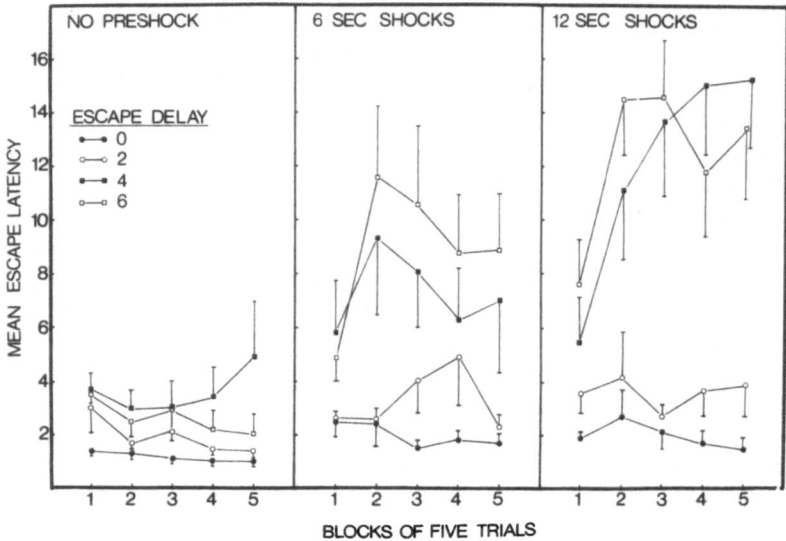

Fig. 9.4. Mean (±S.E.M.) escape latencies among Swiss-Webster mice that received either no prior shock, 60 shocks (150 μA) of 6 seconds duration, or 60 shocks of 12 seconds duration. During test, escape was possible either immediately upon shock onset or after delays of 2, 4, or 6 seconds. (From Anisman, Remington, & Sklar, 1979.)

ble shock were progressively more pronounced with successively longer escape delays. Moreover, levels of shock-elicited activity were found to reliably predict later escape performance. Interestingly, in subsequent experiments it was found that treatments that modified levels of shock-elicited activity also influenced escape deficits in a predictable fashion. For example, in lines of mice where the decline of shock-elicited activity was minimal, the escape deficit was not evident. Likewise, shock parameters that did not provoke particularly marked decreases in shock-elicited activity also evoked minimal deficits of escape (Anisman *et al.*, 1978; Anisman, Grimmer, Irwin, Remington, & Sklar, 1979). As yet unpublished data collected in this laboratory indicate that treatments that enhance the decline of shock-elicited activity (e.g., social isolation or testing older animals) tended to exacerbate the interference effect. Finally, as will be seen later, pharmacological treatments that enhance the decline in shock-elicited activity augmented the interference effect, whereas treatments that prevented the decline in shock-elicited activity antagonized the interference effect (Anisman, Grimmer, Irwin, Remington, & Sklar, 1979; Anisman, Suissa, & Sklar, 1980).

    As noted earlier, Maier and Testa (1975) argue that an FR-2 task is necessary for the interference to be seen in rats because the difficulty of the task permits expression of the helplessness. Maier and Seligman (1976) report that briefly interrupting shock after a hurdle crossing in an FR-2 task eliminated the interference, ostensibly because shock interruption acted as a feedback stimulus thereby making the task associatively less difficult. At the same time, however, shock interruption could also have enhanced shock-elicited activity (as might presentation of a light, buzzer, or tone), thus eliminating the interference. Since a group was not included in which shock interruption was not contingent on a hurdle crossing, the conclusion that associative changes were responsible for the prevention of the interference effect was unwarranted. Indeed, Anisman et al. (1978) demonstrated that shock interruption modified levels of shock-elicited activity. More importantly, using a 6-second escape delay procedure, they demonstrated that interruption of shock 5 seconds after shock onset, but before a hurdle crossing was made, eliminated the interference. Since the shock interruption procedure was independent of the animal's behavior and could not act as a feedback stimulus for appropriate responses, Maier and Seligman's (1976) conclusion is questionable. That is not to deny the possibility that increasing associative difficulty will augment the escape interference. Instead the contention is that changes in the associative difficulty of the task will modify escape behavior simply because the task will require more sustained active responding.

The basic tenet of a cognitive interpretation for the interference effect is that animals can learn correlations between events. Not only can animals learn that certain stimuli or responses are associated with reinforcement, but also that stimuli or responses might be associated with nonreinforcement (see, e.g., Mackintosh, 1973). Proponents of a motor hypothesis do not necessarily take issue with such a possibility; instead they contend that (1) the wide variety of physiological and behavioral effects induced by stress does not allow for adequate assessment of cognitive processes in aversive paradigms, and (2) the behavioral effects of uncontrollable stress can be readily accounted for on the basis of neurochemical change.

4. STRESS AND NEUROCHEMICAL CHANGE

Stress will induce several physiological changes that appear to be essential for the organism to deal with environmental insults. Under most conditions, the organism copes with stress through both behavioral and physiological means. It is assumed that some of the physiological effects are essential for preventing physical and psychological pathology (see Sklar & Anisman, 1981). The latter changes, of course, may also have indirect effects on the expression of behavior. This section will address only the neurochemical changes induced by stress; we have discussed stress effects on hormonal and immunologic changes elsewhere (Sklar & Anisman, 1981). Anisman et al. (1981b) also provide a review of the neurochemical literature.

4.1. Acute Stress

Upon stress inception, the synthesis and utilization of several neurotransmitters, including norepinephrine (NE), dopamine (DA), and serotonin (5-HT) will increase dramatically. We have observed such changes with as few as five shock presentations. This effect is not restricted to footshock stress, but will occur across a broad range of social, psychological, and physiological stressors (Anisman, 1978; Stone, 1975). Within several minutes of exposure to a moderate stress, levels of the neurotransmitters actually increase and remain elevated for several minutes (Welch & Welch, 1970). It seems that intraneuronal degradation of the amines is transiently inhibited, thereby assuring adequate stores of the transmitter at least over the short run.

If the stress is relatively severe or sufficiently protracted, an appreciable increase of amine activity may be expected in order to meet environmental demands. However, utilization of the amines may exceed synthesis, resulting in a net decrease of the neurotransmitter concentrations. In the case of NE, the depletion seen after severe stress is not restricted to any one brain region but has been noted in brainstem, hypothalamus, hippocampus, and cortex (Kvetnansky, Mitro, Palkovits, Brownstein, Torda, Vigas, & Mikulaj, 1976; Stolk, Conner, Levine, & Barchas, 1974; Weiss, Glazer, & Pohorecky, 1976). Some of these variations likely involve stimulation of catecholamine (CA) cell bodies of the dorsal bundle, and in particular the locus coeruleus (Korf, 1976). The depletion of NE is relatively transient, persisting for only a few hours (Maynert & Levi, 1964), although under some conditions effects lasting as long as 24 hours may occur (Weiss, Glazer, Pohorecky, Bailey, & Schneider, 1979).

In contrast to the widespread NE changes induced by stress, DA variations appear to be more restricted. Analyses of DA concentrations and turnover in most brain regions revealed that stress was without effect. However, more discrete analyses subsequently revealed that DA concentrations of the arcuate nucleus of the hypothalamus were reduced by some forms of stress (Kobayashi, Palkovits, Kizer, Jacobowitz, & Kopin, 1976; Kvetnansky et al., 1976), as was DA in some portions of the frontal cortex (Lavielle, Tassin, Thierry, Blanc, Hervé, Barthelemy, & Glowinski, 1978). In addition, DA turnover was increased in the nucleus accumbens (Blanc, Hervé, Simon, Lisoprawski, Glowinski, & Tassin, 1980; Thierry, Tassin, Blanc, & Glowinski, 1976). In light of the connections between the arcuate nucleus and the pituitary, these limited DA changes may be of particular significance in the determination of stress-induced hormonal changes. Moreover, the possible role of the mesolimbic DA neurons in emotional behavior points to the importance of the DA changes in determining behavior in aversive paradigms.

Variations in 5-HT activity are subject to stress effects in much the same way that NE activity is modified. That is, stress will increase the synthesis and utilization of 5-HT; however, the severity of the stress necessary to provoke 5-HT depletion is greater than that required to induce reduction of NE concentrations. Moderate stress will increase utilization of NE newly synthesized and stored in the "functional pools," whereas intense stress will also result in mobilization of NE previously stored in the "reserve pools." Severe stress was found to influence appreciably the activity of 5-HT, whereas moderate stress was without effect (Thierry, 1973; Thierry, Fekete, & Glowinski, 1968; Thierry, Blanc, & Glowinski, 1970). Furthermore, it seems that the effectiveness of stress in eliciting 5-HT depletion is specific to particular nuclei even within discrete brain regions (Palkovits, Brownstein, Kizer, Saavedra, & Kopin, 1976).

Like NE, DA, and 5-HT, the activity of acetylcholine (ACh) neurons is subject to modification by stress. Soon after stress inception, concentrations of ACh decline or remain unaltered (Zajaczkowska, 1975). Within 40 minutes to 4 hours after stress termination, levels of ACh exceed those of control animals (Aprison & Hingtgen, 1970; Saito, Morita, Miyazaki, & Takagi, 1976; Zajaczkowska, 1975). It is not clear whether ACh changes were a direct result of the stress or a secondary compensatory reaction to the catecholamine changes (see Anisman, 1975).

4.2. Coping Style

One factor that appears essential in determining whether or not NE depletion will be incurred following stress exposure is the organism's ability to cope with the aversive stimuli through behavioral means. NE depletion is reliably observed in studies employing uncontrollable footshock, but no such effect is evident when shock is applied in an active avoidance paradigm where control over the stress is possible. As observed by Weiss, Glazer, and Pohorecky (1976), work conducted in this laboratory (Anisman, Pizzino, & Sklar, 1980) indicated that exposure to escapable footshock will not result in depletion of NE: however, exposure to an equivalent amount of inescapable shock, applied in a yoked paradigm, reliably induced NE depletion (see Figure 9.5). By the same token, Anisman, Pizzino, and Sklar (1980) found that if animals initially received controllable shock, the extent of the NE depletion subsequently induced by uncontrollable shock was minimized. Similarly, Stolk, Conner, Levine, and Barchas (1974) report that the NE depletion ordinarily invoked by uncontrollable shock was prevented if rats were permitted to fight during shock exposure. Inasmuch as fighting has also been found to prevent ulceration produced by stress, the possibility exists that fighting acted as a coping response in much the same way that escape does (see Weiss, Pohorecky, Salman, & Gruenthal, 1976).

To date, adequate data are not available concerning the effects of stress controllability on transmitters other than NE. In those studies where DA levels have been assessed using a yoked paradigm (e.g., Anisman, Pizzino, & Sklar, 1980; Weiss, Glazer, & Pohorecky, 1976), amine levels were determined in tissue samples in which DA depletions are not typically detected (e.g., in the entire hypothalamus). With respect to ACh, data are available that provisionally suggest that stress controllability is an essential ingredient for the increase of this transmitter. Specifically, Karczmar, Scudder, and Richardson (1973) found that inescapable shock resulted in increased levels of ACh; however, avoidable/escapable shock had no such effect. Unfortunately, the purpose of

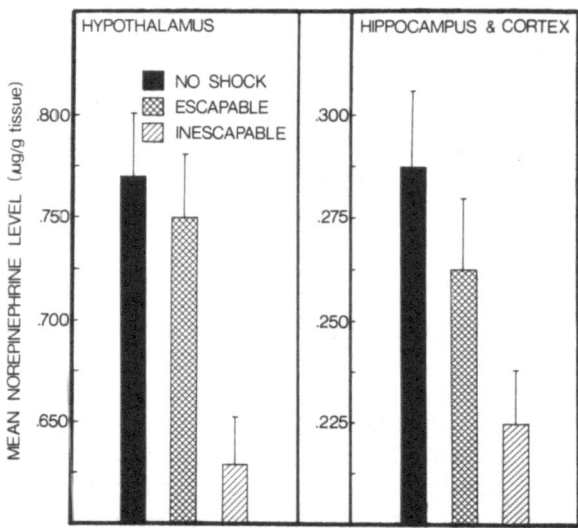

Fig. 9.5. Mean concentration (±SEM) of norepinephrine in hypothalamus and in hippocampus and cortex among Swiss-Webster mice that received either 60 escape trials (150-μA shock), yoked inescapable shock, or no shock. (From Anisman, Pizzino, & Sklar, 1980.)

this study was not to assess the effects of escapable and inescapable shock, and no attempt was made to equate for the actual amount of shock animals received. Thus conclusions about the role of coping factors in determining the ACh changes must be considered cautiously. There are, however, other data that are consistent with those of Karczmar *et al.* (1973). For example, it has been reported that during a decline of performance in a Sidman avoidance task ACh concentrations are increased in midbrain, but lowered ACh levels are evident during behavioral excitation (Aprison & Hingtgen, 1970; Aprison, Kariya, Hingtgen, & Toru, 1968). Whether the ACh changes were a consequence of the apparent "loss of control" or whether they were responsible for the behavioral alterations remains to be determined.

Cherek, Lane, Freeman, and Smith (1980) report data concerning stress controllability effects on ACh and DA receptors. Specifically, after four sessions of 8-hour duration, ACh receptor binding was increased in rats that received yoked shock relative to rats that received avoidable shock. Furthermore, DA receptor binding in the frontal cortex decreased, but increased in other areas. These changes may reflect alterations in availability of receptors owing to increased turnover of the respective transmitters. Thus these data support the contention that stress controllability is an important dimension in determining the activity of ACh and DA neurons.

In sum, it appears that stress controllability is an important feature in determining neurochemical change. It has been our contention (Anisman *et al.*, 1981a,b; Sklar & Anisman, 1981) that these neurochemical alterations reflect only a few of a large series of adaptive changes to aversive environmental events. When confronted by noxious stimuli the organism accommodates through behavioral and physiological means, including increased synthesis and utilization of brain NE. The extent of the neurochemical alterations is dependent on coping factors and the organism's prior stress experience. When behavioral coping is not possible, the rate of synthesis will be exceeded by amine utilization, and depletion of the transmitter will result. Where behavioral responses effectively alleviate the noxious stimuli, amine utilization rates will decline and as a result stable levels of the transmitter can be expected.

A subtle but important caveat is that there are several ways in which one can consider the relationship among stress, coping mechanisms, and neurochemical change. According to one interpretation, the amine depletion will occur when animals have learned that their responses are independent of outcome (helplessness). That is, the neurochemical alterations mirror cognitive changes induced by the stress. A second view has it that increased neurochemical activity will ordinarily result from stress, and if the stress is sufficiently severe and protracted, depletion will result. When behavioral coping is possible, the enhanced amine utilization is reduced, thereby preventing depletion from occurring. In effect, the differential effects of controllable and uncontrollable stress are not so much a result of animals in the latter condition learning that shock offset is independent of their responses as much as of animals in the former condition adapting through behavioral means.

4.3. Chronic Stress

The NE depletion evident after exposure to an acute session of uncontrollable stress is absent if animals are chronically exposed to stress. Such an effect is evident after several different forms of stress including temperature alterations (Ingenito & Bonnycastle, 1967), immobilization (Kvetnansky et al., 1976), and shock (Weiss, Glazer, Pohorecky, Brick, & Miller, 1975; Weiss, Glazer, & Pohorecky, 1976). Moreover, it has also been reported that the DA alterations that occur in the arcuate nucleus after stress are minimized following repeated stress exposure (see Kvetnansky et al., 1976). The return to basal amine values will occur regardless of whether animals receive repeated sessions of uncontrollable stress over successive days (Weiss, Glazer, & Pohorecky, 1976) or receive a single protracted stress session (Kvetnansky et al., 1976). In both instances the activity of tyrosine hydroxylase and dopamine-β-hydroxylase is increased (Kobayashi et al., 1976; Kvetnansky et al., 1976; Thoenen, 1970), suggesting that the increase of amine levels results from this compensatory change in synthesis.

In addition to the increased amine synthesis, Weiss, Glazer, and Pohorecky (1976) report that reuptake of catecholamines is reduced. That is, not only is amine concentration increased, but the transmitter, once released, remains in the synaptic cleft for longer periods, thereby enhancing receptor stimulation. Hendley, Burrows, Robinson, Heidenreich, and Bulman (1977) also observed a similar effect when animals received a single protracted stress session. Clearly, although amine levels are comparable in chronically stressed and in nonstressed animals, synthesis and utilization of the amine, and hence receptor stimulation, are considerably greater in the former group. Since sustain high levels of receptor stimulation itself could have adverse consequences, an additional neuronal alteration occurs. Specifically, Stone (1979a,b) found that following chronic stress the cAMP response to NE was reduced. Stone attributes the reduction to receptor subsensitivity, which occurred in order to compensate for the increased NE release. Accordingly, the impact of the heightened amine synthesis and utilization is diminished and a return to normal behavior should occur.

4.4. Sensitization (or Conditioning) of Stress-Induced Alterations

Although the depletion of brain NE provoked by stress is relatively transient, it seems that the organism's previous history with stress or cues associated with a particular stressor may influence the amine changes. Work in this laboratory, for instance, revealed that immediately after 60 inescapable shocks, NE depletion in hypothalamus and in the hippocampus approached 25%. Within 24 hours of the stress session the depletion was absent. However, if mice were reexposed to only a few shock presentations, which ordinarily had little effect on NE levels, the depletion was reinduced. Figure 9.6 shows the results of work conducted in this laboratory in which the stress reexposure effect is seen in both the hypothalamus and the hippocampus.

Consistent with the results we have observed, Cassens, Roffman, Kuruc, Orsulak, and Schildkraut (1980) found that a CS that had been paired with shock would subsequently increase the accumulation of 3, methoxy-4-hydroxyphenylglycol (MHPG), a major metabolite of NE. Thus it seems that the cues associated with shock are sufficient to provoke rapid mobilization of NE. Likewise, Hingtgen, Smith, Shea, Aprison, and Gaff (1976) found that a CS that had previously been paired with shock would subsequently result in increased ACh levels; Chance *et al.* (1978) and DeVries, Chance, Payne, and Rosecrans (1979)

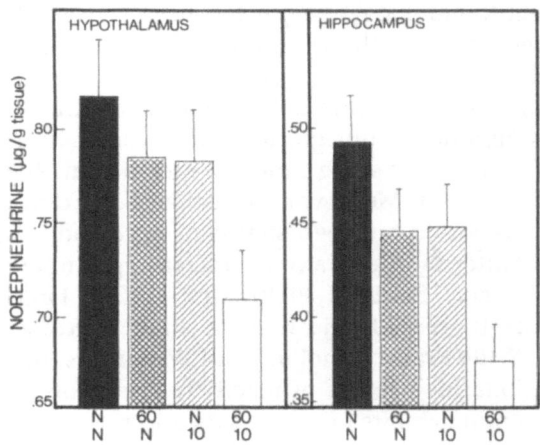

Fig. 9.6. Mean concentration (±SEM) of norepinephrine in hypothalamus and in hippocampus among Swiss-Webster mice that received either no shock (Group N/N) on each of 2 days, 60 shocks (150 μA) on Day 1 and no shock on Day 2 (Group 60/N), no shock on Day 1 and 10 shocks on Day 2 (Group N/10), or 60 shocks on Day 1 followed by 10 shocks on Day 2 (Group 60/10).

report that cues that had been associated with shock influenced enkephalin activity and binding.

It seems that the activity of NE and ACh as well as opiate peptides is
subject to sensitization or conditioning. Clearly, the organism's previous
stress history is a major factor in determining the response to subsequent stress. Profound alterations of transmitter activity can be induced
by a seemingly innocuous stress or by cues associated with a previously
administered stress. Accordingly, sensitization or conditioning of neurochemical factors must be considered in the analysis of stress-induced
pathology, as well as in the analysis of associative and nonassociative
processes.

4.5. Contribution of Organismic and Social Variables

In view of the finding that coping and experiential factors influence
the response to stress, it should be no surprise that several organismic
variables have very profound effects on neurochemical activity. For example, catecholamine activity and levels in rodents vary as a function of
age (Finch, 1973). Moreover, NE depletion is more readily achieved in 9-
month-old than in 3-month-old rats. Furthermore, following a stress
experience, the rate of NE recovery was considerably longer in the older
rats than in the younger animals. Indeed, depletion persisted beyond 24
hours (Ritter & Pelzer, 1978).

With respect to genetic factors, it has been repeatedly shown that
very pronounced between-strain differences occur in levels and turnover of several transmitters (e.g., Ebel, Hermetet, & Mandel, 1973).
Thus the finding that stress differentially influences transmitter activity
across strains should not be unexpected. Stress may have greater effects
on NE and 5-HT changes in some strains of rats than in others (Hendley,
Moisset, & Welch, 1973). Moreover, opposite effects on transmitter activity have been reported between strains of mice and rats; that is, decreasing a transmitter in one strain but increasing it in another (Ray &
Barrett, 1975; Wimer, Reid, & Eleftheriou, 1973). Finally, Schmidt,
Cooper, and Barrett (1980) found that footshock increased cholinergic
function in Zivic-Miller rats but not in F-344 Wistar rats. Inasmuch as the
latter strain exhibits high levels of reactivity and proficient avoidance
and the former strain exhibits low reactivity and poor performance, it is
certainly possible that the behavioral differences are due, at least in part,
to ACh changes produced by stress.

In the area of social factors and amine activity, it has been found
that in mice, individual housing will decrease the synthesis and utilization of NE but will have only small effects on DA (see Modigh, 1976;
Welch & Welch, 1970). The data for rats are less consistent. It has been

reported that NE and 5-HT synthesis are increased in brainstem and telencephalon (Stolk, Conner, & Barchas, 1974) and in whole brain (Nishikawa, Kajiwara, Kono, Sano, Nagasaki, Tanaka, & Noda, 1974). In contrast, however, analyses performed in discrete brain regions indicate that the nature of the DA and NE alterations varies as a function of the region examined. Whereas decreased turnover occurred in some regions, increased turnover occurred in others (Thoa, Tizabi, & Jabobowitz, 1977).

With exposure to stress the neurochemical changes that occur vary as a function of housing condition. Restraint stress, for example, increased NE utilization in individually housed mice but decreased utilization among mice housed in groups (Welch & Welch, 1970). We have found that mice housed in isolation are more susceptible to amine depletion induced by stress than are group-housed mice (Anisman & Sklar, 1981). Finally, Blanc *et al.* (1980) report that in rats isolation resulted in decreased levels of the DA metabolite DOPAC. Upon stress exposure, greater utilization of DA was seen in the frontal cortex of isolated rats relative to grouped animals. The excessive utilization in the isolated rats was accompanied by pronounced motor reductions during and between shock presentations. The behavior of the isolated rats is indeed reminiscent of the behavior pattern described earlier in mice exposed to uncontrollable shock.

It is clear that neurochemical activity in response to stress will not only vary as a function of stress severity and the organism's ability to cope with stress, but will also be dependent on genetic and ontogenetic factors as well as social conditions. Thus equivalent stresses can induce very different outcomes even in a group of animals randomly selected from the same population. Accordingly, the behavioral response to stress might be expected not only to vary as a function of experimenter-imposed manipulations, but to vary among subjects for unknown causes (see, e.g., Maier & Seligman, 1976).

5. PHARMACOLOGICAL MANIPULATIONS AND AVOIDANCE PEFORMANCE

Persistent attempts have been made to identify the neurochemical substrates of learning and memory. The limited success that has been achieved is not particularly surprising, since it is highly probable that processes as complex as learning/memory are subserved by several different neurotransmitters. Moreover, the contribution a particular transmitter makes in one brain region may be very different from that it makes in a second brain region. In aversive paradigms the complexity is increased still further by the various neurochemical changes induced by stress that are unrelated to associative processes. In addition, these neurochemical changes may be influenced by pharmacological or surgical manipulations employed to assess the learning and memory processes. Because we have previously analyzed the potential contribution of NE, DA, 5-HT, and ACh to behavioral change (Anisman & Bignami, 1978, Peters, Anisman, & Pappas, 1978), only a very limited review is presented here. To be sure, although the data tend to be presented somewhat dogmatically, agreement has not been reached concerning the role of various transmitters on memory processes.

5.1. Catecholamines

Phamacological manipulations that influence DA have repeatedly been shown to modify locomotor activity (see Iversen, 1977; Kelly, 1977). Thus it is not surprising that such manipulations have predictable effects on avoidance behavior. For instance, drugs that reduce DA levels or block DA receptors typically disrupt avoidance performance (see, e.g., Davidson & Weidley, 1976). Interestingly, if rats are treated on successive days with the DA receptor blocker haloperidol, performance is severely disrupted; however, when drug treatment is discontinued high levels of performance are noted. It was suggested that rats in the haloperidol condition had learned the response necessary for successful avoidance, but were unable to initiate this response. Indeed, if animals received avoidance training before the drug treatment, thereby enhancing response initiation, the behavioral deficits were absent (Fibiger et al., 1975).

Like DA receptor blockers, the neurotoxin 6-hydroxydopamine (6-OHDA), which depletes both DA and NE, yields severe deficits of avoidance behavior (Lenard & Beer, 1975a,b). This effect is evident when 6-OHDA is applied to either the substantia nigra (Fibiger, Phillips, & Zis, 1974) or the striatum (Neill, Boggan, & Grossman, 1974), regions particularly rich in DA but with little NE. When NE reduction is produced, avoidance performance is, if anything, enhanced (Cooper, Breese, Grant, & Howard, 1973). Thus it seems that DA depletion will disrupt performance, but NE will only marginally affect it. In fact, Lenard and Beer (1975c) suggest that the effects of DA manipulations are due to motor deficits, whereas those of NE alterations reflect hyperactivity or persistent irritability.

With respect to the effects of catecholamine depletion on passive avoidance behavior, inconsistent results have been obtained. For example, whereas Cooper et al. (1973) found intracisternal 6-OHDA to have no effect on 24-hour retention of a step-out passive avoidance task, Rainbow, Adler, and Flexner (1976) found that intraventricular 6-OHDA retarded retention of such a task. In the latter experiment activity data were not presented, and it is possible that hyperactivity influenced performance.

In the case of drug treatments that stimulate catecholamine activity (e.g., amphetamine, L-DOPA), it is generally observed that shuttle avoidance is enhanced, one-way avoidance is unaffected or disrupted, and passive avoidance is retarded (see Peters *et al.*, 1978). In a go–no go task, predictably, performance on the active component is augmented whereas the passive component is disrupted (Frontali *et al.*, 1976). Finally, in the Y-maze discriminated avoidance task response initiation is facilitated, but without a concurrent enhancement of discrimination performance (Barrett *et al.*, 1972, 1974).

In recent years increasing attention has been devoted to the proposition that NE is essential for memory consolidation (see Zornetzer, 1978). It has been shown that a number of pharmacological agents that deplete brain NE (e.g., such dopamine-β-hydroxylase inhibitors as FLA-63, fusaric acid, U-14624, and benzloxyamine), when administered immediately after training, disrupted later retention (Zornetzer & Gold, 1976). Likewise, reserpine, an amine storage granule depletor, has been shown to retard retention of performance (Dismukes & Rake, 1972). Curiously, however, the tyrosine hydroxylase inhibitor alpha methyl-para-tyrosine, which depletes both DA and NE, did not affect performance (Zornetzer, Gold, & Hendrickson, 1974) or affected performance in male but not female rats (Fulginiti, Molina, & Orsingher, 1976). Furthermore, it should be considered that most of the dopamine-β-hydroxylase inhibitors shown to influence retention are fairly toxic; thus their effects may have been due to changes unrelated to memory.

In sum, although there is some reason to believe that NE plays a role in memory processes, the available data do not allow firm conclusions. Although catecholamine manipulations have been shown to influence performance in both appetitive and aversive tasks, it is also the case that NE depletion may induce task-specific effects (Izquierdo, Beamish, & Anisman, 1979).

5.2. Serotonin

The effects of 5-HT manipulations on avoidance behavior have been less extensively assessed than those of the catecholamines. Drugs that deplete 5-HT will augment performance, but such an effect seems to occur primarily in tasks involving a strong inhibitory component (Breese

& Cooper, 1975; Breese, Cooper, Grant, & Smith, 1974; Lorens, 1973). In tasks where inhibitory tendencies are minimal (e.g., one-way avoidance), depletion of 5-HT is without effect (Lorens, Gulberg, Hole, Kolater, & Srebo, 1976). Consistent with a proposition the 5-HT manipulations are without associative consequences, Steranka and Barrett (1974) found that discrimination performance in a Y-maze avoidance task was unaffected by 5-HT depletion, and enhancements in avoidance performance were associated with decreases in shock-induced response inhibition.

Depletion of 5-HT has been found to affect locomotor activity inconsistently, but it reliably enhances responsivity to strong stimuli. Indeed, considerable data show that serotonergic manipulations affect sensitization in habituation tasks involving reactivity to relatively strong stimuli (see Peters *et al.*, 1978). Thus the enhancement of avoidance seen after 5-HT depletion may well represent effects on pseudoconditioning or on anticipatory responding.

5.3. Acetylcholine

It is well-known that drugs that increase levels of ACh have the effect of disrupting shuttle avoidance performance and to a lesser extent one-way avoidance performance, and enhancing passive avoidance (Rosic & Bignami, 1970a). In a go–no go paradigm, cholinergic stimulants increase errors of omission but reduce errors of commission (Frontali *et al.*, 1976; Rosic & Bignami, 1970b). Drugs that block ACh receptors (e.g., scopolamine) will have effects opposite in many respects to that produced by increasing ACh. Specifically, drugs such as scopolamine will enhance shuttle avoidance behavior, where the inhibitory tendency ordinarily prevents high levels of performance, but have no effect or disrupt performance in a one-way avoidance task (Anisman, 1975; Suits & Isaacson, 1968). In a passive avoidance task, performance is ordinarily disrupted by anticholinergics (Meyers, 1965). As might be expected, in the go–no go task errors of omission are reduced, but errors of commission increase (see Frontali *et al.*, 1976). Finally, when animals were tested in a discriminated Y-maze avoidance task, scopolamine was found to increase avoidance responses but without a concomitant change in correct discrimination responses (Barrett *et al.*, 1972, 1974).

In their extensive analyses of the contribution of ACh to performance in aversive tasks, Bignami and his colleagues show that at least some of the effects of anticholinergics depend on the nature of the CS that is employed (Frontali *et al.*, 1976; Rosic & Bignami, 1970b). Thus these investigators conclude that although anticholinergics influence response-modulating systems, the effects of such treatments are complex and might be more appropriately considered in terms of effects on inter-faces between stimulus and response mechanisms.

Another question concerns the temporal changes of avoidance seen after initial training (i.e., retention of avoidance behavior). It will be recalled that a U-shaped retention function is typically observed over the 24-hour period following initial training, with poorest performance oc-curring at the 1- to 4-hour interval. Although some investigators ascribe the behavioral changes to alterations in memory stemming from changes in the internal chemical state of the organism (Klein & Spear, 1970a,b), a nonassociative explanation can also account for the data. That is, the time of poorest performance corresponds to that period where ACh levels are highest and catecholamine levels are either below or at baseline. Thus these neurochemical changes may be responsible for increased response immobility seen at intermediate retention intervals, which in turn result in avoidance deficits.

In accordance with a nonassociative explanation, the U-shaped function is not as readily obtained in a one-way as in a shuttle avoidance task. In the former task the immobility response can be readily sup-pressed, thereby mitigating the behavioral deficit. Furthermore, manip-ulations of cholinergic activity have predictable effects on performance. That is, the anticholinergic drug scopolamine effectively limited the oc-currence of the U-shaped function (Anisman, 1973). Given that the ef-fects of scopolamine appear to influence performance through non-associative mechanisms, it is probable that the U-shaped function is due to processes unrelated to memory change (however, for an alternative explanation see Klein & Spear, 1970a,b).

Finally, Deutsch (1971), in considering long-term memory changes, suggests that alterations of ACh and acetylcholinesterase (AChE) were responsible for some of the nonmonotonic changes in performance. Al-though Deutsch evaluates performance in aversive and in appetitive tasks, thereby bringing some generality to the phenomenon, Signorelli (1976) indicates that some of the behavioral changes evident at the vari-ous intervals were transient. Furthermore, George and Mellanby (1974) indicate that the vehicle in which drug treatments were suspended (pea-nut oil) may have been responsible for the behavioral changes induced by phamacological treatments.

A final note has particular bearing on aversive paradigms. As we saw earlier, it has been demonstrated that neurochemical changes are subject to conditioning or sensitization. Once an animal has been ex-posed to uncontrollable stress, subsequent reexposure to even moderate stress or to the cues associated with stress would result in neurochemi-cal change. These neurochemical changes in turn may induce non-associative behavioral alterations that may influence performance. In effect, behavioral analyses conducted at intervals after the initial stress-produced amine changes have subsided may still be subject to the intrusion of nonassociative influences (see Anisman & Sklar, 1979).

6. PHAMACOLOGICAL MANIPULATIONS AND ESCAPE BEHAVIOR

In the typical escape task most pharmacological treatments do not affect performance unless fairly substantial dosages are employed. In this instance it is likely that toxic effects of the treatment are responsible for the behavioral changes. In the experiments with the disruptive effects of inescapable shock on later performance described earlier, a modified escape procedure was employed. Using the delay procedure, escape behavior was found to be sensitive to various pharmacological manipulations. Accordingly, this section will primarily consider the escape task, in which the response can be executed only after several seconds of shock onset.

Consistent with the proposition that the escape deficits induced by uncontrollable shock are mediated by stress-induced neurochemical changes, we found that several pharmacological manipulations will mimic the behavioral deficits introduced by inescapable stress. For instance, pharmacological treatments that deplete DA and/or NE or block DA receptors will not disrupt performance when escape is possible immediately upon shock onset. However, when an escape delay procedure is employed, such treatments will effectively retard performance. As seen in Figure 9.7, haloperidol, a DA receptor blocker, produces dose-dependent behavioral deficits when a 4- or 6-second escape delay procedure is employed. In the higher doses, deficits will be induced using a 2-second delay procedure, but under no circumstances is performance retarded when escape is possible at shock onset (0 seconds escape delay). In effect, haloperidol decreases the animal's ability to sustain active responding, thereby disrupting performance in motorically demanding tasks. This effect, as depicted in Figure 9.7, is not evident during the initial escape trials but becomes progressively greater as training continues. If the behavioral effect induced by the drug were due to cognitive changes (e.g., inducing helplessness), performance deficits should have occurred throughout training.

As in the case of inescapable shock, we have found that prior escape training limits the disruptive effects of haloperidol (see Figure 9.8). Of course, with a sufficiently high dosage of the drug the initial escape training procedure was insufficient to modify the effects. As yet unpublished data collected in this laboratory indicate that treatments that

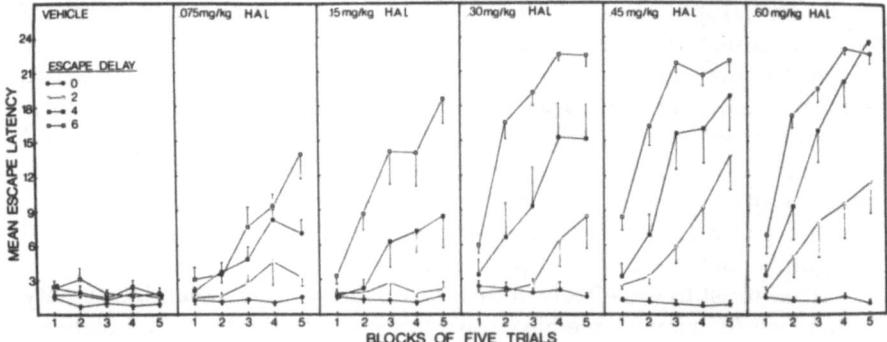

Fig. 9.7. Mean (±SEM) escape latencies among Swiss-Webster mice following treatment with haloperiodol (0.075–0.60 mg/kg) or vehicle. During test, escape was possible either immediately upon shock onset or after delays of 2, 4, or 6 seconds. (From Anisman, Remington, & Sklar, 1979.)

abbreviate the decline of shock-elicited activity also modify escape behavior. For example, brief shock interruption or brief presentation of a light–tone stimulus increased shock-elicited activity and reduced the disruptive effects of haloperidol.

The effects described here with the DA receptor blocker haloperidol were also observed with drugs that increase ACh levels (physostigmine) or reduce DA and/or NE (α-MpT or FLA-63). It is not clear why so wide an assortment of treatments would induce comparable behavioral out-

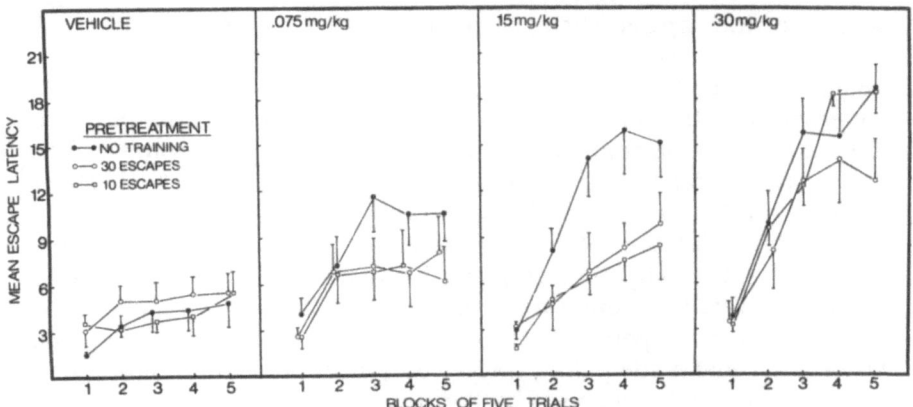

Fig. 9.8. Mean (±SEM) escape latencies in an escape task involving a 6-second delay procedure among Swiss-Webster mice treated with various doses of haloperidol. Twenty-four hours previously, mice had received either 0, 10, or 30 escape trials in the absence of any drug treatment. (From Anisman, Remington, & Sklar, 1979.)

comes. It is highly unlikely that DA, NE, and ACh subserve behavior through similar processes. A more appealing interpretation of these findings is that the integrity of these three transmitters acting in series must be maintained in order for escape behavior to progress readily. Disruption of any one of these transmitters will result in behavioral retardation. Alternatively, these transmitters may play independent, nonoverlapping roles in determining performance (e.g., motoric, arousal, motivational, etc.), and disruption of any one of these serves to antagonize behavior in complex tasks.

In contrast to the effects of drugs that reduce catecholamine activity or increase ACh levels, we have observed that a variety of catecholamine stimulants as well as an anticholinergic will eliminate the disruptive effects of inescapable shock. For example, L-DOPA, apomorphine, and clonidine administered either before inescapable shock or before escape testing will prevent the interference from becoming apparent in subsequent escape from shock tests (Anisman, Remington, & Sklar, 1979; Anisman, Suissa, & Sklar, 1980). Curiously, when administered before the test session scopolamine eliminates the interference, but it has no effect on performance if administered before inescapable shock (Anisman, Glazier, & Sklar, 1981). Inasmuch as the effects of these various agents on avoidance performance seem to be of a nonassociative nature (see the preceding section), it is likely that the effects of the drugs in the escape paradigm are also due to nonassociative changes.

Consistent with the proposition that the escape deficits induced by inescapable shock are due to neurochemical change, Weiss, Glazer, and Pohorecky (1976) report that the behavioral deficits induced by a single session of inescapable shock were absent after exposure to 15 shock sessions. It will be recalled that after such a chronic stress regimen neurochemical adaptation occurred, such that the synthesis of brain NE increased and the amine depletion was not evident. Had the interference been due to cognitive changes (i.e., learned helplessness), then the behavioral deficits should certainly have been evident after 15 stress sessions, and perhaps should have been augmented.

At this point several caveats are in order. First, in assessing the contribution of competing response tendencies to the escape interference, it might be tempting to assess the effects of passive escape training and inescapable shock on later active escape. However, the assumption that a competing response hypothesis would predict comparable behavioral disruption by the two treatments is not warranted. Weiss, Glazer, and Pohorecky (1976) found that neither passive nor active escape training induced NE depletion, although motor inhibition developed in the former group. Accordingly, the neurochemical/nonassociative explanation would, in fact, predict performance deficits in a group exposed to inescapable shock to exceed those engendered by passive escape training.

Second, the motor interpretations based on nonassociative and associative processes are not entirely independent of one another. To be sure, Anisman and Sklar (1979) argue that the reduction of shock-- elicited activity resulting from neurochemical change may be correlated with shock offset. Thus, although not explicitly paired in the experimental protocol, the reduction of shock-elicited activity may be reinforced. Glazer and Weiss (1976a,b) argue that neurochemical changes and learned competing motor tendencies account for different attributes of the interference effect (i.e., short-vs. long-term effects), whereas Anisman and Sklar (1979) entertain the notion that the long-term interference is due to neurochemical alterations owing to stimulus sensitization or conditioning. By no means, however, should it be inferred that a nonassociative effect will not or cannot lead to learned competing tendencies. As Glazer and Weiss (1976a,b) and Anisman et al. (1978) indicate, the parameters of the task, in terms of shock duration, are an essential ingredient in determining whether learned competing tendencies will evolve.

Third, proponents of the helplessness hypothesis have argued that inescapable shock will, among other things, result in associative deficits. That is, animals will suffer in their ability to associate their responses with environmental cues. Jackson, Alexander, and Maier (1980), in fact, report that inescapable shock will impair later acquisition of a discrimination in a Y-maze task. In contrast, however, Irwin, Suissa, and Anisman (1980) report that such deficits were not evident in a series of T-maze discrimination tasks. The source for the divergent results is not readily apparent because of the vast number of procedural differences between these studies. Nevertheless, it may be too early to conclude that stress has direct effects on associative processes. For example, associative difficulties may be secondary to nonassociative effects of stress (e.g., perseverative tendencies, arousal level, etc).

Finally, it is tempting to assume that "helplessness" might simply be a reflection of neurochemical change, or, alternatively, that it produces the neurochemical changes. Inasmuch as pharmacological alterations of NE, DA, and ACh have predictable effects on behavior (i.e., mimicking or eliminating the effects of inescapable shock), concepts such as helplessness are superfluous. Indeed, whereas neurochemical change can be quantitatively measured, helplessness can only be inferred. Thus a more appropriate strategy for assessing the outcomes of stress would be to evaluate the effects of coping (and failure to cope) on ensuing behavioral outcomes and to relate these to endogenous neurochemical and/or hormonal states.

7. ANALGESIA

A number of investigators report that various forms of stress will result in decreased responsivity to subsequent stressors (Amir & Amit, 1978; Bodnar, Kelly, Brutus, & Glusman, 1980; Madden, Akil, Patrick, & Barchas, 1977). Although some investigators (e.g., Jackson, Maier, & Coon, 1979) maintain that stress controllability is an important feature in determining the analgesia, others argue against this notion (Mah, Suissa, & Anisman, 1980). In contrast to Jackson *et al.* (1979), Mah *et al.* (1980) observed the analgesia after both escapable and inescapable shock. Nevertheless, since escape behavior is influenced by shock severity, nonassociative factors related to analgesia may be important in determining performance. Furthermore, in light of the finding that an analgesia can also be elicited by cues previously associated with shock (Chance *et al.*, 1977), behavioral changes seen even at long intervals after initial training might be related to conditioning or sensitization of the analgesic response.

The mechanisms subserving the analgesia have not yet been fully determined. Although stress will result in release of the endogenous opioids, leu-enkephalin and β-endorphin, from the hypothalamus (Chance *et al.*, 1978; Rossier, Guillemin, & Bloom, 1978) and from the pituitary (Rossier, French, Rivier, Ling, Guillemin, & Bloom, 1977), it does not appear that these were related to the stress-provoked analgesia. Specifically, the morphine antagonist naloxone has been shown to have no effect or marginal effects on the stress-induced analgesia (Lal, Spaulding, & Fielding, 1978) or on the analgesia engendered by a CS previously paired with stress (Chance & Rosecrans, 1979a,b). A second possible source for the antinoception is related to biogenic amine changes. That is, DA and NE as well as 5-HT are possible candidates for the stress-induced analgesia (Bodnar *et al.*, 1980; Chance *et al.*, 1977). Indeed, there is reason to believe that more than a single analgesic system exists (e.g., deVries *et al.*, 1979). One of these, induced by repeated shock presentations, may be opioid mediated; the second, induced by limited stress exposure, may involve release of amines. In either case, the role of pain sensitivity would necessarily be a major consideration in assessing nonassociative influences on avoidance and escape performance.

8. SUMMARY

Behavioral response to aversive stimulation is considered an adaptive change to meet environmental demands. In addition, coping with stress occurs through various physiological changes including hormonal, neurochemical, and immunologic functioning. The nature and magnitude of the physiological changes and the concomitant species-typical defensive behaviors will vary as a function of organismic, experiential, and environmental factors. The intrusion of these defensive acts is assumed to influence the expression of behavior in learning paradigms.

The rate at which an avoidance response is acquired depends on the compatibility of the organism's defensive style and the response requirements of the avoidance task. We have looked at several nonassociative behavioral effects of stress as well as neurochemical alterations that occur with aversive stimulation. The contribution of these nonassociative changes to performance was considered across a broad range of avoidance tasks, and the role of neurochemical change to avoidance behavior was assessed on the basis of experiments involving pharmacological manipulations. It seems that analysis of learning and memory processes in aversive paradigms is exceedingly difficult because of the intrusion of nonassociative factors, and conclusions concerning cognitive changes may be inappropriate.

ACKNOWLEDGMENTS

The comments of Lawrence Sklar and Robert Zacharko are gratefully acknowledged.

9. REFERENCES

Abramson, L. Y., & Sackeim, H. A. A paradox in depression: Uncontrollability and self-blame. *Psychological Bulletin*, 1977, *84*, 838–851.

Amir, S., & Amit, Z. Endogenous opioid legands may mediate stress-induced changes in the affective properties of pain related behaviors in rats. *Life Sciences*, 1978, *25*, 1143–1152.

Amkraut, A., & Solomon, G. F. From the symbolic stimulus to the pathophysiologic response: Immune mechanisms. *International Journal of Psychiatry in Medicine*, 1975, *5*, 541–563.

Anisman, H. Cholinergic mechanisms and alterations in behavioral suppression as factors producing time dependent changes in avoidance performance. *Journal of Comparative and Physiological Psychology*, 1973, *83*, 465–477.

Anisman, H. Time-dependent variations in aversively motivated behaviors: Nonassociative effects of cholinergic and catecholaminergic activity. *Psychological Review*, 1975, *82*, 359–385.

Anisman, H. Time-dependent changes in activity, reactivity and responsivity during shock: Effects of cholinergic and catecholaminergic manipulations. *Behavioral Biology*, 1977, *21*, 1–31.

Anisman, H. Neurochemical changes elicited by stress: Behavioral correlates. In H. Anisman & G. Bignami (Eds.), *Psychopharmacology of aversively motivated behavior*. New York: Plenum Press, 1978.

Anisman, H., & Bignami, G. A comparative neurochemical, pharmacological, and functional analysis of aversively motivated behaviors: Caveats and general considerations. In H. Anisman & G. Bignami (Eds.), *Psychopharmacology of aversively motivated behavior*. New York: Plenum Press, 1978.

Anisman, H., & Sklar, L. S. Catecholamine depletion upon reexposure to stress: Mediation of the escape deficits produced by inescapable shock. *Journal of Comparative and Physiological Psychology*, 1979, 93, 610–625.

Anisman, H., & Sklar, L. S. Social housing conditions influence escape deficits produced by uncontrollable stress: Assessment of the contribution of norepinephrine. *Behavioral and Neural Biology*, 1981, 32, 406–427.

Anisman, H., & Wahlsten, D. Response initiation and directionality as factors influencing avoidance performance. *Journal of Comparative and Physiological Psychology*, 1974, 87, 1119–1128.

Anisman, H., & Waller, T. G. Facilitative and disruptive effect of prior exposure to shock on subsequent avoidance performance. *Journal of Comparative and Physiological Psychology*, 1972, 78, 113–122.

Anisman, H., & Waller, T. G. Effects of inescapable shock on subsequent avoidance performance: Role of response repertoire changes. *Behavioral Biology*, 1973, 9, 331–355.

Anisman, H., deCatanzaro, D., & Remington, G. Escape performance following exposure to inescapable shock: Deficits in motor response maintenance. *Journal of Experimental Psychology: Animal Behavior Processes*, 1978, 4, 197–218.

Anisman, H., Grimmer, L., Irwin, J., Remington, G., & Sklar, L. S. Escape performance after inescapable shock in selectively bred lines of mice: Response maintenance and catecholamine activity. *Journal of Comparative and Physiological Psychology*, 1979, 93, 229–241.

Anisman, H., Remington, G., & Sklar, L. S. Effects of inescapable shock on subsequent escape performance: Catecholaminergic and cholinergic mediation of response initiation and maintenance. *Psychopharmacology*, 1979, 61, 107–124.

Anisman, H., Kokkinidis, L., & Sklar, L. S. Contribution of neurochemical change to stress induced behavioral deficits. In S. J. Cooper (Ed.), *Theory in psychopharmacology* (Vol. 1). New York: Academic Press, 1981 (a)

Anisman, H., Kokkinidis, L., & Sklar, L. S. Neurochemical consequences of stress: Contributions of adaptive processes. In S. Burchfield (Ed.), *Physiological and psychological interactions in response to stress*. New York: Hemisphere, 1981. (b)

Anisman, H., Pizzino, A., & Sklar, L. S. Coping with stress, norepinephrine depletion and escape performance. *Brain Research*, 1980, 191, 583–588.

Anisman, H., Suissa, A., & Sklar, L. S. Escape deficits induced by uncontrollable stress: Antagonism by dopamine and norepinephrine agonists. *Behavior and Neural Biology*, 1980, 28, 34–47.

Anisman, H., Glazier, S., & Sklar, L. S. Cholinergic influences on escape deficits produced by uncontrollable stress. *Psychopharmacology*, 1981, 74, 81–87.

Aprison, M. H., & Hingtgen, J. N. Evidence of a central cholinergic mechanism functioning during drug-induced excitation in avoidance behavior. In E. Heilbronn & A. Winter (Eds.), *Drugs and cholinergic mechanisms in the CNS*. Stockholm: Forsvarets Forskning-Sansalt, 1970.

Aprison, M. H., Kariya, T., Hingtgen, J. N., & Toru, M. Neurochemical correlates of behavior: Changes in acetylcholine, norepinephrine and 5-hydroxytryptamine concentrations in several discrete brain areas of the rat during behavioral excitation. *Journal of Neurochemistry*, 1968, 15, 1131–1139.

Ashe, V. M., & McCain, G. Comparison of one-way and shuttle-avoidance performance of gerbils and rats. *Journal of Comparative and Physiological Psychology*, 1972, 80, 291–296.

Barrett, R. J., Leith, N. J., & Ray, O. S. Permanent facilitation of avoidance behavior of D-amphetamine and scopolamine. *Psychopharmacologia*, 1972, *25*, 321–331.

Barrett, R. J., Leith, N. J., & Ray, O. S. An analysis of the facilitation of avoidance acquisition produced by d-amphetamine and scopolamine. *Behavioral Biology*, 1974, *11*, 189–205.

Barry, H., & Buckley, J. P. Drug effect on animal performance and the stress syndrome. *Journal of Pharmacological Science*, 1966, *55*, 1159–1183.

Bignami, G. Nonassociative explanations of behavioural changes induced by central cholinergic drugs. *Acta Neurobiologiae Experimentalis*, 1976, *36*, 5–90.

Bignami, G., & Michalek, H. Cholinergic mechanisms and aversively motivated behaviors. In H. Anisman & G. Bignami (Eds.), *Psychopharmacology of aversively motivated behavior.* New York: Plenum Press, 1978.

Blanc, G., Hervé, D., Simon, H., Lisoprawski, A., Glowinski, J., & Tassin, J. P. Response to stress of mesocortical-frontal dopaminergic neurones in rats after long term isolation. *Nature*, 1980, *284*, 265–267.

Bodnar, R. J., Kelly, D. D., Brutus, M., & Glusman, M. Stress induced analgesia: Neural and hormonal determinants. *Neuroscience and Biobehavioral Reviews*, 1980, *4*, 87–100.

Bolles, R. C. Species-specific defense reactions and avoidance learning. *Psychological Review*, 1970, *77*, 32–48.

Bolles, R. C. Species-specific defense reactions. In F. R. Brush (Ed.), *Aversive conditioning and learning.* New York: Academic Press, 1971.

Bracewell, R. J., & Black, A. H. The effects of restraint and noncontingent preshock on subsequent escape learning in the rat. *Learning Motivation.* 1974, *5*, 53–69.

Breese, G. R., & Cooper, B. R. Behavioral and biochemical interactions of 5, 7-dihydroxytryptamine with various drugs when administered intracisternally to adult and developing rats. *Brain Research*, 1975, *98*, 517–527.

Breese, G. R., Cooper, B. R., Grant, L. D., & Smith, R. D. Biochemical and behavioral alterations following 5, 6-dihyhydroxytryptamine administered into brain. *Neuropharmacology*, 1974, *13*, 177–187.

Brush, F. R. Retention of aversively motivated behavior. In F. R. Brush (Ed.), *Aversive conditioning and learning.* New York: Academic Press, 1971.

Campbell, B. A., & Spear, N. E. Ontogeny of memory. *Psychological Review*, 1972, *79*, 215–236.

Cassens, G., Roffman, M., Kuruc, A., Orsulak, P. J., & Schildkraut, J. J. Alterations in brain norepinephrine metabolism induced by environmental stimuli previously paired with inescapable shock. *Science*, 1980, *209*, 1138–1140.

Chance, W. T., & Rosecrans, J. A. Lack of cross-tolerance between morphine and autoanalgesia. *Pharmacology, Biochemistry and Behavior*, 1979, *11*, 639–642. (a)

Chance, W. T., & Rosecrans, J. A. Lack of effect of naloxone on autoanalgesia. *Pharmacology, Biochemistry and Behavior*, 1979, *11*, 643–646. (b)

Chance, W. T., White, A. C., Krynock, G. M., & Rosecrans, J. A. Centrifugal control of nociception: Autoanalgesic mechanisms. *Proceedings of the Society for Neurosciences*, 1977, *3*, 479. (Abstract)

Chance, W. T., White, A. C., Krynock, G. M., & Rosecrans, J. A. Conditional fear-induced autinociception and decreased binding of [^{3}H] N-Leu-enkephalin to rat brain. *Brain Research*, 1978, *141*, 371–374.

Cherek, D. R., Lane, J. D., Freeman, M. E., & Smith, J. E. Receptor changes following shock avoidance. *Society of Neuroscience Abstracts*, 1980, *6*, 543.

Cooper, B. R., Breese, G. R., Grant, L. D., & Howard, J. L. Effects of 6-hydroxydopamine treatments on active avoidance responding: Evidence for involvement of brain dopamine. *Journal of Pharmacological Experimental Therapeutics*, 1973, *185*, 358–370.

Davidson, A. B., & Weidley, E. Differential effects of neuroleptic and other psychotropic agents on acquisition of avoidance in rats. *Life Sciences*, 1976, *18*, 1279–1284.

Deutsch, J. A. The cholinergic synapse and the site of memory. *Science*, 1971, *174*, 788–794.

DeVries, G. H., Chance, W. T., Payne, W. R., & Rosecrans, J. A. Effect of autoanalgesia on CNS enkephalin receptors. *Pharmacology, Biochemistry and Behavior*, 1979, *11*, 741–744.

Dismukes, R. K., & Rake, A. V. Involvement of biogenic amines in memory formation. *Psychopharmacologia*, 1972, *23*, 17–25.

Ebel, A., Hermetet, J. C., & Mandel, P. Comparative study of acetycholinesterase and choline acetyltransferase enzyme activity in brain of DBA and C57 mice. *Nature*, 1973, *242*, 56–58.

Fibiger, H. C., Phillips, A. G., & Zis, A. P. Deficits in instrumental responding after 6-hydroxydopamine lesions of the nigro-neostriatal dopaminergic projection. *Pharmacology, Biochemistry and Behavior*, 1974, *2*, 87.

Fibiger, H. C., Zis, A. P., & Phillips, G. Haloperidol-induced disruption of conditioned avoidance responding: Attenuation by prior training or by anticholinergic drugs. *European Journal of Pharmacology*, 1975, *80*, 309–314.

Finch, C. E. Catecholamine metabolism in the brains of ageing male mice. *Brain Research*, 1973, *52*, 261–276.

Frontali, M., Amorico, L., de Acetis, L., & Bignami, G. A pharmacological analysis of processes underlying differential responding: A review and further experiments with scopolamine, amphetamine, lysergic acid diethylamide (LSD-25), chlordiazepoxide, physostigmine and chlorpromazine. *Behavioral Biology*, 1976, *18*, 1–74.

Fulginiti, S., Molina, J. A., & Orsingher, O. A. Inhibition of catecholamine biosynthesis and memory processes. *Psychopharmacology*, 1976, *51*, 65–69.

Geller, I. Use of approach-avoidance behavior (conflict) for evaluating depressant drugs. In J. H. Nodine & J. H. Moyer (Eds.), *Psychosomatic Medicine*. Philadelphia: Lea and Fibiger, 1962, 267–274.

George, G., & Mellanby, J. A further study on the effect of physostigmine on memory in rats. *Brain Research*, 1974, *81*(1), 133–144.

Glazer, H. I., & Weiss, J. M. Long-term and transitory interference effects. *Journal of Experimental Psychology: Animal Behavior Processes*, 1976, *2*, 191–201. (a)

Glazer, H. I., & Weiss, J. M. Long term interference effect: An alternative to "Learned Helplessness." *Journal of Experimental Psychology: Animal Behavior Processes*, 1976, *2*, 202–213. (b)

Grossen, N. E., & Kelley, M. J. Species-specific behavior and acquisition of avoidance behavior in rats. *Journal of Comparative and Physiological Psychology*, 1972, *81*, 307–310.

Hendley, E. D., Moisset, B., & Welch, B. C. Catecholamine uptake in cerebral cortex: Adaptive change induced by fighting. *Science*, 1973, *80*, 1050–1052.

Herrnstein, R. J. Method and theory in the study of avoidance. *Psychological Review*, 1969, *76*, 49–69.

Hingtgen, J. N., Smith, J. E., Shea, P. A., Aprison, M. H., & Gaff, T. M. Cholinergic changes during conditioned suppression in rats. *Science*, 1976, *193*, 332–334.

Huppert, F. A., & Iversen, S. D. Response suppression in rats: A comparison of response-contingent and noncontingent punishment and the effect of the minor tranquilizer, chlordiazepoxide. *Psychopharmacologia*, 1975, *44*, 67–75.

Ingenito, A. J., & Bonnycastle, D. D. The effect of exposure to heat and cold upon rat brain catecholamine and 5-hydroxytryptamine levels. *Canadian Journal of Physiological Pharmacology*, 1967, *45*, 733–743.

Irwin, J., Suissa, A., & Anisman, H. Differential effects of inescapable shock on escape performance and discrimination learning in a water escape task. *Journal of Experimental Psychology: Animal Behavior Processes*, 1980, *6*, 21–40.

Iversen, S. D. Brain dopamine systems and behavior. In L. L. Iversen, S. D. Iversen, & S. H. Snyder (Eds.), *Handbook of psychopharmacology* (Vol. 8). New York: Plenum Press, 1977.

Izquierdo, I. A pharmacological separation of buzzer-shock pairing and of the shuttle-shock contingency as factors in the elicitation of shuttle responses to a buzzer in rats. *Behavioral Biology,* 1976, *18,* 75–88.

Izquierdo, I., & Elisabetsky, E. Four memory channels in the rat brain. *Psychopharmacology,* 1978, *57,* 215–222.

Izquierdo, I., Beamish, D. G., & Anisman, H. Effect of an inhibitor of dopamine-Beta-hydroxylase on the acquisition and retention of four different avoidance tasks in mice. *Psychopharmacology,* 1979, *63,* 173–178.

Jackson, R. L., Maier, S. F., & Coon, D. J. Long-term analgesic effects of inescapable shock and learned helplessness. *Science,* 1979, *206,* 91–93.

Jackson, R. L., Alexander, R. H., & Maier, S. F. Learned helplessness, inactivity and associative deficits: Effects of inescapable shock on response choice escape learning. *Journal of Experimental Psychology: Animal Behavior Processes,* 1980, *6,* 1–20.

Karczmar, A. G., Scudder, C. L., & Richardson, D. L. Interdisciplinary approach to the study of behavior in related mice types. In S. Ehrenpreis & I. J. Kopin (Eds.), *Chemical approaches to brain function.* New York: Academic Press, 1973.

Katzev, R. D., & Mills, S. K. Strain differences in avoidance conditioning as a function of the classical CS-US contingency. *Journal of Comparative and Physiological Psychology,* 1974, *87,* 661–671.

Kelly, P. H. Drug-induced motor behavior. In L. L. Iversen, S. D. Iversen, & S. H. Snyder (Eds.), *Handbook of psychopharmacology* (Vol. 8). New York: Plenum Press, 1977.

Klein, S. B., & Spear, N. E. Forgetting by the rat after intermediate intervals (Kamin effect) as retrieval failure. *Journal of Comparative and Physiological Psychology,* 1970, *71,* 165–170. (a)

Klein, S. B., & Spear, N. E. Reactivation of avoidance learning memory in the rat after intermediate retention intervals. *Journal of Comparative and Physiological Psychology,* 1970, *72,* 498–504. (b)

Kobayashi, R. M., Palkovits, M., Kizer, J. S., Jacobowitz, D. M., & Kopin, I. J. Selective alterations of catecholamines and tyrosine hydroxylase activity in the hypothalamus following acute and chronic stress. In E. Usdin, R. Kvetnansky, & I. J. Kopin (Eds.), *Catecholamines and stress.* Oxford: Pergamon Press, 1976.

Korf, J. Locus coeruleus, noradrenaline metabolism and stress. In E. Usdin, R. Kvetnansky, & I. J. Kopin (Eds.), *Catecholamines and stress.* Oxford: Pergamon Press, 1976.

Kvetnansky, R., Mitro, A., Palkovits, M., Brownstein, M., Torda, T., Vigas, M., & Mikulaj, L. Catecholamines in individual hypothalamic nuclei in stressed rats. In E. Usdin, R. Kvetnansky, & I. J. Kopin (Eds.), *Catecholamines and stress.* Oxford: Pergamon Press, 1976.

Kvetnansky, R., Kopin, I. J., & Saavedra, J. M. Changes in epinephrine in individual hypothalamic nuclei after immobilization stress. *Brain Research,* 1978, *155*(2), 387–390.

Lal, H., Spaulding, T., & Fielding, S. Swim-stress induced analgesia and lack of its naloxone antagonism. *Communications in Psychopharmacology,* 1978, *2,* 263–266.

Lavielle, S., Tassin, J. P., Thierry, A. M., Blanc, G., Hervé, D., Barthelemy, C., & Glowinski, J. Blockade of benzodiazepines of the selective high increase in dopamine turnover induced by stress in mesocortical dopaminergic neurons of the rat. *Brain Research,* 1978, *168,* 585–594.

Lenard, L. G., & Beer, B. 6-hydroxydopamine and avoidance: Possible role of response suppression. *Pharmacology, Biochemistry and Behavior,* 1975, *3,* 873–878. (a)

Lenard, L. G., & Beer, B. Modification avoidance behavior in 6-hydroxydopamine-treated rats by stimulation of central noradrenergic and dopaminergic receptors. *Pharmacology, Biochemistry and Behavior*, 1975, 3, 887–893. (b)

Lenard, L. G., & Beer, B. Relationship of brain levels of norepinephrine and dopamine to avoidance behavior in rats after intraventricular administration of 6-hydroxy-dopamine. *Pharmacology, Biochemistry and Behavior*, 1975, 3, 895–899. (c)

Lorens, S. A. Raphe lesions in cats: Forebrain serotonin avoidance behavior. *Pharmacology, Biochemistry and Behavior*, 1973, 1, 487–490.

Lorens, S. A., Gulberg, H. C., Hole, K., Kolater, C., & Srebro, B. Activity, avoidance learning and regional 5-hydroxytryptamine following intra-brain stem 5, 7-dihydroxy-tryptamine and electrolytic midbrain raphe lesions in rats. *Brain Research*, 1976, 108, 97–114.

Mackintosh, N. J. Stimulus selection: Learning to ignore stimuli that predict no change in reinforcement. In R. A. Hinde & J. S. Hinde (Eds.), *Constraints on learning: Limitations and predispositions*. New York: Academic Press, 1973.

Madden, J., IV, Akil, H., Patrick, R. L., & Barchas, J. D. Stress-induced parallel changes in central opioid levels and pain responsiveness in the rat. *Nature*, 1977, 265, 358–360.

Mah, C., Suissa, A., & Anisman, H. Dissociation of antinociception and escape deficits induced by stress in mice. *Journal of Comparative and Physiological Psychology*, 1980, 94, 1160–1171.

Maier, S. F., & Jackson, R. L. Learned helplessness: All of us were right (and wrong): Inescapable shock has multiple effects. In G. Bower (Ed.), *The psychology of learning and motivation* (Vol. 13). New York: Academic Press, 1979.

Maier, S. F., & Seligman, M. E. P. Learned helplessness: Theory and evidence. *Journal of Experimental Psychology: General*, 1976, 105, 3–46.

Maier, S. F., & Testa, T. J. Failure to learn to escape by rats previously exposed to inescapable shock is partly produced by associative interference. *Journal of Comparative and Physiological Psychology*, 1975, 88, 554.

Maier, S. F., Albin, R. W., & Testa, T. J. Failure to learn to escape in rats previously exposed to inescapable shock depends on nature of escape response. *Journal of Comparative and Physiological Psychology*, 1973, 85, 581–592.

Maynert, E. W., & Levi, R. Stress-induced release of brain nerepinephrine and its inhibition by drugs. *Journal of Pharmacology and Experimental Therapeutics*, 1964, 143, 90–95.

McAllister, W. R., & McAllister, D. E. Behavioral measurement of conditioned fear. In F. R. Brush (Ed.), *Aversive conditioning and learning*. New York: Academic Press, 1971.

McGaugh, J. L. Neurobiological aspects of memory. In R. G. Grenell & S. Gabay (Eds.), *Biological foundations of psychiatry* (Vol. 1). New York: Raven Press, 1976.

McMillan, D. E., & Leander, J. R. Drugs and punished responding vs. effects of drugs on responding suppressed by response-dependent and response-independent electric shock. *Archives of International Pharmacodynamics and Therapeutics*, 1975, 213, 22–27.

Meyers, B. Some effects of scopolamine on a passive avoidance response in rats. *Psychopharmacologia*, 1965, 8, 111–119.

Miczek, K. A. Effects of scopolamine, amphetamine and chlordiazepoxide on punishment. *Psychopharmacologia*, 1973, 28, 373–389. (a)

Miczek, K. A. Effects of scopolamine, amphetamine and benzodiazepines on conditioned suppression. *Pharmacology, Biochemistry and Behavior*, 1973, 1, 401–411. (b)

Miline, R. The role of the pineal gland in stress. *Journal of Neural Transmission*, 1980, 47, 191–220.

Modigh, K. Influence of social stress on brain catecholamine mechanisms. In E. Usdin, R. Kvetnansky, & I. J. Kopin (Eds.), *Catecholamines and stress*. Oxford: Pergamon Press, 1976.

Neill, D. B., Boggan, W. O., & Grossman, S. P. Behavioral effects of amphetamine in rats with lesions in the corpus striatum. *Journal of Comparative and Physiological Psychology*, 1974, *86*, 1019–1030.

Nishikawa, T., Kajiwara, Y., Kono, Y., Sano, T., Nagaski, N., Tanaka, M., & Noda, Y. Isolation-induced general behavioral changes and brain monoamine levels in rat. *Kurume Medical Journal*, 1974, *21*, 117–121.

Palkovits, M., Brownstein, M., Kizer, J. S., Saaverda, J. M., & Kopin, I. J. Affect of stress on serotonin and tryptophan hydroxylase activity of brain nuclei. In E. Usdin, R. Kvetnansky, & I. J. Kopin (Eds.), *Catecholamine and stress*. Oxford: Pergamon Press, 1976.

Peters, D. A. V., Anisman, H., & Pappas, B. A. Monoamines and aversively motivated behaviors. In H. Anisman & G. Bignami (Eds.), *Psychopharmacology of aversively motivated behavior*. New York: Plenum Press, 1978.

Pinel, J. P. J., & Mucha, R. F. Activity and reactivity in rats at various intervals after footshock. *Canadian Journal of Psychology*, 1973, *27*, 112–118.

Pinel, J. P. J., & Treit, D. Burying as a defensive response in rats. *Journal of Compartative and Physiological Psychology*, 1978, *92*, 708–712.

Rainbow, T. C., Adler, J. E., & Flexner, L. B. Comparison in mice of the amnesic effects of cyclohexamide and 6-hydroxydopamine in a one-trial passive avoidance task. *Pharmacology, Biochemistry and Behavior*, 1976, *41*, 347–349.

Ray, O. S., & Barrett, R. J. Behavioral, pharmacological, and biochemical analysis of genetic differences in rats. *Behavioral Biology*, 1975, *15*, 391–417.

Rescorla, R. A., & Solomon, R. L. Two process learning theory: Relationships between Pavlovian and instrumental learning. *Psychological Review*, 1967, *74*, 151–182.

Ritter, S., & Pelzer, N. L. Magnitude of stress-induced brain norepinephrine depletion varies with age. *Brain Research*, 1978, *152*, 170–175.

Rosic, N., & Bignami, G. Depression of two-way avoidance learning and enhancement of passive avoidance learning by small doses of physostigmine. *Neuropharmacology*, 1970, *9*, 311–316. (a)

Rosic, N., & Bignami, G. Scopolamine effects on go–no go avoidance discriminations: Influence of stimulus factors and primacy training. *Psychopharmacologia*, 1970, *17*, 203–215. (b)

Rossier, J., French, E. D., River, C., Ling, N., Guillemin, R., & Bloom, F. E. Foot-shock induced stress increases B-endorphine levels in blood but not brain. *Nature*, 1977, *270*, 618–620.

Rossier, J., Guillemin, R., & Bloom, F. E. Foot-shock induced stress decreases Leu[5]-enkephalin immunoreactivity in rat hypothalamus. *European Journal of Pharmacology*, 1978, *48*, 465–466.

Saito, H., Morita, A., Miyazaki, I., & Takagi, K. Comparison of the effects of various stresses on biogenic amines in the central nervous system and animal symptoms. In E. Usdin, R. Kvetnansky, & I. J. Kopin (Eds.), *Catecholamines and stress*. Oxford: Pergamon Press, 1976.

Schmidt, D. E., Cooper, D. O., & Barrett, R. J. Strain specific alterations in hippocampal cholinergic function following acute foot-shock. *Pharmacology, Biochemistry and Behavior*, 1980, *12*, 277–280.

Seligman, M. E. P. On the generality of the laws of learning. *Psychological Review*, 1970, *77*, 406–418.

Seligman, M. E. P., Maier, S. F., & Solomon, R. L. Unpredictable and uncontrollable aversive events. In F. R. Brush (Ed.), *Aversive conditioning and learning*. New York: Academic Press, 1971.

Shettleworth, S. J. Constraints on learning. In D. S. Lehrman, R. A. Hinde, & E. Shaw. *Advances in the study of behavior* (Vol. 4). New York: Academic Press, 1972.

Shurman, A. J., & Katzev, R. D. Escape/avoidance responding in rats depends on strain and number of inescapable preshocks. *Journal of Comparative and Physiological Psychology*, 1975, *88*, 548–553.

Signorelli, A. Influence of physostigmine upon consolidation of memory in mice. *Journal of Comparative and Physiological Psychology*, 1976, *90*, 658–664.

Sklar, L. S., & Anisman, H. Contributions of stress and coping to cancer development and growth. In K. Bammer & B. H. Newberry (Eds.), *Stress and cancer*. Toronto: C. J. Hogrefe, 1981.

Steranka, L. R., & Barrett, R. J. Facilitation of avoidance acquisition by lesion of the median raphé nucleus: Evidence for serotonin as a mediator of shock-induced suppression. *Behavioral Biology*, 1974, *11*, 205–213.

Stolk, J. M., Conner, R. L., & Barchas, J. D. Social environment and brain biogenic amine metabolism in rats. *Journal of Comparative and Physiological Psychology*, 1974, *87*, 203–207.

Stolk, J. M., Conner, R. L., Levine, S., & Barchas, J. P. Brain norepinephrine metabolism and shock induced fighting behavior in rats: Differential effects of shock and fighting on the neurochemical response to a common footshock stimulus. *Journal of Pharmacology and Experimental Therapeutics*, 1974, *190*, 193–209.

Stone, E. A. Stress and catecholomines. In A. J. Friedhoff (Ed.), *Catecholamines and behavior*. Vol. 2. *Neuropsychopharmacology*. New York: Plenum Press, 1975.

Stone, E. A. Reduction by stress of norepinephrine-stimulated accumulation of cyclic AMP in rat cerebral cortex. *Journal of Neurochemistry*, 1979, *32*, 1335–1337. (a)

Stone, E. A. Subsensitivity to norepinephrine as a link between adaptation to stress and antidepressant therapy: An hypothesis. *Research Communications in Psychology, Psychiatry and Behavior*, 1979, *4*, 241–255. (b)

Suits, E., & Isaacson, R. L. The effects of scopolamine hydrobromide on one-way and two-way avoidance learning in rats. *International Journal of Neuropharmacology*, 1968, *7*, 441–446.

Testa, T. J. Causal relationships and the acquisition of avoidance responses. *Psychological Review*, 1974, *81*, 491–505.

Thierry, A. M. Effects of stress on the metabolism of serotonin and norepinephrine in the central nervous system of the rat. In S. Nemeth (Ed.), *Hormones, metabolism and stress: Recent progress and perspectives*. Bratislava: Publishing House of the Slovak Academy of Sciences, 1973.

Thierry, A. M., Fekete, M., & Glowinski, J. Effects of stress on the metabolism of noradrenaline, dopamine and serotonin (5-HT) in the central nervous system of the rat: Modifications of serotonin metabolism. *European Journal of Pharmacology*, 1968, *4*, 384–389.

Thierry, A. M., Blanc, G., & Glowinski, J. Preferential utilization of newly synthesized norepinephrine in the brain stem of stressed rats. *European Journal of Pharmacology*, 1970, *10*, 139.

Thierry, A. M., Tassin, J. P., Blanc, G., & Glowinski, J. Selective activation of the mesocortical DA system by stress. *Nature*, 1976, *263*, 242–263.

Thoa, N. B., Tizabi, Y., & Jacobowitz, D. M. The effect of isolation on catecholamine concentration and turnover in discrete areas of the rat brain. *Brain Research*, 1977, *131*, 259–269.

Thoenen, H. Induction of tyrosine hydroxylase in peripheral and central adrenergic neurons of cold exposure. *Nature*, 1970, *228*, 861–862.

Wahlsten, D. Genetic experiments with animal learning: A critical review. *Behavioral Biology*, 1972, *7*, 143–182. (a)

Wahlsten, D. Phenotypic and genetic relations between initial response to electric shock and rate of avoidance learning in mice. *Behavior Genetics*, 1972, *2*, 211–240. (b)

Wahlsten, D. Behavior genetics and animal learning. In H. Anisman & G. Bignami (Eds.), *Psychopharmacology of aversively motivated behavior*. New York: Plenum Press, 1978.

Weiss, J. M., & Glazer, H. I. Effects of acute exposure to stressors on subsequent avoidance-escape behavior. *Psychosomatic Medicine*, 1975, *37*, 499–521.

Weiss, J. M., Glazer, H. I., Pohorecky, L. A., Brick, J., & Miller, N. E. Effects of chronic exposure to stressors on avoidance-escape behavior and on brain norepinephrine. *Psychosomatic Medicine*, 1975, *37*, 522–534.

Weiss, J. M., Glazer, H. I., & Pohorecky, L. A. Coping behavior and neurochemical changes: An alternative explanation for the original "Learned Helplessness" experiments. In G. Serban & A. Kling (Eds.), *Animal models in human psychobiology*. New York: Plenum Press, 1976.

Weiss, J. M., Pohorecky, L. A., Salman, S., & Gruenthal, M. Attenuation of gastric lesions by psychological aspects of aggression in rats. *Journal of Comparative and Physiological Psychology*, 1976, *90*, 252–259.

Weiss, J. M., Glazer, H. I., Pohorecky, L. A., Bailey, W. H., & Schneider, L. H. Coping behavior and stress-induced behavioral depression: Studies of the role of brain catecholamines. In R. A. Depue (Ed.), *The psychobiology of the depressive disorders*. New York: Academic Press, 1979.

Welch, B. L., & Welch, A. S. Control of brain catecholamines and serotonin during acute stress and after d-amphetamine by natural inhibition of monoamine oxidase: An hypothesis. In E. Costa & S. Garattini (Eds.), *Amphetamines and related compounds*. New York: Raven Press, 1970.

Wimer, R. E., Reid, N., & Eleftheriou, E. Serotonin levels in hippocampus: Striking variations associated with mouse strain and treatment. *Brain Research*, 1973, *63*, 397–401.

Yuwiler, A. Stress, anxiety and endocrine function. In R. G. Grenell & S. Gabay (Eds.), *Biological foundations of psychiatry* (Vol. 2). New York: Raven Press, 1976.

Zajaczkowska, M. N. Acetylcholine content in the central and peripheral nervous system and its synthesis in the rat brain during stress and post-stress exhaustion. *Acta Physiologica Polsky*, 1975, *26*, 493–497.

Zornetzer, S. F. Neurotransmitter modulation and memory: A new neuropharmacological phrenology? In M. A. Lipton, A. D. Mascio, & K. F. Killam (Eds.), *Psychopharmacology: A generation of progress*. New York: Raven Press, 1978.

Zornetzer, S. F., & Gold, M. S. The locus coeruleus: Its possible role in memory consolidation. *Physiology and Behavior*, 1976, *16*, 331–336.

Zornetzer, S. F., Gold, M. S., & Hendrickson, J. Alpha-methyl-p-tyrosine and memory: State-dependency and memory failure. *Behavioural Biology*, 1974, *12*, 135–141.

10

Lateralization of Emotional or Behavioral Responses in Intact and Hemisphere-Damaged Humans and Rats

Godfrey D. Pearlson and Robert G. Robinson

1. INTRODUCTION

Current literature on the relationship of brain lateralization to emotion deals with such diverse topics as the recognition of facial expressions, neuropsychological variables in manic-depressive illness, animal evidence of lateralization, and changes in EEG patterns during human orgasm. These diverse phenomena are frequently treated as though they were different manifestations of some unitary phenomenon— "emotion" or "affectivity." In this chapter we shall propose that these diverse topics can best be integrated by seeing the expression of emotion as a multicomponent process with different experiments testing various parts of this process.

GODFREY D. PEARLSON AND ROBERT G. ROBINSON ● Department of Psychiatry and Behavioral Sciences, Johns Hopkins University School of Medicine, Baltimore, Maryland 21205. This chapter was supported in part by NIH Grants No. RCDA-MH00163 and No. NS15178.

First, we shall briefly review the role of subcortical mechanisms in emotional mediation and then examine human asymmetries of anatomy, biochemistry, and arousal systems in normals. Next, we shall consider human clinicopathological correlations in emotional function in patients with brain lesions, commissurotomy, temporal lobe epilepsy, manic-depressive illness, ECT, and stroke, including our own investigations. We shall then turn to animal studies of hemispheric asymmetry, including our own experiments in this area. Finally, we shall present our view of how emotion is expressed, and discuss how we have tried to base our own investigations of brain mechanisms of lateralization on single-neurotransmitter anatomy as opposed to the conventional, regional anatomic approach.

2. NONCORTICAL AREAS INVOLVED IN HUMAN EMOTION

Papez (1937) offers evidence that the hypothalamus, anterior thalamic nuclei, cingulate gyrus, and hippocampus constitute an interconnected anatomic mechanism that both elaborates the functions of central emotion and participates in emotional expression.

Bilateral lesions of the corticobulbar pathways are known to produce pseudobulbar palsy; this condition is characterized by involuntary, stereotypic pathological laughter or crying, or both (Adams & Victor, 1977). Despite the presence of this abnormal expressive behavior, these patients report that their internal subjective experience of emotions is normal, in contrast to patients with certain types of frontal lobe damage, in whom emotional lability occurs in both subjective experience and expression.

McHugh and Folstein (1975) report affective changes in Huntington's disease, an inherited degenerative illness believed to involve primarily subcortical structures. Some patients with Huntington's disease develop an intermittent mood disorder that seems indistinguishable from idiopathic manic-depressive illness. There is also a severe depression that can accompany idiopathic Parkinson's disease, likely related to reduced dopamine in certain parts of the basal ganglia.

Heilman and Valenstein (1980) postulate that for emotion, the cortex regulates lower-brain structures involved in the activation and control of the hypothalamus (regulating endocrine and autonomic nervous system functions), the brainstem and reticular activating system, and the thalamus, which in turn produce cortical arousal.

In sum, subcortical structures appear to play a role in the production and maintenance of emotional behavior; however, their role may be dominated by the neocortex.

3. HUMAN HEMISPHERIC SPECIALIZATION IN NORMALS

3.1. Anatomic Asymmetries

Information on anatomic hemispheric asymmetries has been summarized by Rubens (1977), Whitaker and Ojemann (1977), and Kolb and Whishaw (1980). The most widely reported, presumably functional asymmetry is that of the planum temporale, a part of the cortical language area whose exact role is unknown but that is significantly larger in length and area on the left than on the right side in the right-handed. This asymmetry is presumed to be related to the functional dominance of the left hemisphere for language. Heschl's gyrus is larger in the right hemisphere, complementary to the larger adjacent planum temporale on the left side. Broca's area is larger on the right side than on the left by approximately one-third, and the superior temporal gyrus is larger on the right side. Although there appears to be no significant weight difference between the two cerebral hemispheres, the occipital horns of the lateral ventricles are larger on the left side (more so in the right-handed). Additionally, the slope of the sylvian fissure is less acute on the left side, as well as greater in length. As Galaburda, LeMay, Kemper, and Geschwind (1978) note, the right hemisphere extends farther anteriorly and less posteriorly than the left hemisphere, with the right frontal and left occipital lobe, respectively, being the wider.

In a study of 36 right-handed male students, R. C. Gur, Packer, Hungerbuhler, Reivich, Obrist, Amarneck, and Sackeim (1980), using Xenon-133, found a relatively greater proportion of gray than white matter in the left hemisphere (most markedly in the frontal and precentral regions). Oke, Keller, Mefford, and Adams (1978) report a lateralization of norepinephrine in the human thalamus, as well as a regional distribution within each side.

Apart from the possible relationship of the asymmetries of the planum temporale to language, the functional significance, if any, of most of these anatomic asymmetries is as yet unclear. R. C. Gur *et al.* (1980) speculate that the greater amount of gray matter in the left hemisphere may reflect a relatively greater emphasis on processing or transfer within regions, as opposed to transfer across regions. This theory may provide an anatomic basis for Semmes's (1968) suggestion that the left hemisphere is compactly organized in structure and function as opposed to the more diffusely organized right hemisphere.

3.2. Arousal and Lateralization

Heilman and Watson (1977a,b) propose that each hemisphere has its own independent cortical-limbic-reticular activating loop. Based on findings concerning hand reaction times following hemisphere-specific stimuli, they propose an asymmetry of interhemispheric activation in which the right hemisphere activates the left.

Some support for this idea was gained from the work of Heilman and van den Abell (1979), in which a warning light presented to the right visual field reduced reaction times to the right hand more than left visual field warning signals reduced either left- or right-hand reaction times. The relevance of the hypothesis that the right hemisphere activates the left was tested by Heilman, Schwartz, and Watson (1978) in a study in which patients with right parietotemporal dysfunction and neglect had the lowest Galvanic skin responses (GSR), whereas aphasic patients with left hemisphere damage had higher GRSs than normals. This finding suggested to the authors that neglect (i.e., right hemisphere damage) is associated with disturbances in bilateral arousal (reductions). In contrast, the heightened GSR in aphasics was felt to explain the "increased emotionality" found in these cases. These authors suggest several possible mechanisms for this asymmetry in cortical arousal, including asymmetries of excitative neurotransmitters. This suggestion is perhaps supported by the finding that intravenous amphetamine, compared to placebo, has differential hemispheric effects on selective attention, using visual-evoked potentials (Reus, Buchsbaum, & Post, 1979.) A second suggestion (Weinstein & Friedland, 1977) is that the corticoreticular loop responsible for activation is more "discretely organized" on the right side, so that a localized lesion would affect more functional units than would the same lesion on the left side. However, this idea conflicts to some degree with Semmes's (1968) notion of a generally more diffuse functional localization in the right hemisphere. With respect to biochemical asymmetries in the systems mediating cerebral activation, Robinson and Coyle's (1979) work with rats showing bilateral reductions in dopamine and norepinephrine following right- but not left-sided cerebral infarction may be important if similar mechanisms exist in humans.

Kinsbourne (1970) considers lateralization data less in terms of inherent hemispheric specialization than in terms of the "priming" of one hemisphere, causing a transient attentional (and therefore perceptual) advantage for the contralateral sensory system such that the hemisphere that is "on" may partially inhibit that of the opposite side. Although this hypothesis was invoked in part to explain the lack of a strict, stable hemispheric advantage found in many early lateralization studies, Colbourne (1979) and M. Schwartz and Smith (1980) could find little evidence for it.

Another approach to attention has been to examine the lateralization of subcortical components of the attention-activation system. Whitaker and Ojemann (1977) have demonstrated some evidence of lateralization of thalamic mechanisms along a verbal visuospatial division, with left thalamic activating mechanisms being dominant. Whitaker and Ojemann suggest that lateral thalamic structures may orient and focus the functional activity of specific regions in the cortex, possibly even in a modality or task-specific way. In support of this work, anatomic asymmetries have been demonstrated in the distribution of norepinephrine in the human thalamus in postmortem specimens taken from subjects with no known neurological disease (Oke *et al.*, 1978). Albert, Silverberg, Reches, and Berman (1976) and Hommes and Panhuysen (1970) report that gross arousal may be lateralized to the left side as suggested by the finding that patients with left hemisphere lesions or amytal injections show a greater reduction of consciousness than do patients with similar insults to the right hemisphere.

In sum, there is some evidence that the right hemisphere may have a dominant role in a particular type of cerebral activation, which is distinct from "gross" arousal. In this role the right hemisphere may function as part of a system involving brainstem, thalamus, limbic system, and cortex; preliminary data suggesting multiple functional, anatomic, and biochemical asymmetries support this suggestion.

3.3. Laterality Studies in Emotion*

In the next two sections we shall examine effects of stimuli selectively presented to one hemisphere or the other.

*Because a significant part of the information concerning human hemispheric specialization is derived from laterality studies, it is germane to mention some qualifications that may modify our interpretations of investigations into hemispheric lateralization.

Colbourn (1979), in a comprehensive survey of difficulties encountered in laterality theory and measurement, asserts that the theory is weak in that the hemispheric processes that underlie the phenomena are not clearly understood. There is no evidence that the degree of a performance asymmetry reflects the actual degree of lateralization of the task or stimulus material in the brain; hence, at best lateralization measures can be used only in a correlational manner. Thus the variability of performance commonly found among psychiatric patients in these types of tasks requires special statistical treatment of

3.3.1. Auditory Studies/Dichotic Listening

In listening experiments it is presumed that a relative superiority of recall for material presented to the right ear is due to a functional dominance of the crossed auditory pathways, as well as to a relative processing or response advantage for the stimulus employed in the cerebral cortex opposite the ear in which the advantage is detected. In support of this assumption Mononen and Seitz (1977) present evidence that when different stimuli are presented to the two ears, ipsilateral (uncrossed) but not contralateral projections to the cortex are inhibited. Teng (1980) and others, however, have criticized dichotic listening experiments by demonstrating that asymmetries in input, attentional bias, and the need for a forced, single, response design may account for many apparent hemispheric asymmetries and poor test–retest reliability.

Given these caveats, Kimura (1967, 1973), King and Kimura (1971), and Bryden (1967) found verbal material was recalled more accurately when presented to the right than to the left ear. In a binaural (dichotic) listening paradigm, King and Kimura (1971) and Haggard and Parkinson (1971) found a slight left ear (i.e., right hemisphere) advantage in the identification of such nonverbal human sounds as laughter or emotional tone of a sentence; however, their studies required verbal matching. Carmon and Nachshon (1973) and Safer and Leventhal (1977) report a slight but significant left ear advantage in the dichotic perception of nonverbal sounds (shrieks, laughter, and particularly crying) or of sentences with emotional content. In these experiments responses were indicated manually to minimize the effects of secondary verbal mediation.

It is also notable that few experiments have included formal au-

---

data; additionally, subjects' sex and handedness should be controlled for rigorously. Experimental design should also attempt to clarify exactly which components of a given task are lateralized, as well as separating stimulus and task factors (Haggard & Parkinson, 1971). Both sensitivity and response bias seem to be subject to laterality effects. The degree to which the subject is required to participate actively in a task, as opposed to merely receiving information passively, can also alter the way information is processed.

Marshall, Caplan, and Holmes (1975) have demonstrated that the particular measure of laterality chosen may well change the result of a study. In work comparing positive to negative affects, it may be difficult to balance emotions so that negative and positive stimuli are comparable in strength. Bradshaw (1980) has shown that confounding factors interfering with lateralization measures include memory duration and loading, familiarity and difficulty of the task, as well as directional biases in attention.

One other methodological issue is that in future work we need to examine a greater number of left-handed people to see how patterns of neural processing occur in them and, hence, if handedness is important in the determination of hemispheric specialization for neuropsychological tasks.

diometric testing of subjects to see whether one or the other ear is more sensitive, or included controls to see whether material that is found strongly lateralized in previous experiments is the same in present subjects.

In a dichotic listening task in normal right-handed individuals, Zurif (1974) found a superior auditory lateralization for prosody in the left ear. This finding is relevant to work by Ross and Mesulam (1979) to be referred to later. In states of heightened suggestibility, Frumkin, Ripley, and Cox (1978) found a highly significant reduction in right ear dominance for verbal material in the hypnotic state compared with the pre- and posthypnotic periods.

In sum, despite methodological difficulties there appears to be a relative right hemisphere preference for processing the emotional tone of sentences, nonverbal sounds with emotional content, and prosody.

3.3.2. Visual Studies/Tachistoscopic Investigations

Tachistoscopic studies involving the presentation of material to one or the other visual half-field are particularly important since there is probably a higher degree of lateralization in the visual than in the auditory pathways. The usual paradigm in this kind of experiment involves the presentation of material to one or the other visual field while the subject is made to fixate on a central point. Ideally, stimulus exposure time is less than that of the average saccade (values of 150 msec are acceptable) in order to exclude the possibility that the stimulus material could accidentally be projected to both hemispheres, and central fixation should be assured by the presentation of a simultaneous identification task at the fixation point (scoring only trials where reports are correct).

Tachistoscopic studies have enabled the presentation of a greater number and variety of emotions, such as facial expressions, than were possible in dichotic listening tests. In such studies the stimulus material usually consists of photographs or schematic pictures of faces (such as cartoons). There is some evidence for separate localization of facial as opposed to emotional recognition (Ojemann, Fried, Mateer, Wohns, & Fedio, 1980). Reynolds and Jeeves (1978) and Hilliard (1973) found a right hemisphere advantage in facial recognition, consonant with the findings of other groups who, in a series of somewhat differently designed experiments, detected an impairment in facial recognition in patients with right as opposed to left hemisphere damage (Benton & Van Allen, 1968; De Renzi, Faglioni, & Spinnler, 1966).

Suberi and McKeever (1977) found a relative left visual field (right hemisphere) advantage in the memory storage of faces with emotional expression, that is, in discriminating emotional from neutral faces independently of the specific emotion expressed. Ley and Bryden (1979) tried to separate the effects of facial recognition from the emotional task. Subjects were asked to judge the similarity of five emotional expressions and the identity of five cartoon characters irrespective of emotional expression, thus separating emotional and facial identification tasks. The authors report left visual field superiorities for each task independently. Ley and Bryden (1981) subsequently report that the largest left visual field effect was found with extremely negative emotional expressions.

Ladavas, Umilta, and Ricci-Bitti (1980) examined male–female differences in the recognition of specific emotions and found that female subjects showed a significant left visual field advantage whereas male subjects showed no such consistent lateral asymmetry. Interestingly, in both sexes accuracy of response depended on the type of emotion presented. Female subjects showed the greatest mean reaction time differences between hemispheres for the emotions disgust and fear (both strongly negative), but responded faster in terms of reaction time with fewest errors to the emotion of happiness. These findings may be important for the design and interpretation of future experiments. Such lateralization differences by sex have been noted in other areas, for example, in McGlone's (1980) comprehensive survey of sex-determined lateralization differences.

Ojemann et al. (1980) investigated the cortical localization of several visuospatial functions by electrical stimulation of the brain in the nondominant (right) hemisphere of 10 conscious patients of unstated sex undergoing craniotomy before the operative treatment of medically intractable seizures. Significant increases in errors of emotional expression identification tasks were evoked by stimulation in four patients at six sites, in the posterior part of the middle temporal gyrus. However, recognition of faces remained intact during stimulation of these sites and did not appear discretely localized, instead appearing diffusely distributed through all parts of the right hemisphere tested (much like the several visuospatial functions tested). This separation of facial and emotional recognition is consistent with the findings of Ladavas et al. (1980)

Kolb, Taylor, and Milner (1980), on the other hand, assert that only the posterior part of the right hemisphere is specialized for the processing of complex visual patterns, including faces and geometric designs. This claim, however, cannot apply to emotional recognition since other work (Kolb & Whishaw, 1980) from the same group shows that lesions anywhere in the right hemisphere (frontal, temporal, or parietooccipital) produced impairments in a task requiring subjects to match photographs of different faces according to the emotion displayed.

Dimond, Farrington, and Johnson (1976) and Dimond and Farrington (1977) performed a series of experiments where films that were humorous (a Tom and Jerry cartoon), neutral (a travelogue), or horrific (a surgical operation) were "projected" via contact lenses to either the right or left visual half-field. The humorous film elicited a greater response when shown to the left hemisphere, measured in terms of heart-rate increase; conversely, the unpleasant film elicited an increase in heart rate when presented to the right as compared to the left hemisphere. No differences were found with the neutral film in either heart rate or rating of emotional intensity between the hemispheres. Subjects judged both the cartoon and the surgical operation more significantly unpleasant and horrific when projected to the right hemisphere, which the authors interpret to signify a "characteristic depressive outlook on the part of the right hemisphere." In addition, the authors report that left hemisphere response was extremely close to that elicited by free vision (i.e., with both hemispheres operating simultaneously); they therefore assume left hemisphere perception to predominate under normal circumstances, implying that the emotional focus of the right hemisphere is normally suppressed. The results of both experiments taken together suggest that the right hemisphere triggers unpleasant emotional experiences, and that the two hemispheres can therefore be viewed as separate generators of either different kinds of behavior or different modes of emotional cognition. Beaton (1979), on the other hand, found no significant difference in the way two films were rated as either "pleasant" or "humorous" when they were shown separately to the two hemispheres. In addition, Dimond et al. (1976) administered test items designed to measure neuroticism and extraversion from the Eysenk Personality Questionnaire separately to the two hemispheres and found no significant difference in scores on these items. The means of response to the questions (verbal vs. nonverbal) were not stated, but the verbal nature of the test makes interpretation here difficult.

Tachistoscopic studies demonstrate a relative right hemisphere advantage in processing information concerning both facial and emotional recognition. These two modalities seem separable functionally and possibly anatomically, with emotional recognition likely varying in its relative strength of asymmetry with sex of subject and type of emotion. The two hemispheres may, however, be separately specialized in the analysis of different types of emotional material, or may display different cognitive interpretations of the same emotional stimuli.

3.3.3. Asymmetries in the Facial Expression of Emotions (Facedness)

Sackeim and Gur (1978) and Sackeim, Gur, and Saucy (1978) report that left-sided composites (i.e., left side of face plus mirror image of left side) were judged more intense than their right counterparts for all emotions except happiness, where the reverse was the case. This work has been criticized by Ekmann (1980), Nelson and Horowitz (1980), and Spinrad (1980) on the ground that rather than cerebral asymmetries, peripheral neurological or anatomic differences or disparity in photographic lighting could have been responsible for the effects. Interestingly, Kolb and Milner (1980) presented normal subjects with two similar right and left composite faces together with the original face from which the composites had been taken and asked them to judge which composite was more similar to the original photograph. Subjects consistently judged the left-sided composite more similar. Although the emotional expressions, if any, on these photographs were unstated, it is possible that subjects were matching to that part of the original falling in their left visual field.

G. E. Schwartz, Ahern, and Brown (1979) examined different facial muscle groups during voluntary and involuntary emotional expression. Positive emotions elicited greater right muscle output, negative emotions greater left muscle output. In the involuntary condition, however, these effects held only for the zygomatic muscle group. (This finding adds some support to Dimond and Farrington's [1977] suggestion that the right hemisphere is more involved with negative affect.) Borod and Caron (1980) found that emotions were preferentially expressed on the left side of the face for both sexes and both handedness groups (77% of right-handed and 65% of left-handed subjects). Interestingly, no lateralization differences were found between positive and negative emotions. Differences in the facial expression of emotions leave unanswered the question whether what is represented is lateralization of a psychological state or only of the neuroanatomic effector mechanisms and pathways.

At this stage it is hard to draw definite conclusions from these studies. It is possible, however, that emotions (particularly negative ones) are expressed primarily on the left side of the face, again possibly reflecting an underlying right hemisphere output specialization.

3.3.4. Lateral Eye Movements and Emotion

These experiments are based on the theory that relative hemispheric activation leads to initial movement in gaze to the left or right. Gaze shift to the left, for example, is presumed to imply right hemisphere activation. This basic premise, however, has been subjected to fairly stringent methodological criticism by Ehrlichman and Weinberger (1978). R. E. Gur, R. C. Gur, and Harris (1975) found that gaze shifts were significantly altered when the experimenter faced or sat behind the subject. Berg and Harris (1980) assert that lateral eye movement phenomena are extremely sensitive to task, subject, and environmental variables.

Still, given these caveats, G. E. Schwartz, Davidson, and Maer (1975) found that right-handed subjects tended to look to the left when answering affective questions, and Ahern and Schwartz (1979) found that significant differences in lateral eye movement were related to positive or negative emotions. On the whole, however, because of major methodological difficulties, this technique does not yet appear to have contributed significantly to our knowledge of emotional lateralization in normal subjects.

3.3.5. EEG Studies

In general, EEG lateralization studies have compared the relative activation of the EEG between the two hemispheres. This technique has the advantage that the brain itself is allowed to "select" how the stimulus is to be processed in terms of relative hemispheric involvement. Unfortunately, there have been numerous methodological flaws in many EEG studies (for a summary, see Donchin, Kutas, & McCarthy, 1977). Among the most relevant flaws are a failure to show that asymmetries are reversible with changes in tasks, a lack of validation of task variables, and a failure to attempt to correlate the behavioral and EEG measures.

Both Harman and Ray (1977) and Davidson, Schwartz, Saron, Bennett, and Goleman (1979) found that positive affects produced greater left hemisphere power on EEG compared to right, whereas with negative affects it was the opposite. This effect was seen particularly in the frontal leads. Leber and Johnson (1980), however, found no evidence for lateralization of emotional tasks in female subjects with parietal EEG recordings. Possibly the different location of recording compared to that in Davidson *et al.* (1979) was responsible for their results. Other investigators have found that such positive affects as experimentally induced euphoric states (Davidson *et al.* 1979; Tucker, Stenslie, Roth, & Shearer 1981) or masturbation-induced orgasm (Cohen, Rosen, & Goldstein, 1976) lead to large increases in EEG amplitude in the right hemisphere.

In an EEG study, Cacioppo, Petty, and Snyder (1979) tried to test three hypotheses about the relationship of right and left hemisphere functions to affect: (1) that there are intrinsic (i.e., localized) differences in emotional perspective between the major and the minor hemispheres (e.g., Dimond & Farrington, 1976); (2) that the right hemisphere is more susceptible to suggestion (e.g., Singer & Singer, 1972); and (3) that affective differences are not a direct property of the hemispheres but result from an interactive process between the two hemispheres the final output of which is determined by the unique characteristics of each hemisphere. Findings indicate that increasing personal relevance of tapes heard by subjects led to a more *polarized* response. The greater the major hemisphere baseline EEG involvement, the more strongly the personal relevance factor influenced the dichotomous character of subjects' verbal responses.

When the minor hemisphere was more activated on the baseline EEG, then increasing the personal relevance of counterattitudinal advocacy elicited negative affective responses. The neutral stimulus group, on the other hand, showed no difference in responses whether the major or minor hemisphere was more involved. Based on these data the authors reject the hypothesis that the minor hemisphere is more susceptible to influence than the major. That the right-hemisphere-active subjects did not evaluative *neutral* communications more negatively suggests that the two hemispheres do not generate affect independently. The powerful change in affective response with increase in personal relevance affords some suggestive evidence for the third hypothesis.

3.3.6. Intracarotid Sodium Amytal Injection

Terzian and Cecotto (1959) and Terzian (1964) were the first to report on the differential behavioral effects of sodium amytal injections into the left and right carotid arteries. Unilateral injections, irrespective of side, gave a rapid ipsilateral decrease in brain EEG activity and a contralateral hemiplegia and hemianesthesia, with or without associated additional contralateral hemidefects. As the paralysis and other effects abated, lateralized behavioral effects occurred. Unfortunately, few attempts have been made to relate these reactions to subjects' premorbid personality, and it is still unclear whether the effects arise from the recovering or the normal hemisphere.

Nondominant hemispheric injections have reportedly been associated with a "euphoric-maniacal" reaction in which patients smile and laugh and express a sense of liveliness and well-being. These patients report appropriate inner emotions during the experiences of these behaviors, including after injections of the opposite side. However, the patients with dominant injections (i.e., on the side where amytal produced aphasia) express a "depressive-catastrophic" reaction characterized by preoccupation with "guilt, nothingness, indignity and worries about the future" (Gainotti, 1979a). Rossi and Rosadini (1967) observed emotional reactions in 54% of their patients; with dominant hemisphere injections depression was seen in 68% of their cases.

Provocative as these observations are, the findings were not confirmed by Milner (1967) and Kolb and Milner (1980), who found no asymmetry in the frequency of affective state or facial expressions following injections of either the right or left cerebral hemispheres. Methodology in these experiments included using each patient as his own control (i.e., both hemispheres were injected although on different days).

Tsunoda and Oka (1967) report with Japanese subjects that euphoria occurred from injections of the verbal (dominant) hemisphere, but none from injections of the nondominant hemisphere. It remains unclear whether the lateralized effects represent a temporary inactivation of the barbiturized hemisphere and hence a "release" of behaviors from the contralateral side, or are due to a removal of inhibiting influences from within the ipsilateral hemisphere leading to behavioral manifestations from that side itself.

4. HUMAN CLINICOPATHOLOGICAL CORRELATIONS

4.1. Lesion Studies

For an overview of affective changes following cortical lesions, see Heilman and Valenstein (1980) and Tucker, Watson, and Heilman (1976).

4.1.1. Emotional Reactions Associated with Brain Injury

Gainotti (1969, 1972, 1979a,b) has reported extensively on patterns of emotional behavior in patients with left and right brain damage. Consonant with the earlier findings of Goldstein (1948) and with results from amytal studies, he reports a significant association between dominant hemisphere damage and the appearance of such "catastrophic reactions" as anxiety, crying, swearing, or refusal to complete tasks. He also found a significant association between nondominant hemisphere damage and a variety of behaviors, including indifference (quite unlike patients experiencing postamytal euphoria) or a tendency to joke and to minimize difficulties seen particularly in those patients with the neglect syndrome.

Within the dominant-hemisphere-damaged group, our own work (Robinson & Szetela, 1981) suggests that more profound degrees of depression are associated with more anterior left hemisphere lesions. This finding is in keeping with Flor-Henry's (1979a) claim that the strongest affective changes occur in the frontotemporal region. Flor-Henry suggests that cerebral mood regulation is mediated most importantly by the nondominant temperoparietal region, and, to a much lesser degree, bilaterally frontally with overall regulation by the dominant hemisphere (Flor-Henry & Yeudall, 1979).

Hecaen (1962) also reports increased incidence of catastrophic reactions (26%) in left-hemisphere-damaged patients, compared with only 13% in right-hemisphere-damaged patients. However, he found that 16% of left-damaged patients and 33% of right-damaged patients showed indifference. On the basis of such data, Hecaen and Angelergues (1963) suggest that sensory information has a different functional organization in the two halves of the brain, right hemisphere data being processed in a more primitive way and retaining their immediacy and "rich affective value."

Unfortunately, few of the studies of the relationship between brain damage and changes in affect have investigated such important factors as premorbid personality and IQ, size and locus of lesion, education, age, and sex in matching subjects and controls. The presence or absence of neglect in right hemisphere lesions may also be an important variable, as well as the exclusion of possible coexisting damage in the opposite hemisphere.

4.1.2. Emotional Perception

Lesion studies on facial and emotional recognition have generally been in agreement with previous tachistoscopic experiments. For instance, DeKosky, Heilman, Bowers, and Valenstein (1980) found that right-hemisphere-damaged patients performed significantly worse when asked to discriminate between emotional or nonemotional faces, and also in naming emotional scenes. Levey, Trevarthan, and Sperry (1972), Benton and Van Allen (1968), and De Renzi and Spinnler (1966) report that the right hemisphere is predominantly involved in facial recognition, although there appeared no relationship of the locus or type of lesion within the right hemisphere (if present) to performance.

A number of studies have dealt with the ability to judge the mood of others following brain damage. Right hemisphere patients, especially those with temporoparietal damage, seem impaired in the comprehension of this modality when compared with left hemisphere patients with similar lesions. Heilman, Scholes, and Watson (1975) found that patients with right hemisphere disease scored no better than chance on recognizing the emotion with which a sentence was read, whereas the left hemisphere group was somewhat impaired but significantly better. The authors posit an "auditory affective agnosia" caused by damage of a right hemisphere area homologous to that of Wernicke on the left side. This finding was confirmed in a second experiment (Tucker et al., 1976) and was extended to demonstrate that right-hemisphere-damaged patients are also unable to read emotionally bland sentences with affective tone. Although Schlanger, Schlanger, and Gerstman (1976) were unable to confirm these findings of reduced comprehension for right-hemisphere-damaged patients, very few of their patients had temperoparietal disease and none was studied for the presence or absence or the neglect syndrome.

Kolb *et al.* (1980) and Gardner, Ling, Flamm, and Silverman (1975) found that left-hemisphere-damaged patients were unable to appreciate affect in written material, and that comprehension of nonverbal humor was impaired in right-hemisphere-damaged patients. To explain their findings, Gardner *et al.* suggest a possible dissociation of comprehension or cognition on the one hand, and appreciation of affect on the other.

4.1.3. Emotional Expression

Ross and Mesulam (1979) studied emotional expression in two patients who had lost the ability to impart affective quality to speech, to use normal prosody in their speech, and to make normal emotional gestures. Using CAT scans, the lesions were localized in the right hemispheres to the analagous cortical area that subserves propositional speech in the left hemisphere, that is, Broca's area. Wechsler (1973) also reports that recall of emotionally charged stories was significantly worse in right-hemisphere-damaged as compared to left-hemisphere-damaged patients, although recall of a neutral narrative text was not.

In sum, right hemisphere lesions can interfere with multiple aspects of emotional perception and expression. These include the perception and discrimination of emotional faces, auditory affective agnosia, and an inability to match emotions or to judge the mood of others. Additionally, there may be an inability to use affective intonation in speech, which can be accompanied by defects in prosody and emotional gesturing.

This range of defects illustrates the range of receptive, cognitive, and expressive affective skills apparently located in the nondominant hemisphere, and provides a significant complement to the work on dichotic and tachistoscopic tasks. These comparisons will be discussed in more detail later. The analogy between linguistic and emotional processes is also apparent, especially in the work of Ross and Mesulam (1979) and Heilman *et al.* (1975).

4.1.4. Pathological/Involuntary Laughter and Crying

There are numerous reports of the occurrence of spontaneous, often stereotypic, uncontrollable outbursts of emotion following neurological lesions (sometimes otherwise silent symptomatically), in which the emotion displayed is usually uncorrelated with external events (Achari & Colover, 1976; Hermann & Chhabria, 1980; Ironside, 1956; Jacome,

McLain, & FitzGerald, 1980; Swash, 1972). Most often there is no subjective mood change to accompany the external behavior, so that these patients can be regarded as having isolated disorders of emotional expression.

In a literature review, Sackeim, Weiman, R. C. Gur, Greenberg, and Hungerbuhler (1981) report that left lesions were statistically associated with crying and right lesions similarly associated with pathological laughing; in seizure patients, pathological laughing was two to three times commoner with left-sided foci.

4.1.5. MMPI Studies

The MMPI literature on laterlization is contradictory with Gasparrini, Satz, Heilman, and Coolidge (1978) and Black (1975), showing a greater elevation of the depression scale in left- as compared to right-hemisphere-damaged patients. Dikmen and Reitan (1974), however, found no differences in MMPI profile.

4.1.6. Commissurotomy (Split-Brain) Studies

Commissurotomy, or severing of the fibers in the corpus callosum and sometimes in the anterior commissure, is performed as a treatment for intractable epileptic seizures. Whitaker and Ojemann (1977) outline some of the difficulties with studies of the brain following commissurotomy in terms of supplying information about the normal function of each separate hemisphere. For instance, many patients still have connections between hemispheres either because the anterior commissure was not sectioned or because hemispheres remain connected by limbic structures. The abnormality for which the operation was initially carried out is most usually due to long-standing disease, and functional reorganization and adaptation to the abnormality may well have taken place.

Gazzaniga and LeDoux (1978) and LeDoux, Wilson, and Gazzaniga (1977) report that words presented to the right hemisphere were rated more negative than the same words presented to the left hemisphere. In another subject with an intact anterior commissure, the same emotional response was obtained when the same word was presented at different times to the right or left hemisphere, suggesting a transfer of emotional response despite surgical disruption of pathways necessary to transfer the cognitive percept (callosum).

4.1.7. Emotional Changes in Temporal Lobe Epilepsy

Flor-Henry (1969, 1974) found an increased association of right hemisphere temporal lobe foci both with neurotic depression and with a manic-depressivelike illness, as compared with left-sided foci which were associated both with increased aggression and a "schizo-phrenialike psychosis." Shukla and Katiyar (1980), however, were unable to replicate Flor-Henry's work on the lateralization of major mental illnesses in 62 patients. Bear and Fedio (1977), studying a very different phenomenon of interictal long-term personality changes in patients with temporal lobe epilepsy, report that patients with right-sided lesions tended to minimize or "deny" problems and displayed emotional tendencies, in contrast to the ideational traits and "catastrophic" over-emphasis of certain social behaviors.

There are many difficulties in extrapolating normal lateralization from the studies of temporal lobe epilepsy; for example, abnormalities originating in one hemisphere can lead the undamaged side to take over the functions originally subserved by the affected side and "mirror foci" can develop, that is, the bilateralization of initially unilateral epilepsy.

4.2. Psychiatric Illness: Emotional Lateralization

There is some suggestive evidence (Flor-Henry, 1969, 1973, 1974, 1979a,b, 1980) that right hemisphere pathology is implicated in manic-depressive illness. Such evidence is based on the association of the latter with right hemisphere temporal lobe epilepsy and on neuropsychological studies that suggest nondominant frontotemporal dysfunctions, as a result of which the right hemisphere takes over language processing (as suggested by Hommes & Panhuysen, 1971).

In hysterical conversion neurosis, Galin (1974), Galin, Diamond, and Braff (1977), Stern (1977), and Ley and Bryden (1981) have all commented on a relatively greater number of left-sided conversion symptoms seen in hospitalized patients. In addition, Ley's studies found that this left-side predominance held up even in body parts other than the hand or arm, suggesting that observed symptom lateralization is not just an unconscious means of preserving the function of the dominant side.

However, the association between schizophrenia and the dominant hemisphere and limbic system is considerably more powerful (Gruzelier, 1979). Studies of both illnesses have been complicated by small numbers of patients and problems of diagnosis, for example, unipolar and bipolar depression, schizophrenia and schizoaffective disorder. In addition, medications such as tricyclic antidepressants may have predominantly unilateral effects (Gruzelier, 1979).

4.2.1. Electroconvulsive Therapy (ECT)

In a review of the literature on lateralized response to ECT, D'Elia and Raotma (1975) conclude that nondominant hemisphere ECT is more effective in relieving the symptoms of endogenous depression, and also produced fewer side effects than ECT given to the dominant hemisphere. The 29 studies chosen for review by these two authors are seen as adequate in evaluative methodology. In three more recent, well-designed studies, Cronin, Bodley, Potts, Mather, Gardner, and Tobin (1970) and Halliday, Davison, Browne, and Kreeger (1968) found a right hemisphere ECT superiority, whereas Fleminger, Horne, Nair, and Nott (1970) found no differences in relief of depression. Although it is a clinical observation that ECT is effective in the treatment of mania (Slater & Roth, 1969), no unilateral treatment studies have been done.

4.3. Stroke Studies: From Our Own Laboratory

During the past several years we have been investigating emotional changes in brain-injured patients, particularly following stroke. As part of this investigation we have been looking at issues of lateralization. Although, as we have seen, there is experimental evidence that there may be a biological basis for the difference in emotions arising from lesions of one hemisphere or the other, most clinicians have assumed that poststroke emotional changes are a secondary psychological response to the impairment. That is, a person is depressed because he or she is paralyzed, and the difference between the emotional reactions to right or left hemisphere injury is the result of loss of different cognitive or sensorimotor functions that are localized in each hemisphere. There are several likely reasons for this general assumpton. One is that there has been no evidence that poststroke depressions are stereotyped in the way that neurobiological responses would be expected to be; another is that there is no generally accepted neurophysiological or neuroanatomic explanation for how a focal cortical lesion might lead to emotional changes (although we have outlined some hypotheses).

In an effort to address these two problems, we have been studying stroke in both clinical and laboratory investigations. We have found some stereotyped characteristics of poststroke depressions and some neuroanatomic and neurobiochemical behavioral correlates, which has led us to propose that depression and paralysis in stroke patients may be outcomes of separate neurobiological processes. In this section we shall summarize our findings from clinical studies.

4.3.1. Relationship of Depression to Time since Stroke

We have examined patients at various times following their stroke using several psychopathological measures. One is the General Health Questionnaire (GHQ), a self-report questionnaire applicable to general medical as well as psychiatric patients. It contains such items as, "Have you been feeling perfectly well and in good health?" with four categories for response: (a) better than usual, (b) same as usual, (c) worse than usual, (d) much worse than usual (Goldberg, 1972). The score on the GHQ was found to correlate well with the scores patients obtained using the Zung Depression Scale (Zung, 1965), the Hamilton Depression Scale (Hamilton, 1960), or the Present State Examination (PSE), a structured psychiatric interview (Luria & McHugh, 1974). Correlation coefficients were $r = 0.86$ with the Zung and the PSE and $r = 0.88$ with the Hamilton.

We examined 83 acute stroke patients and 103 outpatients attending the University of Maryland Hospital. The acute patients were all inpatients on the neurology or medical wards; the outpatients were attending the stroke clinic for follow-up care. We followed these outpatients over 12 months using the GHQ (Robinson & Price, 1982). We found that, as a group, the frequency and severity of depression increased significantly between the first 5 months after the stroke and 6 months to 2 years postinfarct (Table 10.1, Figure 10.1). That is, during the acute stroke period and lasting up to about 5 months, approximately 25% of the overall group was depressed. However, between 6 months and 2 years after the stroke, about 60% of the patients were depressed.

When the data were analyzed by lesion location, only one of the patients with a right hemisphere infarct was depressed during the acute stroke period, whereas 34% of those with left hemisphere infarcts and 15% of those with brainstem infarcts were depressed. These findings remained about constant through the first 5 months. However, from 6 months to 2 years after stroke the frequency of depression rose to about 60% in the outpatient group (a significant change by Chi square, and the actual numerical scores increased significantly by analyses of variance). Approximately 79% of the left hemisphere stroke group were depressed, zero out of seven patients with a right hemisphere stroke, and

Table 10.1. *Relationship between Lesion Location and Prevalence of Depression*

Overall group	Left hemisphere lesion	Right hemisphere lesion	Brain stem lesion
17/81[a]	13/38	1/23	3/20
(21%)	(34%)	(4%)	(15%)
13/59[b]	12/27	1/18	0/14
(22%)	(44%)	(5%)	(0%)

[a] Acute stroke patients who scored in the depressed range on the General Health Questionnaire.
[b] If patients with bilateral injury or left-handedness are excluded.

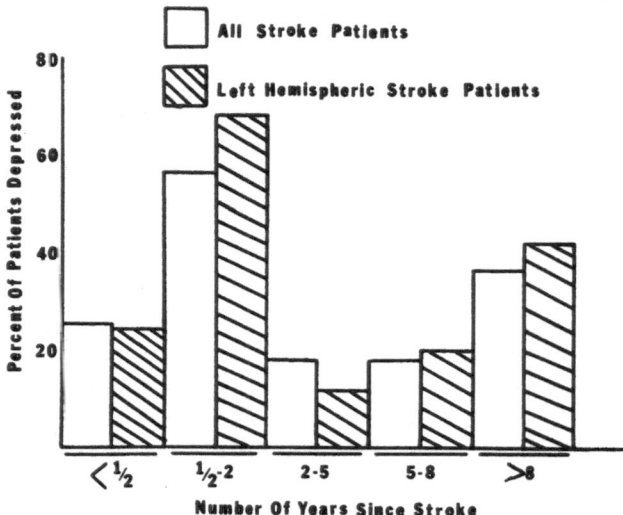

Fig. 10.1. Categorization of patient, depending on the number of years since their stroke had occurred. The percentage of patients who were depressed at various times following the stroke is bimodal in distribution. The first 2 years and the period after 8 years are the periods of highest prevalence of depression. Because there were so few patients whose depressions followed brainstem or right hemisphere strokes, the distribution of depression in these groups could not be plotted.

only two out of 20 with brainstem infarcts (a nonrandom distribution by Chi square test). The frequency of depression decreased significantly from 2 to 8 years after stroke and then increased (although nonsignificantly) again to approximately 40% of the outpatient group who were more than 8 years after stroke. Overall, approximately 30% of the 103 patients who were studied were depressed. Within this group, 51% with left hemisphere infarcts were depressed, 11% with right hemisphere infarcts, and 27% with brainstem infarcts. Thus there seems to be a clear anatomic difference in the frequency of depression, with left hemisphere infarcts causing much more depression than right hemisphere or brainstem infarcts.

When the groups were compared in their demographic variables, there were no significant differences in age, sex ratio, race, marital status, social position, previous medical history or neurological symptoms. We have confirmed these findings in a second group of patients with left hemisphere infarcts examined at the Boston Veterans Administration Hospital (Robinson & Szetela, 1981). This group consisted of chronically hospitalized patients (mean time since infarct was 10 months) many of whom were aphasic; 60% of these patients were depressed. This statistic agrees with our finding in the outpatient study that almost 80% of patients with left hemisphere infarcts from 6 months to 2 years after stroke had significant depression.

4.3.2. Length of Depressive Disorder

Of the 103 patients attending the outpatient clinic, we obtained follow-up evaluations on 83 patients over 12 months using repeated applications of the GHQ (Robinson & Price, 1982; see Figure 10.1). All patients who had evaluations during the 1 to 2 months following the initial evaluation remained depressed (Figure 10.2). There was a slow decline in frequency of depression during the follow-up period, and approximately 65% of the patients who were initially found depressed remained depressed at 7 to 8 months. However, from 9 to 11 months and longer, the frequency of depression dropped off to 16% and none remained depressed at 12 months. Thus there seemed to be a natural course to the poststroke depressive disorders, that is, they lasted approximately 7 to 8 months without treatment. However, it should be noted that the initial evaluation took place at various times throughout the length of the patients' depressive disorders. Therefore, because we were not starting at the beginning of the depressive period, the estimate of 7 to 8 months for the length of depression may be somewhat of an

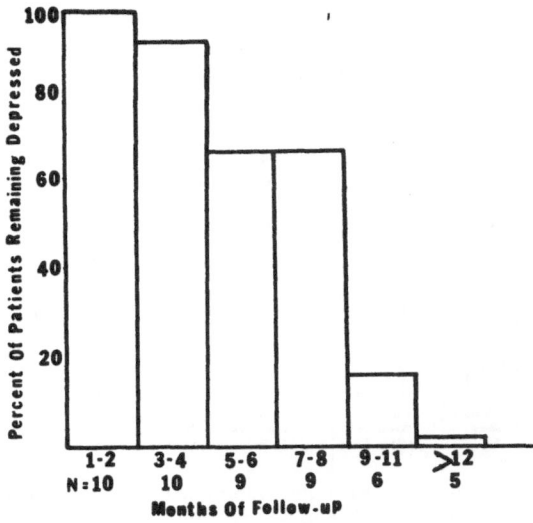

Fig. 10.2. The percentage of patients at the initial interview who continued to be depressed at various follow-up intervals. The number of patients evaluated at each period is indicated. Some patients were interviewed several times, others only once. (From "Post-stroke depressive disorders: A follow-up study of 103 outpatients" by R. G. Robinson and T. R. Price, *Stroke*, 1982, *13*, Fig. 1. Copyright 1982 by the American Heart Association. Reprinted by permission.)

underestimate. Because of the small numbers of patients with depressive disorder and a right hemisphere infarct, it was not possible to determine the length of depression in this group. However, of three patients who were depressed at the time of the initial interview, only one remained depressed 6 months later. Among the patients in the brainstem infarct group, of the three who were initially depressed, none remained depressed at 6 months.

4.3.3. Anatomic Correlates

As noted, there is a strong correlation between the hemispheric side of the lesion and the frequency and possibly the length of the depressive disorder. The highest frequency of depression occurred in those patients with left hemisphere infarcts who were from 6 months to 2 years after stroke. Within this group, we also studied a group with traumatic brain injury and compared them with patients with stroke injury. This study was conducted on the Neurobehavioral Unit at the Boston Veterans Administration Hospital. Eighteen stroke patients were compared with 11 traumatic brain-injured patients for frequency and severity of depression.

The two groups were comparable in their age, marital status, so-

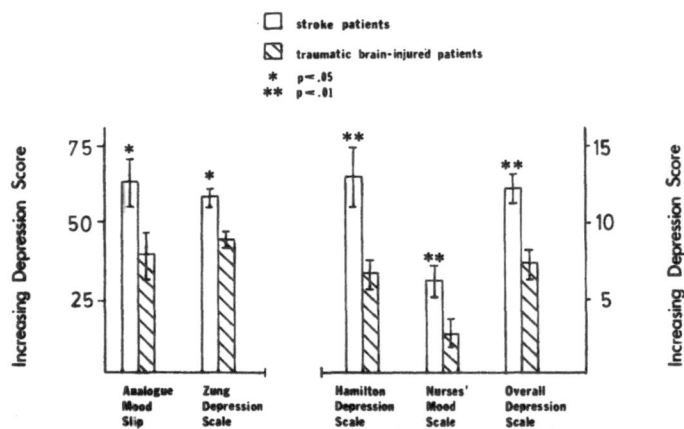

Fig. 10.3. Depression scores for stroke and traumatic brain-injured patients. Scores are expressed such that a higher number indicates a more severe depression. The stroke patients were significantly more depressed than the traumatically brain-injured patients on every depression scale. Using multivariate analysis, $p < 0.01$. Bars indicate SEM. (From "Mood Change Following Left Hemispheric Brain Injury" by R. G. Robinson and B. Szetela, *Annals of Neurology*, 1981, *9*, p. 449, Fig. 1. Copyright 1981 by Little, Brown. Reprinted by permission.)

cioeconomic status, race, sex, time since injury, previous medical history, previous history of psychiatric disorder, and previous family history of psychiatric disorder (Robinson & Szetela, 1981). Their cognitive impairments as measured by the Mini-Mental State Examination score (Folstein, Folstein, & McHugh, 1975) and their physical impairment as measured by the activities of daily living on the Hopkins Functioning Inventory were also comparable. The stroke patients, however, were significantly more depressed than the traumatic brain-injured patients on all depression-measuring instruments (Figure 10.3). The Nurses Rating Scale (Robinson & Szetela, 1981) was filled out by the nursing staff independently of the psychopathological examination.

Analysis of computerized tomographic (CT) scans was done by placing a paper with grid marks over the CT scan slices. We then counted the total number of grids in the brain, excluding the ventricles, and then counted the number of grids within the lesion site. This ratio gave the percentage of brain volume lesioned. The distance of the lesion from the frontal pole was determined by measuring the distance in millimeters from the frontal pole to the anterior border of the lesion for every slice in which the lesion was visible. The numbers were then averaged to produce a mean distance of the anterior border of the lesion from the frontal pole. The stroke and traumatic brain-injured group had more posterior lesions. We then developed matched pairs of stroke and traumatic brain-injured patients by blindly selecting lesion sizes and locations in the two groups that were comparable. We did so without knowledge of the scores on the psychopathological examinations.

When the seven matched pairs of patients were compared for their scores on the various psychopathological examinations, there was no longer any difference between the groups. That is, by controlling for the lesion location, the difference in frequency and severity of depression could be accounted for. We then correlated the distance of the lesion from the frontal pole with the severity of depression. There was a strong negative correlation ($r = 0.76$) (Figure 10.4); that is, the closer the lesion was to the frontal pole the more severe the depression, and the farther the lesion was from the frontal pole the less severe the depression. This finding was confirmed in the group of acute stroke patients where the depression score in 11 patients with CT scans showing a single left hemisphere lesion correlated with the distance of the lesion from the frontal pole ($r = 0.80$). This correlation between depression and distance from the frontal pole is consistent both with Morrison, Molliver, and Grzanna's, (1979) study with rats, in which anterior cortical lesions were shown to be more effective in depleting catecholamine concentrations than were similar lesions in more posterior areas, and with our own laboratory findings that lesions close to the frontal pole cause greater

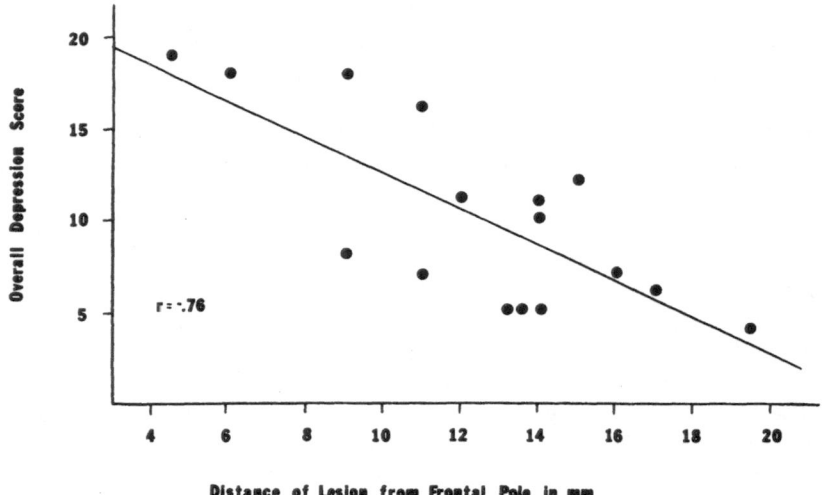

Fig. 10.4. Relationship between severity of depression and mean distance of the lesion from the frontal pole for patients whose lesions extended into the frontal lobe. The closer the lesion was to the frontal pole, the more severe was the depression (slope = −0.76, $p <$ 0.001). (From "Mood Change Following Left Hemispheric Brain Injury" by R. G. Robinson and B. Szetela, *Annals of Neurology*, 1981, *9*, p. 450, Fig. 3. Copyright 1981 by Little, Brown. Reprinted by permission.)

hyperactivity than similar lesions in more posterior areas (Pearlson & Robinson, 1981).

These findings suggest a new concept of cerebral localization in which behavioral functions are not related to specific anatomic areas but are localized in relationship to the underlying neurotransmitter, which mediates or modulates the behavior. The catecholamine-containing pathways within the brain have unique anatomy in that they are diffusely distributed throughout the brain with cell bodies located in the brainstem and arborizing projections from the frontal to the occipital pole. Thus lesions that affect the diffusely distributed arborizing cortical biogenic amine pathways may cause behavioral disturbances whose magnitude varies with the magnitude of the lesion's effect on the underlying pathway. This kind of behavioral localization could explain our findings that more anterior lesions cause more severe degrees of behavior disturbance than do posterior lesions. Thus some types of behaviors may be distributed in a graded fashion throughout the cortex based on the underlying neuroanatomic and neurophysiological principles of the neurotransmitter systems involved.

5. ANIMAL STUDIES AND LATERALIZATION

5.1. Animal Lateralization Studies

Nottebohm (1977) looked extensively at neural control of song in the canary, where the majority of song syllables are produced by the left half of the syrinx, which itself is under the control of the left hypoglossus nerve. Unilateral left brain lesions in adult canaries in the most important control area for song (the hyperstriatum ventrale, pars caudale) dramatically reduced the complexity of the canaries' song structure, whereas unilateral right lesions had a much lesser effect on song (bilateral lesions abolished song altogether). The function of song in the canary is presumed to relate to mate attraction and territoriality, and therefore also to sexual and spatial behaviors (Webster, 1977a). Left hemisphere dominance for song syllables is apparently also seen in the chaffinch and in two species of sparrow. The parrot, however, which is vocally very complex, apparently does not have this type of localization.

Rogers (1980) and Rogers and Anson (1979) studied the effects of injecting a protein synthesis inhibitor into the right or left forebrain of young chicks, finding that auditory habituation and visual discrimination learning were localized to the left hemisphere. Rogers (1980) found that attentional persistence, attack behavior, and copulatory behavior appear to be localized in the right hemisphere and are normally inhibited by the left hemisphere.

With cats, Webster (1977b) presents possible evidence for visuospatial superiority in the hemisphere ipsilateral to the preferred paw in cats given visual discrimination tasks after callosal sections.

Diamond (1980) reports that normally the right cerebral cortex in the rat is thicker. In nonhuman primates, Petersen, Beecher, Zoloth, Moody, and Stebbins (1978) found that five out of five Japanese macaques engaged left hemisphere processing mechanisms (inferred from right ear superiority) preferentially for the analysis of communicatively significant sounds (recorded in the field) of other Japanese macaques. By contrast, only one of five other Old World monkeys had any significant ear advantage to the same sounds. Cain and Wada (1979) found that in six of seven baboon brains examined from two species, the right frontal pole was longer than the left.

Sacchetti, Allaria, Conte, DeRosa, Griffi, Taroni, Resele, and Smeraldi (1979) studied in vitro uptake of norepinephrine, dopamine, and 5-hydroxytryptamine in brains taken from inbred strains of mice, and apparently identified asymmetries in uptake. Nieoullon, Cheramy, and Glowinski (1977) report that a lesion made in the left substantia nigra of the cat interrupted the release of labeled dopamine in the caudate nucleus of the same side, and was associated with a simultaneous increase in the release of labeled dopamine on the opposite side. Leviel, Cheramy, and Glowinski (1979) confirm that dopamine that is released from dendrites in one substantia nigra regulates the activity of the ipsilateral dopaminergic neurons and contributes to the control of the contralateral dopaminergic neurons by influencing the dendritic release of dopamine in the contralateral substantia nigra. The authors suggest that nigrostriatal dopaminergic neurons act to control the dendritic release of dopamine, hence regulating the activity of dopaminergic neurons and other nigral efferent pathways, and controlling the delivery of messages originating from the substantia nigra thus allowing nigrostriatal dopaminergic neurons to coordinate sensory and motor processes bilaterally.

The Denenberg group has extensively studied lateralization behavior in rats. Denenberg (1980) and Denenberg, Garbanati, Sherman, Yutzey, and Kaplan (1978), and Sherman (1980) report on the importance of infantile stimulation (handling) and environmental enrichment in the development of lateralized behavior in the rat. In open field activity experiments, handling appeared to activate the left hemisphere; in spatial preference tasks, it appeared to activate the right hemisphere giving rise to leftward responses. With rabbits, Denenberg, Zeidner, Rosen, Hofman, Garbanati, Sherman, and Yutzey (1981) further suggest that infantile stimulation may act to facilitate the functional competence of the corpus callosum and hence to couple the hemispheres. Denenberg (1980) used general systems theory (Von Bertalanffy, 1969) as a means of understanding the organization of the animals' "whole" behavior. He looked especially at interhemispheric coupling, interhemispheric inhibition, and hemispheric activation (and their combinations) as a means of explaining behavioral asymmetries; he emphasizes that one cannot simply extrapolate from the behavior of a single isolated hemisphere to that of the normal connected pair.

A second group that has studied lateralization in the rat is that of Glick, Jerussi, and Zimmerberg (1977). They report that turning (rotation, circling) behavior in the rat is associated with a naturally occurring 10% to 15% asymmetry in the nigrostriatal dopamine concentrations, as is the tendency of rats tested in T-mazes to show spontaneous preference for either one or the other side. In both of these behaviors, the rat tends to turn toward the side of the brain later found lower in dopamine. Amphetamine increases the nigrostriatal dopamine asymmetry to a value of 25% to 30%, and increases the frequency of rotation toward the side lower in dopamine. These findings support Flor-Henry's (1980) hypothesis that in an environment with no systematic left bias, the introduction of a neural asymmetry increases the efficiency of spatial analysis. Interestingly, this asymmetry is sex linked: Female rats tend to turn more than males (Glick, Schonfeld, & Strumpf, 1980). Such spontaneous rotation and spontaneous side preference also appear to relate to dopamine-stimulated adenyl cyclase activity and to striatal dopamine metabolsim. Whereas the strength of the turning bias appears genetically influenced, its direction seems to be determined environmentally. Glick, Schonfeld, and Strumpf (1980) found that it is possible to train 15-day-old rats to rotate significantly in a specified direction using a T-maze. The age of training is apparently critical, and the effect of training is seen more in males. The effect, if any, of training on striatal dopamine concentrations has not yet been reported. In an attempt to relate the rotational behavior to functional asymmetries in the brain, Glick, Meibach, Cox, and Maayani (1979) injected rats who had a known circling bias first with either labeled d-amphetamine or water and then 15 minutes later with labeled 2-deoxy-d-glucose, and then decapitated them after 30 minutes. Three different functional types of asymmetries were found. One type, found in the frontal cortex, was a simple left–right difference. A second type found in the midbrain was related to directional bias. A third type of functional asymmetry found in the cerebellum correlated with a non-lateralized behavior.

Most recently, Glick, Weaver, and Meibach (1980) found that the direction of spontaneous rotation in rats relates to the lateralization of reward behavior. Following d-amphetamine injections, all rats had lower thresholds for intracranial self-stimulation on the side opposite the direction of rotation, and the entire rate stimulation current functions were higher and were displaced to the left on that side. The authors suggest that the reward-seeking side is lateralized for positive emotions in a manner similar to that postulated for the left hemisphere in humans.

5.2. Experimental Stroke and Lateralization: Our Own Studies

The third group that has extensively studied lateralization in the rat is our own. We began animal investigations in an effort to provide neurobiological data about our hypothesis that postinfarct changes in catecholaminergic neurons may be the underlying cause of psychopathological changes in stroke patients. In the following section we shall outline various aspects of these studies.

5.2.1. Animal Models

5.2.1a. Ischemic Lesions.   Anesthesized male rats weighing approximately 300 grams are placed in a stereotaxic apparatus and a craniotomy is made in the right or left lateral skull extending from the coronal suture posteriorly to the periorbital area anteriorly, and from the ridge separating dorsal and lateral skull superiorly to the zygomatic arch inferiorly. Within this craniotomy site an ophthalmic suture is passed through the dura, behind the middle cerebral artery, and out through the dura again. The artery and overlying dura are ligated and the artery is severed just distal to the ligature using dural scissors. The temporal muscle that had been reflected away from the skull before the craniotomy is sutured to the underlying fascia on the dorsal skull and the skin is closed with suture (Robinson, 1981; Robinson, Shoemaker, Schlumpf, Valk, & Bloom, 1975).

    5.2.1b. Suction Lesions.   Using the same craniotomy as for ischemic lesions, suction lesions can be produced anywhere in the cerebral cortex. Right or left hemisphere lesions are produced symmetrically by using stereotoxic coordinates and a needle that is mounted in an electrode carrier and positioned so that it enters almost perpendicularly to the surface of the brain. Depending on the size of lesion to be made, a large- or small-bore needle is used. The suction needle is lowered to 2 mm below the surface of the brain and then removed. The coordinates for lesioning in the vicinity of the middle cerebral artery are 2.0 mm dorsal to horizontal plane zero and 9.0 mm anterior to ear bar zero. The reflected temporal muscle is then sutured to the underlying fascia and the skin closed, as with the ischemic lesions (Pearlson & Robinson, 1981).

5.2.2. Neurological Examination

    Immediately after recovery from anesthesia, the animals with ischemic cortical lesions of either hemisphere demonstrated a contralateral hemiparesis as evidenced by holding the forepaw close to the body and dragging the rear leg. In addition, the animals had a contralateral hemianesthesia as evidenced by decreased response to light touch (rubbing the fur) and deep pain (pinching the limbs with forceps). The symptoms, however, lasted only the first 24 hours after operation and the animals appeared normal to gross neurological testing after this initial 24 hours. These sensorimotor symptoms presumably resulted from transient ischemia to the peripheral areas surrounding the lesion site but without accompanying cell death. Since in the rat the location of the lesion site is lateral to the sensorimotor areas, ischemia in the areas surrounding the center of the lesion site where cell death occurs is most likely responsible for the transience of the sensorimotor deficits (Robinson *et al.*, 1975).

5.2.3. Behavioral Studies

5.2.3a. Spontaneous Activity. We have measured spontaneous activity in the rat using photocell chambers (Robinson *et al.*, 1975), open field testing (Robinson, 1979), and running wheels (Robinson & Coyle, 1980) (Figure 10.5). We have consistently found that right hemisphere lesions (suction, ischemic, and pharmacological) lead to spontaneous hyperactivity. With all types of right hemisphere lesions this effect begins at approximately postoperative Day 4 or 5. Following ischemic lesions, spontaneous activity decreases after Day 15 and returns to baseline levels by 20 days postoperative (Robinson *et al.*, 1975) (Figure 10.5). However, following suction lesions activity does not return to baseline, but remains elevated from Day 5 throughout the remainder of the 30-day postoperative period (Pearlson & Robinson, 1981). In contrast to the hyperactivity induced by right hemisphere lesions, left hemisphere infarction or suction lesions do not lead to hyperactivity in spite of the fact that right and left hemisphere lesions appear histologically comparable (Robinson & Coyle, 1980). This dichotomy in spontaneous activity has held up whether the animals are tested in a familiar cage-with-running-wheel environment to which they have had 3 weeks of acclimatization, or in a novel environment in which they are placed in the running-wheel cage only after being lesioned (Robinson & Coyle, 1980).

5.2.3b. Shock-Induced Aggression. Following right hemisphere infarction there is a biphasic change in shock-induced aggression (Robinson *et al.*, 1975). The number of aggressive responses on the part of both animals remains above baseline levels until 7 days postoperative, when the number decreases below baseline and remains depressed throughout the 40-day postoperative period (Robinson *et al.*, 1975). This behavior has not been studied following a left hemisphere infarct.

5.2.3c. Intracranial Self-Stimulation. There is a biphasic change in ICSS in the posterior lateral hypothalamus following right hemisphere infarction (Robinson & Bloom, 1978). The maximum number of lever presses per minute decreases below preoperative baseline levels until Day 7, when it increases above baseline and slowly returns to control levels by 20 days postoperative. Similarly, the minimum current necessary for maximum response is increased until Day 7, then decreases from Day 7 until Day 20, and then returns to baseline. These changes in ICSS occur in the electrode placed in the right posterior lateral hypothalamus. Electrodes in the contralateral posterior lateral hypothalamus do not show any significant changes following a right hemisphere infarction (Robinson & Bloom, 1978). This behavior has not been studied following a left hemisphere infarct.

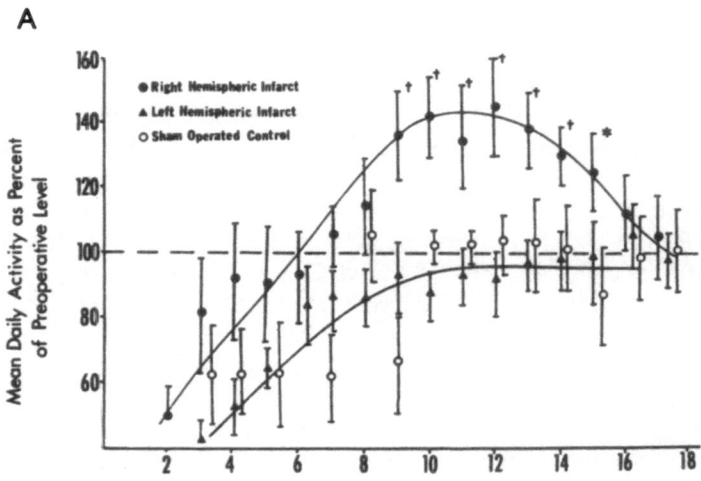

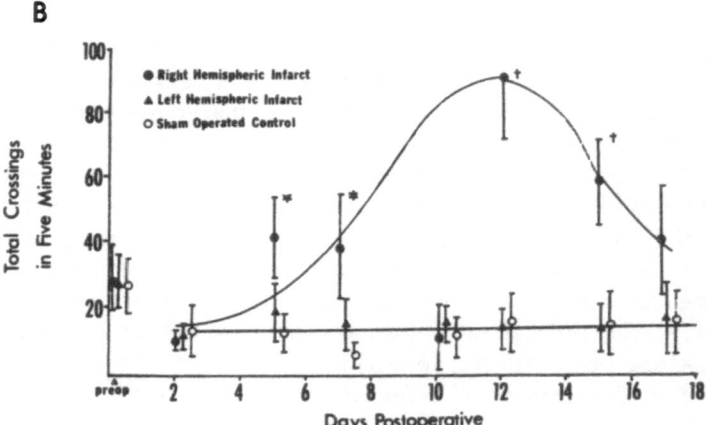

Fig. 10.5. (A) Mean 24-hour running-wheel activity during the 17-day postoperative peri-od. The daily activity of each animal was compared with its mean preoperative value. The absolute values for the preoperative activity were 5,895 ± 1,930 (mean ± standard error of the mean (SEM) for shams, 6,805 ± 1,415 for animals with left hemisphere lesions, and 8,688 ± 1,425 for those with right hemisphere lesions (no significant difference). Bars, SEM. (B) Open field activity during 5-minute observation periods throughout the 17-day postoperative period. Bars, SEM; *$p < 0.05$; $p < 0.01$. (From "Differential Behavioral and Biochemical Effects of Right and Left Hemisphere Cerebral Infarction in the Rat" by R. G. Robinson, *Science*, 1979, *205*, p. 708, Fig. 1. Copyright 1979 by American Association for the Advancement of Science. Reprinted by permission.)

5.2.3d. Food and Water Intake.   There is a slight decrease in both food and water intake in the first 2 days after either a suction or an ischemic lesion. However, food and water intake return to baseline levels by approximately Days 3 to 5, and there is no difference in the response of food and water intake to lesions of either the right or left hemisphere.

5.2.4. Biochemical Studies

5.2.4a. Norepinephrine.   Concentrations of NE in the ipsilateral and contralateral cortex are decreased by 50% to 75% within 12 hours after ischemic lesions of the right hemisphere and slowly recover during a 40-day postoperative period (Robinson, Shoemaker, & Schlumpf, 1980). (Figure 10.6). All contralateral areas return to control levels by 20 days

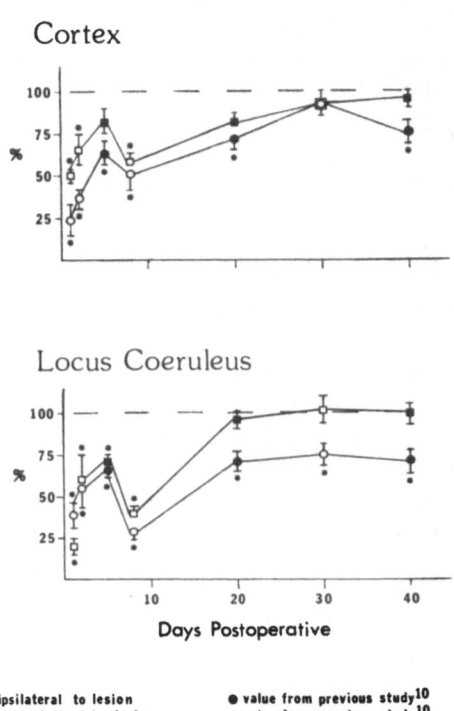

Fig. 10.6. Change in norepinephrine concentrations in ipsilateral and contralateral cortex and locus coeruleus at several times following right middle cerebral artery ligation. (From "Time Course of Changes in Catecholamines Following Right Hemispheric Cerebral Infarction in the Rat" by R. G. Robinson *et al., Brain Research*, 1980, *181*, p. 104, Fig. 1. Copyright 1981 by Elsevier/North-Holland Biomedical Press. Reprinted by permission.)

postoperative; ipsilateral areas show only a partial recovery. The cortex is sampled in two areas: One surrounds the lesion site extending from the cingulate cortex medially to the rhinal fissure laterally; the second cortical sample is taken from an area 3 to 4 mm posterior to the lesion site. Cortical samples are taken both ipsilateral and contralateral to the lesion site. The posterior cortical areas as well as the anterior areas surrounding the lesion site are both decreased in NE concentration both ipsilateral and contralateral to the lesion site. Within the locus coeruleus, there is approximately a 50% to 75% decrease in NE concentrations by 12 hours after the operation. At 2 and 5 days postoperative there is a gradual recovery. However, from Days 5 to 8 there is another decrease in NE concentration. This is the same period when the biphasic change in both shock-induced aggression and ICSS occurs. From Day 8 until postoperative Day 40 there is a slow, gradual, partial recovery of NE concentration in the ipsilateral locus coeruleus and a return to control level in the contralateral locus coeruleus by Day 20. Following left hemisphere infarction there are no significant changes in NE concentrations in either the ipsilateral or contralateral cortex or the locus coeruleus (Robinson et al., 1980). Suction lesions produce similar results in NE concentrations, that is, right hemisphere suction lesions in the vicinity of the middle cerebral artery cause significant depletions in ipsilateral and contralateral cortical and locus coeruleus NE concentrations. However, left hemisphere suction lesions do not cause significant depletions of NE either in the ipsilateral or contralateral cortex or the locus coeruleus (Pearlson & Robinson, 1981; Robinson, 1979; Robinson & Coyle, 1980).

5.2.4b. Dopamine. By 12 hours after right hemisphere infarction there is approximately a 70% depletion in DA concentrations in both the ipsilateral and contralateral substantia nigra and the A10 cell groups (Figure 10.7). Throughout the remainder of the 40-day postoperative period there is only a small amount of recovery. At 30 days postoperative both the ipsilateral and contralateral substantia nigra and the A10 are depleted by more than 50% (Robinson et al., 1980). Thus there is a marked difference in the response of the NE- and DA-containing neurons to injury, the NE neurons being much more capable of recovery and regeneration of normal or almost normal neurotransmitter concentrations whereas the DA-containing neurons are less capable of recovery and remain depleted throughout the postoperative period. Reis, Ross, Gilad, & Joh (1978) also reports the difference in the recovery of these two catecholamine systems. As with the NE concentrations, left-hemisphere infarction does not cause any significant changes in DA concentrations either ipsilateral or contralateral to the lesion site (Robinson, 1979; Robinson & Coyle, 1980).

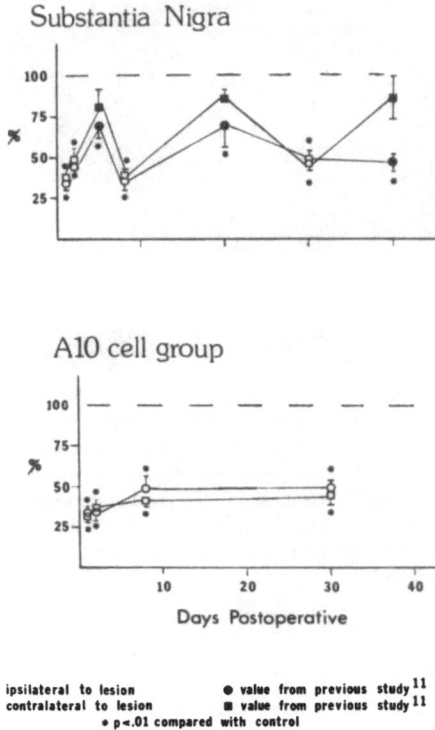

Fig. 10.7. Change in dopamine concentrations in the ipsilateral and contralateral substania nigra and A10 cell group at several times following right middle cerebral artery ligation. (From "Time Course of Changes in Catecholamines Following Right Hemispheric Cerebral Infarction in the Rat" by R. G. Robinson *et al.*, *Brain Research*, 1980, *181*, p. 206, Fig. 2. Copyright 1981 by Elsevier/North-Holland Biomedical Press. Reprinted by permission.)

5.2.5. Histological Studies

5.2.5a. Nissl Stained Tissue. Following either right or left middle cerebral artery ligation, an infarct is found in the frontoparietal cortex. The size of the lesion ranges from 1 to 5 mm in diameter and extends from 50% to 100% through the depth of the cortex but never involves subcortical structures (Figure 10.8). At 5 days postoperative there is evidence of cellular infiltration into the areas surrounding the lesion site; however, we have found no evidence of chromatolysis in the cell bodies of the locus coeruleus or substantia nigra (Robinson & Coyle, 1980). The lesions produced by suction are much less variable than those produced by infarction (one of the reasons we developed this method) (Pearlson & Robinson, 1981) (Figure 10.9). We have quantified lesion size by using

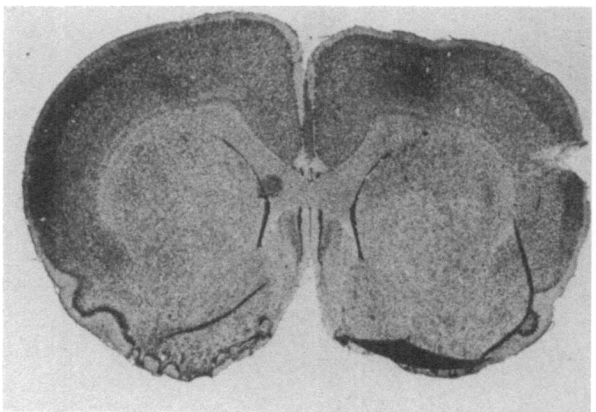

Fig. 10.8. A 25-μm toluidine blue-stained coronal section through the ischemic lesion site in the right hemisphere. Right and left hemisphere lesions had similar histological appearances. The lesions extended to variable depths in the cortex, but none involved subcortical structures. (From "Differential Behavioral and Biochemical Effects of Right and Left Hemisphere Cerebral Infarction in the Rat" by R. G. Robinson, *Science*, 1979, *205*, p. 708, Fig. 1. Copyright 1979 by American Association for the Advancement of Science. Reprinted by permission.)

blind-rater estimations on a 10-point scale. We have demonstrated the reliability of this method and have shown that even if equal-size lesions are compared in the right and left hemisphere, hyperactivity occurs following a right hemisphere lesion but not a left hemisphere lesion. We have quantified the size of the suction lesions, using the vernier scales mounted on the stereomicroscope. The suction lesions we have used are approximately 1.5 mm deep by 1.1 mm high by 1.1 mm wide, or 2 square mm in volume.

5.2.5b. *Fluorescence Histochemical Studies.*   Using the glyoxylic acid method of histochemical fluorescence (Robinson, Bloom, & Battenberg, 1977), we have shown that by 5 days after right hemisphere infarction there is a decrease in the number of visible varicosities in the ipsilateral and contralateral cortex and a decrease in the intensity of fluorescence within the cell bodies of the ipsilateral and contralateral locus coeruleus. By 20 days the locus coeruleus and the substantia nigra appear normal; however, by 40 days postoperative the number of varicosities within the cortex increased above control levels in both the ipsilateral and contralateral cortex surrounding the lesion site.

5.2.6. Pharmacological Studies

5.2.6a. *6-Hydroxydopamine.*   We have injected 6-hydroxydopamine (6-OHDA) either intracisternally or intracerebrally in an effort to deter-

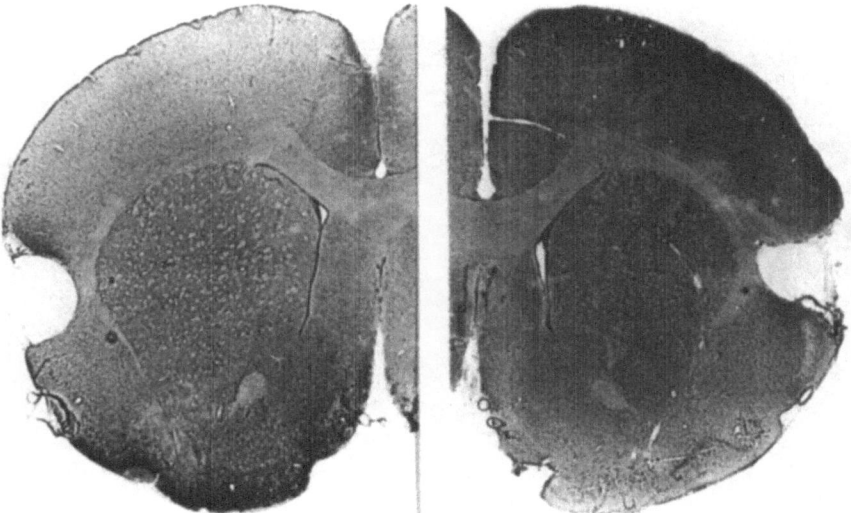

Fig. 10.9. Photomicrographs of 30-μm toluidine blue-stained sections taken through sites of suction lesions from two separate brains, and mounted side by side. Examples of the slight variations in lesion depth are illustrated by the fact that not all lesions extend through the entire depth of the cortex. The discrete focal nature of the lesions and their limitation to cortical tissue are demonstrated. (From "Suction Lesions of the Front Cerebral Cortex in the Rat Induce Asymmetrical Behavioral and Catecholaminergic Responses" by G. D. Pearlson and R. G. Robinson, *Brain Research*, 1981, *218*, p. 238, Fig. 3. Copyright 1981 by Elsevier/North-Holland Biomedical Press. Reprinted by permission.)

mine what role noradrenergic neurons may play in postinfarction hyperactivity. Intracisternal injections, which deplete 80% to 90% of whole brain NE, when given 2 weeks before right hemisphere infarction block the development of hyperactivity. The drug, however, did not decrease activity in control animals who were not given a cerebral infarction (Robinson & Bloom, 1976, 1977). Direct injections of 6-OHDA were made into the cerebral cortex adjacent to the middle cerebral artery 1 mm below the surface of the cortex in a concentration of 2 mg/ml plus 1 mg ascorbic acid and injected at a rate of 0.5 ml/min. Doses as low as 1 mg or as high as 6 mg produced hyperactivity when injected into the right hemisphere but not when injected into the left hemisphere (Robinson & Stitt, 1981). (Figure 10.10). This phenomenon is demonstrable over the entire dose–response curve from 1 ug to 6 ug 6-OHDA (Figure 10.10). This hemispheric asymmetry occurs in spite of the fact that left hemisphere lesions as well as right hemisphere 6-OHDA lesions deplete NE in the ipsilateral cortex and ipsilateral and contralateral locus coeruleus by approximately equal amounts. That is, 30 days after injection, cortical and locus co-

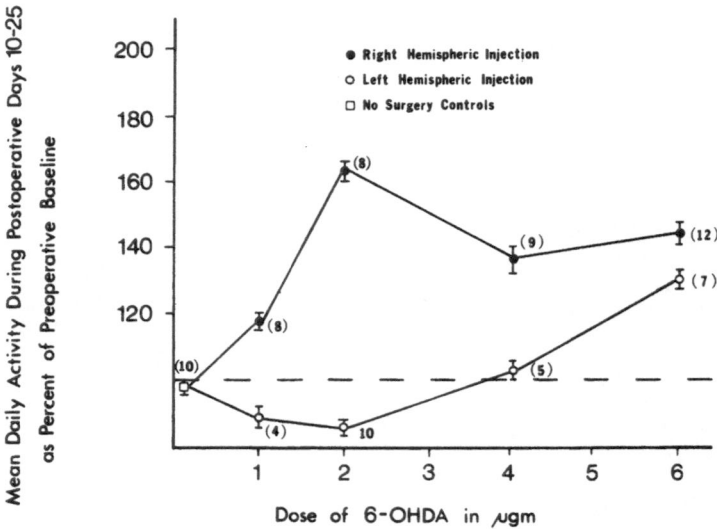

Fig. 10.10. Mean activity during postoperative days 10 to 25 following various doses of 6-hydroxydopamine injected into either the right or left cerebral cortex. Using an analysis of variance these curves are very highly significantly different (F1, 55–126 $p < 0.001$), and by student's t-test the curves are significantly different at every dose tested ($p < 0.001$ at 1, 2, and 4 μg; $p < 0.02$ at 6 μg). (From "Intercortical 6-Hydroxydopamine Induces an Asymmetrical Behavioral Response in Rat" by R. G. Robinson and G. Stitt, *Brain Research*, 1981, 213, p. 388, Fig. 1. Copyright 1981 by Elsevier/North-Holland Biomedical Press. Reprinted by permission.)

eruleus concentrations of NE are depleted by approximately 30% to 40% whether the injection is made into the right or the left hemisphere. However, only right hemisphere injections are followed by hyperactivity, suggesting that the neuronal asymmetry responsible for hyperactivity following right hemisphere lesions may be postsynaptic to the noradrenergic terminals within the cortex.

5.2.6b. *Desmethylimipramine*. This NE-uptake blocker, when given daily by intraperitoneal injections following right hemisphere infarction, will prevent the development of hyperactivity. It does so in spite of the fact that when injected into nonlesioned animals, it did not significantly alter their activity from control levels. These experiments provide further evidence implicating NE neurons as one link in the neural pathways leading to hyperactivity.

5.2.6c. *Lesion Location*. Using the suction technique we have found that there is a graded phenomenon of hyperactivity throughout the right hemisphere (Pearlson, Kubos, & Robinson, 1982); that is, lesions closest to the frontal pole produce the most hyperactivity, whereas lesions of the posterior occipital pole produce the least hyperactivity. This phenomenon is not found within the left hemisphere. This finding, along with our clinical studies, forms the basis for the new concept in cerebral localization we discussed at the end of Section 4.3.3.

6. CONCLUSIONS

In summarizing this chapter, we wish to approach the area of the relationship of the brain to emotion by examining the literature for evidence of emotion as a dynamic process consisting of a series of interconnecting but separable parts that normally function in sequence, some in series and others in parallel.

In this proposed model of emotional processing, internal or external stimuli are "recognized," although not necessarily in the same manner for different stimulus types. These inputs produce a state of activation or arousal and, in turn, give rise to two further stages. The first of these is cognitive in nature and may contribute to "intentionality," that is, the sense that emotions are directed toward objects (feeling angry toward somebody, or happy about something.) The second stage involves internal or subjective experience and an appreciation of appropriate emotional feelings in oneself and others. Finally, there follows an "output" or expressive state.

In turn, each of these stages or states can be recognized as consisting of several component processes. For example, the expressive stage can be considered from the viewpoint of autonomic changes, gesture, facial expression, or the affective components of speech.

In our view the utility of such an approach is twofold. First, the lateralization (if any) of each separate stage can be studied, avoiding the a priori assumption that the stages are unitary in this regard. Second, the disorders can be examined on the basis of failures or dysfunctions of particular stages in the sequence. The issue of lateralization of emotion can be approached in several ways. One is to consider emotion by a method analogous to that employed in the analysis of the neuropsychology of language functions, that is, the increasingly well-documented cerebral localization of the various linguistic subsystems and their anatomic and functional connections. As Whitaker (1971) suggests in the case of the central language system, various linguistic submechanisms can be differentially affected by pathological processes so that abnormal behavior can be used to elucidate lesion locations, system function, as well as component and functional sequence. These in turn may be considered within the framework of an overall interactive explanatory theory.

Table 10.2 presents a broad outline of the proposed dynamic sequence involved in human emotion. We feel this preliminary model can

Table 10.2. Schematic Representation of the Functional Lateralization of Some of the Component Processes of Human Emotion

Process	Findings	Ablative lesion[a]	Irritative lesion[a]
1. Perception/recognition "input"	LEA in perception of emotional tone (Wernicke homologue) (Haggard & Parkinson, 1971)	Auditory affective agnosia (Heilman et al., 1975; Tucker et al., 1977); right-sided inability to choose after right hemisphere disease (De Kosky et al., 1980; Kolb et al., 1980)	
	LEA for prosody (Zurif, 1974)		
	LVFA for faces and emotional expressions (Ley & Bryden, 1979)		
2. Activation/arousal (cortex: limbic: hypothalamus: thalamus: brainstem)	Right hemisphere dominant in corticoreticular loop (Heilman & Watson, 1977a,b)	Neglect syndrome/indifference, right-localized	
	Thalamic behavioral (+ functional) asymmetry (Oke et al., 1978)		
3. Cognition/intentionality	Right hemisphere dominant trigger to unpleasant emotional experiences (Dimond et al., 1976, 1977)	Inability to judge mood of others after right temperoparietal lesions (Heilman et al., 1975)	TLE: sense of personal destiny; R/L interictal personality differences in denial vs. overemphasis (Bear & Fedio, 1977)

(+ comprehension)	Impaired comprehension of humor (Gardner et al., 1975), R-localized $\left\{\begin{array}{l}\text{Abnormal moods postamytal \&}\\ \text{post–brain injury}^{b}\end{array}\right\}$	
4. Internal & external appreciation: subjective feeling	Frontal lobe damage (plus expressive and intentional abnormalities), "true lability"	Free-floating "objectless" anxiety
5. Expressive "output"	Failure of all 3 functions (Ross & Mesulam, 1979)	Involuntary emotional outbursts (Sackeim et al., 1981); gelastic seizures; pseudobulbar palsy
	Right dominance in imparting (Broca homologue) $\left\{\begin{array}{l}\text{affective quality to}\\ \text{speech}\\ \text{prosody in speech}\\ \text{emotional gesturing}\end{array}\right.$	
	Left face dominance in emotional expression (at least for negative emotions (Sackeim et al., 1978; Schwartz et al., 1979)	

[a]The results of ablative and irritative lesions that remove, activate, or distort these processes are also indicated.
[b]See text for details.

serve to generate numerous hypotheses concerning emotional functioning, which will become increasingly testable with the application of new techniques such as CT and PETT scanning. These will aid greatly in the accurate localization of structure and function.

Cortical mechanisms appear to be responsible for the reception and discrimination of emotional stimuli. These functions appear to be localized to the nondominant hemisphere, unlike the complex cognitive functions that accompany emotions; the latter appear to be represented in both cortices. Additionally, the cortex contributes to programming behavior and regulating lower centers. Both cortices appear to contribute to the appreciation and voluntary expression of emotion; these processes appear to be differentially represented on the right and left sides. The right hemisphere, espcially the frontal lobe, seems dominant in contributing to the arousal function of the activating loop that links cortex, limbic system, thalamus, and brainstem. The limbic areas activate and control the hypothalamus, and in turn pituitary (and hence, endocrine) and autonomic functions, which influence both drives and some of the involuntary aspects of emotional function. Arousal appears to modulate both emotional and cognitive functioning.

An important concept not fully represented in Table 10.2 involves the possibility that the right and left hemispheres are specialized in the processing or production of different types of emotion. Suggestive evidence for the "left positive/right negative" dochotomy can be derived, for example, from the studies of Dimond and Farrington (1977). In this light, depressive reactions following left hemisphere stroke or barbiturization as well as the pathological crying associated with left-sided lesions could be viewed as stemming from ablative effects, which "release" emotional mechanism from the undamaged minor hemisphere; the left-sided ictal foci causing pathological laughter would be regarded as irritative in nature.

Concerning the *receptive* or recognition stage, the first step in the proposed sequence, there is considerable evidence both of functional lateralization to the nondominant hemisphere and of separation from other stages of the sequence.

In man, the right (nondominant) hemisphere has been shown in dichotic listening experiments (Haggard & Parkinson, 1971; Zurif, 1974) to be more specialized in the processing of prosody and the emotional tones of sentences, as well as in the perception of emotional, nonverbal sounds in Westerners(Carmon & Nachshon, 1973).Damage to the right hemisphere (in an area analagous to that of Wernicke's on the dominant side) leads to a loss of these functions, an "auditory affective agnosia" (Heilman *et al.*, 1975; Tucker, Roth, Arneson, & Buckingham, 1977).

In the visual mode, the perception or recognition of emotion is closely associated with the recognition of faces, a fact that likely results from the primacy of facial expression in the nonverbal communication of emotion. In tachistoscopic studies, there is a left visual field (right hemisphere) advantage for processing both emotional expressions and faces (Ladavas et al., 1980; Ley & Bryden, 1979). Errors in identifying emotional expressions, but not faces, can be produced by electrical stimulation of the nondominant posterior middle temporal gyrus (Ojemann et al., 1980).

The work of Dimond and colleagues (Dimond & Farrington, 1977; Dimond et al., 1976) may prompt investigations into whether the two hemispheres specialize in the analysis of different types of emotional material, with the nondominant side being associated with more "negative" emotions. In this regard, it is of note that of Izard's (1971) six most reliably discriminated facial emotions, four (fear, sadness, anxiety, and disgust) are "negative" and one (surprise) equivocal, with only a single "positive" emotion (happiness).

The association of defects in emotional recognition with the neglect syndrome (Kolb et al., 1980) suggests an important role for *arousal* in making such discriminations. Heilman and Watson (1977a,b) postulate a right hemisphere dominance in the corticoreticular loops responsible for arousal, which may in turn be associated with the biochemical and functional asymmetries demonstrated in the thalamus (Oke et al., 1978; Whitaker & Ojemann, 1977). A more complex view of arousal as a separate process which is a physiological control function for hemisphere information-processing strategies has been proposed by Tucker (1981). In this model, arousal modulates emotional function and hence, specific types of cognition.

The next stage we wish to examine is that of *cognition*. The area of reciprocal interaction between emotion and cognition is a complex one; observations date back at least as early as Descartes's statement that learning and memory influence the "passions." The work of Dimond and colleagues suggests that the two hemispheres interpret and/or generate different types of affects or emotional judgments, with those of the right side being predominantly negative. The possibility that the dominant hemisphere may normally suppress the opposite side is consonant with a general systems theory of brain activity such as Denenberg's (1980). Tsunoda and Oka (1967) have shown that in Japanese, but not in Westerners, nonverbal human sounds and Japanese (but not Western) music are processed in the dominant hemisphere; they have also shown that these functions become localized in this particular pattern by listening to and speaking, rather than reading and writing, the Japanese language. In Westerners, Gates and Bradshaw (1977) have shown a left hemisphere superiority to musical recall only in musicians, who presumably regard music more as a "language." The implication here is that the language we learn may alter the information processing of the two hemispheres. That this in turn is linked to emotional responses appears to follow from Tsunoda and Oka's (1967) affective findings with intracarotid amytal injections, which are opposite to those reported in most Western studies. If valid, the idea of a linear-sequential structure imposed on information processing resulting from certain types of language usage shows parallels with McLuhanesque ideas.

In the step from reception to *comprehension* of emotional stimuli, the right hemisphere again appears to play an important role. Heilman *et al.* (1975) and Gardner *et al.* (1975) have demonstrated the importance of the nondominant hemisphere in judging the mood of others and in comprehending nonverbal humor, respectively. An intact nondominant hemisphere also seems necessary in order to recall emotionally charged stories (Wechsler, 1973) and to match appropriate emotions with written statements (Kolb *et al.*, 1980).

The latter two tasks imply an interaction between the language-dominant (left) and right hemispheres. Such work as Safer and Leventhal's (1977) in separating emotional tone from semantic content further suggests that the two hemispheres may compete in certain judgments. If the idea of competition between hemispheres is familiar, less widely described is the concept of cooperation or rivalry between the cognitive and emotional "styles," respectively, either within a hemisphere or between hemispheres. One could conceive, for example, of such interactions between the logical, sequential, and "critical" cognitive mode of the dominant hemisphere, and the "depressive," "negative" affective style presumed to characterize the right hemisphere. Relatively simple experiments could be designed to assess the alteration of emotional-processing capabilities and affective "style" of a hemisphere where the ipsilateral or contralateral hemisphere is engaged in various cognitive tasks. Similarly, the interactions between experimentally induced, relatively lateralized affective states and lateralized cognitive functions could be studied. Some preliminary work in this area has been performed by Tucker *et al.* (1981); Cacioppo *et al.* (1979) have examined the effect of the personal relevance of stimuli on both cognitive and affective responses.

Studies in hemisphere-damaged patients could further examine the links between lateralized affective and cognitive functions, and the relationship of both to arousal levels. Thus far, studies in temporal lobe epileptics (Bear & Fedio, 1977) with presumed irritative lesions have highlighted the cognitive style of each hemisphere (e.g., the excessive intellectualization that accompanies dominant hemisphere foci), as have Sackeim *et al.* (1981) in the emotional realm. Bear and Fedio (1977) propose that certain phenomena seen in temporal lobe epileptics—for example, the feelings of intense subjective conviction of personal destiny seen with dominant hemisphere foci—stem from the formation of abnormal cognitive-emotional links caused by a pathological, functional frontolimbic "hyperconnection."

With respect to the next stage, that of the *subjective feeling states* that are part of emotions, information about the opposite affective "tones" seemingly generated by each hemisphere has been obtained from several studies, including Terzian's (1964) with amytal and those of Robinson and Szetela (1981). The true contribution of each hemisphere has yet to be elucidated, because much work remains to be done in differentiating the mechanism of such lesions as those produced by stroke or sodium amytal regarding the relative excitation or depression of the lateralized mechanisms involved in producing affect. In addition to such "objectless" emotional states of unknown etiology as free-floating anxiety, frontal lobe damage is known to cause "true lability," in which emotional feelings arise unaccompanied by the expected cognition, but accompanied by their commonly associated expressive behavior.

In the final *expressive* or "output" stage of emotion, a right hemisphere area homologous to that of Broca in the dominant hemisphere appears to be important in imparting affective intonation and prosody to speech and in executing appropriate emotional gestures (Heilman & Valenstein, 1980; Ross & Mesulam, 1979). The work of Sackeim and Gur (1978), of Sackeim *et al.* (1978), and of Schwartz *et al.* (1979) suggests that the left side of the face (and hence, perhaps the right hemisphere) is more involved in the expression of negative emotions. Experiments by Dimond *et al.* (1977) examining the differential autonomic responses obtained from films shown separately to each hemisphere could shed light on this matter if they were repeated in brain-damaged subjects. The work of Sackeim *et al.* (1981) with involuntary emotional outbursts (which are unaccompanied by the normal internal or subjective appreciation states) again suggests that the expression of opposite mood states is a lateralized phenomenon.

In attempting to examine possible underlying anatomic mechanisms for emotional behaviors, there are difficulties in finding such a basis for two explanatory ideas that have been offered. The first is that each hemisphere generates a separate emotional "tone"; the second is that one hemisphere inhibits the other, as a result of which phenomena are "released." Although we now know of anatomic asymmetries in both human and animal brains, it is difficult to link these to different types of emotions in the form of "positive" or "negative" tones. Additionally, hemispheric cross-connections are bidirectional and one would not easily predict tonic inhibitions of one hemisphere by another. Overall, there seems to be no suitable precedent for looking at brain function in this way.

In our laboratory and clinical work we have attempted to build a conceptual basis of emotional asymmetries from observations on single neurotransmitter systems, rather than on gestalts such as loose or dense packing. We feel that it may be useful to continue to examine the anatomic basis of such single neurotransmitter systems, as it has enabled us to form a dual laboratory/clinical strategy in emotion research in which data from one area cross-fertilize the other. For example, our observation that right but not left hemisphere infarction in the rat produces hyperactivity and changes in catecholaminergic systems has led us to hypotheses concerning the lateralization of emotion in humans. Such symptoms as the apathy and inappropriate cheerfulness that follow certain right hemisphere lesions might result from depletions of catecholamines induced by the unilateral right hemisphere injury that have had bilateral effects. Conversely, the depressed mood following left hemisphere injury may result from disturbances either of other neurotransmitter systems or from the same neurotransmitter system being altered either in a different way or to a different extent.

On the other hand, findings from human studies that the severity of emotional disturbances strongly correlates with the proximity of left hemisphere lesions to the frontal pole could well result from increasing degrees of interruption of the noradrenergic pathway, which has been demonstrated to run from anterior to posterior in the rat cortex in an arborizing fashion by Morrison *et al.* (1979). That such a graded effect indeed occurs with the lateralized hyperactivity phenomenon has now been experimentally proved by us in an animal model (Pearlson, Robinson, & Kubos, 1982).

ACKNOWLEDGMENTS

Helpful suggestions were received from Amy Veroff, Phillip Slavney, Ken Kubos, Alan Duckworth, Fred Bennett, and Milton Strauss. Younus Chaudhry helped with reference preparation; typing was done by Anita Doss and Renee Harrell.

7. REFERENCES

Achari, A. N., & Colover, J. Posterior fossa tumors with pathological laughter. *Journal of the American Medical Association*, 1976, *235*, 1469–1471.

Adams, R. D., & Victor, M. *Principles of neurology*. New York: McGraw-Hill, 1977.

Ahern, G. L., & Schwartz, G. E. Differential lateralization for positive versus negative emotion. *Neuropsychologia*, 1979, *17*, 693–698.

Albert, M. L., Silverberg, R., Reches, A., & Berman, M. Cerebral dominance for consciousness. *Archives of Neurology*, 1976, *33*, 453–454.

Bear, D. M., & Fedio, P. Quantitiative analysis of interictal behavior in temporal lobe epilepsy. *Archives of Neurology*, 1977, *39*, 454–467.

Beaton, A. A. Hemispheric emotional asymmetry in a dichotic listening task. *Acta Psychologica*, 1979, *43*, 103–109.

Benton, A. L., & Van Allen, M. W. Impairment in facial recognition in patients with cerebral disease. *Cortex*, 1968, *4*, 344–358.

Berg, M. R., & Harris, L. J. The effect of experimenter location and subject anxiety on cerebral activation as measured by lateral eye movements. *Neuropsychologia*, 1980, *18*, 89–93.

Black, F. W. Unilateral brain lesions and MMPI performance: A preliminary study. *Perceptual and Motor Skills*, 1975, *40*, 87–93.

Borod, J. C., & Caron, H. S. Facedness and emotion related to lateral dominance, sex and expression type. *Neuropsychologia*, 1980, *18*, 237–291.

Bradshaw, J. L. Sex and side: A double dichotomy interacts. *The Behavioral and Brain Sciences*, 1980, *3*, 229.

Buchsbaum, M. S., Carpenter, W. T., Jr., Fedio, P., Goodwin, F. K., Murphy, D. L., & Post, R. M. Hemispheric differences in evoked potential enhancement by selective attention to hemiretinally presented stimuli in schizophrenic affective and post-temporal lobectomy patients. In J. H. Gruzelier & P. Flor-Henry (Eds.), *Hemisphere asymmetries of function in psychopathology*. Amsterdam: Elsevier/North-Holland, 1979.

Cacioppo, J. T., Petty, R. E., & Snyder, C. W. Cognitive and an affective response as a function of relative hemispheric involvement. *International Journal of Neuroscience*, 1979, *9*, 81–89.

Cain, D. P., & Wada, J. A. An anatomical asymmetry in the baboon brain. *Brain Behavior and Evolution*, 1979, *16*, 222–226.

Carmon, A., & Nachshon, I. Ear asymmetry in perception of emotional nonverbal stimuli. *Acta Psychologica*, 1973, *37*, 351–357.

Cohen, H. D., Rosen, R. C., & Goldstein, L. Electroencephalographic laterality changes during human sexual orgasm. *Archives of Sexual Behavior*, 1976, *5*, 189–199.

Colbourn, C. J. Laterality measurement and theory. In J. H. Gruzelier & P. Flor-Henry (Eds.), *Hemisphere asymmetries of function in psychopathology*. Amsterdam: Elsevier/North-Holland, 1979.

Cronin, D., Bodley, P., Potts, L., Mather, M. D., Gardner, R. K., & Tobin, J. C. Unilateral and bilateral ECT: A study of memory disturbance and relief from depression. *Journal of Neurology, Neurosurgery and Psychiatry*, 1970, *33*, 705–713.

Davidson, R. J., Schwartz, G. E., Saron, C., Bennett, J., & Goleman, D. J. Frontal vs. parietal EEG asymmetry during positive and negative affect. *Society for Psychophysiology Research Abstracts*, 1979, *16*, 202–203.

DeKosky, S. T., Heilman, K. M., Bowers, D., & Valenstein, E. Recognition and discrimination of emotional faces and pictures. *Brain and Language*, 1980, *9*, 206–214.

D'Elia, G., & Raotma, H. Is unilateral ECT less effective than bilateral ECT? *British Journal of Psychiatry*, 1975, *126*, 83–89.

Denenberg, V. H. General systems theory, brain organization, and early experience. *American Journal of Physiology*, 1980, *238*, 3–13.

Denenberg, V. H., Garbanati, J., Sherman, G., Yutzey, D. A., & Kaplan, R. Infantile stimulation induces brain lateralization in rats. *Science*, 1978, *201*, 1150–1152.

Denenberg, V. H., Zeidner, L., Rosen, G. D., Hofmann, M., Garbanati, J. A., Sherman, G. F., & Yutzey, D. A. Stimulation in infancy facilitates interhemispheric communication in the rabbit. *Brain Research*, 1981, *227*, 165–169.

De Renzi, E., & Spinnler, H. Facial recognition in brain damaged patients. *Neurology*, 1966, *16*, 145–152.

De Renzi, E., Faglioni, P., & Spinnler, H. The performance of patients with unilateral brain damage on face recognition tasks. *Cortex*, 1968, *4*, 17–34.

Diamond, M. C. New data supporting cortical asymmetry differences in males and females. *The Behavioral and Brain Sciences*, 1980, *3*, 233.

Dikmen, S., & Reitan, R. M. MMPI correlates of localized cerebral lesions. *Perceptual and Motor Skills*, 1974, *39*, 831–840.

Dimond, S. J., & Farrington, L. Emotional response to films shown to the right or left hemisphere of the brain measured by heart rate. *Acta Psychologia*, 1977, *41*, 255–260.

Dimond, S. J., Farrington, L., & Johnson, P. Differing emotional response from right and left hemisphere. *Nature*, 1976, *261*, 690–692.

Donchin, E., Kutas, M., & McCarthy, G. Electrocortical indices of hemisphere utilization. In S. Harnad, R. W. Doty, L. Goldstein, J. Jaynes, & G. Krauthamer, (Eds.), *Lateralization in the nervous system*. New York: Academic Press, 1977.

Ehrlichman, H., & Weinberger, A. Lateral eye movements and hemispheric asymmetry: A critical review. *Psychological Bulletin*, 1978, *85*, 1080–1101.

Ekman, P. Asymmetry in facial expression [letter]. *Science*, 1980, *209*, 833–834.

Fleminger, J. J., Horne, D. J. D., Nair, N. P. V., & Nott, P. M. Differential effect of unilateral and bilateral ECT. *American Journal of Psychiatry*, 1970, *127*, 430–436.

Flor-Henry, P. Psychosis and temporal lobe epilepsy. *Epilepsia*, 1969, *10*, 363–395.

Flor-Henry, P. Psychosis neurosis and epilepsy, Developmental and gender-related effects and their aetiological contribution. *British Journal of Psychiatry*, 1974, *124*, 144–150.

Flor-Henry, P. Laterality, shifts of cerebral dominance, sinistrality and psychosis. In J. H. Gruzelier & P. Flor-Henry (Eds.), *Hemisphere asymmetries of function in psychopathology*. Amsterdam: Elsevier/North-Holland, 1979. (a)

Flor-Henry, P. On certain aspects of the localization of the cerebral systems regulating and determining emotion. *Biological Psychiatry*, 1979, *14*, 677–698. (b)

Flor-Henry, P. Evolutionary and clinical aspects of lateralized sex differences. *The Behavioral and Brain Sciences*, 1980, *3*, 235–236.

Flor-Henry, P., & Yeudall, L. T. Neuropsychological investigation of schizophrenia and manic-depressive psychosis. In J. H. Gruzelier & P. Flor-Henry (Eds.), *Hemisphere asymmetries of function in psychopathology*. Amsterdam: Elsevier/North-Holland, 1979.

Folstein, M. F., Folstein, S. E., & McHugh, P. R. "Mini-mental state": A practical method for grading the cognitive state of patients for the clinician. *Journal of Psychiatric Research*, 1975, *12*, 189–198.

Frumkin, L. R., Ripley, H. S., & Cox, G. B. Changes in cerebral hemispheric lateralization with hypnosis. *Biological Psychiatry*, 1978, *13*, 741–750.

Gainotti, G. "Catastrophic" reactions and symptoms of indifference following cerebral lesions. *Neuropsychologia*, 1969, *1*, 195–204.

Gainotti, G. Emotional behavior and hemisphere side of the lesion. *Cortex*, 1972, *8*, 41–55.

Gainotti, G. The relationships between emotions and cerebral dominance: A review of clinical and experimental evidence. In J. H. Gruzelier & P. Flor-Henry (Eds.), *Hemisphere asymmetries of function in psychopathology*. Amsterdam: Elsevier/North-Holland, 1979. (a)

Gainotti, G. Affectivity and brain dominance: A survey. In J. Obiols, C. Ballus, E., Gonzales Monclus, & J. Pujol (Eds.), *Biological psychiatry today*. Amsterdam: Elsevier/North-Holland, 1979. (b)

Galaburda, A. M., LeMay, M., Kemper, T. L., & Geschwind, N. Right-left asymmetries in the brain: Structural differences between the hemispheres may underlie cerebral dominance. *Science*, 1978, *199*, 852–856.

Galin, D. Implications for psychiatry of left and right cerebral specialization. *Archives of General Psychiatry*, 1974, *31*, 572–583.

Galin, D., Diamond, R., & Braff, D. Lateralization of conversion symptoms: More frequent on the left. *American Journal of Psychiatry*, 1977, *134*, 578–580.

Gardner, H., Ling, P. K., Flamm, L., & Silverman, J. Comprehension and appreciation of humorous material following brain damage. *Brain*, 1975, *98*, 399–412.

Gasparrini, W. G., Satz, P., Heilman, K. M., & Coolidge, F. L. Hemispheric asymmetries of affective processing as determined by the Minnesota Multiphasic Personality Inventory. *Journal of Neurology, Neurosurgery, and Psychiatry*, 1978, *41*, 470–473.

Gates, A., & Bradshaw, J. L. The role of the cerebral hemispheres in music. *Brain and Language*, 1977, *4*, 403–431.

Gazzaniga, M. S., & LeDoux, J. E., *The integrated mind*. New York: Plenum Press, 1978.

Glick, S. D., Jerussi, T. P., & Zimmerberg, B. Behavioral and neuropharmacological correlates of nigrostriatal assymetry in rats. In S. Harnad, R. Doty, L. Gelstein, J. Jaynes, & G. Krauthamer (Eds.), *Lateralization in the nervous system*. New York: Academic Press, 1977.

Glick, S. D., Zimmerberg, B., & Jerussi, T. P. Adaptive significance of laterality in the rodent. In S. J. Dimond & D. A. Blizard (Eds.), *Annals of the New York Academy of Sciences*, 1977, *299*, 180–185.

Glick, S. D., Meibach, R. C., Cox, R. D., & Maayani, S. Multiple and interrelated functional asymmetries in rat brain. *Life Sciences*, 1979, *25*, 395–400.

Glick, S. D., Schonfeld, A. R., & Strumf, A. J. Sex differences in brain asymmetry of the rodent. *The Behavioral and Brain Sciences*, 1980, *3*, 236.

Glick, S. D., Weaver, L. M., & Meibach, R. C. Lateralized reward in rats: Differences in reinforcing thresholds. *Science*, 1980, *207*, 1093–1095.

Goldberg, D. P. *The detection of psychiatric illness by questionnaire*. London: Oxford University Press, 1972.

Goldstein, K. *Language and language disturbances*. New York: Grune & Stratton, 1948.

Gruzelier, J. H. Synthesis and critical review of the evidence for hemisphere asymmetries of function in psychopathology. In J. H. Gruzelier & P. Flor-Henry (Eds.), *Hemisphere asymmetries of function in psychopathology*. Amsterdam: Elsevier/North-Holland, 1979.

Gur, R. C., Packer, I. K., Hungerbuhler, J. P., Reivich, M., Obrist, W. D., Amarneck, W. S., & Sackeim, H. A. Differences in the distribution of gray and white matter in human cerebral hemispheres. *Science*, 1980, *207*, 1226–1228.

Gur, R. E., Gur, R. C., & Harris, L. J. Cerebral activation, as measured by subjects' lateral eye movements, is influenced by experimenter location. *Neuropsychologia*, 1975, *13*, 35–44.

Haggard, M. P., & Parkinson, A. M. Stimulus and task factors as determinants of ear advantages. *Quarterly Journal of Experimental Psychology*, 1971, *23*, 168–177.

Halliday, A. M., Davison, K., Browne, M. W., & Kreeger, L. C. A comparison of the effects on depression and memory of bilateral E.C.T. and unilateral E.C.T. to the dominant and non-dominant hemispheres. *British Journal of Psychiatry*, 1968, *114*, 997–1012.

Hamilton, M. A rating scale for depression. *Journal of Neurology, Neurosurgery, and Psychiatry*, 1960, *23*, 56–62.

Harman, D. W., & Ray, W. J. Hemispheric activity during affective verbal stimuli: An EEG study. *Neuropsychologia*, 1977, *15*, 457–460.

Hecaen, H. Clinical symptomatology in right and left hemispheric lesions. In V. B. Mountcastle (Ed.), *Interhemispheric relations and cerebral dominance*. Baltimore: Johns Hopkins University Press, 1962.

Hecaen, H., & Angelergues, R. *La Cecite Psychique*. Paris: Masson, 1963.

Heilman, K. M., & Valenstein, E. Emotional disorders caused by CNS dysfunction. *Geriatrics*, 1980, *35*, 77–86.

Heilman, K. M., & van den Abell, T. Right hemispheric dominance for mediating cerebral activation. *Neuropsychologia*, 1979, *17*, 315–321.

Heilman, K. M., & Watson, R. T. The unilateral neglect syndrome: A unilateral defect of the orienting response. In S. Harnard, R. W. Doty, L. Goldstein, J. Jaynes, & G. Krauthamer (Eds.), *Lateralization in the nervous system*. New York: Academic Press, 1977. (a)

Heilman, K. M., & Watson, R. T. Mechanisms underlying the unilateral neglect syndrome. In E. A. Weinstein & R. P. Friedland (Eds.), *Advances in neurology* (Vol. 18). New York: Raven Press, 1977. (b)

Heilman, K. M., Scholes, R., & Watson, R. T. Auditory affective agnosia. *Journal of Neurology, Neurosurgery, and Psychiatry*, 1975, *38*, 69–92.

Heilman, K. M., Schwartz, H. D., & Watson, R. T. Hypoarousal in patients with the neglect syndrome and emotional indifference. *Neurology*, 1978, *28*, 229–232.

Hermann, B. P., & Chhabria, S. Interictal psychopathology in patients with ictal fear: Examples of sensory-limbic hyperconnection. *Archives of Neurology*, 1980, *37*, 607–668.

Hilliard, R. D. Hemisphere laterality effects on a facial recognition task in normal subjects. *Cortex*, 1973, *9*, 246–258.

Hommes, O. R., & Panhuysen, H. M. Bilateral intracarotid amytal injection. *Psychiatrie, Neurologie, Neurochirurgie*, 1970, *73*, 447–459.

Hommes, O. R., & Panhuysen, H. M. A study of bilateral intracarotid amytal in eleven depressed patients. *Psychiatrie, Neurologie, Neurochirurgie*, 1971, *74*, 259–270.

Ironside, R. Disorders of laughter due to brain lesions. *Brain*, 1956, *79*, 587–609.

Izard, C. E. *The face of emotion*. New York: Appleton-Century-Crofts, 1971.

Jacome, D. E., McLain, L. W., Jr., & Fitzgerald, R. Postural reflex gelastic seizures. *Archives of Neurology*, 1980, *37*, 269–271.

Kimura, D. Functional asymmetry of the brain in dichotic listening. *Cortex*, 1967, *3*, 163–178.

Kimura, D. The asymmetry of the human brain. *Scientific American*, 1973, *228*, 70–78.

King, F. L., & Kimura, D. *Left ear superiority in dichotic perception of vocal nonverbal sounds* (Research Bulletin 188). Department of Psychology, University of Western Ontario, 1971.

Kinsbourne, M. The biological determinants of functional bisymmetry and asymmetry. In M. Kinsbourne (Ed.), *Asymmetrical function of the brain*. New York: Cambridge University Press, 1978.

Kolb, B., & Milner, B. *Observations on spontaneous facial expression in patients*. Unpublished manuscript, 1980.

Kolb, B., & Whishaw, I. (Eds.). *Fundamentals of human neuropsychology*. San Francisco: W. H. Freeman, 1980.

Kolb, B., Taylor, L., & Milner, B. *Affective behavior in patients with localized cortical excisions: An analysis of lesion site and side*. Unpublished manuscript, 1980.

Ladavas, E., Umilta, C., & Ricci-Bitti, P. E. Evidence for sex differences in right-hemisphere dominance for emotions. *Neuropsychologia*, 1980, *18*, 361–366.

Leber, W. R., & Johnson, H. J. Cortical and cardiac response patterns during affect-laden imagery. *Psychophysiology*, 1980, *17*, 287–288.

LeDoux, J. E., Wilson, D. H., & Gazzaniga, M. S. A divided mind: Observations on the conscious properties of the separated hemispheres. *Annals of Neurology*, 1977, *2*, 417–421.

Leviel, V., Cheramy, A., & Glowinski, J. Role of the dendritic release of dopamine in the reciprocal control of the two nigro-striatal dopaminergic pathways. *Nature,* 1979, *280,* 236–239.

Levy, J., Trevarthen, C., & Sperry, R. W. Perception of bileteral chimeric figures following hemispheric deconnexion. *Brain,* 1972, *95,* 61–78.

Ley, R. G., & Bryden, M. P. Hemispheric differences in processing emotions and faces. *Brain and Language,* 1979, *7,* 127–138.

Ley, R. G., & Bryden, M. P. Consciousness, emotion, and the right hemisphere. In R. Stevens & G. Underwood (Eds.), *Aspects of consciousness* (Vol. 2). New York: Academic Press, 1981.

Luria, R. E., & McHugh, P. R. Reliability and clinical utility of the "Wing" present state examination. *Archives of General Psychiatry,* 1974, *30,* 866–871.

Marshall, J. C. Some problems and paradoxes associated with recent accounts of hemispheric specialization. *Neuropsychologia,* 1973, *11,* 463–470.

Marshall, J. C., Caplan, D., & Holmes, J. M. The measure of laterality. *Neuropsychologia,* 1975, *13,* 315–321.

McGlone, J. Sex differences in human brain asymmetry: A critical survey. *The Behavioral and Brain Sciences,* 1980, *3,* 215–263.

McHugh, P. R., & Folstein, M. F. Psychiatric syndromes of Huntington's chorea: A clinical and phenomenologic study. In D. F. Benson & D. Blumer (Eds.), *Psychiatric aspects of neurological disease.* New York: Grune & Stratton, 1975.

Milner, B. In C. H. Milikan & F. L. Darley (Eds.), *Brain mechanisms underlying speech and language.* New York: Grune & Stratton, 1967.

Mononen, L. J., & Seitz, M. R. An AER analysis of contralateral advantage in the transmission of auditory information. *Neuropsychologia,* 1977, *15,* 165–173.

Morrison, J. H., Molliver, M. E., & Grzanna, R. Noradrenergic innervation of cerebral cortex: Widespread effects of local cortical lesions. *Science,* 1979, *205,* 313–316.

Nelson, C. A., & Horowitz, F. D. Asymmetry in facial expression [Letter]. *Science,* 1980, *209,* 834.

Nieoullon, A., Cheramy, A., & Glowinski, J. Interdependence of the nigrostriatal dopaminergic systems on the two sides of the brain in the cat. *Science,* 1977, *198,* 415–418.

Nottebohm, F. Asymmetries in neural control of vocalization in the canary. In S. Harnad, R. W. Doty, L. Goldstein, J. Jaynes, & G. Krauthamer (Eds.), *Lateralization in the nervous system.* New York: Academic Press, 1977.

Ojemann, G. A., Fried, I., Mateer, C., Wohns, R., & Fedio, P. Organization of visuospatial functions in human non-dominant cortex: Evidence from electrical stimulation. *Society for Neuroscience Abstracts,* 1980, *6,* 418.

Oke, A., Keller, R., Mefford, I., & Adams, R. N. Lateralization of norepinephrine in human thalamus. *Science,* 1978, *200,* 1411–1413.

Papez, J. W. A proposed mechanism of emotion. *Archives of Neurology and Psychiatry,* 1937, *38,* 725–744.

Pearlson, G. D., & Robinson, R. G. Suction lesions of the frontal cerebral cortex in the rat induce asymmetrical behavioral and catecholaminergic responses. *Brain Research,* 1981, *218,* 233–242.

Pearlson, G. D., Kubos K. L., & Robinson, R. G. Cerebral localization of behaviour as a gradient across the entire hemisphere. In preparation, 1982.

Perria, L., Rosadini, G., & Rossi, G. F. Determination of side of cerebral dominance with amobarbital. *Archives of Neurology,* 1961, *4,* 173–181.

Petersen, M. R., Beecher, M. D., Zoloth, S. R., Moody, D. B., & Stebbins, W. C. Neuronal lateralization of species-specific vocalizations by Japanese Macaques. *Science,* 1978, *202,* 324–327.

Reis, D. J., Ross, R. A., Gilad, G., & Joh, T. H. Reaction of central catecholaminergic neurons to injury: Model systems for studying the neurobiology of central regeneration and sprouting. In C. W. Cotman (Ed.), *Neuronal plasticity*. New York: Raven Press, 1978.

Reus, V. I., Buchsbaum, M. S., & Post, R. M. D-amphetamine: Differential effects on right and left hemispheres. In J. H. Gruzelier & P. Flor-Henry (Eds.), *Hemisphere asymmetries of function in psychopathology*. Amsterdam: Elsevier/North-Holland, 1979.

Reynolds, D. M., & Jeeves, M. A. A developmental study of hemisphere specialization for recognition of faces in normal subjects. *Cortex*, 1978, *14*, 511–520.

Robinson, R. G. Differential behavioral and biochemical effects of right and left hemisphere cerebral infarction in the rat. *Science*, 1979, *205*, 707–710.

Robinson, R. G. A model for the study of stroke using the rat. *American Journal of Pathology*, 1981, *92*, 103–105.

Robinson, R. G., & Bloom, F. E. Pharmacological treatment of a behavioral disorder. In P. Scheinberg (Ed.), *Cerebrovascular diseases*. New York: Raven Press, 1976.

Robinson, R. G., & Bloom, F. E. Pharmacological treatment following experimental cerebral infarction: Implications for understanding psychological symptoms of human stroke. *Biological Psychiatry*, 1977, *12*, 669–680.

Robinson, R. G., & Bloom, F. E. Changes in posterior hypothalame self-stimulation following experimental cerebral infarction in the rat. *Journal of Comparative and Physiological Psychology*, 1978, *92*, 969–976.

Robinson, R. G., & Coyle, J. T. The different effects of right versus left hemispheric infarction on catecholamines and behaviour in the rat. *Brain Research*, 1980, *188*, 63–78.

Robinson, R. G., & Price, T. R. Post-stroke depressive disorders: A follow-up study of 103 outpatients. *Stroke*, 1982, *13*.

Robinson, R. G., & Stitt, G. Intracortical 6-hydroxydopamine induces an asymmetrical behavioral response in rat. *Brain Research*, 1981, *213*, 387–395.

Robinson, R. G., & Szetela, B. Mood change following left hemisphere brain injury. *Annals of Neurology*, 1981, *9*, 447–453.

Robinson, R. G., Shoemaker, W. J., Schlumpf, M., Valk, T., & Bloom, F. E. Experimental cerebral infarction in rat brain: Effect on catecholamines and behavior. *Nature*, 1975, *255*, 332–334.

Robinson, R. G., Bloom, F. E., & Battenberg, E. L. F. A fluorescent histochemical study of changes in nonadrenergic neurons following experimental cerebral infarction in the rat. *Brain Research*, 1977, *132*, 259–272.

Robinson, R. G., Shoemaker, W. J., & Schlumpf, M. Time course of changes in catecholamines following right hemispheric cerebral infarction in the rat. *Brain Research*, 1980, *181*, 202–208.

Rogers, L. J. Functional lateralization in the chicken forebrain revealed by cyclohexamide treatment. *Proceedings of the 17th International Ornithological Congress*, in press.

Rogers, L. J., & Anson, J. M. Lateralization of function in the chicken forebrain. *Pharmacology Biochemistry and Behavior*, 1979, *10*, 679–686.

Ross, E. D., & Mesulam, M. M. Dominant language functions of the right hemisphere. *Archives of Neurology*, 1979, *36*, 144–148.

Rossi, G. F., & Rosadini, G. Experimental analysis of cerebral dominance in man. In C. H. Milikan & F. L. Darley (Eds.), *Brain mechanisms underlying speech and language*. New York: Grune & Stratton, 1967.

Rubens, A. B. Anatomical asymmetries of the human cerebral cortex. In S. Harnad, R. W. Doty, L. Goldstein, J. Jaynes, & G. Krauthamer (Eds.), *Lateralization in the nervous system*. New York: Academic Press, 1977.

Sacchetti, E., Allaria, E., Conte, G., DeRosa, A., Griffi, P. G., Taroni, P. L., Resele, L., &

Smeraldi, E. In vitro NE and DA uptake in inbred mice: Preliminary evidence for lateralization and for strain differences. In J. Obiols, C. Ballus, E. G. Monclus, & J. Pujol (Eds.), *Biological psychiatry today*. Amsterdam: Elsevier/North-Holland, 1979.

Sackeim, H. A., & Gur, R. C. Lateral asymmetry in intensity of emotional expression. *Neuropsychologia*, 1978, *16*, 473–481.

Sackeim, H. A., Gur, R. C., & Saucy, M. C. Emotions are expressed more intensely on the left side of the face. *Science*, 1978, *202*, 434–436.

Sackeim, H. A., Weiman, A. L., Gur, R. C., Greenberg, M. S., & Hungerbuhler, J. P. *Functional brain asymmetry in the experience of positive and negative emotions: Lateralization of insult in cases of uncontrollable emotional outbursts*. Unpublished manuscript, 1981.

Safer, M., & Leventhal, H. Ear differences in evaluating emotional tones of voice and verbal content. *Journal of Experimental Psychology: Human Perception and Performance*, 1977, *3*, 75–82.

Schlanger, B. B., Schlanger, P., & Gerstman, L. J. The perception of emotionally toned sentences by right hemisphere–damaged and aphasic subjects. *Brain and Language*, 1976, *3*, 396–403.

Schwartz, G. E., Davidson, R. J., & Maer, F. Right hemisphere lateralization for emotion in the human brain: Interactions with cognition. *Science*, 1975, *190*, 286–288.

Schwartz, G. E., Ahern, G. L., & Brown, S. L. Lateralized facial muscle response to positive and negative emotional stimuli. *Psychophysiology*, 1979, *16*, 561–572.

Schwartz, M., & Smith, M. L. Visual asymmetries with chimeric faces. *Neuropsychologia*, 1980, *18*, 103–106.

Semmes, J. Hemispheric specialization: A possible clue to mechanism. *Neuropsychologia*, 1968, *6*, 11–26.

Sherman, C. F., Garbanati, J. A., Rosen, G. D., Yutzey, D. A., & Denenberg, V. H. Brain and behavioral asymmetries for spatial preference in rats. *Brain Research*, 1980, *192*, 61–67.

Shukla, G. D., & Katiyar, B. C. Psychiatric disorders in temporal lobe epilepsy: The laterality effect. *British Journal of Psychiatry*, 1980, *137*, 181–182.

Singer, J. L., & Singer, D. G. Personality. *Annual Review of Psychology*, 1972, *23*, 375–412.

Slater, E., & Roth, M. (Eds.). *Clinical Psychiatry* (3rd ed.). London: Balliere Tindall, 1969.

Spinrad, S. Asymmetry in facial expression [Letter]. *Science*, 1980, *209*, 834.

Stern, D. B. Handedness and the lateral distribution of conversion reactions. *Journal of Nervous and Mental Disease*, 1977, *164*, 122–128.

Suberi, M., & McKeever, W. F. Differential right hemispheric memory storage of emotional and nonemotional faces. *Neuropsychologia*, 1977, *15*, 757–768.

Swash, M. Released involuntary laughter after temporal lobe infarction. *Journal of Neurology, Neurosurgery and Psychiatry*, 1972, *35*, 108–113.

Teng, E. L. *Dichotic ear difference is a poor index for the functional asymmetry between the cerebral hemispheres*. Poster session presented at the meeting of the American Psychological Association, Montreal, 1980.

Terzian, H. Behavioral and EEG effects of intracarotid sodium amytal injection. *Acta Neurochirgica*, 1964, *12*, 230–239.

Terzian, H., & Cecotto, C. On a new method for the determination and study of the dominant hemisphere. *Giornale Psichiat e Neuropat*, 1959, *57*, 1–35.

Tsunoda, T., & Oka, M. Lateralization for emotion in the human brain and auditory cerebral dominance. *Proceedings of the Japanese Academy*, 1976, *52*, 528–531.

Tucker, D. M. Lateral brain function, emotion and conceptualization. *Psychological Bulletin*, 1981, *89*, 19–46.

Tucker, D. M., Roth, R. S., Arneson, B. A., & Buckingham, V. Right hemisphere activation during stress. *Neuropsychologia*, 1977, *15*, 697–700.

Tucker, D. M., Watson, R. T., & Heilman, K. M. Discrimination and evocation of affectively intoned speech in patients with right parietal disease. *Neurology*, 1976, 27, 947–950.

Tucker, D. M., Stenslie, C. E., Roth, R. S., & Shearer, S. L. Right frontal lobe activation and right hemisphere performance. *Archives of General Psychiatry*, 1981, 38, 169–174.

Von Bertalanffy, L. *General systems theory*. New York: George Braziller, 1969.

Webster, W. G. Territoriality and the evolution of brain asymmetry. *Annals of the New York Academy of Science*, 1977, 299, 213–221. (a)

Webster, W. G. Hemisheric asymmetry in cats. In S. Harnad, R. Doty, L. Goldstein, J. Jaynes, & G. Krauthamer (Eds.), *Laterilization in the Nervous System*. New York: Academic Press, 1977. (b)

Wechsler, A. F. The effect of organic brain disease on recall of emotionally charged versus neutral narrative texts. *Neurology*, 1973, 23, 130–135.

Weinstein, E. A., & Friedland, R. P. Concluding remarks. In E. A. Weinstein & R. P. Friedland (Eds.), *Advances in neurology* (Vol. 18). New York: Raven Press, 1977.

Whitaker, H. A. *On the representation of language in the human brain*. Edmonton, Canada: Linguistic Research, 1971.

Whitaker, H. A., & Ojemann, G. A. Lateralization of higher cortical functions: A critique. *Annals of the New York Academy of Sciences*, 1977, 299, 459–473.

Zung, W. W. K. A self-rating depression scale. *Archives of General Psychiatry*, 1965, 12, 63–70.

Zung, W. W, K., & Wonnacott, T. H. Treatment prediction in depression using a self-rating scale. *Biological Psychiatry*, 1970, 2, 321–329.

Zurif, E. B. Auditory lateralization: Prosodic and syntactical factors. *Brain and Language*, 1974, 1, 391–404.

11

Neural and Mental Capacities

Robert L. Isaacson and Norman E. Spear

1. INTRODUCTION

The failure to demonstrate our knowledge through our actions may be one of the most important defects of human nature. Indeed, it may be a rate-limiting condition for our species. In many circumstances, we know much more than we demonstrate. Recognition of this fact is the basis of the common complaint of the student who did not do as well as expected on an examination. "I knew the answer but couldn't get it out." The student is often correct. The complaint may not be merely rationalization of a failure to study or learn. The conditions of the test, events of the past few days, a heightened emotional state, or other factors may conspire to prevent what is known from being made concrete through expression. Another time, another day, another place, the test may have been passed.

Although the student's passing or failing a test may be a less important example of the failure of information to direct behavior, other instances in which knowledge fails to gain expression are much more serious. The failure of a diagnosing physician to recognize a symptom of a disease could be disastrous. Engineers, economists, lawyers, and politicians all may be plagued by failures to remember critical information that could have catastrophic results. Indeed, the failure of our actions to reflect our knowledge also leads to difficulties among individuals, groups and nations. The application of our vast funds of knowledge,

ROBERT L. ISAACSON AND NORMAN E. SPEAR • Department of Psychology, State University of New York at Binghamton, Binghamton, New York 13901.

both individual and collective, needs to be more effective than it has been in many aspects of life. To improve our utilization of knowledge we need to understand those circumstances and conditions in which that information is not well used.

To be able to use information, we must be able to retrieve it when needed. It is a fact that at certain times knowledge is not expressed in behavior because we cannot retrieve it. The scholar who fails the examination cannot recall what is needed. The notion of accessing information so that it can be available for "on-line" use has been discussed in Chapters 1, 2, and 6 of this book. Forgetting is not the problem. The investigation of retrieval processes may help us to overcome some difficulties in gaining access to stored information in the future. There are other factors, however, that limit the full expression of knowledge. One of these is the interference with new forms of behavior that arises from the prior learning of other behaviors.

2. HABITS

At times our behaviors do not reflect what we know because of other, competing responses or reactions. We may have learned these competing reactions too well. Certain behaviors acquired through extensive repetition may act to prevent behaviors that could serve us better from occurring.

The commanders of all armies strive to indoctrinate habitual reactions so that their commands will be executed unthinkingly, as if performed by robots. All soldiers are to respond when the leader yells "Charge!" Similar if perhaps less extreme attempts to induce invariant behaviors are undertaken by religions, governments, advertising agencies, parents, and educational institutions.

2.1. William James's Views

The first American psychologist, William James, saw habit as the "enormous fly wheel of society, its most precious conservative agent" (1890, p. 121). Without the perpetuation of habitual acts, executed without thought or reasoning, he felt life would become chaos. The thought of society's members all fulfilling their own goals in individualistic ways never occurred to him as a possible way of life. The current emphasis on self-actualization would have been beyond his comprehension. If he had comprehended it, he would have condemned it as a step toward the dissolution of society. In essence, William James believed that for any society to survive, or even function adequately, people had to behave in ways that were acquired early in life, shaped by economic and social expectations, and such as to assure the continuation of family-based traditions. The children of blacksmiths begot blacksmiths, shopkeepers begot shopkeepers, farmers begot farmers. Even these limited expectations of nineteenth-century families often could not be met, but traditions and habits dictated that a person stay within his or her social class. Individuals seldom, if ever, thought of deviating from their "hereditary" status.

Despite his belief in the social usefulness of habits, a search of James's writings reveals little comment about the mechanisms whereby habits were created or maintained. Habits were accepted as reflecting the plasticity of neural tissue and were thought to be shaped by repeated execution of responses.

No doubt James overvalued the role of habit. That people tended to remain within a socioeconomic class was based *in part* on the development of a specific set of habits. In reality people had little choice. There were very real limitations on social mobility based on family, education, practical skills, and money. It was not habit that doomed a person to slavery, it was the lack of opportunity to be a nonslave. Habits did not make slavery easier to bear, nor did they erase the envy of the poor for the more affluent.

2.2. The Interference Produced by Habits

Yet habits do influence our lives just as they did in the late 1800s. And they often induce behaviors antagonistic to what should be done on the basis of current knowledge and goals. One particularly vexing example occurs when people, driving cars along familiar routes, forget to pick up laundry, flowers, or some other needed item they planned to get. Many times the act of driving home in the usual fashion seems to override the intention to perform the errand. The recognition of the omission may occur after the appropriate intersection has been passed, or may even be "forgotten" until the car is parked at home. (Actually, the role of the habitual act in disrupting intended behaviors is more complicated, and will be discussed later in this chapter.)

In such cases the knowledge of the need to deviate from the usual pathway has not been permanently suppressed or forgotten. It is all too easily remembered after the intersection has been passed or later at home. It was for some reason unavailable at the time it was needed. Behaviorally, the habitual act won out over the unusual need.

It might be asked whether habitual acts are always in opposition to those based on the evaluation of existing knowledge. To some extent, the answer seems to be that they are. If all our behaviors are based completely on previously learned responses, there is no chance for evaluation of the changes in the environment. Habits are efficient means of dealing with stable, repetitive conditions. When X occurs, we do Y. Habits represent stamped-in, unthinking responses to specific signals of the environment. Insofar as they serve to usefully guide our actions, they are valuable. But even when valuable, they are not based on the information available at that moment. If they are useful, it is only because of luck. When habits tend to obscure, defeat, or suppress more useful responses, they interfere with our abilities to cope successfully. A primary requirement for the development of new modes of responding is to be able to express them.

3. AUTOMATIC AND VOLUNTARY ACTS

Habits can come to represent, by virtue of their almost automatic nature, reflexive behavior. Sir Charles Sherrington, one of the great investigators of nervous system function in the first half of this century, believed there was a direct antagonism between thought and reflexive action. He argued that the more reflexive the action, the more automatic the response, and the less mental activity accompanied it (see Sherrington, 1940). Insofar as we can assume that the expression of knowledge is mediated by some thought, it should be distinguished from habitual acts and reflexes. Therefore, reflexive and highly trained responses can be considered "automatic" and have been distinguished from those called "voluntary."

What characterizes more or less automatic behavioral processes, and what prevents the initiation of intentional or voluntary acts? A fundamental principle of living organisms may be the regular and consistent execution of acts that are uniformly initiated by internal and external stimuli as modified by internal mediational mechanisms. A simple example of visually directed behavior is found in the horseshoe crab. It acts like a simple servomechanism that responds differently when circumstances change. Thus the crab's physical orientation to incidental light depends on the time of day as well as on the amount of physical stimulation by photic radiation. Even though contingent on the time of day, the response to illumination is very predictable. It appears that the reactions of many elemental forms of life closely resemble those that could be produced by a machine, one that may be marvelously constructed, complex, regulated by feedback from its actions, and subject to various biases, yet that follows its rules and principles with relatively minor variability. (If it is assumed that low-variability, routine operations are "mindless" and "effortless," the perfect machine would be mindless by such a definition; but what about the imperfect machine?)

As more neural tissue evolves, the opportunity for potential behaviors becomes larger as does the possibility of choice among them. It falls on the newly evolved forebrain tissue to make the wisest choice for the benefit of the organism. Some of these choices may be predictable to an outside observer on the basis of knowledge of the needs or history of the animal. However, predictability may not be a measure of whether a person feels, or can report the feeling of, a choice. At lunch in a particular restaurant, a friend may always select a corned beef sandwich, but if asked why may respond that the entire menu had been carefully examined and only after due thought was the corned beef selected. The predictability of behavior is not always the basis of feelings of choice, but the assumption of potential variability is essential to choice or intention.

However, although predictability of behavior is not an acceptable criterion for the existence of mental activities, the capacity for choice among alternatives must be. Indeed, perhaps the simplest choice is between executing a single action or not doing so. In essence, if we are aware something can be done we must also be aware that it need not be done. To do or not to do, that is the beginning of choice, decision, and mental activity. As the number of alternatives grows, so may awareness. It is likely, however, that we do not possess an infinite capacity for being aware of choices but are limited to an awareness of a limited number of choices at any moment.

Certainly there are substantial individual differences in how many alternatives can be held in memory by different people. This is an important human capacity. Prodigious memories are the hallmark of many great minds. Samuel Johnson had a tremendous memory which by itself did not guarantee his intelligence, but coupled with it allowed unparalleled flights of imagination and creativity. Although great memory capacities alone do not assure intelligence, without memory brilliance cannot be achieved. Individual creative accomplishments depend on memory capacities to a large degree. However, to be effective the products of memory must not be denied access to mental activity or behavior.

4. MOTOR SYSTEMS AND MENTAL ACTIVITY

We still have little idea about how the neural systems responsible for fundamental motor actions are assembled. Many intricate and complex movements are packaged; indeed, for brainstem mechanisms the term "prepackaged" applies.

Anencephalic or microcephalic infants exhibit motor development that is barely different from that of intact offspring until well after birth. Most of the basic activities of the very young seem to occur at appropriate times and degrees despite that there is little or no more brain tissue other than found in the brainstem.

Over the course of development, the motor mechanisms of the nervous system develop additional capacities. It is not so much that new behavioral responses come into existence as that the occasions for exhibiting behaviors change. One aspect of this maturation is reflected in alterations of the neurochemical modulation of the motor systems (e.g., Reinstein & Isaacson, 1981). From the experimental point of view, the net result is a confusing sequence of changing responsiveness to different pharmacological manipulations. An animal is sensitive to a drug at one time, insensitive at a later time, and again sensitive to it still later. It is likely that the changes in drug sensitivity produced by changes in neural systems, both chemical and structural, continue throughout life without ever reaching some permanent plateau.

Over the course of development, new controlling mechanisms come to be exerted on the initial, highly redundant motor systems. The pharmacological redundancy and anatomic flexibility found in the immature mammalian nervous system may reflect a protective device for the newborn at a time when motor activities represent the main order of business. In later development, motor actions come to be less demanding on neural capabilities until in adulthood most motor activities become automatic and can coexist with mental activities. For the toddler, successful vertical motor locomotion across a room or a playpen requires complete involvement of the sensorimotor apparatus and maximal attention to the environment. If the infant tries to divide its attention between walking and "mother" or the "dog," failure and a fall result. In adulthood, a similar movement requires little attention, can be combined with other behavioral or mental activities, and can be easily interrupted. Very little of our brain tissue is required to accomplish simple movements.

The more rapid the required action and the more rapidly adjustments of motor actions need to be made to coordinate with external events, the more forebrain neural tissue is required for the actions. High levels of motor coordination seem to depend on the integrity of the nervous system.

The mentally deficient may have a substantial difficulty in performing motor actions that are readily performed by the nondeficient. Mental deficiency produced by any of a variety of factors is associated with motor dysfunctions. The awkwardness of the mentally deficient is a hallmark of their condition. At the animal level, neocortical damage in the rat has been found to result in certain types of incoordination, and in our laboratories we have noted that animals with hippocampal damage seem to have residual motor dysfunctions; as yet, we have been unable to quantify the anomalies adequately. Thus motor activities that are routine for most may entail a substantial commitment of neural capacities in the mentally handicapped.

In the adult, the learning of new motor skills requires a great deal of mental and presumably neural investment. Learning to ride a bicycle, drive a car, play tennis, or fly an airplane requires an almost total commitment of awareness. Minor environmental events are ignored; if not, the effects of incidental stimulation can be disruptive to the motor actions. As the skill of driving a car becomes mastered, it becomes more automatic and other actions can be undertaken at the same time. Although driving is a well-practiced skill, icy roads, snow, or rain can make driving so demanding that there is little tolerance for distractions. Race-car drivers must give their total attention to their motor skills, which some of them say is the greatest appeal of their sport: It is a time when all else is removed from awareness.

5. BRAIN DAMAGE AND PERFORMANCE

As mentioned above, brain damage or dysfunction produces motor disorders in a general fashion regardless of etiology. A related question is whether the reduction of neural capacities by damage to the brain produces any other general types of mental or behavioral change.

5.1. Lashley's Studies of Neocortical Damage

A good starting point is the work of Karl Lashley, the American pioneer of brain–behavior relationships. His work on the effects of neocortical damage on the acquisition and retention of discrimination problems has already been reviewed (Isaacson, 1976; Chapter 6, this volume) and need not be examined further. In essence: There is little evidence from his studies or those of others that there is any loss of memory for visual habits after neocortical destruction in the rat.

Lashley is best known for his work on the acquisition and retention of mazes, and it is from this work that his laws of mass action and equipotentiality derive. He reached the following conclusions on the effects of brain damage on performance of a number of behavioral tasks:

> For some problems, a retardation results from injury to any part of the cortex, and for equal amounts of destruction the retardation is approximately the

same [for all neocortical regions]. The magnitude of the injury is important;
the locus is not.

There may be a general retardation, arising from any injury to which is added
a specific retardation resulting perhaps from sensory deficiency and associated with lesion to a particular cortical field.

For other habits there may be a complete absence of any effect upon learning
[of cortical damage of any size or in any cortical region]. (Lashley, 1929, p. 60)

In essence, Lashley recognized the task-specific effects of neocortical lesions, a concept that can be applied to the effects of other brain
regions as well (e.g., Nonneman & Isaacson, 1973). He also recognized
that at least *for some problems* disturbances to the neocortical surface
produce a general loss of the capabilities required to deal with the environment. It is this aspect of the lesion-produced effect that is of greatest interest here. In Chapter 6 Meyer and Meyer also point to a general
but hard-to-specify impairment after neocortical damage in any region.

In Lashley's data, the amount of cortical destruction correlates with
the number of errors made in acquisition of the four maze problems and
with the errors made during retention testing in a brightness discrimination (r's from 0.38 to 0.75), suggesting that the deficiencies occurred over
several (but not all) tasks. The highest correlation (0.75) was found between amount of damage and the acquisition of the Type 3 maze.

In connection with the brightness discrimination problem, Lashley
recognized that damage to the subcortical visual systems was related to
the large number of errors made by animals with neocortical lesions.
Excluding the animals with such damage from the analysis reduced the
correlation between amount of cortical damage and errors from 0.45 to
0.22. These correlations are somewhat misleading, since the animals
with cortical damage actually learned the problem more readily than
intact animals, even though *within the lesioned group* the greater the lesion the less rapid was the learning. In discussing this issue, Lashley
cites Herrick's (1926) opinion that injuries to the cortex could potentiate
learning of simple problems by reducing the intrusions of irrelevant
associations. Herrick believed the neocortex provided the means for the
evaluation of the environment for other, new ways of responding, that
is, the development of choices.

Although Lashley recognized the effect of damage to the subcortical
visual systems on performance in the visual discrimination problem by
considering separately the animals with and without thalamic damage,
he attempted a different approach with animals suffering other types of
subcortical damage. Arbitrary numbers were assigned to each subcortical site of damage on the basis of its presumed importance (Lashley,
1929, p. 63). These "important numbers," derived from Lashley's own
opinions, were multiplied by the degree of injury (ranked as 1, 2, or 3)

and these products summed for all subcortical regions damaged. Then these numbers were added to the *ranks* of animals based on surface, cortical damage. The new numbers were now correlated with maze errors. No substantial changes in correlations were found. Clearly, this procedure is inadequate. It is probably impossible to factor out adequately the relative contribution of errors due to neocortical destruction, limbic system damage, and thalamic damage in these old studies; but some further analyses can be made.

Of the 37 animals studied by Lashley in the series of problems reported in his book, 23 had damage to limbic structures. All animals with large amounts of cortex destroyed also suffered damage to limbic structures, most often the hippocampus but sometimes the septal area; some had damage to both structures. Removing these animals from the data reduces the range of neocortical damage (1.5% to 27.6% cortex destroyed). The mean number of errors made by these animals in learning the maze (a substantial overall reduction) is 160.86, but a relatively high correlation remains between cortical damage and errors made in learning the maze ($r = 0.71$). In addition, it is also possible to evaluate the effects of limbic system damage, even though it is correlated with substantial amounts of neocortical damage. Among animals with less than 30% of the cortex destroyed, animals with some damage to the limbic system made an average of 403.8 errors ($n = 9$). Considering the degree of limbic system damage independently of the cortex destroyed indicates that animals with the least amount of limbic system damage (as graded by Lashley) produced 375.13 errors ($n = 8$), those with an intermediate amount produced a mean of 679.9 errors ($n = 9$), and those with the greatest amounts of limbic damage a mean of 1,286.0 errors ($n = 4$). Figure 11.1 represents the performance of animals with limbic system (and cortical) damages.

However, the analysis of performance in terms of errors may not reveal the entire nature of the deficits of the lesioned animals even though it was the method most emphasized by Lashley. In postoperative acquisition of the Maze 3 problem, 67% of the animals with moderate to severe limbic system damage failed to acquire the problem to criterion levels in the 150 trials allowed. Only 7% of the animals with neocortical (only) lesions failed to acquire the problem. The animals with only cortical damage took an average of 54.4 trials to acquire the problem; those with some degree of limbic damage but less than 30% of the cortex destroyed took an average of 94.2 trials. In a postoperative retention test experiment, animals with only cortical damage required 28.6 trials to reacquisition; animals with bilateral hippocampal damage required 82.3 trials. Of the animals with bilateral hippocampal damage, damage to the fornix, or to the septal area, about 30% did not reacquire

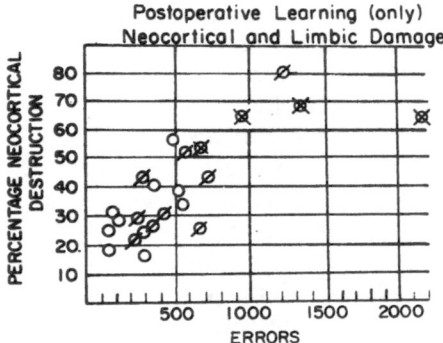

Fig. 11.1 The relationship between the percentage of neocortical destruction and errors made in postoperative maze learning for animals with different amounts of limbic system damage. ○: minimal limbic damage; ∅: moderate limbic system damage; ⊗: greatest amounts of limbic system damage. (Data from Lashley, 1929.)

the problem in the 150 trials provided. Even so, damage to the neocortical surface correlated with trials to acquisition in both the acquisition ($r = 0.67$) and the retention ($r = 0.57$) experiments.

Therefore, Lashley's conclusions concerning a significant role of the cortex in acquisition and retention of the Type 3 maze seem justified, but it also appears that damage to the hippocampus and related limbic structures potentiates and extends the number of errors and the number of trials required to attain his stringent performance criterion (30 errorless trials).

Some years ago, Kimble (1963) found that the structure of the maze played a critical role in determining the number of errors that would be generated by animals with damage to the hippocampal formation. If the maze was built so as to allow animals to run through relatively long unobstructed alleys and easily repeat prior errors, the animals with hippocampal lesions generated extraordinarily large numbers of errors. If the alleys were short, perseverative running through them was reduced and errors would be in the range of those generated by intact animals. The complexity of the problems was not the important factor for error generation; instead, it was the physical nature of the maze. Behavior was altered and became perseverative provided the animal could make long runs. Thus it seems likely that much of Lashley's results do not bear on the issue of whether or not the neocortex's role subserves more or less intelligent behaviors, but instead on how the nature of the physical construction of mazes alters the performance of brain-damaged animals. At least for animals with substantial hippocampal damage, rapidly running through long alleys takes precedence over the behaviors required to attain the food in the goal area. It is difficult for the goal-relevant behaviors to break through the ongoing behavioral acts.

5.2. Maier's Studies of Neocortical Damage

It is clear that certain forms of brain damage can influence the animal's willingness to give up old ways of responding. One approach to this problem was that of N. R. F. Maier, who had the audacity to pit the expression of learned responses (habits) against behavior based on information about the current location of rewards (Maier, 1932). He did so by training rats to make a particular choice in what amounted to a two-choice testing situation. He then showed the animals that the place to which they responded on the basis in the past now did not have food, and that the other place did have food. The animals were then forced to make a choice between the two places: the previously rewarded location now without a food reward, and the previously empty but now food-baited place. Most intact animals chose the location with the food, but animals with brain damage responded to the place where reinforcement had been received in the past. Damage to about 20% of the neocortical surface produced animals that responded only on the basis of past learning. The presumed ability to base performance on "reasoning" had been eliminated. These results can be evaluated in light of Sherrington's views: The less brain tissue available, the less mental activity is involved and the more automatic is behavior. Further evidence supporting this general idea has been presented by Isaacson (1974; 1982).

5.3. Emotional Changes after Brain Damage

It is possible that the great impairment found in animals being tested in mazes arose from a disturbed sensory world affected by the neocortical lesions, which reduced the efficiency of obtaining the rewards provided. This disturbance in the perceived environment and in performance may lead to exaggerated levels of emotional reactions in animals with forebrain damage and a further deterioration of performance. If such were the case, the expression of what the animals had learned would prove impeded by both sensory and emotional factors. On the sensory side brain damage can alter, distort, or even destroy perceptual awareness of environmental events, depending on the size and location of the lesion and on the species being examined. Obviously, such changes would adversely affect the execution of performance based on realization of what is occurring in the environment. Bauer and Cooper (1964) found that some of the consequences of cortical damage in the rat could be attributed to a loss of resolution in the animal's visual system. In essence, their results would indicate that the brain damage distorted the fine-grain resolution of the visual environment and that if this fact were taken into consideration, the rats' retention for acquired visual discriminations was little affected by the damage. Emotional changes that occur in the human and animal after damage to the neocortex are discussed in Chapter 10 with respect to hemispheric differences. We shall return to the matter of emotional changes related to performance when we discuss the behavioral effects of frustration. However, a peculiar instance of the effects of frustration may be relevant.

Several years ago, in unpublished work, Nick Masi and Isaacson tested the effects of serial lesions of frontal neocortex on rats' ability to exhibit skilled manipulative performance with their forepaws. The animals were trained preoperatively on a task devised by Castro (1972) in which they had to reach into small Plexiglas cubes and grasp and retrieve small food pellets. The animals quickly learned to perform the task. After surgery, they were tested once again in this simple apparatus. Some of the animals now made only one or two responses before totally "withdrawing" from the experimental procedures: They simply gave up trying. Animals that kept on with their efforts to retrieve the food pellets managed to improve over a period of several days and reached almost preoperative skill levels. However, the overall results were inconclusive because of the large number of animals that refused to perform the task. The same animals that gave up trying to reach the food pellets in the experimental situation could readily snatch the pellets when held in front of them by a pair of forceps, indicating that they were well motivated to obtain the pellets and would try to do so in conditions in which the task was not that used in preoperative training. It is likely that the brain damage influenced the manipulative abilities of the animals and made obtaining the food pellets in the apparatus more difficult. Coupled with this was a very low threshold for such failures. An adequately designed study would have to build in controls for the extreme effects of frustration in the postoperative period.

To this point we have suggested that neocortical damage can result in changes in motor capacities, sensory abilities, and alterations in reactions to frustrating events. This latter tendency may be greatly accentuated by involvement of the limbic system. Next we shall examine yet another type of effect produced by brain damage.

5.4. Perseverative Behavior

Deficiencies in the ability to shift behavior and/or attention appropriately have been frequently found after various types of cortical and subcortical damage (e.g., Pribram, Douglas, & Pribram, 1969; Pribram, Spevack, Blower, & McGuinness, 1980), although the nature of the perseveration depends on the testing environments and the area destroyed. In addition, at least some lesion-induced perseverative tendencies must be interpreted in light of the prior experiences of the animal and its genetic endowment (Donovick, Burright, & Bengelloun, 1979). In a sense, perseverative motor acts may reflect the consequences of other functional changes and not be a direct cause of behavioral impairments. Nevertheless, perseverative tendencies of action and thought are common sequelae of brain damage in people and in animals.

An example of perseveration after brain damage was reported by Mikulas and Isaacson (1965). In this study, animals with bilateral lesions of the caudate nucleus were tested in a four-choice delayed response problem. As the subjects left the start box they were faced with four closed doors lined up in front of them. One had been signaled as correct before the response could be made. Overall, the performance of these animals was greatly impaired because they perseverated, responding to one of the two end doors of the four as they left the start box. They never acquired the problem because they never gave up this dominant response. At the end of formal training, a change was made in the procedure such that the doors of all four openings were unlocked but required a small effort to push down a card blocking them. The caudate-lesioned animals made their usual, dominant response to the door at one or the other end. They did not, however, push down the door but instead moved to other doors and ultimately pushed down the correct one. The correct door was the only one pushed open by the lesioned animals, and it was always pushed open. This finding indicates that the caudate-lesioned animals had knowledge of the correct door but were unable to express it in behavior under the former conditions of testing. The dominant approach to doors at one side or the other precluded correct performance.

In addition, Mikulas (1966) found that the addition of small cue lights at the choice point disrupted the perseverative responding of the lesioned animals in a T-maze delayed response task. He found that it did not matter whether the cue lights signaled the correct choice or not. The mere presence of the lights was enough to cause the animals to slow down their responses to the end doors and to disrupt the perseverative motor tendencies, thus allowing the performance of the correct response.

An interference in executing a correct response by perseverative responding was also found in mentally deficient patients tested by Isaacson and Perkins (1973). The subjects were tested in a two-object, delayed response discrimination task. The objects in this case were two plastic cubes, both either light or dark at the time the choice was made. The "correct" cube was signaled a few seconds before the subjects could respond by illuminating one of the cubes. The problem was a very simple one; normal adults could solve it in a few trials. Overall, however, the mentally deficient patients performed poorly. Yet this group tendency is misleading, since the patients either learned the task or did not. Those who learned did so as rapidly as the normal control group. The failure of some mentally deficient subjects was because of their use of inappropriate tactics and strategies. Some subjects would engage in simple position stereotypes, but others chose the incorrect cube regardless of its position (right or left) for a hundred or more trials. They operated on the inverse of the correct response. Sometimes they could even tell us the correct solution while still exhibiting incorrect choices. Similarly, monkeys that were made into subjects resembling human phenylketonuria patients by being reared on high-phenylalanine diets were impaired in the learning of object discrimination problems. An analysis of their performance indicated their difficulties stemmed in large part from an inability to stop responding to objects which they had made responses that were unrewarded and to objects for which they had a natural preference. These types of responses were difficult to inhibit and interfered with the learning of the reward contingencies in the experimental situation (Chamove & Molinaro, 1978).

Perkins and I found that one of the best means of interrupting perseverative tendencies in the mentally deficient patients was to allow the subjects to get up and look out the window for a few minutes or to walk down the hall and buy a soft drink. Often on returning to the testing situation there would be a radical improvement in performance, sometimes to 100% correct responding. It was as if these new movements disrupted a set to respond in the particular way they had in the past, something like what happened when Mikulas added the small cue lights in the T-maze. The observation that mentally deficient patients can report the correct solution but persist in incorrect performance indicates a fundamental distinction between verbal statements and performance. This distinction is also found in amnesic patients, who may show progressive improvements in the performance of tasks while claiming they have never seen them before (see Chapters 1 and 2; N. J. Cohen & Squire, 1980).

With the caudate-lesioned animals and the mentally deficient people, the execution of perseverative behavioral acts precluded the performance of appropriate behaviors that would demonstrate the knowledge they actually have.

6. FRUSTRATION-INDUCED PERSEVERATION

Maier (1949) was one of the first to investigate the nature of behaviors that do not seem to be goal-directed occurring under frustrating circumstances. By describing frustration-instigated behavior as non–goal oriented, he did not mean that the organism did not have goals, but instead that when the goals were not reached, behaviors could be initiated that were themselves not goal oriented.

Under conditions of frustration, animals develop perseverative, stereotyped reactions that are highly resistant to modification. The responses are the same not only in terms of identical, repeated choices but also in regard to the typology of behaviors making up the response. The manner of responding, whether jumping, running, or swimming, becomes invariant and persists even when punished. Obviously, human behavior can become perseverative, often irrational, under conditions of high stress or when problems become unsolvable. Behavioral patterns induced by frustration and the inability to solve problems are not predictable on the basis of past performance. They are abnormal fixations of a response that happens to occur in the situation.

Maier found that very few response modification techniques were effective in interfering with the fixated behavior. One that worked was the physical guidance of the animals when making the response. Once a new response was performed, future repetitions could be made. The maximal "effort" was in the initiation of the new response rather than in its subsequent performance. For example, when animals were trained to jump to one of two stimuli presented in windows of a Lashley jumping stand and then presented with an unsolvable problem, they developed a fixation of the response to one window. They perseverated in this response when the problem was made solvable. They would even jump to the window of the fixation when there was no stimulus card in front of the other window. The animals would actually lean out toward the open window, sniff at the food just beyond the window, and then jump to the closed window. They indicated that they "knew" the new problem could be solved, because if the positive card was presented in the window to which they were fixedly jumping they did so much more quickly than when the negative card was presented. (When the negative card was in place it was firmly locked, and when the animal hit the card it fell down into a net suspended below. When the positive card was in a window, jumping against it would knock it down and allow the animal access to the back of the platform, which usually contained a food reward.) The differential latencies of jumps to the fixated side depending on whether the positive or negative card was in place makes it clear that the animals distinguished the two cards and the effects produced by jumping toward each; yet they could not break the inappropriate response, often for a hundred trials or more.

The fixation of the jumping response was dependent on the cues of the situation. If the jumping stand was moved to an unfamiliar room, the fixation vanished: The animals would jump to the postive card regardless of its position. The fixation could be restored by testing the animals in the usual situation, indicating that the emotional responses presumed to be occupying the capacities of the organism and preventing behavioral flexibility are conditioned to environmental cues.

Stresses of several different sorts can induce perseverative responding. Stone and King (1954) report the fixation of an approach into the incorrect alley when rats were made to swim a T-maze underwater. The animals' behavior was similar to that of animals with caudate lesions and of animals under severe frustration. They entered the incorrect arm on every trial and yet the response was progressively aborted, although never abandoned. They would move into the wrong arm but turn around quickly, not bothering to search for a possible escape route at the end; and they would do so as long as training continued. The administration of the neuroleptic chlorpromazine failed to eliminate the perseverative response. Several forms of brain damage, frustration, stress, or mental deficiency all seem able to produce the perseveration of behavioral and mental acts. It appears that perseveration can be exhibited for a number of reasons and is associated with a failure to exhibit appropriate behavior in some circumstances.

To this point we have presented evidence that a number of factors related to changes in neural activities, both inferred and direct, reduce the ability to exhibit fully flexible patterns of behavior. Without such flexibility in thought and action, knowledge cannot be expressed. What has become apparent is the ability of habitual acts, motor actions, brain damage, and emotions to share a common function in reducing the capabilities of the individual for expression. As a consequence, we are in need of a new theoretical structure to encompass this shared ability to incapacitate.

7. A MENTAL CURRENCY

The metaphor we chose to approach this problem is based on money. It is as if at any moment the nervous system has only so much mental currency to spend. The more that is being expended in rapid, highly coordinated actions or emotional reactions, the less is available to be spent giving attention to the environment. To pursue this idea, we propose the use of "action units" as such a currency. We do not wish to dignify this concept by calling it a theory; it is simply a metaphor. Its major goal would be to provide a way in which the behavioral and mental equivalence of actions, states, and behaviors could be recognized. At a common-sense level, the phenomena we wish to include are that when we are engaged in difficult motor acts our thoughts and attention are restricted, that as we attend closely to a particular sensory array our other thoughts and behaviors become restricted, and that as we engage in strenuous thought our abilities to attend, talk, or respond are diminished. There must be a common factor representing these limitations; this factor is what we choose to consider as a limited mental currency.

The limited-currency metaphor suggests that every mental action, including those involving motor actions, perceiving, talking, thinking, as well as the encoding, storage, or retrieval of information, requires the use of action units (AUs). AUs may also be required for the development of associative or cognitive operations, including those required in the generation of hierarchical structures, an ability that Hirsh and Krajden in Chapter 7 attribute to the hippocampus but that may be a more general property of the brain. It will also be assumed that there are only a restricted number of such AUs available at any moment.*

What determines how many AUs are really available for use? In general, AUs will not be available when being used for ongoing emotional, attentional, cognitive, memory, or motor processes. Brain damage, brain dysfunction as in the mentally deficient, and certain drugs are likely to reduce the availability of AUs as well. What distinguishes the present approach from attentional and cognitive theories is its attempt to integrate such varied capacities, abilities, actions, and mental and physical states under a common denominator. Naturally, we believe it is bound to fail because of its overly ambitious character, if nothing else.

7.1. A Limited Capacity

The notion of a limited number of AUs acknowledges our limitations. We have just so much mental capacity to use at any moment. If, under certain conditions, the number of AUs is reduced we become even more limited. If this number becomes sufficiently reduced we may indeed not be able to walk and chew gum at the same time—because so many AUs are occupied that too few are left over for anything else.

Do body activities use up AUs? Although most of the time we are

---

*Our model of action units bears a similarity to certain other ideas, including those of Freud, who suggested that there was only a limited amount of libido available for conscious or unconscious mental activities. The more recent work on the distribution of "attentional resources" (e.g., Kahneman, 1973) is another case in point. Hunt (1980) reviewed attentional theories and presents evidence that mental activities and motor performance can interfere with each other. This interference may, however, be restricted to tasks presumably requiring some common mental function (e.g., Wickens, 1978).

only slightly aware of bodily movements or posture, we can easily think of conditions in which almost all of the AUs are directed toward bodily activities. Again, think of people who have just learned to drive a car when for the first few times they go into heavy traffic. All attention is directed to operating the car. In a few months or years this skill will be automatic and many other mental operations can be carried out concurrently: talking, thinking, singing, looking at the scenery. In AU terms, the operation of the car allows few left over for the beginning driver, but quite a large number for the experienced driver. For the race-car driver, few AUs are available beyond those needed for psychomotor activities in the race.

The same sort of reduction in available AUs occurs when learning any new set of motor skills. At first a large number of AUs must be committed to their execution, but later only a few need be used. It is of special interest that recreational activities tend to be ones that result in reduced availability of AUs. Such activities as racquetball and tennis, skiing, dancing at a discotheque, or even riding a roller coaster all focus attention on sensory events and the body. Sexual activities that may initially involve the use of such mental activities as imagination and anticipation ultimately lead to conditions in which mental activities become focused on the participants' own bodies. In our terms, the available number of AUs is reduced by occupying available AUs with sensory and motor activities.

But continuing mental efforts may also occupy AUs as well. Consider the chess player whose attention is riveted to the board in front of him or the student grappling with calculus. With different people, different types of thought processes may represent dominant themes. How to sell a customer a product, how to make a machine do a somewhat different job than it was designed to do, how to arrange a song for an orchestra, how to play Falstaff or Othello—whatever the goal of the intellectual act, the point is that everyone has times of intense intellectual effort that reduces the number of AUs available for other matters.

7.2. The Rate of Action Unit Sampling

In addition to a limited capacity for AUs, we believe another dimension of behavioral capacity must be recognized: time. Although we have a general idea of the nature of this variable as it interacts with AUs, a precise description of its effects eludes us as yet. Therefore we shall have to be vague, and possibly confusing, in attempting to convey our speculations.

In general, we believe that the finite set of AUs may be assigned or reassigned on a periodic basis. At these moments of sampling (for want

of a better term), unoccupied AUs can be dedicated to new functions—
whether memory storage, retrieval, the direction of attention, or motor
activities. We believe this sampling rate is probably a species-typical
matter but subject to variation within a species. Environmental factors
probably interact with genotype to produce the rate for the individual.
Rates may also fluctuate with drug use, stress, and age. In any case, the
commitment of AUs to any particular purpose can occur only when the
sampling event occurs.

There is reasonably good evidence that many psychological events
(e.g., eye fixations, feature detection, attention span) take a certain
amount of time to occur (see Walker, 1980, pp. 42–69). The actual duration of an act reported by different studies is less important than the idea
that many, and perhaps every, act requires an optimal amount of time
for effective completion. Transitions between acts also require time, generally a much smaller amount than does the act itself. The rate of transitions between acts as well as the duration of the acts themselves may be
related to rhythmic electrical activities that operate to maximize the actions of the brain. Komisaruk (1977) postulates that the slow rhythmic
electrical activities of the brain represent an integrating mechanism of
sensory, motor, visceral, and emotional activities. Processing occurs intermittently during each "cycle" of activity, although somewhat differently for neocortical and limbic rhythms. It may be that the occurrence of
brain rhythms represents a mechanism related to the sampling or ener-
gizing of AUs for mental and behavioral acts.

The idea of a sampling rate attempts to provide the basis of a trade-
off between AUs and the time required to accomplish some goal. If few
AUs are available a task can still be accomplished, but it may require a
longer time. The uncommitted AUs would have to be used repeatedly
over many samplings.

Assessing the effective capacity of an individual would have to take
into consideration the AUs available and the sampling rate. For example, if n AUs are available at any moment and if their rate of change is
limited to m changes per second, that means that ideally some nm action
units would be available per second. This maximum amount is never
achieved in practice. Some AUs *must* be occupied over extended periods
with ongoing activities, thoughts, or actions. These "occupied" AUs are
not available for use. Indeed, some are probably more or less "dedicated" to the initiation or maintenance of ongoing motor activities, even
such simple events as sitting, walking, eating, digesting, or watching
television. The total number of AUs available must be reduced, therefore, by those *dedicated* to specific bodily functions and the number *committed* to continuing thoughts or perceptual processes.

The important matter is the trade-off between the number of AUs available and time. Given a restricted number of AUs, the only way to process a fixed amount of input is by extending the operations over a longer time. Thus if two people approach a task with different numbers of AUs available, both can accomplish the task but at different speeds. Interestingly, some research indicates that the elderly have similar capacities to younger people and are affected only by tasks requiring a high rate of performance (e.g., Schaie & Parham, 1977). At the animal level, Bengelloun, Burright, and Donovick (1976) report evidence that the well-known deficit in passive avoidance tasks in animals with septal area damage actually reflects a need for greater processing time. When the footshocks were appropriately spaced, no deficit was found. Cherry (1975) failed to find a deficit in the acquisition and reversal of a spatial discrimination when responding was self-paced rather than experimenter paced.

7.3. When Do Action Units Become Available?

In our AU model it is assumed that periodically some of the AUs become available for a new use. This could happen in several ways. The most intuitively appealing is one in which the dedication of an AU to an activity must be renewed at each sampling. If the AU has been used between sampling intervals, it will be maintained as dedicated to that purpose; if not, it is available for another use.

The AU notion can readily account for failures of performance due to high levels of motor or cognitive activities that would preclude the detection or perception of environmental events. Indeed, given the idea of processing delays arising from the availability of only a few AUs and the need for repetitive sampling of available AUs, delays in responding during conditions in which the individual is otherwise occupied would be predictable. As a consequence, the interference of motor activities on performance is less mysterious. Can the AU idea make some of the effects of brain damage less mysterious as well?

8. BRAIN DAMAGE AND MENTAL CAPACITIES

Brain damage could directly reduce the number of AUs available or reduce their refreshing rate. It could do so by reducing the likelihood that sensory information from one or more modalities could be processed with AU currency. It could change the efficiency or rate of motor actions such that more AUs were required in their perormance. It could change the intensity or occasions of emotional reactions and by so doing reduce the number left over. Thus the effects of brain damage may be to reduce the number of AUs available both directly and indirectly. In both ways the amount of the reduction should be proportional to tissue loss.

In the case of caudate-lesioned animals described above, normal performance could be restored if the motor sequence was disrupted by the cue lights. Information already available to the animal was not being expressed because of the motor actions that apparently dominated behavior. In our present terms, the effect was indirect; a predominance of AUs were involved with the motor actions and only a few were left to deal with other matters.

In the lesioned animals some amount of the hypothetical mental currency had to be dedicated to the detection of environmental events, but a reduced amount relative to the amount so dedicated by control animals. Thus it is likely that minor, subtle, or very brief changes in the environment would not be detected or processed. Bengelloun, Burright, and Donovick (1977) point out that animals after septal-area damage tend to focus on one aspect of their environment. They are less likely to have "multiple looks" at the environment in Sutherland and MacKintosh's (1971) sense. Therefore, in order for sensory events either to come to interfere with ongoing behavioral acts or to become related to them in any other way, longer or more intense stimulation may be needed.

We do not suggest that the effects of brain damage will be equivalent in all regards. However, it is likely that all forms of brain damage would produce a decrease in mental capacity. In this sense they may have equipotentiality. Some types of damage may produce a greater decrease than others, of course, but some loss, both direct and indirect, should be common to all forms.

We can examine the assumption that the mentally deficient suffer from a reduced number of AUs and that this effect will be reflected in motor, sensory, and cognitive functions. They may also suffer from a decrease in sampling rates. Ferretti (1979) reports similar forgetting curves for mentally deficient and nondeficient people but only when the original input was adjusted to allow for differences in immediate memory capacities. This finding suggests that the rate of renewal of AUs may be the same for the two populations, but the actual capacity is smaller for the mentally handicapped. R. L. Cohen and Sandberg (1980) suggest that the ability to overload the short-term memory system is inversely correlated with intelligence. The problem with low-IQ children may be the relative ease with which this memory system can be overloaded. The cause may be difficulties in efficient encoding but may also be related to a capacity for encoding and other mental operations. Nevertheless, although most of the recent research dealing with memory and intelligence has concentrated on encoding and capacity abilities, the view that the mentally deficient also have a faster rate of loss of material from memory cannot be rejected (e.g., Ellis, 1963).

It is possible that the interruption of perseverative motor or mental actions in brain-damaged animals and the mentally deficient reflects the reallocation of AUs to the analysis of environmental events, removing their commitment to the perseverative acts. With limited currency available, either the perseverative process or attention to the environment could occur, but not both. With attention being paid to the environment, the AUs responsible for the perseverative act could diminish and be replaced with other behavioral tendencies.

9. REPRISE

How do these speculations about action units bear on material discussed earlier in this chapter? Perhaps most enlightening would be to consider an apparent paradox: If repeated acts come to require the participation of fewer and fewer AUs as they become habitual, why is it that we often forget to do other things while engaged in well-established behavioral patterns? Why do we forget to stop by the grocery store when driving home? Should there not be ample AUs available to keep this simple instruction in mind?

The answer may be that when motor actions become automatic, as in driving a familiar route, other streams of mental activities come to engage the AUs. It may be that there are themes of mental activities that await availability of AUs for processing. Thus while driving home the available AUs are engaged with continuing thoughts whose presence prevents the recall of the intended action. It is like the absentminded professor walking across campus oblivious to the Frisbees flying nearby or the greetings of students and colleagues. The lack of contact with the environment is not because of an absence of mental activity, but because of mental activities that are running without interruption. The motor activities do not disrupt the chain of thought because they are so habitual. It is possible that nonhabitual motor acts play a role in interrupting the flow of thoughts that otherwise resist intrusions by low-intensity stimulation. The times at which a person's mind is occupied by a persistent thought pattern are those at which time is required for some unexpected sensory events to be registered, sometimes resulting in the double-take response portrayed by actors in farces. This response should occur when the AUs available are too few to be registered all at once but require sequential processing, which takes time. Therefore, the strolling absentminded professor can be greeted by an acquaintance but not respond until after a few more steps. If the professor had been walking an unfamiliar route, recognition would be instantaneous. Climbing a very difficult mountain trail, however, a delay might occur because of an intensive commitment to the sensorimotor requirements of the task.

The earlier discussion of choices and the awareness of them also bears on the matter of capacity. Choices are limited by the capacity to recognize them, which is assumed to be related to the number of AUs available for their processing. This number is reduced by continuing thoughts, emotions, and sensorimotor activities. What are the optimal conditions for the exhibition of choice behavior? The answer probably varies to some degree on the basis of individual differences, but certainly they should be ones that cause some interruptions of possible perseverative mental or behavioral programs. The goal would be to have as many AUs available as possible at the time a choice is required. That would indicate that, though conditioned emotional reactions and difficult or rapid movements should be reduced, conditions should also be such that perseverative thought patterns are disrupted by motor or sensory events in the environment. A homogeneous and quiet environment may not be the best because it could fail to provide enough extraneous stimuli to disrupt perseverative patterns.

The optimal conditions for choice behavior are likely to be those that allow for the free recall of stored information. In a delayed free recall experimental paradigm the subject who has learned a variety of verbal associates days or weeks earlier first produces a large number of the acquired verbal items but then slows down and finally stops entirely. If all the acquired material is not emitted, the remaining items may be slow in being retrieved or not recalled at all. If that is caused by the perseveration of other materials occupying the action units, then the best remedial treatment would be to provide disrupting sensory or motor activities to free occupied AUs. These distracting conditions should provide enhanced recall of the last, remaining items, but the same conditions should interfere with the expression of the first-recalled items that come out with a rush. The reason is that the initial rush of recalled items represents the actions of organized, essentially perseverative responses of the learned materials. The distracting stimuli would disrupt this organized chain of relevant responses just as they would disrupt the chain of irrelevant responses later on.

The familiar, ineffective procedure of trying to recall a temporarily lost piece of information by "mental effort" becomes understandable in the context of AUs. Expending effort in trying to recall the last item only intensifies the dominant, interfering thoughts that are preventing retrieval. This effort would increase the intensity of the present activities and probably decrease the likelihood of AUs becoming available for the required retrieval.

Throughout our discussion of mental capacities, the use of AUs has been assumed necessary to change a particular way of responding, usually in the contest of perseverative acts. It appears that the changing of behavioral patterns requires a great deal of the AU capacities of the individual, more than required in the simple execution of an acquired response. One reason might be that the previously acquired response must be suppressed *and* the new response must be exhibited. An interesting speculation is that it may require as many AUs to suppress an interfering response as it does to perform it. If that were so, then motor habits in the early stage of acquisition should require more AUs than those that have become well practiced and automatic. Whatever the number required to suppress a response, additional AUs will be needed to launch the new response. The number of AUs involved in both response suppression and initiation would be in proportion to the skill, rapidity, and perceptual-motor coordination demanded by the task. This notion of why response change requires so much mental capacity makes it seem likely that it would be easier to alter well-established, automatic habits than ones being acquired. More AUs would be involved in the learning of the new habit and consequently more would be required for its suppression. Other things being equal, more difficult motor acts would be more difficult to suppress than easy ones.

As mentioned earlier, the behavior of animals with septal lesions tends to be dominated by one or a few cues in the situation. Accordingly, these animals should be able to reverse a discrimination in which the cue to which they had been responding was the one whose significance was changed. The normal animal would be at a disadvantage because other, unaltered stimuli may still call for a continuation of the first acquired response. More rapid acquisition to a reversal of the salient maze cue has been found in animals with septal lesions (Donovick *et al.*, 1979). Cherry (1975) found both faster acquisition and faster reversal of a brightness discrimination problem.

As a further example of the effect of degree of learning on the effort required to produce behavioral change, consider the effect of going to England and driving an automobile. The task should be easiest for the long-term driver with well-practiced abilities. A person who had just learned to drive in the United States or elsewhere in Europe and whose attention was nearly totally committed to the driving act should have more difficulty in driving on the left side. The sudden blaring of horns in the midst of London traffic could lead to a reversion to driving on the right (wrong) side of the street even after months of practice with the new habit. It is also possible that when AU availability is restricted there still would be enough AUs available to suppress an incorrect response, but too few to initiate a more appropriate one. Such an analysis could explain Nonneman and Isaacson's (1973) finding that cats with hippocampal lesions gave up the first acquired response during reversal training as readily as controls but failed to undertake the correct response for prolonged periods.

The effects found in Parkinson's-disease patients following treatment with dopaminergic drugs are also instructive. Typically, the untreated patients are akinetic and have reduced speech. The side effects of L-dopamine treatment can be compulsive movements and thoughts, manic speech, and echolalia. Assuming that Parkinsons's disease represents, at least in part, a reduced activity over the nigrostriatal system *and* a permanent loss of striatal neurons, it would not be suprising that the number of AUs is severely reduced. The latter effect by itself need not necessarily lead to hypoactivity and mutism, but could affect arousal levels. Limited capacities for mental activities could be independent of arousal levels. Therefore, the disease state of the forebrain could be responsible for a reduction in AUs available and the reduction in overall activation due to changes in dopaminergic systems (Hodge & Butcher, 1980) or the balance between nigrostriatal and ventral tegmental-accumbens dopamine systems (e.g., Cools & Van Rossum, 1980). The activation in this instance would activate a chronically inadequate AU system, and the result would be disjointed speech, repetitive acts, and the repeating of sounds.

The rough outlines of the AU idea do not seem to constitute a theory. What is involved is a search for a theory needed to account for both everyday observations and experimental studies that indicate a behavioral and mental equivalence for some purposes among motor actions, thoughts, attention, and emotions, as well as the limited equivalences of brain lesions, drugs, frustration, and stress. Theoretical approaches to such equivalences can be made at several levels, including the black-box empiricism we presented with our action unit currency metaphor, or at a mechanistic or physiological level. Our preference is for the latter type of theory. Unfortunately, we are not yet ready to undertake a neurophysiological analysis of the phenomena that need to be explained. At this point only a more global approach is possible.

10. REFERENCES

Bauer, J. H., & Cooper, R. M. Effects of posterior cortical lesions on performance of a brightness discrimination task. *Journal of Comparative and Physiological Psychology*, 1964, 58, 84–92.

Bengelloun, W. A., Burright, R. G., & Donovick, P. Nutritional experience and spacing of shock opportunities alter the effects of septal lesions on passive avoidance acquisition by male rats. *Physiology and Behavior*, 1976, *16*, 583–587.

Bengelloun, W. A., Burright, R. G., & Donovick, P. J. Septal lesions, cue availability, and passive avoidance acquistion by hooded male rats of two ages. *Physiology and Behavior*, 1977, *18*, 1033–1037.

Castro, A. J. The effects of cortical ablations on digital usage in the rat. *Brain Research*, 1972, *37*, 173–185.

Chamove, A. S., & Molinaro, T. J. Monkey retardate learning analysis. *Journal of Mental Deficiency Research*, 1978, *22*, 37–48.

Cherry, C. T. Variability and discrimination reversal learning in the open field following septal lesions in rats. *Physiology and Behavior*, 1975, *15*, 641–646.

Cohen, N. J., & Squire, L. R. Preserved learning and retention of pattern-analyzing skill in amnesia: Dissociation of knowing how and knowing what. *Science*, 1980, *210*, 207–210.

Cohen, R. L., & Sandberg, T. Intelligence and short-term memory: A clandestine relationship. *Intelligence*, 1980, *4*, 319–331.

Cools, A. R., & Van Rossum, J. M. Multiple receptors for brain dopamine in behavior regulation: Concept of dopamine-E and dopamine-I receptors. *Life Sciences*, 1980, *27*, 127–153.

Donovick, P. J., Burright, R. G., & Bengelloun, W. A. The septal region and behavior: An example of the importance of genetic and experiential factors in discriminating effects of brain damage. *Neuroscience and Behavioral Reviews*, 1979, *3*, 83–96.

Ellis, N. R. The stimulus trace and behavioral inadequacy. In N. R. Ellis (Ed.), *Handbook of mental deficiency: Psychological theory and research* (Vol. 4). New York: McGraw-Hill, 1963.

Ferretti, R. P. *An analysis of passive memory in normal and mentally retarded persons.* Paper presented at the Gatlinburg Conference on Research in Mental Retardation and Developmental Disabilities, Gatlinburg, Tennessee, April 1979. (Cited in R. L. Cohen and Sandberg, 1980).

Herrick, C. J. *The brains of rats and men.* Chicago: University of Chicago Press, 1926.

Hodge, G. K., & Butcher, L. L. Pars compacta of the substantia nigra modulates motor activity but is not involved importantly in regulating food and water intake. *Nauyn-Schmeideberg's Archives of Pharmacology*, 1980, *313*, 51–67.

Hunt, E. Intelligence as an information-processing concept. *British Journal of Psychology*, 1980, *71*, 449–474.

Isaacson, R. L. *The limbic system.* New York: Plenum Press, 1974.

Isaacson, R. L. Experimental brain lesions and memory. In M. Rosenzweig & E. L. Bennett (Eds.), *Neural mechanisms of learning and memory.* Cambridge, Mass.: MIT Press, 1976.

Isaacson, R. L. *The limbic system* (2nd ed.). New York: Plenum Press, 1982.

Isaacson, R. L., & Perkins, M. A. Delayed response performance of mentally retarded patients. *American Journal of Mental Deficiency*, 1973, *77*, 734–747.

James, W. *The principles of psychology.* New York: Henry Holt, 1890.

Kahneman, D. *Attention and effort.* Englewood Cliffs, N.J.: Prentice-Hall, 1973.

Kimble, D. P. The effects of bilateral hippocampal lesions in rats. *Journal of Physiological and Comparative Psychology*, 1963, *56*, 273–283.

Komisaruk, B. R. The role of rhythmic brain activity in sensorimotor integration. In J. M. Sprague & A. N. Epstein (Eds.), *Progress in psychobiology and physiological psychology* (Vol. 7). New York: Academic Press, 1977.

Lashley, K. S. *Brain mechanisms and intelligence.* Chicago: University of Chicago Press, 1929.

Maier, N. R. F. The effect of cerebral destruction on reasoning and learning in rats. *Journal of Comparative Neurology*, 1932, *54*, 45–75.

Maier, N. R. F. *Frustration: The study of behavior without a goal.* Ann Arbor: University of Michigan Press, 1949.

Mikulas, W. L. The effects of lights at the choice point on spatial alternation and position learning by normal rats and rats with bilateral lesions of the caudate nucleus. *Psychonomic Science*, 1966, *5*, 275–276.

Mikulas, W. L., & Isaacson, R. L. Impairment and perseveration in delayed tasks due to bilateral lesions of the caudate nucleus in rats. *Psychonomic Science*, 1965, *3*, 485–486.

Nonneman, A. J., & Isaacson, R. L. Task dependent recovery after early brain damage. *Behavioral Biology*, 1973, *8*, 143–172.

Pribram, K. H., Douglas, R. J., & Pribram, B. J. The nature of nonlimbic learning. *Journal of Comparative and Physiological Psychology*, 1969, *69*, 765–772.

Pribram, K. H., Spevack, A., Blower, D., & McGuinness, D. A decisional analysis of the effects of inferotemporal lesions in the rhesus monkey. *Journal of Comparative and Physiological Psychology*, 1980, *94*, 675–690.

Reinstein, D. K., & Isaacson, R. L. *Behavioral and temperature changes induced by clonidine in the developing rat. Neuroscience Letters*, 1981, *26*, 251–257.

Schaie, K. W., & Parham, I. A. Cohort-sequential analyses of adult intellectual development. *Developmental Psychology*, 1977, *13*, 649–654.

Sherrington, C. S. *Man on his nature*. London: Cambridge University Press, 1940.

Stone, C. P., & King, F. A. Effects of hypophysectomy on behavior in rats. I. Preliminary survey. *Journal of Comparative and Physiological Psychology*, 1954, *47*, 213–219.

Sutherland, N. S., & MacKintosh, N. J. *Mechanisms of animal discrimination learning*. New York: Academic Press, 1971.

Walker, E. L. *Psychological complexity and preference: A hedgehog theory of behavior*. Monterey, Calif.: Brooks/Cole, 1980.

Wickens, C. The structure of attentional resources. In R. Nickerson (Ed.), *Attention and performance* (Vol. 8). Hillsdale, N.J.: Lawrence Erlbaum, 1978.

Index